HEALTH AND BEHAVIOR
A MULTIDISCIPLINARY PERSPECTIVE

H. Russell Searight

Lake Superior State University

ROWMAN & LITTLEFIELD

Lanham • Boulder • New York • London

Executive Editor: Nancy Roberts
Assistant Editor: Megan Manzano
Senior Marketing Manager: Amy Whitaker
Interior Designer: Ilze Lemesis

Credits and acknowledgments for material borrowed from other sources, and reproduced with permission, appear on the appropriate page within the text.

Published by Rowman & Littlefield
An imprint of The Rowman & Littlefield Publishing Group, Inc.
4501 Forbes Boulevard, Suite 200, Lanham, Maryland 20706
www.rowman.com

6 Tinworth Street, London SE11 5AL, United Kingdom

Copyright © 2019 by The Rowman & Littlefield Publishing Group, Inc.
All rights reserved. No part of this book may be reproduced in any form or by any electronic or mechanical means, including information storage and retrieval systems, without written permission from the publisher, except by a reviewer who may quote passages in a review.

British Library Cataloguing in Publication Information Available

Library of Congress Cataloging-in-Publication Data
Names: Searight, H. Russell, author.
Title: Health and behavior : a multidisciplinary perspective / H. Russell Searight.
Description: Lanham : Rowman & Littlefield, [2018] | Includes bibliographical references and index.
Identifiers: LCCN 2018039277 (print) | LCCN 2018039934 (ebook) | ISBN 9781442274082 (Electronic) | ISBN 9781442274068 (cloth : alk. paper) | ISBN 9781442274075 (pbk. : alk. paper)
Subjects: LCSH: Medicine and psychology.
Classification: LCC R726.5 (ebook) | LCC R726.5 .S433 2018 (print) | DDC 610.1/9—dc23
LC record available at https://lccn.loc.gov/2018039277

∞™ The paper used in this publication meets the minimum requirements of American National Standard for Information Sciences—Permanence of Paper for Printed Library Materials, ANSI/NISO Z39.48-1992.
Printed in the United States of America

Contents

Preface xiii

About the Author xvii

CHAPTER 1 Introduction to Health and Behavior: The Systems Perspective 1

Illness Versus Disease 2

The Concept of Diathesis 4
  Diathesis-Stress Models Explain Interaction Between Biological and Psychological Predispositions and the Emergence of Illness 5

Health and Illness Occur in Complex Systems 7
  Bertalanffy's Systems Perspective 8
  Bronfenbrenner's Ecosystems 8
  The Biopsychosocial Model 9
  Reciprocal Causality: A Cause May Be an Effect and an Effect May Be a Cause 10

Examples of Health and Illness and Levels of Complex Systems 11
  Individual Level 11
    DNA 11
    Communication Between Organ Systems: The Brain-Gut Connection 11
    Psychopathology and Health: The Rise and Fall and Rise of Psychosomatic Medicine 12
  Interpersonal Systems: Couples and Families 13
  The Mesosystem—Cultural Values and Religion 14
  Macrosystems 15
    Communities 15
    Changes in National Politics and Economics 15
  Beyond Macrosystems: Our Flat World—International Borders Dissolve 17

Putting It Together: Ms. Ramirez 18

Summary and the Way Forward 19

CHAPTER 2 Research in Health and Behavior: Epidemiology and Beyond 21

Epidemiology: An Overview 21

Food-Borne Illness: Two Examples 22

Example: Sexually Transmitted Diseases 23

Epidemiology: Key Concepts and Terminology 24

Risk Factors and the Diathesis-Stress Model 25

Practical Versus Statistical Significance: Prevalence, Base Rates, and Health Screening Tests   27
    Neurocognitive Disorder of Alzheimer's Type   28
    Screening for Breast Cancer   28
    HIV Self-Testing   29
    Autism Spectrum Disorder   30

Epidemiology: Types of Investigatory Designs   30
    Case Reports   31
    Cross-Sectional Studies   31
    Case-Control Studies   32
        The "Radium Girls"   33
        Thalidomide   33
        Mesothelioma and Asbestos   33
    Cohort Studies   34
        The Framingham Heart Study   34
        Cancer and Nutrition: The EPIC Cohort   35
    Qualitative Research   35

Social Epidemiology   36

Causality and the Bradford Hill Criteria   37

Evidence-Based Health Care   38
    Organizing Published Research to Guide Clinical Decision-Making   39
    Issues and Cautions in Applying EBM Findings   41
    Evidence-Based Health Interventions in Larger Systems   41

Conclusion   42

CHAPTER 3   The Health Care System: History and Current Dilemmas   43

A History of Medical Care   43
    Hippocrates and Galen   43
    Medieval Period Through the Late 1600s   44
    Hospital Medicine   45
    Vaccines   46
    Germ Theory and the Continued Development of Vaccines   46
    Surgery Becomes Safer   47
    Educating Physicians   48
    The Development of Medicine as a Profession   49
    The Growth of Scientific Medicine   50
        Imaging Techniques   50
        Medical Devices to Supplement Physiological Functions   51
        Organ Transplantation   51
        Medications   52

The Consumer Movement and Challenges to the Health Care Professions   53

Health Insurance and Health Care   56
    Federal Health Insurance: Medicare and Medicaid   59
        Medicare   60
        Medicaid   60
        S-CHIP   61

    The Uninsured 61
        Emergency Medical Treatment and Active Labor Act 62
        Health Care Reform: The Background of the Affordable Care Act 63
            The Affordable Care Act (ACA) 63
            Problems with the Affordable Care Act 64

The US Health Care System: International Comparisons 65
    Switzerland 66
    Great Britain 67
    Canada 68

International Health Care: Differences in Underlying Values 70

Conclusion 71

CHAPTER 4 Health Disparities and Diversity 73

Disparities: An Overview 75

Economic Disparity 75

Educational Disparities 77

Gender 78
    Gender in Developed Countries 78
    Gender in Developing Countries 79

Sexual Orientation 80
    Mental Health 82
    Interactions with the Health Care System 83
    Transgender and Gender-Nonconforming Youth and Adults 83

Disparities by Race/Ethnicity: The Evidence 84
    Pregnancy and Infancy 85
    Childhood Health Conditions 85

Medical Conditions Disproportionately Impacting Minorities 86
    Differences in Types and Severity of Health Conditions 86
    Discrimination Toward African Americans—Associations with Health Status 87
    Risk Factors and Disease Complications 87
    Patterns and Quality of Care 88
    Physician-Patient Interaction 89
    Mortality 90

Linguistic Diversity 90

The Role of Cultural and Historical Factors in Health, Illness, and Treatment 92
    American Medicine as Culture 92
    A Brief History of Health Care for African Americans in the United States 93
    Hispanic and Latino Culture and Health Care 96
    Asian Culture: Views and Treatment of Illness 98

Conclusion 99

CHAPTER 5 Health Communication and Behavior Change 101

Brief Overview of Theories of Health Communication and Behavior Change 102

Health Belief Model 102
- Susceptibility 102
- Severity 103
- Benefits 103
- Barriers 103
- Cues to Action 104
- Self-Efficacy 104
- Analysis of the Health Belief Model 104
- Does Fear Change Health Behavior? 106

Theory of Reasoned Action and Theory of Planned Behavior 107
- Behavioral Intention 107
- Attitudes 107
- Subjective Norms 108
- Perceived Control 108
- Theory of Reasoned Action/Planned Behavior: Analysis and Research 109

Social Cognitive Model 110
- Example of Applied Modeling—Telenovelas 111

Social Marketing 112

Diffusion of Innovation 114

Individually Focused Models of Behavior Change 116
- Transtheoretical Model 117
- Relapse Prevention 120
  - Relapse Risk Factors 121
  - Abstinence Violation Effect 122
  - Problems with the Abstinence Standard 122
  - Relapse Prevention Strategies 122
- Motivational Interviewing 123
  - Philosophy of Motivational Interviewing 123
  - Specific MI Skills 124
- Harm Reduction 125
- Cyber Media and Health Behavior Change 126

Conclusion 127

CHAPTER 6 In the Clinic: Communication, Adherence, and Symptoms Without Disease 129

What Is Primary Care? 130

The Importance of the Clinical Interview 131

Overview of the Medical Office Encounter 132

The Difference Between Good- and Poor-Quality Physician-Patient Interaction 132

Electronic Medical Records: Benefits and Drawbacks 134
Values of Patients and Health Care Providers 134
Communicating Medical Mistakes 134
Medically Unexplained Symptoms 135
    The Psychiatric Approach to Medically Unexplained Symptoms 136
        Malingering 136
        Factitious Disorder 137
        Conversion Disorder 137
        Illness Anxiety Disorder (Hypochondriasis) 137
        Somatic Symptom Disorder 138
    Medically Unexplained Symptoms in the Primary Care Office 139

Cultural Issues 141

The Medicalization of Society 141

Adherence 142
    An Overview of the Problem of Non-adherence 143
    Reasons for Non-adherence: Patient Factors 144
    Health Care Professionals' Communication Style and Patient Adherence 145
        Physician Social Power and Adherence 145
        Timing and Modality 147
        Does Fear Increase Adherence? 147
        Characteristics of the Illness and Treatment 148
    Social Support 148
    Interventions for Increasing Adherence? 149
        Mobile Apps for Improving Adherence 149
    Adherence as the Result of a Complex Biopsychosocial Decision 150
    The Macrosystem's Role in Adherence 150
        A Vaccination Program Arouses Suspicion 150
        Making Health a Requirement for Employment 151
        Economic Causes of Non-adherence 151

Conclusion 151

CHAPTER 7 Stress and Coping 153

What Is Stress? 154
    Walter Cannon and the Fight-or-Flight Response 155
    Hans Selye and the General Adaptation Syndrome 156
    Allostatic Load 156
    Psychoneuroimmunology 157
    Tend and Befriend 158
    Transactional Model 158

Assessing Stress 159
    Perceived Stress Scale 159
    Social Readjustment Rating Scale 159
    Hassles and Uplifts 160

Mediators and Moderators of Stress   160
Characteristics of the Stressor   161
Emotional State   161
Coping Styles   162
History of Exposure to Stressors   163
Personality Traits   163

Does Stress Cause Physical Illness?   165
Cardiovascular Disease, the Type A Personality, and Depression   165
   Cardiovascular Disease and Anxiety and Depression   166
   Hypertension   166
   Cancer   167

The Macrosystem   168
Environmental Factors   168
Couples and Relationship Conflict   169
Workplace   170
Community   171
Social and Economic Costs of Early Traumatic Experiences   172

Diversity   172
Gender   172
Stress Across Cultures   173

Specific Strategies for Stress Reduction   174
Progressive Relaxation   174
Autogenic Training   175
Biofeedback   175
Meditation   176
   Transcendental Meditation   176
   Benson's Relaxation Response   177
   Mindfulness   177
Cognitive Intervention   177
Acceptance and Commitment Therapy   178
Journaling: Writing to Manage Stress   180
Positive Psychology   180
   Background   180
   Positive Psychology Interventions   181

Conclusion   182

CHAPTER 8   Chronic Pain as a Psychosocial Condition: Causes, Consequences, and Treatment   183

Pain Defined   183

When Does Pain Become Chronic?   184

Chronic Pain—A Brief History   184

Common Pain-Related Disorders   185
Fibromyalgia   185

Low Back Pain   186
Headache   186
Cancer   188

Explanations of Chronic Pain   188
Operant Model   188
Cognitive Perspectives   189
Gate Control Model   190
Neuromatrix Model   192
Pain as a Social Metaphor   193
Pain and the Workplace   193

Cross-Cultural Aspects of Pain   194

The Macrosystem: The Politics of Chronic Pain and Its Treatment   195
Pain, the Work Ethic, and the Politics of Disability   195
The Politics of Gate Control Theory   197
Intractable Pain and Physician-Assisted Suicide   198
Pain as a Fifth Vital Sign and the Rise of Opiates   198

Assessment of Pain   200
Rating Scales   200
Pain Diary   201
The Clinical Interview for Pain   201

Chronic Pain: Treatment Approaches   202
Surgery   203
Implantable Spinal Stimulators   203
Medications   204
Trans-Electrical Nerve Stimulation   205
Acupuncture   206
Physical Therapy   206
Behavioral and Psychological Treatment for Chronic Pain   207
   Behavioral Approaches to Treatment   207
   Progressive Relaxation Training   209
   Biofeedback   209
   Hypnosis   209
   Cognitive Behavioral Therapy   210
   Third-Wave Cognitive Behavioral Therapy   211
Multimodal and Multidisciplinary Pain Programs   212

Conclusion   213

CHAPTER 9   Smoking and Smoking Cessation   215

Health Risks of Smoking and Tobacco Use   215

History of Cigarette Smoking   216

Demographics of Smoking   217

Smoking Initiation   218

Mental Health Conditions and Smoking   218

The Macrosystem: Public Health, the Cigarette Industry, and Tobacco-Control Policies   220
   Tobacco Taxes and Related Legislation   220
   Public Education   221
   Smoking Bans   222
   The Tobacco Industry   223

Mental Illness and Tobacco Use   224

Ethnicity, Culture, and Smoking   224

Smoking Cessation—Common Issues   225
   Background for Smoking Cessation   225
   Assessment Prior to Undertaking Smoking Cessation   226
   Nicotine Withdrawal   227

Interventions   228
   Pharmacotherapy   228
   Cognitive and Behavioral Strategies   229
   Stages and Successful Smoking Cessation Strategies   231
      Preparation   231
      Action   232

Vaping and E-cigarettes   232

Conclusion   233

CHAPTER 10   Obesity, Exercise, and Eating Disorders   235

Obesity's Role in Health and Illness   236

Risk Factors for Being Overweight   236

Body Weight, Stereotypes, and Discrimination   237

Weight-Loss Interventions   238
   Low-Calorie Diets   239
   Behavioral and Cognitive Behavioral Approaches   239
   Weight-Loss Medication   240
   Bariatric Surgery   240

The Macrosystem   241
   Cultural Factors in Food Consumption: The French Paradox   241
   The Food Industry   242
   Policies for Increasing Nutritional Awareness   242
   Sugar Taxes   243
   Marketing and Economic Factors   244

Exercise   244
   A Brief Historical Perspective   244
   Exercise and Mental Health   245
   Exercise and Cognitive Functioning   246
   Developmental Benefits of Exercise for Prevention of Mental Health Conditions   247
   Macrosystems and Physical Activity   247

Eating Disorders   247
   Anorexia Nervosa   248
      Physical and Medical Effects of Anorexia Nervosa   248
      Comorbid Conditions   248

        Course Over Time   249
        Causes   249
        Treatment   250
    Bulimia Nervosa   250
        Psychological and Physical Effects of Bulimia Nervosa   250
        Comorbid Conditions   251
        Course Over Time   251
        Causes   251
        Treatment   252
    Binge Eating Disorder   252
    Eating Disorders: Immediate Social and Macrosystem Influences   253
        Family and Social Factors   253
        Mass Media   253
        Cross-Cultural Studies of Eating Disorders   253
        Eating Disordered Culture   254

Conclusion   255

CHAPTER 11   Sleep and Sleep Disorders   257

Why Do We Sleep?   257

The Stages of Sleep   258
    Non-REM Stages   258
        Stage 1   258
        Stage 2   258
        Stage 3   259
        Stage 4   259
    REM Sleep   259

Circadian Rhythm   260

Sleep Through the Life Span   260

Reasons for Disrupted Sleep   262

The Macrosystem: Diversity and Sleep   264
    Culture   264
    Gender   265
    Ethnicity   265
        The Cross-Cultural Significance of Sleep Paralysis   266

Sleep Disorders   266
    Insomnia   266
        Definition and Prevalence   266
        Health Conditions Associated with Insomnia   267
        Medications Causing Insomnia   267
        Psychological Causes of Insomnia   268
        Insomnia Treatment   269
    Obstructive Sleep Apnea   271
    Narcolepsy   272
    Restless Legs Syndrome   273
    Excessive Daytime Sleepiness   274
    Hypersomnia   274

Childhood Sleep Disorders   274
   Bedtime Refusal   274
   Sleep (Night) Terrors   275
   Nightmare Disorder   276
   Somnambulism (Sleepwalking)   276

Conclusion   276

CHAPTER 12   Psychosexual Disorders   279

The Sexual Response Cycle   279

Sensate Focus   280

Erectile Dysfunction   281

Female Sexual Interest/Arousal Disorder   282

Hypoactive Sexual Desire in Men   284

Problems with Ejaculation   285
   Premature (Early) Ejaculation   285
   Delayed Ejaculation   286

Female Orgasmic Disorder   287

Genito-Pelvic Pain/Penetration Disorder   288

Cross-Cultural Issues in Sexuality   289

Conclusion   290

CHAPTER 13   The Future Direction of Health and Health Care   293

The Interface of Physical and Mental Health   293

Collaborative and Integrated Health Care   295

Increased Attention to the Psychosocial in Medical Care   297
   Psychosocial "Vital Signs"   297
   Brief Models of Counseling for Busy Physicians   298
   Professionalism and Patient-Centered Care   300

Health Care Navigators   300

Internationalization: The Flat World Continues to Flatten   301

The Aging of the Population and the Maximization of Life   302

Conclusion   303

References   305

Index   347

Preface

A Bit About the Author's Journey Through Health and Behavior

If in five years you remember few of the details of this book but know and appreciate that health and illness are influenced by social, cultural, economic, political, psychological, and family factors, I will be happy to conclude that this book did what I intended it to do. Most of the topics covered are ones that I have addressed as a clinician working with patients; a researcher studying questions ranging from emotional responses to viral illness to the impact of national and state policy on patient care; and a teacher of primary care resident physicians, nurses, and future psychologists. After reading this textbook, I hope you will find your own niche in the medical world.

There has never been a point at which I stopped learning. As a psychologist entering the medical system, and later as a student of public health, I found that it was a challenge to keep up with changes in medicine, health promotion, mental health, and the larger health care system. As a clinician who has spent close to 20 years in medical clinics and general hospitals, teaching future health care professionals and seeing patients alongside my physician faculty colleagues, I came to appreciate that while I was fairly adept at diagnosing and treating common mental health problems, I was seeing only a tiny sliver of the multiple systems that impact health and illness.

I knew that overeating and smoking cigarettes were undesirable, but other than giving direct advice or considering underlying deep-seated personality dynamics such as oral dependency, I had little understanding of how these "lifestyle" problems arose and became habits. And I knew even less about how to go about changing them.

I also naively thought that my medical colleagues missed mental health conditions such as anxiety disorders and major depressive disorder in at least 50 percent of their patients (Kessler, Heath, Lloyd, Lewis, & Gray, 1999) because they were not adequately trained. I had little appreciation of how difficult it is to disentangle a mood disorder in patients presenting with a complex web of physical complaints that might include poor sleep and diminished energy but also lower back pain, tension headaches, poorly controlled hypertension, and type 2 diabetes.

One of the major problems in medicine today is that patients often do not follow through on providers' recommendations to lose weight, increase activity level, undergo medical testing, refill their prescriptions, or take medication regularly. Non-adherence in this era of concern about soaring medical costs is a major issue. It is estimated that 20 to 60 percent of patients stop taking prescribed medication without consulting their physician. At first, as a psychologist, other than trying to determine whether non-adherent patients were clinically depressed, I felt that I did not have a lot to offer in these situations. If these non-adherent patients exhibited major depressive disorder, their physician typically would write a prescription for an antidepressant medication such as fluoxetine (Prozac) or citalopram (Celexa). Research suggests that, at best, 50 percent of these patients would actually take the medication as indicated (Sansone & Sansone, 2012).

As an instructor of physicians, I felt that I learned more than I was ever able to teach. One of my roles in that setting was observing doctors-in-training as they saw their patients. My objectives were to make sure that physicians could communicate clearly to patients and develop and/or maintain a solid, trusting doctor-patient relationship. However, after a few years, I realized that I was learning as much as, if not more than, the doctors-in-training I was supposed to be teaching.

I learned that a physician who begins the patient visit with an open-ended question such as "What brings you in today?" rather than the closed-ended "I see you are here for your headaches—is the pain on the left or right side of your forehead?" is actually likely to have a briefer and more satisfying patient visit. I learned that the physician who perused the patient's record and presumed they knew what was wrong with the patient when they walked into the examination room was much more likely to have to deal with a "doorknob question." Doorknob questions are the ones that arise when the physician believes that the meeting is over and already has a hand on the doorknob, ready to leave the room. The patient may say something like "I don't know if this is important, and it was not the reason I came in today, but I really have been having some very bad pain in my chest, and it seems to spread to my left arm."

Physicians often express frustration with having to spend time addressing medical conditions that could have been prevented. The emergence of type 2 diabetes in an obese patient or chronic bronchitis in a smoker is known as a "lifestyle" illness because of the role that individual habits play in contributing to the cause and maintenance of the condition. From listening to patients over the years, I came to appreciate that spouses, children, extended family members, and social networks (including friends as well as communities of faith) also played a major role in their health. Similarly, having seen many patients who came to the office because of a workplace injury or because they needed documentation to permit several days away from work or to have accommodations in the workplace for their chronic illness, I appreciated the role that the workplace and the need for income played in health and illness.

I also observed the "missed connections" occurring when a white European physician worked with a patient of color. When a patient of African American background would seem suspicious and ask questions about a recommendation for a particular treatment, such as surgery, I was sensitive to the undercurrent of mistrust of white institutions—particularly those that have had a history of exploiting and mistreating people of color.

As a member of the hospital staff, I periodically heard from physicians about patients who were refusing treatment or situations in which patients were being maintained on life support when the medical staff saw little likelihood of improvement. There was occasional physician frustration when family members refused to withdraw life support in a "hopeless" case. While having a durable power of attorney or written advance directives would seem like rational preparation for serious illness, most patients and their families do not have these documents—leaving decision-making to family members if the patient is incapacitated. Family members in these situations would occasionally remind the health care team that while they appreciated their expertise, the choice of life or death was up to God, and they did not want to interfere in a divine plan.

One of the hospitals with which I was affiliated was having increasingly serious financial problems. Yet, when I walked by the emergency room waiting area, there was no shortage of patients who had been waiting hours for care. I learned that because of a federal law, the Emergency Medical Treatment and Labor Act (EMTALA), all of those patients had to eventually be seen and treated and/or stabilized. Even though they might not have the money or insurance to cover the visit, federal law required that all patients who presented in the emergency department must be evaluated and stabilized. The hospital had no way to recover the full cost of providing these patients with care but was still legally required to do so. For those without insurance, the emergency department was a clinic in which patients were guaranteed to be seen by a physician. While a victim of an auto accident was rushed from an ambulance through the emergency department's door, the patient in the next emergency room cubicle might be there because their anti-hypertensive medication prescription ran out that week.

Hovering above patients in the clinic or the hospital, there was always the cloud of health insurance. If the patient did not have coverage, they might be prescribed a medication or referred for an essential test that they could not afford. Even if they did have coverage, it was often necessary to convince an insurance reviewer that the company should cover a specific test or treatment. I was periodically struck by what appeared to be irrational policies of many insurance companies. While paying for the medical costs associated with chronic obstructive pulmonary disease, the same insurance company refused to cover smoking cessation counseling and medications. I also saw physical practices refusing particular types of patients—not because of their medical condition, but rather because the patient was insured by a company that often did not cover the cost of the patient's care. This pattern was often true for the two major government-funded insurance plans in the United States—Medicare and Medicaid. I was also often frustrated that our health care system would pay for invasive treatments such as lower back surgery but not for integrated biopsychosocial pain management programs, which research has indicated are very effective. I came to appreciate that economic and political factors often override scientific evidence.

Through reading and direct experience, I also came to appreciate that the United States is one of the few countries in the world that did not have a form of universal health care coverage. In working with physician colleagues who had been trained in Europe and other countries, they seemed confused and aghast that Americans oftentimes had to sell their homes to pay medical bills.

I have been teaching a course on health psychology to undergraduates for more than 10 years. Previously I had taught a graduate course, "Clinical Health Psychology," to future clinical psychologists. In my undergraduate class, psychology majors are well represented. However, I also have had students from other disciplines, including nursing, exercise science, pre-medicine, and education. After I had taught the class for several years as a "traditional" health psychology class, the number of non-psychology students prompted me to do some critical reflection about the course content. I asked myself, "If I were to interact with the health care system today as a patient, a health care professional, or in a role in which periodic interaction with medical professionals was necessary, what would be helpful to know?" The results of those questions changed how I taught the course and led to the development of this book.

I hope that this book gives you several new "lenses" from which to view health, illness, and medical care. I also hope that you come away from your reading with information and perspectives that improve the quality of your own life.

There are many people who made this book possible. For the organization and multi-systems approach to health that is at the book's core, I owe a debt of gratitude to students in my "Health Psychology" course at Lake Superior State University. The psychology majors in this course tolerated a psychology professor who focused on topics such as international health care policy, health care funding, cross-cultural medicine, and medical interviewing, which may have been considered very tangential to a psychology class. I want to thank the many students from exercise science, athletic training, kinesiology, and nursing who were the impetus for expanding the range of this course to examine broader health systems issues.

Despite my best intentions and enthusiasm for the topic, this book would have never seen the light of day without the help and support of many people. I wish to thank Ms. Molly White, formerly of Rowman & Littlefield, who encouraged the project in its very early stages and championed the book proposal. I am very grateful to Ms. Nancy Roberts, who as executive editor communicated a wonderful combination of patience, understanding, and encouragement. The final product is also a tribute to the editorial talents of assistant editor Ms. Megan Manzano, as well as the work of Ms. Patricia Stevenson as senior production editor.

My greatest debt of gratitude is to my wife, Dr. Barbara Searight. While encouraging me to complete the book, Barbara also embodied the compassion to support a multiyear project in which I was often not the available and attentive husband that she deserves. Her love, support, and understanding were above and beyond what anyone could expect, and I will always be grateful to her as I have for the nearly 30 years we have been married. She has made me a far better person than I could ever be without her.

About the Author

H. Russell Searight is professor of psychology at Lake Superior State University in Sault Ste. Marie, Michigan. He received his PhD in clinical psychology from Saint Louis University and a master's in public health (MPH) from Saint Louis University School of Public Health. He has published widely on a range of topics including management of psychiatric conditions in primary medical care, bioethics, and medical education.

CHAPTER 1

Introduction to Health and Behavior
The Systems Perspective

What does behavior have to do with illness and health? We typically think about medicine as dealing with biological and chemical abnormalities. Viruses, bacteria, broken bones, blocked arteries, osteoporotic decay, severed arteries, and so on are what we typically think about when we think about the domain of medicine. However, it has become increasingly clear that narrowly focused biomedical explanations do not account for many illnesses and the management of chronic diseases. The questions below are just some examples of questions that cannot be readily answered simply through knowledge of viruses, bacteria, or anatomy:

1. *After exposure to cold virus some people get colds, others do not. Why?*
2. *Men who are married live longer than men who are not. Why?*
3. *People who are regular churchgoers have lower blood pressure. Why?*
4. *Women live longer than men. Why?*
5. *In many regions of the world that are becoming increasingly industrialized, there is a period where the national life expectancy actually declines. Why?*
6. *Even when socioeconomic factors are controlled, African American patients with heart disease receive less aggressive treatment than whites. Why?*
7. *Among college students, many are well aware that the first part of their break between semesters finds them in bed sick. Final exams are over. Why should you get sick now?*
8. *While medication treatments are readily available for many chronic health conditions such as chronic obstructive pulmonary disease or type 2 diabetes, a very high percentage of patients with these conditions do not take their medication as prescribed. Why?*

As I hope will become evident, the answers lie in the fact that behavior and health interact at multiple levels—from the cellular aspects of the immune system to the international issues of large-scale human migration across continents.

In order to best describe health and illness, this book relies on a biopsychosocial perspective. While "traditional" health and behavior topics, such as pain, stress, and coping, and conceptual models of health behavior change are included, the book also attempts to highlight the role that social forces such as income inequality and culture play in individual health and well-being. In addition, there are ongoing political and economic forces impacting our health care delivery system. The ongoing political debate about health care and the government's role in ensuring that citizens have health insurance in the United States and in other countries such as the United Kingdom highlights the role that these larger forces play in our ability to seek treatment when necessary and the types of treatment we receive. Before "diving in" to these issues, I would like to introduce several key concepts: the distinction between illness and disease, the interlocking and interactive systems that influence our health, the interaction between our biology and the environment, and how our health influences but is also influenced by multiple levels of interaction ranging from the individual patient to international relations.

Illness Versus Disease

The World Health Organization defines health as a "state of complete physical, mental and social well-being and not merely the absence of disease or infirmity." While this definition may seem unrealistically optimistic, it does recognize that physical and psychological distress can be present with or without physical disease. Most of this book focuses on illness rather than disease. Illness is the patient's subjective experience and is a psychosocial construction addressing perceptions of physical sensations, what symptoms are, whether those physical symptoms are cognitively appraised as meaningful, the intensity of the experience, and the extent to which it impacts daily functioning. Illness also reflects a cultural dimension and acts as a form of interpersonal influence and communication (Kleinman, 1988).

The concept of the sick role is usually associated with the sociologist Talcott Parsons, who described how entry into this role is associated with changes in how others perceive them. Additionally, Parsons (1951) indicated that the role has rights and responsibilities. One responsibility is to seek assistance; however, other responsibilities, such as the typical rules for productive involvement as a worker or family member, are suspended.

Disease—a physiochemical or anatomical abnormality—is the traditional domain of the physician. Disease can exist with or without symptoms, the physical or psychological signs that experientially tell us something is "not right." While our optimal state is health without illness or disease, there are three other categories: disease with illness ("rightful suffering"), disease without illness ("successful coping"), and illness without disease ("physical distress without physical abnormality") (Cockerham, 2015).

Illness is usually organized in the form of a narrative (Kleinman, 1988; Searight & Noce, 1988)—a story of distress, what it means, motivation to seek assistance, and the type of help considered appropriate. Humans use explanatory models to "make sense" of physical distress and usually generate an explanation for the cause of symptoms and a judgment about whether symptoms are serious. Physician office visits are places in which patients bring a unique story about how the disease is disrupting their life. The physician also is attempting to develop a story from the patient's narrative. The physician listens for specific points of the patient's narrative (onset of pain, presence or absence of fever, vomiting, sore throat, etc.). The anamnesis, as it is formally known, is the physician's extraction of meaning from the patient's narrative (Kaplan-Myrth, 2007).

Symptoms do not exist outside of interpersonal relationships and culture. In the farm country of the Midwest, the temporal rhythm of daily life centers around the crop cycle (Stein, 1982). During the planting and harvesting seasons, physical discomfort that might prompt non-farmers to seek medical care is ignored and labeled as the result of hard work. During the winter months, when the demands of farming are reduced, the aching, swollen knee becomes a symptom. However, members of the farm family do not seek medical care to feel better or directly improve the quality of their lives; seeing the physician is for the purpose of getting the human machine fixed so that work can continue. The meaning and purposes of treatment are also tied to the culture of farming. Factors that influence these symptoms can include location and cost of care, social status, gender, and ethnicity. In a place where economic stability depends on the household labor force, there are worse times for one to be sick than others. Periods of planting and harvesting are essential to crop production; it is likely that a family member will "postpone" their acceptance of the sick role (which would confirm their being ill) until after these "critical" times have passed (Stein, 1982).

Culture and our own unique life experiences lead to a personal story that we develop about our symptoms. These personal narratives include a description of the symptoms themselves, their perceived significance, a causal explanation, the event or experience that led the individual to consider the physical or emotional distress to be significant, the actions taken to address the distress, the effectiveness of these actions, and a resolution that may include continued illness. For example, in interviews with participants in a cardiac rehabilitation program who had sustained a heart attack within the past six months, patients typically had situational explanations. Their heart attack was caused by events ranging from "rushing around at Christmastime and going in and out of the house into the cold air" to the stress caused by a new work supervisor in a fast-food restaurant (Searight & Noce, 1988).

While disease exists on a gradient (blood pressure, blood glucose ["sugar"], red blood cell count), sickness is largely categorical—once one passes the threshold for being "sick," one views oneself differently than before and is viewed differently by others. In the United States, one key element of the sick role is the social expectation that the patient should be motivated to leave the role. If one is not motivated to leave the role, such as a patient who does not want to "get better" and return to work, and this lack of desire to leave the role is perceived by others, the sick role provides fewer social benefits and negative evaluations by others ("he's a hypochondriac"; "something is always wrong with her"; "I think she just wants to be taken care of").

Many symptoms exist without corresponding physical disease. While it may seem that it would be difficult to justify the sick role with symptoms alone as an entry ticket, the World Health Organization's view that health is freedom from any distress has seeped into society and, more specifically, into the health care system. Medicalization, the growing use of medical diagnoses and treatments to address multiple types of discomfort, such as that arising from physical appearance (cosmetic surgery), working the swing shift and not getting enough sleep (shift-work syndrome treated by modafinil), or being comfortable in being appropriately assertive in social situations (Kramer & Brody, 1994), has extended the definition of sickness considerably.

In Western countries, access to health care and significant increases in the public's use of various types of media to understand their own health have made entering the sick role increasingly easy. We are constantly bombarded with information about medical conditions and their treatment through the popular media and the internet. Many of these syndromes do not have a clear biological cause. In primary care settings, patients fitting the category "symptoms without clear disease" are very common; only about 10 to 15 percent of patients seen in primary care practices have symptoms that have a clear-cut cause (Kroenke & Mangelsdorff, 1989).

As will be discussed in more detail later in the book, within the span of 7 to 10 days, most of us will experience some form of physical discomfort: a runny nose, itchy red eyes, a headache, an aching sensation in our lower back. Most of the time, these are not labeled as "symptoms" but simply as an unpleasant part of life. However, this everyday discomfort can become a symptom when we focus our attention on it and ascribe meaning to it. If I have a low threshold for physical symptoms—partly because of growing up in a family in which parents were frequently talking about their own symptoms or in which there were significant health problems—discomfort otherwise considered "normal" may be interpreted as catastrophic. If I come from a family in which multiple uncles had life-ending heart attacks in their early 40s, these achy sensations in my chest are more likely to be interpreted as symptoms of something possibly serious rather than indigestion from the three chili dogs I just ate. Symptoms do not exist in isolation—the person experiencing the distress gives the symptoms unique meaning.

The Concept of Diathesis

A diathesis is a predisposition to an illness. Heritability refers to the amount of variation in some physical characteristic or trait that can be attributed to genetic rather than environmental factors. For schizophrenia, the heritability is about 80 percent. At the individual level, concordance is the probability that if one biologically related family member has the condition, another member will also have the condition. For example, in schizophrenia the concordance rate for schizophrenia for identical twins is approximately 40 percent—if one twin has the condition, it is about 40 percent likely that the other one will have the condition. A genetic predisposition for schizophrenia is physiologically expressed through elevated activity of the neurotransmitter dopamine. For type 2 diabetes, usually having its onset in middle adulthood, heritability ranges from 20 to 80 percent. In terms of concordance, if one parent has the condition, it is about 40 percent likely that one of their offspring will develop type 2 diabetes (and 70 percent likely if the condition affects both parents).

Physiologically, the process of type 2 diabetes typically begins with resistance to the hormone insulin. Thus, many of the cells, including those of the muscles and liver, do not optimally use insulin, and the body needs more insulin to help glucose enter the cells. Initially, the pancreas can produce more insulin, but over time it becomes unable to do so and blood glucose levels increase. However, it is important to recognize that a diathesis is a predisposition and not an ultimate cause. The expression of the diathesis with type 2 diabetes is influenced by lifestyle factors such as weight and physical activity. If one maintains healthy weight and optimal exercise levels, the genetic predisposition may not manifest itself as disease. Similarly, when considering the concordance rate for schizophrenia among monozygotic twins—who have identical genetic makeup—the fact that the rate is about 40 percent and not 100 percent suggests that other factors are involved in determining whether a genetically predisposed individual will develop schizophrenia. Compared with type 2 diabetes, less is known about the specific environmental or lifestyle factors associated with the expression of the diathesis for schizophrenia. In the case of schizophrenia, it is likely to be a much more complex array of influences.

The Pima Indians, a group of Native Americans residing in both Arizona and northern Mexico, illustrate the complexity of the genetic-environment interaction as well as the strong influence of lifestyle factors in the development of type 2 diabetes. US Pima Indians have almost 5 times the rate of diabetes as their counterparts in Mexico. While the genotypes of the two groups of Pima Indians are not identical, their genetic cluster is similar and distinct in genetic background from other Native American tribal communities.

The Mexican Pima live in a fairly remote area in the Sierra Madre mountains centering around the village of Maricopa. It was not until the early 1990s that a paved road made the village more accessible. The Maricopa Pima still rely on a relatively traditional diet based upon cultivation of beans, potatoes, corn, and other vegetables. Up until the early 1900s, the Arizona Pima had a lifestyle similar to their Mexican counterparts. Through building an elaborate system of canals, the Arizona Pima were able to develop productive farms growing corn and beans in the Sonora Desert. However, beginning around 1900, water was diverted by newly arriving white settlers. As a result, the lifestyle that the Arizona Pima had led for approximately 2,000 years underwent abrupt change. This was reflected in dietary change as the Pima went from a low-fat, high-carbohydrate diet to a diet in which more than 40 percent of calories were from fat. By the 1950s, increases in obesity and type 2 diabetes among the Arizona Pima were noted.

Diathesis-Stress Models Explain Interaction Between Biological and Psychological Predispositions and the Emergence of Illness

Type 2 diabetes is a chronic disease that typically emerges in middle-aged adults and reflects the interaction of lifestyle and genetic predisposition. As the rates of type II diabetes increased, public health researchers began comparing body mass index and indices of diabetes between the Arizona and Mexican Pima. Body mass index and percent body fat were similar between the Mexican Pima and nearby "Blancos" (nonindigenous residents). However, the Arizona Pima had a type 2 diabetes rate of approximately 38 percent compared with the 7 percent of the Mexican Pima and the 2.6 percent of the "Blancos" (Ravussin, Valencia, Esparza, Bennett, & Schulz, 1994; Esparza-Romero et al., 2015).

In comparing body mass index (an index of weight), Pima women in Mexico average 25.1 compared with 35.5 for women in Arizona. Among male Pima, the body mass index in Mexico was 24.8 compared with 30.8 in Arizona. Average blood pressures were slightly higher for the Arizona Pima, but the magnitude of difference was small. As the Arizona Pima moved from a traditional to a more Westernized diet, type 2 diabetes and body weight increased. In addition to diet, both male and female Pima in Mexico were involved in more than 40 hours a week of physically demanding work, such as farming, milling, and fence building (Ravussin et al., 1994; Esparza-Romero et al., 2015).

Currently, the Arizona Pima have one of the highest rates of type 2 diabetes in the world. It appears that the Pima have a particularly strong genetic predisposition to type 2 diabetes. The differences between Pima living in Arizona and Mexico also demonstrate how powerful environmental and lifestyle factors can be in eliciting or overriding this predisposition. It has been suggested that environment, in this case diet and activity, can override pre-existing genetic factors. By 2010, there was more interaction with non-indigenous populations, and the Mexican Pima began to show some elevation in rates of type 2 diabetes (Esparza-Romero et al., 2015).

While we often think about a diathesis as a genetic or biological predisposition, such as in the case of type 2 diabetes or schizophrenia, a diathesis can also be a schema, a psychological representation of a difficult experience that influences how we react to current stressors. To illustrate how an implicit cognitive pattern can be a diathesis, Hilsman and Garber (1995) assessed children's views of their academic performance and grades prior to receiving report cards. Students with a pre-existing explanatory style higher in self-blame and lower in perceived academic competence exhibited more depressive symptoms five days after receiving poor grades on their report card (Hilsman & Garber, 1995).

For example, a schema centering around loss and including the associated, painful emotions may arise from the experience of a parent's death while a child is young. It is likely that because of the psychological representation of the loss that this child will become an adult who may be particularly sensitive and reactive to interpersonal losses (death, breakup of a relationship, friend moving away). Additionally, this loss schema may predispose them to be vigilant to any remote signs of relationship conflict.

For the past 25 years, investigators have been examining adult attachment styles—the perceptions of others and pattern of interpersonal behaviors exhibited in close, romantic relationships. It is well established that children somewhere between 18 and 36 months exhibit a distinct pattern of behavior in relation to their primary caregiver. This pattern is typically shown when the caregiver leaves a child in an unfamiliar situation. Based upon observation, Ainsworth and colleagues (Ainsworth, Blehar, Waters, & Wall, 1978) described three patterns of attachment—anxious, secure, and avoidant. These patterns tend to reflect the history of the relationship between the child and the primary caretaker. If the primary caretaker was unpredictable in responding to the child's needs, the anxious, ambivalent types of behavior likely emerge. Parents who promoted the child's needs to explore their immediate environment while being consistently available—particularly when the child was distressed—led to a secure attachment style. Caregivers who were consistently nonresponsive typically led to an avoidant child who had little expectation that their caregivers would be physically or emotionally available to them.

Since longitudinal studies of at least 20 years duration would be necessary, it is difficult to determine whether adult patterns of attachment are a direct developmental outcome of childhood attachment patterns. However, research suggests that these patterns may be stable. It is noteworthy that the percentage distribution of the three attachment styles among infants and adults in the general population is approximately the same (Hazan & Shaver, 1987). Among adults, attachment patterns tend to emerge in late adolescence or early adulthood when romantic relationships are being formed. This internalized representation of close relationships will be enacted with others as well—particularly health care professionals. Since one is typically in a physically and emotionally vulnerable position when seeking health care, these attachment styles are particularly likely to be enacted in this context (Hunter & Maunder, 2015).

Additionally, there is growing evidence that adult attachment styles are associated with adult health, including obesity and alcohol use (Hunter & Maunder, 2015). Adults with fearful/anxious styles are more likely to be overweight and were also more likely to exhibit disordered eating (Hunter & Maunder, 2015). Attachment style also appears to influence the ability to be successful in smoking cessation; adults with a secure attachment style are most likely to stop smoking (Hunter & Maunder, 2015). McWilliams and Bailey (2010) found that among adults, insecure attachment styles were associated with cardiovascular disease such as stroke, high blood pressure, and heart attacks. Additionally, anxious attachment styles were associated with chronic pain and ulcers. Securely attached adults did not exhibit elevated risk for any medical conditions (McWilliams & Bailey, 2010).

Health and Illness Occur in Complex Systems

Contemporary Systems Theory, as applied to human interaction, is usually traced back to World War II. At that time, many scientists were working on defense-related projects. The ideas of circular causality, self-correction, and feedback loops emerged from this work, much of it with precursors to modern computers, and were later applied to humans. While Ruesch and Bateson's (1949) declaration that "psychological man is dead and social man has taken his place" was probably overstated, the social disruption associated with World War II illustrates how large-scale international processes can have unintended influences "downstream." For example, domestic patterns and perceptions of marriage and childbearing in the United States changed dramatically as a result of challenges posed by the war. During the war, many women went to work for the first time outside of the home. Employment of women outside of the home had never taken place on a scale of this magnitude (Mintz & Kellogg, 1989). When the war ended, families and couples were impacted by this change in several ways. First, the divorce rate rose—many commentators believe that women, by participating in the competitive workforce, came to realize that they did not have to be financially dependent upon a husband (Mintz & Kellogg, 1989). Second, however, almost in direct contradiction to the first point, technology developed during the war led to the development of labor-saving and technologically sophisticated devices to make housework easier and even more attractive. Advertisements featuring women smiling in a gleaming up-to-date kitchen encouraged women to leave the workforce so that the returning male soldiers could have jobs. Madison Avenue made this transition attractive—even glamorous (Searight, 2016).

Bertalanffy's Systems Perspective

There are multiple variations on systems theory, each of which stresses different aspects such as hierarchies of content and role, processes, change, and forces for stability. One of the best-known and most all-encompassing systems models is based upon the work of Ludwig von Bertalanffy. Bertalanffy was a biologist whose work was applied to multiple disciplines, including psychology, sociology, ecology, and political science. Bertalanffy's view was that the world was organized as a system conceptually similar to an inverse pyramid, with cells at the bottom, then organ systems, then human beings who live in social systems. We both influence and are influenced by social systems, including our families, places of employment, government, and even international economic conditions. Depending upon our interests and/or the issue involved, we can choose the system on which we focus our attention. When we have a fever, cellular processes involved in our immune system are particularly relevant. When we are seeking health care, our immediate community becomes the level of interest. If we are concerned about how we are paying for health care and whether we can pay for health care, we are likely to be following changes in governmental policy very closely.

Systems theory also appreciates that many processes are circular or trigger a corrective process. For example, the last time you had a fever, your body's immune system was engaged in correcting an aberration involving your immune system. While most of the time living systems are in a steady state, any aberration that changes the equilibrium will initiate a correction. The medication that we take for a bacterial infection that caused cold or flu is an agent that returns our body from disequilibrium to a steady state (Bertalanffy, 1968, 1969).

Bronfenbrenner's Ecosystems

Bertalanffy highlighted processes that occur within systems as well as the general concept that it is almost always possible to go up or down in the system hierarchy to understand some phenomenon. However, Urie Bronfenbrenner (2005), a developmental psychologist, developed categories to organize and name the social systems with which we interact. Bronfenbrenner (2005) describes five ecological systems that differentially influence individual development. Microsystems include our families and friends, religious community, and even cultural norms that are transmitted through our family. A mesosystem is actually a type of buffer between our community, culture, and immediate social group (e.g., live-in boyfriend or girlfriend; parents and child) and the microsystem. The next level, the ecosystem, may include our community, which in turn includes local political issues, the availability of jobs, and the availability of areas in which one can safely exercise. Finally, the macrosystem may include our country, larger-scale social policy, legislation that bears on our well-being and health, and the national political and economic climate. Bronfenbrenner does not include global issues in his model. However, as anyone who follows the news is aware, infectious disease epidemics can travel very rapidly due to the speed and frequency of air travel. Economic policies in Japan and China may impact local industry, which in turn impacts health-related indices such as unemployment. Historically, in the United States when people lost their job, they also lost their health insurance. The recently enacted Patient Protection and

Affordable Care Act in the United States ("Obamacare") is a governmental policy developed in part as a response to this problem.

The Biopsychosocial Model

In the mid-1970s, the physician George Engel declared that the biomedical focus of medicine was overly limiting and no longer appropriate; he offered an alternative—viewing patients within a biopsychosocial context. Engel challenged medicine's emphasis on reductionist, exclusively biological causes of illness: "It [biomedicine] . . . assumes disease to be fully accounted for by deviations from the norm of measurable (somatic) variables" (Engel, 1977, p. 131). The hallmark of traditional medicine is "rational treatment . . . directed only at the biochemical abnormality [which] . . . does not necessarily restore the patient to health" (Engel, 1977, p. 132). Engel recognized that, in many respects, physicians needed to evaluate more than physical symptoms and physiological abnormalities. They needed to pay attention to the impact of the patient's conflictual marriage, economic worries, or coping with job loss, which was far more challenging than assessing the heart's functioning with a stethoscope and an electrocardiogram and analysis of a patient's blood iron levels or hemoglobin A1C (measure of blood sugar over several months).

As a physician, Engel certainly appreciated the biological contribution to illness, and in his seminal articles through which he introduced his colleagues to this new medical model, he relied upon schizophrenia and type 2 diabetes as examples. However, as discussed earlier in this chapter, a biological predisposition is elicited and maintained through an interaction of cognitive, emotional, familial, and community factors. The psychological trauma of the illness itself may, in turn, impact the already impaired immune system (Leserman, Drossman, & Hu, 1998), leading to an infection warranting hospitalization.

The biopsychosocial model recognizes that most illnesses—particularly those associated with lifestyle factors but even infectious illnesses—have biological, psychological, and social causes. There is also an appreciation that factors such as stress—external demands that overwhelm someone's available coping skills—can be triggered by multiple person-centered or environmentally centered events. Personality factors include traits such as perfectionism, emotional reactivity, and cynicism.

Factors in the immediate environment, such as the availability of close relationships that are generally supportive, will interact with these personality styles and coping skills and larger-scale social events, including those triggered by governmental policy. While most clinicians are familiar with the interpersonal dimensions and factors in the immediate environment that impact health and wellness, health care professionals must also be cognizant of larger-scale factors such as economic and social policy.

A recent example that illustrates how larger-scale economic and demographic changes impact individual health is the current rise of methamphetamine use. Many commentators have noted that methamphetamine has become particularly common in the rural Plains and Midwestern regions of the United States (Reding, 2010). Several factors have been suggested as causes—the availability of inexpensive chemicals such as ammonia that are available in large quantities in rural areas since it has been used as a component of fertilizer, the consolidation of large family farms into large corporate agriculture businesses, population migration to cities, and the relative ease and low cost of manufacturing methamphetamine (Reding, 2010).

Methamphetamine's rise in economically depressed areas was also associated with the closure of many factories. With the scarcity of well-paying, stable industrial jobs, residents of these now economically deprived areas often had to turn to employment in service industries (Reding, 2010). These positions are generally part-time, with varying shifts and low pay. Access to inexpensively manufactured stimulants helped people maintain employment at several part-time or seasonal jobs in which demand for workers fluctuates.

Reciprocal Causality: A Cause May Be an Effect and an Effect May Be a Cause

Physicist Werner Heisenberg described how the act of observing may change the phenomenon being observed (Eastwood, 2017). This may sound abstract and philosophical, but this principle actually has several very practical implications for health care. While many of Engel's ideas embodied in his biopsychosocial model were present long before the late 20th century, Engel brought the physician—and, by extension, the health care system—into this web of reciprocal causality. Engel (1977) is often credited with originating the emphasis on patient-centered care that has become increasingly prominent in the past 15 years. Patient-centered care emphasizes attention to the "whole person" in the physician-patient encounter. There are situations in which clinical observation may improve those outcomes.

While the reciprocal interaction between patient and provider plays a significant role in clinical outcomes, technology may inadvertently, through the act of observation, create or worsen medical problems. Deyo (2002b) provides a number of interesting examples of the "cascade effect" initiated by medical technology: "a chain of events initiated by an unnecessary test, an unexpected result, or patient or physician anxiety, which results in ill-advised tests or treatments that may cause avoidable adverse effects and or morbidity" (Deyo, 2002b, p. 23).

An example is the use of electronic devices that monitor fetal heart rate during childbirth. During the process of labor and delivery, fetal heart rate changes are often inferred to be an indicator of fetal distress, which would lead to various medical interventions to increase the pace of delivery. As Deyo (2002b) notes, the effective use of fetal monitoring requires that the mother's movements in bed be restricted. The physician's directive to lie still may trigger increased anxiety in some women (if you have ever had a CT scan or imaging procedure in which you were required to lie perfectly still while holding a specific position for multiple minutes, you may appreciate how difficult this can be).

Because of reduced activity and increased anxiety, the pace of labor may become slower, which, in turn, leads to medical interventions to speed up the pace. One strategy to speed up labor is to use medication such as oxytocin or to artificially break the membrane. With this accelerated labor comes increased contractions and accompanying pain, leading to a request for epidural anesthesia (an injection of pain-dulling medication into the lower spine). While rupturing of the membranes and loss of fluid may lead to higher pressure within the baby's skull, the epidural anesthesia may lead to reduced blood pressure in the mother. This combination of abnormalities is likely to trigger a surgical delivery of the baby—a cesarean section. Overall, there is little evidence that the use of fetal monitors improves outcomes of labor and delivery (Deyo, 2002b).

Engel (1977) emphasized that the interactions between systems were dynamic and complex and may include unintended effects. As with the clinical cascade (Mold & Stein, 1986; Stein & Mold, 1988) that leads to a disproportionate number of cesarean deliveries, it is necessary to "take into account the patient, the social context in which he lives, and the complementary system devised by society to deal with the disruptive effects of illness" (Engel, 1977).

To illustrate for the reader how health involves multiple systems simultaneously, this chapter concludes with some examples of health-related issues at several systems levels.

Examples of Health and Illness and Levels of Complex Systems

Individual Level

DNA

While genes can influence our behavior, there is growing evidence that this association is bidirectional; this phenomenon, "epigenetics," is likely to become an area that will be given a good deal of attention in health psychology. While the structure of DNA cannot be readily altered, the expression of genes can be influenced by age, environmental factors such as stress (Heim & Binder, 2012), and the influence of specific diseases.

The process of turning off and on specific gene sequences can be influenced by our behavior and the environment that we select—a good example of reciprocal causality. One of the major effects of physical exercise is on epigenetic modifications that can be beneficial to cancer-prone patients. Modifications in DNA methylation patterns as a result of physical exercise can increase the expression of genes involved in tumor suppression and decrease the expression of oncogenes involved in cancer (Moosavi & Ardekani, 2016).

Communication Between Organ Systems: The Brain-Gut Connection

One of the most common gastrointestinal problems seen in clinical settings is irritable bowel syndrome (IBS). IBS, typically more common among women than men, is associated with abdominal pain, cramps, the experience of feeling "bloated," diarrhea, and/or constipation. It is a chronic condition, but it is not life threatening and does not increase the risk of colon cancer. The condition tends to affect those under the age of 45 and also those who have a family history of the condition. Those with IBS who consult physicians also appear to have a higher prevalence of anxiety and depression. Additionally, there is some evidence that, particularly among women, histories of sexual physical abuse are much more common among those with irritable bowel syndrome versus comparably aged women without the condition (Drossman, 1998; Leserman et al., 1998).

Research on IBS over the past 20 years has focused on interaction between the intestinal tract and the central nervous system—"the brain-gut connection"

(Drossman, 1998). There is evidence that persons with IBS interpret and react to sensations in the colon and rectum differently than persons without the condition. While this account is perhaps a bit graphic, it illustrates nicely how these two organ systems often believed to be distinct actually interact. A balloon was placed in the sigmoid rectal region and then inflated. Those who had IBS were much more likely to report distress and pain when the balloon was inflated (Drossman, 1998). However, among those without a history of the condition, this distention and accompanying stimulation from the inflated balloon did not elicit enough neural activity to be experienced as pain.

Psychopathology and Health: The Rise and Fall and Rise of Psychosomatic Medicine

During the 1930s through the 1950s, a historical period in which psychoanalysis was at its peak of popularity in the United States, psychological explanations for physical illnesses were the subject of considerable attention by both psychiatrists and general physicians. The psychiatrists Alexander and French asserted that management of impulses and associated anxiety via defense mechanisms accounted for cardiovascular and respiratory diseases. The treatment of choice for these conditions was psychoanalysis. In the early 1950s, when psychosomatic medicine was at its peak, Alexander (1950) presented a list of physical conditions that he believed to be psychologically based or "psychosomatic" diseases: hypertension, thyroid abnormalities, bronchial asthma, rheumatoid arthritis, peptic ulcer, ulcerative colitis, and dermatitis (chronic skin inflammation). In the psychosomatic worldview, psychologically threatening life events often precipitated these conditions. The physical expression through asthma or hypertension was a sort of safety valve—a defense against expression of anger, helplessness, or fear. Psychoanalytically oriented investigators extended this list to include conditions such as cancer. There were critics of this approach who asserted that the psychoanalysts were overreaching and neglecting the role of physiological and anatomical factors.

One of the most dramatic examples of this overreach that also illustrates the extent to which psychosomatic medicine captured medical practice is the case of composer George Gershwin. Gershwin began reporting symptoms at the age of 23 (Kinetz, 2001). However, physicians could not find any physical explanation for his abdominal pain and constipation and referred him for psychoanalytic psychotherapy. "Talk" therapy apparently did not alleviate the symptoms. Gershwin's symptoms became worse, he began complaining of headache, and his behavior became more erratic. Gershwin was briefly admitted to the hospital because of the headaches and was discharged after a very brief stay with a diagnosis of "likely hysteria." A month later he appeared at the hospital. This time Gershwin was unconscious. Surgeons found a large tumor in the right temporal region of the brain. He died soon afterward at the age of 38 (Kinetz, 2001).

In the 1960s and 1970s, as medicine became more sophisticated and the influence of psychoanalysis declined in psychotherapy, the scope of psychosomatic explanations was reduced considerably. However, conditions such as stomach ulcers were still viewed as the result of stress. Specialists in the digestive system, gastroenterologists, often recommended to patients—many of them males experiencing stomach ulcers—that they needed to "take it easy." The "ulcer-prone" personality was characterized as having very high standards but being outwardly submissive. "[The man who develops ulcers] may appear quite considerate, kindly and soft-hearted, probably because he fears and avoids the clashes which would result from assertive hostile behavior towards others" (Alp, Court, & Grant, 1970, p. 776).

Later research found that this "psychosomatic holdout" was actually associated with a specific bacterium—*Helicobacter pylori*. Ulcers were the result of bacterial infection. This finding effectively refuted the idea of an ulcer-prone personality. However, research indicated that while bacteria were the principal cause of stomach ulcers, it was found that the bacteria increased in concentration in response to stress (Guo et al., 2009). Importantly, many of us are infected with *H. pylori* but do not develop ulcers. The presence of *Helicobacter* by itself is not predictive of the development of stomach ulcers. Later research found that specific life stressors as well as socioeconomic status and smoking were all independent predictors of ulcer development in the presence of *H. pylori* (Levenstein, Rosenstock, Jacobson, & Jorgensen, 2015). Another risk factor for stomach ulcers is regular use of aspirin. Again, stress appears to have an additive effect with aspirin in increasing the ulcer risk (Levenstein et al., 2015).

Early psychosomatic medicine's explanations for cancer as the result of repressed emotion, and the idea of a "cancer-prone" personality, are no longer widely accepted (Wellisch & Yager, 1983). However, there is growing evidence that responses to stressful life events may correspond to cancer development. For example, after divorce, separation, or death of a spouse, breast cancer incidence increases among women; pre-existing depression is a risk factor that appears to predate the onset of cancer. It has been suggested that the stress response, which will be discussed later in the book, is involved in this linkage (Antoni et al., 2006).

Interpersonal Systems: Couples and Families

Intimate relationships have a set of implicit rules. These are often the result of several years of either explicit or implicit negotiation and compromise. Once these rules are established, negative feedback often maintains them—activated to prevent small changes from escalating into larger ones that could transform or dissolve the relationship. For example, excessive alcohol use among those in a relationship both influences and is influenced by relationship dynamics. If a husband is escalating his alcohol use—perhaps as a result of stressors at work—his wife may attempt to counter his alcohol use by providing more direct attention to him or engaging him in activities such as going to the movies, socializing in non-alcohol-related settings, or even sexual activity (Skoyen, Kogan, Novack, & Butler, 2013). The importance of these dynamics in alcohol use is reflected by the finding that an evidence-based approach to treating someone with an alcohol abuse problem in a relationship is conjoint relationship therapy (O'Farrell & Fals-Stewart, 2003).

While alcohol abuse patterns among women have not been as well studied, there are suggestions that women who are increasing their alcohol use also experience relationship problems and that drinking is associated with positive expectations for intimacy. In otherwise emotionally "barren" relationships, drinking may be a way to reduce emotional distress and increase emotional expression. Importantly, treating women with alcohol problems would ideally include attention to relationship dynamics and trying to find more healthy ways to develop emotional closeness and expressiveness (Kelly, Halford, & Young, 2002; Skoyen et al., 2013).

John and Julie Gottman, through their research into couples' patterns of interaction and dyadic relationship over multiple years, describe patterns of interaction that appear to be associated with increased physical distress. In managing conflict—particularly in a relationship—a not uncommon dynamic is the demand-withdraw interaction pattern. Gottman (2013) found that particularly in the first several years of marriage, men tend to find the emotion associated with conflict or potential conflict to be very uncomfortable in that it elicits strong physiological reactivity (increased heart rate as well as muscle tension). In order to manage this discomfort, men often will "stonewall" and shut down. This shutting down may take the form of leaving the room, appearing to be minimally engaged while actually not being engaged at all ("Yes, dear"), and waiting for an opportune moment to end the exchange.

A pattern of suppression where one spouse attempts to be outwardly supportive while exerting considerable emotional energy to avoid appearing distressed (smiling through gritted teeth) may be experienced as demeaning or intrusive. Skoyen and colleagues (2013) note that this approach may actually backfire. This is particularly likely if the spouse attempting to be helpful comes across as a "parent" trying to placate her partner as a strategy for reducing drinking, smoking, or other health-risk behaviors. Research on men who had sustained a myocardial infarction suggested that this pattern often provoked anger in the ill partner and made him less open to recommended changes in diet and activity level (Carter, 1984). By contrast, when observing a spouse drinking or overeating, a positive response that is experienced as supportive but not controlling ("Looks like you had a rough day today"), without any criticism or mention of the health-related behavior, will often preempt this cycle (Skoyen et al., 2013).

The Mesosystem—Cultural Values and Religion

Mesosystems transmit information from the larger culture, including values, rituals, and expectations for behavior. For example, religious beliefs and cultural expectations about one's responsibilities to others are transmitted by parent to children. Given that this transmission begins before children have language, these family-mediated cultural dimensions are often unquestioned—they are simply the way that the world is (Searight, 1999).

Multiple studies have found that various health risks seem to be reduced among persons who are actively involved in a community of faith such as a church, synagogue, mosque, or Buddhist temple. While spiritual aspects may play a significant role in longevity, these dimensions have been difficult to study. One exception has been the research on prayer and its health benefits—nearly all of which has been conducted with Christian populations. Regular prayer appears to be associated with decreased risk of congestive heart failure and pneumonia, as well as better mental health. In terms of health benefits associated with religious involvement, positive effects have been found for immune functioning, heart surgery recovery, hypertension, and major depressive disorder (Powell, Shahabi, & Thoresen, 2003). Some studies have also found a positive linear relationship between the degree of religious involvement—frequency of church attendance—and health status (Strawbridge, Cohen, Shema, & Kaplan, 1997). While certainly not negating the spiritual dimensions, lifestyle and social factors do appear to mediate the relationship between religious involvement and health, including diminished alcohol use (particularly among men), reduced smoking, and greater marital satisfaction (Strawbridge et al., 1997).

Macrosystems

Communities

Social epidemiology, a relatively recent subfield of epidemiology that will be discussed further in the next chapter, examines large-scale social factors such as residential segregation, income, and governmental support programs and their association with health and illness. For example, there is reasonable evidence that the rise of no-smoking ordinances for work settings (Fichtenberg & Glantz, 2002) and other public places has been associated with population-level reductions in smoking among high-risk groups such as pregnant women (Nguyen, Von Kohorn, Schulman-Green, & Colson, 2012) and has increased the number of attempts to quit smoking in the population as a whole (Albers, Siegel, Chen, Biener, & Rigotti, 2007).

While perhaps intuitively obvious, the community in which one resides can be a force for or against health promotion. Researchers have found that in neighborhoods that were more pedestrian friendly and in which residents had access to exercise facilities, people were less likely to be overweight or obese and more likely to engage in regular physical activity (Brownson et al., 2000). Geographic features associated with increased physical activity include access to community walking trails and gyms as well as outdoor settings perceived as physically safe. Among elderly residents, higher neighborhood crime was associated with greater physical inactivity. In neighborhoods perceived as safe, older residents were twice as likely to be physically active (Brownson et al., 2001).

Changes in National Politics and Economics

In late 1991, the Soviet Union broke up into 15 separate states. The Soviet economy was based upon communism, with government ownership of most factories and farms. This system was associated with an almost complete absence of unemployment as well as job security. The dissolution of the Soviet Union was associated with major changes in health status.

In Russia, over the past 25 to 30 years, life expectancy actually declined and is now slowly returning to the levels it reached under communism. In 1965, the average life expectancy in Russia was 72 years. Between 1987 and 1994, life expectancy dropped substantially. In 1992, Russians' average life expectancy was 56 years. Beginning in 1994, this trend began to reverse (Cockerham, 2015; Leon et al., 1997). By 2010, life expectancies were rising again, with an average of 63 years. The major demographic group that experienced an increase in early deaths was middle-aged adults. Alcohol consumption has been cited as a significant cause of the increased mortality among this group of Russians (Shkolnikov & Nemtsov, 1997; Shkolnikov, McKee, & Leon, 2001). Within this group of middle-aged adults, men who were manual laborers, and thus most likely to be affected by economic changes, were the population subgroup with the greatest overall mortality (Cockerham, 1997). Factors that have been cited for this decline include economic instability, increased rates of tobacco and alcohol use, deteriorating nutrition with increasing consumption of high-fat food, depression, and a less accessible health care system (Notzon et al., 1998). Additionally, larger-scale social factors included increased unemployment, job turnover, increased crime, and increased income inequality (Walberg, McKee, Shkolinov, Chenet, & Leon, 1998).

In the early 1990s, a new, puzzling, mental health condition began to affect Japan's young adults. Hikikomori is a pattern of extreme social withdrawal in which young adults confine themselves to their bedrooms in the family home and refuse all social, educational, and work-related contact (Saito & Angles, 2013; Teo, 2010). This refusal typically extends to family members as well. It is common for mothers of these young adults to leave a tray of food outside the bedroom door each day. These young adults will not even leave their room to have dinner with the family or leave home for normal recreational activities. They spend a great deal of time online and typically sleep during the day and are awake at night. In a collectivist culture such as Japan, the actions of an individual reflect on their families. Their presence would be an embarrassment to the family, and recognizing the shame that they bring upon others, young adults with Hikikomori make themselves invisible. These young adults, incarcerated in their rooms, have often completed high school but not gone further with their education or career. Others have dropped out of college. It is estimated that in Japan, among adults between 20 and 40, there are at least 600,000 cases of Hikikomori (Koyama et al., 2010). Many Japanese mental health professionals point to the fact that reports of Hikikomori began in the 1990s—a time in which Japan began undergoing significant economic turmoil. While Japan's economy had demonstrated strong economic growth beginning in 1950, the economy essentially collapsed in the early 1990s. Real estate and stock prices became greatly inflated; then their value declined markedly in a short period of time. Between 1975 and 2010, the manufacturing economy in Japan shrunk considerably. There has also been an increase in irregular employees (part-time or temporary workers). In 1991, the figure was reportedly 20 percent, and almost 35 percent by 2010 (Suwa & Suzuki, 2013). This change reflects shifts in the work world from manufacturing to information-oriented fields. When taken together, larger economic factors intensified competition for jobs among young adults and created a much greater sense of financial insecurity for the future.

Changes in policy and accompanying legislation also impact the health of US citizens. While the United States may have one of the most sophisticated health care systems in the world, it also has a greater percentage of the population that does not receive basic preventive care. The systems used to pay for health care are likely to play a major role in this difference. Countries with universal coverage (typically a single government-sponsored health insurance plan that covers all citizens), including Canada, Great Britain, and even the relatively economically poor Caribbean nation of Cuba, have lower rates of fetal mortality and higher rates of vaccination among their citizens (World Health Organization, 2010).

Beyond Macrosystems: Our Flat World— International Borders Dissolve

Recent globalization is changing patterns of disease transmission as well as health care. As Friedman (2007) points out, we do indeed live in a flat world. This flat world includes countries that have not eradicated many illnesses, such as tuberculosis or measles, and also may be the site of new viruses that are often transmitted from animals to humans.

Recent infectious disease epidemics have often been initiated by migration associated with war and poverty. Current warfare and economic stressors in the Middle East and Africa have created a large population of refugees—the biggest since World War II. Present-day Europe has become a major center for financial and war-related refugees from the Middle East and Africa. In contrast to years past, many of these refugees are using cellular phones, geographic positioning systems, and more modern forms of transportation such as speedboats to help them reach countries such as Germany, France, and Sweden. This surge in migration is also associated with diseases that have been generally eradicated or are under control in the West being reintroduced by refugees from parts of the world where these conditions still are relatively common. Diseases transmitted via vectors (mosquitoes, rats, birds) typically found in Asian countries have appeared in southern Europe. Conditions such as cholera may also be rising, expedited by the less-than-optimal sanitation and crowded conditions of many refugee sites, such as "the Jungle" in Calais in Northern France. An excerpt from a recent news account described the site:

> I see why it's called the Jungle.
>
> This refugee camp in Calais is a sprawl of hundreds of flimsy tents, plywood shacks and ramshackle shelters made of tarp, jammed together atop sand dunes next to the English Channel. It houses about 6,000 Afghans, Sudanese, Iraqis, Iranians and other men who fled terror in their homelands only to find reluctance and indifference here in France.
>
> Men bathe at water taps next to a row of battered chemical toilets. Tattered laundry flutters in the breeze. Large gray rats scurry among the tents, while dead rodents litter the sand nearby.
>
> The Jungle, often described as one of the worst refugee camps in France, is primitive and squalid. Charred timbers show where a fire blazed in May after a dispute broke out among the different nationalities—angry, frustrated and forced to co-exist in this bleak 90-acre space. (Shankland, 2016)

While writing an early draft of this section, in mid-July 2016, a news story announced that the first US resident had died of the Zika virus in Utah. While the news story kept the identity of the deceased patient anonymous, the implication was that the person had been infected during travel outside the United States.

Our world is flat in other ways too—many Americans, because of rising prescription costs, buy their medications online from other countries. While writing this book, I received a notice in the mail for discounted prescription medication from a company in Canada. The company contrasted its low prices for common prescription medications for high blood pressure, depression, type 2 diabetes, and other conditions with the significantly higher prices charged in the United States.

In reading the material more carefully, I learned that if I ordered medication through this Canadian company, my pills would actually be manufactured and sent from India. While the practice is discouraged and possibly illegal, the cost of many medications could be 75 percent less if imported from India compared with being purchased here in the United States. Some states have even encouraged their citizens to use international pharmacies to keep subsidized insurance costs down (Luthra, 2018).

Finally, US citizens needing particular types of surgery, including organ transplants, have been increasingly traveling to other countries to have these procedures done more quickly and at a fraction of the cost of the operation in the United States. In 2007, Michael Shopen, an American man, traveled to Belgium for hip replacement surgery. While the procedure would have cost about $100,000 in the United States and was not going to be covered by his health insurance, the total cost of treatment abroad, including medications, physician fees, and round-trip airfare to and from Belgium, was $13,660 (Rosenthal, 2013). A heart bypass operation costing $144,000 in the United States can be had for $25,000 in Costa Rica and slightly more than $5,000 in India. Lap band gastroplasty ("stomach stapling"—often used for weight loss), while costing $30,000 in the United States, is only $3,000 in India and $6,500 in Mexico (MediConnect, 2018).

Putting It Together: Ms. Ramirez

Ms. Ramirez, a 47-year-old Hispanic female, is seen at her local neighborhood clinic. She has been experiencing some numbness and tingling in her hands and feet; Ms. Ramirez also reports that her vision is not as good as it once was. About five years ago, Ms. Ramirez was diagnosed with type 2 diabetes. Her mother also had type 2 diabetes and actually had a leg amputated because of poor diabetic control and other complications of the disease. Today, laboratory tests suggest that Ms. Ramirez's diabetes is under very poor control. It is likely that her symptoms of numbness, tingling, and difficulty with vision are the result of uncontrolled diabetes.

When asked how often she checks for blood sugar at home, Ms. Ramirez says, "Well, I used to do it all the time, but I heard that checking too much will make your fingers go numb and even turn black. I did not have any problems with my sugar until I saw my cousin killed by getting hit by a car—right in front of me. I was just crying and wailing for a long time. Two weeks later I went to the doctor, who told me my sugars were high. That terrible shock of seeing my cousin killed—it affected my whole body and gave me diabetes."

When asked about her diet, Ms. Ramirez indicates that her husband is very particular about what he eats, and she feels that she should eat the same as he does. "I probably do eat a lot of things I shouldn't." The couple also has two children ages 10 and 12.

Ms. Ramirez had previously been prescribed medication for diabetes as well as high blood pressure. She indicates that she lost her job about eight months ago and cannot afford to buy health insurance through the government ("Obamacare") online insurance exchange. Upon further questioning, she reports that she has been taking medicinal tea that was recommended by a curandera, an indigenous

TABLE 1.1. Ms. Ramirez: A Biopsychosocial Systems Perspective

Level of the Biopsychosocial Model	Health Risk Factors
Biological—Genetic	Genetic diathesis for type 2 diabetes
Biological—Pathophysiology	Hyperglycemia (excess blood sugar); insulin resistance
Individual: Physical Symptoms	Blurred vision; numbness and tingling in hands and feet
Individual: Psychological	Depression; external locus of control; fatalism
Family	Minimal support from husband; dietary habits set by husband
Cultural	Etiology of diabetes: "susto"—a frightening experience Treatment—herbal tea from curandera
Community	Health care access is challenging
National and State Policy	Does not have health insurance despite government mandate

healer, in the community. When the physician raises the possible need for initiating insulin, Ms. Ramirez becomes frightened and agitated. "Nooo way! When my mother started taking that insulin, she got worse—it was soon after she started that medicine that she had to have her leg amputated."

Summary and the Way Forward

While the emphasis in clinically oriented health psychology has been on individual health risks, diagnosis, and treatment, each of us is embedded in a much larger matrix consisting of interpersonal relationships, culture, and economic and political forces. Focusing on individual health as a set of coping skills, traits, biological predispositions, and values artificially encapsulates us in a bubble, which, in reality, is illusory. While this book will certainly include attention to individual psychosocial dimensions of health, each chapter includes attention to the impact of larger systems—including family, culture, history, politics, and economics—on well-being. Several of the early chapters focus almost exclusively on larger systems issues such as population epidemiology and the health care system in the United States and internationally. As we continue through the book to topics that are more individually focused, such as stress and pain, each chapter will include attention to economic, cultural, and/or political dimensions. It is hoped that after finishing the book, you will have greater knowledge of the psychosocial aspects of health but also, as a citizen and/or professional, that you will appreciate the role of larger systems on individual health and illness.

CHAPTER 2

Research in Health and Behavior
Epidemiology and Beyond

The prevalence of and factors associated with disease may not, at first glance, seem very exciting. However, for any of you who like a good mystery story, the field of epidemiology is full of them. Watching a new disease arise—seemingly out of nowhere—and observing what geographic areas and which social groups are affected are all part of the epidemiologist's work. "Catching the bad guy" in this context means finding out the cause of the illness—usually a virus or bacteria—developing a model of its transmission, and then trying to stop the disease from continuing to spread. Even before there was an understanding of bacteria, viruses, and various parasites, early public health observers recognized that people sharing the same living space, water supply, and/or food sources were often the ones that became ill.

Several new cases of persons with severe cramps and diarrhea appear in the local hospital's emergency room. They are different in many respects—children, young adults, older adults, male and female. However, the epidemiologist is looking for a commonality, something that the patients all have in common. Laboratory tests indicate that everyone with this pattern of symptoms tests positive for a strain of the bacterium E. (Escherichia) coli. This bacterium is often associated with food or occurs when food handlers are not practicing good hygiene.

However, we consume food from multiple sources—the lettuce that we didn't wash before making last night's salad, the fast food restaurant across town, the university cafeteria, the food truck outside your workplace, and that crab dip from your friend's party last night. What did all of those suddenly sick people share in terms of the food they consumed? As some of the examples below will illustrate, the source of an E. coli outbreak can be undercooked meat, food that is left sitting at room temperature for too long, or kitchen utensils that have not been washed completely.

Epidemiology: An Overview

Probably the most common reason to conduct epidemiological research is to determine the cause of an illness. However, epidemiological studies have also been useful in determining the safety of medication; the benefits of various treatments, including surgeries; the effects of diet on long-term health; and the risks associated with specific behaviors such as consuming alcohol, smoking cigarettes, or extended use of street drugs. Finally, when new, usually large-scale interventions or health education campaigns are introduced, epidemiologists can determine whether these have population-wide and long-term benefits.

From reading the newspaper, many of you are likely familiar with outbreaks of food-borne illness that have occurred in your hometown. Typically, the local emergency room sees a very large number of patients with common gastrointestinal symptoms such as nausea, vomiting, diarrhea, and so on. While in the past, the source of a pathogen could be determined (water from an unclean source), our understanding of infectious disease during the past century has resulted in the ability to isolate the specific bacterium or virus involved. In the United States, many food-borne pathogens are attributable to organisms such as salmonella found in the hamburger from a fast food restaurant or grocery store. Other outbreaks may occur in settings such as daycare centers. In these settings, contamination with fecal material containing the protozoan *Giardia lambia* is often responsible. *Giardia* may be transmitted through food by childcare workers who do not adequately wash their hands after changing infants and preparing children's food. Another setting for transmission of *Giardia* is wading pools in which toddlers in diapers share the same water.

Finding the cause of new or unexpected infectious diseases is necessary for preventing further outbreaks. Epidemiology is, indeed, detective work. Today, up to half of all food purchases occur in restaurant settings. Nearly 50 percent of food-borne illnesses are traced to restaurants. Eating at fast food restaurants five or more times a week elevates the risk of food-borne illness by 30 to 40 percent. This pattern was not found for "full-service" restaurants. Foods that place patrons at greater risk of illness include eggs, poultry, and beef—particularly "rare" beef (Angulo & Jones, 2006). The epidemiologist looks for possible clues to the cause of new outbreaks of established diseases or, on rare occasions, discovers completely new syndromes, such as a number of emerging infections in the United States, including the Zika virus.

Food-Borne Illness: Two Examples

In 2013, Fayetteville, North Carolina, reported an outbreak of 103 cases of salmonellosis—food poisoning caused by the bacteria salmonella (Goetz, 2013). Medical officials concluded that all of those affected had eaten at a local Holiday Inn. However, since the Holiday Inn had three different dining facilities, the precise source of transmission was still not available. Eventually it was determined that the dishwasher was not working properly, and the water was not of an appropriate temperature. Additionally, remnants of food remained on apparently "clean" plates. Once the dishwasher was repaired, there were no further episodes of the disease.

On August 11, 2013, 81 people in Minneapolis developed salmonellosis and reported diarrhea, abdominal cramps, and fever. While health officials suspected food-borne illness, the source was not immediately obvious. However, the disease only seemed to affect persons who had attended a street fair for Ecuadorian Independence Day. Eventually it was determined that the majority of those who became ill had consumed undercooked guinea pig—a traditional food in Ecuador. Others attending the festival fell ill as a result of cross-contamination (Gillespie, 2013).

Example: Sexually Transmitted Diseases

Transmission of infectious disease often follows a triangle model in which there is a host that harbors the disease, an agent causing the disease, and an environment that supports disease transmission. Additionally, time is an important factor, since in many cases disease transmission from an infected individual only occurs for a limited duration (Merrill, 2016). In some instances, the microorganism is excreted from the individual's system; in other cases, the pathogen is effectively removed through treatment. When the disease is highly infectious and treatment is available, public health officials attempt to locate and treat all exposed persons as quickly as possible to reduce the spread of the illness.

In 1996, there was an outbreak of syphilis among affluent teenagers in Conyers, Georgia, an Atlanta suburb in Rockdale County. Syphilis is a relatively low-prevalence sexually transmitted disease—particularly among young women. Among females ages 14 to 19, other sexually transmitted diseases are much more common, including human papillomavirus (29.5 percent), chlamydia (7.1 percent), and gonorrhea (2.5 percent) (Forhan et al., 2009). About 90 percent of all syphilis cases are males. In the case of the Conyers teenagers, nurses at the local public health department were caught off guard, since syphilis is most common among persons with histories of multiple sexual partners. However, in Rockdale County, the teenagers exposed to syphilis were as young as 13, with those infected ranging from 13 to 17 years old.

The local health department engaged in a process called contact tracing. Physicians are required by law to report positive sexually transmitted disease test results to the local health department. The goal of contact tracing is to prevent the spread of infection. Patients testing positive for syphilis are interviewed in detail about their sexual contacts. They are asked specifically about the identities of their sexual partners as well as anyone else believed to have been sexually active with any of their partners. The goal of contact tracing is not to be punitive but to treat as many people as possible to prevent the spread of the disease.

In Rockdale County, through contact tracing, a clear pattern emerged in that there were four to six females—some of whom were under the age of 16—who had a large number of slightly older males as sexual partners (Goodman & Goodman, 1999). Typically, sexual intercourse was preceded by use of marijuana and/or alcohol. Often, the sex was public and communal, and the adolescent girls would have multiple partners in sequence and simultaneously. By the end, it was determined that more than 200 young people had been exposed to syphilis.

In addition to alcohol and drugs, there were several other risk factors present. Parental oversight and monitoring was often absent. The teenagers often met in homes after school where the parents worked late. Their upper-middle-class social status gave them ready access to money for marijuana and alcohol. Among the core group of teenage girls who participated regularly, interviewers concluded that poor self-esteem and possibly depression were present. These personality and social factors have been associated with higher-risk sexual activities.

The epidemiological detective work in Rockdale County began with the local health department noting that a sexually transmitted disease—syphilis—was occurring in an atypical population. As the number of adolescents appearing for sexually transmitted disease testing increased, the department recognized that a significant and unusual pattern of sexual activity was occurring. Through contact tracing and in-depth interviews, the picture of high-risk sexual behavior associated with the syphilis reports became clearer. In addition, as more information was gathered, risk factors such as the absence of parental oversight and the adolescents' desire to "fit in" (Rothenberg et al., 1998) became evident, as did the absence of other structured and supervised activities for adolescents in the community.

Epidemiology: Key Concepts and Terminology

Epidemiologists study the prevalence, incidence, and factors associated with a disease. Prevalence refers to the number of cases (typically expressed as a percentage) at a point in time; for example, "1 of 68 or 14.6 per 1,000 children in the United States currently have been diagnosed with autism spectrum disorder" is a statement of prevalence (Centers for Disease Control, 2016a). The finding that during a 12-month period, 20 percent of US high school–age females meet criteria for major depressive disorder is also a prevalence statement (National Institute of Mental Health, 2018).

Incidence refers to the number of new cases of the disease in a population during a specific time period. This period is often expressed as months or years. It's common to hear about the incidence of flu cases each fall and winter. An example of incidence is a report of increased diagnoses of narcolepsy (a sleep disorder characterized by an overwhelming and sudden urge to sleep during times of wakefulness) from 2004 to 2013 among military personnel—the overall increase was from 14.6 to 27.3 cases per 100,000 person-years during this time (Lee & Radin, 2016). Incidence figures do not include the reasons for increases or decreases in disease over time, but marked changes in incidence typically precipitate a search for possible underlying reasons for the variation.

Exposure refers to any specific factor associated with an outcome (typically a disease). Exposures are usually dimensions of the environment that are believed to be causal agents of the disease. However, it may also refer to any factor that shows a systematic increase or decrease in a specific outcome. For example, exposure to coal dust increases the likelihood of respiratory disease. A medication such as an antibiotic may be associated with a decrease in bacterial growth.

Epidemiology differs from clinical medicine or clinical mental health treatment in that the focus is on populations rather than individuals. The population may range from all residents of the United States or a specific state or county. Additionally, populations may be defined by age (e.g., individuals from ages 15 to 64 years), sex, or other specific feature (e.g., all women who used hormone replacement therapy between 1970 and 1990).

In epidemiology, cause-effect relationships are very difficult to establish with certainty. There are multiple reasons for this; however, a major limitation is that epidemiological research occurs in the "real world" during a point in time, not in a laboratory. As a result, there are many factors that cannot be controlled but that may interact with the exposure and/or disease. Instead of speaking of causes, epidemiologists typically refer to "risk factors"—any variable or dimension that is associated with increased likelihood of the disease. For example, hours of exposure to ultraviolet light at a tanning studio is associated with an outcome such as skin cancer.

While conventional behavioral science statistics such as analyses of variance and correlations as well as multiple regression and path analysis are used in studying health and behavior, epidemiology relies heavily upon two types of statistics—relative risk and the odds ratio. Relative risk provides information about the ratio of risk of disease in those exposed to a risk factor compared with those who were not exposed to that risk factor. Relative risks are often used for treatment studies and in studies where groups of individuals are followed over time. For example, in the Framingham study, over a 30-year period, the relative risk of developing type 2 diabetes increased from 1.37 in the 1980s to 1.81 in 2000 (Abraham, Pencina, Pencina, & Fox, 2015).

The odds ratio is a measure of the degree of association between exposure and an outcome—typically a disease (Szumilas, 2010). Odds ratios express the odds that an outcome is associated with an exposure relative to the odds of that outcome occurring without the exposure (Szumilas, 2010). Results are interpreted as follows: OR = 1, the exposure has no impact on the odds of the outcome; OR > 1, an exposure is associated with increased odds of the outcome; OR < 1, an exposure is associated with lower odds of the outcome (Szumilas, 2010). For example, the likelihood of developing an unusual type of cancer, mesothelioma, is more likely among those who worked with asbestos than those who did not.

When results in epidemiological studies or treatment are presented in the popular media, the emphasis is on relative risk. For example, the incidence of liver disease in the general population is 0.2 percent per year for men and .03 percent per year for women. Among men, consuming 14 to 27 drinks per week increased the risk by two (0.4 percent), and for women there was close to a fourfold increase in risk (0.12 percent) (Becker et al., 1996). As is evident from this example, a large relative risk is often associated with a very small increase in absolute risk.

However, reliance on relative risk is often confusing to the public. When relative risks are presented in the news, the description frequently makes it sound as if it is much more likely that a person can contract a particular illness from a specific source than is actually the case. For example, if a particular disease affects 4 out of 1,000 people, and a particular treatment or lifestyle change reduces the risk by 50 percent, the absolute risk reduction is 2 out of 1,000. Given that the absolute risk of the disease was low in the first place, the reduction associated with treatment appears almost minuscule.

Epidemiological research often involves very large samples. With larger samples, a relatively small difference between groups may be statistically significant. The use of inferential statistics has been criticized by clinicians as well as public health officials, because while there may be a difference between two groups, the absolute magnitude of difference may be quite small.

Risk Factors and the Diathesis-Stress Model

Whenever there is an in-depth discussion about heart disease, obesity, or type 2 diabetes, it is common to hear about risk factors for illness. Smoking is a risk factor for lung cancer, obesity a risk factor for type 2 diabetes, high cholesterol a risk factor for heart attacks. What does this actually mean? A risk factor is something that is significantly more common among persons who have that particular illness.

It can be an exposure but also could be a pre-existing biological or psychological diathesis. Importantly, a risk factor does not necessarily cause a disease; it is simply more common among persons who have that particular health condition. For example, men are much more likely to develop a condition called hemophilia, where the blood does not clot. In many cases, the gene for hemophilia is carried on the male sex chromosome. However, it would be incorrect to say that being male causes hemophilia—being male does increase the risk of having the condition.

Within psychology and psychiatry, there is ongoing debate on the extent to which biology (nature) versus the environment (nurture) determines behavior. As suggested by the biopsychosocial model, these two dimensions interact with individuals having a biological predisposition for a particular characteristic that is elicited by the environment. Additionally, for those illnesses that are chronic or ongoing, the environment can affect the condition's severity and course. A good example of this is the association between schizophrenia—a condition in which a biological predisposition is necessary to develop the condition—and the patient's family climate. While Engel recognized that environmental factors could elicit psychotic symptoms in the presence of a predisposition to schizophrenia, at the time of his writing, relatively little was known about the explicit environmental factors associated with the condition. Among persons who develop schizophrenia, the severity and frequency of symptoms, even when treated with medication, can be influenced by their family environment. Young adults with schizophrenia who return from the hospital to environments high in expressed emotion, a pattern of interpersonal conflict, and criticism are much more likely to have relapses of symptoms that require hospitalization (Hooley, 2007).

A predisposition can also be a historical pattern that illness shows over time. Major depressive disorder and other psychiatric conditions are not diagnosed until the threshold in the form of a specific number of symptoms—five out of a possible nine for two weeks' duration—has been reached. In modeling major depressive disorder from a diathesis stress perspective, it was found that recurrence of the condition depended upon the number of past episodes, and the likelihood of remission (the condition no longer being present) was heavily influenced by the duration of past depressive episodes (Bulloch, Williams, Lavorato, & Patten, 2014). These past patterns of symptoms can be considered risk factors for future episodes of major depression.

Risk factors may also include a psychological diathesis example: the type A personality (Friedman & Rosenman, 1959; Merrill, 2016), particularly those individuals with a high level of free-floating hostility, appears to be at greater risk for heart disease and high blood pressure. Another less well-known personality style that is associated with disease is the type D, who tends to be socially withdrawn, ruminative, worried, and depressed. These type D characteristics are also a risk factor for heart disease (Emons, Meijer, & Denollet, 2007; Merrill, 2016). Individuals with generally consistent positive characteristics, such as being flexible, maintaining composure, being curious, and not hanging on to grudges tend to show reduced risk and have been labeled "hardy type A's" (Kobasa, Maddi, & Kahn, 1982). While personality may be thought of as something formed by environment—particularly family experiences—research by Costa and McCrae (1992) and Eysenck (2017) suggests broad personality features such as extraversion, conscientiousness, social innovation, and a tendency toward worry and rumination have a hereditary basis (Engler, 2013).

Environmental stressors may include a wide range of factors, including physical exposures such as sunlight or lead or ingesting exposures such as smoking cigarettes or drinking alcohol. As illustrated by the young adolescents of Rockdale County, behavioral choices can bring one into contact with exposures such as sexually transmitted diseases. Similarly, exposing children who are predisposed to asthma to secondhand cigarette smoke increases the length and severity of asthmatic episodes (Hollenbach, Schifano, Hammel, & Cloutier, 2017).

However, while the idea that we have control over our health through our lifestyle is certainly appealing, there are critics of this view who believe overemphasis on lifestyle is a form of risk reduction. Our genetic makeup places some limitations on our ability to change our risks. For example, it is estimated that the heritability of body mass index (a figure used to classify persons as overweight or obese) is about 40 percent. Similarly, abnormal glucose tolerance, a precursor to type 2 diabetes, has a heritability of 61 percent (Poulsen, Kyvik, Vaag, & Beck-Nielsen, 1999). Serum cholesterol's heritability is approximately 37 percent (Smith et al., 1998).

As these examples illustrate, the extent to which disease is heritable varies widely. It is estimated that, overall, cancer's heritability is 15 to 30 percent, with particularly high heritability for skin melanoma at 56 percent (Lichtenstein et al., 2000; Mucci et al., 2016). However, some subtypes of breast cancer in women may be highly heritable, with genetics accounting for 80 percent of the likelihood that women will develop the condition. Genetic testing is useful in helping women determine their prognosis for breast cancer. In some instances, when risks are very high, a prophylactic (preventive) mastectomy (surgical procedure to remove the breasts) is a reasonable treatment.

However, it is estimated that the proportion of cancer cases linked to avoidable risk factors is as follows: 30 percent for tobacco, 20 to 50 percent for diet, 10 to 20 percent for infection, 5 to 7 percent for ionizing and ultraviolet light exposure, 4 percent for the year of occupational exposures (e.g., asbestos, pesticide), and 1 to 5 percent for pollution (Doll, 1998; Merrill, 2016).

Practical Versus Statistical Significance: Prevalence, Base Rates, and Health Screening Tests

In the social sciences, inferential statistics are widely used. The possibility of differences between an experimental and control group on some dimension is assessed through statistical procedures such as analysis of variance (ANOVA) and t-tests. The degree of association between variables is determined through correlation and regression analyses. A significant difference between groups or significant association occurs when we reject the null hypothesis of little difference or no association. In doing so, we establish a probability level such as .05, indicating that the probability that we have incorrectly rejected the null hypothesis is 5/100 or 1/20.

As samples increase in size, a very small difference between one group and another may be statistically significant, but the magnitude of difference can be quite small. These statistically significant differences may have no practical meaning. A review of studies of treating chronic back pain with exercise found that 18 of the studies indicated a positive effect for exercise. However, of these, only seven reports demonstrated differences that were clinically meaningful (Keller, Hayden, Bombardier, & van Tulder, 2007).

Health screening and even specific medical laboratory tests often yield ambiguous findings. When a medical test or screening measure indicates that a person has a condition that is not confirmed by subsequent investigations, this is termed a false positive. False positives occur when patients are told they have a condition or a probable indicator of the condition when that disease is, in reality, not present. Additionally, there are often subgroups within a population that may be at higher or lower risk for a particular condition.

As more dependent variables are added, the probability of finding an effect increases, but so does the likelihood of a false positive (saying the difference exists when it does not) (Simmons, Nelson, & Simonsohn, 2011). Clinically, this also occurs with patients with vague physical complaints in which the physician responds by ordering a panel of laboratory tests. Given the laws of probability, the more tests that are conducted, the greater the likelihood of finding a result that is statistically significantly different from what is considered "normal." For example, while there is a 5 percent chance of an abnormal test when one laboratory test is performed, this figure rises to 26 percent with 6 and 46 percent with 12 laboratory tests (Deyo, 2002b). As Deyo (2002b) facetiously notes, "The only normal person is someone who hasn't had enough tests" (p. 30). This issue has arisen in human genome research when testing for multiple genetic markers simultaneously (Fernando et al., 2004). A danger is that a difference may not be a true or meaningful difference but an artifact of running multiple statistical tests. Indeed, a clinical cascade process such as that described in Chapter 1 can occur in these circumstances. Several examples of issues in health screening are presented below.

Neurocognitive Disorder of Alzheimer's Type

The problem of mis-labeling a patient with a serious condition such as Alzheimer's dementia has arisen in multiple studies attempting to develop a screening test for early detection of the disorder. In diagnosing Alzheimer's disease, commonly used brain imaging procedures are not specific, and most diagnoses are based upon assessment of the patient's cognitive functioning. Anthony and colleagues (Anthony, LeResche, Niaz, von Korff, & Folstein, 1982) examined the ability of the Mini Mental Status Examination to detect Alzheimer's dementia. The Mini Mental Status is a brief, verbally administered test assessing attention, concentration, short-term memory, language, and visual spatial skills. The investigators found a false positive rate of 39 percent—meaning that the test concluded that nearly 40 percent of the time the person's score fell in the range associated with Alzheimer's dementia when the patient did not have the condition. It was noted that those in this false-positive group were disproportionately persons who had less than nine years of formal education and were over the age of 60 (Anthony et al., 1982).

Screening for Breast Cancer

When the base rate or prevalence of a condition is relatively low, medical tests are more likely to yield false positives. The frequency and meaning of false positive test results has been a source of contention in the debate about routine screening for breast cancer. While routine mammography (a type of X-ray of the breasts) for women is a standard preventive care recommendation, this guideline has been subject to some controversy. Mammograms are conducted to determine whether there are any unusual masses or high-density areas in breast tissue. At present, it is recommended that women ages 50 to 74 receive a screening mammogram every two years. While some women—particularly those with a history of breast cancer in the family—begin to receive regular mammograms at a younger age, the guideline is somewhat nonspecific about early screening, indicating only that the patient's values regarding specific benefits and harms (Nelson et al., 2009) should be considered.

The lifetime prevalence of breast cancer for women in the United States is approximately 12 to 13 percent. To reduce the death rate from breast cancer, it is important to detect masses that are in early stages and often not recognized in a physical exam—either by patient or by physician. It is estimated that mammography reduces deaths from breast cancer by 50 percent (Olsen & Gøtzsche, 2001). Mammography is generally fairly sensitive to the presence of breast cancer tumors. However, mammography also shows the presence of any unusual or structural abnormality within breast tissue.

A high percentage of abnormalities detected through mammography are false positives, meaning that post-mammography evaluation did not find evidence of a cancerous tumor. However, these negative findings are not without risk to the patient. Using a combination of clinical examination and mammography, rates of correct detection of breast cancer were 95 percent. Mammography alone was associated with a correct detection rate of 89 percent. The conclusion is that these screening tests are sensitive to breast cancer but unfortunately are not very specific. However, if a woman starts getting tested every year at age 40, the cumulative risk of having at least one false positive is 50 percent for mammography (Elmore et al., 1998) and 25 percent for a clinical breast exam performed by a health care professional.

A sizeable proportion of women with false positives experienced increased emotional stress and anxiety as well as sleep problems (Eddy, 1983). In some instances this life disruption lasted for up to 12 months after receiving the false positive result. Additionally, false positives result in surgical procedures, with women who do receive mammography 30 percent more likely to undergo surgery (Lerman et al., 1991; Montgomery & McCrone, 2010). For every single patient who avoids death from breast cancer, approximately 10 to 20 are treated unnecessarily as cancer patients and receive surgery, radiation, and/or chemotherapy. The reduction in death rate associated with mammography is small—an estimated 0.05 percent; it is difficult to quantitatively evaluate the benefit versus the risk of overtreatment and anxiety associated with false positives.

HIV Self-Testing

A common issue with HIV is that many of those who are positive for the condition are unaware of their health status. In addition, because of emotional discomfort and/or perceived stigma, many individuals at risk for the condition will not seek testing from their health care provider. HIV has a much lower prevalence rate in the general population than most forms of cancer. Early self-testing for HIV raised significant concerns, with 85 percent of those using the test failing to carry out the specific steps of testing correctly and 56 percent getting invalid results (Lee et al., 2007). There was also apprehension that among those who had relatively recently contracted the infection, testing would yield a false negative—providing an unwarranted level of security. The concern about false positives as well as the absence of immediate access to counseling in the case of a true positive further delayed the development and approval of HIV self-testing kits. While some forms of self-testing were available as early as 2005, the US Food and Drug Administration did not approve HIV home testing until July 2012. Currently marketed self-tests for HIV have low rates of both false positives and false negatives (Johnson et al., 2017).

Autism Spectrum Disorder

When a screening program is initiated, obtained prevalence rates are frequently much higher than the existing standard. Some have argued that the increased number of children diagnosed with autism spectrum disorder is an artifact of screening. Early studies found a very high rate of false positives when a screening measure for autism was completed by parents and a family physician. The most commonly used screen for autism is the Checklist for Autism in Toddlers (CHAT) (Baron-Cohen, Allen, & Gillberg, 1992). Items on the CHAT are answered "yes" or "no." Examples of items: for the physician (during the appointment), "Does the child make eye contact with you?" and, for parents, "Does your child take an interest in other children?" While the sensitivity of the scale was very high (95 percent), the specificity of the CHAT was low (38 percent). Therefore, if a child does indeed have autism, the screening measure would detect the condition. However, a number of children who did not demonstrate clear evidence of autism on follow-up were misclassified as autistic by the initial screen. Also of note is that those children who were false positives often demonstrated other developmental issues such as language disturbance (Baird et al., 2000).

Epidemiology: Types of Investigatory Designs

The types of questions that are asked by epidemiologists will lead to the general approach that they use for a study. If one is interested in questions about possible cause—"What causes bladder cancer?" or "Can the presence of more hiking trails in the community reduce the risk of cardiovascular disease?"—an analytic approach is used. If one simply wants to know how many cases of the condition exist, whether a condition is more common among men or women, or whether there is an association between the weekly consumption of fruits and vegetables and cases of bowel cancer, then a descriptive study is undertaken.

Occasionally, the epidemiologist is basically starting at ground zero. There are increased numbers of persons with a disease that is atypical for this demographic group or unusual in a particular geographic area. After determining the number of cases, the epidemiologist then begins looking for factors associated with the illness that discriminate between patients and non-patients.

Case Reports

Case reports are descriptions of disease or health risks in one or a small number of individuals. While typically not providing much quantitative information, case reports are useful when there is evidence of a new disease arising in a given population or the return of a disease that was thought to be eliminated. They are also useful for detecting drug side effects. A thoroughly presented case report can be of great value in educating medical students and practicing physicians (Vandenbroucke, 2001).

Case reports of emerging diseases are frequently published in the Centers for Disease Control's *Morbidity and Mortality Weekly Report* (MMWR). These case reports are also often listed on the Centers for Disease Control's website. One of the reasons for publishing these findings on small numbers of cases is to alert health care professionals about the possibility of a new disease and also to encourage both clinicians and public health specialists to report similar cases.

In 1981, the Centers for Disease Control's *Morbidity and Mortality Weekly Report* published a description of five cases of pneumocystis pneumonia—a serious infection associated with compromise of the immune system. The 1981 report suggested that the disease was acquired through sexual contact. Several case reports of men with an unusual type of skin cancer, Kaposi's sarcoma, accompanied by impaired immune system functioning were reported soon thereafter. By the end of the year, 159 cases of this new condition were reported in the United States. These were the early reported cases of the AIDS epidemic of the 1980s and 1990s.

Case reports are useful as "sentinels" of new diseases or the reoccurrence of conditions that were believed to be eradicated in the United States. As in the case of AIDS, these early reports signaled the spread of a new disease.

Cross-Sectional Studies

A cross-sectional design provides information about disease- or health-related characteristics in a specific population or subpopulation at one point in time. When a report tells us that the prevalence of schizophrenia in the general population is 1 percent, this is an example of cross-sectional information. Since the investigators are only collecting information at one point in time, this type of study is relatively easy to carry out. In a study of sleep disorders in cardiovascular disease, the investigators gathered data on a large sample of individuals who used polysomnography at home to measure sleep quality. In addition, data were obtained about the presence of cardiovascular problems, including histories of heart attack, heart bypass surgery, heart failure, or stroke (Shahar et al., 2001). Patients showing the highest levels of disordered breathing during sleep exhibited significantly higher rates of cardiovascular disease, with odds ratios ranging from 2.1 to 2.5.

In some cases, cross-sectional studies are repeated at regular intervals of multiple years. While the data may not all be obtained from the same individuals at each measurement point, these repeated cross-sectional studies do often provide information on changes in population health status over time. Not surprisingly, body mass index, often used as a measure of obesity, has become larger at each measurement point in the past several decades for both adults and children (Flegal & Troiano, 2000).

While useful, and from a research point of view relatively easy to carry out, cross-sectional designs do not provide information about changes in rates of developing a particular disease. It is also not possible to say whether a disease occurred after exposure or vice versa. In cross-sectional studies, variables are measured at a given point in time. While useful in describing associations, this design does not permit a delineation of cause-effect relationships. Additionally, acute illnesses, such as newly emerging infections, are likely to be underestimated, and chronic illnesses such as obesity are overestimated in cross-sectional studies. Cross-sectional studies do permit the examination of multiple exposures at one point in time.

Case-Control Studies

Case-control studies are typically retrospective and used to determine the exposures associated with a particular outcome. Several steps are necessary for a good case-control study. First, the study identifies some cases—these are individuals with the condition—as well as a group of controls. Ideally, the controls are similar to cases in all respects except that they do not have the outcome of interest, which is typically a disease. Next, the investigator examines whether the cases and controls differ on hypothesized causes. Exposure rates of cases are compared with those of the controls (in order to reduce bias, it is recommended that the person who is gathering the data on risk factors—particularly if it involves interviewing patients—be unaware of the disease status) (Lewallen & Courtright, 1998). One problem that arises with case-control studies involving interviews is that of participant bias, and unless there is a blinded process, an interviewer can inadvertently contribute to distorted recall (e.g., "Are you absolutely sure that you did not drink the well water during this time period?"). When we have a particular health condition, it is normal for us to look backward and try to find a cause. Additionally, factors such as social stigma can contribute to distorted reports of exposures. For example, if women who gave birth to a child with significant physical or cognitive problems are queried about their alcohol use during pregnancy, it is understandable that they may underreport their alcohol consumption (Merrill, 2016).

Case-control studies are generally fairly efficient, and findings can be obtained quickly. They are also useful for relatively rare diseases (Lewallen & Courtright, 1998). It is important to control for possible confounds—these are exposures that are also associated with the outcome but are not unique to the outcome. Case-control studies are particularly useful in trying to isolate causes of relatively rare conditions. The odds ratio that is computed provides information about whether the exposure of interest was over- or underrepresented in those who developed the disease versus those who did not. While cause-effect relationships are often inferred from case-control studies, the strength of the association is not as valid or well-established as in a cohort design. Additionally, the case-control study, like the cross-sectional study, does not provide direct information about changes in the incidence of the disease over time.

Conceptually, a case-control model was employed in the food-poisoning study involving undercooked guinea pig described earlier in this chapter. The investigators initially learned that all of those affected had attended the Ecuadorian street festival. A case-control study would have compared those who ate at particular vendors with those who did not. Typically, the case and the control should have the same characteristics in terms of age and gender as well as other variables such as health status. Several examples of historically significant case-control studies are summarized below.

The "Radium Girls"

In the early 1920s, a group of young women all working in the same setting began losing their teeth, developed multiple painful sores in their mouths, and became increasingly weak due to profound anemia; some also developed a large, disfiguring tumor on their chins. Soon the women began dying. It wasn't until some years later when one of the deceased was exhumed that the cause of this mysterious syndrome was found.

During World War I, it became apparent that there was a need for sturdy watches that could be read in the dark. German scientists had developed a luminous paint by mixing in radium. Because of their availability and their well-developed fine-motor skills, teenage and young adult women were hired to paint luminous dials on watches and clocks. After work hours, some of the young women would paint their fingernails with the luminous paint (Blum, 2011). Soon, however, problems arose. In the mid-1920s, scientists began to study this syndrome, and some concluded that it was due to radium exposure. There were also some reports from radiologists of sickness and losing fingers that some attributed to their unprotected work with X-rays. The original reports of harm were suppressed by the owner of the company where the women worked. However, at the same time, there were many health experts who viewed radiation as beneficial—many patients benefited from soaking in "radium springs." A number of the women sought legal assistance, and at the end of the 1920s several of them received monetary awards (Martland, 1931).

Thalidomide

In the late 1950s, a number of children in Europe were born with deformed or stunted limbs as well as heart and kidney problems. It soon became apparent that these defects were much more common among women who took a drug called thalidomide during pregnancy. Thalidomide became available in the mid-1950s in Germany, where it became widely established as a medication to reduce morning sickness. It is important to remember that in the early 1960s, knowledge of teratogens, substances that can cross the placental barrier and harm the developing fetus, was not well developed. It was not unusual for pregnant women to smoke cigarettes, consume alcohol, or continue taking psychotropic medications. Once these specific effects of thalidomide were established by the early 1960s, its use for morning sickness was discontinued. However, by that time, in Germany alone, it is estimated that 10,000 children were affected by thalidomide.

Mesothelioma and Asbestos

Mesothelioma is a relatively rare type of lung cancer. The condition can also occur in the abdomen and heart. Until the mid-1940s, it was believed that mesothelioma was a secondary form of cancer associated with a primary source elsewhere in the body. In the in the mid- to late 1960s, scientific papers appeared suggesting that there was a distinct linkage between asbestos exposure and mesothelioma. However, in addition to the debate about whether it was a "primary" cancer, there were confounding variables present. Men working with asbestos were much more likely to be smokers than the general population. However, studies that controlled for this confound still found a linkage between mesothelioma and asbestos exposure. Strengthening this association were studies that the children and spouses of asbestos workers also were at elevated risk for developing this atypical form of cancer. Eventually, it was recognized that the tiny particles associated with asbestos were inhaled. Women and children often had this exposure through contact with asbestos fibers that were left on the workers' clothing when they returned home (Smith, 2005).

Cohort Studies

A cohort is a large group of people assembled at one point in time and then followed over days, months, or years to determine the incidence of particular health conditions, factors that protect one from developing an illness, or the course of an illness over time. Additionally, cohorts may be followed longitudinally to determine the longer-term effects of a treatment. Cohort studies are one of the more definitive ways to determine cause-effect relationships outside of a laboratory setting.

Some of the problems with cohort studies are that there may be dropouts from the original cohort over time. On occasion, this results in a biased cohort—for example, in a treatment study, participants who experienced negative side effects drop out. To maintain an adequate number of participants, with the expectation that some will drop out for various reasons, it is typically necessary to have a fairly large cohort. As is probably evident, cohort studies require time and money to continue data collection. Finally, with outcomes that are rare or unusual, cohort studies are not the best approach, since it is certainly feasible that the unusual condition may not emerge in a pre-specified group over time (Merrill, 2016).

Cohort studies can be prospective or retrospective. In prospective studies, exposure is known and the cohort is followed over time to assess for disease. Several of the early studies linking cigarette smoking to lung cancer were conducted in this way. If information on both the outcome and exposure are available, the investigator can retrospectively assess their association (Merrill, 2016).

The Framingham Heart Study

Much of our knowledge about cardiovascular health, including heart attack risk and stroke, comes from a cohort in Framingham, Massachusetts. The original 1948 cohort consisted of 5,209 respondents from a random sample of two-thirds of the adult population of Framingham. One of the early studies was published in 1959 and was based on a six-year follow-up. At that point in time, risk factors associated with development of heart disease in the cohort included educational status (those with less formal education were at higher risk) and cigarette smoking. Investigators noted that cholesterol levels were higher among current and former smokers, but at that point, they could not disentangle the unique effects of cholesterol on heart disease (Dawber et al., 1959). A later 1970 report from the

Framingham cohort highlighted the unique predictive value of elevated cholesterol for coronary heart disease among men (Kannel, Gordon, & Schwartz, 1971). As of June 2017, about 1,200 articles had been published based upon Framingham data (Framinghamheartstudy.org).

Cancer and Nutrition: The EPIC Cohort

The European Prospective Investigation into Cancer and Nutrition is a large cohort study conducted across multiple countries. The original cohort, recruited from 1993 to 1999, consisted of 521,457 adults fairly equally distributed across 10 countries. One of the research centers in the United Kingdom was able to recruit a subgroup of 27,000 vegetarians and vegans. To date, the study has found that reduced salt intake and high potassium intake from fruits and vegetables are associated with healthier blood pressures; dietary fiber has a protective effect against bowel cancer; and obesity increases the risk of multiple types of cancer. Increased fat increases the risk of breast cancer in particular. Further analyses indicated that four behaviors added 14 years to one's lifespan: not smoking, being physically active, exhibiting moderate alcohol intake, and eating at least five fruits and vegetables per day (Khaw et al., 2008).

Qualitative Research

Qualitative studies are often used when investigators want to better understand a phenomenon but the state of knowledge is such that it is difficult to develop specific quantitative hypotheses to test. Qualitative studies are also useful when investigators explore participants' reasoning around a particular pattern of quantitative findings. Qualitative methods may include direct observation, but in health research the most common qualitative techniques are semi-structured interviews.

Blackhall, Murphy, Frank, Michel, and Azen (1995) published a large-sample quantitative study on cross-cultural views of end-of-life decision-making and found significant differences between ethnicities in whether a patient should be told of a terminal diagnosis as well as in preferences for decision-making about treatment. Findings indicated that Korean Americans and Hispanic Americans were more likely than African or European Americans to indicate that patients should not be told of their condition and that decision-making should be carried out by the family rather than the patient themselves. It was necessary to conduct detailed interviews with members of various ethnic groups to better understand the reasons for these differences. Several themes emerged. First, it was seen as disrespectful to burden an elder. This was particularly true for the Korean Americans who indicated that senior family members should be treated with great respect and not burdened with unpleasant information and burdensome decision-making (Frank et al., 1998).

Second, in some instances, it was believed to be harmful even to discuss the possibility of needing end-of-life care, even when the patient was healthy. Also, from a spiritual perspective, some respondents believed that by establishing advance directives planning for the possibility of terminal illness, one was interfering with the work of God (Searight & Gafford, 2005; Searight & Meredith, in press).

Social Epidemiology

Social epidemiology examines macro-level social factors and their association with health (Honjo, 2004). These factors may include economics, political issues, and quality of community living, including access to grocery stores, parks, or public transportation. As a relatively recent subfield, social epidemiology has emphasized the impact of income inequality on health status. Social epidemiologists view larger-scale social factors such as poverty or residential segregation as exposures. In contrast to the epidemiological design discussed above, in which information is gathered about a specific disease and a specific exposure, social epidemiology draws upon census data and aggregated health information for specific subgroups of a population, such as those residing in a particular neighborhood. Nearly all social epidemiological studies are cross-sectional.

A consistent finding has been that in the United States, multiple diseases as well as specific risk factors for illnesses are often significantly more common in lower socioeconomic groups. In addition, factors such as patterns of housing discrimination are, independent of poverty, associated with poorer health. Persons with household incomes below the poverty level are more likely to develop diabetes, arthritis, major depressive disorder, neurocognitive problems, back pain, and hypertension, as well as being at greater risk of death. Geospatial analysis has found that regions associated with greater poverty and housing discrimination are associated with more complications of diabetes, such as vision problems and amputations (Kimmel, Fwu, Abbott, Ratner, & Eggers, 2016; Lee et al., 2016).

Colorectal cancer is the third most common cause of death for US residents and appears to exhibit a particularly strong association with poverty. The overall incidence of the condition is higher among those who have less education and live in neighborhoods of lower socioeconomic status. In addition to exhibiting greater risk factors such as unhealthy diet and smoking, persons developing colorectal cancer are more likely to have advanced illness by the time they seek help (Liss & Baker, 2014).

For many of these diseases, there is a dose-response relationship between level of poverty and likelihood of developing health problems—as a population falls further and further below the poverty level, the risk of many illnesses and death increases linearly. The mechanisms through which factors such as poverty influence health are still being determined. It is certainly likely that those in lower socioeconomic groups live in neighborhoods with greater crime, which, in turn, increases the likelihood of being a victim of theft and/or assault. Additionally, persons living in poverty have reduced access to social resources such as quality schools, free preschools, and safe parks and places of recreation (Honjo, 2004).

Social epidemiologists have also developed unique quantitative indices that attempt to summarize aspects of economic disparity. For example, the "Robin Hood index" reflects "the portion of aggregate income that must be redistributed from rich to poor households in order to attain perfect equality of incomes" (Kawachi & Kennedy, 1997; Kawachi & Subramanian, 2014). A lower Robin Hood index indicates greater equality in income distribution, while a higher score reflects greater income disparity within the population. The Robin Hood index has demonstrated robust positive associations with multiple illnesses and causes of death. This pattern of association was still present even after median household income, poverty rates, prevalence of cigarette smoking, and the impact of urban/rural residences were statistically controlled (Honjo, 2004).

Causality and the Bradford Hill Criteria

Throughout this chapter, the issue of establishing causal connections between specific exposures and disease outcomes has been treated with caution. Because epidemiology does not occur in a controlled laboratory environment, it is difficult (if not impossible) to definitively establish that a particular agent causes a particular illness. Also, because a myriad of social, psychological, and behavioral factors influence health and illness, there may be a number of risk and protective factors that may be associated with a disease but are not directly causal. Odds ratios and risk ratios give us information about patterns of association but in and of themselves do not specify causes.

Today, most scientists accept that there is a causal relationship between cigarette smoking and a risk of developing lung cancer. However, there is a pronounced time lag of decades between initiating cigarette smoking and the development of respiratory conditions such as chronic obstructive pulmonary disease (COPD). In a classic article, Richard Doll and A. Bradford Hill (1950) recognized that there had been a significant increase in cases of lung cancer in the United Kingdom. They analyzed a very large cohort of physicians and nurses in terms of smoking behavior and subsequent development of various illnesses. Through a systematic analysis of possible causal factors, they concluded that "there is a real association between carcinoma of the lung and smoking" (p. 746). To be able to make this causal statement, Doll and Hill systematically reviewed specific patterns of association from multiple sources and looked for convergence and consistency of findings.

Hill later elaborated on these criteria, and they became established as a list of factors to consider in making the argument that an association is causal. As the number of these criteria increases in a given study, the more likely it is that an exposure causes a particular disease.

1. Consistency—There is a pattern that consistently links the illness with the exposure, and persons who do not receive the exposure do not develop the illness. Has the pattern shown consistently across different populations?
2. Strength of Association—The magnitude of the relative risk; the higher the relative risk, the more likely that an association is causal.
3. Temporal Sequence—The exposure clearly precedes the development of the illness. In the case of lung cancer it was clear that smoking—often decades earlier—occurred before the development of the disease.
4. Biological Gradient (a dose-response relationship)—A stronger or longer duration of exposure should increase the probability that the outcome will occur. Likewise, reduced exposure should be associated with a reduced probability of disease. In the case of smoking, this was the case—the more cigarettes smoked, the greater the likelihood that cancer would develop.
5. Specificity—Is it clear that the hypothesized cause is linked with the disease, as opposed to other causes? As noted above, this was initially an issue in

determining that asbestos exposure was associated with mesothelioma, since those who worked with asbestos were more likely to smoke. Hill, however, did recognize that specificity was a challenging standard: "It has always been possible to acquire cancer of the scrotum without sweeping chimneys or taking to mule spinning in Lancashire" (Hill, 1965, p. 297).

6. Coherence—There should be a logical and coherent explanation of the mechanism by which an effect is produced (Merrill, 2016). Is the proposed cause-effect relationship logical?
7. Biological Plausibility—Based upon the principles of biology and chemistry, is the proposed explanation reasonable? Hill (1965) pointed out that biological plausibility is often relative to the state of knowledge in a particular field. With respect to lung cancer, exposures to some of the agents in cigarettes in "pure" form have also been associated with increased risk of cancer. Based upon 29 case-control and seven cohort studies, it was shown that exposure to specific carcinogens (e.g., Benzene; cadmium polonium-210) increases the risk for lung cancer as well as several other types of cancer, including cancers of the lip, throat, and esophagus, as well as the bladder.
8. Analogy: Are there other conditions that may have different exposures but follow a similar pattern? It is established that use of chewing tobacco increases the risk of oral cancers (Johnson, 2001).
9. Experimental Evidence: This information may be present. Hill emphasized that if one removed the exposure, one should see a corresponding reduction in or absence of the illness. While research in the 1950s was not entirely clear about the impact of smoking cessation, we now know that persons who quit smoking reduce their risk of several types of cancer as well as cardiovascular disease.

In reviewing Sir Bradford Hill's criteria, one can also see how smoking advocates, such as the tobacco industry, could make a case that a causal association between cigarette smoking and lung cancer has yet to be proven. The tobacco industry has highlighted the distinction between risk factor and cause. Additionally, most public health investigators would agree that cigarette smoking is probably multifactorial and influenced by genetic, personality, and social factors. The cigarette industry has responded by indicating that if smoking is indeed determined by multiple factors, how can one be sure that tobacco, specifically, is the cause of lung cancer? These critics would invoke Hill's criterion of specificity and argue that with respect to smoking and cancer, the specificity standard has not been clearly met.

Evidence-Based Health Care

The use of research-based evidence to guide decisions about medical and public health intervention is actually a relatively recent phenomenon. Evidence-based medicine is the use of research evidence to guide clinical decision-making. A formal definition of evidence-based medicine (EBM) by Sackett (1997), who is considered to be one of the founders of the movement, is as follows: "The conscientious, explicit, and judicious use of current best evidence in making decisions about the care of individual patients." Historically, many medical treatments, including mental health interventions such as psychotherapy, were often based upon clinical experience and handed down to new generations of clinicians according to what was consensually accepted practice. In many respects, health care was considered an "art," and research was often seen as minimally relevant to clinicians.

Evidence-based medicine centers around five essential principles: (1) Clinical decisions should be made based on the best available scientific evidence. (2) The clinical problem or symptom should guide the search for existing research. Clinical "lore" regarding the symptom's relationship to a diagnostic syndrome, as well as optimal treatment, is insufficient and often misleading for clinical decision-making. (3) Epidemiological and biostatistical information is considered the appropriate source of evidence. (4) The utility of research is based upon whether it is used to benefit patients and make health care decisions. (5) Response to treatment should be assessed on an ongoing basis (Davidoff, Haynes, Sackett, & Smith, 1995).

A study of physicians found that for every 10 patients seen in office practice, three clinical questions arose (Ely et al., 1999). Clinical practitioners, however, despite having evidence, must be able to critically assess research findings. In particular, practitioners are tasked with determining the validity of research findings—particularly whether research data are "strong enough" to guide clinical practice. Hill's criteria are often useful but may be considered too laborious for a busy health care professional. Key issues in assessing the quality of clinical evidence are the consistency of elements across studies and the quality of existing research. There are several questions that guide assessment quality: (1) Were participants in the study randomly assigned? (2) Is there an alternative or placebo condition to which the treatment under study is being compared? (3) What is the source of the information? (Journals that are refereed [meaning that manuscripts submitted for possible publication are evaluated by several authorities in the field before publishing them] are considered to be of higher quality.) A related issue is publication bias. For example, an investigator who has received grant money from a pharmaceutical company may have an implicit bias when conducting a study on a medication's effectiveness.

Organizing Published Research to Guide Clinical Decision-Making

While there are several definitions, the recently developed field of medical informatics focuses on the use of technology to improve health care delivery. While the field may include electronic medical records and other technological methods to organize and transmit patients' clinical information, it also encompasses access to current health care information with the goal of improving the efficiency and quality of patient care. In keeping with EBM, one goal of medical informatics is to assist physicians and other health care professionals in translating published research into clinically usable knowledge.

There are a growing number of sources—many of them online—that physicians can turn to when they have questions about the status of research regarding a specific condition and/or treatment. Probably the best-known of these are the Cochrane Reviews. The evidence-based movement, in some disciplines called empirically supported treatment, has spread to mental health care, physical therapy, dentistry, nursing, occupational therapy, and public health.

In order to provide clinicians with up-to-date current knowledge, strategies continue to be developed to monitor, organize, and distill key findings from an overwhelming number of published research studies from multiple sources. In 1992, during the early years of EBM, it was estimated that a physician would need to read about 17 articles per day every day of the year to cover the major journals in their subfield (Davidoff et al., 1995). Given the explosion of knowledge and health, it is likely that today's physician would need to be able to cover 50 articles per day.

Early efforts to compare results from multiple studies used a "box score" approach in which the numbers of studies that did and did not demonstrate an effect were tabulated and reported; the intervention supported by the greatest number of studies "won." There were multiple problems with this approach—among them the absence of attention to the quality of the studies being analyzed to determine "winners" and "losers." Fortunately, there have also been new approaches to analyzing published research that organize and summarize key findings in an area.

Meta-analysis is a statistical procedure for combining the results of multiple studies on a specific research question. For example, a meta-analysis of therapy for women at risk of breast cancer found that 15 years after initiation of estrogen treatment, there was a 30 percent greater likelihood of developing breast cancer if one took estrogen versus not taking it (Steinberg et al., 1991). Rather than using statistical significance, meta-analyses report results in terms of a single quantitative index—the effect size (Sullivan & Feinn, 2012).

Another approach to organizing research findings from multiple studies is the systematic review. Systematic reviews may include meta-analyses. However, one of the distinctive features of systematic reviews is that they include a detailed and comprehensive search strategy that is developed in advance with the goal of reducing bias and identifying all relevant studies on a specific topic (Sullivan & Feinn, 2012). Systematic reviews often begin with a specifically phrased clinical question (e.g., "Is biofeedback effective for nonspecific abdominal pain?"). Typically, those developing systematic reviews set stringent criteria for including a study in the analysis, such as the presence of a control group; standardized, established measurement techniques; and so on. When these criteria are applied, it is not unusual for an initial pool of studies to shrink by more than 50 percent.

As mentioned earlier, a well-known set of high-quality systematic reviews are the Cochrane Reviews. The Cochrane Reviews are one of the best sources of current clinical evidence. Cochrane reviews are written in a clinical question format—for example, "Can antibiotics help in alleviating the symptoms of a sore throat?" The reviewers then gather and organize all studies on the topic. In addition, they apply a set of research-quality criteria, such as the presence of a control group, sample size, and so on, to the set of studies. If available research is of questionable quality, Cochrane reviewers will indicate that any conclusion must take this qualifying factor into account.

For many years, it was clinical practice to have children undergo removal of the tonsils if they had a history of recurrent infectious sore throat or periodic inflammation of the tonsils. However, a Cochrane Review concluded that tonsillectomies are not as "curative" as many clinicians believed. When compared with groups that did not undergo tonsillectomy, those who did have their tonsils removed exhibited only 0.6 fewer episodes of sore throat—3.6 episodes for the no tonsillectomy group versus 3.0 episodes for those who underwent the procedure (Burton, Pollard, Ramsden, Chong, & Venekamp, 2014).

Cochrane Reviews have also been conducted on behavioral and psychosocial aspects of patient care. A study of physician advice on smoking cessation concluded that its effect was very modest and only increased cessation rates by 1 to 3 percent when compared with no advice. Evidence-based treatment for conditions such as chronic pain and headache includes many behaviorally oriented interventions (Penzien, Rains, Lipchik, & Creer, 2004). For irritable bowel syndrome, mentioned in Chapter 1, a Cochrane Review concluded that several types of psychotherapy, including interpersonal therapy and cognitive behavioral therapy, appear to be more effective than standard treatment for the condition. However, among the studies that did post-treatment follow-up, these benefits did not appear to be long-lasting (Zijdenbos, de Wit, van der Heijden, Rubin, & Quartero, 2009).

Issues and Cautions in Applying EBM Findings

Critics of EBM note that studies employed in these analyses may reflect a publication bias in that treatments that demonstrate no benefit or that are harmful to patients are often not published. As a result, heavy reliance upon the available literature for patient care decisions may make available findings appear stronger than they actually are. Another concern is that clinical trials tend to be carried out in situations in which there is tight experimental control. For example, patients only have one condition and do not have comorbid conditions, or a specific age group or sex may be may be over- or underrepresented among the participants. As a result, it may be difficult to generalize journal findings to more complicated situations of direct patient care. Davidoff and colleagues (1995) have responded to these critiques by indicating that they had not intended to encourage cookbook medicine and that evidence can help clinicians in the diagnostic and treatment process but certainly cannot replace the judgment of health care professionals.

Evidence-Based Health Interventions in Larger Systems

In the 1970s, Campbell (1979) suggested that government programs should be routinely evaluated to determine their effectiveness. In some instances, when it's known in advance that a program is going to be phased in, the target population can serve as its own control (Campbell, 1991). For example, in January 1974, President Nixon signed the Emergency Highway Energy Conservation Act. Prior to that time, speed limits on US interstate highways were as high as 80 mph. Nixon's reason for signing legislation to reduce fuel consumption was that foreign countries had placed an embargo on oil shipments to the United States. One of the unintended outcomes of this fuel conservation legislation was that the number of auto accident fatalities dropped by 16.4 percent (Friedman, Hedeker, & Richter, 2009). When the act was repealed in the mid-1990s, the overall increase in accidents was 3 to 4 percent. Investigators suggested that the relatively small increase in auto fatalities after the law was repealed was, in part, attributable to increased auto safety, including use of seat belts, airbags, and child restraints, as well as enforcement of drunk-driving laws (Friedman et al., 2009).

The Campbell Collaboration, similar to the Cochrane Reviews, focuses on finding the best evidence in areas such as education and social welfare. A thorough systematic review of an intervention designed to reduce teen pregnancy examined both abstinence-only programs and programs that included contraception or discussion of contraception, as well as larger-scale programs in which information about prevention of pregnancy and sexually transmitted disease was integrated into a series of activities. For years, program results indicated that when evaluated as a group, these programs were not successful in preventing teen pregnancies (Scher, Maynard, & Stagner, 2006).

While there is currently debate about the effects of the Affordable Care Act (Obamacare), there are available data that suggest its possible long-range impact may reduce the number of uninsured and provide other economic benefits. In 2006, Massachusetts implemented a program somewhat similar to the national Affordable Care Act. The goal was for all residents of Massachusetts to have health insurance. One of the objectives was to reduce use of the emergency department for non-urgent medical problems. While, globally, emergency department use in Massachusetts increased slightly after health care reform, there was some evidence of small declines in emergency room use for non-urgent problems. Sommers et al. (2014) concluded that there was a reduction in mortality and deaths from conditions amenable to health care (Sommers, Long, & Blacker, 2014). Additionally, a 2016 study found that health care reform's implementation was associated with reduced personal bankruptcies and improved credit scores among Massachusetts residents (Mazumder & Miller, 2016).

Conclusion

One of the major "selling points" for research in health and behavior is that it typically addresses "real-world" problems, often with relevance for population health and even mortality. As is the case in most of the social sciences, the level of control needed to say with certainty that a causal relationship exists is often not present. However, the likelihood of causality increases as the number and strength of risk factors associated with the disease increases. As will be discussed in detail later in the book, the risk factors for the common causes of death in Western countries have a strong behavioral component. Even though there is strong support for evidence-based interventions, the difference between the laboratory and complex social systems, in which health and illness occur, will continue to require health professionals with excellent conceptual and analytic skills.

CHAPTER 3

The Health Care System
History and Current Dilemmas

When was the last time you had an interaction with the health care system? If you were in a physician's office, did you have to prove to the receptionist that you had health insurance? How long did you wait after your specified appointment time to actually see the health care provider? How much time did the provider spend with you? Did you get all of your questions and concerns addressed? If you were referred for laboratory work such as having your blood drawn or having some type of imaging procedure such as an X-ray or MRI, did you understand why you were undergoing the procedure?

If you had the unfortunate experience of being admitted to a hospital, how many days did you spend there? Did you understand why you were undergoing the tests that you had while you were hospitalized? When you were discharged, did you understand what you were supposed to do for follow-up? Did you happen to see the bill after you were discharged? Did it surprise you?

When was the last time you had to have a prescription filled? Did you have insurance that covered part of the cost? Did you have to pay for the prescription on top of your insurance coverage?

Have you ever not seen a health care provider when you were ill, not gotten a recommended medical test or a prescription filled because you could not afford it?

This chapter focuses on our health care system. It begins with a history of medicine from the ancient Greeks to the present. We will then examine how health care is funded in the United States. These funding sources, in many respects, determine whether you receive health care and the type you receive. Finally, to help you better understand the US health care system and some of the current political debates about the topic, we will briefly look at health care systems in several other countries.

A History of Medical Care
Hippocrates and Galen

The ancient Greeks are considered the founders of modern medicine. Hippocrates (460–370 BCE) was an early holistic healer. Hippocrates believed that in order to appropriately treat patients, the doctor needed to know a great deal about them, including their social circumstances, where they lived, where they traveled, and their personal history of disease (Bynum, 2008). At this point in history, the workings of the human body were inferred. Anatomy and surgery had not yet developed. Hippocratic medicine was based on the concept of a balance between four humors of the body. Each of these humors—blood, yellow bile, black bile, and phlegm—was associated with four basic elements: air (blood), fire (yellow bile), earth (black bile), and water (phlegm). Each of these humors was associated with an organ—blood associated with the heart, yellow bile with the liver, black bile with the spleen, and phlegm with the brain—and the focus of humoral medicine was on balancing these substances within the body. Treatments included diet, exercise, and massage, based on the patient's condition. Inflammation was a sign of an imbalance in the humors with a disproportionate amount of blood. Bloodletting, intentionally bleeding the patient, was the indicated treatment.

Galen (129–200 CE), while generally in the tradition of Hippocrates, was able to study some anatomy through treating the wounds of Roman soldiers (Bynum, 2008). He also dissected animals such as pigs and sheep and concluded that the blood vessels carry blood rather than air, as had been previously believed. Galen expanded Hippocrates's view of the four humors by emphasizing the role of the body's organs in humoral imbalance. Galen's views prevailed through the early 1600s throughout most of European medicine (Bendick, 2002).

Medieval Period Through the Late 1600s

While the medieval period is often portrayed by historians of medicine as an era in which medical progress halted due to the Catholic Church becoming the dominant force in Europe, this view is probably an oversimplification. Galen's work, available in Arabic, was influential in many areas of the Middle East and North Africa. In addition, academic science and medicine continued to advance; for example, early medical textbooks such as Avicenna's *Canon of Medicine*, an encyclopedic work completed in 1025, influenced European physicians in the 1700s (de Bustinza, 2016). Hospitals also developed in the Arabic world by the 11th century. These institutions even included specialized units for persons with psychiatric illness and eye diseases (Bynum, 2008). Islamic or Arabic medicine also included surgery as part of medicine—which would not occur in Europe for some centuries.

While there was some development of hospitals in Europe during the Middle Ages, these institutions were under the auspices of the Catholic Church, and medical treatments were limited. Often, interventions centered around prayers to the appropriate saint.

European physicians of the medieval era had only a limited understanding of the human body. The Church and social norms of the Middle Ages did not support human dissection. While a few public dissections of the body for educational purposes occurred in the early 1300s, systematic study of the structures and mechanics of the human body did not occur until two centuries later. The best known of the early students of anatomy was Vesalius (1516–1564), who documented aspects of the human body that were not always consistent with Galen's descriptions. Although there was still considerable public, and even professional, sentiment against human dissection, detailed woodcuts were made of the internal organs for teaching purposes (Bynum, 2008).

Other physicians, such as Paracelsus (1493–1541), focused on the chemistry, rather than the anatomy, of the human body. Paracelsus studied the medical effects of mercury, lead, and arsenic. He believed that in order to heal, the body must be poisoned on a small scale. He found that mercury, while having many negative side effects, such as loss of one's teeth, neurological damage, and, in some cases, death, was effective in treating syphilis, and it continued to be used until the early 20th century.

In England, Thomas Sydenham (1624–1689) emphasized the careful clinical observational methods developed by Hippocrates. The ability to consistently characterize a disease, he emphasized, would lead directly to treatments. Sydenham believed that diseases could be classified in the same way that Linnaeus developed organizational categories for organisms (Dewhurst, 1966). Sydenham concluded that Peruvian bark, which contained quinine, was consistently effective in addressing fevers; it later was established as an efficacious treatment for malaria. Sydenham, like Hippocrates, also argued that exercise, fresh air, and an appropriate diet could both prevent and treat illness.

Hospital Medicine

In France during the late 1700s, hospitals for teaching and research were established. These hospitals permitted physicians to study large numbers of patients, describe commonalities in symptoms, generate diagnostic categories, and make connections between physical signs and diagnosis (Bynum, 2008). As noted above, European hospitals had been in existence for some time—typically supported by the Church. The French orientation to hospital medicine focused on being able to understand and describe diseases and experiment with new treatments by intense observation of patients in a controlled environment over time. The developing field of neuropsychiatry, in particular, benefited from this method. The French physician Charcot studied many cases of conversion hysteria in depth. French hospitals often included an amphitheater so that case conferences and demonstrations of patient pathology could occur in front of a live audience of physicians. Charcot put on many dramatic demonstrations of inducing and removing symptoms with hypnotic techniques (Hustvedt, 2011).

The ability to follow large numbers of patients in depth over time allowed the French hospitalists to determine consistencies in symptoms, which led to descriptions of diagnostic syndromes as well as to making connections between physical signs and underlying pathology. As Bynum (2008) notes, prior to the development of physical diagnosis by the French hospitalists, physical contact between the physician and patient was limited. While the physician might check a pulse and look inside the patient's mouth, there was no systematic approach to physical assessment of patients. French hospitalists developed the four key aspects of physical diagnosis, which are still routinely taught in medical schools around the world: inspection, palpation, percussion, and auscultation (Bynum, 2008). Careful observation of the patient's physical appearance could alert the physician to maladies, such as red flushing in the face indicating fever. It also might include coarser observation, such as seeing the patient to be significantly underweight. Palpation, systematic touching or pressing at points of the body, allowed the physician to determine the presence of unusual growths. Percussion, usually taking the form of tapping on the chest or abdomen, continues to be a routine part of physical examination, which still sometimes confuses patients. Percussion was particularly useful in determining whether there was unusual fluid in areas such as the heart or lungs or if the heart was enlarged. Auscultation refers to listening to sounds coming from inside the patient's body. This technique was advanced by the work of Laennec (1781–1826), who developed the first stethoscope.

Patients of French hospitals were often drawn from poor segments of society, and because of their life circumstances, they were often seriously ill. The patient's social status undoubtedly reduced some of the objections to conducting autopsies. These autopsies permitted physicians to make further associations between organ and tissue pathology and symptoms.

Vaccines

Inoculation dates back to ancient China. The pox material that arose during smallpox was often granulated and then introduced into the body through various methods (Bynum, 2008), including deliberately scratching the skin with the material. The Chinese had also observed that those who had had the disease would not develop it again (Riedel, 2005). Edward Jenner (1749–1823) became aware of reports that most young women who milked cows for a living ("milk maids") and developed cowpox would not develop the more virulent smallpox. In 1796, Jenner scraped a pustule from a local milkmaid and inoculated a young boy. The boy developed a fever, but after about 10 days, he was back to normal and never developed full-blown smallpox. Jenner then inoculated the boy again, and he did not develop any symptoms. While not really discovering smallpox inoculation, Jenner is credited with establishing it in the scientific and medical community (Riedel, 2005). Later observations found that immunization often did not always provide lifelong immunity.

Germ Theory and the Continued Development of Vaccines

Particularly among the early British physicians who were interested in public health, hygiene and crowding were considered macro-level causes of disease. However, as was the case with John Snow and the Broad Street Pump, the actual source of the disease was not known. Von Leeuwenhoek's development of the microscope was the key to understanding the specific cellular-level changes associated with contagious conditions. However, the acceptance of cellular-level processes did not occur until the 1830s. In the late 1830s, Schleiden and Schwann concluded that the basic unit of both plants and animals was the cell (Riedel, 2005).

With the understanding of the cell as a foundation, medicine could move to its next major conceptual breakthrough—germ theory (Stern & Markel, 2005). Louis Pasteur already had a reputation as a scientist when the French government asked him to study an infestation of silkworms that was damaging the silk industry. At that time, anthrax was affecting cattle. Pasteur dramatically demonstrated how inoculation with a weakened form of anthrax provided the cattle with immunity from future episodes. Bacteria can be seen under a microscope. However, viruses are significantly smaller, and, in Pasteur's day, they were only known by their effects. Through working with rabbits, he found he could weaken substances containing the rabies virus. He also capitalized on the fact that rabies had an incubation period, so there was a time lapse between being bitten by a rabid dog and contracting the disease. At that time, rabies often resulted in a horrific death. Pasteur vaccinated a boy relatively soon after he had been bitten by a rabid dog, and the patient survived.

While there were many contributors to our understanding of microorganisms as disease-causing agents, Pasteur is now considered to be one of the founders of germ theory (De Kruif, 1996).

Robert Koch (1843–1910), who also worked with anthrax, studied the microorganism involved in cholera. Koch is regarded today as the founder of bacteriology for his work in articulating the biological mechanisms involved in anthrax, tuberculosis, and cholera (De Kruif, 1996). While he is often credited with discovering *Vibrio cholerae*, the cholera-causing organism was actually discovered by the Italian scientist Filippo Pancini (1812–1883). However, Koch may be best known for articulating four related principles, known as Koch's postulates, which are the necessary requirements for concluding that a microorganism causes an infectious disease (Bynum, 2008).

In the United States from 1916 until the 1950s, outbreaks of polio occurred in various parts of the country each summer. In the 1930s and 1940s, there were a number of highly publicized outbreaks. The most virulent episodes occurred in the 1940s and early 1950s (Oshinsky, 2005). While polio had varying degrees of seriousness, paralysis of the legs and—less commonly—the diaphragm occurred. President Franklin Roosevelt was infected with the virus as an adult, probably while swimming, and experienced significant paralysis of his legs for the remainder of his life. When the muscles of the diaphragm were paralyzed, the patient could not breathe. It was necessary to place the patient in a large machine, the iron lung, which was an early form of artificial ventilation (Oshinsky, 2005).

While the exact mode of polio's transmission was not initially known, the seasonal pattern suggested that the disease was probably communicable and led to the closure of many public swimming pools. Eventually, it was determined that polio was transmitted through waterborne fecal material as well as droplets of saliva in the air. In the late 1940s, the poliovirus was isolated. With the virus known, it was possible to develop a vaccine. Jonas Salk developed a vaccine with a "killed" poliovirus that was injected (Oshinsky, 2005). Albert Sabin, by contrast, argued that permanent immunity from polio could only occur if a live, yet weakened, virus was used for inoculation. While Sabin's weakened virus had been preferred for some time, this live virus at times became strong enough to produce the actual disease. Over time, Salk's "killed" virus became the standard for inoculation.

Surgery Becomes Safer

While surgery was gradually merging with modern medicine rather than being practiced by scientifically untrained barber surgeons, infection was a constant threat to surgical outcomes. In fact, a hospital was actually a dangerous place to receive health care. In the 1850s, Semmelweis described a simple intervention that, when consistently employed, greatly reduced the maternal death rate in Vienna's hospitals (Obenchain, 2016). It did not involve any complex surgical procedure or use of medication; physicians simply needed to wash their hands before delivering babies. In the Semmelweis era, the likelihood of mothers dying in labor was 10 to 20 times greater if they delivered in a hospital than if they delivered at home with the assistance of a midwife. Puerperal fever was associated with elevated body temperature and severe abdominal pain (Hallett, 2005). These symptoms would have their onset within 24 hours of the delivery. Unfortunately, many women did not get to see the baby that they had just delivered. When Semmelweis himself, and the medical students and physicians under his supervision, washed their hands in an antiseptic solution before deliveries, the death rates of Semmelweis's patients dropped dramatically. Those physicians who continued to deliver babies wearing blood-encrusted laboratory coats, often as a badge of honor, continued to have high rates of maternal death. In part because Semmelweis was an interpersonally "difficult" colleague, his ideas were largely resisted. Eventually, however, clinical experiments in the later 1800s proved Semmelweis correct (Obenchain, 2016).

Recognition of microscopic cellular bacteria and viruses as well as a better comprehension of the process of infection—particularly once the skin was broken—led to a better understanding of the reasons that surgical procedures had such poor outcomes. Joseph Lister used carbolic acid to demonstrate that wounds arising from compound fractures could essentially be sealed. Prior to that time, the solution for compound fractures, when bones pierced the skin, was amputation (Ellis, 2002).

A second factor promoting surgery was the development of anesthesia. Initially ether was used, with the first demonstration of it being during a surgical procedure in the mid-1840s (Bynum, 2008). Ether was soon followed by the use of chloroform. Importantly, anesthetics permitted physicians to operate for longer periods of time by keeping patients sedated and pain-free (Fenster & Fenster, 2001). The multi-hour complex operations that we have today would not have been possible without the development of effective and safe modes of anesthesia.

Educating Physicians

In the mid-1840s, while European medicine had developed into a more scholarly discipline, in the United States, health care was basically an unregulated field. Physicians generally learned their skills by serving as apprentices. Relatively few physicians actually attended medical schools, and the medical schools that existed were generally for-profit organizations—many of which were essentially "diploma mills." American medicine was highly commercial. Salesmen promoted various potions and tonics and competed with homeopaths and even proponents of physical fitness. The public was not particularly deferential toward physicians during this era, and "shopping around" for medical care was commonplace.

Patented medicines, some of which were no more than placebos, were also common. Medical malpractice litigation began in the 1840s, primarily focusing on badly set broken bones—a procedure that was relatively easy to assess objectively. US courts began to promulgate a standard according to which patients were entitled to expect a certain level of professional medical skill. By the late 1800s it became increasingly apparent that the public required some type of protection from medical providers marketing elixirs that had no scientific basis. To demarcate between appropriately professional and unprofessional practitioners, the American Medical Association in 1848 developed a code of ethics. Beginning in the middle of the 19th century, the American Medical Association also began advocating for a system of medical education based in science. The availability of early vaccines and changes in surgical procedures designed to reduce infections provided a stronger basis for the AMA's position on education.

In 1910, as a representative of the American Medical Association, Abraham Flexner visited all active medical schools in the United States. Of the 155 centers that he visited, very few met his standards for adequate laboratory hospital facilities and adequately trained teachers. Flexner also strongly encouraged states to set standards for regulating medical education through licensure of physicians who had completed their education in a school of acceptable quality (Beck, 2004). This standard was further accelerated by Flexner's report, in which it was recommended that anyone entering a medical school have a college education.

Philanthropists donated money to establish quality medical schools in the United States—among them Johns Hopkins University. One of the newly established medical school's faculty members was William Osler (1849–1919), who had received additional training in Europe. Osler asserted that it was best to teach students through direct interaction with patients (Dornan, 2005). His approach involved bedside examinations and interviews with patients with medical students at the bedside (Dornan, 2005). Osler also, based upon his experiences in Europe, further impacted US medical education by initiating the internship—a period of one year of general, predominantly inpatient, medicine followed by residency in the specialty area. Like Hippocrates, Osler was a strong believer in viewing the patient in context and advocated for patient-centered medicine almost a century before it was fashionable. He is well known for many pithy quotations about medical practice, such as "The good physician treats the disease; the great physician treats the patient who has the disease." Additionally, Osler emphasized careful observation and interviewing of patients: "Listen to your patient; he is telling you the diagnosis" (Drossman, 2013).

The Development of Medicine as a Profession

Professional organizations such as the American Medical Association encouraged physicians to be above the salesman-customer interactions of the modern marketplace. With new licensing laws now publicly certifying physicians as qualified, there was no need to advertise. For physicians, marketing oneself was seen as harking back to the promoters of snake oil medicine. "Advertising is not resorted to by honest, upright, and self-respecting members of our profession" (Tomes, 2016, p. 28).

As medicine became more professional, the pool of patients for medical care increased as well. Even before World War I, death rates from infectious diseases were declining. The American life span grew dramatically from 40 years at birth in 1852 to 60 years in 1930 (Tomes, 2016). With developments in public health and greater attention to clean food, water, and living conditions, as well as the availability of vaccines and increased attention to sterile techniques in medical practice, the US death rate began dropping. By 1921, heart disease, rather than tuberculosis, became the single most common cause of death in the United States (Tomes, 2016). These new sources of mortality were characterized as "diseases of affluence" (Tomes, 2016, p. 43) and became linked to an ethic of personal self-indulgence and a lack of self-discipline (Tomes, 2016).

Articles in popular magazines encouraged readers to be alert to possible early signs of disease—shortness of breath for heart attacks; headaches for high blood pressure. Early warning signs of cancer consisted of a veritable list of possible physical changes and symptoms, including the appearance of lumps in various parts of the body and even recurrent indigestion. It was implied, and occasionally stated explicitly, that those who did not heed these recommendations would die prematurely (Tomes, 2016).

However, while advertising and overt marketing were frowned upon, the business aspects of medicine were given more attention within the medical profession. Some popular publications presented the old-style, Norman Rockwell type of physician as outmoded. Not only were the new physicians of the era much more attentive to the economic and business aspects of medicine, but they were also becoming specialists. Specialization grew during the first decades of the 20th century. While the early physicians of the late 1800s were, in many respects, medical jacks-of-all-trades, the modern physicians of the 20th century specialized in specific organ systems (Tomes, 2016).

Tomes (2016) describes many physicians' offices of the early 1920s as being types of medical showrooms. To keep patients as satisfied customers, physicians were advised to be sure that the patient left the office with something—a medical device, such as those that monitor blood pressure or blood sugar, or a prescription. The number of physicians was growing, and, like automobile manufacturers, there was an undercurrent of competition for patients.

However, with the development of medications and medical technology, physicians controlled health care information like members of an insular guild. As a result, patients relied heavily upon the advice of their physicians about the treatments they should receive. As Tomes (2016) notes, "Patients were being simultaneously asked to spend more on medical services and told that they could not possibly appreciate the real value of these services" (p. 76).

The Growth of Scientific Medicine

If patients of the late 1930s were unable to grasp the basics of medicine, their knowledge deficit became significantly more pronounced over the next 50 years. Beginning in the late 1940s, medicine began a period of unprecedented growth that continues today. Advances included new surgical procedures, mechanical devices such as dialysis machines, medications, and approaches to imaging of tissue and organ systems.

Imaging Techniques

Wilhelm Röntgen (1845–1923), a physicist, while not actually discovering X-rays, is usually credited as being the first to demonstrate their use for imaging parts of the body. Soon after his description of this application, X-rays were put to diagnostic use. Because X-rays are absorbed differently by tissue structures of different density, an image can be created. However, the densities of adjacent areas of soft tissue are often very similar—thus limiting the ability of X-rays to visualize different pathologies. The use of contrast agents, substances of varying colors injected prior to an X-ray application, permitted visualization of blood vessels and the gastrointestinal system, as well as eventually other regions of the body, such as the heart and brain (Kevles, 1997).

Houndsfield and Cormac used computer-processed X-rays to show "slices," or tomographic images, of specific body regions, for which they were awarded the Nobel Prize in 1979 (Kevles, 1997). While it took some years to convert this discovery to a usable medical technology, current CT scans can acquire and construct an image almost simultaneously.

Magnetic resonance imaging (MRI) relies upon magnetic radio waves creating a magnetic field, which causes protons to align. As the protons move back to the original position, radio waves are sent out that are then converted into pictures (Comer, 2015). Usually only the part of the body being studied is exposed to a strong magnetic field, but whole-body MRIs are also possible. This procedure can show abnormalities within the body that other methods do not detect.

The most recently developed method of studying processes within the body is Positron Emission Tomography, often called a PET scan. This technique uses radioactive glucose that is injected into the body. PET scans are useful in observing metabolic processes within the body, both in research and diagnostically, for detection of metastatic cancer and some types of dementia.

Medical Devices to Supplement Physiological Functions

Kidney dialysis machines were developed by Wilhelm Kolff in the early 1940s. His early prototypes were not effective with acute kidney failure, but in 1945, Kolff had his first successful outcome. While he was developing early dialysis machines, Kolff viewed the machine as being a temporary substitute for impaired kidney function. He assumed that the patient's kidneys would eventually recover. The first outpatient kidney dialysis center in the United States was established in 1962.

Using machinery to supplement breathing dates back to the late 1920s when the "iron lung" was developed. These machines were widely used in the polio epidemics of the 1940s and 1950s. Some patients spent their entire lives encased in the machine. The iron lung was based on the physical principle of negative pressure. The mechanism of the iron lung involved decreasing the surrounding air pressure to stimulate inhalation (breathing in). The machine then re-pressurized and the process was repeated (Drinker & McKhann, 1986).

Because of technology developed during World War II, positive pressure ventilators, using the same principles used in assisted ventilation today, were developed. These ventilators increase the patient's airway pressure through a tube placed within the patient's trachea.

Organ Transplantation

The kidney was the first organ to be successfully transplanted. Early transplant efforts were stymied by the recipient's immune response, which resulted in rejection of the transplanted organ. The first successful kidney transplant occurred between identical twins in the mid-1950s. Successful transplantation of other organs—liver and heart—followed in the 1960s. However, heart transplants conducted through the 1970s were not highly successful, and most patients died. With availability of medications to control immune-system responses leading to organ rejection, cardiac transplants began to be successful. By the mid-1980s, heart transplants began to increase (Fox, 2017). A continuing issue with organ transplants is the availability of donor organs versus the need for transplants. At present, it is estimated that there are a total of more than 100,000 patients on organ transplant waiting lists in the United States. It is estimated that 22 people die each day awaiting a transplant (OrganDonor.gov, 2018).

Medications

For most of medical history, physicians had a limited armamentarium of medications. The same medications were used to treat multiple conditions. Barbiturates and bromides were particularly popular. Originally discovered in the late 1920s by Alexander Fleming from mold growing in his petri dishes, penicillin was not evaluated for therapeutic use until the late 1930s and was not put into widespread use until about 1945 (Bynum, 2008). It was shown to be effective against many bacterial infections, including syphilis, gonorrhea, and bacterial pneumonia. In its early days, penicillin was prescribed widely—including for conditions for which it was not appropriate—and in incorrect doses. Over time, antibiotic-resistant bacteria emerged, a problem that continues, contributing to the development of multiple types of antibiotics.

Beginning in the 1950s, there was a major acceleration in the development of medications. The effects of these medications also began to define as well as alter pre-existing definitions of diseases. During the 1930s, fundamental issues such as the definition of hypertension and whether elevated blood pressure was even a problem were debated. John Hay, a professor of medicine at Liverpool University, is quoted as saying, "There is some truth in saying that the greatest danger to a man with a high pressure lies in its discovery, because then some fool is certain try to reduce it" (Hay, 1931; Moser, 2006). The antihypertensive drug hydrochlorothiazide was introduced in the 1950s and became available for patient use by 1958. Early clinical trials found that even among those with mild hypertension, these medications reduced death rates (Moser, 2006).

Medications for alleviating pain have a long history dating back to the cultivation of the poppy plant in 3000 BCE. Morphine became available in various forms in the early to mid-1800s. There was, however, limited awareness of the drug's addictive potential. For example, in the early 1900s, heroin was widely available in pill form (Rosenblum, Marsch, Joseph, & Portenoy, 2008). Addiction soon became a problem, and heroin was formally made illegal in 1924. Leaves of the coca plant had been widely used in South America. In the United States, cocaine, derived from the coca plant, had both anesthetic and stimulant properties. Cocaine was also unregulated, readily available, and sold in various forms, including as an ingredient added to drinks and cigarettes. By 1920, its addictive potential became clear, and many states passed laws prohibiting distribution and use. Additionally, at around the same time, the US government passed the Pure Food and Drug Act, requiring that the contents of medications be clearly labeled.

It was not until the early 1970s that prescription medications such as Percocet and Vicodin became available. Because of the previous history of patients becoming addicted to drugs such as heroin and cocaine, physicians were initially reluctant to prescribe these new pain medications. However, in 1980, a report in the prestigious

New England Journal of Medicine indicated that of 11,000 patients treated with narcotics, very few became addicted (Porter & Jick, 1980).

Psychiatric medications to treat conditions such as anxiety, depression, and schizophrenia became available in the 1950s. A pharmaceutical company had been investigating sedating drugs for use during surgery and discovered chlorpromazine, which became widely used to treat schizophrenia. Minor tranquilizers such diazepam (Valium) became available at about the same time (Smith, 1991). While drugs such as diazepam are formally considered antianxiety drugs and are prescribed with much greater caution today, in the past they were widely prescribed by primary care physicians for a range of nonspecific "nervous" symptoms. By the 1970s, Valium was one of the top-selling medications in the United States. The first of a generation of antidepressant medications, known as tricyclics, also became available at about the same time. The medications were originally being investigated for treatment of schizophrenia, for which they were found not to be beneficial, but they did seem to be helpful for depression.

The Consumer Movement and Challenges to the Health Care Professions

Beginning in the 1960s, there were multiple challenges to the established status quo in the United States, including the civil rights movement, students questioning the governance and relevance of their universities, and the feminist movement. The authority of experts, including members of the professions, was also challenged. Ralph Nader's attention to consumer rights challenged the faith that the general public automatically placed in institutions such as business, industry, educational systems, and health care. Nader's (1965) journalistic exposé of lax safety standards in the automotive industry was part of a much broader challenge to large, economically powerful institutions that minimized or actively concealed risks of harm to the public.

A rare public description of how specialized and scarce medical resources are allocated occurred in the early 1960s around the issue of kidney dialysis. When dialysis first became available in the 1960s, the number of machines was very limited. In Washington State, this treatment scarcity led to the establishment of a "God Committee"—a surgeon, pastor, lawyer, banker, state government official, labor leader, and "housewife," along with two physician advisors. The group was charged with recommending which patients should and should not receive dialysis (Blagg, 1998; Pence, 2017). This group of citizens and professionals had to determine whether a housewife with two children, an accountant who is the primary or sole breadwinner of the family, a single male adult, among other applicants, were more or less deserving of dialysis (Pence, 2017). The members of the committee were depicted in a popular magazine as faceless silhouettes. The media attention given to the committee raised issues about access to life-saving technology that made many Americans acutely uncomfortable (Jonsen, 2007). It also challenged the idea that in terms of health care, all Americans were equal. In one of its meetings depicted in a *Life* magazine article, the "God Committee" selected two of five applicants for kidney dialysis—a businessman active in his church and an aircraft worker with six children—as deserving of treatment. A chemist, accountant, and housewife were essentially consigned to death. Needless to say, there was considerable controversy regarding the values associated with the committee's decision to preserve versus discontinue life among the five candidates.

There were also significant legal challenges to the view that physicians knew what was best for their patients and could provide surgical interventions based solely upon what they viewed as in the patient's best interest. Though the legal basis for patients' informed consent for surgical procedures had been present for 50 years, paternalistic medicine was directly challenged by two exposés in the 1960s and early 1970s. Henry Beecher (1966) documented what appeared to be a common practice of conducting biomedical research, including studies involving risky exposures on vulnerable populations, such as the mentally ill, prisoners, and children, in the absence of the participants' informed consent. In 1972, a whistleblower within the Public Health Service brought to public attention the Tuskegee syphilis study, in which treatment had been deliberately withheld from sick patients to study the course of the illness (Thomas & Quinn, 1991).

On multiple fronts, activists attempted to change the hierarchical doctor-patient relationship into a more egalitarian partnership. The development of community health centers, beginning in the mid-1960s, often espoused an egalitarian view of the doctor-patient relationship (Zuvekas, 1990) in which physicians and patients were encouraged to refer to each other by their first names (Tomes, 2016). In some centers, the label "patient" was replaced with "client" (Tomes, 2016).

The women's movement also changed the role of patients from passive recipients of advice to critical evaluators of the medical services received (Charles, Whelan, & Gafni, 1999). Among the targets of feminist critics of conventional medical practice (McCabe, Varricchio, Padberg, & Simpson, 1995) were paternalistic oncologists dictating to women that they needed breast biopsies and mastectomies. In the 1960s, the customary medical procedure for suspected breast cancer was to perform a biopsy and mastectomy as part of the same procedure. Breast cancer advocates argued that there should be a two-step process in which a biopsy was performed and women were provided with the results. With this information, the patient could determine whether a mastectomy was in her best interest. Oncologists were also encouraged to provide women with information about alternative treatments to radical mastectomies (Tomes, 2016).

The medico-legal standard of a decision of "a reasonable medical practitioner" was critically evaluated. In the 1970s, a new legal standard, the material risk approach, emphasized the role of the patient in medical decision-making. Rather than deferring to physicians' judgment, patients should be informed of any risk that would be significant to a reasonable person (Tomes, 2016). This disclosure would include the risks and benefits of radical mastectomy, partial mastectomy, and lumpectomy, as well as current data about the success rates of these procedures. Given this information, women were encouraged to choose for themselves the treatment that best matched their needs (Tomes, 2016).

As the public began to critically evaluate and make choices about the health care they received, patients came to be increasingly viewed as consumers. Similar to the view of Nader and other consumer advocates, recipients of health care had basic rights that should be protected. In the late 1960s, health activists developed the

Patient's Bill of Rights (Tomes, 2016). This was predominantly a set of principles that emphasized a transparent relationship between patients and physicians as well as patients and hospitals. In 1972, the American Hospital Association endorsed a version of the Patient's Bill of Rights. While there were many critics of these standards, including those who viewed the document as providing a very limited degree of patient support (Tomes, 2016), the document did provide a basis for legal and policy challenges to the medical profession.

In 1978, the long-standing prohibition against advertising by physicians was legally challenged by a US Supreme Court decision. While the initial ruling was for attorneys, the Federal Trade Commission extended the legality of direct marketing to physicians (Starr, 2008). Prior to the court ruling, direct advertising was prohibited by the American Medical Association. However, even after the court ruling, surveys conducted in the 1980s indicated that more than a third of the general public considered physician advertising to be unprofessional and unethical (Schlesinger, 2002).

With direct marketing of pharmaceuticals and medical care to the public, the consumer orientation of patients has become progressively stronger. Research indicates that patients with a consumer orientation are better educated and report less faith in and dependence upon physicians (Schlesinger, 2002). In 2001, it was found that 38 percent of survey respondents had obtained or sought information about a personal health issue from a source other than their physician (Schlesinger, 2002).

Patients' increased tendency to view medical care from a marketplace perspective corresponded with a decline in public confidence in the professions. According to surveys, between 1965 and 1995, the loss of professional recognition and respect for medicine was "more pronounced than that experienced by other social institutions," with medicine becoming "one of the least trusted social institutions" (Schlesinger, 2002). As will be explored further below, health care professionals have been caught between two conflicting forces. Insurance companies' concerns with cost-containment led patients to wonder whether physicians' decisions about their care were overly influenced by economic considerations. Periodic news stories of fraudulent Medicare and Medicaid billing did not help matters. Physicians essentially had to please two constituencies—their funders and their patients. As physicians increasingly became employees of large hospital corporations, they also found their practice regulated by non-physician health care administrators.

There have been a number of criticisms of the influence of business models on patient care. Groopman (2010; Hartzband & Groopman, 2016), a physician, argued that receiving medical care differs considerably from buying a car. When the marketplace orientation is taken to its logical extreme and a patient's body is discussed in terms of its component parts and the cost of surgical intervention for each, even consumer-oriented patients are offended or disturbed (Groopman, 2010; Hartzband & Groopman, 2009). While tentative, research in cognitive psychology suggests that when physicians view their work in economic terms, many of the virtues of health care, such as pride in one's work, duty, and collegiality, become subjugated to self-interest (Groopman, 2010). When health care administrators view physicians' work in terms of productivity and dollars billed, health care professionals become assembly-line workers (Hartzband & Groopman, 2016).

Health Insurance and Health Care

The provision of health care in the United States and other countries is strongly influenced by economics. Specifically, medical services may be paid for by a centralized government system, direct payment from patients, private insurance companies, and/or patients' employers. As will be discussed further, many countries such as Canada and Great Britain have a centralized government-funded health care system. In these countries, physicians and hospitals are paid directly by a government office for services rendered to patients. Other countries, such as the United States, feature a mix of government-funded health care services, private insurance, and direct patient payment. The type of funding mechanism plays a major role in access to health care and, to a varying extent, the types of medical services that a patient may receive.

Many commentators note that the role of employers in funding health care is uniquely American and has contributed to a complex system, with policies that often appear contradictory. Health insurance as a condition of employment in the United States actually dates back to 1798 with the establishment of the US Marine Hospital. Seamen had the cost of services deducted from their paychecks (Scofea, 1994). Hospitals became more common in the 1800s but were mostly run as charitable services, often associated with religious institutions. As is evident from the earlier part of this chapter, the armamentarium of treatments—either in hospitals or as outpatients—was limited. Recovery generally depended on the body's own responses. In the late 1800s, several industries such as railroads and timber companies developed health care plans for their employees. In some instances, such as railroads, these plans included hiring physicians and establishing company-owned hospitals (Starr, 2008).

One of the first plans was at Baylor University Medical Center in the 1920s. The hospital had accumulated many unpaid bills and offered the local teachers' union a plan. For the cost of six dollars a year, subscribers could, if needed, receive a 21-day hospital stay with all costs paid. However, in an early example of a deductible, this insurance agreement would take effect only after the initial week of hospital care, for which the insured would pay five dollars a day (Starr, 2008). Eventually, the Baylor plan became Blue Cross—a national health insurance plan operated by a not-for-profit organization. The focus of this early health insurance system was to protect patients from bankruptcy as well as to support religious hospitals. Beginning in the 1960s, other for-profit companies began offering health insurance, and the number of subscribers to what was then known as Blue Cross Blue Shield diminished. Eventually, Blue Cross Blue Shield also became a private corporation. It is important to recognize that private insurance companies are profit-making enterprises. There are shareholders to whom they must report and quarterly figures indicating a profit or loss.

While developing Social Security in 1935, President Franklin Roosevelt was interested in including government-provided health insurance with this income-support program. However, the American Medical Association at the time was highly critical of any type of government-sponsored health insurance plan (Blumenthal, 2006). Historians suggest that Roosevelt recognized that health insurance would be very controversial and could negatively affect congressional support for income insurance for the elderly and unemployed (Blumenthal, 2006; Starr, 2008).

Yet, soon after, the federal government passed legislation that resulted in the emphasis on employer-sponsored insurance that continues to be a key part of health care funding. During the early 1940s, the government had placed limits on employers' ability to increase wages. However, at the same time, because of the war, the available labor force was limited and industries were competing for workers. Employers were looking for nonwage benefits to attract workers. Health insurance became one of these benefits. Labor unions were also more powerful compared with today. The government established a policy that labor unions could not change their health benefits program until the labor contract that was in effect had expired. Employer-based health insurance was further institutionalized in the 1950s when the Internal Revenue Service ruled that health insurance was not taxable as income to employees (Blumenthal, 2006). These regulations have led to the ongoing issue of health care for employees being a key component of union contracts.

By 2000, employer-based insurance covered two-thirds of nonelderly Americans. However, during the past 50 years, health care costs have risen significantly. In 1960, health care accounted for about 5 percent of gross domestic product in the United States. Today the figure stands at around 16 percent. As health care costs continued to escalate, employers for some time, absorbed the increased cost. As Blumenthal (2006) notes, the United States had become dependent upon employers to protect US citizens from rising health care costs and catastrophic illness. As a result, health care for many Americans is influenced by the financial success of American business and industry. This point has been made very clear by the economic problems associated with the US auto industry. As the cost of employer-based health insurance increased dramatically—from 1999 to 2011, health care premiums increased by 160 percent—the cost could no longer be absorbed and began to be passed on to employees (Claxton et al., 2012).

In the last 25 years, whenever unions renegotiated with businesses and industries, health insurance was often a major sticking point. In the mid-1980s, as chairman of Chrysler, Lee Iacocca highlighted how the additional cost of health insurance had to be passed along to consumers; from a price perspective, this made American cars less competitive. At that time, Chrysler was paying on average about $6,000 per employee per year for health insurance (Rosenbaum, 1984). In the United States, worker wages were often higher than those of comparable workers in other Western countries. However, in countries with universal coverage or government-sponsored health care, the cost of health insurance was borne by the government rather than the employer, so both overall wages and the price of the product (e.g., automobiles) could be maintained at a lower level. Chrysler attempted to negotiate lower premiums by agreeing to use plans that strongly encouraged the use of less expensive generic (as opposed to brand-name) medications and began requiring insurance companies to establish the necessity of some surgical procedures (Rosenbaum, 1984). Health insurance premiums, as well as patient deductibles and co-pays, have been rising more rapidly than wages. For example, between 2009 and 2014, health care premiums increased by 28 percent compared with an increase in wages of only 7.8 percent (Springer, 2016). Over the past decade, employers have begun to drop coverage altogether, particularly smaller companies, and they have required employees to pay higher premiums. Insurance companies have reduced restrictions on care but simultaneously increased premiums, co-pays, and deductibles, so patients maintain choice but bear more of the cost (Starr, 2013).

By the 1970s, it became increasingly clear that cost containment was going to be necessary to prevent health care premiums from continuing to rise. In 1973, President Nixon signed the Health Maintenance Organization Act, which encouraged the development of health maintenance organizations that were paid a flat sum in advance for providing health care services to a specific group. By 1989, more than 50 percent of working Americans with private health insurance were enrolled in some form of health maintenance organization (Starr, 2008).

The term *primary care physician* became much more popular during this era, in that access to a referral for a specialist such as an orthopedist could only be provided in terms of coverage if one went to one's primary care physician first, who certified the need for it. Also, networks of health care providers developed—these networks were typically groups of physicians and related hospitals who agreed to accept payment for specific procedures provided by the company. Insurers would negotiate reduced costs for their members with doctors, hospitals, and pharmacies based upon the notion that the majority of patients would be covered under that specific plan. There was also a pattern of capitation. In this system, a physician group was given a flat amount of money each year by a health insurer to take care of all in-network patients. If there was money left at the end of the year, the health care providers kept it. In reality, however, because of costs and patient demand for specialty care and expensive tests and hospitalizations, providers often had to reimburse the insurance company. Since these were generally governed by private businesses, there was little incentive for preventive care. Patients often will ask why smoking cessation medications such as Chantix or Wellbutrin are not covered by their health insurance company. From a business model, it does not make sense to fund treatments that will reduce the likelihood of an illness appearing 20 years later. The insurance company, as a corporation, is focused on short-term profits and loss. The benefits of smoking cessation, the absence of lung and related cancers, would not occur until far into the future.

However, by the late 1990s, there was considerable consumer backlash associated with HMOs. Stories of "drive-through" deliveries of babies became more common. Data appeared to support the fact that HMOs were associated with fewer hospital days for new mothers. In 1990, about 4 percent of insured patients spent only one day in the hospital after delivering a baby. In 1994, this figure was 48.1 percent for HMO patients. The odds of a patient staying only one day for a delivery was nearly twice as great for an HMO versus a non-HMO patient (Volpp & Bundorf, 1999). Withholding care that was deemed unnecessary by HMOs resulted in profit. Often HMOs placed significant restrictions on the health care providers from which the patient could receive treatment. In some situations, patients were required to use hospitals that were up to 30 miles from their home rather than a nearby facility that did not have a contract with a particular HMO. Complaints such as these prompted a congressional hearing on HMOs. Particularly devastating testimony at this hearing came from Dr. Linda Peeno, a physician who had been a medical reviewer for several HMOs:

> I wish to begin by making a public confession: In the spring of 1987, as a physician, I caused the death of a man.

Although this was known to many people, I have not been taken before any court of law or called to account for this in any professional or public forum. In fact, just the opposite occurred: I was "rewarded" for this. It bought me an improved reputation in my job, and contributed to my advancement afterwards. Not only did I demonstrate I could indeed do what was expected of me, I exemplified the "good" company doctor: I saved a half million dollars!

Since that day, I have lived with this act, and many others, eating into my heart and soul. For me, a physician is a professional charged with the care, or healing, of his or her fellow human beings. The primary ethical norm is: do no harm. I did worse: I caused a death. Instead of using a clumsy, bloody weapon, I used the simplest, cleanest of tools: my words. The man died because I denied him a necessary operation to save his heart. I felt little pain or remorse at the time. The man's faceless distance soothed my conscience. Like a skilled soldier, I was trained for this moment. When any moral qualms arose, I was to remember: I am not denying care; I am only denying payment. (Peeno, 1996)

As a result of public backlash, states enacted numerous laws regulating the activities of health maintenance organizations. The number of health insurance plans with the label "HMO" declined dramatically. A lesson learned from the decline of the HMO is that Americans highly value individual autonomy and choice (Mechanic, 2004). At the same time, there is a history of respect for science and scientific authority that leads American patients to be sure that they are receiving the most modern and sophisticated treatment available (Tomes, 2016).

However, the cost of providing health care continues to rise. This cost has been passed along to patients and their employers in the form of higher insurance premiums as well as deductibles (the amount that the patient must pay directly before their insurance takes effect) and co-pays (the amount of the cost of an office visit or prescription for which the patient directly pays—often 15 to 20 percent). Some of the components of managed care remain.

Professional provider organizations (PPOs) are a group of physicians, hospitals, and medical laboratories who agree to accept a discounted rate of payment from insurance companies (de Lissovoy, Rice, Ermann, & Gabel, 1986). Often, patients can go to providers that are outside of the PPO network but must pay substantially more of the bill. Another remnant of the managed-care era of HMOs is the centrality of the primary care physician. In the earlier days of private insurance, patients could direct themselves to a specialist. Often, specialists, who charge significantly more for their services, would be treating problems readily treated by a less expensive family physician, internist, or pediatrician. To prevent what was perceived as unnecessary use of specialists, patients were required to receive a referral from their primary care physician. Without the referral, the insurance would not cover the cost of the specialist visit. Mechanic (2004) has pointed out that the managed-care aspect of HMOs has not disappeared completely; it was replaced by "managed-care lite" (p. 76).

Federal Health Insurance: Medicare and Medicaid

In 1965, President Johnson amended Social Security with the addition of Medicare and Medicaid.

Medicare

Medicare is a form of universal coverage that extends benefits to everyone over age 65 in the United States. In 1972, under the Nixon administration, Medicare was expanded to include those under 65 who were receiving Social Security disability benefits typically for chronic illnesses such as end-stage renal disease. Medicare is, in many respects, a form of universal coverage for senior citizens. Medicare is an entitlement program, meaning that everyone receives this form of insurance, and it is not related to one's income. If you receive a slip with your paycheck, you should be able to see how much of your salary or wages are taken out for Social Security and state, federal, and local taxes. You will note that there is typically a percentage of your salary taken out for Medicare. You may have heard on the news that there are concerns that in the not-so-distant future, funding for Medicare may run out. This possibility is raised because as the life span lengthens, the ratio of working adults to those over 65 is likely to become narrower.

Medicare Part A is available to everyone over 65 as well as some nonelderly individuals with disabilities that prevent regular employment, and it is funded through payroll taxes (Cohen, 1985). Part A covers hospital services. Part B covers physicians and other services. Part B is not mandatory and is funded through a combination of federal contributions and premiums funded by the recipients themselves. In addition, Part B does include copayments and deductibles. Furthermore, physicians may bill the patient above the Medicare-established fee—a practice called "balance billing." This additional charge cannot exceed 15 percent of the Medicare-established rate (Lavarreda & Brown, 2013). While not often officially called "Part C," there are two available forms of coverage to address the cost of deductibles and other charges not covered directly by Medicare Part B. Medigap is one form of supplemental coverage, which is a form of private insurance. This coverage can also be obtained through a managed-care plan such as Medicare-plus. With the growing price of medications, and the limited coverage in Medicare Part B, many seniors were forgoing medication treatment because of cost. In 2006, Part D was implemented for prescription drug coverage; however, patients are required to choose a private drug plan, which are often limited in number and also have a rather complex set of rules (Lavarreda & Brown, 2013).

Medicare is not without its problems. Notable areas that are not covered are long-term care and home health services. In addition, as medical technology and pharmaceuticals have improved dramatically over the past two decades, there has been a corresponding cost increase that is likely to continue to be passed along in the form of co-pays and deductibles. Even though supplemental insurance can be purchased for these extra costs, it is likely that the cost of these supplements will see a corresponding rise as well.

Medicaid

Medicaid was developed to provide health care to those with low income who are eligible for programs such as aid to families with dependent children and Supplemental Security Income. Funding of Medicaid is shared between states and the federal government, with the federal contribution being between 50 and 77 percent (Lavarreda & Brown, 2013). Medicaid is a means-tested public assistance program such that a family's income must be below a certain level to receive this form of health insurance. Administration of the program and income standards for eligibility are established at the state level. Availability of additional health care services, such as vision care, prescription medications, and physical therapy, is established at the state level. Medicaid has been associated with increased health care utilization among lower-income patients. Again, somewhat similar to trends in Medicare, Medicaid is often outsourced to private insurance companies. Medicaid was successful in increasing access to medical care. Infant mortality rates, after the introduction of Medicaid, were cut in half. In pre-Medicaid 1963, 20 percent of Americans living below the poverty line had not seen a physician; by 1970, this rate had shrunk to 8 percent (Coontz, 1992). Among those with Medicaid, the number of physician visits per year is essentially the same as that among higher-income people.

One problem with Medicaid is that payment levels are often very low and many physicians will not accept patients whose sole payment will be through Medicaid. This became a particular problem with obstetricians, and Congress eventually increased the fees for obstetrics care. Another criticism is that, in part because of its origins in public assistance programs, the means tests that are conducted in welfare offices have been seen as demeaning (Lavarreda & Brown, 2013).

S-CHIP
A related program, State Children's Health Insurance Program (S-CHIP), was enacted in 1997 to cover low-income children who otherwise might not be covered by Medicaid. In addition to allowing states to set the income eligibility criteria significantly higher than for Medicaid, the federal government provided a significant level of matching funds to states to support S-CHIP because of family income being too high. S-CHIP in its early days actually served children who were previously insured through private programs, not the uninsured children whom the program intended to target. However, over time, the program was able to demonstrate that children enrolled in S-CHIP were more likely to receive health care and that with chronic conditions in particular, such as asthma, the program was successful in permitting access to quality care (Lavarreda & Brown, 2013). This model of expanding Medicaid eligibility upward in terms of income levels was a key feature of a later development in government health insurance—the Affordable Care Act (Obamacare).

The Uninsured
Despite the population coverage provided by employer-sponsored health insurance as well as government programs, a significant number of Americans remained without health insurance. In the current century, this figure has hovered between 16 and 17 percent of the population. For example, in 2008, one out of seven Americans did not have health insurance (Obama, 2016). With the implementation of the Affordable Care Act discussed below, the percentage of those without health insurance declined by 43 percent. As of 2015, 9.1 percent of Americans were reportedly without health insurance.

Some of those without insurance have been able to receive a range of health services through federally funded neighborhood clinics. Historically, health centers in low-income areas have received support from the federal government

(Zuvekas, 1990). These clinics typically apply for grants, and if they are determined to be a federally qualified health center that shows they are serving underserved populations, they are able to receive governmental financial support (Zuvekas, 1990). They are provided with other benefits as well, such as the ability to purchase vaccines for children and drugs at reduced cost. These neighborhood clinics also tend to provide an array of services, including dental, vision, and mental health. The author, for a number of years, provided mental health services at a federally qualified center in south St. Louis, Missouri. Children, in particular, who would not have been able to access mental health services in the private sector were able to receive assessment and limited counseling.

Emergency Medical Treatment and Active Labor Act
For those without insurance, emergency departments have become a source of medical care. In 1986, the federal government passed the Emergency Medical Treatment and Active Labor Act (EMTALA). Any hospital that receives federal Medicare or Medicaid funds and operates an emergency department is required to provide care for all patients who present to the emergency room (Friedman, 2011). All patients must be medically evaluated, stabilized, and transferred to another facility or treated. Patients cannot be turned away because of the absence of insurance or ability to pay. The basis of this legislation was the practice of emergency department "dumping." In one instance, a pregnant woman in labor appeared at the hospital but was turned away. The second hospital conducted an assessment, and fetal monitoring indicated that the fetal heart rate was irregular and there was other evidence of fetal distress. Despite these circumstances, the woman was sent to the local county hospital, where an emergency cesarean section was conducted. The baby was stillborn (Friedman, 2011).

While evidence is somewhat mixed, there are suggestions that in some regions of the country, particularly where there are few other options for uninsured patients, the emergency department is a source of care for non-urgent problems (Johnson et al., 2012). This issue raises concerns about the appropriate use of emergency department resources, but at the same time, it is recognized that for persons without insurance or other financial resources, the local emergency department may be one of the few places to get medical care.

Some commentators have asserted that in the United States, the health care system ends up attempting to compensate for a social service safety net with many holes. Social factors such as inadequate housing, food, and poor working conditions are often underlying problems of many medical conditions—a point that most physicians recognize. Homelessness is a driving force behind the use of the emergency department among patients with non-urgent problems. Researchers found that homeless individuals were at least three times more likely to use an emergency department within the past year. A survey of homeless individuals found that about 40 percent had used the emergency department at least once in the previous year (Kushel, Perry, Bangsberg, Clark, & Moss, 2002). Those providing health services try to respond to these broader social issues but are not equipped to do so. Meanwhile, individuals with social problems account for some of the "overcrowding" characteristic of many urban emergency departments (Schanzer, Dominguez, Shrout, & Caton, 2007).

Health Care Reform: The Background of the Affordable Care Act

Health care reform was attempted in the 1990s under President Clinton. During the economic recession in the early 1990s, many Americans became unemployed and lost their employer-based insurance. As he campaigned for president, Clinton indicated that he was going to be supporting legislation for a universal health plan (Starr, 2008; 2013). In the Clinton plan, the proposed Health Security Act, the central component for both expanding coverage and containing costs, would require employers to enroll all their employees in a managed-care plan. Since most people with jobs already had health insurance, the Clinton plan, if enacted, would have required that employees give up their insurance and possibly their current health care providers to join an HMO network. The plan also included price controls on insurance premiums, which were not well received by the insurance industry. President Clinton placed his wife, Hillary Clinton, in charge of health care reform. At that time, Ms. Clinton had not had any significant government/legislative experience, and her central role in this effort was criticized by Republicans. The Clinton plan never even made it to a congressional vote and was basically scuttled.

However, in 2006, the state of Massachusetts enacted what essentially is a plan of universal coverage for residents of the state. It included an expansion of Medicaid and subsidies for the purchase of private insurance as well as a mandate requiring all citizens to have health insurance (Kominski, 2013). The Massachusetts program, signed into law by then governor Mitt Romney, has been seen as a success in extending health care to a significant percentage of the population that was previously uninsured.

The Affordable Care Act (ACA)

The major focus of the Affordable Care Act ("Obamacare") was to provide insurance to the one in six Americans who did not have any type of health coverage. The ACA was guided by a set of core principles.

1. Everyone in the country will have health insurance of some type.
2. Some of this greater coverage will be due to increased availability of Medicaid. Specifically, families whose gross income was previously too high for Medicaid would be more likely now to be eligible.
3. For those not eligible for government-supported health insurance or who did not receive coverage through their employer, insurance could be purchased from an exchange that offered varying degrees of coverage from private insurers. These health insurance companies provided different packages of care, sometimes labeled as "bronze," "silver," and "gold," according to their level of coverage and price. Typically, the difference between the plans was that the cost to individual patients was lower through either a low deductible or lower co-pays for services and medications.
4. A fine would be assessed on citizens who did not have insurance.
5. The government would include some regulation of private insurance companies—specifically, patients could not be turned down by a private company because of pre-existing health conditions.
6. There was an emphasis on increasing efficiency and decreasing waste in the health care system.

Tax credits were made available to families earning between 133 percent and 400 percent of the federal poverty level. The formula for tax credits was designed to keep insurance premium costs between 2 and 8 percent of total family income (Kominski, 2013). To address a segment of the population that frequently did not carry health insurance, the ACA allowed young adults to stay on their parents' insurance until the age of 26. The fine for not having health insurance was initially $95 per person for four or more persons, not to exceed 1 percent of household income. By 2016, this had increased to $695 per person, or 2.5 percent of household income (Kominski, 2013). In addition to not discriminating against those with pre-existing conditions, the ACA required insurance companies to cover basic maternity care.

Some of the financial protections included no annual or lifetime limits on the amount that an insurance company would pay for an individual's care. Previously, many private insurance companies had a "cap" on coverage—a dollar amount for each patient beyond which the insurance company would not pay for health services. Private insurance companies may spend no more than 15 to 20 percent of premiums on administrative costs, which include advertising and lobbying, although the federal Medicare program spends only about 1 to 2 percent of its costs on administration (Groopman & Hartzband, 2017). Insurance companies must also go through a review process for any premium increases.

Problems with the Affordable Care Act

In order to ensure passage of the ACA by Congress, President Obama and those working with him made several concessions that diminished the act's effectiveness. The insurance industry, pharmaceutical companies, and hospital executives would have actively worked to defeat the legislation if significant restrictions were placed on their domains. Initially, the ACA was to include significant restrictions on the price of medications. However, the insurance industry, as well as health care institutions such as hospitals, were given considerable latitude in setting prices, premiums, and deductibles (Emanuel, 2014). As a result, the economic benefits from the ACA have been limited. In some instances, Americans were forced into paying more for a health insurance plan and abandoning their prior plan because it did not meet standards of coverage specified by the ACA. It was estimated that soon after the ACA was implemented, about 20 percent of those who were carrying insurance had their policies canceled (Blumenthal & Collins, 2014).

Cost variations for medical procedures are very common. With the exception of programs such as Medicare or Medicaid, which establish preset prices for treating specific conditions or for procedures such as gallbladder removal, there are no standard charges across hospitals. Groopman and Hartzband (2017) describe how an echocardiogram test was priced at $8,000 at one local hospital, $6,000 at a second institution, and $4,000 at a third hospital. It is often difficult to know the real cost of medical services since insurance companies are frequently "middlemen" whose arrangements with hospitals result in discounts; however, these discounted costs have become the standard such that the "real" cost of many medical procedures is actually unknown.

In order for private health insurers to be successful, they need to have a large number of relatively healthy people—often young adults—in their pool of premium payers. The premiums paid by these healthy individuals, who rarely use health services, in essence fund the care of those who are much sicker and often suffering from age-related illnesses. Unfortunately, young adults have not signed up in the numbers often needed to make health insurance profitable from a business perspective.

While many health insurance companies initially supported the ACA because of the possibility of increased revenues through selling more policies, reports indicate that many of these companies have taken significant financial losses. Some of the restrictions in terms of levels of service provided, together with the absence of caps on payments for services and requirements to take those with pre-existing conditions, may not make this program particularly attractive to insurers. Indeed, as this chapter is being written, there are reports that insurers are moving out of areas and no longer offering coverage in regions of the country that have proven unprofitable. The result has been that many citizens have fewer choices for their health insurance. In addition, as has been the case in the past, the cost of premiums continues to rise, and the amount of direct out-of-pocket expense to patients is increasing as well. It is also likely that there will still be a percentage, albeit smaller, of Americans who are uninsured. Implementation of the ACA revealed a coverage gap between those who earn too much to be eligible for expanded Medicaid but do not have employer-based insurance. For many of these individuals and their families, the cost of health insurance through the exchange is prohibitive.

The US Health Care System: International Comparisons

During the last forty years, as the United States has grappled with health care reform, some policy makers have studied health care delivery systems in other countries. As the United States is changing in terms of how health care is organized, countries such as Canada, Great Britain, and Japan are often cited as either models of health care to which the US should aspire or models of health care to be avoided.

As is evident from our discussion in this chapter, the US health care system is not systematically organized. Instead, US citizens experience a somewhat haphazard arrangement of public and private health care institutions that often do not interact with one another. The significant role of employers in funding health care was, in many respects, an accident of history (Starr, 2008) that has continued even though it has placed growing economic demands on US companies as well as workers.

As Hinote & Wasserman (2016) note, the US health care system is full of contradictions. While the United States spends more on health care than any country in the world, it lags behind many others on key health indicators. The United States devotes 17.1 percent of its gross domestic product to health care—a figure that has continued to rise during the past three decades. After the United States, Switzerland's total spending on health care is 11.8 percent, Germany 10.7, France 11.6, and the United Kingdom approximately 8.8. In the United States, per capita health care expenditures are approximately $9,000, while the comparable figure for Japan is $3,700, and for Canada it is $4,500 (Mossialos, Wenzl, Osborn, & Anderson, 2017).

The World Health Organization ranks the United States 24th in terms of health attainment, with an overall worldwide ranking of 37th for quality of health care. Among 12 industrialized countries, the United States has the highest infant mortality rate and the shortest life expectancy at birth (Mossialos et al. 2017). There are a number of countries, such as Switzerland, Canada, Australia, Japan, and France, in which the life expectancy at birth is from two to seven years longer than in the United States.

When indices of receiving health care are examined, the United States also falls behind many other countries. When compared with the United States, patients in Australia, Canada, New Zealand, and the United Kingdom are more likely to report that they received a recommended medical test. A similar pattern exists for filling prescriptions.

At the same time, US medical care is often seen as the best in the world. It is not unusual for political and business leaders from countries around the world to come to the United States for health care if they are seriously ill. The United States has some of the most advanced medical technology available. Importantly, this sophisticated technology is readily accessible to patients with the resources to cover the cost. The ratio of MRI machines in the United States per one million people is 35.5. With the exception of Japan, the comparable ratio in other developed countries does not exceed 13 per million. Similar international disparities exist with CT scans. The number of MRI exams completed per 1,000 citizens is twice as high in the United States as in Canada and the Netherlands, and almost 4 times as high as in Australia (Mossialos et al., 2017).

All of the countries that we discuss below have universal coverage, meaning that all citizens have some form of health insurance. Several of these countries, such as Great Britain and Canada, have "single-payer" systems, which means that the government provides health care, and it is paid for through taxes.

Switzerland

One of the relatively few countries in the world that resembles the United States in terms of its health insurance system is Switzerland. The Swiss have a complicated group of funding sources for medical care. In contrast to the United States with Medicare and Medicaid, Switzerland does not have any forms of government-based insurance. All Swiss citizens are required to have basic health insurance coverage. The government subsidizes the cost of insurance for persons below a specific income. For those with the means to pay for them, there are a number of optional forms of insurance a patient can carry in addition to the "base" insurance required of all citizens. However, the co-pays and out-of-pocket expenses in Switzerland are about 60 percent higher per year than in the United States. Administrative costs for health insurance are significantly lower than in the United States. While costs are significantly lower, outcomes have been reported as better than the United States for cerebrovascular disease and diabetes (Herzlinger & Parsa-Parsi, 2004). Swiss physicians report dissatisfaction with the tight regulations over their practice by insurance companies. This oversight is particularly demanding with regard to prescribing medications. However, their average health care expenditures overall are significantly lower than in the United States. Total US expenditures in 2007 were approximately $7,000 compared with $4,500 in Switzerland (OECD Health Statistics, 2017).

Great Britain

In the spring and summer of 1948, the citizens of Great Britain received a flyer with the following announcement:

> [The new national health service] . . . will provide you with all medical, dental, and nursing care. Everyone—rich or poor, man, woman, or child—can use it or any part of it. There are no charges except for a few special items. There are no insurance qualifications. But it is not a charity. You are all paying for it, mainly as taxpayers, and it will relieve your money worries in times of illness. (Webster, 2002, p. 240)

Inaugurated on July 5, 1948, the National Health Service (NHS) was the third-largest nonmilitary organization in Britain, with 360,000 medical staff, 3,100 hospitals, and 550,000 hospital beds. During World War II, it became apparent that Britain's health care system was extremely fragmented. There were public hospitals, voluntary hospitals, and an array of clinics that were differentially administered. Webster (2002) notes that in one area of Britain there were 93 hospitals administered by 46 separate local authorities.

British citizens' response to the availability of health care was overwhelming and much greater than policy makers had anticipated. Webster (2002) notes that in 1951 the average number of prescriptions per person per year was 5.2. Additionally, the availability of free or greatly subsidized medical devices, such as false teeth and eyeglasses, was eagerly taken advantage of by citizens who had gone without many necessities during the war years.

One of the key features of the health service is the central role of general practice physicians. Initially general practitioners were in solo office practices. However, today's NHS general practitioner is part of a health care team that successfully manages the majority of patients without referral to specialists. In the original model, general practitioners were independent contractors and not on a salary. However, this model has changed, with general practitioners generally operating out of a community-type clinic and managing a number of patients. In terms of a biopsychosocial approach to health care, National Health Service general practitioners were far ahead of their American counterparts. In the late 1950s, psychoanalyst Michael Balint began holding seminars/case conferences with general practitioners in London. The physicians brought particularly frustrating cases to the group. Typically, the patients presented had significant psychosocial issues in addition to ongoing medical problems. Over time, the focus shifted to the physicians' emotional responses to patients and their impact on doctor-patient interaction (Balint, 1957). What we now call "Balint training" is a common component of family practice residency education in the United States.

Despite the centrality of general practitioners in the NHS system, technological advances as well as medication costs have led to economic strain for Britain's health care. As costs continued to escalate, government oversight of care increased. For example, by the early to mid-1980s, the government began the practice of regulating medications that could be prescribed. The service periodically goes through revision and reorganization. In 2005, when there appeared to be an increased emphasis on consumers, the NHS established a policy whereby when referred for specialty care, patients are provided with the names of four different providers and permitted to choose (Klein, 2006). Target data about outcomes associated with individual regional health centers has also been made public along with patient satisfaction ratings. It is now possible to go online and examine the performance of local hospitals as well as NHS clinics.

There have also been periodic discussions of privatizing the National Health Service. However, the institution remains the third-largest employer in Britain, and despite periodic criticisms, it is not a service with which British citizens would readily part.

A key problem with the British system has been access to services. For example, a newspaper article claimed that 500 patients died in 2015 in Britain because of excessive waiting times in NHS hospital emergency departments. Of these 500 patients, 150 were not admitted because of the unavailability of a hospital bed (Campbell, 2015). Surgical procedures that are considered elective are also associated with long wait times. For gallstone removal, patients must wait an average of 91 days; for knee replacement, 107 days; for cataract removal, 24 days. Overall, many patients had been waiting more than 18 weeks for one of seven procedures (Campbell, 2017). Because of this issue, about 10 percent of British patients carry private insurance so that they can receive care outside of the NHS.

Thus, while patients are not directly responsible for the cost of their health care, waiting for diagnostic tests and surgery is a major problem in the NHS. As the population ages and demands for health care increase, it will continue to be difficult for the National Health Service to respond to consumer demand without further raising taxes. More disturbing to many Americans, the NHS does engage in rationing care (Vize, 2015). The shortages of health care providers have resulted in a process of triaging patients based upon factors other than the seriousness of their illness. For example, it has been reported that regular cigarette smokers and patients with obesity are often refused surgical procedures. Additionally, there is an implicit rationing system for patients with kidney failure and other conditions such as cardiovascular disease based upon patients' age (Doyal, 1997; Vize, 2015).

Canada

The Canadian system is, to some extent, modeled on Britain's NHS. It is a centralized system providing all citizens with government-sponsored health care that is paid through taxes. Health care is approximately 10 percent of Canada's gross domestic product. While the origins of Canada's system have at times been debated, there is clarity about the importance of the work of Tommy Douglas, who was premier of Saskatchewan (MacKinnon, 2004). Douglas introduced a free provincial medical hospital and dental care plan in 1945 for older and indigent residents of the province. In 1947, he introduced a hospital insurance plan in which premiums were $5 a person and $10 per family. By the end of 1947, 93 percent of the population was covered by this system. In 1949, Douglas introduced what was termed "Medicare" to the province as a whole. In the Saskatchewan model, all bills were prepaid; patients never saw a physician's bill. The plan was available to everyone regardless of age or any pre-existing condition. The health care would be administered by the provincial government. Within a year of the bill passing, Saskatchewan physicians went out on strike for 23 days. In 1964, Premier Lester Pearson of Canada indicated that financial assistance would be given to any province that had a system like Medicare (Clarke, 1996).

Canadians appear to be healthier than Americans. Survey data indicate that overall prevalence rates of hypertension, diabetes, and asthma are significantly lower in Canada than in the United States (Lasser, Himmelstein, & Woolhandler, 2006). The Canadian system emphasizes primary over tertiary care. It is more prevention oriented. The Canadian system has markedly lower administrative costs and markedly lower out-of-pocket costs for patients. However, the cost of health programs has been increasingly passed on to the provinces. The federal contribution diminished from 50 percent in 1971 to 23 percent in 1997. Coverage is available for all medical necessities; however, there are, as in Great Britain, significant wait times for elective procedures. Some of these procedures are questionable in terms of being elective. The wait for cardiac bypass surgery has been approximately two months, treatment for lung cancer 60 days, obtaining a CT of the brain 73 days, hip replacement 210 days, and knee replacement 291 days (Fraser Institute, 2017).

In addition, there are gaps in coverage for dental care, long-term care such as nursing homes, and medications. While one is free to choose one's primary care physician, choices are often limited, and the number of providers and specialists does reduce availability compared with the United States, in which 40 percent or so of patients report that they can get a same-day appointment with their physician. The comparable figure for Canada is about 25 percent due to shortages of medical personnel—particularly in some of the more remote parts of the country. There appears to be growing criticism by Canadian citizens about the wait times for various procedures. Since the majority of Canada's population lives within 100 miles of the US border, some Canadians come to United States for health care; another concern is that despite being a single-payer universal coverage system, there continue to be health disparities linked to income. The poorest 20 percent of the population is about a third more likely to report that they have an unmet medical need compared with the remaining 80 percent. Providing adequate health care for Canada's indigenous people has been a particular area of concern (Lasser et al., 2006).

Receipt of preventive services such as vaccination is higher among Canadian children than their US counterparts. Even though there may be delays in seeing the benefits of vaccinations, the single-payer approach allows the government to directly benefit from preventive care. In contrast, in the United States, heavily dominated by commercial insurance companies in which quarterly profits and losses are closely monitored, it is unlikely that a private insurance provider would benefit economically from many types of preventive care, since the benefits may not appear for 10 to 30 years. This difference between the United States and Canada has been particularly pronounced for human papillomavirus vaccination rates (Ogilvie et al., 2010). The HPV vaccine is helpful in preventing the development of cervical cancer later in life. To be completely vaccinated, children who are 11 to 12 years of age should get two shots of HPV vaccine, and for those 14 or older three shots are necessary over the span of six months. In Canada, vaccines are administered in schools to preadolescent girls. Provincial HPV vaccination rates range from 40 percent in the

Northwest Territories to 91 percent for Newfoundland (Raco, 2017). In the United States, the average for children and adolescents completing the vaccine is 49 percent (Centers for Disease Control, 2018e). The Canadian system, through medical practice as well as public health, emphasizes prevention.

In summary, Canadians have universal coverage and do not have to worry about incurring bankruptcy due to medical bills. The system emphasizes preventive care. In comparison to the United States, access to specialists, technology, and elective procedures requires a significantly greater delay. In some instances, this delay has led to preventable deaths.

International Health Care: Differences in Underlying Values

From a political perspective, governments that have a parliamentary system, such as Canada and Great Britain, are less likely to experience some of the "gridlock" around passing health-related legislation that has characterized the process in the United States. In the parliamentary system, in order for a party to have support as a majority, it will need to form coalitions with other political parties. For example, while the Green Party in Canada typically receives a smaller percentage of the vote than Liberal and Conservative parties, as well as the New Democratic Party, the Greens still have political influence—often through coalitions with a party with more parliamentary representatives. Additionally, with a coalition, there is less dissonance in passing legislation since there is no sizable party to oppose it. The US system, dominated by two political parties, does not require this level of cooperation. In European countries, labor unions continue to have more power than in the United States; the unions were a significant force for supporting single-payer, universal coverage in both Britain and Canada.

There also appear to be differences in values. Countries with government-sponsored health care have a tradition of social solidarity with the view that health care is a public good that should be equitably distributed. In the United States, in contrast, individualism tends to be much more important, leading to a tendency to be self-focused rather than emphasizing the common good when health care issues arise (Gilson, 2003). Another expression of this solidarity was noted earlier. Compared with the United States, most Western countries devote a greater proportion of government resources to education, food assistance, housing, childcare, and elder care. In these countries, preschools are heavily subsidized and free, and there are generous government-supported benefits and employment insurance for new parents.

In other countries that have a history of being part of the United Kingdom, such as New Zealand and Australia, there is a collectivist ethic that influences health care decisions. In the United States, in situations in which a patient is unable to voice his or her wishes for continued care, family members often will demand that "everything be done." As noted in the discussion about Great Britain and dialysis, there is greater emphasis on collective justice and fairness relative to individual rights. In contrast with the United States, countries with an emphasis on social solidarity place a greater value on equitable distribution of health resources, and the medical system is less likely to continue treatments with a low probability of success (Cassell, 2005).

What would an optimal health system look like in the United States?

1. An employer mandate—all companies must provide insurance for all employees.
2. An individual mandate requiring everyone to buy insurance. As in Switzerland, employers and private companies could offer discounted plans or receive government subsidies for citizens earning below a certain amount.
3. While it is possible that a universal plan could be offered by the government—similar to the United Kingdom or Canada—there would likely be a protracted struggle in attempting this option. Given the history of private insurance in the United States and the combined economic/political power of for-profit insurance companies, this would be difficult. Also, pharmaceutical companies and manufacturers of medical devices would oppose any plan that tightly regulated what they could charge patients.
4. Obamacare and the plan initiated in Massachusetts both relied upon the incremental addition of an already existing plan—Medicaid—to support universal coverage. If Medicaid were expanded to higher-income groups, it is likely that the stigma associated with this means-tested insurance would diminish.

Some commentators have suggested that Obamacare is an intermediate step between free-market health care and a universal system (Geyman, 2015). However, the tension between the American economy and freedom of choice for medical care and social costs, including greater taxation, may make it difficult to implement such a system. Furthermore, European countries with histories of strong social welfare policies, such as Britain, are currently experiencing significant economic challenges accompanied by threats to the continued generosity of the medical and social safety net.

Conclusion

While the amount of space devoted to the history and finance of the health care system may seem excessive, it is hoped that this context will help you better understand many of the dilemmas that arise in health care today. As you can see, political and economic as well as cultural forces have, in many respects, shaped both our expectations for health care and the type of care actually received. When there is a disconnect between what we want or expect and what actually occurs, it is often the case that these larger-system factors are playing a role. During the two years that I have been working on this book, health care has been a "hot" political topic in the United States. It will be interesting to see where our health system goes from here.

CHAPTER 4

Health Disparities and Diversity

I will begin this chapter with a confession. As an older White European heterosexual male, much of the content of this chapter is content of which I was unaware until I had been practicing for some years. When I began studying public health, after about 15 years of doing research, teaching and practicing as a clinical psychologist, learning about disparities opened my eyes to the complex cultural issues that arise when representatives of the dominant culture and minorities meet in the health care setting. I was particularly disturbed that as a psychologist I had not heard of the Tuskegee syphilis study, which is discussed below. The historical legacy of this government research in which Southern African American males were treated unethically and probably harmed certainly explained the overtone of suspicion I sometimes experienced when interacting with families of seriously ill African American patients in the hospital. Several recent authors have described "Two Americas" (Sanger-Katz, 2014). This is certainly evident when we examine receipt of health care.

Health disparities are a significant and persistent issue in the United States. When discussing diversity, several caveats are in order. Disparities between groups are founded on the assumption that a social group is distinct or unique in some way. Typically the point of comparison for people of color and various ethnicities is White Northern Europeans. As will be discussed below, the "standard" of White European in the United States has an accompanying set of values. When we talk about how an ethnic community is "different," the distinction is between the minority community in question and the dominant White European norms (McGill & Pearce, 2005) of the United States. Cultural generalizations such as "Asian Americans have a collectivist orientation" not only are stereotypes but also include an implicit comparison with the dominant culture.

Many anthropologists are critical of the term "race," since it implies a type of genetic homogeneity. From a genetic perspective, while biological variability does occur, its effect is relatively small. There is no support for the concept of distinct biologically based racial groups—95 percent of the variation that exists is *within* racial groups rather than between our socially constructed racial categories. Montoya gives this perspective: "Races are not biological categories discernible through genetic frequencies. . . . The ways genetics is used to explain population differences for medical purposes are at odds over what constitutes a person" (Montoya, 2011, pp. 17–18).

Publicly announced associations between race and disease can also be used to serve discriminatory ends. Duster (2004) suggests that the idea that sickle cell anemia among African Americans led to a declining birth rate is attributable to "genetic ideology." Duster (2004) argues that media-based public health campaigns encouraging African Americans to get tested for genetic conditions such as sickle cell disease may also implicitly convey that reproduction should proceed with caution.

Gender, historically, has been equated with sex—determined by whether there were two X chromosomes or an X and Y at the 23rd site. This idea is undergoing revision. Gender is now more commonly used to describe one's social identity, with "sex" referring to one's chromosomal composition. The movement against gender labels, often termed gender nonconformity, challenges our view of people being sorted into two fundamental categories based on biology. A recent review found more than 20 different possible gender-related categories.

Additionally, whenever one speaks about a particular group such as African Americans, Hispanics, Asians, White Europeans, and so on, these, in reality, are not homogeneous groups. There is often diversity within a commonly used category of race/ethnicity. Latinos are also not a homogeneous group. In the United States persons of Mexican and Puerto Rican background account for about two-thirds of the Latino population. However, the term *Latino* is also used to describe persons from Central America. Another example of the limitations of these broad census-type labels is the common category "Asians and Pacific Islanders." This broad categorization obscures important information relative to health status. In California, Vietnamese and Korean women experience higher rates of cervical cancer compared with Whites of European background, while Chinese and Japanese women have lower rates of the condition (McCracken et al., 2007; McDougall, Madeleine, Daling, & Li, 2007).

Degree of acculturation is also an important factor modifying the association between minority status and health. For example, in the United States, it is well established that African Americans have significantly higher blood pressure, on average, compared with non-Hispanic Whites. However, in Africa the hypertension rates are about the same as for European Americans in the United States (Cooper, Rotimi, & Ward, 1999). Among African Americans within the United States, higher rates of hypertension are disproportionately in lower-income groups. Japan is noted for having relatively low rates of breast cancer. However, Japanese women who immigrate to the United States have higher rates of breast cancer than women remaining in Japan (Ziegler et al., 1993).

However, despite the reality that these distinctions are socially constructed and not biologically based, health care is strongly influenced by these categories. In our own research on end-of-life care and cultural differences, one of our conclusions is that there appears to be a greater array of preferences when it comes to end-of-life care outside of White European communities (Larkin & Searight, 2014).

Eliminating health disparities has been a major public health focus in the United States for the past 30 years and was given renewed attention by the Affordable Care Act. While there has been some success, disparities by demographic category still exist. The benefits of health care in the United States, where more of the gross domestic product is devoted to health care than in any other country in the world, are not equally distributed. It would seem that requiring all citizens to have health insurance would reduce disparities. While there are hopeful signs, it is too soon to determine whether reduced disparities will progress to an absence of disparities.

As noted earlier, chronic diseases now account for more than 70 percent of deaths and about 85 percent of annual health care costs in the United States (McGinnis & Foege, 1993). This is in contrast to the early 1900s, when chronic disease accounted for less than 25 percent of all deaths. However, despite these improvements, ethnic minorities continue to experience a higher disease burden, particularly of chronic illness. Some have argued that the growing rates of obesity may lead to a plateauing of life expectancy in the United States. Across the country, there are major differences in access to health care depending on where one lives—and the differences are not solely rural or urban or based on the distance to the closest hospital. Even within specific cities in the United States, there are significant differences in life expectancy by geography. Within Washington, D.C., there is a gap in life expectancy of 20 years depending on the neighborhood in which one resides (Virginia Commonwealth University, 2016).

Residential segregation is associated with reduced likelihood of receiving optimal breast cancer care (Haas et al., 2008) and greater likelihood of survival on hemodialysis (Kimmel, Fwu, & Eggers, 2013). Other research suggests that this pattern may reflect structural components of the neighborhood. Some of this disparity appears to be due to racial and ethnic disparities that exist even when income is controlled. For example, areas with more black and Hispanic residents tend to have fewer physicians and are also more likely to have hospitals in which emergency departments have been closed (Malone and Dohan, 2000).

This chapter begins with a review of research on health care disparities. In the second part of the chapter, we will examine some of the cultural factors that influence minorities' use and experience of the US health care system.

Disparities: An Overview

"The medical arena is just a microcosm of society in general" (Whitman, cited in Edwards, 2014). Social patterns of inequality as well as stereotypes around sexual orientation, gender, socioeconomic status, and ethnicity all influence the experience and treatment of both acute and chronic health conditions. Patients with HIV or type 2 diabetes often struggle psychologically and socially, with the social disapproval stemming from a view that these illnesses were caused by the patients themselves (Edwards, 2014). Women with conditions such as angina (chest pain typically associated with heart attacks) or chronic pelvic pain have been inappropriately dismissed as hysterical and prone to emotional excitement (Elderkin-Thompson & Waitzkin, 1999; Scull, 2009; Smith et al., 2000). There has been a long history of undertreating various types of pain among persons of African American and Hispanic background. This undertreatment often stems from prejudices such as viewing these patients as drug-seeking or as being able to bear higher levels of pain than White Europeans (Washington, 2006). While access to care is certainly a reason for disparities, stereotypic assumptions about specific ethnic groups present in the general population are also encountered among health care professionals.

Economic Disparity

Income disparities, even when other factors are controlled, are an independent risk factor for illness and mortality. It has been estimated that at least 119,000 deaths per year in the United States can be attributed to income inequality (Galea et al., 2011). Income inequality has been operationalized with a statistic called the Gini coefficient, which ranges from 0 to 1 (Yitzhaki, 1979). Higher scores indicate greater income inequality, and a score of "0" indicates perfect equality. In most industrialized societies, Gini coefficients are relatively high and particularly high in societies undergoing rapid economic transformation (Barro, 2000). However, there is variability; the Gini coefficient is significantly lower in Sweden and Norway than in the United States and United Kingdom, meaning that these Scandinavian countries have less income inequality.

A country's or region's degree of inequality is predictive of a number of health outcomes (Kondo et al., 2009) and strongly associated with death rates among children and young adults. Income inequality was strongly associated with all causes of death, particularly communicable-disease mortality. With each point increase in the coefficient, there was a 3 to 6 percent increase in mortality (Ward & Viner, 2017). In 2010, the Gini coefficient for the United States was .38, and for Canada .32 (DeSilver, 2018). When the United States was compared to Canada, Canada demonstrated no correlation between income inequality and mortality. Even the most economically unequal Canadian provinces were more egalitarian than the most egalitarian US states (Ross et al., 2000).

Income inequality in the United States has grown significantly in the past four decades, and its association with health status is likely attributable to multiple issues. From a psychosocial perspective, even when other factors are controlled, health status is likely to be a function of one's place in the social hierarchy. Marmot and colleagues' (Marmot et al. 1991) Whitehall study of British civil servants found that even those professionals with job classifications slightly below the top had poorer health outcomes than those at the highest level. There was a linear gradient showing an inverse association between one's British civil service grade and cardiovascular disease and bronchitis. This pattern is particularly noteworthy since it was found in England, where everyone has the same health insurance coverage through the government-based National Health Service (NHS). Even movie stars can be impacted by disparity. Among movie actors and actresses, Oscar winners were found to live 3.6 years longer than those who were nominated but did not win. Multiple Oscar winners lived 2.7 years longer than single winners (Redelmeier & Singh, 2001).

Another factor contributing to this pattern is that maladaptive behaviors such as smoking, drinking, and violence/aggression also occur more frequently in the lowest socioeconomic strata. Obesity and mental health service utilization show a similar pattern. However, there is evidence that persons experiencing greater deprivation delay medical care. For example, in Scotland, which also has universal insurance coverage, residents of regions with greater socioeconomic deprivation exhibited more severely progressed glaucoma (Ng et al., 2010), a pattern also found with colorectal and skin cancer (Powe, 1995; Robinson, Altman, & Rademaker, 1995; Wells & Horm, 1992). In one study, each standard deviation increase in the index of deprivation was associated with 57 percent excess mortality (Smith, Hart, Watt, Hole, & Hawthorne, 1998). Recent research has shown associations with brain development and poverty. Even in infancy, lower socioeconomic status (SES) was associated with smaller cortical gray and deep gray matter volume (Kim et al., 2018; Kolb, 2018).

These negative psychosocial and physical effects synergistically impact those with the lowest level of economic resources (Lynch, Smith, Kaplan, & House 2000). While Lynch et al. (2000) emphasize that the same political processes leading to income inequality diminish personal resources but also exert impact through educational access and quality, health care, and working conditions, Marmot (2005) emphasizes that the key factors affecting well-being include independence and a sense of personal control over one's work and the ability to fully and meaningfully participate in society.

Among Black and White women, a similar gradient was found in rates of unintended pregnancies. Unintended pregnancies were related to perceived social standing—the lower the self-rated social standing, the greater the likelihood of an unintended pregnancy (Bryant, Nakagawa, Gregorich, & Kuppermann, 2010). Discrimination is also likely to play a role in the income-mortality association. Whites are more likely to demonstrate a strong association between income and greater occupational attainment. However, even at higher levels of socioeconomic status and education, African Americans still experience poorer physical health outcomes (Winkleby, Jatulis, Frank, & Fortmann, 1992).

Active striving for upward mobility among members of disadvantaged groups appears to be associated with poorer health consequence. Particularly for men in the African American community, cardiovascular health has been linked to the extent to which one desires material success and is striving to achieve these goals. When the obstacles of low SES life are significant, striving often does not lead to success but instead leads to high blood pressure. As Kawachi and Subramanian (2014) note, keeping up with the Joneses may be harmful to your health unless keeping up can be done with modest effort. Among young adults and adolescents in the rural South, those who exhibited higher levels of confidence and were more likely to be enrolled in college also exhibited higher indicators of allostatic load (body mass index, blood pressure, and stress hormones) (Brody et al., 2013; Myers, 2010).

Originally described among African American men, John Henryism is a pattern characterized by facing challenges with high determination and "high effort coping" (James, 1994). Early research found a fairly strong relationship between John Henryism and blood pressure among middle-aged African American males (Subramanyam et al., 2013). Of interest, research has found better health status among African American females who exhibited high levels of John Henryism (Dressler, Bindon, & Neggers, 1998). Among upper-SES African American males, John Henryism was associated with better health (Bonham, Sellers, & Neighbors, 2004).

Social epidemiologists argue that these factors impact health by disadvantaging some populations with respect to income, social status, political power, environmental risks, and neighborhood assets. In addition, access to quality health care is likely to be a factor.

Educational Disparities

Some quantitative epidemiological studies have concluded that much of the relationship between income inequality and poor health is attributable to lower levels of education—specifically, not completing high school. According to Galea et al. (2011), failure to complete high school accounts for approximately 245,000 deaths in the United States per year. Noncompletion of high school's association with increased mortality has been explained by a constellation of factors, including reduced access to material resources, increased negative life events, a lack of health insurance, and jobs with a greater risk of injury (Larson & Muller, 2002). Completing college adds another five years to one's life expectancy beyond high school graduation. However, the benefits of education are not shared equally. Among African Americans, increased education does not have the same corresponding increase in socioeconomic status that it does for Whites (Cook, 2015). While many causes of mortality, including infant mortality, decline with increased levels of education, the infant mortality rate among White American women with the lowest level of education was still less than that of women from other ethnicities with the lowest levels of education.

Gender
Gender in Developed Countries

Gender is a psychosocial identity—what it means in terms of one's social identity, to be a man or a woman. Sex is biologically based and chromosomally determined. When we refer to the term "sex" to describe differences, we are referring to biology. When we discuss differences between genders, we are describing nonbiological differences and socially constructed views of what is male and female.

One of the clearer differences in health status by sex is that women live longer than men. As of 2013, US women's life expectancy was 81.2 years, with a corresponding value of 76.4 years for US men (Centers for Disease Control, 2013). This sex difference in mortality appears to begin at conception among males. For males, recessive, sometimes harmful, characteristics such as hemophilia are transmitted via the X chromosome. For males, the sex Y-chromosome is paired with a larger X chromosome. Females have a pair of X chromosomes; recessive characteristics on the X chromosome will not be expressed. However, with the smaller Y chromosome for males, characteristics of the X chromosome are more likely to be expressed, and many of these traits, such as hemophilia, can be harmful. Despite their relative longevity, however, women have more health care visits, use more health services, and report poorer health. Even when issues associated with pregnancy and reproduction are controlled, women still report more sick days and hospital days. There have been multiple attempts to explain these differences in health care utilization.

Psychosocial explanations emphasize gender differences in managing stress. As will be discussed in the chapter on stress, females are more likely to manage emotional reactions through social-affiliative strategies such as talking with friends or dealing with the individuals involved directly (Griffith, Dubow, & Ippolito, 2000). Men tend to be less flexible in how they respond to stress, focusing on situations as problems to be solved. However, despite these differences in coping styles, women exhibited higher rates of many mental health problems, such as major depressive disorder and many of the anxiety disorders. However, some have challenged the argument that women are more likely to develop psychological disorders and emphasize that there are gender differences in managing stressors. Men may be more likely to externalize distress in the form of using substances and possibly acting out, while women are much more likely to internalize, and the distress may not be as visible. This pattern begins in childhood. Men's life span may be artificially shortened by their greater involvement with high-risk activities including smoking and drinking, as well as physically aggressive behavior.

From a physical health perspective, one possible explanation for these gender differences is that in developed countries, men experience more serious, life-threatening conditions at younger ages, while women are more likely to experience chronic but less lethal conditions associated with poor-health-related quality of life. Some observers have also suggested that these differences in health risk–related behaviors such as smoking and binge drinking have become more common among women as views of what is masculine and feminine have changed. For example, lung cancer rates have been declining among men but increasing among women (Zang & Wynder, 1996); there are suggestions that women may be more sensitive to the carcinogens in cigarettes compared with men (Zang & Wynder, 1996). Women report more autoimmune and rheumatoid disorders (Whitacre, 2001), while men are more likely to have cardiovascular disease and smoking-related conditions such as various cancers and COPD, which may be increasing among women. Another factor is that women are much more likely to be diagnosed with "medically unexplained illnesses" (Johnson, 2008). These are conditions that do not have a clear cause. However, there are sets of symptoms that consistently cluster together as syndromes. These include conditions such as irritable bowel syndrome, chronic fatigue syndrome, and fibromyalgia (Johnson, 2008).

As will be discussed in Chapter 10, covering eating disorders, beginning at a young age, women are socialized to pay greater attention to their bodies, which may result in greater concern about health. Some research suggests that women tend to have greater health-related knowledge and use health services more often than men (Bertakis, Azari, Helms, Callahan, & Robbins, 2000)—particularly mental health services, which women are significantly more likely to use (Mackenzie, Gekoski, & Knox, 2006).

However, there do appear to be disparities in receipt of health care among patients with cardiovascular disease. Women were significantly less likely to receive the evidence-based treatment and statins compared with men (Virani et al., 2015).

As women begin to account for more than half of the incoming class in many American medical schools, researchers have examined whether the gender of the physician makes a difference in patient outcome. Among a large sample of older patients treated in the same hospital, patients cared for by female, versus male, physicians had better outcomes (Tsugawa et al., 2017). The authors raise the possibility that female physicians seem to be more likely to provide patient-centered care, including attention to psychosocial issues, and better knowledge of their patients may lead to better outcomes. However, as far as health care professionals are concerned, medicine, like other fields, shows a gender gap for physician earning (Apaydin, Chen, & Friedberg, 2018). Even when hours of work per week are controlled, male primary care and specialty physicians earn more than females (Apaydin et al., 2018).

Gender in Developing Countries

The description immediately above describes women in industrialized developed countries. As noted by Marmot (2005), one's position in a social hierarchy plays a significant role in health and well-being. In many developing countries such as those in Africa and parts of South East Asia, women have significantly less social power and control over their lives than is the case in the more developed Western countries. Given this power imbalance, it should not be particularly surprising that women in developing—as opposed to developed—countries often have poor health. This power differential in African countries is associated with high rates of domestic violence and predatory sexual practices. Women also appear to have less power in determining the circumstances associated with having sex, which often results in a higher frequency of sexual activity and less protection with condoms. Collectively, these factors likely contribute to the increased rates of HIV infection for women versus men in these societies (Jewkes, Dunkle, Nduna, & Shai, 2010). Women are at particular risk for HIV for a range of reasons. Many of these explanations have to do with the developmental status of women's reproductive system and lack of control over sexual situations (Jewkes et al., 2010). Hormonal changes associated with menopause increase the likelihood of vaginal tears and lesions. Similarly, while most societies that legally permit child marriages do place some limits on the female's age for consummation, these guidelines are not consistently followed. For young girls, the immature development of the genital and reproductive system increases the risk of tears and lesions during sexual intercourse. This damage, in turn, raises the risk for HIV acquisition and transmission among young married women. In some countries, such as Uganda, rates of HIV infection among married women are more than 80 percent (Nour, 2009).

In the Pacific, the Trobriand Islands also have particularly high rates of HIV infection among young women and adolescent girls. There is a culture of pronounced sexual coercion, where young girls often have sexual relations with significantly older males (Lepani, 2012). The males, because of their longer histories of sexual activity, are the carriers of HIV. Since many of these girls begin sexual activity before menarche, there is greater risk of vaginal tearing and transmission of sexually transmitted diseases (Lepani, 2012). Many women have also died because of diseases associated with HIV, such as HPV, which is, in turn, associated with elevated rates of cervical cancer (Yang, Bray, Parkin, Sellors, & Zhang, 2004).

In many countries that are undergoing rapid industrialization, married partners are often away from one another for months or years at a time. They may live in cities far from their home—often in spartan, company-provided dormitories. In these countries, women are also victims of sexual trafficking as well as "survival sex." When their partners are working in distant urban areas, women employed in China's free enterprise zones may be at risk for sexual harassment by supervisors (US Department of State, 2013).

Sexual Orientation

Compared with ethnicity and race, there have been far fewer studies of health care disparities associated with sexual orientation. This no doubt stems from multiple issues, such as the continued discrimination against gay and lesbian couples as well as the fact that one's sexual orientation is not a visible indicator of minority status.

At present, the size of the lesbian-gay-bisexual population in the United States is believed to be somewhere in the 3 to 5 percent range (Gates, 2011). Census data in the United States as well as health statistics have only recently included attention to sexual orientation. According to national health statistics data from 2000 to 2013, 96.6 percent of adults identified as straight, 1.6 percent as gay or lesbian, 0.7 percent as bisexual, and 1.1 percent as "something else" or "I don't know," or they refused to answer (Ward, Dahlhamer, Galinsky, & Joestl, 2014). While self-identification is certainly important for a range of reasons, including supporting the identity of minorities, it is useful to keep in mind that sexual behavior and categorical labels are often not congruent. In some areas, such as Latin America, where the stigma for gay men continues to be very high, men who are sexually active with other men may not label themselves as "gay." From a health perspective, the sex of one's sexual partners does become important in terms of risks associated with being sexually active with the same or opposite sex.

This discrepancy may not always be attributable to social sanctions. In one study, 75 to 90 percent of women who reported that they were having sex only with women had had prior sexual activity with men. Without this knowledge, health professionals would neglect asking lesbian women about contraception and certain sexually transmitted diseases. For health care providers, a useful question to ask new patients as part of a standard history is "Do you have sex with men, women, or both?"

As far as health risks are concerned, cigarette smoking and alcohol use is higher among those who identify as gay or lesbian. Those identified as gay or lesbian evidence a prevalence of cigarette smoking of 27.2 percent, with those who are bisexual at 29.5 percent, compared with 19.5 percent of those who identified as "straight" (Ward et al., 2014). Binge drinking, defined as having five or more drinks in one day in the past year, was higher among gay men and lesbian women (35 percent) or those who are bisexual (42 percent) versus those identified as heterosexual (26 percent) (Ward et al., 2014). In addition, sexually transmitted diseases—syphilis, chlamydia, and gonorrhea—are more common among men who have sex with men (Centers for Disease Control, 2016c). Of those in the United States living with HIV, more than 50 percent are men who have sex with men. They also account for more than two-thirds of new cases each year. However, between 2008 and 2014, HIV rates declined by almost 20 percent among gay and bisexual men. Among gay men, rates of HPV-related anal cancers are significantly higher than in other segments of the population (Quinn et al., 2015).

Because many women who are lesbian are less likely to use contraception and have never been pregnant, they may be at higher risk for certain types of cancers, including ovarian, endometrial, and cervical cancer. Another factor that may contribute is that BMI levels may be somewhat higher among women in same-sex relationships. Cervical cancers appear to be higher among lesbian and bisexual women compared with heterosexual women. The greater rates of smoking as well as higher BMIs among lesbian women have been suggested as potential contributors to this difference (Pantalone, Haldeman, & Martell, 2018). Data regarding mammography rates being higher or lower among lesbian women are mixed. For breast cancers, rates are lower among lesbian and bisexual women than for heterosexual females. However, research suggests that lesbian women with breast cancer experience more distress and receive less social support than heterosexual women.

Of interest is the fact that those identifying as gay or lesbian were more likely to have received an influenza vaccine in the past year (Ward et al., 2014). In terms of HIV testing, 69 percent of those self-identifying as gay or lesbian, 54 percent self-reported as bisexual, and 42 percent identified as straight reported being tested in the past year (Ward et al., 2014). Among adult males, nearly 80 percent of those who identified as gay reported undergoing HIV testing (Ward et al., 2014).

There are suggestions that intimate partner violence may be higher in same-sex relationships than it is in opposite-sex relationships (Finneran & Stephenson, 2012). There are a number of acute and chronic health conditions associated with partner violence, including chronic pain, substance abuse, obesity, and sexually transmitted diseases (Pantalone, Haldeman, & Martell, 2018). Mental health sequelae of domestic violence victimization include major depressive disorder and posttraumatic stress disorder. There is some evidence that women in same-sex relationships have more negative health outcomes associated with interpersonal violence than those in opposite-sex relationships. When asked about their last physical violence experience, 39.5 percent of women abused by their opposite-sex partner reported physical injury, while 48.7 percent of women abused by their same-sex partner reported this outcome. When asked about domestic violence, 27.5 percent of women abused by an opposite-sex partner reported physical injuries, with 35.7 percent of women abused by a same-sex partner reporting physical injuries after a violent episode (Coston, 2014). Of interest is that women physically abused by other women were twice as likely to seek out psychological help after the episode; however, they were less likely to seek out medical care for physical injuries (Coston, 2014). The disparity in seeking out medical care is consistent with the reduced trust and apprehension about seeking medical treatment that continues to be common in the lesbian and gay communities. There is also evidence that members of sexual minorities are more likely to be victims of hate crimes (Duncan & Hatzenbuehler, 2014). Data for 2011 indicate that 20.5 percent of hate crimes were based on sexual orientation (Swan, 2016; Tumolo, 2014).

Mental Health

The levels of psychological distress are almost 3 times as high among those who identified as bisexual compared with those who identified as straight (Ward et al., 2014). Among gay men and lesbian women, rates of many psychiatric disorders such as major depressive disorder and substance use are higher than among heterosexuals. However, it is noteworthy that among those who are "out" about their orientation—particularly to family members who are supportive—rates of mental health conditions are significantly lower.

Gay men and lesbian women are more likely to use mental health services. It is possible that the greater likelihood of seeking psychological care may be influenced by associated factors such as greater educational level, higher income, and greater likelihood of being self-employed (Coston, 2014). Women in same-sex relationships are more likely to seek out psychotherapy than women in heterosexual relationships.

Interactions with the Health Care System

Both males and females in same-sex relationships appear to be less likely to have health insurance (Ward et al., 2014). The highest rates of health insurance are found among married adults in heterosexual relationships, followed by men and women in same-sex relationships.

It also appears that gay men and lesbian women have more difficulties with access to care. Persons who self-identified as straight were significantly more likely to have a source of usual medical care compared with those who reported being bisexual. Among adult women, those who self-reported as being gay or lesbian or bisexual also were less likely to have a usual source of medical care. Additionally, of persons who identify as bisexual, 15 percent failed to obtain needed medical care compared to 10 percent of those who self-identified as heterosexual (Ward et al., 2014).

There is evidence that because of concerns about health care providers' response, many gays and lesbians have not disclosed their sexual orientation to their primary care physician. An early study by Smith, Johnson, and Guenther (1985) of lesbian and bisexual women found that 40 percent of them thought that being open about their sexual orientation would negatively affect the quality of their health care. Fewer than 20 percent had actually disclosed the orientation to a physician. More than 70 percent indicated they would like to discuss sexual problems with the physician if they could find one comfortable with gay and lesbian patients (Orel, 2014; Willes & Allen, 2014). Health care providers' "heteronormative assumptions" are seen by many gays and lesbians, at minimum, as annoying, and they are often experienced as disrespectful, such as when a lesbian woman is lectured on the importance of birth control to avoid pregnancy.

Surveys of physicians conducted in the mid-1990s found that nearly two-thirds of them had observed health interactions in which the patient's sexual orientation was associated with substandard care. Twenty-five years later, while disclosure is somewhat greater, only about half of bisexual and transgender individuals indicated that their physician was aware of their orientation. A 2014 study did find that a majority of respondents indicated that their physician did note their sexual orientation. Still, close to 30 percent of gay men and lesbian women indicated that they were concerned about physicians perceiving them negatively (Harrison & Silenzio, 1996; Ward et al., 2014).

Among gay men, a tendency was for the physician to focus on sex as a key part of their identity. For example, some gay men reported that if the physician knew of their orientation, they repeatedly encouraged them to get an HIV test. Many physicians provided this directive even when patients indicated that they were not sexually active (Manning, 2014).

Transgender and Gender-Nonconforming Youth and Adults

Gender dysphoria, or gender identity disorder, occurs when a child or adolescent typically experiences distress associated with a contradiction between his or her biological sex and experienced gender. The percentages of "gender-nonconforming" adults seeking "gender-affirming" surgery range from .005 percent to .014 percent for affirmed females and .020 percent to .003 percent for affirmed males (Vance, Ehrensaft, & Rosenthal, 2014). In large metropolitan areas, there are a growing number of health care settings that are specifically sensitive to transgender issues. There has been greater openness to medical interventions involving sex hormone therapy so that secondary sex characteristics can match the individual's affirmed gender. It is recommended that cross-sex hormones not be initiated until about age 16, with testosterone being used for affirmed males and estrogen for affirmed females. While there has been concern that estrogen treatment used with male-female persons may increase rates of breast cancer, to date, this concern has not been borne out (Vance et al., 2014).

Transgender and gender-nonconforming adolescents and adults are less likely to have preventive health checkups and report significantly poorer health status (Rider, McMorris, Gower, Coleman, & Eisenberg, 2018). However, about 20 percent of transgender persons lack health insurance (Grant et al., 2010).

Transgender women have particularly high rates of HIV infection; it has been estimated that 22 percent of transgender women in the United States have HIV (Centers for Disease Control, 2016c).

Research indicates that rates of self-harm, depression, and anxiety are significantly higher among adolescents and adults with gender nonconformity. However, when a child or adolescent's status as gender nonconforming is supported, emotional distress is greatly reduced. Mental health issues have been a principal concern for transgender persons—41 percent of transgender or gender-nonconforming individuals reported a suicide attempt; rates were higher among those reporting physical or sexual assault or harassment (Grant et al., 2010).

The reliance upon binary male-female gender categories is being challenged by adolescents and young adults who are nonbinary in their identity. The primary care physician is likely to be the first medical provider consulted by a young adult who is gender nonconforming. It is particularly important to be sensitive to the young adult's affirmed gender and use the person's preferred name and gender pronouns. It is suggested that those working with adolescents be familiar with chest binders used by identified males to diminish the appearance of breasts. When these are too tight, they can produce a rash as well as rib pain. Affirmed females may develop hoarseness because of repeated efforts to elevate the pitch of the voice (Vance et al., 2014).

Disparities by Race/Ethnicity: The Evidence

African Americans currently comprise about 12 percent of the US population; 16 percent are Latino, and 9 percent are Asian/Pacific Islanders. Within the next 40 years, it is estimated that the Latino population will come to comprise approximately one-third of the US population, while the non-Latino White population will decline by approximately 20 percent—from 65 percent to 46 percent, even with equitable access to care. If the current pattern of health within specific racial and ethnic communities persists, a growing percentage of the population will have chronic health problems. With respect to health care quality, the Association for Health Research and Quality concluded that African Americans as well as Native Americans received worse care than Whites for about 40 percent of measures; Asians received worse care than Whites for more than 20 percent of measures, while Hispanics received a poorer quality of care on 60 percent of these benchmarks. Those who were of low income received worse care on 80 percent of core measures (Agency for Healthcare Research and Quality, 2015). Disparities in care have an economic cost, including additional health care expenditures in later life as well as lost work productivity and early death.

Pregnancy and Infancy

In the United States, disparities are evident even before birth. African American women are nearly three times as likely to report that a pregnancy was unplanned or unintended compared with White women. Minority women—particularly African American and Native American—are less likely to receive prenatal care, and when they do, it is often not until the third trimester of pregnancy. Compared with White women, African American women are significantly more likely to die during childbirth (Curtin & Hoyert, 2017).

Since the 1990s, the mortality rate of infants weighing 3.3 pounds or less at birth has been about 25 percent. Beginning in 2002, the mortality rate for low-birth-weight Black infants began increasing and has continued to increase, while mortality for White infants has been declining (Bruckner, Saxton, Anderson, Goldman, & Gould, 2009). African American infants are twice as likely to die from sudden infant death syndrome (SIDS) as White infants (Moon & Task Force on Sudden Infant Death Syndrome, 2016). However, despite awareness of the "back to sleep" campaign, African American women are more likely to place infants on their stomachs to sleep, not convinced by the well-publicized link between sleeping position and SIDS. Instead, they often view SIDS as a random event that cannot be prevented except through vigilant care of their infant (Moon, Oden, Joyner, & Ajao, 2010).

Childhood Health Conditions

Approximately 12 percent of White European children live at or below the poverty level, contrasted with 38 percent of African American and 35 percent of Latino children. African American children are significantly overrepresented among children with elevated lead levels, which are associated with cognitive problems such as learning disabilities as well as hyperactivity in children. The difference between African American and White children is reduced somewhat when income is taken into account (Moody, Darden, & Pigozzi, 2016). Elevated lead levels are typically associated with exposure to lead paint and dust from older housing. In Chicago, particularly in neighborhoods with buildings constructed in the 1950s or earlier, both Hispanic and Black children had significantly elevated lead levels compared with White children (Sampson & Winter, 2016).

Another condition found among children that is associated with environmental exposures is asthma. Even after controlling for income, asthma is far more common among African American children. Roughly 14 percent of African American children have asthma compared with 7 to 8 percent of Hispanic and White children and 5 percent of Asian children. There also appears to be an income gradient associated with childhood asthma, with more cases in families with incomes below the poverty level (Washington, Curtis, Waite, Wolf, & Paasche-Orlow, 2018).

Medical Conditions Disproportionately Impacting Minorities

Differences in Types and Severity of Health Conditions

Among men, the top three causes of death in the United States do not differ by race and ethnicity. Heart disease, cancer, and unintentional injuries are the most common, although cancer is the most common and heart disease is the second most common among persons of Hispanic background. Beginning with the fourth most common cause of death, there are increasing differences (Centers for Disease Control, 2013). The fourth most common cause of death for Native Americans and Hispanic men is diabetes; for Blacks, stroke; and for Whites, chronic lower-respiratory disease. The fifth most common cause of death for African American men is homicide, and for Native Americans, liver disease. While suicide is the sixth leading cause of death for Native Americans, it is the seventh for Hispanics and Whites. Homicide is the ninth leading cause of death for Hispanic and Native American men; it does not appear in the top 10 for white men (Centers for Disease Control, 2013).

For women there is consistency across ethnicities in the top two leading causes of death—cancer and heart disease. The third leading cause of death is stroke for Hispanics and African Americans, but for Whites it is chronic lower-respiratory disease, and for Native American women it is unintentional injuries. The fourth most common cause of death for Native American women is chronic liver disease, with diabetes the fourth most common for Hispanics and African Americans. For White women, Alzheimer's disease is the fifth most common cause of death, and it is the sixth most common cause of death for Hispanics and African American women (Centers for Disease Control, 2013).

Native Americans have diabetes rates that are twice those of Whites, and they are almost three times as likely to have end-stage renal disease as Whites (Centers for Disease Control, 2013). Asian-Pacific Islanders are more likely to die from stomach cancer than non-Hispanic Whites. In Hawaii, native Hawaiians have more than twice the rate of diabetes compared with Whites (Centers for Disease Control, 2013). As the Hawaiian example illustrates, the common demographic practice of combining Asians with people of Pacific Island heritage unfortunately obscures differences between these groups.

Tuberculosis was thought to be well controlled in the United States. However, in 1991, a number of cases of TB were reported in New York City; among these cases almost 80 percent were persons of African American background (Bruckner et al., 1991). In the United States, African Americans, Hispanics, and Native Americans are more likely to develop TB compared with Whites (Cantwell, McKenna, McCray, & Onorato, 1998). However, when social indicators are controlled, including residential crowding, TB's association with ethnicity becomes much less pronounced (Cantwell et al., 1998).

The relative ranking of causes of death is also influenced by age. For example, among African Americans ages 25 to 44, HIV is the third leading cause of death. There have been periods of time in which HIV has been diagnosed in Blacks at 10 times the rate of Whites (Centers for Disease Control, 2013).

In the United States, as was the case with the Pima Indians, there is considerable evidence that the level of acculturation is associated with health status. This pattern has been found among Mexican and Asian Americans. Cancer among Japanese who moved from Japan to the United States is significantly higher than for residents of Japan (Dunn, 1975). As noted earlier, African Americans have significantly higher rates of hypertension than Black residents of Africa.

Discrimination Toward African Americans — Associations with Health Status

African Americans—particularly men—are at high risk for the development of hypertension; their rate of hypertension is about 30 percent greater than for Whites (Dolezsar, McGrath, Herzig, & Miller, 2014). In studies comparing persons of White European background with African Americans, African Americans develop high blood pressure earlier in life and its severity is greater (Flack, Ference, & Levy, 2015; Straub, 2016). Some researchers have linked the greater rates of hypertension among African Americans to both implicit and explicit racism. A recent meta-analysis found that perceived discrimination was associated with a greater risk of hypertension. In addition, this association was stronger for African American men who were older and less well educated (Dolezsar et al., 2014).

Among African Americans, exposure to speeches addressing racial issues and staged scenarios involving being accused of shoplifting increased cardiovascular activity (Hoar, 2015). In these situations, lower-SES African American men tended to display a greater level of reactivity than women and upper- and middle-class African American males. Other research finds that for both African American men and women, greater perceived levels of discrimination are associated with globally poorer health as well as increased rates of major depressive disorder. Among African American men, perceived discrimination is associated with greater likelihood of smoking and increased consumption of dietary fat. Among both African American men and women, discrimination was associated with fewer hours of sleep (Sims et al., 2016). Brown and colleagues (Brown et al., 2000) found that when cross-sections were compared over time, subjective reports of racial discrimination at one time led to more psychological symptoms at a later point. Importantly, mental health problems did not influence reports of racial discrimination. The racial discrimination appeared to occur prior to increased rates of psychological distress (Brown et al., 2000).

Risk Factors and Disease Complications

Three-quarters of Mexican American women are considered overweight or obese. They are also 40 percent more likely to have cervical cancer. With respect to diabetes, findings suggest that glycemic control is worse for ethnic minorities, and they experience more diabetes-related complications. These include cataracts neuropathy and kidney disease. Approximately 57 percent of African American females are obese, compared with 46 percent of Hispanic women, 39 percent of White females, and 12 percent of Asian women (May, Freedman, Sherry, Blanck, & CDC, 2013; Flegal Kruszon-Moran, Carroll, Fryar, & Ogden, 2016).

Gestational diabetes, which occurs during pregnancy, is significantly more common among Hispanic, Native American, and Asian women when compared with White or Black women. It has been suggested that since both Asian Americans and Native Americans genetically originated in Asia, there may be a common genetic risk factor for developing the condition (Caughey, Cheng, Stotland, Washington, & Escobar, 2010).

In terms of preventive care, African American and Hispanic patients age 65 and older are less likely to receive vaccinations for influenza and pneumonia. A common preventive test for men over the age of 50 is a colonoscopy, used to determine whether there are cancerous or precancerous growths in the GI tract. Whites, as compared with African Americans, were about 20 percent more likely to undergo one of these procedures.

Patterns and Quality of Care

The AHRQ figures reported at the beginning of this chapter highlight global differences in the quality of care received by minorities in the United States (Agency for Healthcare Research and Quality, 2011).

Black infants are much more likely to die during the first month of life. A study of births and deaths for very low-birth-weight infants found that Black and White mothers' deliveries occurred in hospitals with widely differing quality of care. While low-birth-weight White infants were more likely to be born in hospitals with lower risk of neonatal mortality, low-birth-weight Black infants were born in hospitals with higher risks of neonatal death. It was estimated that if the Black infants had been born in one of the hospitals used primarily by Whites, more than a third of the difference between survival rates would have been eliminated (Howell, Hebert, Chatterjee, Kleinman, & Chassin, 2008).

In a study of Medicare patients in more than 3,000 hospitals, it was found that Black patients had a higher risk than Whites of acquiring hospital-related infection or experiencing an adverse drug event during their hospital course (Metersky et al., 2011).

Among patients with cardiovascular disease, African Americans were less likely to receive cardiac catheterization, less likely to receive medications to decrease blood pressure and risk of stroke, and less likely to undergo coronary artery bypass graft (CABG) surgery (Kressin & Petersen, 2001). These effects were similar, yet less pronounced, when Hispanics were compared with Whites.

African American and Hispanic patients tended to receive poorer-quality care across a range of conditions, from cancer to mental health (Schneider, Zaslavsky, & Epstein, 2002). Additionally, African Americans were more likely to receive "less desirable" services, such as amputation of a limb rather than aggressive treatment to preserve it (Lavery, Ashry, van Houtum, et al., 1996). Even when insurance status is controlled, African American and Hispanic patients are less likely to be offered rehabilitation compared with Whites.

While disparities between African Americans and Whites are not as great when it comes to cancer or cardiovascular disease, they are still present. African American women are less likely to receive breast-conserving surgery and radiation treatment as opposed to mastectomies, which were less common among White women (Washington, 2006). Among those with non-small-cell lung cancer, African Americans were 50 percent less likely to undergo surgery that can increase survival time. In examining chemotherapy practices, African Americans were four times as likely to receive a low (often subtherapeutic) dose of chemotherapy (Griggs, Sorbero, Stark, Heininger, & Dick, 2003). Additionally, African American patients undergoing cancer chemotherapy, when compared with Whites, were less likely to receive information about possible treatment side effects.

Differences in prescribing pain medication are also pronounced by ethnicity, with Hispanic and African American patients significantly less likely to receive pain medication in the hospital emergency department (Todd, Samaroo, & Hoffman, 1993). Among pharmacies in predominantly non-White neighborhoods, only 25 percent had appropriate opiate supplies, with 72 percent of pharmacies in predominantly White neighborhoods having adequate opiates in stock. This disparity persisted even when economic and crime activity statistics were controlled (Morrison, Wallenstein, Natale, Senzel, & Huang, 2000).

Even when they have the same type of insurance as Whites, African American patients with Medicare reported more difficulties getting care quickly, experienced office staff as less helpful, and reported less satisfaction with interactions with representatives of their health plan (Fongwa, Cunningham, Weech-Maldonado, Gutierrez, & Hays, 2008).

Physician-Patient Interaction

Health care providers in the United States are disproportionately of White European backgrounds and often of higher socioeconomic status, while many ethnic minority patients are from poorer socioeconomic communities. It has been suggested that providers may feel more comfortable communicating with those of similar backgrounds who, in turn, are more likely to trust their physician (Saha, Komaromy, Koepsell, & Bindman, 1999). Research has suggested that physicians' implicit racism is likely to be associated with less patient-centered interaction (Green et al., 2007).

Greenwald, McGhee, and Schwartz (1998) conducted a study in which they asked participants to categorize names as "black" or "white." The investigators then asked the participants to categorize a number of valenced words such as "bomb" or "joy" as pleasant or unpleasant. Next, the two tasks were put together. When "black" was paired with an unpleasant word, participants' reaction times were faster than when "black" was paired with a pleasant term. This pattern of implicit associations has been found with a variation on the IAT involving Black and White faces (Sabin, Rivara, & Greenwald, 2008). Participants seemed to implicitly associate "black" with "bad" and "white" with "good." Some of the participants were disturbed when they learned about the pattern and its possible implications. The cardiology study mentioned in an earlier chapter comparing diagnoses of standardized Black versus White male and female patients concluded that some form of implicit physician bias was operative in making decisions about cardiac care, since the clinical data presented for Whites and Blacks was identical (Schulman et al., 1999). A later study using a similar research design found that while physicians indicated that they had no racial biases in how they viewed patients, implicit associations suggested otherwise. Implicit preferences or beliefs included viewing

Black Americans as less cooperative with medical procedures and less cooperative in general. As level of implicit bias increased, there was a corresponding increase in these beliefs (Green et al., 2007).

There is evidence that these implicit biases translate directly to patient care. In examining clinical interactions between physicians and patients, interactions with Black patients received lower ratings on interpersonal dimensions of care, and they were associated with less positive patient affect and more verbal dominance by the clinician (Cooper et al., 2012).

Several studies examining physician-patient interaction found that physicians are less likely to adopt a patient-centered approach to patients who are Black or Hispanic. Studies of HIV patients in New York and Portland found that even when the Hispanic patients were fluent in English, there was significantly less conversation about psychosocial issues compared to interactions with White patients (Beach et al., 2010). Attention to psychosocial issues is particularly important with HIV care (Beach et al., 2010).

Physician and patient ethnicity does appear to have an effect on quality of care (Cooper et al., 2003). In a large sample of patients with diabetes, it was found that among African American and Hispanic patients, medication adherence was greater when African American patients were paired with African American physicians (Traylor, Schmittdiel, Uratsu, Mangione, & Subramanian, 2010). Among Hispanic patients, adherence rates were higher when the physician spoke Spanish (Traylor et al., 2010).

Mortality

As would be expected from the health information reviewed, mortality occurs earlier in some ethnic/racial minorities. When ethnicity and gender are examined together, Hispanic women have the longest life expectancy at 83.7 years, followed by Whites at 81, and African Americans at 77.8. For males, life expectancy for Hispanics is 78.94 years; African American men, 71.6; and White males, 76.44 years (Centers for Disease Control, 2013). When examined together, the life span of African American males is the shortest of any ethnic/sex combination. The single largest contributor to these differences in mortality appears to be cardiovascular disease rates. Also of note is that Hispanics appear to have a longer life span than Whites. This is likely attributable to multiple factors, including strong social support networks, healthier diet, and higher levels of physical activity.

Linguistic Diversity

In the United States, 15 percent of the population speaks a language other than English at home (Ingraham, 2018), with approximately 20 million residents having limited English proficiency. This pattern is likely to influence health care. Many medical visits now include an additional person—a language interpreter. (Before going further, a bit about terminology: Translation typically refers to written text, while interpretation is usually for oral exchanges and involves going beyond words to convey meaning that includes specific cultural references [Searight, 2017].)

There is consistent evidence that when health care providers and patients do not speak the same language, quality of patient care suffers. Patients receive less health education and are less likely to receive preventive care, such as mammograms; have clear, documented informed consent for surgical procedures; or receive appropriate pain medication in the emergency department. They also report significantly less satisfaction with their health care (Ku & Flores, 2005; Flores, 2006). Furthermore, patients with a history of language-discordant care have more hospitalizations and diagnostic tests, are more likely to leave the hospital against medical advice, and are likely to have more adverse events with greater severity during hospitalization (Ku & Flores, 2005). In outpatient settings, patients with limited English proficiency miss more appointments, have poor adherence to instructions, and are less likely to follow up with referrals (Ku & Flores, 2005; Flores, 2006).

A well-known case in which a health care professional misinterpreted the words of a Spanish-speaking patient resulted in a significant adverse outcome for the patient and costly litigation to the health care institution in which the event occurred. In this case, Willie Ramirez, an 18-year-old male, collapsed at a friend's home. At some point soon after he collapsed, Ramirez said he felt "intoxicado." When he was brought into the emergency department, Ramirez was comatose. The term *intoxicado* was also used by family members in their interaction with hospital emergency department personnel. Medical personnel interpreted the word to mean "intoxicated" and assumed that Ramirez was under the influence of drugs and saw his symptoms as consistent with drug overdose. However, *intoxicado*, depending on the syllable that is accented, can also mean "nauseated," which is what Ramirez and his family were attempting to convey. After two days, it was recognized that Ramirez had a cerebral aneurysm. It was argued in the courtroom that if the term had been correctly interpreted, a neurologist could have seen Ramirez and prevented the paralysis that resulted from the burst aneurysm. As a result, the patient won a $71 million lawsuit against the hospital (Price-Wise, 2008).

An early study of interpreter accuracy in medical settings (Flores et al., 2003) examined language interpretation in the pediatric emergency department and concluded that an average of 31 interpretation errors occurred per doctor-patient encounter, with 63 percent of these errors having potential clinical significance. While hospital interpreters made fewer clinically significant errors (53 percent versus 77 percent), the rate of errors by hospital interpreters was still quite high. Common errors included omission of information, false fluency (overestimating one's skills and knowledge in a second language), substitution (replacing physician's or patient's words with terms that are similar but not exactly the same), editorialization (offering commentary or the interpreter's personal opinion about the physician-patient exchange), and adding material that the patient did not say. Two examples of seemingly small modifications of wording that could have significant consequences for medical care are as follows:

Physician: Take this medication three times each day.
Interpreter: Take this medicine in three days.

Physician: Put the hydrocortisone cream on the baby's face twice a day.
Interpreter: Put the ointment on the baby for two days. (based on Flores et al., 2003)

Among nonnative speakers, particularly if the second language was acquired primarily through formal classroom language instruction in secondary school or college, false fluency can be an issue. Traditional instruction in a foreign language often neglects many conversational nuances. In another emergency department case, a two-year-old girl presented with a broken collarbone after falling off her tricycle. The child's mother described the child's injury with the phrase *se pego*—a Spanish phrase with different meanings depending on which syllable is emphasized. The physician, who spoke Spanish, misinterpreted the phrase as "she was struck." The Child Protective Services office was notified and took the girl into custody. However, the mother's use of *se pego* conveyed that the girl struck her shoulder on the pavement when falling off her tricycle (Searight & Armock, 2013).

While the quality of care is certainly better when an interpreter participates in health care visits for patients with limited English proficiency, the presence of an interpreter does add time to the clinic visit—on average, visits are 15 to 20 percent longer. Research has found that with Spanish-speaking patients, interpreted encounters were nine minutes longer, and Russian-speaking patients required an average of six additional minutes (Kravitz, Helms, Azari, Antonius, & Melnikow, 2000). However, when taking into account additional medical tests, unnecessary hospitalizations, and medical mistakes associated with language discordance, this extra time in the clinic is likely to save time in the long run.

The Role of Cultural and Historical Factors in Health, Illness, and Treatment

American Medicine as Culture

While linguistic issues, unconscious health care prejudice, economic factors, and health care access are all contributors to population disparities, culturally based views of health and medical care also play a role. The reductionist, biologically based explanation of illness and health that characterizes American medicine often contradicts long-standing culturally based explanations of the cause of disease and its appropriate treatment.

In many respects, health care is a culture in and of itself. Historically, medicine as an academic discipline as well as an area of clinical practice was primarily the province of White males. While the tenets and beliefs of White Northern Europeans and their descendants are often not considered to be a "culture," their values permeate American medicine (Bellah, Madsen, Sullivan, Swidler, & Tipton, 2007; Stein, 1990).

It is expected that things will go well in Anglo-American families, and when illness strikes, it is often primarily seen as inconvenient—something that disrupts one's daily routine. Problems, particularly health-related issues, are often minimized; there is a belief that all problems can be overcome through individual effort. The strong value that Western medicine places on traits of perfectionism and conscientiousness reflects this view. McGill and Pearce (2005) describe how this value of individual autonomy can be taken to extremes:

> The father of an Anglo-American man developed a melanoma on his back. Eventually, it bled so much that he had to change his shirt many times a day, yet he never

sought medical attention. Finally, a tumor developed under his arm that was so painful and disabling that he was "forced to get to a doctor." He soon died.

Listening to this description, the son's . . . therapist suggested that it was too bad that the father had not gotten some help and relief earlier. The patient responded . . . "No, my father made his choice and died his own way." (McGill & Pearce, 2005, p. 524)

A value that many Americans share with the culture of medicine is the emphasis on technological problem solving. The growing use of weight-loss medications and surgeries for obesity—a recent phenomenon in our evolutionary history—illustrates this principle very well. Obesity is inconvenient and harms one's social standing; however, while lifestyle issues are likely to have contributed to it, medical technology can eliminate it.

The pragmatism that characterizes American medicine is also consistent with this value system. Both patients and physicians have a strong to need "do something" (Searight, 1994), with science and technology seen as the source of solutions to all health-related problems. In addition, medicine values systematic problem solving—step-by-step protocols are highly popular, even in the case of ambiguous situations in which alternative diagnoses are systematically ruled out (Searight, 2010). Medical culture is also characterized by efficiency and often a sense of urgency. Health care practice tends to be oriented toward realistic immediate treatment options, even when a specific diagnosis is not yet clear. This pragmatic pattern is less common in many parts of Europe, where there is a tendency not to prescribe medication and to prescribe less of it than in the United States (Payer, 1988). This value often becomes a conflict when a patient with cold or flu symptoms is not given an antibiotic when it is not clearly established that their illness has a bacterial cause (Fletcher-Lartey, Yee, Gaarslev, & Khan, 2016). In US medical practice, "doing nothing" is not acceptable; aggressive treatments that "fix" the patient are highly valued (Stein, 1990). The stereotype of the surgeon as a "cowboy" who alone can save the patient through invading the body is often mocked by non-surgical physicians for excessive intervention: "When in doubt, cut it out" (Stein, 1990, p. 41). However, the surgeon also represents the "ultimate" intervention.

This value of independence is evident in the development of advanced directives and living wills. These documents permit the individual to ensure that their treatment choices are known even when they cannot convey them. People of White European background are most likely to have a written advance directive, compared with most ethnic minorities in the United States (Searight & Gafford, 2005).

A Brief History of Health Care for African Americans in the United States

African Americans are significantly less likely to participate in medical research, donate organs, or have an advance directive. Studies have found that compared with White patients, African Americans were less likely to trust a physician and more likely to report concerns about personal privacy and the possibility of being the subject of experimentation when receiving hospital treatment (Boulware, Cooper, Ratner, LaVeist, & Powe, 2016; Washington, 2006).

The African American community in the United States has an extended history of negative interactions with the White European–dominated health care system that has contributed to a climate of mistrust. This suspicion has its roots in multiple historical incidents in the past 250 years in which African Americans were maltreated by the medical system. Many people of White European background, including health care professionals, are not aware of this history and are often puzzled by African American patients' health care decisions.

During the late 1700s to mid-1800s African American slaves were often used for medical experiments. J. Marion Sims, often seen as the founder of American gynecology, was known for operating on slave women without anesthetic (Washington, 2006). At the time, many physicians had the erroneous belief that African Americans did not experience pain. Sims deliberately purchased slave women for experimentation with surgical techniques. He would deliberately induce fistulas in slave women so that he could develop and demonstrate surgical procedures for his colleagues. He performed 30 surgeries on one of the slave women, Anchara, who is depicted in a well-known painting in which she is on an operating table with Sims and his colleagues standing around her. After leaving the South, Sims eventually settled in New York City. A statue was erected in his honor and for about the past 80 years has been in Central Park. Recently, as Sims's abuse of "patients" became better known, the statue was removed from that area (Neuman, 2018).

During the 1800s and early 1900s, most medical schools were private proprietary businesses (Starr, 2008; Tomes, 2016). In order to teach anatomy, human cadavers were needed. Many early medical schools had on their staff a "porter" who was in charge of acquiring cadavers. Particularly in the Southern United States, there is evidence that the majority of cadavers were those of African Americans whose graves were dug up by what were called "night doctors" or "resurrectionists." Washington (2006) notes that "by 1788, few Blacks were permitted to remain in their grave." Some families even built high wrought-iron fences around their relatives' graves to deter grave robbers. During the era of segregation, African Americans were treated at separate health facilities, which were not of the same quality as those for Whites.

One of the most troubling cases of discrimination was the Tuskegee syphilis study. Between 1930 and 1972, 600 African American men participated in a longitudinal study of syphilis. The overall study's purpose was to describe the long-term course of the disease. The men were promised free meals, medical care, and burial. The men with syphilis died at twice the rate of uninfected men of the same background. The study was overseen by the US Public Health Service. Approximately 10 years into the study, it was determined that penicillin was an effective treatment for syphilis. However, the affected men in the Tuskegee study were deliberately denied treatment. The men in the study, however, did have regular visits to the clinic during which some of them had painful lumbar punctures and all had their blood drawn (Reverby, 2011). The men in the study were led to believe that these medical tests were, in fact, treatment. Amazingly, this study continued into the early 1970s, when Peter Buxton, a social worker associated with the US Public Health Service, brought this to the attention of his superiors (Baker, 2009). After receiving no response from PHS administration, he took the story to the *New York Times*.

The study was abruptly stopped and congressional hearings followed. The surviving men did not receive an apology until the 1990s, from President Clinton.

More recently, it was found that a version of this study was conducted in Guatemala in the 1940s (Reverby, 2011). The US Health Service deliberately infected prisoners, soldiers, and patients in psychiatric hospitals, as well as prostitutes and children in orphanages. The focus was to determine whether antibiotics have a protective effect against syphilis.

In both the United States and Guatemala, study participants did not give informed consent. Many of the Tuskegee participants were minimally literate and unfortunately were deceived by the presentation of blood draws and lumbar punctures as forms of therapy.

Recently, the story of Henrietta Lacks became well known due to the award-winning book by Rebecca Skloot (2010). Ms. Lacks was a married African American woman with children. She went to Johns Hopkins Medical Center seeking treatment for vaginal pain; physicians found that the pain was likely due to cervical cancer. The physicians at Johns Hopkins took samples of the cancer cells without Ms. Lacks's consent. In the laboratory, the cells were found to be very robust and rapidly multiplied. Unfortunately, Ms. Lacks's cancer spread very rapidly, and she died six months after diagnosis (Skloot, 2010).

The cells that were cultured from Ms. Lacks proliferated and were used in various laboratory studies, including studies of the poliovirus and associated vaccine. The cells were also used to examine the effects of radiation. The cell line, termed "Hela" cells, is still available from commercial biological supply companies. The Lacks family did not receive any reimbursement for the use of Ms. Lacks's cells, although commercial biological labs have made significant profits from them (Skloot, 2010; Truog, Kesselheim, & Joffe, 2012).

By the late 1980s, many in the African American community were aware of the narrative of Tuskegee. In 1987, a new measles vaccine, the Edmonton-Zagreb vaccine, was given in intentional overdoses, sometimes at up to 500 times the typical level. The virus was given to African American and Hispanic children in Los Angeles without parental consent. Parents were unaware of the dosage being given as well as the experimental nature of the treatment. Another instance of using minority children for research without consent occurred in New York State in the mid-1980s. During the early days of the AIDS epidemic, groups of infants—a majority being African American—were tested for HIV without parental consent. The results of the test were also withheld from the parents (Washington, 2006).

In the 1960s and 1970s, various forms of birth control became readily available. Up until that time, there were fairly stringent laws about providing contraception. Among the agencies that publicized access to birth control were federally funded neighborhood clinics—often serving minority populations. In many African American communities, the contraception availability met with suspicion. In the late 1960s, a contraceptive clinic was intentionally burned while a crowd of African American residents yelled "Genocide!" (Randall, 1995).

Particularly in the Southern states, state legislatures at times have attempted to pass laws requiring sterilization of women receiving welfare benefits. These surgical sterilizations were often performed on poor African American women (Washington, 2006). Sometimes the women were informed of the procedure; sometimes they were not directly informed. The procedure was an "add-on" to an indicated surgery. In the early 1970s, medical students at Boston City Hospital openly criticized the policy of performing "elective" hysterectomies on Puerto Rican and African American women. Medical professionals often did not adequately explain alternative methods of birth control to lower-income African American women. In parts of the South, these involuntary surgeries were known as "Mississippi appendectomies" (Washington, 2006).

A state prison near Philadelphia was the site of a number of dermatological experiments. Many of these studies were conducted to assess how various cosmetics and cleaning agents affected the skin. More than 100 experimental drugs were tested on the inmates over four years; the vast majority were Black. Among the substances tested was dioxin, which is now known as a carcinogen (Washington, 2006).

As is evident, many in the African American community have reason to be suspicious of health care institutions. This history may also play some role in the frequent use of alternative medicine among African Americans (Mackenzie, Taylor, Bloom, Hufford, & Johnson, 2003).

Hispanic and Latino Culture and Health Care

Again, a reminder—people of Spanish-speaking background come from a range of cultures and countries, including Mexico, Puerto Rico, and countries of Central and South America, as well as Spain. As a result, it is certainly impossible to describe uniform health beliefs among the Spanish-speaking population.

However, health care providers often encounter patients who have, to varying degrees, accepted the explanatory models of illness that are common in some of these countries. For example, in some Hispanic communities, obesity—particularly among women—is often seen as a sign of health. Galanti (2002) tells the story of a Panamanian young man who brought his somewhat overweight girlfriend to meet his family. Several times, family members commented directly on her weight; they seemed pleased that she was "fat." The young woman was obviously embarrassed. Her boyfriend explained to her that in their culture an overweight woman is seen as someone who can produce a number of babies, and the family was delighted that he was dating "a real woman" (Galanti, 2002; Poss & Jezeweski, 2002).

There are certain values that guide many decisions, including health-related questions, within Hispanic communities. *Familisimo* emphasizes that loyalty and obligation to the family are particularly important (Davidson, Rosales, Shillington, et al., 2015). Compared with White Europeans, Hispanic patients are more likely to turn to family members, trusted coworkers, and, in some instances, indigenous healers, before seeing a health care professional. Any significant health care decision about a family member is typically made collectively. In emergency situations, health care professionals may find it frustrating to have to wait until the family can be convened before they can treat a minimally responsive patient. Additionally, even when a patient of Hispanic background is cognitively able to decide for themselves, they may prefer that extended family members make the decision and communicate with the physician on their behalf.

Health care providers may initially be viewed with some guardedness in many Hispanic communities. *Personalismo* is a core value; it means establishing rapport that includes *respeto*—the inherent worth of each individual (Calzada, Fernandez, & Cortes, 2010; Juckett, 2013). For a Hispanic patient seeing a physician for the first time, it is recommended that the provider establish a personal connection before addressing the patient's presenting problem. This will help build "confianza"—a type of trust found in a personal relationship. It has been suggested that health care providers ask about the patient's family in an interested and supportive manner to develop this relationship (Juckett, 2013).

One common cause of many health conditions is *susto*. Susto is an experience of intense fear usually associated with a significant life event. Many conditions, including chronic pain, have been attributed to susto. Emotionally intense traumatic events are common in susto narratives. One account of the onset of type 2 diabetes centers on a driver who almost hit a patient's vehicle and then got out and threatened him with a pistol (Poss & Jezewski, 2002). In another instance, the patient witnessed an accidental death. Part of the etiology of how susto causes an illness is a separation between the body and soul triggered by trauma (Poss & Jezewski, 2002).

Among infants, illness may be attributed to the "evil eye" (Mikhail, 1994). Relatives or friends may cast the evil eye when they look upon the infant with admiration and a sense of jealousy. The evil eye can produce symptoms such as vomiting, fever, and excessive crying.

Another belief that also occurs in Asian culture is the view that health represents a balance of hot and cold forces within the body. Illness may be caused by rapid changes in the hot/cold balance within the body. "Cold" illnesses would include cancer, colic, headache, and menstrual cramps. "Hot" conditions include hypertension, sore throat, pregnancy, and "*bills*," which is an angry outburst (Juckett, 2013).

Many of these illnesses are treated traditionally with herbal products such as wormwood for bills; wormwood is also used to purify or sweep the body of PTSD symptoms (Juckett, 2013). Other natural products that are used include cilantro, for anxiety and stomach cramps, and borriga—a flower that is made into a tea—to treat bronchitis (Juckett, 2013).

Several types of native healers may be consulted. In Mexico, curanderos operate from the hot and cold theory and often recommend herbs (Juckett, 2013). They may also recommend environmental changes to the patient. Among Latino patients, antidepressant medication adherence is found to be significantly lower than for non-Latino Whites, with non-adherence rates as high as 40 percent (Juckett, 2013; Price, 2014).

Price (2014) conducted a study of antidepressant medication use among Latino women that highlighted differences in biomedical and cultural perspectives. There was considerable ambivalence about taking the medication. Some of the women did not view depression as an illness and instead used the phrase *Estado de anima* ("It's a part of life") (Price, 2014). There was also concern about others finding out about the diagnosis of depression. This could conceivably bring a stigma or shame on the patient's relatives. Some women viewed the medications as an artificial way to make them "happy." This perspective was often in contradiction with their religious faith. Some of the women interpreted Catholicism to mean that carrying one's burdens without the aid of medication was demonstrating faith in God (Price, 2014).

Asian Culture: Views and Treatment of Illness

As mentioned at the outset of this chapter, Asia is a very large geographic area with multiple ethnic groups. Therefore, again, it is not possible to talk about a view of health and illness that is common to all people of Asian background.

However, of interest is that the balance of hot and cold that is characteristic of some Hispanic cultures is also found in traditional Asian medicine (Ko, Mak, Chiu, & Poon, 2004). The meaning of hot and cold is somewhat different; however, the idea of having a balance between these forces for health is a shared concept. Yin is "cold" and Yang is "hot." However, these terms have a broader meaning, such as the quality or essence of bodily processes (Galanti, 2002). This balance can be maintained through choice of food and/or one's emotional state. If there is an imbalance—too much Yin or too little Yang—illness occurs.

Treatments also vary. In contemporary China, Western-style medicine is practiced along with traditional Chinese medicine. In the Chinese hospital that I visited, there were two hospital pharmacies—one with Western-style prescriptions and the other for traditional medicine such as herbs and various plants.

There are some conditions that do not have a direct Western equivalent. For example, *hwa byung* is a Korean condition in which epigastric pain is attributed to an abdominal mass caused by unresolved anger that can result in the patient's death (Lin, 1983). Among men, *shen kui* is anxiety or panic attributed to the loss of semen (So & Cheung, 2005). An "unnatural" loss of semen will harm the body's Yin-Yang balance.

In addition to herbs and foods, the balance of hot and cold forces can be restored through application of intense heat—in the form of either cupping or coining. In coining, a coin (such as a quarter) is heated to a high temperature and then rubbed against the patient's back. This will produce temporary burn-like lesions. Unfortunately, in the United States, some parents have been hotlined for child abuse when these marks are seen as part of a physical examination. Cupping is a technique in which cup-like objects with an opening are heated and placed on the patient's back. The heated cups leave a distinct ring-like burn mark. It is believed that the hot cup pulls the cold air out of the body.

In Asian cultures, there is a particular set of "rules" associated with childbirth. *Zuo yuezi*, or "doing the month," refers to the months immediately after delivery (Pillsbury, 1978). During that time, the mother must not have any contact with nonfamily members; she must stay inside and is not permitted to wash her hair or brush her teeth. It is permissible for the new mother to sponge bathe with a mixture of boiled wine and water. She is to avoid stress, which includes talking. She should not consume cool or cold drinks but only warm foods and drinks, such as tea. Among those who adopt this worldview, later adverse effects of not "doing the month" correctly may include osteoporosis, complicated menopause, and arthritis.

Conclusion

There continue to be marked health care disparities in the United States. While cost appears to be a factor, other issues include access as well as continued subtle forms of discrimination. The Affordable Care Act, depending on its actual implementation, could address the issue of cost. However, ready access to care with patient-centered providers is a greater challenge. Many of the "problems" that health care institutions experience in providing care to minorities can often be attributed to issues such as language, culture, and history. In this increasingly flat world, it is important that all health care providers have a background and sensitivity about how to approach cultural issues with patients. Personally, I have found that being respectfully curious about patients' lives and values often leads to increased openness on the part of the patient and enhances the development of trust.

CHAPTER 5

Health Communication and Behavior Change

We are constantly bombarded with information about health. Commercials on TV describe the latest drug treatment for conditions that we sometimes did not even know were medical conditions (e.g., restless legs syndrome). Public service announcements, both on television and in printed matter, are another source of this information. Social media conveys a good deal of informal health information. The public service ads encouraging us not to drink and drive or advocating for pregnant women to take folic acid or for regular seatbelt use or child car seats are usually carefully crafted. Many of these notifications are developed in the same way that ads for automobiles, candy bars, soft drinks, and perfume are crafted.

However, changing health-related behavior in many respects is much more challenging than getting us to buy pizza. Benefits of behavior change are not likely to show up for many years to come. In fact, the benefits may be the absence of a poor outcome. Additionally, some of the behaviors needed are not particularly attractive—bypassing jumbo hamburgers, daily intense workouts at the gym, smearing on sunscreen, and avoiding tanning booths are a difficult sell.

At the level of our own individual behavior, most of us know how difficult it is to begin and sustain an exercise program. Even though we make those New Year's resolutions, our attendance at the gym seems to drop off by about the third week of January. It's also difficult to bypass the french fries in favor of a salad when the scent of hot fried potatoes is in the air.

Models of health communication and behavior change are continuing to be developed. This tradition of thoughtful and planful approaches to encouraging healthy behavior dates back to approximately the 1950s. For those of you who have taken a psychology class and have been exposed to different theoretical models (humanistic, behavioral, psychodynamic) or sociology (Marxism, symbolic interactionism), the various models of health communication and behavior change should be conceptually familiar. They often include elements from marketing as well as from social psychology.

The next time you see an ad targeting health promotion, remember that it was not generated from simple intuition or brainstorming but was likely the product of systematic analysis of a problem and application of specific dimensions known to be associated with behavior change.

Brief Overview of Theories of Health Communication and Behavior Change

When crafting health-related messages to induce behavior change, many health communication experts rely upon specific theoretical models describing the process and/or necessary factors to create changes in both attitude and behavior. This chapter will examine models at the macro and micro levels. Macro-level messages are ones conveyed through community health education strategies. These may include billboards, magazine ads, television commercials, online pop-ups, or notices sent en masse to smartphones. These educational notices rely upon communication models such as the health belief model, theory of reasoned action/planned behavior, and the social cognitive perspective. When there is a need for significant change in behavior, such as when an outbreak of a new or previously eradicated disease occurs, models such as the spread of innovation model describe how segments of the population respond to new information. Additionally, when new health-related devices are made available, such as fitness-tracking devices or phone apps for health-related behaviors such as smoking cessation, diet, or general stress reduction, diffusion theory explains the process by which these are incorporated into populations.

Theories of health-behavior change, such as the transtheoretical model, motivational interviewing, and relapse prevention, are predominantly individual-level interventions. However, concepts from these models have been incorporated into larger-scale public health educational efforts. You will also notice that there seems to be some overlap in concepts between some of these theories. In particular, the principle of self-efficacy or the belief that one can carry out an action successfully has been explicitly incorporated into public health education as well as individual behavior-change counseling. Additionally, most of the theories address the issue of what we need to change internally or externally so that targeted health behaviors can be implemented and maintained over time.

Health Belief Model

Between 1950 and 1960, the US Public Health Service was focusing on prevention of disease. However, it rapidly became clear that there seemed to be reluctance to undergo screening for early detection of possible serious illness. Importantly, this public reluctance to accept screening tests occurred even when the tests were free. At that time, medical tests of importance included those for tuberculosis, polio, and rheumatic fever. A key dilemma for the social psychologists who attempted to address this public health problem was how to motivate people to be screened for an illness when they were not currently experiencing any significant symptoms (Rosenstock, 1974). Concepts from the health belief model (HBM) are regularly used in public service announcements as well as in many commercial health enterprises such as pharmaceutical marketing. The dimensions of the HBM (susceptibility, severity, benefits, barriers, cues to action, and self-efficacy) will be discussed individually.

Susceptibility

A key element in determining whether we will undertake a preventative health behavior such as mammography is an individual's perception of actual threat from the disease. If one views oneself as moderately to highly susceptible, one is much more likely to undergo screening. For example, a 35-year-old woman whose mother had breast cancer would likely think of herself as susceptible to the condition and begin receiving mammography in her mid- to late 30s rather than later, as is the standard recommendation.

Severity

This dimension is essentially a value judgment. For acute illnesses or injuries such as influenza, a broken leg, or a terrible toothache, severity alone is likely to motivate action. However, the health belief model generally focuses on screening for conditions—some of which might occur two decades later or may not occur at all. In cases in which the outcome is severe and the patient has directly observed family members experiencing the symptoms, the perceived severity, in some instances, may be so great that the patient does not want to undergo screening. Genetic screening for Huntington's disease is an example of a situation in which some individuals who know they may be carrying the autosomal dominant gene have refused to undergo testing (Codori & Brandt, 1994). One of the reasons is that they are likely to have seen a relative die of this progressive disease in which patients, in the later stages of the disease, become psychotic and unable to carry out basic life skills. By contrast, a woman with a genetic predisposition for breast cancer who has observed her mother suffering from the condition may be particularly motivated by the severity of the illness to undergo testing to prevent this outcome.

In studies that quantify the dimensions of the HBM, the perceived susceptibility and perceived severity have been added together as an index of *perceived threat*. Often the outcome to which one is susceptible is not so much the illness itself but the consequences of the illness. For example, a recent ad encouraging persons to get tested and treated for HIV pictured a man sitting on the toilet with the word "diarrhea" prominently displayed. While HIV may seem somewhat abstract, diarrhea is certainly concrete.

Benefits

Another motivating factor is the extent to which receiving screenings is seen as beneficial. For someone without a history of cardiovascular disease in their family, issues such as weight, blood pressure, and cholesterol may not be seem particularly relevant. The benefits of scheduling an office visit with the physician every six months, monitoring blood pressure, and monitoring fat intake and diet may not be seen as worth the effort. In studies of patients undergoing genetic testing for Huntington's disease, the benefits appear to be reduced psychological distress. There is some debate in the literature about whether those who test positive suffer severe psychological consequences. However, it has been suggested that those who do undergo testing are more resilient and better able to face the consequences of a positive genetic testing result (Codori & Brandt, 1994).

Barriers

There may be obstacles to undergoing screening, but there may also be factors that prevent taking actions to prevent disease. For example, women may be fearful of asking a new sexual partner to wear a condom. Barriers to requesting that a partner use a condom include the interpersonal consequences of an implication that a partner is unfaithful. In relationships with a history of domestic violence, women were significantly less likely to ask their partners to use a condom (Wingood & DiClemente, 1997). Barriers may also be concrete and practical. In research on diabetes management, concrete issues such as transportation to the pharmacy and money to pay for insulin were cited as common barriers (Pun, Coates, & Benzie, 2009).

Cues to Action

These are either internal or external events that heighten awareness of the need to take action. For example, a chipped tooth might be a cue to schedule that overdue dentist's appointment. A sign in the local pharmacy announcing the availability of flu shots may elicit a memory from last year when you had a terrible case of the flu. As these examples suggest, there is some overlap between action and perceived threat. Indeed, it has been suggested that cues are effective only when they make us aware of our susceptibility and, secondarily, appreciate the severity of a condition that could be prevented (Rimer & Brewer, 2015).

Self-Efficacy

About 25 years after its initial formulation, self-efficacy was added to the HBM (Rimer & Brewer, 2015). As noted in the introduction, preventive health behaviors require that we take action. If someone does not believe that they can take meaningful action, such as avoiding tanning salons when they have become a central part of one's social life, activation of the other dimensions of the HBM are unlikely to result in behavior change.

Analysis of the Health Belief Model

To summarize, individuals are likely to enact a health-related behavior when these conditions apply:

1. They view themselves as susceptible to the condition.
2. If they acquired the illness, the consequences would be aversive.
3. The benefits outweigh barriers.
4. They believe that if they take action, it will make a difference—particularly in terms of susceptibility and/or severity.
5. There is a clear course of action to be taken that could reduce severity and/or susceptibility; there are benefits to carrying out preventive behavior.
6. These benefits may be immediate in the form of some type of emotional relief or security, and long-term in that the outcome (e.g., lung cancer) does not occur.

While the HBM suggests that we engage in a cost-benefit analysis as we evaluate possible benefits and barriers, this process may be more intuitive than logical—particularly when we have had personal experience, such as observing the death of a family member from cardiovascular disease.

The HBM is generally supported by research. However, some of the dimensions, such as cues to action, are often difficult to operationalize (Skinner, Tiro, &

Champion, 2015). In addition, there appear to be demographic and cultural aspects as well as possible personality dynamics that may differentially impact the influence of some of the HBM dimensions (Skinner, Tiro, & Champion, 2015).

A meta-analysis of studies addressing multiple types of health behavior concluded that the susceptibility and severity dimensions of the HBM were the strongest predictors of actual behavior (Carpenter, 2010). Similarly, in a meta-analysis of vaccination, risk and susceptibility were modest yet significant predictors of receiving vaccination, with a small contribution from severity (Brewer et al., 2007). While it might seem that health behavior would be strongly influenced by the perceived severity of the condition, this association has not been consistently found. When examining patients with HIV compared with persons with a less severe condition, those with HIV were less likely to adhere to treatment (Catz, Kelly, Bogart, Benotsch, & McAuliffe, 2010).

In another application of the theory to exercise, prior to beginning an exercise routine lasting for multiple months, the participants were encouraged to directly discuss short-term costs of regular exercise. Participants then listed the long-term benefits and immediate short-term costs as well as benefits associated with multiple types of physical exercise. It was found that those who engaged in this procedure showed 11 more hours of exercise per month than the control group (Hall & Fong, 2015).

Age also appears to influence the relative importance of the HBM dimensions. Among younger patients with diabetes, perceived barriers or costs had a much greater influence than they did among adults with the condition (Harvey & Lawson, 2009; Harvey, 2015). Among adults, however, benefits and susceptibility to diabetic complications best predicted adherence to a chronic disease regimen.

In a descriptive, largely qualitative study, Abadie (2010) studied a subculture of adults ("professional guinea pigs") in the United States who earned a significant part of their living expenses through being participants in clinical pharmaceutical trials. When considering entering a trial for pay, members of the guinea pig subculture weighed a number of factors, with particular attention to severity. Most participants operated from a hierarchy of possible risks, with completely experimental drugs at the top and drugs that were already on the market seen as less risky. Why did individuals participate in trials in which there was substantial risk involved? While not a consistent pattern, there was a tendency for compensation to increase along with risk (Abadie, 2010). At times, it was difficult to completely evaluate the risk because of the lack of available information about a procedure or medication being tested. When there was uncertainty, participants discussed a possible trial with one another and also included attention to benefits such as the quality of the setting in which the study took place. Some studies required that the participants be in a hospital-like environment for several weeks. An important factor in these studies was whether one's friends were also enrolled in the trial. In addition to the compensation, participants included institutional amenities, such as the availability of cable TV and the quality of the food served, in their risk-benefit analysis (Abadie, 2010).

In a society such as the United States, risks are not equally distributed and often fall to those who are financially poor and with few sources of support. The volunteers became quite adept at calculating hourly income potential from their participation. Most of the "guinea pigs" believed that the general public saw these trials as being a much greater risk than they actually were (Abadie, 2010).

However, critics have pointed out that the overall predictive value of the HBM is limited. In a study of asymptomatic women and compliance with mammography, it was found that physician input was more predictive of undergoing the test than any of the HBM dimensions (Aiken, West, Woodward, & Reno, 1994). Critics have also argued that the model really does not give adequate attention to cultural, social, and economic factors. Given that the perceived etiology and expected treatment of many chronic illnesses such as hypertension and type 2 diabetes vary across cultures, it is likely that perceived susceptibility and severity would be influenced as well.

Does Fear Change Health Behavior?

Susceptibility and severity appear to be core motivational components of the HBM. When applying the theory to changing health behaviors such as smoking or sedentary lifestyle, the HBM would suggest that increasing fear and anxiety would make it more likely that people would engage in preventive health behavior. There have been mixed findings about the role of fear in behavior change (Witte & Allen, 2000). While increasing fear to a moderate to high level may result in behavior change, this is probably not the most effective strategy for smoking cessation, regular seat belt use, or consistent application of sunscreen. From the perspective of motivational theory, moderate levels of arousal would be most likely to produce behavior change. High levels of fear, anger, or anxiety interfere with the ability to take in and retain information, so some of the message—for example, how to choose the safest car seat for your child—may be lost. Research does suggest that fear levels are moderated by self-efficacy; high levels of fear may be effective when self-efficacy for the targeted behavior is also high (Witte & Allen, 2000).

However, fear-arousing messages are used in many public health campaigns. These include smokers who have multiple visible health problems, such as a stoma, or who have emphysema and require oxygen. The Montana meth advertisement program pictures emaciated young adults engaging in prostitution and theft to support their drug habit. A closer inspection of a picture of a young woman seemingly at a tanning salon shows that her tanning bed is actually a coffin. The idea is that by graphically conveying the consequences of certain health behaviors, behavior will be altered. Severity is typically the most common element of health beliefs used in advertising. There is evidence that fear-arousing content does get people's attention. However, it may do so in a way that activates defensiveness. Among smokers, less attention was paid to a high-threat message such as a picture of a diseased lung versus a low-threat message such as a picture of a person holding a cigarette. This pattern of differences was not found for nonsmokers (Kessels, Ruiter, Jansma, 2010). Most studies show that messages that increase self-efficacy are more effective than those that increase fear (Ruiter, Kessels, Peters, & Kok, 2014). There is evidence that as the intensity of the fear appeal increases, defensiveness increases as well. Witte and Allen (2000) caution that fear appeals may actually backfire. Continuation of risky health behavior in response to a fear-arousing message is more likely when self-efficacy is low. Recent research also suggests that when people are asked to reflect upon core values or positive characteristics of themselves, they appear to be more open to fear-inducing messages. For example, women who engaged in a self-affirming exercise first were less resistant to negative messages on cigarette packs than those who did not engage in the self-awareness exercise (Ruiter, Kessels, Peters, & Kok, 2014).

When comparing four approaches to health communication, Meyerowitz and Chaiken (1987) found that of four different mechanisms—enhancing factual content, increasing fear, altering misperceptions, or enhancing self-efficacy—adoption of personal health-promoting behavior was best predicted by approaches that increased perceived self-efficacy. Bandura (2010) has also indicated that strategies to increase personal empowerment are much more effective than deliberately increasing fear.

Theory of Reasoned Action and Theory of Planned Behavior

The theories of reasoned action and planned behavior (TRA/TPB) date back to the 1960s. Fishbein's original theory of reasoned action stemmed from his research on how attitudes, intentions, and social influences and behaviors were related in early research. Fishbein (1967) found that attitudes toward the specific behavior—obtaining a mammography—were much better predictors of whether one would have the screening test than attitudes toward cancer. In a later modification of the theory, Ajzen (1991) added the concept of perceived behavioral control.

Behavioral Intention

According to Fishbein (1967), the best predictor of the target behavior itself is behavioral intention. It is assumed that unless something unforeseen occurs, people will behave according to their intentions. The ability of intention to explain the behavior depends in part upon whether the behavior is under voluntary control. In research on the theory, behavioral intention is the most common outcome assessed. It is assumed that attitudes, subjective norms, and perceived behavioral control—to varying degrees—predict behavioral intention.

Attitudes

Other direct determinants include attitudes toward the behavior, such as behavioral beliefs; these include beliefs about the target behavior itself (receiving a colonoscopy) and the evaluation of behavioral outcomes. For example, "I need to undergo a colonoscopy to detect any early signs of G.I. cancer; if they do not find anything, that's great. If they do find something, it will be early enough that I can get it successfully treated." As noted above, one's attitude toward screening and evaluation of the longer-term outcome are distinct. The negative attitude toward obtaining a mammography might include the discomfort associated with it as well as the possibility of a finding suggestive of breast cancer. While it has been suggested that the attitudes are the equivalent of the HBM's barriers and facilitators, the subdivision of attitude into behavioral beliefs (about the imminent preventive action) and evaluation of behavioral outcomes (remaining healthy or developing the disease eventually) is more complex than the two dimensions of the HBM.

Subjective Norms

As a social psychologist, Fishbein recognized the influence of a peer group as well as close family members in influencing health behavior. This dimension is composed of two parts—normative beliefs and motivation to comply. Normative beliefs are the extent to which valued others support a specific health behavior. The second part, motivation to comply, describes the relative importance that we place on these members of our social network, be they friends, family, or coworkers. Essentially, do we care what others think of us?

If you are trying to quit smoking, and if your social network, including your spouse, are all smokers, quitting smoking may threaten your relationship with your normative group. Since smoking cessation may result in losing valued social interaction, motivation may be minimal.

Marketing professionals, including social marketers attempting to change health behavior, often will attempt to increase motivation by indicating that if we participate in some form of health promotion, we will join a valued peer group. Ads for gyms and weight-loss products typically show attractive people who appear to enjoy exercise. The implication is that if we join the gym or adopt the weight-loss diet, we can join this social circle of fit and happy people. As mentioned earlier, elements of the TRA/TPB commonly occur in public service announcements. A strategy that uses desired peer affiliation as a motivator is the "Don't Be That Guy" campaign against sexual assault on college campuses. The ads report survey data indicating that 83 percent of college men respect their partner's wishes about sexual activity. The implication is that respecting women's wishes places you in an honorable majority. Another creative approach depicts a young man who is present while other college-age men are sexually harassing a young woman. The hero of the ad tells the other guys to stop it and comments, "They were way out of line." The message encourages young men to join the peer group of those who protect young women rather than take advantage of them.

Perceived Control

This dimension was added later and resulted in the TRA being renamed the theory of planned behavior (TPB). Control is subdivided into control beliefs and perceived power. Someone may have a particular behavior that he or she can control, in part because of internal factors (knowledge base, skills, motivation, emotional state) but also because of external factors (social support, access to resources) and an absence of barriers (Harvey, 2015). While perceived control deals primarily with internal factors, perceived power is more dependent upon the context. For example, someone who is trying to quit smoking can use medication, remove all smoking stimuli from their home and car, and substitute new behavior for episodes in which they previously would smoke. However, in the presence of a room full of family members who are smoking and chiding the individual about quitting, internal skills and knowledge may not be enough to maintain cessation. There are significant similarities between the elements of perceived control and Bandura's concept of self-efficacy.

Theory of Reasoned Action/Planned Behavior: Analysis and Research

The TRA/TPB helps to model causal relationships, and for those wishing to alter particular behaviors, it highlights several specific dimensions that can be modified, including attitudes toward the behaviors and subjective norms. The different elements of the model show different associations with specific health behaviors, and they differ among demographic groups. For example, intention to undergo colonoscopy among middle-aged adults was primarily dictated by norms. Exercise intentions, however, were predicted by both attitudes and perceived control (Montano & Kasprzyk, 2015). Since peer influence is more important among young adolescents, a health campaign that targets subjective norms would probably be more successful with this group than with older people

As an example of an attempt at attitudinal changes, the Canadian government issued requirements for cigarette packaging that included very graphic pictures of the results of smoking, such as pictures of blackened lungs, patients on oxygen, and a person with a tracheostomy. In a survey of smokers, 90 percent reported they had seen the labels, and of those who said they had seen the labels, it was found that three months later 23 percent reported quitting and 25 percent indicated they had cut down on cigarette use (Hammond et al., 2007). Those who reported reading and thinking about the label after the initial interview were more likely to have a change in their behavior, which suggests that the graphic labels may have altered attitudes about smoking (Hammond et al., 2007).

Attitudes and norms demonstrate a stronger association with intention than intention does with actual behavior (Albarracin, Johnson, Fishbein, & Muellerleile, 2001). A number of studies have examined condom use from the perspective of the TRA/TPB. A meta-analysis found that intentions to use condoms were influenced most by attitudes and secondarily by subjective norms. Perceived behavioral control demonstrated a weaker association with actual condom use (Albarracin et al., 2001).

In a meta-analytic study of exercise behavior, the addition of past behavior to the TPB weakened most of the associations between TPB dimensions and the target behavior. Self-efficacy was also found to be a particularly strong predictor of actual exercise activity (Hagger, Chatzisarantis, Biddle, 2002). Past behavior is a notable omission from many of these models. Past behavior, particularly the more recent it is and the closer it is to the target behavior, is actually one of the overall best predictors of future actions.

The association between intentions and actual behavior was summarized across 10 studies, with an average correlation of .63 (Ajzen & Fishbein, 1977; Warshaw & Davis, 1985). While moderate, this association would not be considered particularly strong. If we think of our lives, our behavioral intentions for regularly working out and avoiding junk food on January 1 may be particularly strong; despite our intentions, by about the third week of January the behavior change that we maintained for a week has often evaporated.

Another criticism is that the link between intention and behavior becomes more problematic when the behavior is not entirely under the individual's control. For example, studies have found that in many ethnic minority neighborhoods, access to desirable produce at a reasonable price is often quite limited (Galvez et al., 2008). In these circumstances, an intention to eat the recommended five fruits and vegetables a day may be compromised by accessibility.

Social Cognitive Model

Albert Bandura is still probably best known for his study with children on the modeling of aggression. Children observing a model being aggressive with an inflatable "bobo" doll were more likely to engage in aggression than children who observed a model engaged in non-aggressive play (Bandura, Ross, & Ross, 1961). Beginning with modeling, Bandura's social cognitive perspective has become progressively more sophisticated over the years. Humans exist in a transactional context that includes cognition and emotion as well as behavioral patterns and environment—all of which are mutually influential. Rather than viewing the environment as a static force, Bandura has argued that one can create environments that maintain desired behavior—a process called "reciprocal determinism" (Bandura, 1978).

As it gets closer to final exam week, many students I know consider their risk of becoming distracted from studying and deliberately set up an environment that minimizes outside influences. Some students turn their cell phones and laptop computers over to a friend with instructions to keep them until finals are over. In addition, they find a semi-permanent location in the library that is free of distractions and "mark their territory" with a coat or other possessions. They may also set up times with peers or instructors to review course content. These are all self-directed acts, based upon the student's self-knowledge, through which they establish an environment that will support the achievement of goals.

Efforts to change our behavior through the use of models are routinely used by advertisers. Television ads show children being extremely happy in the presence of their favorite sweetened cereal. Models that share characteristics of the target population are likely more effective. For example, a peer-modeling video of children enjoying fruits and vegetables did appear to positively impact fruit and vegetable consumption among primary school children (Lowe, Horne, Tapper, Bowdery, & Egerton, 2004). Adolescents are more likely to model the behavior of their peers regarding smoking or alcohol use compared with the influence of parents, other adults such as teachers, or even teenagers from another culture (Kelder, Hoelscher, & Perry, 2015). Similarly, in school-based adolescent smoking prevention programs that employ modeling principles, the health educator targets teenagers who have status in the school since they are more likely to persuade others to appreciate the negative effects of smoking and provide ongoing support for the social norm that smoking is "not cool." Finally, by their actions, the model reinforces advantages of maintaining abstinence (Kelder, Hoelscher, & Perry, 2015).

With respect to health behavior, Bandura believes that there are several core determinants for health promotion and disease prevention. These are knowledge, perceived self-efficacy, outcome expectations, and facilitators and impediments to change. Social cognitive theory argues that behavior is a function of personal cognitive factors, physical and social environment, and behavioral factors. Among the personal cognitive factors is one's ability to self-regulate emotion and behavior. In addition, Bandura argues that knowledge—understanding specific health behavior, such as how to appropriately take blood sugar readings on a daily basis—and the ability to predict outcomes are also part of this process. However, while reciprocal determinism has been influential, Bandura's major contributions to health education are the concepts of self-efficacy and observational learning from a model. D'Amico and Fromme (1997) found that younger siblings model some health-related behaviors of older siblings.

The importance of beliefs and self-efficacy was illustrated in a weight-loss study. Foster and colleagues (Foster, Wadden, Vogt, & Brewer, 1997) asked persons beginning a weight-loss program about their expectations of weight loss. On average, those entering the program had a body weight of 99.1 kilograms (218.47 pounds). For them to achieve their "dream weight" would require losing 38 percent of their current body weight. To achieve a weight that was not ideal but with which they could be happy required a weight loss of 31.4 percent of current body weight. An "acceptable" weight loss would require a reduction of 25.1 percent, and a weight loss considered "disappointing" was a 17.4 percent weight loss. A common physician recommendation is a 5 to 10 percent weight reduction. There is evidence that even in the absence of significant reductions in body weight, increased physical activity and monitoring of diet is associated with improvement in a number of health risk indicators such as blood pressure and blood glucose. However, it is easy to see why many people would drop out of a weight-loss program and consider themselves unable to lose weight. The goals being set are unrealistic and would likely result in diminished self-efficacy for future weight-loss attempts.

As a clinician, I have seen many patients who wish to quit smoking. The majority of those patients had made previous attempts at quitting. Those who were successful for 6 to 12 months in the past clearly had the necessary behavior for cessation in their repertoire. As part of an interview, I highlight this and also ask patients to consider in detail how they successfully achieved cessation in the past. By highlighting past successes, previously unrecognized coping skills are emphasized and self-efficacy is enhanced (Searight, 2018). Similarly, when a health care provider knows the patient well and can articulate past successes (successfully following a diabetic diet; weight loss) they can help the patient "get back on the wagon." Asking the patient to describe how they have handled previous challenges and how they managed to pull themselves out of a slipup highlights the patient's strengths and should help them feel confident about mastering future challenges. Social cognitive theory has been able to successfully predict smoking cessation, food choices, lowering cholesterol, dental hygiene, condom use, and regular exercise (Bandura, 2004).

Example of Applied Modeling—Telenovelas

Bandura's work has influenced an innovative approach to behavior change in Latin America, Africa, and India—the use of TV serials to model family planning, literacy, and HIV prevention. Latin American telenovelas, similar to US soap operas, have had the most success in addressing behavior change and will be the focus of this discussion. The first telenovela for educational purposes was the Peruvian show *Simplemente Maria*, which aired in 1969. Maria was a young woman who migrated to the city, worked very hard as a domestic, used her spare time for sewing, and was a positive role model for social improvement. Maria obtained permission from her employers to attend an adult literacy class. After the serial had been running for a while, reports emerged of young domestic workers who became interested in sewing and were asking about literacy courses. Based upon this success, Sabido (2003) began the process of systematic application of social learning concepts for developing educational telenovelas. Sabido included Jungian archetypes—the wise old man, the earth mother, the hero—in the stories as well. The archetypes, according to Jungian theory, are universally recognized character types.

To maintain audience interest, it was important to include key characteristics of telenovelas—there had to be a melodramatic plot, typically involving a romantic relationship, and a secondary plot as well. Sabido (2003) and his colleagues conducted a needs assessment and concluded that topics such as status of women, family harmony, literacy, and communication between husbands and wives were all areas of interest, and they developed shows around these themes. In his telenovelas, Sabido has three sets of characters: those who support the value being highlighted (e.g., women's rights, family planning)—thus, positive role models; those who oppose the value—negative role models; and a group of characters who were "doubters," neither strongly positive nor negative (Singhal & Rogers, 2012). The formula is as follows: one of the doubters adopts the preferred value relatively early in the course of the serial, a second doubter does so about two-thirds of the way through the show's run, and the holdout doubter is punished and, at times, killed.

A serial from India, addressing female equality, featured a young village woman who spoke openly about female equality and was involved in a women's organization; it also featured a male who endorsed female equality. Negative role models included a teenage servant in an arranged marriage who died in childbirth and a father who did not allow his daughter to continue school. Female literacy is a major dimension of women's status and well-being around the world. In developing countries, female literacy is associated with overall better health status for women as well as regular use of prenatal care (McTavish, Moore, Harper, & Lynch, 2010).

In Brazil, where telenovelas are particularly popular, it has been argued that exposure through television to smaller, less burdened families, even in the absence of a deliberate thematic message, has contributed to a reduction in childbirths and (probably) more consistent use of contraception. In several states within Brazil, during a 10-year period after mass introduction of television, the fertility rate dropped from 5.4 to 4.2 children. When young women were asked before and television's large-scale adoption about the number of children desired, the average dropped from 2.2 to 1.8 (La Ferrara, Chong, & Duryea, 2012).

Social Marketing

Social marketing is the use of marketing principles found in advertising and business to improve health or sustainability behavior, such as recycling, or to advance a larger social objective. Andreasen (1995) provides a more detailed definition of social marketing: "the application of commercial marketing technologies to the analysis, planning, execution and evolution of programs designed to influence the voluntary behavior of target audiences in order to improve their personal welfare and that of society" (p. 7).

Similar to commercial marketing, social marketing is based on four principles—product, price, place, and promotion. The product is what is being sold—running shoes, cars, frozen dinners. Examples of health-related "products" are smoking cessation, use of infant car seats, wearing a bike helmet, and avoiding drinking and driving. Marketers are very aware that to be effective, particularly in getting people to buy something non-essential, core values should be linked to the product. In the United States, there are five core values that marketers associate with their products—freedom, independence, autonomy, control, and individual identity (Siegel & Donner, 1998).

In commercial marketing, there is instant gratification with tangible products. Pizza companies guarantee 30-minute delivery; Amazon can have a product on your doorstep in less than 24 hours in most parts of the country, and in less than six hours in large metropolitan areas. "Promotion" refers to how a product is presented. Commercial marketing emphasizes short-term benefits, and the product is presented as an expression of one's core values. For example, television commercials frequently depict a pickup truck driving down a major canyon or going cross-country on a wooded trail, typically with the message that this feat should not be tried by the viewer. The truck reflects independence and rugged individualism: "I can go wherever I want to and not be tied to the road like all of those other drivers." Again social marketing emphasizes long-term social benefits—lifestyle change presented as an expression of personal values or, similar to the TRA/TPB concept of social norms, engaging in a behavior that makes you part of a valued interpersonal group. I have yet to see a health club market itself with the message that regular workouts lead to reductions in blood pressure or blood glucose. Instead, the health club patrons in ads appear attractive, with no excess weight.

In terms of targeting valued characteristics or outcomes, health promotion messages have lagged behind marketers of products that threaten health. The Marlboro Man and the independent, fashionably dressed Virginia Slims woman were around for decades before antismoking groups began wrapping their message in the five core values. For example, antismoking ads that show the results of a tracheostomy, close-ups of facial wrinkles, or yellow stained fingers may have more impact on a young adult than statements about risks of lung cancer or heart disease. The Legacy Foundation's "Truth" campaign taps into the value of autonomy—being able to experience personally valued life events (Durkin, Biener, & Wakefield, 2009). A woman with a weathered face fights back tears as she describes not being able to live long enough to see her grandchild grow up.

With respect to price, in traditional marketing, the cost is typically financial. In social marketing directed toward health-related behavior, the costs are less tangible and involve time, energy, and the social emotional resources required to learn new skills or make lifestyle changes (Smith, 2000). In addition, the outcome—if it is better cardiovascular health or the absence of cancer—will not be seen for many years. This is one of the key dilemmas in health behavior—how to motivate behavior change in the present to prevent long-range outcomes such as disease that occurs 20 years later. There will also be a reasonable percentage of people for whom engaging or not engaging in behavior will be unrelated to outcome. From the epidemiological perspective, the health marketer is working in the realm of probabilities—some of them fairly low. Again, not all smokers will develop lung cancer. Finally, for health behavior, a good outcome is often the absence of a bad outcome. For commercial diets that include branded food such as Weight Watchers, advertising clearly makes these foods appear as desirable as "non-diet" foods. In addition, the ads emphasize that you do not have to "give up" the foods that you like to lose weight. These companies include "diet" versions of chocolate cake, pizza, spaghetti, and hamburgers. Therefore, the price of change becomes less steep. Similarly, the public health department in Peel, Ontario, had a campaign to discourage pregnant women from drinking alcohol, and it developed a list of alcohol-free "mocktails" accompanied by recipes. The drinks all had names similar to specialized cocktails made in upscale bars. Examples include chocolate monkey, blueberry allure, and slurp berry sling (Peel Ontario Department of Public Health, 2018). The message here is that one does not need to give up drinking exotic drinks when one is pregnant—just hold the alcohol.

"Promotion" also refers to how the marketer makes people aware of their product. In addition, it may entail explaining how a particular company's product is superior to that of the competition. Many social marketers have teamed up with commercial marketers and use the same media, and in some instances it may be endorsed by a commercial company. For example, the Komen Foundation for breast cancer awareness and treatment is one of the leaders of "cause marketing." Cause marketing is a company's attempts to appear "socially responsible" by aligning with a health or human service organization. This is included in the marketing activities of the commercial business. For example, Yoplait yogurt has included information about the Komen Foundation on the lids of its yogurt containers ("Save Lids to Save Lives").

"Place" refers to the setting in which the consumer receives information about the product. Typical marketing involves billboards, TV, the internet, radio, magazines, newspapers, and stores. Social marketing also relies upon market segmentation—this means identifying target audiences for the health care message. For example, for promotional messages about safe sex, driving carefully, and substance abuse, bars that are frequented by young adults would be optimal venues. Television programs such as news broadcasts are probably good venues for health marketing directed to middle-age adults—it is noted that pharmaceutical companies often advertise on news channels. For city dwellers and lower-income groups, notices on public transportation may be the optimal venue.

Diffusion of Innovation

New information practices need to be acquired if they are to be implemented. Diffusion of innovation theory describes the process by which a new finding or new technology becomes established. There is considerable evidence that scientific findings alone do not automatically change behavior health care practices. Consider that Semmelweis's straightforward intervention of hand washing before having contact with patients required at least 20 years to become frequent practice in hospital settings. The regular inclusion of airbags in automobiles also follows a similar multiyear trend. At first, there is an invention, it is picked up by a relatively small number of people, the innovation becomes better known, and it progressively becomes used more commonly. This model appears to explain how new technology such as iPhones or even computers become part of daily life. In medicine, it takes 17 years to turn medical research into practices that benefit patients (Weingarten, 2000).

In the late 1800s, Tarde, a French judge, became interested in the adoption of change based upon the language and clothing of those who appeared in his court. Innovations that advanced society occurred as a result of the populace imitating figures that inspired them. He argued that it typically began with those of higher income and that, through exposure over time to role models, new ideas would spread (Kinnunen, 1996). Tarde believed that the key factor was social interaction—at that time in history, conversations—as well as actions. In looking at the process of change, Tarde described three phases. In repetition, an inventor exerts social influence over an imitator. Next, there is often a period of rebellion and critical questioning that Tarde called opposition (Kinnunen, 1996), in which the new practice is critically evaluated and in which others consider other options. Finally, after an individual chooses a particular perspective or reconciles opposing perspectives, he or she enters the final phase, called adaptation. In the United States, early research on the acceptance of innovation focused on how new farming practices were adopted. Ryan and Gross (1943) described how a particular hybrid seed corn became adopted by communities in Iowa through a process resembling Tarde's description.

Much more recently, Gladwell (2006) described three key players in moving from innovation into larger-scale acceptance. Connectors are those with a wide range of social ties who interact very well with others. Importantly, they know a diverse range of people—people in different occupations, of different family backgrounds, and so on. As a result, there is a connection between groups of people who would not normally interact. Mavens, such as Steve Jobs of Apple, know about a particular product issue in depth, but at the same time they like to help others and, in particular, like to help others make decisions. Finally, salesmen are those who have very engaging personalities but also are excellent at persuading; they sell the new product, idea, or research.

In addition to the people involved, other factors play a role in how readily innovation is incorporated (Rogers, 2004). Cost—time, energy, and money—is a major factor. The common sales technique for a new medical device that requires a cash outlay is to determine how long it would take for the purchaser to recoup the sales price. The new practice also has to be clearly superior to that of competitors. Generally speaking, new practices are replacing older ones, and because there will be some cost, the relative advantage of change has to be clear. Simple and straightforward innovations are much more likely to be adopted than those that are complex. If there is extended training involved, the likelihood of adoption is diminished. How compatible is a new adoption with current practice? Electronic medical records have been difficult for many medical practices to implement because the way that information is recorded differs significantly from formats used in previous, written hardcopy medical records. Observability deals with the extent to which the benefits from the innovation can be quantified and are clearly visible. If the use of an electronic medical record quickly reduces time for prescription refills, this would be a factor in adoption. The ability to pilot test a new innovation before it is adopted on a large scale is also considered desirable. Unfortunately, this practice often does not occur. For example, a new computer program is implemented wholesale for a large medical group. The implementation almost always will uncover some "bugs" in the program or issues that are not compatible with how the practice operates. This may lead users to quickly abandon the innovation. If the innovation had been tried as a pilot, and these issues had surfaced and been addressed, the likelihood of adoption would have been greater (Brownson, Tabak, Stamatakis, & Glanz, 2015).

Over time, there appear to be four stages by which innovations are adopted. First, there has to be Knowledge or awareness of the new practice and how it is applicable to a current problem. Next is the Attitude Formation stage. Here, individuals and organizations must be persuaded that the new practice is something that should be seriously considered. Decision is next, the early stage of adoption when some person or unit decides to actually implement the new program. Finally, the Evaluation stage determines whether the innovation was indeed effective and desirable. This last stage is influenced by a range of factors, including interpersonal relationships as well as the amount of energy and funding invested in the innovation (Brownson et al., 2015).

New practices are not adopted by everyone immediately following the discovery of an innovation. In terms of social systems, innovators probably comprise about 2.5 percent, and they are then followed by early adopters, who comprise 13.5 percent. Next, a significant number of people, the early majority (34 percent) will incorporate the new practice, followed by the late majority (34 percent), and then, finally, the laggards (16 percent) (Brownson et al., 2015). This model actually simulates a normal curve, and the relative percentages are likely influenced by a number of the factors noted above. Today, media plays a significant role in this process—early adopters are highly engaged with media—particularly social media. Bandura and others have criticized the presentation of diffusion for overemphasizing the perspective of promoters. If an innovation is indeed likely to improve one's life in some way, the terminology of "early adopters" and "laggards" for those who delay is probably appropriate. However, when an innovation is of questionable value or has been sold by deception or invalid information, it is probably more correct to speak of those early adopters as more gullible and those who resist innovation as being astute (Bandura, 2009).

Individually Focused Models of Behavior Change

The health belief model (HBM), theory of reasoned action/planned behavior (TRA/TPB), social cognitive model, social marketing, and diffusion of innovation model, are typically used at the macrosystems level. You will find elements of these approaches in public service announcements and local public health campaigns directed to residents of your community, state, or country. The conceptualizations of change described in the upcoming section are based on individual models—commonly derived from mental health and substance abuse treatment. However, models such as motivational interviewing and the transtheoretical model have been used by many different health care professions, including medicine, nursing, nutrition, physical therapy, substance abuse counseling, and psychotherapy. These approaches have been translated into brief, problem-focused counseling techniques that can readily be learned and implemented and that have a reasonably strong evidence base.

Transtheoretical Model

Prochaska and DiClemente, the developers of the transtheoretical model (TTM), also known as the stages of change, studied a broad array of approaches to psychotherapy. They found more than 300 psychotherapy theories and then narrowed them to 25 approaches. The TTM was initially developed as a way of trying to integrate the psychotherapy field. Most of these theories described why people changed during the course of therapy but provided little useful information about the process or how people change. From closer examination of these approaches to therapy, 10 processes of change were isolated. These mechanisms represented very different approaches to understanding psychopathology and changing behavior. Consciousness-raising, involving insight and self-awareness, was drawn from Freudian theory, the importance of environmental contingencies and deliberate use of them to change behavior was drawn from Skinner's operant model, and the importance of a relationship in helping others came out of Rogerian theory (McConnaughy, Prochaska, & Velcier, 1983). To better understand which processes were drawn upon for change, Prochaska and DiClemente (1982; Prochaska, DiClemente, & Norcross, 1992) studied former smokers who had changed on their own and compared them with a group that had been receiving professional treatment. In addition, they assessed how frequently people were attempting to stop smoking and compared those who changed on their own with those who received professional guidance. Finally, they examined differences between current and former smokers. Through the accounts of their participants, it was evident that the transition from regular smoking to being a nonsmoker involved a series of stages (Prochaska et al., 1992). Each of the 10 dimensions is more or less important at different points in the change process.

Precontemplation, the first stage, is where the individual has no intention of changing the behavior in the next six months. This category includes both those who are aware of the problem but have no interest in changing and those who do not see health risk behavior as being at all problematic. Examples would be regular smokers, consumers of high-fat diets, or those not engaging in regular exercise. In the next stage, contemplation, there is an intention to initiate change activity within the next six months. In this stage, people are very aware that their behavior is a problem and are giving serious thought to addressing it but have not yet made a firm commitment to action. Contemplators are open to information and advice about strategies for change but are often ambivalent about acting. While seriously considering change, a smoker in this stage is still thinking about the costs and benefits of continuing smoking as well as the pros and cons of smoking cessation.

Many students set fitness goals for themselves several months before they intend to act. It is not unusual for a college student in October to articulate a goal for the next semester: "I can't do it now, but next semester, I am going to the gym five days a week."

In the preparation stage, there is a plan to take action within the next 30 days. In this stage, there is a concrete plan for behavior change, such as joining a health club, setting up a physician's appointment, or getting rid of alcoholic beverages in the house. For those with fitness goals, it might be signing up for a spinning class that begins at the end of the current month or purchasing a good pair of running shoes. While some small steps may already be made in the desired direction, such as not eating after 7 p.m., these efforts do not substitute for a specific and realistic action plan. If you have typically had six to eight beers with friends on Friday night, what are your specific plans for the upcoming Friday? Have you told your friends that you will not be drinking with them or, if it is too difficult to be with them and not drink, have you told them you will not be joining them for a while? As a psychologist, I find it helpful to ask patients about challenges they might face so the patient can prepare for them: "What would happen if your friends got mad at you for not joining them in Friday-night drinking? What if they came by your apartment with a six-pack and tried to get you to join them?"

I have suggested an addition to the preparation stage called Kaizen (Imai, 2012; Searight, 2007). Kaizen was developed by the Japanese during World War II (Imai, 2012). At that time, there was a need to rapidly improve production in factories. However, there was not adequate time to assess the situation and develop a completely new system. Workers were encouraged to consider small steps that were under their control and that could improve productivity. In Kaizen, one begins with small, almost trivial, steps in the direction of the goal: for example, "I'll order the medium-sized French fries at McDonald's instead of the large." For those who are completely inactive, a one-hour five-day-a-week exercise regimen is likely to be overwhelming, and it is likely that there will be no movement beyond precontemplation or contemplation. For those who have been completely inactive, I suggest walking in place for five minutes while they watch TV. Then, each week, adding one minute to the time spent walking in place. This small-steps approach is likely to make the process of behavior change less overwhelming.

It is often very difficult to change a habit without putting another behavior in its place. The preparation stage is the optimal time to decide on this new behavior. For smoking cessation, chewing gum or eating hard candy might be the replacement. Preparation is also the time in which a smoking quit date is set. It is also helpful, as in the above example of Friday-night binge drinking, for people to examine the role that a particular health-risk behavior plays in their relationships with others.

In the action stage, the change is in effect but has been present for less than six months. This is the stage in which people actually modify behavior and/or their environment. They are in the active process of change. The focus is on preventing relapse and sustaining a new behavior in the face of environmental or social pressures to return to drinking, smoking, or letting days go by without exercising. Prochaska (1994) emphasizes that the criterion must be clear. Reducing the number of cigarettes is not an appropriate standard for being in the action phase—complete cessation is the endpoint. (However, later in this chapter, we will briefly discuss harm reduction—the proponents of which might not agree with Prochaska.)

In entering the maintenance stage, the action stage has been successful and the change has been in place for six months. Now, the focus is on continuing to sustain the new behavior. Depending on the objective, maintenance may last from six months to five years. For example, after a year of continuous abstinence from smoking, close to half (43 percent) of ex-smokers return to regular smoking. The relapse rate after five years, however, was only 7 percent (Prochaska, Hall, Delucchi, & Hall, 2014).

The termination stage is characterized by a complete absence of relapse risk. Even when there are aversive mood states such as sadness and anger, returning to smoking or drinking does not occur (Prochaska et al., 2014; Prochaska et al., 1992). The standard of absolutely no temptation is a challenging one. In discussions with former smokers who have been abstinent for 10 years or more, it is not uncommon for them to say, "On occasion, I do miss smoking, and a couple of times, I have felt like lighting up a cigarette." Therefore, depending on the behavior, termination might not ever be completed. Of those who had serious alcohol problems in the past, fewer than 20 percent had reached the criterion of zero temptation and total self-control (Prochaska et al., 2014; Snow, Prochaska, & Rossi, 1992).

The stages present the course of change, but they do not explain what is happening when people consider, initiate, and maintain new behavior. While the 10 processes described by Prochaska do not impact all of those who successfully change health behavior, they are useful for clinicians to consider as they work with patients. Precontemplation, consciousness raising, and emotional relief are the major processes driving behavior change. Environmental reevaluation, considering the impact of the problem behavior on others, is also part of preparation.

Self-reevaluation (i.e., "What kind of person am I now and what kind will I be if I stop drinking?") characterizes both the contemplation and the preparation stages (Prochaska et al., 2014). During the action stage, self-liberation, the repeated recognition of being successful at changing behavior ("I am really beating smoking this time") helps keep the habit from returning. Applications of learning theory will maintain the change. In maintenance, cues for problem behavior are removed (no ashtrays or cigarette lighters in the house), and there is now a set of behaviors that is replacing the former habit—for example, instead of smoking after dinner, taking a 15- to 20-minute walk.

The TTM also incorporates self-efficacy. In this model, self-efficacy reflects confidence in being able to handle high-risk situations. Temptation is the "pull" of a situation to engage in unhealthy acts (Prochaska et al., 1994) and is typically associated with strong positive or negative emotion and/or social pressures that trigger craving for food, a cigarette, or a beer (Prochaska et al., 1994).

As mentioned earlier, most of us have some ambivalence about self-change. Change involves altering the balance of pros and cons of adopting the desired behavior or stopping the undesired behavior. The process has been quantified—moving from precontemplation to action requires an increase in the pros or benefits of changing of one standard deviation. Moving from precontemplation to action also requires a 0.5 standard deviation decline in the "cons" of changing. Moving through the stages successfully requires that the benefits outweigh the barriers by 2:1 (Prochaska et al., 1994).

The ability to classify individuals into their current stage with TTM-based questionnaires has often been supported. The TTM was initially developed with patients desiring smoking cessation, but it has been successfully applied to a broad range of conditions, including diet, exercise, substance use, medication adherence, anxiety disorders, condom use, and domestic violence (Prochaska et al., 1994). Interventions used within TTM research have generally shown positive effects. However, it has been difficult to isolate the therapeutic elements associated with specific stages.

Velicer et al. (1995) examined the stage distribution of current smokers. They found that 40 percent were in precontemplation, 40 percent were in contemplation, and 20 percent were in preparation. Armitage (2009) suggests that there may be two essential phases of change, with a motivational phase followed by a volitional or implementation stage. The theory also suggests that change would be more likely to occur if clinicians matched their communication to the patient's stage of change. For example, in the precontemplation stages, the health provider might ask, "Have you given any thought to cutting down on your drinking?" In the contemplation stage, the focus would be on ambivalence: "What would the benefits be if you stop drinking? What would you have to give up, or what problems would be created if you stop drinking?" There have been some studies suggesting that matching communication to stage may move persons into the next phase of change. For example, this general pattern was found for smoking (Dijkstra, Conijn, & De Vries, 2006). When examining stage-based tailored communication for mammography, receiving an initial mammogram did seem to be more likely with stage-based messages. However, there appeared to be no advantage for stage-based over typical educational communication about receiving a second mammogram (Clark et al., 2002). In a study of smoking among pregnant women, Aveyard et al. (2006) also found equivocal evidence supporting the TTM. While the group of pregnant smokers who received the TTM stage intervention was more likely to move into the next stage, this benefit may have been due to the fact that the TTM intervention was more intense; also, it was found that the women changed their intention to smoke but did not cease smoking. In sum, while the idea of stage-managed communication is intuitively attractive, overall the studies have not yielded consistent findings.

Relapse Prevention

Lapses are an inherent part of the change process. During the maintenance stage, and even during the action stage, lapses are not uncommon. The lapse is a single violation of the goal behavior. A relapse, however, is a return to the behavior pattern that was the focus of change. Long-term success rates for many types of behavioral change, such as smoking and diet, have been notoriously low. The overall abstinence rate one year after smoking cessation does not exceed 10 percent. In the original conceptualization, the nonsmoker who has been successful for the past eight months experiences an unexpected stressor (job loss, demotion, marital turmoil, significant parent-child conflict) that challenges newfound abstinence. Faced with this loss of equilibrium, the individual may, without much reflection, return to previous coping styles such as smoking, drinking alcohol, or overeating: "I don't know what happened. In just three minutes it seemed like I'd eaten a whole pizza; I don't even remember eating it. It is like some force just took me over." Many descriptions of lapses have this dissociative quality—an outside force takes over, and before recognizing what is happening, the ex-smoker stops at the closest store, buys a pack of cigarettes, and begins smoking. After 10 or so cigarettes, the ex-smoker "wakes up" and realizes what they have done. What happens next determines whether a lapse becomes a relapse.

Rather than being linear events, lapse, relapse, and continued maintenance appear to be governed by discontinuous change and catastrophe models. These nonlinear models appear to predict relapse in alcohol use much better than their linear counterparts do (Hufford, Witkiewitz, Shields, Kodya, & Caruso, 2003; Marlatt & Donovan, 2005). Inhibition is disrupted by alcohol—one of many small changes that can trigger a process ending in relapse. Typically, this process is bimodal—the lapse leads to relapse or abstinence.

Relapse Risk Factors
There have been multiple classification schemes of risk factors for relapse. In his original formulation, Marlatt (1985) described three general categories: emotional, environmental, and interpersonal. Emotions may be negative states such as depression, boredom, sadness, or other intrapersonal experiences. However, positive emotional states can be relapse triggers as well. While this includes events such as celebrations ("I got a big raise; I deserve a beer"), it also includes simply testing one's willpower ("I bet I can smoke one cigarette and then stop"). Social situations, particularly those involving conflict with another person, such as an argument with a spouse, lead to negative moods and can also precipitate relapse. Marlatt (1996) found that about half of relapse episodes involved interpersonal conflict and negative emotion. Social pressure either directly ("You think you are better than us—you won't even drink a beer with the guys anymore") or indirectly, such as being around others who are drinking or smoking, accounts for about 20 percent of relapse episodes.

As suggested above, the TTM's view of lapse and relapse is probably overly simplistic. More recent views of relapse highlight the dynamic complexity involved. Individual histories, which include prior unsuccessful quit attempts, family history, genetic predisposition, and pre-existing psychiatric conditions, interact with current challenges, including environmental cues, cognitive distortions ("I have no self-control at all"), current social support, craving ("I want so much to smoke—this feeling is not going away, I really miss smoking"), and the ability to enact coping strategies (Borland, Partos, Yong, Cummings, & Hyland, 2012; Kirchner, Shiffman, & Wileyto, 2012). Similar to the concept of learned helplessness, lapses are likely to lead to relapse when the individual concludes from the lapse experience that they are unable to master the challenge of abstaining from cigarettes, marijuana, or alcohol. In particular, when the lapse is attributed to internal ("my fault—not the situation"), stable ("it will always be this way and I will always feel this way"), and global dimensions ("I have absolutely no self-control"), lapses are more likely to become relapses (McCormick & Taber, 1988).

Abstinence Violation Effect

Habits such as smoking or drinking differ from other types of behavior change because a commonly held standard of success is abstinence. While increasing the number of days one goes to the gym from three times last week to five times this week or reducing the fat in one's diet by 70 percent for the course of two weeks would be considered a success, drinking, drug use, and smoking cannot usually be done in moderation, and abstinence is the only appropriate goal. When an ex-drinker does slip up and drink a beer, they have automatically become unsuccessful and the likelihood of this lapse turning into a relapse is high.

There are several characteristics of abstinence violation that are likely to lead to relapse. Personal attributions for the lapse can determine whether the episode remains an isolated "slip" versus a return to habits such as smoking. Attributing the lapse to factors that are internal ("I don't have any willpower at all"), stable ("This just proves it; once an alcoholic, always an alcoholic"), and global ("I'll keep drinking no matter what type of situation I'm in") will lead to longer-term relapses in which the goal of abstaining has been abandoned completely (McCormick & Taber, 1988). If the lapse is seen as evidence that one has "blown it for good" (Latimer, Ernst, Hennessey, Stinchfield, & Winters, 2004), behaviors such as drinking or smoking are actually likely to escalate to negative thoughts and feelings.

Problems with the Abstinence Standard

Baumeister and Vonasch (2015) question the zero-tolerance approach for substance-abuse treatment. While establishing a "bright line" can help self-regulation in the early part of the action stage when motivation is higher, when relapse does occur, the abstinence/zero-tolerance cognitive set does not include strategies for coping with lapses or relapses. Baumeister (Baumeister & Tierney, 2012) also notes that the relative strength of our ability to self-regulate varies throughout the day. For someone who is trying to stop drinking, a particularly demanding day at work may deplete available self-control energy, making a lapse more likely.

Eating disorders such as binge eating are conditions in which a bright line of abstinence is not possible. Obviously, one needs to consume a particular number of calories to maintain life, and food, the key stimulus, is ubiquitous. However, without a preestablished coping response for excessive eating ("What do you do when you briefly lose control and have a short binge?"), an all-or-nothing cognitive style is likely to be activated, diminishing self-efficacy. Since eating has been a way of coping with stress in the past, it is likely to return in the current situation. This lapse is interpreted as a failure at self-control and underscores the view that in the face of food, self-regulation is not possible.

Relapse Prevention Strategies

There are techniques that cognitively compartmentalize lapses so that they do not trigger a return to the problem behavior. As suggested above, with alcohol, if a person has violated their definition of success as complete abstinence, relapse is likely to follow. However, the response might be more objective: "I drank this beer. Why? Well I've had a bad day at work and somebody offered it to me. Next time work does not go so well, I need to be sure I'm not with people who are drinking." Being able to examine the situation objectively and recognize that one was caught off guard gives the individual information about high-risk situations. Since it is impossible to predict the various situations that one will find oneself in, lapses are opportunities to learn about additional environmental triggers. Again, the overall goal here is to predict situations that may trigger relapse (Latimer et al., 2004). The individual can then decide whether to simply avoid the situation (probably the best advice in the early stages of abstinence) or develop a more specific strategy about how they will manage temptation to drink or smoke if they remain in the situation.

Motivational Interviewing

Motivational interviewing, while arising historically at about the same time as the stages of change, is a distinctly unique approach. William Miller, the founder of this approach, had been training substance-abuse counselors in a combination of behavioral self-control strategies and empathic relating. Empathic relating was a definite departure from most approaches to substance abuse counseling, which emphasized confrontation and was often seen as "shame based." Persons with substance abuse had been viewed as manipulative and as "in denial" about their substance use as a problem. Miller (1983), instead, believed that addressing ambivalence about substance use in a genuine and supportive manner was more effective. Motivational interviewing has been found to be effective in reducing problem drinking, gambling, and risky sexual behavior and increasing exercise, diet, and medication adherence (Miller & Rose, 2009; Rollnick, Miller, & Butler, 2008).

Philosophy of Motivational Interviewing

Unlike the TTM, motivational interviewing (MI) does not classify patients according to a stage. While there are standard principles and common questions, counseling is individualized to the patient's values and lifestyle. While recognizing that there are pros and cons of changing, motivational interviewing maintains greater flexibility and actually focuses upon patients' ambivalence about changing rather than trying through education to move them to a new stage. While traditional patient education requires the clinician to do a good deal of work while the patient passively absorbs information, MI places the responsibility and motivation for change with the patient (Rollnick & Miller, 1995). Rather than confronting irrational thinking, correcting a deficient knowledge base, or persuading the patient that changing is in their best interests, MI requires that the patient consider and articulate their reasons for and against change. MI believes that patients are more likely to accept and act upon health-related information if they personally "own" it (Resnicow & Blackburn, 2005).

MI advocates often describe its "spirit." In addition to the classic Rogerian triad of warmth, empathy, and unconditional positive regard, the health care provider is not in the role of expert but, instead, is in a collaborative partnership with the patient. In early research, Miller (1983; Miller & Rose, 2009) found that therapist empathy was particularly predictive of whether clients were drinking six months later as well as whether there was success in smoking cessation (Boardman, Catley, Grobe, Little, & Ahluwalia, 2006).

However, it is also very important to listen to the client's account of the role of drinking, smoking, or other behavior in their life and, in particular, be attentive to "change" talk ("Although I always drive myself home from the bar, I've been wondering lately if that is such a good idea"). Given the ambivalence about changing, it is also important to listen for "sustain" talk. However, Miller and Rollnick (2002) also recognized that people are ambivalent and "change" talk often alternates with "sustain" talk ("I just can't see giving up beer; I really like it, and it's the only thing that helps me relax"). Confronting "sustain" talk directly is not productive, however; change is much more likely when the person with the problem verbalizes the reasons for change themselves.

Specific MI Skills
There are four basic skills that characterize MI.

1. Express Empathy: This dimension is the foundation for the other techniques. Unless the patient believes that you are genuinely concerned about his or her goals and values, the encounter will not be beneficial. There are multiple ways to convey respectful concern. In addition to reflecting and summarizing the content of the client's verbalizations, the interviewer typically asks permission before providing any type of recommendation: "Would you be interested in hearing how smoking could affect your baby?" (Miller & Rollnick, 2002).
2. Develop Discrepancy: The interviewer indirectly or directly learns about the patient's key values. Often these key values are inconsistent with current behavior. This contradiction, cognitive dissonance, creates discomfort when the client's actions and their stated values or goals are clearly contradicting one another (Miller & Rollnick, 2002).
3. Roll with Resistance: "Resistance" is actually a term that MI would prefer not to use, since it implies a personality-behavioral deficit residing within the patient and creates problems in the patient-provider interaction. In traditional substance abuse counseling, the focus would be on confronting or "breaking down" resistance. However, in MI, it is typically an indication that the clinician is moving too quickly or that the "sustain" pole of the client's ambivalence has been activated. It is counterproductive to argue for change with a patient (Miller & Rollnick, 2002). If the health care provider attempts to address defensiveness by pointing it out, the patient will become more defensive.
4. Support Self-Efficacy: It is important to highlight patient strengths. Asking about accomplishments and/or other habits that the patient has successfully changed in the past can make the patient aware that they have been successful at other life challenges and that they can apply the same perseverance to eliminating a high-fat diet or reducing alcohol use (Miller & Rollnick, 2002). When the patient is ready to discuss possible solutions, it is often useful to have several options from which they can choose. Providing an array of choices reinforces patients' investment in changing and also continues with the theme of maintaining patient autonomy (Searight, 2018).

Because of patient ambivalence, when the provider acts as an "expert" it often threatens their autonomy, and patients may "dig in their heels" and resist suggestions that they might actually generate themselves, if permitted. Besides reflection of ambivalence, there are several other techniques that evoke subtler discrepancies. The provider may ask the patient to rate their level of motivation to change on a scale from 0 to 10 (0 being completely unmotivated and 10 being the highest level) (Miller & Rollnick, 2002). Use of a rating system is also helpful in that it shows the patient that motivation for change exists on a continuum. For example, "On a scale from 0 to 10, how important is it for you to lose weight?" If the patient says a "4," the clinician—particularly if the patient has been less open to change—can ask, "Why not a 1 or 2?" (Rollnick, Miller, & Butler, 2008; Searight, 2018). By responding with a lower number, the patient will acknowledge that they have some motivation for change. Another follow-up question highlighting variations in motivation is to ask what it would take to get the patient to a higher number; the response often reveals barriers (Resnicow & Blackburn, 2005; Rosengren, 2017).

The fulcrum of change is the patient's awareness and self-generated statements highlighting the discrepancy between their core values (family, long life, remaining active) and their behavior. Through the interviewer's questions and summary statements, the patient becomes uncomfortably aware that their values and health behavior are incongruent: "On one hand, you really like the feeling of relaxation and freedom from worry that you experience when you have had five or six drinks; at the same time, you worry that as you get older, drinking at this level is raising your blood pressure and you remember your dad having a stroke." This cognitive dissonance leads the patient to the conclusion that the amount he is drinking is not consistent with his values or life goals. He either gives up core values or changes his behavior. While the Socratic questions lead patients to conclude that their current behavior and goals are discrepant, the patients themselves must make the argument for change (Miller & Rollnick, 2002).

Harm Reduction

Harm reduction (HR) is a controversial approach to high-risk behavior such as heavy drinking, intravenous drug use, and sexual activity. The goal is not abstinence but typically focuses on reducing the quantity of a substance used or how it is used. From a public health perspective, harm reduction is focused on the adverse consequences of drug use for society at large. By quantifying "harm" in dollars (lost wages, arrests, deaths, jail time) associated with drug use, it is apparent that reduced use, rather than a likely unrealistic goal of eliminating drugs, would be beneficial (Marlatt & Witkiewitz, 2002). Another strategy, particularly with the use of drugs such as heroin or putting oneself at risk for sexually transmitted diseases, is to alter the conditions under which the harmful activity occurs. For sex, readily available condoms reduce the risk of sexually transmitted diseases, including HIV. Among those using intravenous heroin, access to clean needles and syringes reduces the risk of infection and disease transmission. When there is acceptance of harm reduction by regional and national governments, the previously concealed high-risk behavior is now open and can be regulated by public and private health agencies. Harm reduction still supports abstinence as a desired end point, but it views drug or alcohol use as on a continuum from less to more harmful (Marlatt & Donovan, 2005; Marlatt & Witkiewitz, 2002).

One of the best known and most controversial HR examples is "Needle Park" in Zurich, Switzerland. From 1986 to 1992, as a response to increased intravenous drug use, the city government implemented a series of harm reduction policies (MacCoun, 1998). Attempting to contain drug use within a specific area of the city rather than having roving small groups of heroin users on the streets, Zurich passed a policy indicating that a specific downtown park was a zone in which IV drug users would not be arrested and clean needles would be made available. In 1992, the city government put an end to the policy. The park had become run-down, with used syringes on the ground, and was the site of frequent heroin overdoses. However, Switzerland continued to be fairly liberal in providing drugs such as methadone to take the place of heroin and prevent withdrawal (Cohen, 1992).

Particularly with young adults who consume alcohol, abstinence may not be a realistic or even necessary goal. For those with excessive drinking, moderate drinking may be an achievable outcome. This would include those who have experienced some negative consequences for drinking (spouse upset, calling in to work with a hangover) but not a major life crisis such as an arrest or divorce, do not consider themselves addicted, have no close relatives with histories of alcohol problems, and have not demonstrated tolerance or withdrawal (Miller & Munoz, 1982). Some research has suggested that with lower levels of alcohol consumption, harm reduction approaches appear to be as effective as abstinence, including focused interventions in reducing alcohol consumption and the social consequences of drinking (Marlatt & Witkiewitz, 2002).

Cyber Media and Health Behavior Change

Nearly all of the theoretical models described in this chapter predate widespread use of the internet as well as the mass availability of cellular communication devices. This technology has radically changed how people find and apply health information, as well as how they engage in self-directed behavior change. By 2015, 68 percent of Americans owned a smartphone and more than 40 percent owned a tablet computer (Anderson, 2015). More than half of all adults report using the internet to find health information, with nearly 30 percent doing so in the past month (Wong, Harrison, Britt, & Henderson, 2014). Research suggests that up to half have looked for a physician or specific health care professional. And at least 10 percent have followed health advice obtained from the internet. Persons with greater difficulty accessing health care in their community appear to be more likely to use the internet for medical information (Amante, Hogan, Pagoto, English, & Lapane, 2015). At present, there are few quality controls for online health information. Persons with health conditions appear to be looking for valid expert-based advice. There is concern that persons with lower levels of health literacy may not be able to critically evaluate information being provided. Of those who do use the internet for health care information, more than half have indicated that their approach to a personal health issue has been influenced by internet-based information (Amante et al., 2015).

There are a growing number of mobile phone apps for behavioral self-change. Most of the available health apps are oriented toward recording exercise activity and diet, and monitoring chronic health conditions such as diabetes and hypertension. Many of these apps use prompts for taking medication regularly and have also been used for recording health-related information, such as blood pressure or blood sugar readings, on a daily basis, as well as activity level and weight. Of available studies on diabetes, the majority have reported positive changes in glycosylated hemoglobin, which is a measure of longer-term diabetic control (Tran, Tran, & White, 2012; Quinn et al., 2008). Most of the studies of exercise apps indicate significant increases in activity level as well as statistically significant decreases in body mass index.

A recent study evaluated a group of 40 health-related smartphone apps. Of these, 75 percent were directed toward exercise and 15 percent focused on diet. Content was rated as somewhat better on paid apps than those available for free (Direito et al., 2014). Evidence-based techniques for modifying health behavior were present in about 60 percent—the most common was self-monitoring of physical activity and diet, "intention formation," in 50 percent; setting specific goals, 38 percent; and review of behavioral goals, 23 percent (Direito et al., 2014). None of the apps reviewed included relapse prevention, which is important for maintenance of behavior change. The evidence-based approaches were more common in paid versus free apps (Direito et al., 2014).

The number of apps developed specifically for mental health has also grown quickly. Public health researchers note that from the perspective of the World Health Organization, the global burden of major depressive disorder and other psychiatric conditions such as anxiety disorders is continuing to rise. It is neither practical nor realistic to assume that all individuals with these conditions can readily access psychotherapy. As a result, self-directed programs have developed to provide some of the key components of therapy and/or to monitor symptoms. The Department of Defense created PTSD Coach. The app has been widely used and provides concrete strategies for dealing with overwhelming emotion, such as strong affect triggered by flashbacks (Kuhn et al., 2014). Another app, FOCUS, was developed to proactively assist persons with schizophrenia. The app will ping several times a day and ask questions about sleep, mood, and medication adherence. Based on the patient information, FOCUS will recommend strategies to address any problems. Patients using FOCUS for a month reported significant reduction in psychotic and depressive symptoms (Ben-Zeev et al., 2014). Apps are also available for relapse prevention, including those that can be accessed at high-risk times.

Conclusion

If nothing else, this chapter illustrates that providing health advice in a manner that will evoke behavior change is not simply a matter of education about health risks. Both the macro- and micro-level models, in some way, address individually or culturally held values. Values are the fundamental motivator for change. These values, however, may include a desire to be a member of a socially valued group or someone who is in control of all aspects of his or her life. With the addition of cyber-communication, it is very likely that new models will emerge. The ability of smartphone apps to provide health feedback and guidance in "real time" opens the door to new possibilities in this field.

CHAPTER 6

In the Clinic
Communication, Adherence, and Symptoms Without Disease

If you consider the last time you saw a physician, think about several issues: (1) How much time did the doctor spend with you? (2) Was this a primary care physician— someone you refer to as "my doctor"? (3) Did you feel as if the physician addressed your concerns? (4) How rushed or harried did your physician seem to be? (5) If you were given directions to follow—take medication on a particular schedule, follow up for a test—did you understand what you were supposed to do? (6) If you disagreed with the physician about some aspect of your treatment or felt it was unrealistic because of time, finances, or your social situation, did you raise this concern?

When you think about your family members, friends, and acquaintances, do they all react the same way to physical symptoms? For example, are you or a family member essentially immobilized when you have a head cold with a stuffy nose, cough, and sore throat? Do you recognize that, other than rest and maybe over-the-counter pain relievers, there is not much you can do except allow time to pass for the symptoms to go away? However, do you or those you know find these symptoms too debilitating or become worried that they are the early signs of something more serious? Are you worried enough that you make an appointment at the clinic as soon as possible? Some of you may have been raised by parents who were particularly sensitive to their own or your physical discomfort. In some families, a bit of sneezing, snuffles, and saying "I don't feel good today" would be enough for a child to be allowed to stay home from school that day. Since my father was a physician and my mother was a nurse, the required symptoms to stay home from school for my siblings and me typically involved a fever of 106, extreme nausea, and delirium. All of us seem to have an internal threshold for discomfort that is unique but likely influenced by our family and culture.

The Affordable Care Act encourages patients and physicians to establish medical "homes"—a central "first stop" for health care (Gilfillan et al., 2010). This "home" will likely be a primary care provider's office and/or clinic staffed by multiple primary care physicians, including pediatricians, internists, and family physicians. In addition, these primary care practices increasingly include other professionals, such as social workers, nurse practitioners, psychologists, and nutritionists.

Primary care physicians rely heavily upon interviews and physical examinations in their evaluation of patients, and while ordering tests or referring to specialists is common, most primary care diagnoses are based upon an office interaction between physician and patient (Lazare, Putnam, & Lipkin, 1995). As a result, dimensions such as communication skills, patient agendas for the office visit, adherence with medical recommendations, and managing patients whose symptoms reflect biopsychosocial dysfunction as opposed to narrower physiochemical abnormalities have all become very relevant. As will be discussed in this chapter, the training of future physicians has undergone significant changes, with the addition of interpersonal skills and the role of psychosocial factors influencing patient care, receiving greater attention in the past decade. While technical knowledge and skill continues to be a foundational piece of medical education, this content is being placed in a broader psychosocial context including the physician-patient relationship (Emanuel & Gudbranson, 2018).

What Is Primary Care?

Primary care providers are generalists and can treat the majority of problems brought to their offices. While somewhat arbitrary, primary care medicine includes family medicine, internal medicine, and pediatrics. Because of their focus on women's health, gynecologists may be considered primary care providers. While the majority of providers are physicians, nurse practitioners and physician assistants also practice primary care medicine.

While all medical specialties include attention to social and behavioral science, the primary care sector has actually been most strongly influenced by the issues that are covered in this book. Family medicine in particular is one of the newest primary care fields that replaced the older general practitioners (GPs). While the influence of the biopsychosocial systems model has been debated (Searight, 2016), residency education for primary care physicians includes attention to psychological, family, and community variables. As noted in Chapter 1, Engel's (1977) description of a new paradigm for medical practice was published relatively soon after the establishment of family medicine as a distinct medical discipline. Engel (1977) himself noted the contribution that a biopsychosocial approach could make to this new primary care medical field. Engel highlighted a frequent observation by physicians that many patients had symptoms without evidence of any physiological abnormality. Conversely, patients could have strong evidence of an anatomical abnormality (e.g., a "slipped disc" in the vertebrae) but no symptoms. Additionally, it was often difficult to isolate the biochemical, bacterial, viral, or anatomical abnormality associated with many common presenting symptoms such as fatigue, gastrointestinal distress, and headache. Given that the boundaries between health and illness—sick and well—are often arbitrary, it should not be surprising that seemingly "rational" treatment based on biomedical logic did not necessarily return patients to health.

Engel's work was influential in some medical schools in which medical students, when seeing patients under supervision, would be required to describe to their supervising faculty issues at the biological, psychological, social, and even community levels that were contributing to the patient's illness (Engel, 1977). As an example of this model, third-year medical students who were spending a month learning family medicine—in addition to receiving lectures and going to a clinic—participated in a community activity, including riding along with local police officers.

While the term "secondary care" is not typically used in medical circles, the next level up from primary health care are specialists. These specialist physicians typically focus on a particular organ system (neurology—central nervous system; otolaryngology—ears, nose, and throat; ophthalmology—eyes; orthopedics—skeletal; cardiology—heart and cardiovascular system) or a specific type of disease (oncology—cancer; rheumatology—diseases such as arthritis; psychiatry—mental illness). One of the reasons that development of the primary care sector has been encouraged is that many patients with relatively minor conditions such as seasonal allergies would refer themselves to a more costly specialist even though the condition could be appropriately evaluated and treated much less expensively and efficiently by primary care providers. However, referrals to specialists are very common in the primary care sector, and if you have ever broken a bone, it is likely that you were referred to an orthopedist, or if you had some heart irregularity, your primary care physician would have sent you directly to a cardiologist.

Tertiary care typically takes the form of specialized approaches to evaluation and treatment found at university medical centers or in subspecialty clinics in large metropolitan areas. For example, pediatric cardiologists would be heart specialists who have devoted specific study and training to understanding how these diseases manifest in children. Some subspecialists perform very specific surgical procedures, including neurosurgeons who conduct microscopic brain surgeries; dermatologists who specialize in skin grafting among burn victims; or oncologists who have specialized training in various forms of therapy for cancer.

The Importance of the Clinical Interview

As suggested above, the vast majority of ailments are evaluated and treated in the primary care sector. Primary care physicians, while certainly availing themselves of technology, are very well trained in maximizing the amount of information that can be obtained through patient interview and physical examination. The majority of diagnoses, despite our high-tech medical equipment and the plethora of medical tests that can be run based upon a sample of your blood or urine, are based upon the history and physical examination. In reality, only about 12 percent of encounters involve a diagnosis made solely from the physical examination; in 11 percent, the diagnosis is made based on laboratory tests alone; and in more than 75 percent of encounters the diagnosis is made from the history. This history is gathered through patient interview (Rich, Crowson, & Harris, 1987). Some physicians and some researchers have rated the history as the key to diagnosis in at least 90 percent of medical encounters.

While mental health professionals are trained in detail about how to interview patients and how to word questions to obtain the most reliable and valid information, the skills involved in effective physician-patient communication have only recently been included in medical school curricula. In post–medical school residency training, primary care residents are more likely to receive some education in this area compared with specialists. However, recent changes in medical education have emphasized effective doctor-patient communication as a foundational medical competency for all physicians.

Overview of the Medical Office Encounter

A patient-centered interview typically begins with an open-ended question from the provider: *"What brings you in today?" "How can I help you today?"* A less patient-centered interview might begin with a closed-ended query: *"The nurse's note says you are having headaches. How long have those been going on?"* When practicing physicians are encouraged to begin their encounters with open-ended queries, they often respond with concerns about time. Efficiency is an important value in medical systems, with the average length of an outpatient medical encounter somewhere in the range of 13 to 20 minutes. As physicians become employees of larger clinical networks, productivity pressures increase. Hartzband and Groopman (2016) note that medicine is unfortunately moving toward "Taylorism," in which medical practice has come to resemble a tightly regulated automotive assembly line with efficiency being the goal.

Research findings should allay physicians' concerns about open-ended queries opening up a "can of worms." When asked "What brings you in today?" 75 percent of patients completed their description of the presenting problem in under 60 seconds; 90 percent of all patients completed their description in under two minutes (Roter et al., 1995).

Skillful interviewers, even when they must structure the interaction with a patient who is verbally digressive, still use open-ended questions (*"Tell me more about your headache"*) (Mauksch, 2017). After obtaining some clarity about the presenting problem, the physician is likely to focus on questions that are more specific to a diagnosis. At this point, the physician is often engaging in an internal process of hypothesis testing and looking for confirmatory or dis-confirmatory evidence of different conditions. For example, a patient reporting that they sleep 8 to 9 hours a night but are tired during the day raises questions about the possibility of sleep apnea, major depressive disorder, or hypothyroidism. The physician's subsequent questions often try to eliminate some of these possibilities. In the case of the tired patient, follow-up questions might focus on the patient's mood or, if the physician is considering sleep apnea, asking the patient whether their husband or wife has complained about the patient's snoring. Next, the physician typically carries out some type of physical examination. The visit concludes with a diagnosis and treatment plan or some tentative diagnoses and a plan for follow-up and perhaps laboratory testing to clarify the clinical picture and rule out possible conditions.

The Difference Between Good- and Poor-Quality Physician-Patient Interaction

As noted above, the majority of useful diagnostic information comes from the clinical interview. However, there is research indicating that many health care providers have less than optimal skills in conducting clinical interviews. A classic study of internists found that physicians interrupted patients in the initial 18 seconds of the patient's description of their presenting problem (Beckman & Frankel, 1984). Once they lost the conversational initiative, patients were typically unable to regain much control over the interview and subsequent interaction. If their concerns for the physician had not been mentioned by the 18-second mark, it was unlikely that the patient's problem would be addressed in the encounter that day.

Levinson and colleagues (Levinson, Roter, Mullooly, Dull, & Frankel, 1997) conducted a study in which physician-patient interactions were videotaped. Based on the video, physician behavior was rated, and then the group of physicians studied was followed for up to an average of approximately 10 years. The investigators examined whether there were differences in the number of malpractice lawsuits against these physicians based upon their interviewing styles and interpersonal skills with patients. It was found that those physicians who were less likely to be sued made more facilitative comments during the interview (encouraging the patient: *"Tell me more about that"*). These physicians also asked patients directly about their own understanding of their symptoms (*"What are your thoughts about what might be causing your back pain?"*) and provided more interpretive statements (*"Since your father died of a heart attack in his mid-40s, you are really worried about what your chest pain might mean"*). Other techniques used by interpersonally sensitive physicians included more orienting statements, which provided the patient with a verbal roadmap of the office visit (*"First, I would like to ask you some more questions about your pain; then I will do an overall exam and pay particular attention to that area of your back where the pain is worse"*). The good-quality physician-patient encounters also included more humor and laughter (Levinson et al., 1997).

Other research has indicated that for physicians with strong interpersonal skills, patients report greater satisfaction and are more likely to adhere to treatment for chronic conditions such as type 2 diabetes or hypertension. Good-quality communication also reduces the likelihood of frequently changing physicians ("doctor shopping"). Of importance to time-stretched practitioners, patient-centered interviewing techniques led to more efficient encounters, since the physician was better able to elicit the patient's key concern for the office visit at the beginning.

Physician behavior associated with negative patient outcomes and/or ratings included interruptions, being overly formal, and ignoring or not inquiring about psychosocial issues (Levinson et al., 1997). Other physician behavior associated with negative outcomes included being overly directive and providing the patient with their diagnosis during the exam rather than after the examination (Roter et al., 1997). Finally, patients who felt overloaded by information provided by the physician at the end of the encounter—particularly when it involved a significant amount of medical jargon—led to less patient satisfaction. In my own experience, it has not been unusual to see a patient leaving the exam room after seeing a physician, appearing confused, and saying to the nurse or receptionist, "I'm not exactly sure what I'm supposed to do next."

Research suggests that as more women enter the field of medicine, the interpersonal aspects of the physician-patient encounter may improve. On the whole, female physicians appear to exhibit better skills in the interpersonal aspects of the interview than male clinicians. Female physicians have been found to spend more time with patients, are more egalitarian and less paternalistic, provide more counseling, and ask more about psychosocial issues (Roter, Hall, & Aoki, 2002). In turn, their patients are more likely to disclose psychosocial concerns (Hall & Roter, 2002).

Electronic Medical Records: Benefits and Drawbacks

A key component of the Affordable Care Act (ACA) was the large-scale implementation of electronic medical records (EMRs). ACA proponents argued that widespread adoption of EMRs would lead to cost savings through a centralized "medical home" database that permitted better patient tracking, increased medication adherence, and reduced numbers of unnecessary and duplicate medical tests. A centralized EMR could also be used to track patient response to treatment with the possibility of establishing a system of financial rewards to physicians who kept patients out of the hospital.

However, despite the promise of improved efficiency associated with EMRs through features such as computerized order entry (ordering laboratory tests, X-rays, referrals to specialists), early feedback suggested that this innovation was associated with lower levels of work-related satisfaction among physicians (Shanafelt et al., 2016). Several studies described physicians making far more eye contact with their laptop screens than with the patients during clinical encounters (Margalit, Roter, Dunevant, Larson, & Reis, 2006). Additionally, the conversational tone of skilled medical interviewing has been replaced with the "check the box" templates that are part of EMRs and the clicking of computer keyboards.

Values of Patients and Health Care Providers

In examining the values of physicians and patients, particularly about what constitutes a quality physician-patient interaction, differences are clear. Physicians tend to value technical diagnostic information, clinical experience, and efficiency. Patients, by contrast, value listening, explanations of their condition, and information about treatment and therapeutic options. Some studies have found that at least a third of the instructions or recommendations provided by physicians to patients are not understood. Patients do, however, appreciate options (*"For your back pain we could try reduced activity pain medication or we could try physical therapy—what do you think would help the most?"*).

These values are articulated very clearly in the growing number of websites in which patients rate physicians. There are few comments about health care providers' technical knowledge but a great many observations about physicians' interpersonal sensitivity. While they may not always have a complete understanding of the mechanics of the medical examination, laboratory tests selected, or medications prescribed, patients can assess whether they are genuinely being listened to and if the physician is responsive to their concerns. The following are two paraphrased examples recently taken from patient websites rating physicians: "Dr. X is very friendly and takes the time to learn about her patients"; by contrast, Dr. Y "rolled her eyes at me, was very cold and made me feel like a hypochondriac."

Communicating Medical Mistakes

Research on physician-patient communication is a relatively recent development. An even more recent issue is how physicians should handle medical mistakes. As noted earlier, medical error is a significant cause of death and disability. What should physicians do when they make a mistake? Concern about legal repercussions and certainly the professional pride of physicians has often historically contributed to a pattern of not acknowledging these errors to patients. However, recent writing on the subject suggests that physician apologies may actually protect against litigation. Nearly 30 states now have laws encouraging physicians to apologize for mistakes and have even gone as far as making disclosure of mistakes to patients inadmissible in court.

Jauhar (2008) courageously described one of his medical errors in a *New York Times* article. A 30-year-old East Asian man presented to the hospital's emergency department with chest pain. In addition to his age, the history and available medical information did not indicate any of the traditional risk factors for heart disease. After being admitted to the hospital, multiple tests were completed. Jauhar's (2008) diagnosis was pericarditis—an inflammation of the muscle around the heart. Other physicians who were caring for the patient during the hospitalization accepted Jauhar's (2008) diagnosis. As a routine part of the evaluation, the patient had an angiogram that showed a complete block of the left anterior descending artery.

Jauhar's (2008) reaction:

> Heat rose to my face as colleagues wandered in to inquire about what was going on. "How could we have missed this?" I asked aloud. I was well aware of the disturbing prevalence of heart disease among South Asians, whose risk is up to four times that of other ethnic groups. I knew that heart attacks in this population often occurred in men under 40 who often did not exhibit classic coronary risk factors. I knew all this but somehow my mind had suffered a block.
>
> "Don't beat yourself up," a colleague said sympathetically. "Every doctor I know would have done the same thing . . . [as you did]." . . .
>
> What now? I knew I had to explain myself, but how much should I say? Like all doctors, I had made errors before but never one this big—and in my own specialty, too. Should I just tell my patient the facts? Should I apologize? . . .
>
> I found [the patient] lying on a stretcher. The pain in his chest was gone he happily informed me. However, the groin, where the catheter had been inserted, now hurt. "They substituted one pain for another," he said, laughing.
>
> I grasped the rails of the gurney. "I thought you had pericarditis," I said carefully. "I was obviously wrong. I'm sorry."
>
> He seemed embarrassed. "No, no. The past is finished," he replied. "I am more interested in the future."

The patient chose to have his follow-up care from Dr. Jauhar, saying, "You have been terrific. . . . Thank you." According to Jauhar, "I nodded silently, feeling empty. 'You are much too generous,' I said."

Medically Unexplained Symptoms

Much of outpatient clinical practice involves addressing symptoms that do not have a clear etiology. The term "medically unexplained symptoms" (MUS) is frequently applied to a cluster of co-occurring symptoms for which a specific physiological or anatomical abnormality has not been established (Isaac & Paauw, 2014). Despite the absence of a clear cause, patients with these conditions experience considerable physical and psychological distress. Additionally, the symptoms typically disrupt work and family functioning.

Before proceeding, it is important to address the common issue that arises when conditions with MUS are discussed. In teaching, I find that students often respond with the view that these physical symptoms are made up by patients or are somehow not real. This is a misconception. While there are patients who do exhibit "fake" symptoms, the vast majority of patients with MUS are not fabricating their complaints. It is critical to appreciate that these patients genuinely do experience the physical distress that they are reporting. As can be imagined, their encounters with the medical community are often frustrating. Patients with somatic symptom conditions often feel that their complaints are not taken seriously. As a result, these patients are very sensitive to any suggestions that there may be a psychological or psychosocial basis for their symptoms.

There are a number of conditions now diagnosed with fairly high frequency in which there is a consistent pattern of symptoms but for which causes are controversial or unknown (Nimnuan, Hotopf, & Wessely, 2001; Nimnuan, Rabe-Hesketh, Wessely, & Hotopf, 2001). These have been called "functional" syndromes and include fibromyalgia (pain at multiple tender points on the body), irritable bowel syndrome (abdominal pain, constipation, and/or diarrhea), noncardiac chest pain, and chronic oral facial pain (temporomandibular joint dysfunction [TMJ]).

Psychiatrists have developed diagnoses for patients who have physical complaints that are believed to include psychological factors as a cause. In keeping with the Diagnostic and Statistical Manual of Mental Disorders (American Psychiatric Association, 2013), the psychiatric approach includes specific categories based upon the type of symptoms and how they are manifested. Additionally, for some of these DSM-5 conditions, causal explanations have been offered. Despite the fact that these conditions are viewed as psychiatric disorders, it is relatively rare for these patients to take their symptoms to a mental health professional. Instead, patients experience these as physical conditions and view their primary care physician as the appropriate source of help. As will be discussed further below, primary care providers do not often make a distinction between physical symptoms that have a physiological cause and physical distress that is caused by psychological factors. To present both sides of this issue, we will begin with an overview of how somatic symptom disorders are classified, diagnosed, and (when possible) treated from the perspective of DSM-5.

The Psychiatric Approach to Medically Unexplained Symptoms
Malingering

An important component of differential diagnosis in psychiatry is ruling out possible conditions that could be present before arriving at a specific diagnosis. To begin with, there are two conditions in which "symptoms" are voluntarily produced by the patient. In malingering, the patient is essentially lying about their symptoms. The goal for pretending to have symptoms is typically something concrete such as winning a workmen's compensation claim or, among prisoners, being moved to the infirmary, which may feature better food than the general inmate population gets. Malingering is clearly goal-directed, and the patient is not experiencing physical symptoms. Officially, malingering is not considered to be a valid clinical condition.

Factitious Disorder
In factitious disorder, the patient does indeed have symptoms, but they are deliberately caused by the patient themselves (American Psychiatric Association, 2013). Making oneself ill may involve an intentional medication overdose or deliberately causing a wound and then rubbing it with feces or urine to develop an infection. In these situations, there is no concrete benefit or goal. Patients with factitious disorder derive a sense of psychological gratification from being in the patient role. In large cities, these patients may appear with their baffling symptoms at multiple hospitals. Eventually, however, they are often detected, and when this occurs, the patient leaves the hospital suddenly. A variant of factitious disorder is Munchausen syndrome, in which patients present with unusual symptoms but also will have somewhat dramatic stories describing how their condition arose. Patients with Munchausen syndrome also may travel from hospital to hospital with their symptoms and often-changing stories.

Conversion Disorder
While classic conversion disorder, with patients suddenly going blind or having paralyzed limbs in response to a traumatic event, seemed to be quite frequent among Sigmund Freud's Viennese patients, this dramatic presentation is in reality relatively uncommon. In conversion disorder, patients will have the sudden onset of a dramatic sensory and/or motor problem such as the inability to see, motor paralysis, or aphasia (inability to speak). Typically, the symptom occurs very soon after a traumatic event and frequently has a symbolic association with the event itself. For example, someone who has witnessed a close family member killed may develop conversion blindness. Demographically, conversion symptoms are more common among women under the age of 35.

While the types of conversion disorder described by Freud appear to be relatively rare today, the expression of emotional distress through physical symptoms soon after a traumatic event is relatively common. Pseudo seizures are seizure-like activity without any evidence of electrical abnormality in the brain. Some factors that often distinguish pseudo seizures from neurologically based seizures include the absence of falls with injuries, patients' self-reports that they are aware of their surroundings, and the absence of a post-seizure state of confusion.

Illness Anxiety Disorder (Hypochondriasis)
Most people are familiar with the term "hypochondriac." In the DSM-5, hypochondriasis was replaced by the diagnostic label "Illness Anxiety Disorder" (American Psychiatric Association, 2013). People with this condition are very preoccupied with the fear of having a possibly life-threatening illness and often believe they have a serious disease such as cancer that has not yet been detected. Patients with illness anxiety disorder tend to catastrophize about relatively common unpleasant physical experiences. For example, someone with periodic tension headaches may erroneously conclude that they have a brain tumor. People with this condition have varying degrees of insight and, at times, may temporarily recognize that their fears may be

unfounded. However, their ability to appraise physical sensations objectively waxes and wanes.

Persons with this condition appear to have a greater history of sexual abuse and other psychosocial trauma (Salmon & Calderbank, 1996). Adults with illness anxiety disorder report that they were frequently sick as children and missed a good deal of school. Illness anxiety tends to be a chronic condition. Barsky (2001) and colleagues (Creed & Barsky, 2004) found a high percentage of patients still had illness anxiety symptoms at a 5-year follow-up.

For patients with some insight into their condition, cognitive therapy has had some success (Barsky & Ahern, 2004). The key distortions in thinking to be targeted are the patient's exaggerated and unrealistic fears of illness. The cognitive therapist focuses on helping the patient reinterpret these benign physical sensations not as signs of illness but as normal.

Somatic Symptom Disorder

In the most recent version of the DSM, this diagnosis was modified considerably from its previous definition. Somatic symptom disorder refers to a condition in which the patient experiences one or more physical symptoms that are present for at least six months. The symptoms are associated with a pronounced cognitive emotional or behavioral reaction. The onset of this pattern must be before the age of 30. In previous editions, the DSM listed a number of common nonspecific symptoms associated with this condition, including headaches, backaches, chest pain, tingling sensations in hands and feet, and so on, which did not have an established physiological cause. In the current revised criteria for this condition, the previous requirement that the symptoms could not be attributable to an established physiological cause was eliminated (American Psychiatric Association, 2013). The new diagnosis, as written, would apply to patients who had conditions with clear etiologies, such as cancer, and had particularly strong emotional reactions to their condition.

This diagnosis is broad and nonspecific and includes conditions that are explainable biologically but are psychologically disruptive and impair the patient's daily functioning (American Psychiatric Association, 2013). Terminology has been a significant issue with these conditions since these patients do indeed experience physical suffering. Patients with unexplainable symptoms are particularly sensitive to being told that their chest pain, headaches, or dizziness are "all in their head." A recent study suggested that among patients with a functional somatic condition, a preferable label would be a diagnosis that included the word "physical" (Picariello, Ali, Moss-Morris, & Chalder, 2015), such as "persistent physical symptoms" (Marks & Hunter, 2015). Both patients and health care providers reported a good deal of frustration in encounters in which physical symptoms did not have a clear medical cause (Peters et al., 2015). Complicating matters further is the observation that patients with this condition are particularly sensitive to even slight suggestions that their symptoms are not "real" but instead are (at least partially) attributable to psychological distress (Burbaum et al., 2010). The approach to management of these patients is to schedule regular office visits occurring at least once or twice per month. Each visit should be an opportunity for the patient to share concerns as well as for the physician to conduct a brief examination and reassure the patient. Over time, the physician may get to know the patient better and begin to gradually link physical symptoms with events in the patient's life. While not curing the condition, this approach is likely to lead to a reduction in emergency room visits, hospital days, unnecessary testing, and reduced costs.

Medically Unexplained Symptoms in the Primary Care Office

While the formal prevalence of these psychiatric conditions involving somatic symptoms, when combined, is below 10 percent, physical complaints without a specific cause characterize the majority of patients seen in primary care offices. However, in reviewing the medical records of primary care patients, diagnoses such as somatic symptom disorder or illness anxiety disorder would be very uncommon.

Complicating the picture further is that physical symptoms without an established cause are common in the general population (Leger, Charles, Ayanian, & Almeida, 2015). In the past week it is very likely that you have had one of the following: headache, muscle ache, insomnia, runny nose, watery eyes, or insomnia. Up to 95 percent of the general population experiences at least one physical symptom every 2 to 4 weeks. The majority of readers likely had at least one symptom in the past 5 to 7 days. Among those of you who experienced symptoms, it is unlikely that you sought professional medical help. The headache and the watery eyes were seen as "part of life," and you knew that they would go away on their own in a few days. You were not distressed enough about these physical sensations to "package" them as symptoms that you would bring to a health care provider.

Somatosensory amplification is a trait centering on sensitivity to bodily changes. This trait includes being aware of one's heart rate, being highly sensitive to an upset stomach, or having a strong startle reaction to loud sounds. Individuals with this trait also continuously monitor physical sensations (Barsky, Wyshak, & Klerman, 1990). It is likely that somatosensory amplification is associated with sympathetic nervous system arousal. This physiological predisposition, when paired with a family climate that is oriented toward sensitivity to physical symptoms, may result in developing a debilitating level of somatosensory amplification. There are suggestions that adults who develop this condition grow up in families where at least one parent has ongoing physical symptoms (Van Tilburg et al., 2015). In this family climate, children become inducted, through a process resembling hypnosis, into being hyperaware of their own physical sensations.

Primary care physicians in office practice often have days in which the majority of the patients that they see have symptoms without a clear cause. A total of 14 complaints account for about 40 percent of patient general medical office visits (Kroenke & Mangelsdorff, 1989). In only a distinct minority of cases (typically under 10 percent) can a specific physical cause be found for the patient's symptoms. Additionally, most of these conditions are self-limiting—meaning that they generally get better on their own without formal treatment. (See Figure 6.1.)

As discussed earlier, psychosocial factors play a particularly prominent role in seeking care for physical symptoms (Strosahl, 1998). The presence of anxious and depressive symptoms (not necessarily the magnitude for a formal diagnosis) is likely to "drive" patients to seek care for nonspecific complaints. The high prevalence and high resource utilization of patients with medically unexplained symptoms has led to

10 Most Common Complaints in Primary Care: Established "Organic" Causes

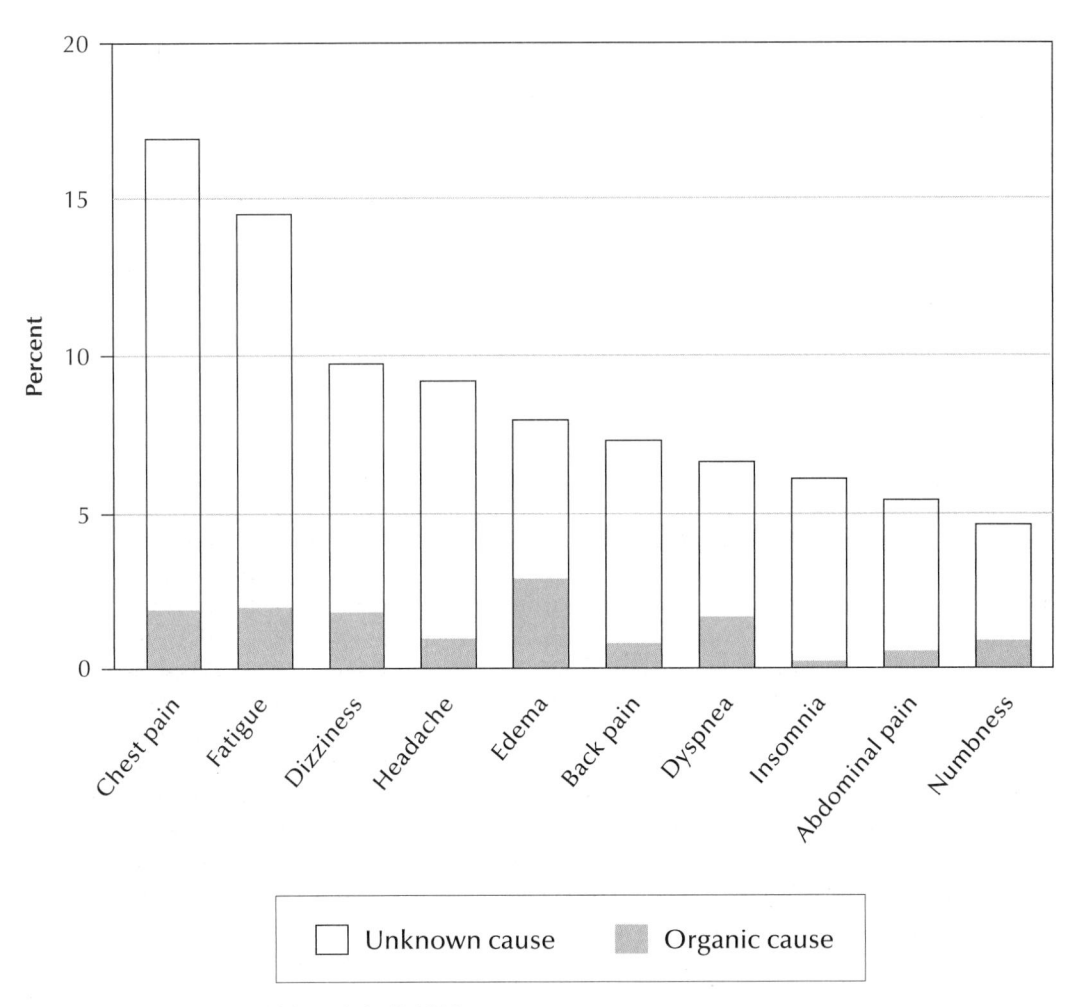

FIGURE 6.1 Kroenke and Mangelsdorff, 1989.

the development of various sets of criteria and algorithms to help distinguish patients with functional conditions from those whose symptoms have a detectable physiological cause. An informal set of criteria that mirrors the DSM-IV criteria for somatization disorder is as follows: (1) onset before the age of 30; (2) symptoms that are not explainable medically or for which the level of distress is considered excessive for the illness; (3) symptoms representing different organ systems and including four pain sites, two gastrointestinal symptoms, a sexual symptom, and one pseudo-neurologic symptom (dizziness, numbness in the hands) (American Psychiatric Association, 1994). Research has demonstrated a linear relationship between the number of medically unexplained symptoms and corresponding symptoms of depression and anxiety (Katon & Walker, 1998).

Other clues to patients who have a significant psychosocial component to their physical symptoms include frequent emergency room and clinic visits—often with relatively minor symptoms and when the resolution of a physical complaint is rapidly followed by the appearance of a new physical complaint. The distinction between primary and secondary gain, discussed further in Chapter 8, is also applicable to patients with long histories of medically unexplained symptoms. Primary gain is the role that the symptom serves—a physical expression of psychological distress. Secondary gain, however, results from the social consequences of having physical symptoms. This might include not going to a job that one dislikes, not having to mow the grass, or in some instances seeking compensation from the government for disability or workmen's compensation from an employer. As is the case with chronic lower-back pain, the longer these symptoms are associated with reduced expectations for the patient in their workplace and family, the more likely it is that the symptoms are maintained through reinforcement (Fordyce, Fowler, Lehmann, & Delateur, 1968).

Cultural Issues

As was discussed in the earlier chapter on diversity, outside of Western cultures, emotional distress is often transformed into physical symptoms. This physical expression often occurs in cultures in which there is stigma associated with mental illness. For example, the anthropologist Arthur Kleinman describes in some detail how "neurasthenia," a condition in which the principal symptom is feeling run-down and tired, was an expression of depression during the Maoist era in China (Ware & Kleinman, 1992). Historically, this was a time in which expression of negative emotion was harshly sanctioned and considered a sign of disloyalty to the collective society. Outward expression of sadness would imply that there was something wrong or unsatisfying about one's station in life or dissatisfaction with employment, which could result in harsh sanctions such as imprisonment. Another ethnic group prone to expressing emotional distress somatically is people of Latin American background. In the United States, Hispanic Americans may be particularly likely to express emotional difficulties through physical symptoms (Comer, 2015).

The Medicalization of Society

Medicalization refers to the process by which psychological distress or undesired personal characteristics are relabeled as illnesses (Conrad, 2008). As discussed earlier, a major historical change is that medical information, previously only available to a restricted audience of professionals, is now widely disseminated to the general public. With the rise of health information available on the internet along with direct-to-consumer marketing of both pharmaceutical and medical services, physicians are no longer the sole source of information about illness and its treatment. With the availability of internet communities, people who have conditions such as "sick building syndrome," multiple chemical sensitivity syndrome, or functional illnesses such as fibromyalgia can have a readily available support network through internet sites. While individuals suffering with these conditions may not receive support or validation from family members or the medical community, online blogs and chat rooms of those with similar conditions provide this affirmation. Within these virtual communities, a common theme is disparaging health care professionals, who are often seen as dismissive of patients' concerns. Because of the severity of their symptoms, many individuals with these conditions may be socially isolated. Finding an online community of fellow sufferers helps these isolated individuals find a social support network (Barker, 2008).

The rise in direct marketing of pharmaceuticals to the general public also contributes to medicalization in several ways. Conditions that were previously seen as "part of life" can now be effectively treated with medication or surgery (Barsky & Borus, 1995). For example, becoming bald (alopecia) is an unfortunate problem among many adult men. However, advertisements indicate that it can be eradicated with pharmaceutical agents or surgical procedures such as a hair transplant. Similarly, obesity, rather than being treated through diet and exercise, can be "cured" in a short period of time with bariatric surgery. Most pharmaceutical ads include a litany of symptoms—many of them nonspecific—with the implication that many people in the general public have this problem and that they should ask their physician about whether a new medication being advertised is "right for you." Among those high in somatosensory amplification, these ads are likely to trigger an even greater sensitivity to benign physical symptoms.

Adherence

With the shift from acute illness with time-limited treatment to chronic diseases requiring long-term medication and dietary regimens, adherence has become a major focus of contemporary health care. Practices such as following dietary guidelines, taking multiple medications several times per day, self-assessment of blood glucose, and maintaining a diet and exercise program require patients to make substantial lifestyle modifications. Many readers are probably familiar with the term "compliance" defined as the *extent to which a person's health behavior, such as taking medications as prescribed, coincides with health care professionals' recommendations* (Haynes, Taylor, & Sackett, 1979). However, while the term "compliance" continues to be used within health care, a more recently applied term, "adherence," has become preferred. "Compliance" reflects a unidirectional model of care based on the physician as the authority and the patient as a passive recipient of medical information. Noncompliant patients who do not follow medical advice are very frustrating for health care providers. Informally, health care providers have, at times, described these patients with a range of pejorative labels, such as "passive aggressive," "irresponsible," "crazy," and "GOMER" (an acronym that stands for "Get Out of My Emergency Room"). "Noncompliant" has a trait-like quality suggesting a behavior pattern that is a permanent part of the patient's personality, with the added implication that the patient is to blame for their health problems. Particularly when treatment is unsuccessful, medical professionals can blame the "noncompliant" patient.

However, the more contemporary term "adherence" has a less judgmental tone, suggesting that the health care professional and patient are equally responsible for the patient's well-being. From the perspective of adherence, the ideal physician-patient relationship is a partnership (Myers & Midence, 1998). When recommended professional advice is not followed, rather than blaming the patient, the focus becomes the patient's interaction with the physician as well as the biopsychosocial aspects of care.

Economically, non-adherence is costly and a major factor in driving up the price of health care in Western countries. The World Health Organization suggests that increasing adherence may have a far greater impact on the health of the population than any specific medical treatment. In the United States, non-adherence costs between $100 billion and $289 billion per year (Viswanathan et al., 2012). At least 10 percent of all hospitalizations in the United States are associated with non-adherence (Peterson, Takiya, & Finley, 2003). If patients regularly followed medical recommendations, the financial benefits would cover the cost of health care for close to 45 million Americans.

An Overview of the Problem of Non-adherence

Depending on the behavior of interest, non-adherence is very widespread—about 25 percent of patients do not keep medical appointments that they schedule. If someone else makes the medical appointment for them, only about 50 percent of patients will keep it. Approximately 30 to 50 percent of US adults do not take medication regularly as prescribed (Marcum, Sevick, & Handler, 2013). Between 20 and 30 percent of new prescriptions are never filled (Fischer et al., 2010). In a review of more than 40 years of adherence research, DiMatteo (2004) concluded that the difference in health outcomes between high- and low-adherent patients was about 26 percent. Adherence with oral medication for a chronic condition such as diabetes ranges from 36 to 90 percent (Fukuda & Mizobe, 2017). Overall, non-adherence with diabetes care is associated with higher cumulative health care costs and greater rates of neuropathy, retinopathy, and nephropathy (kidney damage) (Fukuda & Mizobe, 2017). About half of all patients prescribed antidepressants discontinue medication prematurely despite increased rates of symptom relapse and hospitalizations associated with non-adherence (Sansone & Sansone, 2012).

In the United States, about half of pregnancies are unintended (Finer & Zolna, 2011) and 38 percent of women ages 15 to 44 are not using any form of contraception (Daniels, Daugherty, & Jones, 2014).

Some selected examples of common types of non-adherence: only 41 percent of women received the recommended routine mammography; 30 to 70 percent of children use inhalers appropriately for asthma (Capanoglu et al., 2015); among those with type 1 diabetes, 50 percent are non-adherent with the recommended diet (Davison et al., 2014); for those infected with tuberculosis, up to half of those with the condition do not take medication as prescribed. A common treatment for amblyopia or "lazy eye" is to wear a patch over the good eye. The goal is to train the "lazy eye." Rates of regular use of the eye patch over a four-week period are only about 50 percent (Newsham, 2000). As a result, it is difficult to determine whether patching is a useful intervention.

With respect to lifestyle factors that increase risk of morbidity and mortality, 19 to 20 percent of the general population are regular smokers, 5 to 7 percent are binge drinkers, and 31 percent had no physical activity in the past month. Only about 25 percent of Americans adhere to dietary recommendations for 5 to 9 fruits and vegetables per day (Moore & Thompson, 2015).

Causes of non-adherence include patient-centered factors such as personality traits, mental health conditions, communication styles of health care providers, cost of health care, and the treatment regimen itself.

Reasons for Non-adherence: Patient Factors

A description of patient or provider factors associated with non-adherence is, to some extent, artificial since both parties are embedded in a web of dyadic as well as larger systems interactions. However, for the sake of clarity, the discussion of non-adherence below looks at patients and physicians separately.

In terms of demographics, age appears to influence adherence. Younger and older adults are less likely to be adherent. Age-wise the optimally adherent patient is probably 30 to 50 years old. With respect to gender, the patterns are somewhat complex. In the general population, women, as compared with men, are more likely as a group to be taking regular medication (Manteuffel et al., 2014). Some studies have found no gender differences in adult males and females in terms of adherence. However, with respect to medications for chronic conditions such as high blood pressure or asthma, men appear to be more adherent (Manteuffel et al., 2014). Studies of HIV medication suggest that this gender difference may also be influenced by age. With respect to retroviral therapy, women, particularly those age 30 and under, appeared to be less adherent than comparably aged men (Puskas et al., 2017).

Cognitive functioning—particularly working memory and executive functioning—appears to play a role in medication adherence. Among older adults, a delay between the intention to take and actually taking medication led to significant declines in adherence. Even distractions as brief as five seconds are associated with substantial memory impairment among older adults (McDaniel, Einstein, Stout, & Morgan, 2003; Insel, Morrow, Brewer, & Figueredo, 2006). With more complex medication regimens, executive functioning becomes more important. When the ability to inhibit distractions is compromised, forgetting to take medication becomes more likely (Anderson, Jue, & Madaras-Kelly, 2008).

Personality psychology has established that in order to predict complex behavior such as adherence, characteristics of both the person and the situation need to be taken into account. Mischel and Ayduk's (2004) CAPS model (cognitive and affective personality system) provides a useful explanation of how personality may influence adherence. Rather than viewing behavior as the result of a dominant personality trait, Mischel (1999) argues that people assess their own competencies as well as goals and values as they pertain to a specific situation. As a result, it becomes difficult to describe an "adherent personality." Adherence is likely to be subjectively different based on the challenges required and the overall context of the patient's life. For example, someone with type 2 diabetes may be quite adherent with taking medication regularly but because of the social and emotional significance of family meals, may not be adherent with a diabetic diet.

However, there do appear to be some knowledge factors as well as personality dimensions that increase or decrease adherence with medical regimens. Cognitively, knowledge of their illness (Dennison et al., 2011) as well as acceptance of the diagnosis of a chronic condition make patients more likely to engage in behavior needed to control their symptoms.

The Big Five personality factors (openness, conscientiousness, extraversion, agreeableness, neuroticism)—a set of traits that are believed to be genetically based and fairly stable through the lifespan (Costa & McCrae, 1992)—demonstrate intuitively predictable patterns with medication adherence. For example, persons high on the trait conscientiousness are more likely to be adherent. However, if neuroticism (associated with anxiety and rumination) is also high, the impact of conscientiousness on adherence is greatly reduced (Axelsson, Brink, Lundgren, & Lötvall, 2011). Patients who are high on neuroticism are likely to view the obstacles to treatment as being significant (e.g., medication side effects) and are also more likely to be pessimistic about its effectiveness (Ye, Krupka, & Davidson, 2012). Lower levels of agreeableness (optimism, friendliness, positive social skills) also appear to be associated with reduced medication adherence (Ye et al., 2012).

One of the most common, yet treatable, factors leading to non-adherence is the presence of a mental health condition (DiMatteo, Lepper, & Croghan, 2000). Major depressive disorder increases non-adherence by a factor of three (DiMatteo et al., 2000). Patients with somatoform disorders tend to have a high degree of sensitivity to medication side effects and are likely to discontinue them. Among patients who have significant depressive symptoms, self-efficacy—confidence that one can carry out a prescribed medical treatment—is likely to be impaired. Self-efficacy is likely to be a particularly important factor with more complex interventions such as the combination of regular insulin injections and a diabetic diet, or retroviral therapy for HIV (King et al., 2010).

Rather than understanding non-adherence as an expression of personality traits or reflecting the impact of significant mental illness, Marcum, Sevick, and Handler (2013) suggest that non-adherence is a medical condition in and of itself. While some of the dimensions described can be influenced by external factors, such as economics and interaction with health care providers, in keeping with their view of non-adherence as a categorical diagnosis, Marcum et al. (2013) place the locus of the problem squarely within the patient. The "etiology" of non-adherence is likely to be one of the following: (1) the patient does not understand the relevance of medication adherence to continued health and well-being; (2) the patient has concluded the benefits of taking medications do not outweigh the costs; (3) the complexity of medication management exceeds the information processing capacity of the patient; (4) the patient is not sufficiently vigilant; (5) the patient holds inaccurate, irrational, or conflicting normative beliefs about medications; and (6) the patient does not perceive medication to have therapeutic efficacy (Marcum et al., 2013).

Health Care Professionals' Communication Style and Patient Adherence

Physician Social Power and Adherence

Social influence theory, when applied to physician-patient interaction, highlights dynamics that are likely to be associated with adherence. While critics have suggested that physician authority is diminishing, physicians continue to maintain several types of social power relative to patients (Nimmon & Stenfors-Hayes, 2016; Linder-Pelz, 1982). There are suggestions that physicians who are successful in persuading patients to be adherent are able to optimize specific types of power based upon the personality characteristics of the patient, their readiness to change, and the type of illness and treatment regimen involved. There are several categories of social influence; thoughtful health care providers match the influential style to the clinical situation. Legitimate power occurs when patients agree that the physician's role is to give them particular types of advice. Additionally, receiving attention from someone with legitimate power is typically reinforcing after other types of rewards, which may be attention from the physician or a prescription. Referent power is the health care provider's temporary and deliberate attempt to place themselves in a context similar to that of the patient ("Yes, I had a sprain like the one you have, and it was really painful"). Informational power is based upon the fact that the physician should have thorough and current knowledge about conditions that fall within their realm of practice. Again, as noted earlier, while it may seem like this distinction is being increasingly eroded with the internet, health care professionals have the ability to critically evaluate new findings and determine their applicability to specific patients. Coercive power refers to concrete rewards or the physician's control of access to something that the patient values, such as a school physical for sports or a "sick note" verifying that the patient is ill and cannot work.

The types of power that are particularly important in treating acute versus chronic illness are somewhat different. For short-term adherence—following a course of antibiotics to address a viral infection—expert, coercive, legitimate, and reward power are prominent. For long-term adherence such as a type 2 diabetes diet or regular taking of blood pressure medication and reducing dietary sodium, referent, informational, and expert power seem to be more significant (Lewis, DeVellis, & Sleath, 2002).

Meta-analyses have found that physicians rated as having good patient communication skills have patients who are more adherent. There is also good evidence that training physicians in communication skills is helpful and indirectly improves patient adherence. Specific aspects of communication that appear to increase patient adherence include deliberately developing rapport and trust, encouraging patients, involving patients in decision-making, and having open discussions about the risks, benefits, and barriers (DiMatteo, Haskard-Zolnierek, & Martin, 2012). In outpatient settings, characteristics of communication styles associated with better adherence include health care providers who are "friendly" rather than detached and "businesslike." "Friendly" physicians are seen by patients as emotionally supportive and encouraging. Physicians who are sensitive to nonverbal communication—particularly when patients are hesitant to follow a recommendation—also have improved rapport. Adherent patients are more likely to say that their doctor completely answers their questions (Noble, 1998). In sum, "liking" one's health care provider appears to be more important than the provider's technical skills. Physicians who were rated as "unapproachable" had patients lower in adherence. Patients are more likely to take medication as prescribed when they view their relationship with the physician as positive.

Timing and Modality

While office encounters are of limited duration, the timing of the physician's recommendations and directions is particularly important. Effective communication for adherence involves capitalizing on the primacy and recency effect. Primacy indicates that people are much more likely to remember the beginning of a verbal exchange, while recency suggests that they are more likely to remember the last part of the message that was conveyed (Murdock, 1962). Physicians with good communication skills summarize very clearly at the end of the visit and include a description of the patient's condition as well as treatment options and a clear plan for follow-up visits.

In part because of the ready availability of good-quality printed patient education information, but also because of the time demands placed on physicians, patients are often given written information about treatment options for weight loss, diet, or types of exercises that may benefit musculoskeletal complaints. Written information, when presented alone, is far less likely to be followed by patients than when written information is combined with the physician's explanation. Without this personalized message directly from the physician, many of the general printed guidelines routinely made available to patients are less likely to be effective if the patient views them as generic. However, if the physician verbally emphasizes how those particular exercises would be of benefit to the specific patient based on the patient's lifestyle, adherence will likely be better, as will patient satisfaction. It has been suggested that the combination of verbal and written information may improve adherence—particularly when verbal directions are given prior to written instructions (Raynor, 1998).

Does Fear Increase Adherence?

There has been a long-standing debate about the extent to which it is beneficial to "scare" patients as a strategy for increasing adherence (e.g., "If you cannot control your blood sugars better, you are eventually going to have to get your leg amputated"). As noted in the previous chapter, fear induction is not usually seen as conducive to a good physician-patient alliance. There are a few situations in which inducing fear may be helpful, and recent research actually suggests that up to a certain point, fear induction can be beneficial for provoking behavior change (Tannenbaum et al., 2015). Inducing fear may be helpful when the patient is unconcerned about serious illness, there is a specific course of reasonable action that can be taken to address the illness, the action can be implemented immediately, and the patient experiences a supportive relationship with the health care provider.

An example of deliberately increasing anxiety to push someone into making health behavior changes is the confrontation that is often used for getting persons with substance abuse problems into treatment (Liddle & Dakof, 1995). The elements of an effective confrontation include a direct message ("I'm concerned about your drinking"); family and friends describing what they see the patient doing in terms of directly observable behavior and describing the impact of the patient's behavior on themselves ("I worry a great deal when you do not come home until 3 a.m."); setting a clear limit and being prepared to keep to it ("If you do not enter treatment, you can no longer live here"); and having an action plan that can be immediately implemented. The emphasis is on getting the individual into treatment immediately. If too much time elapses, the patient, as well as family members, may back off on their commitment as the patient attempts to negotiate the terms of treatment. This "patient-controlled negotiation" is part of the problem and should not be entertained. There is a singular focus—getting the patient into treatment immediately. ("I hear that you have a project at work that you want to complete. It is critical that you enter treatment now rather than in two weeks.")

Characteristics of the Illness and Treatment

Research suggests that the type of illness plays a critical role in determining adherence. Conditions such as hypertension, in which patients often experience no symptoms at all ("the silent killer"), are associated with lower treatment adherence rates. By contrast, acute illnesses involving pain or discomfort, or that disrupt one's daily routine, are much more likely to be associated with compliance. An example of a disruptive acute illness would be bronchitis.

There are five factors that appear to be associated with greater adherence: severity of the condition, personal susceptibility, sense of self-efficacy in carrying out the treatment, the intention to carry out the treatment in the immediate future, and treatment complexity (deVries et al., 2014). The reader may recognize many of these dimensions from the health belief model. An example of treatment complexity would be the greater adherence that occurs when medication is dosed once per day versus medication that is taken multiple times per day. Not surprisingly, research indicates that adherence is better with medications that are taken once per day or, in some circumstances, injections that are given every 14 to 30 days. An example is Depo-Provera (medrosyprogesterone acetate), a type of birth control given as an injection to young women. Injections have also been used with persons with severe mental illness such as schizophrenia, who may not appreciate the significance of their illness and would be unlikely to take a pill once or twice a day.

Social Support

Spouse or family support is typically associated with greater compliance and greater success at reducing health risk behavior. There is evidence that being married and/or living with another person does increase the likelihood of medical adherence (DiMatteo, 2004).

While some studies view support as unidimensional and do not differentiate between various types of support, there is evidence that not "all help is helpful." Instrumental support typically involves taking on a task such as transporting a friend or family member to a physician's appointment or picking up a prescription for someone. Emotional support typically involves listening and being empathic. Studies of family dynamics focus on the variable of cohesion, characterized by acceptance, nurturance, and warmth. By contrast, conflict is characterized by criticism and frequent arguing. DiMatteo's (2004) meta-analysis concluded that practical support was most strongly associated with adherence. Adherence was significantly greater in cohesive and significantly lower in conflictual families.

In cases of chronic illness or recovery from a catastrophic event such as a heart attack, it is important that family members work collaboratively with the patient rather than dictating recommendations to them. There is also evidence that for smoking cessation and weight control, small group interventions—particularly those that occur in the workplace—maybe more effective than individual treatment (Moher, Hey, & Lancaster, 2005).

Interventions for Increasing Adherence?

Several interventions show promise in improving adherence. Any form of pharmacotherapy that reduces the number of times per day that medication is taken will lead to increased adherence (Kripalani, Yao, & Haynes, 2007). Additionally, pillboxes, often with alarms to remind the patient to take the medication, are increasingly common; there is evidence that the frequency of physician office visits also improves adherence. Research suggests that patients' adherence to medication is significantly better the week before and after a physician appointment; it is likely that some type of external monitoring could achieve the same effect (DiMatteo, 2004).

Health education directed toward improving adherence is based on the assumption that patients have knowledge deficits regarding the nature of their illness, its course, and the need for daily medication or other interventions such as diet. However, while education is a common approach, when used alone, its effects are modest at best (Morrissey et al., 2017; Nieuwlaat et al., 2014). Single episode interventions also have limited effectiveness. In their meta-analysis Visawanthan et al. (2012) concluded that educational interventions with behavioral support through continued patient contact over several weeks or months were effective for increasing medication adherence for several chronic illnesses. Finally, while some interventions demonstrated at least low to moderate efficacy for increasing adherence, these techniques did not markedly improve disease outcomes (Kripalani et al., 2007).

Mobile Apps for Improving Adherence

The number of apps for mobile devices that address diet, exercise, and provide reminders to take medication has skyrocketed in recent years. Recent research has suggested that mobile devices may have potential to improve adherence. Most research has examined the impact on adherence among patients with either diabetes or cardiovascular disease. Mobile apps can provide regular automated reminders to check blood glucose, as well as educationally focused text messages and data transmission of health parameters. In some studies, blood sugar readings have been transmitted directly to health care providers through mobile devices (Hamine, Gerth-Guyette, Faulx, Green, & Ginsburg, 2015).

Optimally, mobile devices would be able to transmit data to the electronic medical record. In theory, this practice could increase patient adherence markedly. For example, patients could transmit blood pressure or blood glucose readings for the past several weeks prior to an office visit. With this information, the physician would have real-time data that they could review in advance of the face-to-face encounter with the patient that is likely to be reliable and valid and could guide decision-making about changes in medication. Currently, there are well over 300 mobile apps for medication adherence. However, the quality of these mobile phone apps is questionable, and very few have been specifically studied with respect to effectiveness in increasing medication adherence (Santo et al., 2016).

Adherence as the Result of a Complex Biopsychosocial Decision

The human papillomavirus (HPV) vaccine is a relatively recent preventive inoculation originally directed toward females from age 9 to mid-20s. The vaccine was developed to provide protection from the human pappilomavirus. HPV is a precursor to cervical cancer, and large-scale vaccination of young women is a strategy to reduce the incidence of the condition. The vaccine, however, has not been without controversy. Despite the linkage being unsupported, the publicity associated with vaccines and autism has raised public concern about possible negative effects of all vaccines.

A recent study of young women considering whether to obtain the HPV vaccine illustrates how, in contemporary society, young educated adults do not automatically defer to medical recommendations. The women who were interviewed assessed the health risk information critically but also placed it in a broader social and economic context. For example, the actuarial risk data offered by physicians was not seen as meaningful (one in ___ unvaccinated women will develop cervical cancer). Instead, the women developed their own individualized risk assessment that took into account their health history, sexual relationships, and personal sexual practices. Rather than accepting the statistical probability provided by epidemiology, these women examined their "personal [risk] probability" (Roberts & Mitchell, 2017, p. 315). The public service health message "Spread the Word, Not the Disease" (Roberts & Mitchell, 2017, p. 316) also placed the responsibility for preventing transmission of HPV on women. In addition to chafing at this implication, the interviewees verbalized suspicion about the financial relationship between the prescribing physicians and the pharmaceutical companies marketing the vaccine.

The Macrosystem's Role in Adherence
A Vaccination Program Arouses Suspicion

Cultural factors influence perceptions of Western medicine's legitimacy and efficacy. As suggested by the discussion of the African American community's history with the White European–dominated medical establishment, conventional health care may be viewed with a suspicion. An unintended outcome of the US government's killing of Osama bin Laden in Pakistan was increased local suspicion of vaccinations and targeted killing of public health workers. In order to determine bin Laden's whereabouts in Pakistan, the US Central Intelligence Agency (CIA), through several intermediaries, sponsored a community vaccination program. The goal for the program was to obtain DNA samples with the hope that one of the samples would verify that bin Laden's family was living in Abbottabad. It is not clear whether bin Laden was located through this method or whether a community health nurse, as part of a door-to-door vaccination effort, left a tracking device in the bin Laden compound. While the vaccine campaign probably contributed to the successful discovery of bin Laden, the methods used heightened local suspicions of vaccinations and related public health campaigns (Bhutta, 2013). There is evidence of a decline in receipt of the polio vaccine in the region, an effort that previously had the support of Muslim clerics (Bramadat, 2017). In December 2012, several local health volunteers who were providing polio vaccine were shot and killed by the Taliban.

Because of safety concerns, the anti-polio campaign was halted in some regions of Pakistan (Bramadat, 2017).

Making Health a Requirement for Employment
A recent controversy has been the adoption of corporate policies mandating health behavior. Some companies have developed rules to prevent hiring current smokers as well as to maintain cigarette abstinence among employees who previously smoked. These companies have implemented rules making current smokers who apply for a position ineligible for hiring. By implication, current smokers already employed could possibly be ineligible for promotion if they continue to smoke (Schmidt, Voigt, & Emanuel, 2013). Companies that have implemented policies of this type include Union Pacific Railroad and Alaska Airlines as well as multiple health care organizations. Privately owned hospitals and clinics justify this policy on the basis of their mission to promote health. Hospital administrators argue that that their employees should be role models and, as such, should behave in ways that exemplify the organization's publicly stated values of health promotion.

A second line of support for discriminating against smokers in the workplace is economic. It has been estimated that annual health insurance and medical costs for each smoking employee are $4,000 more than for nonsmokers (Schmidt, Voigt, & Emanuel, 2013). Those who oppose such regulations point to the fact that most adults began smoking in their teens and developmentally were not able to fully appreciate the consequences of their behavior. Additionally, adolescents often do not have an appreciation of the addictive power of cigarettes. For many teens, this initial experimentation with cigarettes leads to a regular pattern of use accompanied by pronounced physiological withdrawal if they attempt to stop smoking. Based on this line of reasoning, from a personnel perspective, having a policy that prevents hiring or considering promotions for adults who smoke might be considered discrimination based on a pre-existing medical condition.

Economic Causes of Non-adherence
Finally, to completely understand medication non-adherence, it is important to look at economic realities. Not having adequate income to pay for physician visits and medications as well as any medical tests plays a major role in non-adherence in the United States. Particularly in countries that do not have universal coverage, the cost of care is a significant determinant of non-adherence A meta-analysis suggested that lower out-of-pocket expenditures as well as having insurance that does not require a patient co-pay, or only requires a small charge, is associated with better medication adherence (Nair et al., 2010). While the emphasis in adherence research is on developing strategies to address the psychological reasons for not taking medication regularly, these larger-scale economic and social factors, which are very important, are often neglected.

Conclusion

As I hope the reader has come to appreciate, the world of primary care medicine is a complex web involving communication skills, detecting and diagnosing mental health problems, and understanding and addressing barriers to patient adherence. The increased attention to physician-patient interaction, physician interpersonal skills, and the role of patients' values, culture, and personality all play a significant role in treatment seeking and carrying out health care providers' recommendations. The large population of patients who do not have a diagnosable condition but who frequently appear at outpatient medical clinics and hospital emergency departments is an ongoing challenge for primary care providers. Rather than diagnosing these patients with a mental health condition such as somatic symptom disorder or illness anxiety disorder, well-trained primary care providers can successfully manage these patients. While it is unlikely that inappropriate treatment seeking can be eliminated by patients with "functional" conditions, a reduction in this pattern would yield significant cost savings as well as free up finite health care resources for other patients.

However, it would be a serious mistake to place the blame for non-adherence on health care providers and their patients. The health care system in the United States inadvertently contributes to the problem of non-adherence. In the absence of universal health insurance coverage, the cost of obtaining prescriptions, medical tests, and appearing for follow-up visits makes medical care inaccessible for many Americans.

Innovations such as the electronic medical record were touted as devices that would increase patient adherence by improving physician communication. However, the market forces governing the implementation of electronic medical records has, thus far, prevented this coordination of care. Additionally, research conducted in the early years of implementation suggests that the use of computers with standardized templates may contribute to an experience of impersonal health care by both physician and patient.

CHAPTER 7

Stress and Coping

"This class stressed me out." "I am so stressed that I can't think straight." "He asked me if I could help him and I just screamed at him. It wasn't him—I was just under a lot of stress."

What do these commonly used phrases mean? What does it mean when we read stories about college students being under undue levels of pressure? What does stress mean? The term is sometimes used as a synonym for significant mental illness: "He was so stressed out he had to go to a hospital," or "The stress got to him and he went to his doctor, who started him on Prozac." At other times, the pressure is briefer and goes away as soon as the demanding situation—like that midterm exam—is completed.

How do you know whether you are "stressed"? For most of us it is a cognitive, emotional, and physiological experience. We experience muscle tension—perhaps so great that we feel some pain in our shoulders. We usually have some self-talk ("I have so much to do, I am so tired and overwhelmed—I don't think I can get it done"). We go to bed at night but are unable to relax and fall asleep and instead toss and turn trying to find that comfortable position that seems elusive.

Our friends might notice that we seem irritable; the tone of our voice is "snappy"—a bit angry and sarcastic. When they ask what's wrong or can you go to the movies this weekend, you snap at them: "Who do you think I am—the entertainment director? I have got so much to do—you wouldn't really understand."

The common factor here is that our perception of our ability to manage a situation—be it an exam, the sorority dance that we ended up being the chairperson for, or the 10 tables for which we are responsible as a waiter or waitress—requires more energy, time, and concentration than we expected and it feels overwhelming. Once the overwhelming theme begins, everything else seems to pile on top of it, and even brushing our teeth seems like another onerous chore.

For some students, the stress of college is simply a carryover from high school (Jayson, 2014). Approximately 40 percent of young women reported that they felt overwhelmed during their senior year of high school compared with approximately 20 percent of men. This high school student's experience is not unusual:

> Carolyn Walworth, 17, often reaches a breaking point around 11 p.m., when she collapses in tears. For 10 minutes or so, she just sits at her desk and cries, overwhelmed by unrelenting school demands. She is desperately tired and longs for sleep. But she knows she must move through it, because more assignments in physics, calculus or French await her. She finally crawls into bed around midnight or 12:30 a.m.
>
> The next morning, she fights to stay awake in her first-period U.S. history class, which begins at 8:15. She is unable to focus on what's being taught, and her mind

drifts. "You feel tired and exhausted, but you think you just need to get through the day so you can go home and sleep." (Richter, 2015)

There is also evidence that over the past 50 years, the self-reported emotional health of both male and female college students has declined and currently appears to be on a downward trajectory. The simultaneous demands of schoolwork, employment, maintaining friendships, and involvement in university activities lead many students to feeling overwhelmed. Over the past year, about one-third of US college students reported difficulty functioning because of symptoms of depression, and close to 50 percent reported being overwhelmed by anxiety (Novotney, 2014). Of the growing number of students who seek help at university counseling centers, close to 30 percent report having considered suicide at some point in their life (Novotney, 2014). As the number of students requesting help at college counseling centers has increased, many centers have had to establish wait lists, since the demand for services is often greater than the number of available counselors. The most commonly cited reason for dropping out of college is mental health problems. Some studies have reported that 25 to 30 percent of university students seeking counseling are currently, or have been, taking medication for a mental health condition (Mistler, Reetz, Krylowicz, & Barr, 2013).

What Is Stress?

"Stress" is a nonspecific term. It is not a formal mental health diagnosis. It can arise from multiple sources. Stress underlies most mental health conditions as well as many non-psychiatric medical conditions. When someone says, "I am so stressed!" it is not really clear what they mean. Are they depressed? Are they anxious? Not sleeping well? Feeling that they had too much to do? Just broke up with a boyfriend/girlfriend? Just totaled their car? In and of itself, stress provides few specifics. In its original use, stress meant a sense of pressure or strain. Early descriptions of stress were for severe conditions such as "shell shock," which we would now call post-traumatic stress disorder.

Over 60 percent of Americans believe that stress is diminishing both physical and mental health (American Psychological Association, 2015). "Stress management" is a popular topic for workshops directed to college students, employees in large corporations, government sector workers, and the public at large.

From a diathesis stress perspective, stress is a multisystemic phenomenon involving biological, psychological, and situational factors. As an intrapersonal phenomenon, stress is the cognitive, emotional, and physiological reaction to some type of an external threat. Sometimes the threat is more imaginary than real. Mark Twain famously said, "I've been through some terrible things in my life—some of which actually happened."

The physiological response to external threats is shared by humans with other animals and probably has evolutionary significance. The ability to increase norepinephrine (adrenaline), focus our attention, and redistribute blood flow has, when confronted with a threatening animal, no doubt saved many human beings from an unpleasant death. From an evolutionary perspective it is logical that our bodies would exhibit significant changes that help us escape the threat.

Stress has been conceptualized in multiple ways. Several of the classic explanations will be discussed as well as more recent and complex biopsychosocial explanations. Physiologically speaking, there are three systems involved—the sympathetic-parasympathetic nervous systems, the hypothalamic-pituitary axis, and the immune system.

Walter Cannon and the Fight-or-Flight Response

The peripheral nervous system is the network of neural connections between the brain and spinal cord and the rest of the body. It is divided into a somatic nervous system and an autonomic nervous system (Carlson, 2013). The somatic system permits voluntary muscle and limb activity. The autonomic nervous system, by contrast, regulates multiple physiological processes of which we are typically unaware unless one of these processes functions abnormally. We rarely pay attention to our heart rate or respiration rate except when these become abnormal (Abraham, Conner, Jones, & O'Connor, 2016). The autonomic nervous system includes both the sympathetic and the parasympathetic nervous systems. The sympathetic nervous system is the part that is "turned on" under conditions of threat. At those times, our blood pressure and respiration rate increases, pupils constrict, adrenaline (norepinephrine) is produced, and chemicals are released that make our blood coagulate much more quickly (Carlson, 2013). After the threat has been removed, the parasympathetic nervous system is activated and brings our physiological activity back to the normal range. Walter Cannon, one of the founders of stress theory, argued that stress operates primarily by upsetting our physiological homeostasis. During our evolutionary history, those who had responsive autonomic nervous systems were likely to survive by being able to outrun threatening animals as well as warriors intent on doing harm. However, today, the threats are much more likely to be psychological. While we may feel that that final exam is a life-or-death issue, the threat is likely to be to our self-esteem or to an internalized goal as opposed to one involving physical harm. However, from Cannon's perspective, the physiological reaction to confronting a saber-toothed tiger and a final exam in calculus is essentially the same. Our physiology is based on physical threats rather than psychological ones. Moreover, persons with diagnosed anxiety disorders turn on this physiological pattern in response to situations that bear little risk of either physical or psychological harm. For example, among those suffering from social anxiety disorder, the prospect of speaking before a group of people will elicit an intense fight-or-flight response. The fear of "looking stupid" and being evaluated can be every bit as potent physiologically as a semitrailer bearing down on us.

The sheer power of our physiological reactivity can be illustrated by Cannon's (2002) explanation of voodoo death. Cannon noted that in many cultures, such as among indigenous peoples of Africa and South America, a condemnation or a curse from a high-status healer (the "medicine man") was enough to cause death in a seemingly healthy individual. Cannon (2002) describes several cases in which people ate food considered taboo in a specific culture. After doing so, they died within 24 to 48 hours. Cannon believed that the intense fear associated with the curse escalated sympathetic nervous system activity, which, in turn, caused a reduction in blood volume. The reduced blood volume led to declines in blood pressure. In addition, there was an increase in adrenaline, which caused some of the smaller arteries to constrict. This vasoconstriction in turn led to inadequate blood supply to important organs. As a result of reduced blood flow, there was damage to the heart as well as the central nervous system. The reduced blood volume increased heart and respiration rates. Further weakening the individual is the fact that, because of the overwhelming fear, the "cursed" individual has probably not eaten or taken in adequate fluid. Together, the reduced blood flow and increased heart activity can lead to death—often proximately caused by cardiac arrhythmia (irregular heart rate). From Cannon's (2002) perspective, the fight response (extreme anger) is not possible in the situation, and the flight aspect (fear) predominates—eventually culminating in death.

Hans Selye and the General Adaptation Syndrome

Hans Selye was both a physiological researcher and a physician. Selye (1973) observed that patients with very different diseases showed similarities in terms of their clinical symptoms. Selye's research with rats found that nonspecific external events such as exposure to cold or relatively small doses of various drugs, including adrenaline and morphine, as well as frequent handling of the animals by experimenters, led to a nonspecific physiological response. During the first stage, which Selye called *shock*, occurring 6 to 48 hours after the injury or exposure, there is a decrease in the size of the spleen, lymph glands, and liver, as well as reduced fat tissue. In addition, body temperature declines and ulcers may develop in the digestive tract. Approximately 48 hours after the injury, the adrenal glands become enlarged, body growth stops, and in lactating females, milk production ceases. However, Selye found that if the exposure continued through ongoing small doses of a drug, minor injuries, or further handling, the rats responded with *resistance*, and their organs—in terms of both their functioning and their appearance—returned to normal. After 1 to 3 months, this adaptive resistance was lost and the animals died (Selye, 1973). Selye argued that the hypothalamic pituitary adrenal axis is the central driver of the stress response, which also includes increased release of cortisol.

In Selye's three-stage model, humans respond to different types of threats with the same physiological pattern (Taylor, 2014). In the alarm stage, we are preparing ourselves to address the threat. If the threat continues, we enter the resistance stage, in which we attempt various coping responses as our immune system begins to malfunction. The final stage, exhaustion, is the result of multiple unsuccessful attempts to manage the stressor. Instead of dying, human beings often develop various illnesses. These may include an array of stress-related conditions, including tension headache, recurrent abdominal pain, some forms of back pain, hypertension, and sleep disturbance. As Selye emphasized, these various ailments share an underlying common foundation in our three-stage response to external stress.

Allostatic Load

Allostasis refers to the body's reaction to stress through homeostatic mechanisms, including body temperature, autonomic nervous system activity, immune functioning, and hypothalamic pituitary axis activity (McEwen & Stellar, 1993). All of these mechanisms attempt to preserve normal body functioning. However, if there are repeated stressors or a single prolonged stressor, the long-term physiological strain increases the risk for disease. McEwen, one of the developers of this theory, suggests that there are several factors that increase our allostatic load—repeated exposure to stressful life events or multiple stressors simultaneously, inability of the physiological system to adapt, a prolonged stress response, reduced immune function, increased hypothalamic pituitary activity, increased autonomic nervous system activity, and the absence of successful coping responses. In some circumstances, even though the threatening event has been terminated, the allostatic response may be maintained—particularly if perceived coping skills are inadequate. There are links between allostatic load and multiple illnesses, including obesity and cardiovascular disease. In addition, among older adults, higher allostatic loads are associated with greater deterioration in skills such as memory, concentration, and attention (Seeman, Singer, Rowe, Horwitz, & McEwen, 1997). The important contribution of allostatic theory is that exposure to repeated stressors in the past, even though they may no longer be present, have a cumulative effect that does not entirely disappear over time.

Psychoneuroimmunology

The field of psychoneuroimmunology examines responses to stress at the cellular level. There is growing evidence that exposure to stress influences immune-system functioning and that this mechanism increases susceptibility to infectious disease. For example, in an early study, Kiecolt-Glaser and Glaser (1995) found that among persons caring for someone with Alzheimer's disease, wounds required nine additional days to heal as compared with a control non-caregiver group. In another seminal study, Cohen (Ader & Cohen, 1993) found that exposure to a cold virus was more likely to result in the development of symptoms in the presence of psychological stress. Even when a number of other variables were controlled, including smoking, this association between stress and cold symptoms remained.

Psychoneuroimmunology usually focuses on immune-system activation when bacteria, viruses, or cancer cells are detected in our body. Specialized cells, monocytes and lymphocytes, represent our defense against these "invader" cells. When a source of infection enters the body, specialized lymphocytes of two types—T cells and B cells—are activated. T cells respond to infectious bacteria or viruses by releasing killer cells. When in the presence of an infectious agent, B cells stimulate the release of antibodies. One type of monocyte, the macrophage, directs the infectious agent to a T helper cell. The sympathetic nervous system and the hypothalamic pituitary axis also influence the immune system. Longer-term sympathetic nervous system activity activates the immune system. However, activation of the hypothalamic pituitary axis increases release of cortisol, which in turn reduces the number of white blood cells and adversely affects lymphocyte function (Taylor, 2017). Since stress suppresses immune functioning, infections associated with bacteria or viruses are more likely to occur and will be of greater severity and longer duration when we are under stress (Abraham et al., 2016).

Tend and Befriend

Taylor (2017) notes that besides responding to threats with fight or flight, humans and other animals also have a tendency to seek out others when under stress. This affiliative style in humans is likely to be a product of evolution. If women, while pregnant or caring for children, responded to threat by attempting to fight, their efforts would likely be unsuccessful. However, females who "blend in" while attending to the well-being of their children are more likely to survive, as are their offspring (Taylor, 2017). In hunting-and-gathering societies, men and women's roles are segregated. Women, while men are hunting, are engaged in child-rearing and foraging. Compared with males, women have greater social support networks as well as a tendency to turn toward others when under stress. In affiliative groups, females can fend off aggressive threats from males (Taylor, 2006). While norepinephrine facilitates the fight-or-flight response, the hormone oxytocin, also released in response to stress, has been described as increasing affiliative behavior. Estrogen also appears to play a role in increasing positive social interactions. High levels of oxytocin, in addition to promoting social behavior, appear to promote a sense of physical relaxation and emotional calm (Taylor, 2017). Animal studies have shown that increased oxytocin is associated with initiation of maternal behavior toward younger mammals (Pedersen, Ascher, Monroe, & Prange, 1982). Among women who have major depressive disorder, there is evidence of impaired regulation of oxytocin.

Transactional Model

While the allostatic model does include attention to cognitive and behavioral coping, up to this point, stress has been described predominantly from a biological perspective. We know intuitively, however, that the same event, such as a final exam, may be viewed as an anxiety-inducing threat or as a challenge responded to with calm and focus. Lazarus and Folkman (1984) indicated that when confronted with a potentially stressful situation, we engage in several types of appraisal. Primary appraisal is our judgment about whether the situation or event is positive, negative, or neutral. If the situation is interpreted negatively, it is viewed as a potential harm, a threat, or a challenge. When the situation is viewed in terms of the threat of future harm, blood pressure is likely to increase. However, when the same event is interpreted as a challenge, this physiological reaction is less pronounced. Getting fired from a job certainly could be considered a threat when someone is worried about finances and the current job market is poor. However, many people who have been fired will report that it was "a blessing in disguise" because it led them to a new career (Taylor, 2017). If the event is viewed as a potential threat, a secondary appraisal process begins (Dewe, 1991).

Secondary appraisal involves assessment of one's own coping resources: "Do I have what it takes to manage the situation successfully?" Thus, in the transactional model, events are experienced as more or less stressful depending on the balance of primary and secondary appraisal. If action is taken (studying for an exam, beginning the process of writing a term paper), there is also ongoing reappraisal—updates on our success in meeting the challenge. (If you have ever had to write a 15-page paper, how many times, while you were putting the paper together, did you stop and count the number of words and pages produced before getting back to work?)

Assessing Stress

While stress has a strong physiological component, the majority of stress assessment measures are pencil-and-paper self-report scales.

Perceived Stress Scale

The Perceived Stress Scale (PSS; Cohen, Kamarck, & Mermelstein, 1983) asks about frequency of the respondent's experience in the past month. Items address "feeling stressed," "perception of coping," and perceived control over important life activities. Respondents rate the frequency of these experiences from 0 (never) to 4 (often). In a study of smoking cessation, among those who were not able to quit smoking for more than 24 hours, PSS scores were consistently high over a 6-month period. Scores were lower among those able to maintain abstinence and continued to decrease as the period of abstinence became longer. Relapse from cessation was associated with increased levels of stress (Cohen & Lichtenstein, 1990).

Social Readjustment Rating Scale

Probably the best-known stress questionnaires are those that query about specific life events. In the 1960s, Holmes and Rahe (1967) asked a large sample of men and women from various backgrounds to indicate from a list the degree to which they would have to actively adjust to a number of specific life events. The specific life events came from the test developers' professional experience. The resulting questionnaire, the Social Readjustment Rating Scale, assigned point values—"life change units"—for a series of specific life events.

At the top of the scale was death of a spouse (100 points). At the bottom of the scale was "minor violation of the law" (11 points). Other events, such as divorce (73 points), pregnancy (40 points), change in work responsibilities (29 points), vacation (13 points), and Christmas (12), were also on the lower end of the scale. The three most commonly reported events were vacation, death of a loved one, and illness or injury (Sarafino & Smith, 2011). Holmes and Rahe found that in a group of naval personnel, high scorers were more likely to develop both psychiatric and physical illness in the next year.

It is important to recognize that one can obtain a high score through either several "big" life events or many smaller ones. Holmes and Rahe emphasize that it is not so much whether an event is "good" or "bad" but the fact of change in our life that creates distress. These changes can be positive, such as getting married or getting a new job, or negative, such as divorce or death of a parent. Events such as Christmas or vacation are included because our routine tends to change at those times.

There have been a number of criticisms of the life events perspective. The wording of some items is ambiguous: "trouble with in-laws" (29 points) can vary considerably; "change in living conditions" (25 points) may be desired, such as moving into a bigger house, or undesired, such as no longer being able to pay the rent and having to move to a smaller apartment. Additionally, the respondent's appraisal of the specific situation is not considered—the same event is seen as having universally equal impact. These items are also presented as if they are independent events—but, in reality, a key event may lead to a series of other stressful events in a domino-like effect. In the case of a divorce, there is likely to be a change in one's financial status, living situation, relationship with in-laws, and daily responsibilities. The respondent's appraisal of the situation—is it a challenge or a threat?—is also not taken into account. Additionally, some of these events are controllable and predictable while others are not. Versions of the Social Readjustment Rating Scale have been developed for specific populations, such as college students, with life events that are more appropriate to the demographic group (Clements & Turpin, 1996). For example, the Student Stress Scale includes items such as "first semester in college," "failing an important course," and "dropping more than one class."

Hassles and Uplifts

After reading the items on the Social Readjustment Rating Scale, you might conclude that you do indeed experience stress, but it is not from these major events. Instead, it is the buildup of little things—minor irritants that make life difficult: spilling coffee on your new shirt; breaking a shoelace; an unexpected bill from the dentist; a pop quiz in a class. In addition, you are well aware that on some days these events bother you more than others.

However, you are also aware that some small things can make you almost immediately feel better—a compliment on your shirt, hearing your favorite song on the radio, getting a good grade on an exam, or having your favorite dish for dinner. It was originally thought that these positive events might buffer or offset the irritants. Influenced by the transactional model, Kanner and colleagues (Kanner, Coyne, Schaefer, & Lazarus, 1981) developed the Hassles and Uplifts Scales. The original Hassles Scale contained 117 items, while the Uplifts Scale featured 135 items. In early research with the instruments, it was found that common hassles were concern about weight; worrying about the health of a family member; the rising price of consumer goods; home maintenance; having too many things to do; and traffic jams. Commonly reported uplifts were relating well with spouse or significant other; relating well with friends; completing a task; feeling healthy; and getting enough sleep. Subsequent research has found that hassles do predict health status. However, uplifts have not been found to be consistently predictive of health status (DeLongis, Coyne, Dakof, Folkman, & Lazarus, 1982; DeLongis, Folkman, & Lazarus, 1988). While correlated with scores on the Social Readjustment Rating Scale, studies have found that hassles may be a better predictor of health status than Holmes and Rahe's large-scale life events (Sarafino & Smith, 2011). One of the major issues with the assessment of hassles is that the perception of the specific events is likely to be strongly influenced by current mood states. In particular, persons experiencing depression and anxiety are likely to rate these irritants as more severe and causing greater life disruption.

Mediators and Moderators of Stress

As suggested by the discussion of the Social Readjustment Rating Scale and the Hassles Scale, the effects of stress are often not direct. The impact of stressors is often mediated by intervening dimensions (Abraham, Conner, Jones, & O'Connor, 2016).

For example, the appraisal of a pop quiz as a challenge for which one is prepared is likely to lead to more successful performance than if it is viewed as an unpredictable threat. Stress often exerts effects indirectly on health through high-risk behaviors such as smoking, drinking excessively, and unsafe driving. Research suggests that physical health deteriorates following a divorce (Amato, 2000). While this outcome could be due to the direct effects of this emotionally distressing event, it is also known that alcohol and cigarette consumption increase during this time as well.

A moderated effect is one that directly alters the stressor or its relationship with the outcome (Abraham et al., 2016). Sometimes a moderator is referred to as a buffer, since it reduces the impact of the emotionally or physically threatening life event. We will discuss moderators further below, but one of the most common is coping style. While recognizing the realistic limits of the situation, persons who approach stressors with active rather than passive coping generally experience better emotional adjustment.

In the sections below we will review some of the common mediators and moderators of stress.

Characteristics of the Stressor

There are a number of factors that can influence appraisal. First is valence—is the situation something that is wanted or undesired? Is the threat ambiguous or clearly defined? An instructor who gives you a very specific study guide for exams versus a professor who tells you to "know everything" for an upcoming exam elicits very different reactions. Duration—how long will the stressor last?—is another important dimension. Many of us can tolerate a range of threats, such as loud noise or extreme temperature, if we know in advance that these are time-limited stressors. Control—if the situation is perceived to be controllable and I have the knowledge or skills to exert this control, the event will likely be experienced as less stressful. Similarly, unpredictable events are much more stressful than predictable ones. For example, being able to predict as well as having knowledge of the extent and duration of physical discomfort appears to be associated with better adjustment after surgery (Johnston & Vögele, 1993). It is increasingly common for hospitals to have classes or to develop video programs to describe and illustrate what will happen to surgical patients during the procedure and immediately afterward (Taylor, 2017). In addition, the recovery process for many procedures, such as hip replacement, requires that the patient begin walking—albeit with assistance—soon after the surgery. Physical therapists encourage patients to walk progressively longer distances, which also emphasizes the patient's role in the recovery process.

A final dimension is centrality—how close are we to the stressful event? A tornado warning for a distant state is likely to be far less stressful than one issued for the county adjacent to the one in which you reside.

Emotional State

Fredrickson (2001, 2005) points out that our emotional state, independent of the external event, can be a productive force for managing stress. Fredrickson (2001, 2005) has described a "broaden-and-build" approach designed to increase and capitalize upon positive emotion. She notes that when under stress, our thought processes become narrowly focused—which limits our ability to see a broad range of possible adaptive responses. However, positive emotion broadens our thought processes, including the number of possible cognitive interpretations and accompanying actions. Research has supported positive emotion as associated with a greater variety of possible actions as well as greater openness to new information. In their research, Fredrickson and colleagues found that persons experiencing positive emotion listed a greater number of activities that they would currently like to engage in compared with those experiencing negative or neutral emotions (Fredrickson, 2005).

At the level of the sympathetic nervous system, Fredrickson found that positive emotion, in essence, "undoes" the physiological effects of negative emotion. In one study, participants were required to perform a very demanding task—they were given 60 seconds to prepare a speech. As would be expected, responses included increased heart rate and blood pressure. Immediately after this task, participants were classified into groups and they watched one of four films characterized by themes of joy, contentment, neutral emotion, and sadness. Those observing the joy or contentment-themed films recovered more quickly (heart rate and blood pressure returned to baseline) than those observing the other two types of films (Fredrickson, 2005). In sum, the ability to have a foundation of positive emotion appears to assist recovery from stressful life events (Fredrickson & Branigan, 2005).

Coping Styles

In the transactional theory, Lazarus and Folkman (1984) described coping skills as being an important moderator of stressful situations. Two basic coping styles include emotion focused and problem focused (Lazarus & Folkman, 1984). Problem-focused coping involves taking active steps to change the situation itself. In emotion-focused coping, the focus is less on instrumental action than on managing feelings or obtaining support to improve one's ability to manage an uncontrollable situation. For example, persons who are able to access social support tend to cope better with uncontrollable events such as the death of a loved one. Another dimension that interacts with emotion- and problem-focused coping is whether the stressor is directly engaged. In avoidant coping, the individual behaviorally and psychologically disengages from the stressful situation. This ineffective strategy often includes simply not thinking about the situation (Carver, Scheier, & Weintraub, 1989). Other avoidant strategies include distraction such as redirection of attention to television and use of drugs or alcohol. Passive strategies include fantasizing about an unrealistic outcome (winning the lottery) or hoping that the problem will simply go away. In most situations, avoidance is associated with poor well-being.

However, adaptive use of emotion-focused strategies depends on the situation. In a situation in which there are concrete steps that one can take to improve outcome, instrumental activity is most adaptive. However, in situations that are beyond our control, managing emotion adaptively will lead to better overall well-being. For example, in a study of women with breast cancer, Taylor, Lichtman, and Wood (1984) found that cognitive control—thinking about the situation differently—was associated with better psychological adjustment. Importantly, women who attempted to find meaning in the cancer experience tended to exhibit better adjustment. For these women, the emphasis was on how to address the cancer in the here and now rather than searching for reasons that it occurred (Taylor, Lichtman, & Wood, 1984). From a cognitive perspective, it is often helpful to redefine the situation to find some positive value. Qualitatively, Taylor (1983) also found that many women saw some benefit in their disease, such as being able to better appreciate life and their relationships as well as developing greater sensitivity and compassion toward others.

History of Exposure to Stressors

As noted in Chapter 1, the biopsychosocial perspective highlights how risk factors at multiple levels may predispose individuals to specific illnesses. The allostatic load model considers the cumulative effect of stressors during the life course. This load may, in many respects, be a diathesis. While we often think of diatheses as being genetic, these predispositions may also take the form of long-standing cognitive schema formed at a young age (Teasdale, 1988). For example, a three-year-old child whose father abandons the family may carry an unarticulated expectation that relationships are not enduring and may unexpectedly end at any time. When coupled with the egocentricity characterizing preschoolers' cognitive processes, the child may take on the blame for the father's departure ("I was bad and made Daddy leave us"). As an adult, this grown child may be inordinately fearful about doing something that could cause a romantic relationship to end.

Recent research, on multiple fronts, has posited a causal relationship between stressful early childhood experiences and adult health outcomes. The majority of the studies today have examined general psychosocial adjustment and the emergence of adult psychiatric disorders. There have even been associations found between utero experiences and adult outcomes. One of the most dramatic examples is the "Dutch famine" study in which fetal malnutrition during the Nazi occupation of the Netherlands was found to be predictive of increased risk of coronary heart disease 50 years later (Roseboom, de Rooij, & Painter, 2008).

Other research led to the development of a brief checklist, the Adverse Childhood Experiences Survey (ACES). The items ask specifically about personal histories of childhood emotional, physical, and sexual abuse as well as emotional and physical neglect. Other ACES dimensions include characteristics of the parental household, including observing partner abuse, parental substance abuse and mental illness, parental separation/divorce, and having an incarcerated family member (Centers for Disease Control, 2016b). Large-scale studies have found that in addition to being predictive of psychiatric disorders such as major depression and substance abuse, these childhood events are a risk factor for adult physical inactivity, obesity, ischemic heart disease, cancer, chronic lung disease, and liver disease. There also appears to be a dose-response relationship such that the greater number of adverse childhood experiences, the higher the risk of developing these illnesses as an adult (Felitti et al., 1998).

Personality Traits

We often describe acquaintances as pessimists ("He is an eternal pessimist—he can never see anything good in anyone") or optimists ("She sees the world through rose-colored glasses; everything is wonderful"). When operationalized and assessed, pessimism and optimism appear to have strong effects on health. Pessimists have higher mortality rates (19 percent higher than optimists), increased levels of major depressive disorder, weaker immune functioning, and a greater inclination to ruminate (Carver & Scheier, 2014; Carver & Connor-Smith, 2010). Optimists, by contrast, tend to experience more positive emotions and are more likely to appraise life difficulties as challenges rather than threats, as well as report a greater sense of control. Optimists exhibit less of a blood pressure increase in response to stress, are less likely to die of a heart attack, have shorter hospital stays, quicker recovery from surgery, fewer minor health problems, and improved immune functioning (Carver & Connor-Smith, 2010). Optimists are also more likely to be proactive in protecting their health and seeking medical care when appropriate (Scheier & Carver, 2003). As might be expected, optimists are more likely to use active coping strategies as opposed to avoidance or disengagement (Scheier & Carver, 2003).

Another personality dimension that appears to buffer the experience of external stressors is hardiness. Hardiness includes three traits—commitment, challenge, and control. Commitment is a belief that if you persist, you will be successful. Those high in control believe that they can effect change in the situation through their own actions. Finally, challenge is a belief that the situation is not a threat but an opportunity for further personal development (Kobasa, 1979). Hardiness has been found to be associated with lower rates of stress-related illnesses, better adjustment among women who have multiple roles, and reduced rates of depression among institutionalized elderly persons (Funk, 1992). There is also evidence that hardy individuals have better skill at regulating their emotions. They are able to assess the controllability of situations and, when appropriate, disengage from attempts to control uncontrollable situations while turning their attention to how to best manage their emotion. Hardy individuals are also more likely to have an internal locus of control, which has been associated with better health status, including lower systolic blood pressure (Lawler & Schmied, 1992). After the unexpected death of a partner, persons with an internal locus of control appeared to function better and reported fewer somatic symptoms.

If you have a reasonably sized social circle and observe your friends, you will notice that they react differently to the same type of threat. While individual differences in appraisal certainly play a role, there are also individual variations in autonomic nervous system response, hypothalamic pituitary axis variability, level of cortisol release, and immune system reaction. Among adults, those who are higher in trait reactivity release more cortisol and report a greater number of negative life events (Boyce et al., 1995; Taylor, 2017). In addition, reactivity is associated with greater hostility, more interpersonal conflict, and lower levels of social support (Smith, 1992). Reactors also have a greater likelihood of developing respiratory disease with corresponding impairment in immune system activity (Cohen et al., 2002; Taylor, 2017). Trait reactivity is present as early as preschool age and is likely to be an inherited predisposition. Young children high in reactivity are more likely to develop illnesses after family crises compared with children with less reactivity (Obradović, Bush, Stamperdahl, Adler, & Boyce, 2010; Walker, Garber, Smith, Van Slyke, & Claar, 2001).

While procrastination has been associated with stress, there is debate about whether this dimension is a situational characteristic versus a more enduring trait.

State-based measures of procrastination have found it to be associated with a greater number of health problems (Sirois, Melia-Gordon, & Pychyl, 2003). Lay and colleagues (Lay & Schouwenburg, 1993; Lay & Silverman, 1996) present research suggesting that procrastination is an enduring personality characteristic. The trait perspective comes from research in which students reported feelings of anxiety and also completed the scale assessing delay behavior at several points during the five days prior to an exam. While trait procrastination was predictive of unproductive delay behavior before the exam and on the exam day, it was unrelated to anxiety (Lay & Silverman, 1996). This perspective challenges the view that anxiety about performance is a key underlying dimension driving procrastination. Schouwenburg and Lay (1995) have also found strong associations between high trait procrastination and low trait conscientiousness. Specifically, procrastinators scored significantly lower on the dimensions of competence, self-discipline, and deliberation.

Does Stress Cause Physical Illness?
Cardiovascular Disease, the Type A Personality, and Depression

In the late 1950s, the cardiologists Friedman and Rosenman began to study personality factors associated with heart disease. It has been said that these physicians were puzzled by the fact that the chairs in the waiting room often were worn out—particularly the edge of the seat. Friedman and Rosenman concluded that there was a personality style, which they called the type A, that was at greater risk for heart attacks (and more likely to wear out waiting room chairs). Their original longitudinal study found that type A personalities were twice as likely to develop coronary heart disease as those without these characteristics. The core characteristics of the type A that Friedman and Rosenman described were competitiveness, time urgency (trying to get more done in less time), aggressiveness, and impatience. Jenkins, Rosenman, and Friedman (1967) went on to develop a specific questionnaire—the Jenkins Activity Schedule—to assess these dimensions. Physiologically there have been suggestions that type A individuals have a decreased parasympathetic response to offset greater sympathetic arousal (Suarez & Williams, 1989).

In the six decades since the original research, subsequent findings have led to a more nuanced and complex view of the impact of personality characteristics on heart disease. All of the characteristics originally described are not equally predictive, and subsequent research found that some of the traits described by Friedman and Rosenman are actually unrelated to development of cardiovascular disease.

When the type A personality style was initially described, the core defining factors were considered to be speed, multitasking, and intense job involvement. However, as research continued it became increasingly clear that "free-floating" hostility demonstrated the most pronounced association with coronary heart disease. Persons with higher levels of hostility are more likely to experience cardiac death, heart attack, and angina, even after controlling for traditional cardiac risk factors such as smoking and obesity. The cardiovascular diseases that are precursors to heart attack and stroke, such as hypertension, carotid atherosclerosis, and ischemia, are also associated with higher levels of hostility (Sirois & Burg, 2003).

Interventions targeting the type A behavior pattern have been found to be successful in reducing the reoccurrence of a heart attack. One study found that over a 5-year period these interventions had resulted in reductions in coronary recurrence rates (Sirois & Burg, 2003).

Cardiovascular Disease and Anxiety and Depression
While the type A is a multifaceted personality trait, mental health conditions associated with stress, such as anxiety and major depressive disorder, also appear to play a significant role in risk for heart disease as well as recovery after a heart attack. Anxiety is positively associated with elevated blood pressure and coronary heart disease. Patients who had higher levels of anxiety after an acute heart attack were much more likely to have further heart complications while in the hospital (Moser & Dracup, 1996) and rehospitalization for cardiac problems (Strik, Denollet, Lousberg, & Honig, 2003).

Physiological linkages between anxiety and depression and heart disease have been suggested. Elevated levels of cortisol and elevated heart rate are found among persons with major depressive disorder. As you may recall, the stress hormone cortisol is associated with dysregulation of both the autonomic nervous system and the hypothalamic pituitary adrenal axis.

While much of the focus has been on anxiety, major depressive disorder is also highly predictive of cardiovascular disease and its severity. Among patients with major depressive disorder who had unstable angina (chest pain while at rest associated with reduced blood flow to the heart muscle) survival rates were approximately 10 percent less than for those without a psychiatric condition (Lespérance, Frasure-Smith, Juneau, & Théroux, 2000). While unlikely to be the sole cause of this association, abnormal platelet (small disk-like structures that are a component of blood) activity is present in depression as well as angina. New research on major depressive disorder suggests that, in addition to platelet activity, at least in some cases, an abnormal inflammatory response occurs in both cardiovascular disease and major depressive disorder.

Studies suggest that up to 50 percent of patients develop major depressive disorder after suffering a heart attack. Untreated major depressive disorder is a major predictor of death in the months and years following an initial heart attack; patients with significant levels of depressive symptoms were significantly more likely to die during the 5-year follow-up (Lespérance, Frasure-Smith, Talajic, & Bourassa, 2002). There appears to be a dose-response relationship between the levels of depressive symptoms and 5-year mortality among persons experiencing a heart attack (Lespérance, Frasure-Smith, Talajic, & Bourassa, 2002). Moreover, after a heart attack, patients with depression are less likely to return to work and experience a poorer quality of life compared with non-depressed cardiac patients. Among those undergoing cardiac bypass graft surgery, depression present immediately prior to surgery is associated with greater disability after surgery (Sirois & Burg, 2003).

Hypertension
High blood pressure or hypertension is a condition that arises when there is extra pressure put on artery walls by the flow of blood. There are two factors associated

with elevated blood pressure—the volume of blood pumped out by the heart and the condition of the arteries. When arteries are narrowed—usually by cholesterol deposits—blood must be pumped harder and blood pressure increases. A normal blood pressure is less than 120/80. The top figure, called the systolic blood pressure, is the amount of pressure associated with blood when the heart beats. The diastolic blood pressure (bottom number) is the amount of pressure that occurs between beats. Hypertension has two levels depending upon the blood pressure readings—stage 1 (140–159/90–99), stage 2 (160 and above/100 and above). A category that falls between normal and hypertensive stage 1 is called pre-hypertension (120–139/80–89). This third category, while not officially labeled "hypertension," is associated with increased health risks. Most cases of hypertension are called "essential," meaning that the precise cause is not known, but it is likely to be an interaction of genetic, physiological, biological, and social factors.

There is a rough dose-response relationship between blood pressure and risk for vascular disease such as stroke or heart attack. There is some evidence that among middle-aged and older males, pre-existing anger and anxiety are predictors of the development of hypertension (Rutledge & Hogan, 2002). Both anger and anxiety as risk factors for hypertension have been detected in children (Nichols, Rice, & Howell, 2011), suggesting that these chronic emotional states may have a genetic predisposition as well.

Even among individuals who have not had any cardiovascular event such as a stroke or heart attack, stage 1 hypertension is associated with cognitive impairment—particularly in the area of short-term memory. While both obesity and hypertension have an association with impaired cognition, both of these diseases had a cumulative effect such that among men with both hypertension and obesity (a common combination), the level of cognitive impairment was greater than for either condition alone (Elias, Elias, Sullivan, Wolf, & D'Agostino, 2003). This cognitive impairment associated with hypertension is likely to be a major factor in greater cognitive impairment occurring when a patient has both Alzheimer's disease and high blood pressure at the same time. Additionally, a recent study found that even among people with schizophrenia, the presence of hypertension worsens the condition. It has been suggested that in this population, treatment of hypertension may be associated with improvement in some psychotic symptoms as well as in overall functioning (Morra & Strauss, 2016).

Cancer

Since the days of psychosomatic medicine, there has been an interest in determining whether there is a cancer-prone personality. Eysenck (1994) described a "type C" personality, characterized by difficulty managing stress, suppression of negative feelings such as anxiety, and anger while maintaining outward self-control (a "bland surface" was Eysenck's term), which was associated with a greater likelihood of developing cancer. A study based upon data from 16 prospective cohorts suggests that the link between deficits in stress management and cancer may be a disruption in natural killer cell functions as well as dysregulation of the hypothalamic pituitary axis. Batty and colleagues (Batty, Russ, Stamatakis, & Kivimäki, 2017) concluded that even when other risk factors such as smoking and obesity were controlled, persons with higher levels of pre-cancer psychological distress were more likely to die from cancer. For colorectal and prostate cancer, there was a direct association with a clear dose-response relationship—the greater the degree of distress, the higher the risk of death due to cancer. While not as strong, there were also associations between psychological distress and pancreatic and esophageal cancer as well as leukemia. While depleted immune functioning may be involved in the development of tumors, conditions such as leukemia are likely to be mediated by hypothalamic pituitary dysfunction (Batty et al., 2017).

Once diagnosed, cancer survival may also be influenced by psychological factors. Spiegel, Kraemer, Bloom, & Gottheil (1989) randomly assigned women who had just been diagnosed with metastatic breast cancer to one of two groups—standard medical care or standard medical care with the addition of group psychotherapy. The group therapy patients lived an average of 18 months longer (Spiegel et al., 1989). There has been difficulty replicating Spiegel's highly publicized study. It has been suggested that many of the psychosocial contributions provided by Spiegel's therapy groups are now a standard part of cancer care (Sapolsky, 2004).

The Macrosystem
Environmental Factors

Several environmental factors are likely to amplify the effects of demanding situations on emotional and physiological indicators of stress, including noise levels and the experience of physical crowding. Repeated exposure to high-intensity noise has been associated with permanent elevations in blood pressure. Of interest, noise is less stressful when it is predictable and the individual has control over it (Carter & Beh, 1989). Studies in laboratory settings in which individuals are exposed to high-intensity sound for specific periods of time find that if the subject can control the time of the sound—for example, by pushing a button—it is less stressful than the same level and duration of sound presented at random intervals (Hanson, Larson, & Snowdon, 1976).

Calhoun's (1962) classic study of rats overcrowded in a "behavioral sink" demonstrated the effects of high population density. Calhoun systematically added more and more laboratory mice to a large dish-shaped container. He found that as density increased, there were a number of behavior changes, with increased aggression, reduced maternal care for offspring, and even cannibalism (Calhoun, 1962).

University dormitories, while not behavioral sinks, are often settings with very high population density. In recent years, architects and interior designers have worked to increase the "homelike" appearance of college dorms and have developed strategies to increase the perception of greater physical space. For college dormitories, there is evidence that subdividing long corridors into smaller sections with about 20 residents per section, versus one extended corridor with 36 to 40 residents, increased residents' experience of control over their living space (Baum, Mapp, & Davis, 1978) and reduced the perception of crowding (Baum & Davis, 1980). After 6 to 8 weeks of long corridor living, residents were more likely to report a higher sense of helplessness (Aiello, Baum, & Gormley, 1981; Rodin & Baum, 1978).

Couples and Relationship Conflict

Intimate relationships, while certainly fulfilling and a source of social support, can increase stress, particularly when there are problems. Relationship status as it impacts health and disease may have somewhat different meaning and mechanisms for men versus women. Marital status by itself is associated with reduced mortality among men (Rendall, Weden, Favreault, & Waldron, 2011); however, the quality of the relationship is much more important to mortality among women. Marital conflict appears to be more strongly predictive of poor health for women than men. There have been two explanations for this gender difference. Kiecolt-Glaser and Newton (2001) suggest that because identity is represented relationally for women, they are more impacted by interpersonal conflict. However, other gender researchers suggest that the issue of conflict is secondary to women having lower status and less power (Wanic & Kulik, 2011).

When examining relationship satisfaction, women in more satisfying relationships reported fewer risk factors for metabolic syndrome (a frequent precursor to type 2 diabetes) and lower levels of atherosclerosis (thickening of the walls of the arteries) (Troxel, Matthews, Gallo, & Kuller, 2005). However, women in distressed relationships had poorer cardiovascular outcomes over time, with increased rates of heart attack and stroke. Marital distress has been found to be associated with depressed immune functioning, greater cardiovascular arousal, and increase in the release of corticosteroids (Kiecolt-Glaser et al., 1987; Kiecolt-Glaser, McGuire, Robles, & Glaser, 2002). These effects appear to be more pronounced for women than men; for men, marriage appears to have a health-protective effect (Gottman & Notarius, 2002). In the days following an argument, the spouses reporting a more positive mood exhibited lower cortisol levels and, among older, but not younger, adults, more rapid wound healing (Kiecolt-Glaser & Wilson, 2017).

As might be expected, the end of a relationship due to either divorce or death is also experienced as stressful. Death of a romantic partner, even when other factors are controlled, increases the risk for mortality, with a particularly pronounced window of increase in death during the first three months of bereavement. However, when compared with men, women may fare better (Boyle, Feng, & Raab, 2011) after the loss of their husband than men after the loss of their wife. It has been suggested that when a man loses his wife, he has also lost the person who encourages positive health behaviors; completes household tasks; and, importantly, is their primary and often sole source of social support. Women usually have larger social support networks. However, during the past decade, this gender effect in response to bereavement has become less pronounced, with recent studies finding no differences (Vable, Subramanian, Rist, & Glymour, 2015).

Since divorce often occurs in the context of significant relationship conflict, it is not surprising that divorce and separation are associated with poor immune functioning, increased risk of vascular and respiratory disease, and increased risk of liver problems (likely associated with increased alcohol use). Kiecolt-Glaser and Wilson (2017) have documented that the disruptions in immune functioning may still be present one year after divorce. Finally, divorce is also associated with increased mortality. When followed over time, persons 65 years or older who are divorced have an increased likelihood of death compared to still-married men and women. However, other research findings suggest that in terms of health-related issues, divorce among younger adults is associated with greater risk of early death compared with older adults.

Research on divorce and its impact on children as well as adults suggests that some of the distress may be remediated by remarriage. However, there are fewer studies in this area, and results investigating the impact of remarriage upon mortality have been inconsistent. Mason and Sbarra (2012) concluded that those who remained divorced, compared with those who remarried, were more likely to die sooner. However, other investigators have not found this pattern. Given that second and third marriages tend to be of shorter duration and have a greater likelihood of ending in divorce than first marriages, it is likely that this relationship may be complex.

Workplace

Workplaces in which workers have minimal control over the conditions of their employment, such as assembly lines or call centers, are frequently experienced as highly stressful. Historically, the relationship between lack of control in the workplace and stress was highlighted by a 1970s case study in the automotive industry. In the early 1970s, at the Lordstown, Ohio, auto plant, during production of the Vega, assembly line workers were subjected to an abrupt increase in productivity demands by management. Instead of the assembly-line norm of 55 cars per hour, management required that 100 cars per hour be produced. Each line worker had, on average, 36 seconds to perform their task rather than the previous time frame of 60 seconds. Many line workers—particularly younger employees—reported that they felt they were being treated like machines. While still the source of some debate, many observers believed that there was deliberate sabotage of the cars by disgruntled and alienated workers. Specifically, autos had upholstery that was deliberately split, body paint was scratched, bolts were missing, and it was reported that a worker intentionally dropped a vehicle's ignition key into the gas tank. Fires were also deliberately set on the assembly line—including one instance of setting a glove on fire and locking it in the trunk as the car went down the line (Ashforth, 1989; Orchard, 2013).

Workplace schedules that involve shiftwork—either consistently working at night or changing shifts on a frequent basis—are associated with a greater number of health complaints, including headaches, GI distress, major depressive disorder, and heart disease (Taylor, 2017).

Another source of workplace stress is role ambiguity or conflict. This pattern often occurs when more than one person is supervising a worker and the two (or more) supervisors have widely differing expectations regarding job duties and standards of evaluation. Role ambiguity often goes along with role conflict when someone receives unclear information about either the standards of performance or the specific work tasks themselves. Employees in workplaces high in conflict and ambiguity are more likely to have elevated blood pressure (Taylor, 2009). A particularly difficult workplace role is when one is held responsible for situations or outcomes over which one has little direct control. Middle-management positions often include this frustrating balance of accountability with little power. There is evidence that this combination is also associated with elevated rates of cardiovascular disease (Taylor, 2009).

Relationships in the workplace are also important. Supportive relationships with one's coworkers reduce stress and risk of cardiovascular disease. Persons who are isolated from coworkers tend to experience more work-related stress (Taylor, 2009). These supportive relationships can even buffer the effects of a particularly stressful job (Taylor, 2009).

Uncertainty about continued employment—particularly when coworkers may be losing their jobs—appears to be particularly stressful. Unemployment is associated with increased reports of physical symptoms as well as depression (Taylor, 2009). Studies of workers who are at risk for losing their job, because of possible plant closings or threatened layoffs, have been found to exhibit increased blood pressure and serum cholesterol (Taylor, 2009).

One's place in the work hierarchy also contributes to stress. One of the best examples of this effect is the Whitehall study in which civil servants at various levels in the United Kingdom were studied closely over time. The health status of those at the upper levels was consistently better than those in the lower grades of civil service (Marmot et al., 1991). This is particularly noteworthy since the study was conducted in England where there is universal health care coverage. This effect appears to be more pronounced in work settings in which there are few avenues for workplace advancement.

Community

An example of the powerful effects of social support is Roseto, Pennsylvania. In Roseto, settled by Italian immigrants, residents were not succumbing to common causes of death found in towns several miles away. While the most common cause of death in the United States is heart disease, residents of Roseto were essentially dying of old age. Interestingly, Roseto's residents were frequently cigarette smokers who ate a diet high in fat, demonstrated relatively little exercise activity, and had other risk factors such as hypertension and diabetes. However, death rates from coronary artery disease were significantly lower in Roseto compared with surrounding communities (Bruhn & Wolf, 2013). The community was cohesive, with extended families forming the foundation and often related to one another through intermarriage to form "clans." The Catholic Church was a centerpiece of family life. Additionally, there were many social and civic organizations. Among Roseto's men, 80 percent were members of at least one of these organizations. Political figures, such as the mayor, were elected because of their family ties, with political affiliation secondary. As the community began to change and family size declined along with the influence of ethnic-religious traditions, heart disease among younger males began to increase. After careful study, Bruhn and Wolf (2013) concluded that the lower level of stress-related illness was associated with Roseto's dense social support network featuring extended families with shared religious and cultural values. This same tightly knit group also found collective meaning in overseeing the town's civic activity (Hinote & Wasserman, 2016).

Social and Economic Costs of Early Traumatic Experiences

Research on adverse childhood experiences (ACEs) continues to show the enduring and large-scale impact that early trauma has on significant proportions of the adult population (Liu et al., 2013). ACEs, while having adverse effects on adult physical and mental health, also negatively influence socioeconomic status. Among those reporting only one ACE, the likelihood of unemployment was significantly higher compared with those indicating no adverse childhood experiences (Liu et al., 2013). Investigations by social epidemiologists have examined ACEs' impact on larger-scale economic outcomes and concluded that the concept of cumulative allostatic load occurs at the population level as well. The CDC estimates that the total lifetime economic cost associated with child maltreatment is $124 billion. This includes $83.5 billion for productivity loss, $25 billion for health care, $4.6 billion for special education, $4.4 billion for child welfare, and $3.9 billion for criminal justice. The lifetime cost for each victim of child maltreatment that lives into adulthood is comparable to that for chronic health conditions such as type 2 diabetes (Substance Abuse and Mental Health Services Administration, 2018).

Diversity

Gender

Consistent gender differences have been found in preferences for emotion- versus problem-focused coping. Women tend to demonstrate more coping flexibility and to use both coping styles depending on the situation. Men tend to rely on problem-focused coping and exhibit different physiological reactions to stress compared with women. Men appeared to release more stress-related biochemical markers such as norepinephrine and epinephrine, while women showed an elevated glucosteroid response (Taylor, 2009; 2014). Role overload characterizes life for many working women with children. While there has been some progress in gender equality, this has been somewhat limited in the home environment. Married women who have three or more children and who are employed work (including housework and childcare) a total of 90 hours a week on average, with men working 60 hours a week. This disparity appears to be offset by the earnings of the female partner—to put it bluntly, the more money the female partner earns, the more equity there is in household and childcare responsibilities between partners.

Research findings on stress among women who are and are not employed outside of the home suggest a complex pattern. The presence of children at home does increase norepinephrine levels among women as well as cortisol production (Taylor, 2009; 2014). Women who are employed outside of the home who also have significant domestic responsibilities do appear to be a greater risk for major depressive disorder. At the same time, however, there is research that indicates that women who are employed outside of the home, particularly those with children, also report greater self-esteem and satisfaction with life. Factors that appear to reduce the experience of stress associated with dual roles include having assistance with housework and childcare, as well as a supportive partner (Taylor, 2009; 2014). As noted in the discussion of the workplace, a key variable in reducing experiences of stress associated with demanding roles is having a sense of control.

Stress Across Cultures

There are suggestions that sources of stress as well as the experience of being under stress may differ for collectivist versus individualist societies. In comparing a Japanese and British sample, the British respondents reported a substantially higher sense of personal control. While controllability appears to be a significant factor in the experience of stress, research suggests that this association is much more prominent in Western society. When the emphasis is on autonomy and personal achievement, controllability is likely to be particularly important. However, in cultures valuing loyalty to coworkers and extended family, it may be that personal autonomy and controllability may not be a particularly salient value. O'Connor and Shimizu (2002) found that psychological adjustment and perceived stress were associated with controllability in the British sample, but this association did not occur among the Japanese.

In the earlier discussion of stress and heart attack risk, the hostile, time-urgent type A personality was found to be at greater risk for heart disease. However, this finding and the concept of type A personality itself were developed based on samples of American men of White European background. Helman (1987) suggests that the type A behavior pattern is a culture-bound syndrome reflecting Western values. The linear, task-focused perspective with an emphasis on efficiency, in which the goal is to get more done in less time, is in sharp contrast to polychronic cultures in which relationship maintenance and social interaction are prioritized. Polychronic societies place more emphasis on the immediate here and now versus being controlled by quantifiable clock time that may be wasted or lost (Helman, 1987).

In Japan, there is a condition called karoshi, also known as "Salary Man Sudden Death Syndrome" (Herbig & Palumbo, 1994). The underlying physiological cause of most of these deaths is a cardiovascular event such as a subarachnoid hemorrhage, stroke, or heart attack. Cases of karoshi began to appear in the Japanese press in the 1990s, simultaneously with the collapse of the Japanese economy. Two pillars of economic security for Japanese workers were demolished during this financial crisis. A seniority-based wage system was replaced with an outcome-based system that depended upon objective measures of productivity. A further casualty was the guarantee of lifetime employment. As karoshi cases and suicides increased, the government responded with half-hearted attempts to regulate workers' hours. While limits of 48 hours for the workweek were recommended, the government proposed monthly limits of 100 overtime hours. Karoshi is also being reported in South Korea, China, and Taiwan. A recent Japanese case involved a 31-year-old woman who was employed as a broadcast journalist. She died of congestive heart failure after working 159 hours of overtime during the month immediately before her death.

"Resignation syndrome" is another example of a stress-related illness associated with culture, politics, and government. In Sweden over the past 8 to 10 years, immigrant children and young adolescents have become comatose without any physical injury or disease involved. In most cases, the onset occurs soon after the patient's family receives notification that they have been denied political asylum in Sweden (Aviv, 2017; Sallin et al., 2016). As a result, these families would be required to return to the country from which they emigrated and often face ongoing discrimination and persecution (Aviv, 2017; Sallin et al., 2016). In one case, a young adolescent girl lost the ability to walk within 24 hours of the family's residency application being rejected by the Swedish government (Aviv, 2017). Between 2003 and 2005, more than 400 cases of resignation syndrome were reported in Sweden. The refugee families were primarily from the former Soviet republics or former Yugoslavia. Many of these families were members of an ethnic group, the Uighur. This cultural group has been described as highly collectivist; thus, children may be particularly reactive to their parents' distress (Aviv, 2017). Children have remained in the comatose state for months or even years. In most cases, the patient gradually improves weeks to months after the family receives a residency permit and reads the enclosed letter aloud in the child's presence.

Specific Strategies for Stress Reduction

Many of you have probably tried some of the techniques that will be discussed below. Some of you may use them on a regular basis. A common factor shared by all of them is the ability to "quiet" the autonomic nervous system. All of these techniques appear to be effective in reducing physiological arousal and promoting a sense of personal control. Selecting a technique is mostly a matter of personal preference and practical issues such as having a place to practice.

Progressive Relaxation

Progressive relaxation involves systematically tensing and relaxing specific muscle groups one at a time. The alternate tensing-relaxing process is often paired with deep breathing, whereby tensing is paired with inhaling and relaxing with exhaling to focus attention on the specific muscle groups being tensed and relaxed. It is also important that the practitioner be able to discriminate the experience of muscle tension versus muscle relaxation. Many individuals are not aware of their physical experience, so they will require repeated focused attention and may benefit from the addition of biofeedback, which is discussed below.

In performing progressive relaxation, it is important to sit quietly in a chair and be in a setting where you won't be disturbed for 15 to 30 minutes. It is usually not recommended that the person lie down because of the possibility of falling asleep. Initially, it is helpful to breathe slowly and deeply, in and out—try to do so through the nose rather than the mouth. After 30 to 60 seconds of regular deep breathing, focus on a specific muscle group, such as the feet or ankles. One way to tense these muscles is to push your feet down into the floor, holding this posture for about five seconds and then relaxing. Typically, this relaxation procedure is conducted in a way that makes you move systematically through your body so that you will be tensing your legs, chest, arms, hands, shoulders, and face. The protocol is still the same—tense for approximately 5 seconds and then relax. Fairly soon, you should be able to consistently pair your breathing with tensing and relaxing muscle groups. Progressive muscle relaxation is based on a counter-conditioning model in which a physically relaxed body is incompatible with physiological arousal and the sympathetic nervous system is "dampened down." In the classical form, patients are taught to pay attention to 16 different muscle groups as they are specifically tensed, the posture held and relaxed. Over time, the 16 muscle groups are gradually condensed into seven and then to four (Smitherman, Penzien, Rains, Nicholson, & Houle, 2015). Ideally, patients who practice regularly will have the experience of reduced physiological arousal that they can access themselves, on demand. In order for progressive relaxation to be effective, it is important to practice regularly—in the first three weeks, the protocol should be practiced twice a day.

When progressive relaxation is a part of your repertoire, it will be possible to use a "mini" version throughout the day. The mini version involves doing this exercise for 1 to 3 minutes throughout the day or when feeling overwhelmed.

Progressive relaxation is often used as the initial step in a procedure called systematic desensitization, used to treat phobias. Patients goes through the progressive relaxation protocol, and then while in a relaxed state the therapist describes threatening scenes associated with the phobia—for someone fearful of spiders, the description would become more threatening as weeks of treatment progressed: "You open your front door and see a spider web attached to your house." Week 2: "You look down at the pavement, and there is a brown recluse spider." Week 3: "A small spider is climbing up your leg." This procedure is believed to be effective because it conditions a new state—relaxation—to the previously anxiety-arousing stimulus or situation.

When practiced regularly, progressive relaxation has been found to be associated with improvements in insomnia (Greeff & Conradie, 1998), reductions in seizures (Puskarich et al., 1992), and improved immune functioning (Kiecolt-Glaser et al., 1986).

Autogenic Training

Autogenics takes advantage of the relaxation experienced when a sensation of warmth is felt in the body. For example, if you have ever spent a few minutes in a hot tub or Jacuzzi, that sense of warmth from the water often relaxes tense muscles. Autogenics was developed by a German physician, Johan Schultz (Schultz & Luthe, 1969). Schultz noted that patients seemed to recover better from hospitalization and surgical procedures if they practiced this technique. Autogenics also combines elements of self-hypnosis through sub-vocal suggestion. Again, similar to progressive relaxation, you would be sitting in a chair with your back supported, eyes closed, and breathing slowly and evenly. While you are doing this, you would "begin to imagine your legs becoming warm and heavy." You would systematically focus on different parts of your body but with the same type of autosuggestion ("my right arm is feeling warm and heavy"). Again, to be successful as an intervention, autogenics needs to be practiced on a regular basis. Autogenic training has been found to be beneficial for migraine and tension headaches, mild hypertension, and insomnia (Stetter & Kupper, 2002).

Biofeedback

Biofeedback involves using one of these relaxation procedures while sensors are conveying information to an electronic device that produces an audio tone or visual display (Brown, 1977). The tone or visual display differs (the tone may become louder or higher-pitched; electronic bars on the screen may move higher or lower) based upon the individual's muscle tension, respiration rate, body temperature, or galvanic skin response—a measure of the skin's electrical conductivity. This electrodermal activity changes as a function of external or internal conditions such as stressors. When, for example, muscle tension in the forehead is reduced, the biofeedback apparatus will typically show a decline in the size of bars on the graph or change tone from high-pitched to a lower pitch. Biofeedback appears to be particularly helpful for individuals who do not have well-developed abilities to "read" their body and may not know when they are having increased sympathetic nervous system activity. Additionally, the visual or auditory feedback from the machine demonstrates to the patient that they have some control over their reactivity. Biofeedback has been demonstrated to be an effective treatment for migraine and tension headaches, anxiety, and in some instances chronic pain. For migraine, thermal biofeedback is frequently used, while EMG feedback—a measure of muscle tension—is used to treat tension headache (Smitherman et al., 2015).

It is important to recognize that the active component in biofeedback is the ability to control sympathetic nervous system activity. The instrumentation provides ongoing information about levels of muscle tension or temperature in the hands. The advantage of using biofeedback with patients is that it demonstrates to them that they do indeed have some control over their physical sensations and also helps them learn how reduced muscle activity feels (Smitherman et al., 2015).

Meditation

It is estimated that almost 10 percent of the US workforce uses some form of meditation daily (Kachen et al., 2017). Yogic breathing, known as pranayama, has a long history and underlies most contemporary approaches to meditation (Brown & Gerbarg, 2009). One form of yoga breathing involves inhaling through one nostril for 2 seconds and holding the breath for 8 seconds; this is typically done for a period of 10 to 15 minutes. When compared with an attentional control condition, research has found that yogic breathing is associated with short-term reductions in various markers of inflammation (Twal, Wahlquist, & Balasubramanian, 2016) as well as reductions in depression and anxiety (Brown & Gerbarg, 2009). Focusing on the rhythm of breathing, which is a stress reduction technique by itself, is also the basis of most forms of meditation (Brown & Gerbarg, 2009).

Transcendental Meditation

Transcendental meditation (TM) is typically associated with Maharishi Yogi, who developed the technique in India and made it popular in the United States and Europe in the 1960s and 1970s. Transcendental meditation involves the use of a mantra, a simple word or phrase such as "calm," "peace," or "be happy," which the practitioner repeats sub-vocally, while in a quiet place, in a seated position, with the eyes closed. Practitioners typically meditate for 20 to 30 minutes per day.

A study of TM with college students found that after three months of practicing, compared with a control group, there was a significant reduction in global psychological distress, anxiety, and improved coping ability (Travis et al., 2009). Results of a meta-analysis found clinically significant reductions in both systolic and diastolic blood pressure associated with regular practice of transcendental meditation (Anderson, Liu, & Kryscio, 2008).

Benson's Relaxation Response

A similar approach to meditation was developed by the cardiologist Herbert Benson (Benson & Klipper, 1992) and made popular in a book titled *The Relaxation Response*. Benson's approach involves a protocol similar to transcendental meditation but without a specific mantra. Benson's focus is on activating the parasympathetic nervous system to counter the increased sympathetic activity associated with stress. Benson's approach has been associated with decreases in blood pressure in hypertensive patients (Benson, Marzetta, Rosner, & Klemchuk, 1974) and significant improvement in premenstrual symptoms (Goodale, Domar, & Benson, 1990).

Mindfulness

In the past 20 years, a particularly prominent approach to meditation has been mindfulness. The underlying principles of mindfulness meditation are rooted in Buddhism. The central Buddhist tenet is that human beings create their own suffering through clinging to a belief that there is permanence in an ever-changing world. Our consciousness is also fluid and changing. However, we often merge or fuse with our thoughts and feelings rather than recognizing these experiences as transient—much like clouds floating across the blue sky. In mindfulness meditation, one is taught to be an observer of one's own experience (Kabat-Zinn, 2003). Conceptually, mindfulness encourages us to detach our central observing "self," our identity, from the waves of thoughts and feelings that we experience. These thoughts and feelings are not who we are but are transient experiences that we can observe, much like watching a movie on a screen. Typically beginning with slow, rhythmic inhalation and exhalation, mindfulness meditation focuses on the here and now. The beginning of most meditation sessions involves focusing on the breath itself. Next, the individual reflects upon their internal experiences—these may be physical sensations, sound in the room, or one's own thoughts. During mindfulness meditation, if thoughts or images arise—as they most certainly will—these can be labeled ("a thought about work") and then be the focus of consciousness while the deep breathing continues.

Many versions of mindfulness can be conducted throughout the day. Fitness trackers or cellular phones may include programs to remind the user to breathe and be mindful at regular intervals during the day. Mindfulness has been found to be helpful with reducing anxiety, depression, and pain (Goyal et al., 2010). While there are reports of successful application of mindfulness to substance abuse, sleep, and dietary choices, the overall evidence to date is inconclusive for these conditions (Goyal et al., 2014).

Cognitive Intervention

Cognitive therapy's emphasis on recognizing and disputing irrational thoughts has been demonstrated to be useful both as an approach to therapy and as a self-directed set of modules. Cognitive therapy is based upon the assumption that emotional reactions, including depression and anxiety, stem from faulty interpretation of personally relevant situations. Common cognitive errors or distortions include catastrophizing (interpreting a minor setback as inevitably leading to a terrible outcome), magnification (honing in on a minor flaw and exaggerating its significance), and rigidly dichotomized all-or-nothing reasoning ("I was late to my child's baseball game—I am an awful father"). These thought patterns are typically automatic. The first stage in cognitive therapy is to recognize these implicit, ongoing patterns. Once these cognitive distortions are recognized, individuals are encouraged to examine the objective evidence that supports or disputes their conclusions (Herbert & Forman, 2013). While considerable research supports cognitive therapy for treatment of major depressive and anxiety disorders (Beck, 1979; Clark & Beck, 2011), this approach has been effective in reducing type A behavior (Jenni & Wollersheim, 1979) and was as beneficial as yoga in reducing stress-related behavior as well as physiological indices of stress (Granath, Ingvarsson, von Thiele, & Lundberg, 2006). As will be discussed in a later chapter, cognitive therapy has also been helpful in reducing self-reported pain (Morley, Eccleston, & Williams, 1999).

In cognitive treatment, a key element is becoming aware of thoughts and their rationality. This observing stance is also found in mindfulness. Mindfulness interventions have been integrated with cognitive therapy. Importantly, the mindfulness perspective emphasizes that these thoughts are impermanent and can be examined in a detached third-person manner. Research suggests that cognitive therapy components, such as a focus on rumination and worry, add to the effectiveness of mindfulness interventions in addressing well-being (Gu, Strauss, Bond, & Cavanagh, 2015).

Acceptance and Commitment Therapy

Acceptance and commitment therapy (ACT) is considered a third-wave behavior therapy. (Operant learning is first wave and cognitive-behavioral is second wave.) As a descendant of the strongly quantitative and research-oriented behavioral therapy, ACT incorporates many aspects of mindfulness. Drawing upon concepts from Buddhism, the emphasis is on acceptance of thoughts and feelings rather than trying to change these experiences (Hayes, Strosahl, & Wilson, 2012). Rather than extinguishing a response (such as anxiety around an upcoming exam), the focus is on accepting discomfort and symptoms while maintaining focus on lifetime goals and core values. While cognitive therapy focuses on developing the ability to refute irrational thoughts and target cognitive errors, ACT does not encourage systematic refutation of maladaptive thinking but instead emphasizes carrying out behavior that is consistent with core values (Hayes, Strosahl, & Wilson, 2012). ACT does include an element of exposure found in traditional behavior therapy in techniques such as desensitization, but it is not guided by counter-conditioning. Instead, using concepts such as mindfulness, patients are taught to cognitively detach from their thoughts and feelings and to become observers of these psychological processes.

Kabat-Zinn's (1994) perspective on mindfulness is a basis for ACT: "paying attention in a particular way: on purpose, in the present moment, and nonjudgmentally" (p. 4). Importantly, negative experiences, such as the physical sensation of pain, sadness, and significant anxiety, are phenomena that one can examine much like a specimen under the microscope. These experiences are approached with an element of curiosity and a desire to understand them. To achieve the proper distance, it is necessary to engage in a process called defusion—once we are aware of our emotion and the accompanying thoughts, we are in direct contact with them ("I'm scared of this exam—my heart is beating fast, my neck muscles are tight, my stomach is queasy. I'm worried that I will forget everything I've learned and fail this test"). Most of us in a situation like this try to psychologically run from those experiences ("I need to stop feeling scared—if I can't get control of this fear, I am sure I will mess up the exam"). This focus, fear of failure, occupies consciousness, and if we are not able to practice detachment, our observing self loses the stance of observer and, instead, fuses with the experience. There's an important distinction between the experience itself and our observation of it (Hayes, Strosahl, & Wilson, 2012); this ability to observe thoughts and feelings in a detached manner is called defusion (Hayes & Shenk, 2004).

Herbert and Brandsma (2015) provide the example of someone who is so depressed he can't get out of bed. A typical behavior therapist will focus on action—give yourself a reward for getting out of bed, and you'll notice you'll feel better shortly thereafter. A traditional cognitive therapist would ask a client to consider the consequences of not getting out of bed, such as getting fired from a job. An additional faulty belief is that one would not be able to function at all if one is tired. In ACT, this thought is externalized and the question is raised as to whether it is relevant at all—one can get out of bed with these thoughts and feelings.

ACT also points out that the stereotyped ways we respond to fear, sadness, and feeling overwhelmed are variations on attempts to avoid these experiences (Hayes, Strosahl, & Wilson, 2012). Fear of failure is one of the underlying reasons for procrastination: "The project must be perfect; otherwise, I have failed." Perfection is a tall order, triggering anxiety that is managed by distraction with a less important activity.

However, ACT points out that trying to avoid the fear of failure only tends to intensify the fear. Similarly, trying to avoid the gradual increase in pain associated with a tension headache is likely to make the pain worse, since the observer has "fused" with the pain and given it power by focusing on avoiding it. Instead, proponents of ACT suggest that the individual become an observer of the pain or anxiety and examine these experiences from the point of view of a curious scientist ("Where is the pain in my head? Where am I feeling anxiety in my body?" "How bad is this discomfort on a scale from 1 to 10?" "What happens with the rest of my body when pain or anxiety tries to get hold of it?"). Research indicates that ACT has been effective in reducing patients' pain experience (Hughes, Clark, Colclough, Dale, & McMillan, 2017) as well as depression and improving quality of life (Glover et al., 2016).

Self-compassion, also a concept originally from Buddhism, provides another perspective on avoidance. Self-compassion refers to viewing oneself from the perspective of kindness, not engaging in self-blame when distressing situations arise, and recognizing failures as learning experiences that are part of being human (López, Sanderman, & Schroevers, 2016). Self-compassion also reduces the tendency to engage in avoidance of unpleasant experiences. There does appear to be an inverse association between self-compassion and avoidant coping styles. Persons who relied on avoidance as a means of managing stress and depressed moods were found to be lower on self-compassion (Krieger, Altenstein, Baettig, Doerig, & Holtforth, 2013).

Journaling: Writing to Manage Stress

Some readers may have experience in keeping a journal. Writing and reflecting upon one's experiences can actually be important for reducing stress and improving immune function. However, the approach to writing appears to play a major role in journaling's stress-reduction benefits. James Pennebaker and colleagues (Pennebaker, Kiecolt-Glaser, & Glaser, 1988) randomly assigned college students to write in a journal for four days in a row. One group was assigned to write about their shoes, while the other group was assigned the task of writing about a personal life trauma. In analyzing the completed journals, the focus of the trauma-related journal entries included the death of a loved one (27 percent); relationship breakups (20 percent); and major fights with a family member or friend (16 percent).

Initially, the trauma journal group showed increased negative mood and blood pressure. However, at 6 weeks and again at 4 months after completing the writing assignment, those who wrote about traumatic events were less likely to have fallen ill and reported fewer physical symptoms. Of particular interest were the number of visits to the campus health care center during that time. On average, the control group was slightly more likely to have health center contact than those writing about either their feelings about the trauma or the factual content of the trauma. However, the greatest reduction in health center visits was among the group of students whose journal writing both expressed their feelings and attributed meaning to the experience. The most effective approach to journaling involved enhanced self-understanding, as reflected in this comment: "It helped me think about what I felt during those times. I never realized how it affected me before" (Pennebaker & Smyth, 2016, p. 21). In other research, Pennebaker found that meaningful journaling was associated with improved immune functioning that was present up to 6 weeks after the study had ended (Pennebaker & Smyth, 2016).

Positive Psychology

Background

Positive psychology is based upon a perspective that is distinctly different from traditional stress management. Instead of developing approaches to reducing negative emotions, distorted cognitions, and physiological reactivity, positive psychology focuses on increasing life satisfaction, meaning, and happiness (Seligman, Steen, Park, & Peterson, 2005). Research on the rising incidence of depression—particularly in developing countries—suggests that by 2020 major depressive disorder will likely be the third most common chronic disease worldwide. Given the large population of individuals anticipated to develop major depressive disorder, individual treatment will not be adequate to address the surging need. Rather than reducing anxiety and depression through various self- or therapist-directed interventions, the positive psychology movement has argued that we can increase the incidence of an incompatible response—namely happiness.

While we often think of happiness as stemming from experiences of pleasure, such as eating our favorite food or lounging in a hot tub on vacation, this positive feeling is unlikely to be enduring (Seligman et al., 2005). Happiness of a more meaningful type, called eudaimonia, is generally associated with deeper life satisfaction (Huta & Waterman, 2014). For example, once basic needs for food, shelter, and so on are met, a higher income is not associated with greater life satisfaction. Research on lottery winners indicates that they return to their pre-lottery-winning levels of happiness within a year. We have also been led to believe that having more choices leads to greater life satisfaction and happiness. Research indicates that more choices, such as a greater number of flavors of ice cream to sample, decreases happiness (Schwartz, 2015). Individuals who are called "maximizers" often have the most difficulty with the aftermath of decisions—primarily because of the regret accompanying second-guessing their choices. Maximizers place a strong value on making the absolute best decision. However, satisfiers are basically accepting of their decisions and do not spend a lot of time second-guessing themselves; as a result, they experience minimal regret (Schwartz, 2015).

Positive psychology also focuses on educational interventions. Adherents of this approach believe that beginning in early childhood, we can be inoculated against developing psychological disorders by cultivating resilience (Seligman, Ernst, Gillham, Reivich, & Linkins, 2009). One aspect of resilience is recognizing and developing one's signature strengths. A meaningful, satisfying life typically comes from being able to use these signature strengths toward something outside of ourselves, such as family, community, or a career. Pursuing eudaimonia has been found to be associated with lower levels of cortisol, reduced cardiovascular risk, and better-quality sleep (Ryff, Singer, & Love, 2004).

Positive Psychology Interventions

Seligman and his colleagues in positive psychology have developed specific interventions that are associated with greater life satisfaction and happiness. Positive psychology interventions may focus upon highlighting individual strengths, understanding, developing character traits, and expressing gratitude and appropriate forgiveness to others (Bolier et al., 2013; Seligman et al., 2005).

One activity is deliberately recognizing positive daily life experiences. When we are confronted with multiple demands of work, school, and family, the rewarding aspects of life sometimes are glossed over. In order to emphasize and recognize these, it is recommended that a spreadsheet or notebook be kept, and, toward the end of the day, a log of the day's events should be entered. In addition, each day should receive a rating from 1 ("one of the worst days of my life") to 10 ("one of the best days of my life"). After completing this exercise for 2 to 4 weeks, review the log and pay attention to the events associated with "good days." Then make a deliberate effort to increase the frequency of these activities. Often, actions that are part of "good days" have a social component such as calling a friend, helping someone with their homework, or simply spending time with family (Seligman et al., 2005).

Another reflective technique is called "You at your best." Most of us have days or episodes in our life that reflect our best possible self. In order to capture these experiences, it is helpful to keep a journal or diary and note which personal strengths were being used at that time when we were at our best. It is possible that your compassion and sensitivity to others and being a good listener characterize "you at your best," or it could be accomplishing a task that resulted in recognition or making a meaningful contribution to an organization of which you are a part. Research, to date, suggests that "you at your best" is the intervention that is most likely to be continued by participants after the experimental study period ends (Seligman et al., 2005).

Expressions of gratitude appear to be a particularly powerful intervention. It has been suggested that these expressions be done systematically by writing a letter to someone who has made a major impact on your life but has not been properly thanked. When possible, it is important to deliver the letter in person and even to read it to the recipient and give them a copy (Seligman et al., 2005). At the physiological level there is evidence that heart rhythms become more regularized when expressing gratitude versus frustration.

Being able to forgive is a complex process and far more difficult than simply increasing our sense of self-worth and confidence. Genuine forgiveness includes a conscious effort as well as disengaging from the anger, fear, frustration, and resentment that we often carry around after some insult or infraction from another (Toussaint, Worthington, & Williams, 2015). The ability to disengage from these negative feelings appears to be associated with significant improvement in well-being. There is also considerable evidence that holding onto grudges and being unforgiving may be associated with increased physical illness, anxiety, and depression (Toussaint et al., 2015).

A recent meta-analytic review suggested that positive psychology interventions demonstrate small, yet significant, effects for reducing depression and improving subjective well-being (Bolier et al., 2013). The majority of studies to date have been carried out in general populations, often with college students, rather than in clinical populations. Among the most researched interventions are performing acts of kindness, writing about positive experiences, and practicing gratitude, as well as using signature strengths (Bolier et al., 2013).

At present, the research evidence supporting some of these positive psychology interventions is modest at best. It is likely that in the future these interventions will be refined through isolation and amplification of their active components. Additionally, the general thrust of positive psychology, building resilience, and being proactive, rather than developing strategies to react to stress with less intensity, has rapidly become well established.

Conclusion

Stress is one of the most common topics in introductory psychology and health psychology. While stress is not the same as mental illness, it certainly contributes to psychological disorders. Research indicates that as college and university students, you are likely experiencing frequent periods of feeling overwhelmed and having difficulty relaxing. If dimensions such as controllability, perfectionism, time urgency, and procrastination are contributing to your stress level, it may be helpful to examine the reasons behind such strong influence. Stress management techniques such as meditation, progressive relaxation, and the positive psychology interventions described in this chapter are ones that can be readily applied to your life and do not necessarily have to take a good deal of time. Several other topics discussed in future chapters, such as sleep, diet, and exercise, are particularly helpful in maintaining health and reducing anxiety.

CHAPTER 8

Chronic Pain as a Psychosocial Condition
Causes, Consequences, and Treatment

If you've ever had a bad toothache, you know how disruptive pain can be. It is a terrible, helpless feeling, and it becomes difficult to pay attention to anything else other than the throbbing that is going on in your mouth. Other types of pain hit us in bursts and sometimes at unpredictable times. The onset of migraine—with the nausea, extreme sensitivity to light, and pulsating pain in your forehead—can become so incapacitating that you cannot do anything else except go to a dark room, lie down, and try to sleep so it goes away. However, there are times when we have at least been temporarily successful in ignoring pain. Many of you who are high school or collegiate athletes have probably sustained an injury during the course of a basketball, football, or volleyball game and "played through it." Once the game was over, and you looked at your swollen, throbbing ankle, the pain became all too real.

In this chapter we are not going to focus much on acute pain because it generally resolves on its own. However, chronic pain is a major problem in the industrialized world and a significant source of disability and absence from work. Chronic pain can exist in the absence of an injury and even without any type of apparent tissue damage. In talking about chronic pain with students, the response I get is that patients often make up their reports of pain and those with ongoing chronic pain are "hypochondriacs." I want to emphatically make the case that this is not true. While there are malingerers—patients who fake having symptoms to obtain disability payments or time off of work—patients with chronic pain conditions do indeed experience pain even in the absence of a broken bone or pulled muscle. The medical community began to recognize this aspect of pain approximately 40 to 50 years ago. Since that time, psychologists and other behavioral scientists have been active members of clinical pain management teams. Given the increase in chronic pain in Western countries over recent decades, the involvement of behavioral scientists in this field is only likely to increase. However, pain and its treatment have also become the source of political debate.

Pain Defined

Pain is one of the most common reasons people seek medical care. About 80 percent of all physician office visits in the United States are associated with pain. It is estimated that between 11 and 12 million Americans are substantially impaired by pain, and between two and three million are completely disabled by chronic pain (Gatchel, 2005).

The International Association for the Study of Pain provides a useful definition: "An unpleasant sensory and emotional experience associated with actual or potential tissue damage or described in terms of such damage" (Merskey, 1994).

When Does Pain Become Chronic?

Most of us have experienced acute pain. You spent a weekend helping a friend move—two days of lifting multiple boxes, appliances, and furniture. Upon awakening Monday morning, you feel stiff and your lower back is incredibly sore. While unpleasant, you typically are able to carry out most of your regular duties. During the course of the week, your back gets better, and 10 days later, you do not notice any pain at all. Acute pain usually resolves on its own and, by definition, lasts less than 3 months.

While your pain resolved, the experience of those with chronic pain is that the pain never resolves or gets worse. While back pain may have begun with a period of heavy lifting, in order to be considered chronic, the pain must continue for at least 3 months after its onset. Some definitions of chronic pain delay the use of the label "chronic" until the pain has been present for 6 months. Some studies have suggested that up to half the population experiences chronic pain by the 3-month definition. Within this group, 10 to 30 percent report clinically significant chronic pain (Carley et al., 2015; Johannes, Le, Zhou, Johnston, & Dworkin, 2010). With either time frame—3 or 6 months—chronic pain is present every day and disrupts the person's lifestyle, including the ability to work productively and be an active, participating member of the family. Pain conditions are also expensive. Gaskin and Richard (2012) estimated that the expense of treating pain is $261 billion to $300 billion annually. When adding in the pain-related cost to society, such as diminished productivity and lost work hours, the cost rises to between $560 billion and $635 billion (Gaskin & Richard, 2012).

Chronic Pain—A Brief History

One of the results of Renaissance science in the 1600s was the rupture between the mind and the body. Hippocrates, the ancient Greek philosopher-scientist who is often considered the founder of modern medicine, was holistic in his orientation and described how physical processes influenced behavior. However, Renaissance medicine and philosophy established biomedical reductionism (Gatchel, 2005) and split the domains of mind and body. René Descartes was probably the most ardent adherent of this dualistic worldview and argued that the physical or somatic world and the mind were completely different domains and did not affect one another.

Descartes viewed pain as a series of physical events. From his perspective, the skin—when it is exposed to flame—initiates activity in the hand that is transmitted to the brain; once received by the central nervous system, motor activity is initiated and the hand pulls away (Gatchel, 2005). This physical chain of events did not allow for psychological or environmental influences for pain. Interpretation of the pain or others' responses to the individual in pain were not considered relevant in the Cartesian worldview.

During the late 1800s and early 1900s, somewhat more sophisticated models of pain preserved the idea of physical pain sensors in the skin transmitting signals directly to the brain. Von Fry posited the existence of different types of sensory receptors in the skin, with specific receptors responsible for temperature, pressure, and pain (Gatchel, 2005). A view that is somewhat closer to contemporary models of pain is that of Goldschneider, who described patterns of nerve impulses that are coded and in turn interpreted by the brain as pain (Gatchel, 2005).

In the mid-1960s, there were two competing models of pain. Skinner's operant behavioral view had become increasingly influential in the mental health field. His view that behavior was a function of its consequences was incorporated into Fordyce's operant view—a black box behavioral perspective on pain (Fordyce et al., 1973). Gate control theory, developed by Melzack and Wall (1965), integrated sensory and anatomical aspects of pain with cognitive and emotional dimensions. While reformulated from the original gate control conceptualization from the mid-1960s, this model continues to be a commonly employed explanation of pain.

Pain is one of the most common symptoms brought to primary care physicians. A common problem in evaluating pain is that the majority of cases do not have a clear-cut cause. Again, this is not to say that the patient is not genuinely experiencing pain. However, pain is often present in the absence of any current orthopedic, muscular, or skin abnormality.

Common Pain-Related Disorders

Fibromyalgia

With a prevalence rate of 2 to 4 percent in the general population, fibromyalgia is characterized by pain and sensitivity to pressure that typically affects multiple areas of the body. Additionally, persons with this condition often experience significant daytime fatigue and sleep problems. Historically, the condition has been diagnosed based upon a specific number of "tender points" out of a total of 18 different body sites. Patients with this condition will not find sleep refreshing and have cognitive problems with short-term memory and concentration that may be fatigue-related. Symptoms typically last for at least 3 months and are constant during that time (Wolfe, 1989). The condition has been treated primarily by rheumatologists. However, the cause and, to some extent, the definition of fibromyalgia have been controversial. While a consistent cause has not been established, many people do develop the condition after a viral illness or the development of surgical complications. Recently three genes were found that appear to predispose people to fibromyalgia. A serotonin transporter gene seems to be involved with heightened sensitivity to the sensory input and decreased central nervous system inhibition of pain (Offenbaecher et al., 1999). However, this gene (5-HTT) also appears to be common in major depressive disorder and irritable bowel syndrome. Mental health conditions are common among persons with fibromyalgia. Major depressive disorder has been found in more than 60 percent of fibromyalgia patients, and anxiety disorders—including panic disorder, social anxiety disorder, and posttraumatic stress disorder—are present in approximately 20 percent of patients with fibromyalgia (Binkiewicz-Glińska et al., 2015).

Low Back Pain

The most common pain disorder in the United States is lower back pain, with an estimated prevalence of about 3 to 4 percent of the general population. This condition is responsible for a large number of lost workdays and is one of the most common reasons for seeking workmen's compensation. While the US population increased by 12 percent between 1970 and 1990, the number of people with lower back pain increased by 168 percent during the same period (Gatchel, 2005).

Among America's labor force, approximately 2 percent of workers are essentially disabled by the condition. Lower back pain is responsible for approximately one-third of all lost workdays in the United States. The peak age for chronic low back pain is between ages 20 and 40. Certain demographic factors are associated with the condition, including lower income and lower levels of education (Rustøen et al., 2004). In terms of gender, chronic low back pain is equally represented among men and women until about age 60, when women are more likely to have chronic pain (Andersson, 1999). Being overweight is another risk factor for low back pain. Since a significant number of back injuries initially occur on the job, lower back pain is one of the more common diagnoses for persons receiving workmen's compensation and for those seeking long-term disability payments. Research suggests that when present for at least a year, the condition remains stable up to 25 years (Itz, Willems, Zeilstra, & Huygen, 2016).

Lower back pain illustrates one of the key dilemmas in evaluating and treating chronic pain conditions. A classic study examined persons with and without back pain symptoms and found a significant number of people with no symptoms showing evidence of herniated discs on an imaging study such as a CT scan or X-ray. This finding has been repeatedly replicated, and in fact disc hernias appear to be about as common among those without back pain as those with lower back dysfunction (Deyo, Loeser, & Bigos, 1990). Similarly, no specific pattern of musculoskeletal abnormality has been found to be associated with back pain (Dahl, Wilson, & Nilsson, 2004).

Only a small percentage—20 percent at most—of cases of chronic low back pain are associated with verifiable physical pathology. In addition, abnormalities of the lower back (slipped discs) are often found among people with absolutely no symptoms. There is also no consistent association between X-ray findings and physical exam findings among lower back pain patients and the patients' reports of pain or level of disability. The common pattern of the onset of chronic lower back pain is for someone to have a musculoskeletal injury, often due to heavy lifting or a fall. While the musculoskeletal damage heals, the pain does not resolve.

Headache

Tension and migraine headaches are the second and third most common medical conditions worldwide. Tension headaches have a characteristic pattern—there must be an average of 10 episodes, occurring 1 to 14 days per month, for an average of 3 months (Smitherman, Penzien, Rains, Nicholson, & Houle, 2015). The duration of tension headaches is widely variable, ranging from 30 minutes to 7 days. Specific symptoms include location on both sides of the head, a pressing tight band–type quality, mild to moderate intensity, and not aggravated by physical activities such as walking or running. Nausea and vomiting are generally absent, as is sensitivity to light and sound (Smitherman et al., 2015). Tension headaches are slightly more common among women, with a sex ratio of 5:4, females to males.

By contrast, migraine headaches may occur with or without unusual visual experiences—spots of light or "fortification illusions," which are a zigzag pattern of lines that appear to be at the top of a wall (Richards, 1971). In medieval times, it was believed that these experiences, termed "auras," had spiritual and mystical significance.

Auras typically last less than an hour and are indicators that a headache will soon follow. However, while distinctive and dramatic, only about a third of migraine sufferers report having an aura. Migraine episodes last between 4 and 72 hours. Symptoms include a pulsating experience of moderate to severe intensity that occurs on one side of the head. The headaches are made worse by physical activities, and during the time of the headache there is nausea and vomiting as well as sensitivity to light and sound. Migraine affects about 12 percent of Americans per year and about 30 percent of Americans during their lifetime (Smitherman et al., 2015). Women are three times as likely to have migraine as men. While migraines may have their onset in late childhood or adolescence, the peak prevalence developmentally is between the ages of 30 and 39 (Smitherman et al., 2015). Migraine is a major cause of disability in the world. The typical person with migraine will have up to four days of headaches per month. Because of the severity of migraine headaches, there is often a need for bed rest and greatly restricted activity.

Among those who develop chronic headache, medication overuse is a significant precipitant (Abrams, 2013). The diagnosis of medication overuse headache is applied when someone has experienced 15 or more headache days per month and has used acute migraine medication or opioids at least 10 days per month.

While it is no longer accepted that migraine is a psychosomatic condition, as was the case in the past, prevalence rates of both major depressive disorder and anxiety disorder are significantly higher among those with migraine. Lifetime prevalence of major depressive disorder among those with migraine may be up to three times higher than in the general population (Breslau et al., 2000), and if one has either condition, the risk of having the other condition is elevated (Breslau, Lipton, Stewart, Schultz, & Welch, 2003). Therefore, depression may predate the onset of a headache condition—this is particularly true for chronic tension headaches. The second most common conditions are specific anxiety disorders, with anxiety overall more common than depression—particularly among those with migraine (Smitherman et al., 2015; Zwart et al., 2003). The observation that mood and anxiety disorders and migraine are bidirectional suggests that there may be some common causal mechanism. Triptans, a class of medications often used to treat migraines, act upon the serotonin neurotransmitter system, which is also involved in depression.

While direct causal relationships are difficult to determine, patients often report there are triggers for their migraine headaches. Common triggers include menstruation, change in dietary habits, and sleep disturbance—either too much sleep or inadequate sleep. Although changes in weather, odors such as strong perfume, and loud noise have been reported by many patients, research does not consistently indicate these as migraine triggers.

Cancer

Pain is common in multiple types of cancer. It is estimated that 50 to 70 percent of patients with cancer will experience pain. Patients with cancer-related pain report greater anxiety about increased pain than about the disease itself (Gutgsell, Walsh, Zhukovsky, Gonzales, & Lagman, 2003). Cancer may also spread to other areas of the body—a process called "metastasizing." Cancer pain may stem from the illness but also its treatment, with close to 60 percent of cancer patients undergoing treatment reporting pain (Gutgsell et al., 2003). In patients with advanced cancers, physicians are often presented with the dilemma that treating the patient's pain with opioid medication will bring some relief; however, opioid medication also has side effects in higher dosages, which include heavy sedation and decreased respiration rate. When pain is present in terminal illness, which is the case in an estimated 50 percent of the terminally ill (Weiss, Emanuel, Fairclough, & Emanuel, 2001), the goals of treatment are often palliative—reducing physical discomfort while maintaining their ability to interact with others and less concern with addiction.

Explanations of Chronic Pain

Operant Model

Wilbert Fordyce (Fordyce, Fowler, Lehmann, & Delateur, 1968; Fordyce et al., 1973) developed a treatment approach to chronic pain based upon operant learning principles. While Fordyce does recognize the possible role of pain receptors in the skin and central nervous system, his model, like B. F. Skinner's view that our internal experiences are not able to be objectively evaluated, de-emphasizes the subjective experience of pain. The central principle of the operant modes is that behavior is under the control of the environment (Fordyce, Shelton & Dundore, 1982). Environmental factors can increase or decrease the frequency of behavior. In the operant view, pain behavior is directly observable and measurable.

Some examples of directly observable behavior include physical bracing or a stiffening of the torso when movement is initiated, talking about the pain, and reduction of activity and spending time in passive activities such as watching television rather than interacting with spouse or children. Pain behavior has become associated with not returning to an unpleasant job and/or receipt of compensation through workmen's compensation or disability payments. During the time frame between 3 and 6 months after the original injury, pain behaviors come to be governed by these environmental contingencies. The phrase that is often used to describe these "rewards" of illness is *secondary gain*. The term *secondary gain* comes from Freudian theory. If an individual develops a conversion symptom, such as paralysis of the hand, in response to some significant stressful life event, the primary gain is that, because of the symptom, the patient is temporarily relieved from experiencing the emotional distress associated with the traumatic event. Secondary gain occurs when the patient receives social and/or environmental reinforcement for their symptoms. Secondary gain may take the form of workmen's compensation, attention from high-status medical personnel, and a reduction in expectations for the patient to participate in family chores or to interact with and discipline children. When secondary gain becomes established, it becomes very difficult to make behavior changes.

Pain behavior can be measured and modified. The behavioral model applies principles to reducing pain behavior, but the issue of whether the patient actually experiences more or less pain as a result of intentional changes in pattern reinforcement is sidestepped. Fordyce et al. (1982; 1984) present data for patients with cancer-related pain in which hospital nurses were trained in the operant model. When a patient reported pain (either through contacting the nurse in the hospital using the call button or when a nurse checked on a patient as part of their daily routine), if the patient verbalized the pain, the nurse would briefly check to determine whether anything serious was present. If it was not, the nurse would not interact further with the patient. However, if the patient verbalized non-pain content, the nurse would interact with them socially. Over time, pain-related verbalizations declined (Fordyce et al., 1982; 1984). Did these patients generally experience a reduction in pain, or did only their behavior change? From the black box behavioral point of view, behavioral change is the equivalent of a decline in pain.

Cognitive Perspectives

The experience of pain is also strongly influenced by the meaning that we attribute to it. As a physician during World War II, Beecher treated a number of seriously wounded soldiers. In his judgment, about half reported being in moderate or severe pain. However, only about a third of these patients would take medication when offered. In contrast, in a civilian population, 75 percent of those undergoing surgery reported being in significant pain, and more than 80 percent wanted to take medication for it. Beecher argued that for soldiers, the injury meant the end of their involvement in the war and their return home. Those undergoing surgery were likely to be anxious since they were about to undergo an event that would significantly change their lives (Abraham, Conner, Jones, & O'Connor, 2016; Beecher, 1956).

Even lower-level cognitive processes, such as attention, influence the experience of pain. Virtual reality scenes—particularly those that are interactive—have consistently been shown to be associated with reduced self-reported pain in experimental laboratory conditions (Malloy & Milling, 2010). In addition, interactive video games have been used to engage and distract burn victims when they are having their dressings changed. Changing the dressings for serious burns is a very painful experience. An immersive virtual reality video game, Snow World, in which the player is in a snow-covered region throwing snowballs at penguins, appears to reduce the pain when dressings are changed. While large-sample studies have not been conducted, Snow World's ability to engage patients' attention appears to successfully distract them from pain. Some investigators have found that there are corresponding patterns of brain activity as measured through functional MRIs associated with this temporary pain relief via immersive distraction (Wiederhold & Wiederhold, 2007).

Catastrophization—a common cognitive error seen in persons with anxiety and depression—also appears to be strongly associated with impaired functioning among persons with chronic pain ("Once this pain comes on I can't do anything; my whole life is going to be nothing but pain!"). There are a number of cognitive errors or distortions that characterize the thinking of pain patients. For example, some patients overgeneralize and believe that pain will become a stable part of their life, will lead to an inability to enjoy anything, and will set a life course devoid of satisfaction. Particularly when pain arises from a work-related injury, there may also be a theme of victimization ("It isn't fair that they did this to me") (Straub, 2016). This is also a common theme for those who have unsuccessful back surgeries.

A common misconception among those with chronic pain conditions is that they need to limit their physical activity and that physical activity exacerbates pain. As patients become less active they become physically deconditioned. This deconditioning leaves individuals feeling tired and "too exhausted to do anything." In reality, physical activity will often reduce the patient's pain experience and provide more energy.

Another aspect of catastrophization deals with the sensation of pain itself. The amount of distress actually caused by the pain is overestimated or exaggerated (Burns, Kubilus, Bruehl, Harden, & Lofland, 2003). Researchers have found that those who catastrophize also tend to engage in rumination—a process of preoccupation and ongoing worry about pain that is experienced as uncontrollable (Eccleston & Crombez, 2007). Rumination involves a search for a cause and often a corresponding plan of action. However, in the case of chronic pain, this search is unproductive and does not lead to problem resolution but, instead, triggers a circular, escalating pattern of cognitive rehearsal (Reynolds, Searight, & Ratwik, 2014).

Patients with chronic pain also tend to magnify the significance of the pain and its implications for their overall health and experience helplessness—a complete loss of control over one's life. Persons who catastrophize report greater pain for a longer period after surgery—specifically, catastrophization predicts the development of pain or its increased severity after undergoing surgery (Burns et al., 2015). This cognitive style, in turn, is predictive of poor functional outcomes.

Gatchel (2005) notes that anger may be associated with ongoing pain. This negative affect may emerge as distrust of one's employers if the pain resulted from a work-based injury. This anger and distrust may also extend to the insurance and health care systems—making patient adherence significantly less likely. This hostility may even intensify after undergoing surgery that does not alleviate the patient's pain. Kerns, Rosenberg, and Jacob (1994) found that internalized anger was strongly associated with reported intensity of pain.

Gate Control Model

Another theory of pain developed around the same time as the operant approach is the gate control model of Melzack and Wall (1965). Gate control theory includes attention to psychological variables such as feelings, thoughts, and behaviors and their influence on experienced pain. This explanatory model, while later requiring some revision, recognizes the role of emotion, thought, and even environmental influences on an individual's subjective experience of pain. The type, intensity, duration, and disruption of functioning are influenced by factors other than the level of tissue damage alone. Importantly, Melzack and Wall's conceptualization challenges the concept of "objective pain." Since there were multiple factors that could contribute to pain, patients' reports were considered a valid representation of their reality. While some of the physiological and anatomical factors involved in the pain gate as described by Melzack and Wall (1965) have been disputed, the model is very helpful in explaining how psychological and social factors play a role in patients' pain experience.

Pain occurs when tissue damage such as a burn or cut triggers chemical activity at the site of the injury. Pain receptors, called "nociceptors," are associated with two types of nerve fibers: a-Delta, which transmit impulses quickly, and c-Delta fibers, which transmit more slowly. The a-Delta fibers transmit directly to the motor and sensory areas of the brain, while the c-Delta fibers transmit to the brain stem and forebrain. Pain associated with activation of the a-Delta fibers is experienced as intense and often "stabbing" or "sharp," while the type of pain associated with the c-Delta fibers is a "dull ache" (Melzack & Wall, 1965). Nociception involves chemical, mechanical, or thermal stimulation corresponding to some injury or other aversive event. Over time, the pain receptors can become hypersensitive as a result of "priming" (Kandasamy & Price, 2015). After the initial stimulation resolves, subthreshold stimulation will lead to the experience of pain. This sensitivity to subthreshold pain appears to be a key distinguishing factor between persons with chronic pain syndrome compared with those who do not have this conditioned hypersensitivity. Those who do not develop chronic pain did not experience this stimulation as pain. Over time, even the thought of initiating activities that have in the past been uncomfortable will trigger pain. For example, for someone with chronic shoulder pain, simply looking up and thinking about reaching for something on an upper shelf may trigger pain. As pain receptors become hypersensitive, corresponding regions of the body may become inflamed (Pergolizzi et al., 2009).

Gate control theory is based on the principle that there is a gating mechanism in the dorsal horn of the spinal cord. The a-Delta and c-Delta fibers carrying stimulation from nociceptors transmit signals to the dorsal horn of the spinal column. There is no physical gate; the gate is actually a set of physiological processes. The presence and intensity of the pain signal depend upon whether the gate is open or closed. Multiple factors, such as signals from the nerve fibers, can control the pain gate.

Descending signals from the brain also open the pain gate. Influences such as attention, cognitive interpretation of the pain, and emotional experiences such as depression, anger, and anxiety can all open the pain gate.

Gatchel (2005) adds additional factors that can impact the pain experience, such as inadequate nutrition, lack of exercise, poor sleep, smoking, and a sedentary lifestyle. While the neuroanatomical and physiological aspects of gate control theory have been challenged, the model is very helpful in that it links environmental, cognitive, emotional, and physical experiences to pain and recognizes that these experiences can amplify pain and, by implication, if addressed, can reduce pain intensity.

The gate control model also recognizes that pain can exist without an injury such as a muscle strain, burn, or a broken bone. A dramatic example that is consistent with gate control theory is the phenomenon of phantom limb pain. After having a limb amputated, many patients experience intense pain in the region where their limb was prior to amputation. The gate control model suggests that the region of the brain associated with the now nonexistent limb maintains a neural representation of the absent limb (Nikolajsen & Christensen, 2015). A type of therapy done with mirrors or virtual reality in which the patient's amputated limb is visually "replaced" with a virtual or perceived limb seems to be associated with reductions in pain (Murray et al., 2007).

Gate control theory also explains how social factors such as reinforcement from others or reinforcement from avoiding an unsatisfactory work experience can play a role in patients' pain experience. As a clinical psychologist who has worked with pain patients, I have found the gate control model to be particularly helpful as an explanation to patients of their experience. Many patients with chronic pain are sensitive to any implication that their pain may be "psychosomatic" or "all in their head." By describing the involvement of neurophysiological processes in lay language, as well as pointing out to patients how factors such as mood, attention, and activity can influence pain, there is often greater receptiveness to psychological and behavioral intervention.

Neuromatrix Model

Building upon gate control theory, the neuromatrix model views pain as a multi-dimensional process. Pain is produced by a network of nerve impulses that may be triggered by nociception via external stimuli such as fire or a sharp object but also through central nervous system patterns. The neuromatrix model explains how pain may persist after an injury is healed. The brain continues to exhibit patterns of activity that are associated with the experience of pain. That same pattern of nervous system activity may also be triggered or amplified by environmental stressors—particularly external cues that were previously associated with the injury. The neuromatrix is believed to have genetic origins but is also modifiable through sensory experiences (Melzack, 2001).

Recently, the model was further revised. In this revised model, there are networks of neurons throughout the body that contribute to our experience of the unified physical self. The pain experience is constructed from sensory, emotional, and cognitive dimensions. In the matrix, pain can be triggered by external stimulation as well as a recurring pattern of neural transmission. Melzack (2001) uses the term "neurosignature" to describe this pattern.

The neuromatrix perspective also includes attention to the "fight-or-flight response." In reaction to the array of neural signals associated with pain, the sympathetic nervous system is activated or, in many cases, may be chronically aroused. The anticipation of pain will activate a subcortical chain of events that results in prolonged release of the stress-related hormone cortisol. To ensure that there is adequate glucose to support the increased release of cortisol under stress, protein will become less available to the muscles, and inhibition of calcium replacement may occur. Together, these factors are associated with the type of muscle and joint pain that is characteristic of fibromyalgia. The sustained sympathetic nervous activity also may lead to the experience of pain diffusion-discomfort beginning at a site such as the lower back and spreading into the neck and shoulders.

Both gate control and the more dynamic neuromatrix model are helpful in that they explain how conditions such as major depressive disorder, life stressors, and behavioral patterns such as reduced physical activity can amplify pain experience.

Pain as a Social Metaphor

As is evident by this point, pain does not exist in a social vacuum. Describing relationships that are in distress and turmoil with the term "pain" has been a literary strategy used to make ephemeral emotional states into a more concrete experience to engage the reader. The family therapist Jay Haley (1987) comments on how, when used metaphorically, pain can be a signal to a partner to lower their expectations as well as a commentary on their relationship quality. Imagine a situation in which a married couple is sitting together in their living room at about 10 p.m. The husband rises from his easy chair and says, "I'm ready for bed." His wife says, "Yes, I should get to bed, too, but I am having this awful headache." Haley (1987) suggests that there is more going on here than nociception and neuromatrices. In addition to directing her husband to avoid initiating physical intimacy, she may be metaphorically saying, "This is a painful relationship."

Poets and songwriters often use the term "pain" as the equivalent of emotional distress. As Haley suggests, this emotional distress is often related to intimate conflict. In looking back at an unhealthy relationship, it's not uncommon for people to say, "That was a painful relationship." We also talk about the pain of being rejected when someone ends a romantic relationship: "When she broke up with me, it was so devastating, so *painful*, I thought I would never get over it." When someone close to us forgets our birthday or criticizes us, we often will say that the person "hurt" our feelings.

Research conducted over the past 20 years suggests that the pain of rejection actually bears a number of physiological similarities to physical pain resulting from an injury. Functional MRI studies that examine patterns of brain activity demonstrate that the sensory component of pain is the same for rejection by romantic partner as it is for physical pain. The secondary somatosensory cortex and dorsal posterior insula region of the brain have been shown to become activated in a similar manner for physical pain as well as for the experience of social rejection. A common stimulus used for social rejection is to ask individuals to vividly remember an unwanted breakup. The experience is further amplified by having the participant view a picture of their ex–romantic partner while brain activity is recorded (Kross, Berman, Mischel, Smith, & Wager, 2011). This consistent pattern of finding these similarities gives "new meaning to the idea that social rejection 'hurts'" (Kross et al., 2011, p. 6273). Further support for this perspective comes from studies in which participants who took a centrally acting analgesic (acetaminophen) reported declines in social pain compared with a group that also experienced social pain but were given a placebo (DeWall et al., 2010). While speculative, some clinicians note that among some patients with chronic pain, the onset appears to be associated with loss of a job or relationship—both forms of social rejection (Pollock, 1961).

Pain and the Workplace

The addition of a systems perspective, in which gate control and/or neural matrix explanations are embedded in the pain sufferer's life context, provides an account of how social and environmental factors—ranging from marital conflict to ongoing litigation surrounding an injury that initiated the pain—may also influence pain experience. According to the communal coping model, verbal statements of pain (catastrophization) may lead to sympathy from others as well as social support (Sullivan et al., 2001).

As noted in the discussion of lower back pain, many injuries that begin the chronic pain trajectory occur in the workplace. When compared with non-chronic pain controls, persons with ongoing lower back pain have fewer years of formal education—making it difficult to secure alternative employment. For persons feeling overwhelmed in their roles in the workplace, chronic pain can eventually serve as the basis for financial subsidies such as workmen's compensation or Supplemental Security Income (SSI), which often plays a role in reinforcing pain behavior.

Because of the ambiguity inherent in low back pain, there may be difficulty acquiring compensation through workmen's compensation or related sources. As a result, litigation is often initiated to obtain either a settlement from the workplace for injury associated with hazards in that setting or workmen's compensation. There is some debate about the role that ongoing litigation plays in patients' reported pain and functional status. One of the results of chronic pain is unemployment. Unemployment, in turn, often reduces social contact and feelings of confidence, and it increases family distress around finances. Loss of one's job due to pain triggers a ripple effect throughout the patient's life. This ripple effect, in turn, may solidify their identity as a pain patient, and it may further amplify the stress associated with being unable to work, causing marital conflict, financial problems, and so on.

Cross-Cultural Aspects of Pain

Still considered a classic in medical anthropology, Zborowski (1952) described differences in responses to pain among several ethnic and cultural groups. In his examination of Italian, Jewish, Irish, and Anglo Americans ("Old Americans"—typically White and Protestant), Zborowski concluded that culture plays a role in attitudes and expression of pain.

By today's standards, Zborowski is certainly guilty of stereotyping. He characterized Jewish and Italian patients as particularly sensitive to pain and as "exaggerating" its intensity. In the clinic and hospital settings, members of both ethnic groups were outwardly emotional; however, at home, Italian pain patients exhibited authority and were focused on the discomfort and desire to relieve pain. In contrast, Jewish patients, according to Zborowski (1952), focused more on the meaning of the pain. Analgesic medication was much more acceptable to the Italian patients and less acceptable to the Jewish patients because of concerns about addiction. American patients of British background were much more restrained in their expression and focused on providing factual information to health care personnel; they downplayed pain, which they endured with stoicism. A similar study by Zola (1966) included Irish American patients. Zborowski's (1952) earlier descriptions of Italian and Anglo-American patients were generally supported. Zola (1966) described Irish patients as engaging in stoic denial of their symptoms and not even recognizing pain (Cockerham, 2015). Contemporary medical anthropologists have been critical of Zola and Zborowski for presenting what may be considered ethnic stereotypes. However, it is likely that culture does play a role in expressing and experiencing pain, although there is likely to be a good deal of individual variation within an ethnic community.

The meaning of pain and coping styles can play a major role in how pain is experienced. Recent research suggests that even at the neural level, the meaning associated with pain can alter patterns of brain activation. In a study using functional magnetic resonance imaging (fMRI) to assess experienced pain intensity, a small group of practicing Catholics were compared with a group of nonreligious individuals in their response to painful electric stimulation (Dedeli & Kaptan, 2013; Wiech & Tracey, 2009). Both groups were shown pictures of the Virgin Mary or an unknown woman while receiving the painful shocks. The religious group reported significantly less pain when viewing pictures of the Virgin Mary, while the nonreligious group's reports of pain did not vary according to the picture. Brain imaging procedures indicated that the right ventrolateral prefrontal cortex was activated among the religious group when they were viewing the Virgin Mary. This differential activation pattern did not occur in the nonreligious group. This brain region is involved in inhibitory activity; the authors suggest that when contemplating the picture of the Virgin Mary, religious individuals were able to detach from the pain experience (Wiech & Tracey, 2009).

In India, during the Hindu festival of Thaipusam, some individuals pierce their cheeks, chest, and back with multiple spears. Research indicates that individuals participating in these rituals report low pain intensity. Most individuals engage in some type of meditative practice while engaging in these painful activities and exhibit evidence of dissociation or depersonalization (Jegindø, Vase, Jegindø, & Geertz, 2013). The state of detachment is often a desired goal, and the experience of pain can be embraced as part of one's spiritual path toward a state of inner peace. Rather than trying to engage in the avoidance and reduction of pain, acceptance, rather than struggling to change the experience of pain, is desirable (Whitman, 2007).

Among indigenous groups in North America, the Sun Dance is a common healing ritual that, by most standards, involves considerable pain (Searfoss, 2013). In some instances, the Sun Dance involves piercing the skin. Young men are tethered to a pole and dance while attached by rawhide tags that are pierced through the skin.

The Macrosystem: The Politics of Chronic Pain and Its Treatment

Pain, the Work Ethic, and the Politics of Disability

Chronic pain has been a political issue since World War II. The politics of pain reflect values surrounding the American work ethic, views of personal responsibility, and the role of government in supporting persons who, because of illness, are not productively employed (Wailoo, 2014). Two types of compensation have been targeted specifically—Veterans' Compensation and the availability of Supplemental Security Income (SSI) for chronic pain conditions.

Supplemental Security Income is a fixed amount of money each month that is provided by the federal government for persons who have been judged unable to work due to a medical or psychiatric disability. To receive compensation, the patient must have documentation of their disability and, importantly, how it relates to the patient's ability to function in a work setting.

Earlier in the chapter, the observations of Henry Beecher were mentioned. Beecher's view was that there were considerable differences in an individual's pain experience based upon the anticipated consequences. Beecher's (1956) observations suggested to many lawmakers that pain was highly subjective and frequently exaggerated by patients. In part because of the number of World War II veterans reporting chronic pain, the field of pain medicine became firmly established in the late 1940s and 1950s.

There were mixed opinions about soldiers' pain. Veterans groups argued that these wounded soldiers, who had served their country well, were not receiving adequate medical attention. However, some legislators and physicians were concerned about the increase in disability claims, suggesting that many of those reporting ongoing pain "did not want to get well." There were also questions about whether soldiers' pain was service related or whether the onset of pain was due to some event after discharge from the service or a pre-existing condition when entering the military (Wailoo, 2014). Politicians raised an issue that medical science could not answer with any objective "gold standard": "How do physicians determine whether pain is genuinely debilitating?" Between 1945 and 1960, the number of veterans receiving disability rose dramatically from a half million to three million.

As noted in Chapter 3, throughout much of the 20th century, physicians' groups such as the American Medical Association were vigilant about any type of change in the US health care system that included any elements of socialism (Hoffman, 2008). Socialism in the 1950s was, in many respects, a code word for "Communism" and became associated with the Soviet Union's political and economic systems. Government-funded health systems that provided care at no cost, like the Veterans Administration for those who had served in the military, had, for many physicians, a socialist tinge and were viewed with suspicion (Wailoo, 2014).

The narcotic oxycodone, marketed as Percocet, became available in 1950. It rapidly became a widely prescribed drug. Echoing the theme of a diminishing work ethic, critics expressed concern that the medication promoted a "blissed-out state" that eliminated personal responsibility (Wailoo, 2014).

While becoming more common, the chronic pain diagnosis continued to be questioned by many physicians because of its subjectivity and worry that the diagnosis would give support to "freeloaders" who did not want to work. Reliance upon patient self-report and overt pain behavior as the basis of a chronic pain diagnosis seemed woefully inadequate for physicians accustomed to objective indicators such as X-rays and laboratory test results. Moreover, certifying patients as disabled on such flimsy evidence made many physicians uncomfortable.

According to Wailoo (2014), over time, pain became a symbol of the underlying philosophical debate between liberals and conservatives about government versus individual responsibility. Wailoo (2014) describes chronic pain as a type of medical volleyball passed back and forth between political liberals who stressed the importance of compassion and helping through an array of social services and political conservatives who could not tolerate state-sponsored "coddling" of individuals by encouraging the government to take care of them.

The Politics of Gate Control Theory

Gate control theory was compatible with the politically liberal perspective on pain (Wailoo, 2014), since it validated subjective pain as "true pain." The gate control model was also a boon to disability attorneys in that it legitimated pain existing in the absence of tissue damage.

As suggested earlier, gate control theory effectively challenged the Cartesian split of mind and body. The developers of the model, Melzack and Wall, were critical of the reliance upon medication and surgery as pain treatments because these interventions reflected this outdated dualism. From the gate control perspective, pain perception is actually a very complex process involving our past experiences, expectations, and even our social-political culture. Pain is not a single unitary phenomenon associated with a single site in the brain but a complicated experience influenced by multiple characteristics, including psychological features, perception, mood, and social context. Importantly, for advocates of the liberal position and attorneys representing chronic pain patients in workmen's compensation and other litigation, pain was a unique phenomenon for each individual and could not be assessed with a traditional medical evaluation.

By the late 1960s, the courts, influenced by this line of reasoning, had moved to a more consistently liberal position on pain. Gate control theory shifted the burden of proof from patients to prove that they were not malingering, to physicians, who now must prove that the patient did not experience legitimate pain (Wailoo, 2014). Given the role of subjectivity in pain experience, proving that the patient was not experiencing pain was next to impossible.

Gate control theory probably went further into the social-psychological realm than Melzack and Wall (1965) had intended. By opening the door to the role of psychological and social factors in pain, gate control theory argued against a "one-size-fits-all" approach to treatment. Indirectly, the gate control model supported and encouraged development of new treatments—some of which were not scientifically tested. Chronic pain interventions ranged from drugs to surgery to hypnosis to novel strategies that address patients' psychological and physical state. Bonica, a well-recognized pain specialist, pushed the boundaries even further by going to China and returning with descriptions of acupuncture as an effective pain control method. He described his observation of patients undergoing surgery with acupuncture as the only anesthesia (Bonica, 1974).

With the election of Ronald Reagan, policy makers and attorneys who had either explicitly or implicitly adopted the gate control model met a new adversary (Wailoo, 2014). Reagan was a major critic of any federal programs that contributed to "coddling" citizens and believed that personal responsibility and work ethic needed to be reinstated. Reagan invoked a woman named Linda Taylor as prototypical of those who abused government support—she was described as a welfare queen driving a Cadillac (Kohler-Hausmann, 2007). Under Richard Schweiker, Reagan's secretary of health and human services, a stringent review of Supplemental Security recipients was initiated, and standards for establishing disability became more challenging. The goal was to "weed out" persons who were "milking" the system and, by the new criteria, render them ineligible for disability benefits.

Melzack and Wall's gate control theory began to be criticized as a "fuzzy" explanation that was not based on firm empirical evidence. Because the model legitimated the pain of patients who had no observable injury or disease process, gate control theory was seen as being a tool of political liberals who wanted to establish a welfare state (Wailoo, 2014). While previous US presidents, including Carter and Nixon, wanted to address medical and welfare fraud, Reagan and his allies went further and evaluated underlying motivations of disability applicants. In doing so, the psychodynamic concept of secondary gain became pain medicine's "welfare queen." To Reagan conservatives, the gate control model had sanctioned and supported those who were too characterologically weak to maintain full-time employment. Dr. Brenda Brenna adopted the language of learning theory and learned helplessness to describe a subculture in which reports of ongoing pain were a pathological social norm: "chronic pain is often a conditioned socioeconomic disease" (Brenna, 1980, in Wailoo, 2014).

Intractable Pain and Physician-Assisted Suicide

In the 1980s, the distress associated with pain—particularly that caused by cancer—became a public concern. While medical technology often added months or even years to the lives of those with chronic and terminal illnesses, the quality of this life was questioned, since these patients were frequently in pain. Libertarians, who believed that government should minimally restrict the lives of citizens, emphasized that people should be able to be self-determining in their right not to suffer and should have access to methods to end their lives. Dr. Jack Kevorkian became a public advocate for the right to control the conditions of one's death and developed a "suicide machine" for administering the morphine and other medications that quickly and painlessly ended patients' suffering (Silvers, Rhodes, & Battin, 2015; Wailoo, 2014).

One of Kevorkian's major points of defense in his early cases was that people should not have to live with excruciating pain. While Kevorkian was eventually imprisoned for his efforts, his highly publicized work was at least implicitly supported by those who believed they should not have to suffer and not have to tolerate a life being kept alive by a medical system that did not appreciate their suffering. Oregon became the first state in the United States to legalize physician-assisted suicide and was eventually followed by other states, including Washington and, more recently, California.

However, physician-assisted suicide raised a philosophical tension within the politically conservative community (Wailoo, 2014). Conservatives emphasized small government and that the government should not be intruding into private lives. However, many of these conservatives also believed in the sanctity of life. For many adherents of this political perspective, the view that people should be able to end their lives at will was a red line that should not be crossed.

Pain as a Fifth Vital Sign and the Rise of Opiates

Beginning in the 1980s, as a result of multiple influences, including aggressive marketing of pain medication and the growing influence of consumerism in health care, there came to be a consensus that patients were being undertreated for pain. Physicians, it was argued, had become so preoccupied with the possibility of addicting patients to medications that they either would not prescribe opiates or did so sparingly—leading to needless patient suffering. Pain or fear of intractable pain was one of the primary reasons that patients requested physician assistance in ending their lives prematurely. The US Conference of Catholic Bishops came out in favor of palliation of pain with an article titled "Kill the Pain Not the Patient: Palliative Care vs. Assisted Suicide" (Doerflinger & Gomez, 2017). The article contained this admonition: "The question, 'What is the maximum dose of morphine for a cancer patient in pain?', has one answer: 'The dose that will relieve the pain.'"

Pain became the fifth vital sign, along with temperature, pulse rate, respiration rate, and blood pressure (Ballantyne & Sullivan, 2015). It became routine practice for nurses and physicians to ask patients to rate their pain on a scale from 0 (none at all) to 10 (worst possible). Many argued that the concern about possible addiction had been overstated, leaving many patients suffering needlessly with pain. The rationale was that if medications could bring pain under better control and relieve patients' distress, narcotics should be given to patients upon request (Ballantyne & Sullivan, 2015).

This view was consistent with American pragmatism. Medications should be used in the service of reducing suffering and increasing human productivity. With the growing consumer orientation, hospitals emphasized alleviation of pain in their patient satisfaction questionnaire, the results of which are frequently posted on the internet.

Beginning in 1981, pharmaceutical companies began marketing medications directly to the general public (Ventola, 2011). Eventually, opioids such as oxycodone, morphine, tramadol, and fentanyl, which stimulate opioid receptors in the brain and spinal cord, became readily available and were marketed directly to consumers in the United States. Part of the marketing message to physicians was that these medications were safe; pharmaceutical companies also tended to understate the possibility of dependence upon these drugs. While it was correct that the majority of people did not become addicted to these medications, there were patients who did, and many of these medications were diverted for recreational use. Multiple forces led to increased government oversight of physicians' prescribing practices for pain medication. A conflict arose between the government's concern about diversion and inappropriate use of pain medication and physicians' perception that government was encroaching upon their professional judgment and practice.

However, a few unscrupulous physicians were prescribing medication such as oxycodone to patients in large quantities with minimal assessment of the patient's medical condition. These so-called pill mills became common in many states, such as Florida. Local newspapers periodically reported about break-ins at local pharmacies in which the burglars were primarily interested in prescription opioids. The issue and the popularity of the drug OxyContin became public when conservative talk show host Rush Limbaugh confessed to having a significant addiction to painkillers (Wailoo, 2014). The availability of drugs through internet pharmacies—often without a prescription—was another source for both users and illicit sellers of opiates. Data gathered between 1965 and 2000 found that compared with tranquilizers, stimulants, and sedatives, the number of people using pain medication had grown by a factor of five (Wailoo, 2014). Since 2000, there has been a gradual decline in documented prescriptions for opiates. Pharmaceutical manufacturers, sensitive to the issues involved, developed opioids with chemical properties that deterred abuse (Pezalla, Rosen, Erensen, Haddox, & Mayne, 2017). Additionally, many states now have registries that monitor physicians' prescriptions of opioids.

Patients with chronic pain oftentimes will report that they developed a dependence upon these medications when they were appropriately prescribed for pain by their physician. However, over time, physicians, concerned about external sanctions for their prescribing practices, became less likely to readily refill opioid prescriptions. Since some patients with chronic pain had developed tolerance and dependence upon medication, when the medications were reduced or terminated, rebound pain arose.

As the availability of opioids was reduced, the street value of the drugs increased. Persons who previously used prescription opioids turned to heroin, often laced with the drug fentanyl, as an alternative. From 2010 to the present, while deaths associated with drugs such as oxycodone declined, deaths from heroin overdose increased and continue at an accelerated rate (Pezalla et al., 2017). While individuals abusing oxycodone developed knowledge of the optimal dosage for a "high," this did not translate readily to heroin. For those new to heroin and using it as a substitute for prescription opioids, dosing, as well as the effects when combined with the drug fentanyl, were often unknown. As a result, it is likely that many patients overdosed on heroin because of limited knowledge about the drug.

The remaining sections of this chapter focus on clinical assessment and treatment of chronic pain.

Assessment of Pain

Rating Scales

The use of a self-report scale for pain from 1 (completely pain free) to 10 (worst pain ever experienced) is very common in evaluating patients' pain. These self-report measures are used in hospital settings, physical therapy, and comprehensive pain management programs. Some patients are better able to report the pain experience if there are visual anchors that they can point to; the visual analog scale is commonly used for this task.

One of the most commonly used scales is the McGill Pain Questionnaire (MPQ; Melzack, 1975), constructed by the developers of gate control theory. The MPQ consists of groups of three types of adjectives—sensory, affective, and evaluative (cognitive). The sensory dimension includes terms such as *hot, burning, scalding, tingling, itching,* and *stinging*. The emotional dimension is assessed with terms such as *annoying, troublesome, miserable, unbearable,* or *fearful, frightful,* and *terrifying*. The evaluative dimension is represented by terms such as *annoying* or *troublesome*. A miscellaneous set of terms addresses the temporal dimensions of the pain—*brief, momentary, periodic, intermittent, steady,* and so on. The sensory dimension itself was also able to differentiate between tension and migraine headache sufferers. Tension headaches were described as "tight," while migraines were reported to be "blinding," "nauseating," and "sickening" (Hunter & Philips, 1981).

The MPQ includes a schematic outline of the body, on which patients indicate pain sites. Additionally, patients rate the intensity of their pain. The scale is sensitive to changes in pain associated with treatment. For clinicians, the quality of the pain reported may be useful in guiding treatment. For example, patients who report a large number of emotionally laden adjectives as descriptors of their pain are more likely to have a condition such as major depressive disorder or to be experiencing high levels of anxiety (Kremer, Atkinson, & Ignelzi, 1981). Hopefully, this MPQ information would prompt a clinician to further assess for mental health issues. If the patient's levels of anxiety or depression are treated, it is likely that the intensity of their pain experience will decline.

Pain Diary

To obtain a clearer picture of frequency, situational aspects, and degree of functional impairment associated with pain, it is helpful for the patient to keep a pain diary. There are a number of formats available for patients' daily accounts. Typically, patients note the presence or absence of pain, its intensity, activities in which they were engaged at the time of the pain, whether they took medication, and the pain's duration. Other useful dimensions might be to add who was present during the episode and how long it took to get relief from pain if medication was taken. The version used by the American Cancer Society includes a section in which patients are to indicate non-medication cognitive behavioral strategies that they tried and their relative effectiveness. The diary is very useful in that if pain primarily occurs at home or in the workplace or in the presence of their spouse and/or their children, it raises issues to guide clinical intervention. In addition, careful analysis of the pain diary data is likely to uncover possible sources of reinforcement for pain behavior. In recent years, a number of electronic versions of the diary have been developed; there are suggestions that the electronic version may be used more frequently than the older pencil-and-paper version (Gaertner, Elsner, Pollmann-Dahmen, Radbruch, & Sabatowski, 2004).

The Clinical Interview for Pain

A detailed clinical interview is very helpful. Key dimensions are outlined below.

1. Pain onset, frequency, and intensity
2. Factors or situations that increase or decrease pain
3. Sleep patterns
4. Daily activities
5. Medical history
6. Family history, with particular attention to pain-related issues in one's family of origin
7. Past treatment and its effectiveness, current treatment and effectiveness
8. If treatment includes medication, which medications, what dosage and schedule, taken how frequently?
9. Occupational history and educational history
10. Current status with regard to workmen's compensation, litigation, or other financial issues related to pain

11. If the patient is not currently working, when was the last time he or she was working on a regular basis? What is the patient's perspective on returning to work?
12. Alcohol and drug use history
13. Mental health history; history of traumatic events
14. Current cognitive and emotional status; suicidal ideation or behavior
15. How do they perceive their involvement in treatment? Active? Passive? (Edwards, Dworkin, Sullivan, Turk, & Wasan, 2016; Searight, 2010)

In terms of mental health history, although it was thought that chronic pain was a symbol or expression of psychological distress, including repressed emotions, during the psychosomatic era, this view is no longer held today. When studying the onset of major depressive disorder and chronic pain, one lingering view from psychodynamic theory is that chronic pain is a type of introjected object (Engel, 1959; Mikail, Henderson, & Tasca, 1994). As such, it is a representation of a difficult issue in the patient's life, such as loss of a parent. However, while this explanation may characterize a few pain patients, it probably does not characterize the majority. One piece of evidence that contradicts the view that pain is simply an expression of psychological conflict is that among low back pain patients, it was found that the mood disorder emerged after the patient had been in pain for several months (Krishnan et al., 1985), rather than before or concurrently, as the psychosomatic hypothesis would suggest.

Research does suggest that psychiatric conditions are very common among lower back pain patients, with major depressive disorder present in about 40 percent, anxiety disorders in 15 to 25 percent, substance abuse in approximately 20 percent, and personality disorders in 30 to 50 percent of patients (Andersson, 1999; Atkinson, Slater, Patterson, Grant, & Garfin, 1991; Polatin, Kinney, Gatchel, Lillo, & Mayer, 1993). Again, when examining lower back pain, among patients who have had a significant reduction in pain, relapse is best predicted by psychological distress (Katon, Egan, & Miller, 1985; McWilliams, Cox, & Ennis, 2003). Among patients who had surgical intervention, returning to work was best predicted by depression and occupational stress rather than the intensity of pain itself (Pincus, Burton, Vogel, & Field, 2002).

Chronic Pain: Treatment Approaches

It is important to recognize that only about one-third of those with ongoing pain seek medical help. As is the case with irritable bowel syndrome, discussed in Chapter 1, dimensions such as anxiety and social support are likely to be factors that drive help-seeking. Additionally, with chronic conditions, the decision to seek medical care at a particular point in time—particularly if it had not been sought previously for the condition—is likely to be meaningful. Often, help-seeking is associated with a life stressor or accumulation of several stressful life events. Considering dimensions such as life change units from the Holmes and Rahe scale (1967), as well as the accumulation of "hassles," will often shed light on immediate precipitants for seeking help for a chronic pain condition. Additionally, as has already been discussed, secondary factors such as the need for medical certification for compensation through disability insurance or continued time off of work are likely to play a role in help-seeking among some chronic pain patients (Searight, 2010). As will be evident in the review of treatments below, it is likely that a combination of therapies, tailored to specific patients, will be most helpful.

Surgery

The United States, with its orientation toward aggressive treatment, performs far more lower-back surgeries than any other developed country (Weinstein et al., 2006). While lumping all back surgeries into one group is certainly questionable practice, data suggest there is reason to be concerned about the potential success of surgical intervention for low back pain (Itz et al., 2016). While there is variation in success rates, research indicates that an unusually high number of patients have poor surgical outcomes. For example, a procedure called spinal fusion, in which two adjacent vertebrae are melded together, often leaves patients with new unpleasant physical sensations as well as recurrent back and leg pain (Deyo, Nachemson, & Mirza, 2004). There is even a diagnostic label, "failed back surgery syndrome," for those who undergo back surgeries and are left with continuing or increasing pain. It is estimated that up to 40 percent of post-surgical patients may fall into this category (Itz et al., 2016). While physiological issues such as nerve damage or infection are certainly features of these poor outcomes, research has indicated that postsurgical outcome for back pain and knee pain is also predicted by psychological and environmental factors (Deyo et al., 2004; Itz et al., 2016). As noted earlier, it is not uncommon to have some lower back abnormalities that appear in X-rays but have never caused any distress or impaired functioning. These spinal abnormalities are so common that they are often considered "normal" and of little clinical significance (Deyo, 2002a; 2002b). Some research suggests that overreliance upon spinal X-rays leads to a number of unnecessary and often unsuccessful back surgeries (Deyo, 1994; 2002a; 2002b; Deyo, Nachemson, & Mirza, 2004). There is no one-to-one relationship between anatomical and physiological abnormalities and level of reported pain with X-rays showing herniated discs or bulging discs in many people with no reported complaints. Therefore, reliance upon spinal X-rays as a "gold standard" of "real" back pain is not supported.

In an interesting epidemiological study of back surgeries in the state of Maine, Keller et al. (1996) studied the preoperative and postoperative outcomes of patients undergoing surgery for spinal stenosis (narrowing of the spine, which is typically age-related) or herniated discs. Rates of surgeries for the condition ranged from nearly 40 percent below the state average to 72 percent above the state average (Deyo, 2002a; 2002b; Deyo, Nachemson, & Mizra, 2004). In the regions with very high rates of back surgeries, patients had fewer symptoms and fewer spinal abnormalities but also had poorer outcomes from the surgery than patients in the low surgical rate regions (Atlas, Keller, Wu, Deyo, & Singer, 2005; Atlas, Keller, Robson, Deyo, & Singer, 2000; Deyo, 2013). Only about half of back pain surgeries result in significant pain reduction (Chan & Peng, 2011).

Implantable Spinal Stimulators

Based upon the concept of a "pain gate" in the spinal cord, electrical stimulation has been used as a treatment. Stimulation of the dorsal spinal column occurs via small electrical devices inserted through an epidural needle with electrodes attached to a battery-powered electrical device. Conceptually, the placing of electrodes is based upon the concept that stimulation may close the pain gate. After some initial instruction, patients then control the strength and duration of stimulation. Patients typically use the stimulator for one or two hours at least three times per day. While there is some evidence of effectiveness, the mechanism of spinal cord stimulation is probably not entirely due to its originally posited mechanism and instead may be associated with increased regional blood flow. Success rates are somewhat difficult to assess, but up to half of patients who receive the implant stimulator may benefit from it (Kumar, Toth, Nath, & Laing, 1998). A study of patients who had "failed back surgery syndrome" found that compared with standard medical management, spinal cord stimulation was associated with reduced back pain intensity and improved quality of life (Kumar et al., 2008). It is important to recognize that most medical treatments of chronic pain do not eliminate pain but reduce its intensity. As discussed earlier, a good outcome is considered to be an increase in activity and/or return to work.

Medications

Peripherally acting analgesics such as aspirin inhibit the neurochemicals that increase inflammation that sensitizes nociceptors at the pain site. By contrast, centrally acting analgesics block central nervous system opiate receptors and alter pain perception. Opiates are a subgroup of narcotics that are directly or indirectly synthesized from or analogs of the opium poppy. This category includes drugs such as codeine, oxycodone, and methadone. These medications may be helpful in the short term—particularly for pain following any type of surgical procedure or dental work. However, they are not intended to be used long term, since tolerance and dependence readily develop. In cases of tolerance, the patient requires more of the same medication to obtain the same analgesic effect. However, over time, a new level of tolerance will develop and the process will begin again. Medications only reduce pain by about 30 to 40 percent in fewer than half of patients (Gatchel, 2005; Gatchel, McGeary, McGeary, & Lippe, 2014). In addition to concerns about dependence, opioids cause side effects such as nausea, constipation, and hyper analgesia in which pain receptors become overly sensitive to any sensation.

For fibromyalgia, several types of antidepressant medication appear to be beneficial. These include selective serotonin reuptake inhibitors such as fluoxetine (Prozac) and sertraline (Zoloft), both antidepressants that act upon the serotonergic system. Newer antidepressants such as duloxetine (Cymbalta) that act upon the noradrenergic and serotonergic systems, as well as older tricyclic antidepressants such as amitriptyline, have also been found to be useful. Disrupted sleep, particularly disruption in stage-4 sleep, is often associated with diffuse pain even among persons without fibromyalgia. It is possible that patients with fibromyalgia derive benefit from antidepressants through their effect of improving sleep.

For pain that is debilitating and not responsive to other interventions, morphine pumps have been surgically implanted. These pumps deliver pain medications through an implanted catheter. Depending on the patient, medication may be delivered continuously in a single high dose. There are suggestions that not all patients benefit equally from spinal stimulation or the implantable morphine pump.

After periods of time ranging from 7 to 39 months, approximately 60 to 70 percent of patients report significant reductions in pain with implantable morphine pumps (Angel, Carey, & Gould, 1996). Some patients have reported enough reduction in pain to return to work. In one small sample, among 13 patients, 12 returned to work full-time after implantation (Duse, Davià, & White, 2009).

Patients tend to show a pattern in which the amount of morphine is gradually increased over time. Side effects are typically not due to the medication but to the device itself. While there is general acceptance of the use of morphine pumps for pain associated with conditions such as cancer, there is less consensus about the appropriateness and overall effectiveness for many other specific chronic pain conditions. With regular use, patients have reported long-term reductions in pain lasting up to three years while the pump is in continuous use (Atli, Theodore, Turk, & Loeser, 2010). While the morphine pump reduces pain, it does not eliminate it.

There is evidence that patients would benefit from a psychological evaluation prior to both spinal stimulation and implantable pumps; these devices appear to be less successful in patients with several characteristics, including an elevated level of sensitivity to bodily sensations (somatosensory amplifiers), untreated psychiatric conditions, and a history of substance abuse problems. Additionally, patients with any type of cognitive compromise, such as Alzheimer's dementia, are usually not good candidates for these procedures.

Some patients also benefit from local anesthetic injections—particularly in cases where there are specific "tender spots" in areas such as the shoulders. The most commonly used are drugs such as lidocaine. Some patients do show long-term benefits even after the chemical effects of the medication have worn off.

Trans-Electrical Nerve Stimulation

Trans-electrical nerve stimulation (TENS) involves stimulating a specific region of the body on the skin with electric vibrations. The electric current is provided by a small portable device and electrodes are attached to the skin—typically at the pain site or on the spinal area. TENS is based on the principle of counter-stimulation. A familiar example of counter-stimulation is that many of us, when accidentally striking an area of the body such as the elbow or knee, respond by immediately rubbing the area. With the TENS unit, the frequency (number of vibrations per second) is typically set at either high or low. The intensity (amplitude) of the stimulation appears to be the critical factor in terms of pain relief. Typically, when a patient is initially using a TENS unit, the intensity is varied to find the optimal level to reduce pain.

Multiple explanations have been offered for TENS's effectiveness. It is likely that the electrical stimulation works through more than one mechanism. Within the context of gate control theory, TENS may exert its effect through stimulation of large-diameter afferent nerve structures transmitting signals to the central nervous system (Catley, Gibson, Wand, Meads, & O'Connell, 2015). However, there is also evidence that TENS stimulation decreases the sensitivity of the dorsal horn spinal cord to inflammation and may also alter levels of neurotransmitters such as gamma amino butyric acid (GABA), which are known to inhibit nociceptors. TENS activity also appears to increase activity of endogenous opioids—often called endorphins.

In terms of its effectiveness, it is difficult to isolate nonspecific or placebo effects of TENS because a true double-blind study is at best difficult to conduct. A true "sham" TENS-like unit that would be credible to research participants is challenging to develop (Catley et al., 2015). As a result, the relative effectiveness of TENS has been difficult to establish. There are suggestions, however, that patients do develop tolerance to the electric stimulation (Vance, Dailey, Rakel, & Sluka, 2014).

Acupuncture

Probably the most common reason to seek acupuncture is to treat chronic pain (MacPherson, Sinclair-Lian, & Thomas, 2006). About 1 to 2 percent of the US population reports having had acupuncture treatment (Dorsher, 2011). Acupuncture involves stimulating specific points on the body through surface pressure or with needles, which may be heated or transmit electrical vibrations. Recently, laser stimulation of acupuncture points has been used (Dorsher, 2011).

Acupuncture is based upon an ancient Chinese view of pathophysiology. *Qi*, energy along with blood, spreads along 12 meridians of the body. Each meridian is associated with a particular organ such as the kidney, heart, bladder, and so on. Proponents of acupuncture assert that pain arises because of blockages in blood flow in particular regions of the body, and exact placement of the acupuncture needles along specific meridia restores normal circulation. While the meridian theory has a long history—dating back more than 2,000 years in China—the mechanism(s) involved in acupuncture have not been specifically established through research.

There is also evidence that the needle insertion is associated with the release of endogenous opiates—endorphins (Dorsher, 2011). When compared with no treatment or a simulated "sham" acupuncture procedure, acupuncture was better than the alternatives for back and neck pain, osteoarthritis (also known as degenerative joint disease), chronic headache, and chronic shoulder pain (Madsen, Gøtzche, & Hróbjartsson, 2009; Vickers & Linde, 2014; Witt et al., 2006). Acupuncture needles were approved in 1996 by the Food and Drug Administration as a medical device. Given current concern in the United States with opioid prescribing, the medical community has recently shown increased interest in the procedure. Research suggests a small, yet significant, benefit for acupuncture for back and neck pain and for chronic headache when compared with a sham treatment (Dorsher, 2011; Vickers & Linde, 2014).

Physical Therapy

Physical therapy (PT) involves specialized exercises to increase muscle strength and flexibility. Typically, the patient meets two to four times a week with a physical therapist and then has assigned exercises to perform in between sessions. PT appears to be better for certain types of pain than others. For patients with rheumatoid arthritis, for example, PT appears to maintain flexibility. For acute back pain, physical therapy was associated with reduced symptoms and improved functioning (Cherkin, Deyo, Battié, Street, & Barlow, 1998). PT's effectiveness for chronic pain is more equivocal. There are suggestions that the addition of cognitive behavioral psychotherapy may improve physical therapy outcomes.

Behavioral and Psychological Treatment for Chronic Pain

As discussed earlier, with the recognition that pain is independent of tissue damage, psychological and social factors have been given greater attention. However, at the same time, the view that pain should be accepted and not "cured" conflicts with the culture of American medicine. Thus, it is important that clinicians working with patients from a psychosocial perspective do not contribute to false hopes that complete relief from pain is a likely outcome. Importantly, newer cognitive behavioral interventions, such as acceptance of pain while engaging in valued life activities (work, exercise, interaction with family), do not focus on alleviation of pain as the outcome but instead consider increased activity to be the most important treatment goal.

One of the key issues in working with chronic illness such as pain-related conditions is defining a desirable outcome. Realistic criteria for success should be established early in the course of treatment. It is important to recognize that becoming completely pain free is unlikely. Instead, the goal for patients is to increase activity and social interaction, and when appropriate, return to work. In a medically oriented system focused on toward "cure," chronic pain patients as well as patients with other chronic illnesses are often challenging for physicians. Physicians themselves are oriented toward cure rather than improvement, and anything less may feel like a treatment failure.

Behavioral Approaches to Treatment

Fordyce et al.'s (1984) approach to the treatment of chronic pain emphasizes overt behavior and environmental contingencies. Again, as discussed earlier, Fordyce et el. emphasize that pain behavior has been reinforced, often inadvertently, by family members and aspects of the environment such as the patient's work situation. Many psychosocial-oriented pain treatment programs are reluctant to work with patients who have ongoing litigation related to their pain. Again, the potential financial reinforcement for pain-related behavior would work against the focus of treatment, which is to increase non-pain-related behavior. Gatchel (2005) differs from many clinicians in that he does not consider active litigation—such as workmen's compensation, insurance litigation associated with an auto accident, or seeking government assistance through Supplemental Security Income (SSI)—related to pain a deciding factor in whether the patient should be referred for multidisciplinary pain management. However, other research has found consistent evidence for reports of higher levels of pain-related behavior when legal action is pending (Blyth, March, & Cousins, 2003). Gatchel (2005) asserts that even in cases where financial claims have been resolved in the patient's favor, the disability associated with reported pain persists, and that even patients who have ongoing financial litigation have benefited from appropriate treatment.

In its initial, "pure" form, Fordyce et al.'s (1984) approach to treating chronic pain was conducted in an inpatient setting over several weeks. Consistent with an operant learning approach, the goal of treatment was to improve the patient's functioning. In this behavioral model, rather than patients in physical therapy exercising to the point of being tired or in pain, patients are instructed to work toward and are reinforced for exercising to a particular quota (e.g., walking 25 yards rather than walking until the patient is in pain or uncomfortable). Physical therapy was particularly important in this regard in that the patient's ability to walk a certain number of steps, and to stand for a period of time, and so on, were in many respects key outcomes of this approach. If the patient could walk only 30 steps without grimacing and needing to sit down at the beginning of treatment, and after 30 days could walk 250 steps successfully, this would be considered a treatment success. Again, the patient's internal experience of pain was deemphasized.

The behavioral perspective also looks at the role of pain medication. If patients take narcotics whenever they begin to feel low-level pain, the medication becomes a powerful reinforcer. As Fordyce and Steger (1979) note, the patient must engage in pain behavior to receive the medication. Instead of having patients take their medication when they experience pain, Fordyce puts the patient on the equivalent of a fixed interval schedule whereby they receive their medication every 4 or 6 hours rather than when reporting pain. Therefore, the reinforcement value of medication is not related to self-reports of pain. In some instances, this approach also involved reducing the amount of active narcotic in the patient's pain medication over the span of several weeks by giving the patient's medication in a solution rather than pill form. Close to 60 percent of patients maintained the reduced level of medication at 10 months after treatment (Fordyce & Steger, 1979).

In contemporary pain programs, which are largely outpatient based, family members are encouraged to participate. Spouses of pain patients do report more depressive symptoms compared with spouses of patients with other chronic illnesses (Flor, Turk, & Scholz, 1987). Both a pain diary—completed by a family member—and a family-focused pain interview can be useful for assessing family members' perceptions of and reactions to the patient's pain behavior. Careful review of the pain diary can give the clinician useful information about the situational parameters of pain—if it occurs at particular times of the day, in interaction with specific family members, and so on—and use this information to focus on interactions that may be particularly stressful. In the behavioral treatment program, spouses are educated about the relationship between pain behavior and social reinforcement. Spouses may be discouraged from focusing conversation on the patient's pain. Additionally, the pain diary will provide information about how family members respond to the patient's pain behavior.

Pain behavior may also be modeled. It is not uncommon for patients with chronic pain to have grown up in a family in which one or both parents have ongoing chronic pain. Somatic expression of psychological difficulties has been found to be more common among parents of children with chronic abdominal pain compared with non-patients (Walker, Garber, & Greene, 1991). Similar to the familial explanation of somatization, it is likely that individuals growing up in an environment that is pain focused have a lower threshold for what is considered to be significant pain.

Behaviorists recognize that it is difficult to simply decrease the frequency of long-standing behavior. Behavioral change is likely when desirable behavior alternatives are available and reinforced. A Cochrane Review of behavioral intervention for low back pain found moderately positive effects on pain intensity with smaller effects for functional status and specific behavioral outcomes (van Tulder et al., 2002).

Progressive Relaxation Training

Progressive relaxation was described in detail in an earlier chapter. Progressive muscle relaxation often pairs rhythmic breathing with encouraging patients to focus attention on the breath. While doing so, patients focus attention on different muscle groups. While progressive relaxation often involves alternately tensing and relaxing muscle groups, this aspect of the protocol may be omitted with some pain patients. Early research showed some benefit for progressive relaxation in treating chronic pain in terms of self-reported pain and depressive symptoms in functioning (Turner, 1982). Progressive relaxation has been found useful in reducing migraine and tension headaches by approximately 40 to 50 percent. Its applicability to other types of pain is not as well studied. A slightly different variation on this involves autogenic training—beginning with a deep rhythmic breathing process, patients are encouraged to visualize and attempt to somatically experience a sense of warmth that progressively moves through the body.

Biofeedback

As noted in chapter 5, biofeedback involves the use of specialized devices that measure and generate analog visual or auditory patterns of signals. The patient commonly has electrodes attached to specific regions of the body and often are measuring electrical activity in the muscles. The patient can then see on the screen when muscles are tense versus relaxed. Reducing muscle tension through EMG biofeedback is an approach that is used with multiple pain conditions. It has been well studied with chronic lower back pain and appears to be effective. The major benefit of biofeedback appears to be that many lower back pain patients are not aware of muscular tension. While biofeedback typically does not eliminate pain, the reduction in muscle tension, in turn, reduces pain. Biofeedback may be particularly effective with patients who have been trained in progressive relaxation or some other breathing or meditative approach and can view signals indicating that muscle tension is increasing or decreasing. Biofeedback helps patients who are not very aware of their physical reactions to become more aware of them. By using specific techniques to become more physically relaxed and inducing reduced sympathetic nervous system activity, patients can see on the screen their relative success.

Biofeedback has demonstrated some success with migraine headache. While temperature-focused biofeedback has often been used—in which a thermometer is typically attached to the patient's finger and biofeedback machine while the patient relaxes and imagines the sensation of warming of the hands—this approach does not appear to be more effective than EMG (muscular biofeedback) (Nestoriuc, Martin, Rief, & Andrasik, 2008).

Hypnosis

There are a number of anecdotal accounts, including very dramatic ones, of hypnosis being used as the only source of analgesic during a surgery or childbirth. In these instances, hypnosis probably does not eliminate pain but may redirect attention. It has been noted that in persons who are highly suggestible, hypnosis has been associated with physiological changes in brain and spinal cord activity. In self-hypnosis, patients are to practice the induction on their own. Patients may be given the audio recordings of the session to facilitate practice. The following is an excerpt from a hypnotic induction for pain:

> You may already be aware that the pain intensity, and the distress that pain can produce are two different things.... It is possible to be aware of a painful sensation, but not be bothered by it.... Maybe it helps to remember that these sensations don't really mean you need to do anything.... You really don't need to pay attention to them, and you certainly don't need to feel bothered by them. (Jensen, 2010, p. 244)

Compared with biofeedback, hypnosis was found to be equally effective in terms of its immediate effect on pain intensity as well as daily average pain when self-hypnosis was included as part of the protocol (Jensen 2009). One of the major issues in establishing the effectiveness of hypnosis is that the samples that are typically used in these studies are small and the length of follow-up is brief. Again, patients who are likely to benefit from hypnosis, similar to those who benefit from acupuncture, are those who are highly suggestible and motivated.

Cognitive Behavioral Therapy

Before addressing traditional cognitive therapy for pain, there is evidence that very basic cognitive functions such as attention can be temporarily modified so that patients are distracted from painful stimuli. Virtual reality therapy, often associated with its use for treatment of phobias through computer-generated exposures, has been applied to pain. The video game Snow World is a virtual reality visual and auditory scenario in which the patient is in an environment with deep snow. As a game, Snow World includes having the patient throw snowballs at penguins, for which they get points. Snow World was developed deliberately for burn patients (Kato, 2010). Patients engage in the game when their dressings are being changed, which is a particularly painful procedure.

Cognitive behavioral therapy for pain has a strong educational component. For example, patients may be educated about the gate control model, which may include an explanation of gate control theory. The overall objective is to help patients appreciate that pain is a physical as well as a psychological event. Pain, similar to mood states, may result from interpretation of the situation rather than the situation itself.

Patients are introduced to the basic cognitive behavioral model with an emphasis on how the pain experience is interpreted. Maladaptive beliefs about pain are challenged in a systematic way so that patients can apply this Socratic method of logic to their own thought processes. For example, many patients with chronic pain reduce activity level considerably. However, reduced activity level often will trigger a downward spiral, culminating in more intense pain. Reduced activity contributes to deconditioning, which, in turn, leads to a greater sense of fatigue and physical weakness—often convincing the patient that they "have done too much." This self-perpetuating cycle only serves to intensify the patient's pain experience.

Patients are also taught how thought processes such as catastrophization can amplify the pain experience. For example, low levels of discomfort may trigger apprehension about what is anticipated to come; this anxiety and worry are associated with muscle tension, which is likely to amplify pain experience. Similar to the overexertion-deconditioning dynamic, increased back pain associated with involuntary "bracing" or tightening of the muscles of the lower back increases both discomfort and apprehension. This belief that pain signals harm, when it is effectively addressed in cognitive therapy, appears to be associated with improvement in terms of increased functioning in decreased self-reported pain (Turner, Holtzman, & Mancl, 2007).

Patients are also educated about the difference between active and passive coping. Coping involves doing something that may distract them from the pain (playing a game, conversing with a family member, watching television) or engaging in some physical activity such as walking. Passive coping typically includes pain medication and reduced activity. A passive coping style would be saying something like "Oh no! Here it comes again. There's nothing I can do about it, and I will be at the mercy of the pain the rest of the day. I won't be able to sleep tonight." Active coping would involve encouraging the patient, at the first sign of discomfort, to have a set of preplanned activities that they can turn to that will, at minimum, distract them from the pain. One of the key elements of successful cognitive therapy for pain appears to be increased self-efficacy—the patient believes that they have some control over their physical experiences.

Cognitive behavioral therapy has been found to be effective in lower back and temporomandibular joint pain compared with customary treatment or no treatment (Eccleston, Morley, Williams, 2013; Svensdottir, Eriksen, & Reme, 2012). However, when compared head-to-head against any other type of active psychosocial treatment, CBT's effect size, while significant, diminishes and is more modest (McCracken & Vowles, 2014).

Cognitive therapy's effectiveness for pain appears to be greater when it is combined with another form of treatment. Researchers found that the combination of medication for migraine prevention, such as beta blockers, with cognitive behavioral intervention demonstrated significant improvement in migraine symptoms. With the addition of cognitive therapy, migraine prevention rates rose from 12 percent with medication alone to 50 percent among those using cognitive therapy as well as medications to address migraine (Smitherman et al., 2015). Similarly, patients with tension headache had the best outcomes when cognitive behavioral treatment was combined with an antidepressant (amitriptyline) medication. Among those receiving combined therapy, almost two-thirds reported significant reduction in tension headaches, whereas the rates for antidepressant medication alone were in the 30 to 40 percent range (Smitherman et al., 2015).

Third-Wave Cognitive Behavioral Therapy

In the past 15 years, the field of cognitive behavioral therapy has changed its focus from attempting to actively identify and refute irrational thoughts to a stance of accepting experience. With an emphasis on following through on behaviors associated with core values despite how we feel, acceptance and commitment therapy would seem to be a useful fit for patients with chronic pain.

The basic principles of ACT were outlined in Chapter 7's discussion of stress. Another feature that would seem to make ACT a good fit for chronic pain is the emphasis on experiential avoidance. The role of cognition in persons with long-standing chronic pain was discussed above. However, one of the key features of ACT is that it is important to act in accordance with core values regardless of extraneous thoughts and feelings. One common cognitive theme in chronic pain patients is the unrealistic goal of being free from pain before engaging in daily activities: "I cannot work or enjoy my family if I have any pain; I would like to be more active, but I cannot because of the pain." As Dahl and Lundgren (2006) note, a limiting cognitive attribution is the belief that "I must be free of pain before I can get on with my life." Over time, many individuals with chronic pain engage in experiential avoidance to try to minimize pain. However, this avoidance typically includes anxiety and fear associated with physical discomfort as well as reduced activity.

Trying to avoid the gradual increase in pain associated with a tension headache is likely to make the pain worse since the observer has "fused" with the pain and given it power by attempting to avoid it. Instead, it is suggested that the individual become an observer of the pain and examine it from the point of view of a curious scientist—for example, "Which part of my head is actually hurting? Is the pain sharp, stabbing, dull? How bad is this one on a scale from 1 to 10?"

Evidence for ACT for chronic pain has been promising. The effect sizes are in the medium to large range and the treatment has been associated with improved physical and social functioning as well as a reduced number of pain-related medical visits (McCracken & Vowles, 2014). Among patients who adopt ACT's central principles, there is evidence of increases in their acceptance of pain and overall acceptance of their thoughts and feelings, as well as placing emphasis on actions consistent with core values. These changes in cognition are associated with decreased anxiety and depression as well as reduced disability (McCracken & Vowles, 2014).

Multimodal and Multidisciplinary Pain Programs

A comprehensive multidisciplinary program will include a physician who typically is the medical director; nurses, some of whom function as physician extenders; and others who may provide limited treatment such as injections and nerve blocks under the supervision of a physician. A psychologist would initially provide a detailed psychosocial evaluation. Based upon the needs of the particular patient, a psychologist may provide cognitive behavioral treatment for pain, biofeedback, mindfulness meditation, or other techniques used for stress reduction. Additionally, the psychologist may treat accompanying mental health disorders. Physical therapists typically work with patients each day with the goal of increasing their level of physical activity. Through exercises in instruction biomechanics, patients may also learn to reduce their pain experience. Occupational therapists address vocational issues and in situations where patients do not return to work, assist the patient in developing a repertoire of meaningful activity. As is evident, this team-based approach requires regular and consistent interaction between all professionals working with the patient. Typically, there are team meetings at least once a week. In addition to providing multiple perspectives on the patient's functioning and recovery, regular multidisciplinary meetings ensure that the patient is receiving consistent information about treatment and their goals from all professionals working with them.

One obstacle to implementing this comprehensive approach has been patterns of insurance reimbursement. Rather than funding a multidisciplinary package, insurance companies often will authorize or not authorize specific treatment services based on the terms of each patient's insurance policy and the insurance reviewer's opinion about clinical need. While costly and requiring multiple health care providers, multidisciplinary pain programs appear to have the best outcome for chronic low back pain. In comparison with surgery, there were no differences among those receiving multidisciplinary rehabilitation in reported pain, disability, and work functioning. However, surgery was associated with a greater risk of negative effects (Kamper et al., 2015).

Åkerblom and colleagues (Åkerblom, Perrin, Fischer, & McCracken, 2015) reported on a multidisciplinary chronic pain program that was based upon ACT. In addition to having the patient meet regularly with a psychologist trained in ACT, physical therapists and nurses all incorporated ACT principles into their clinical work. Patients on the average showed significant reductions in pain intensity of about 50 percent, depression was nearly eliminated, and pain-related anxiety was also was nearly eliminated.

In terms of return to work, interdisciplinary models are far less expensive than surgery, ongoing use of spinal cord stimulators, or medication. For example, when return to work is used as a criterion, interdisciplinary pain treatment results in 45 to 50 percent of patients returning, with only 20 percent for those receiving back surgery and 13 to 25 percent for those receiving spinal cord stimulation (Turk & Burwinkle, 2005).

Gatchel and colleagues (Gatchel, Polatin, Mayer, & Garcy, 1994) examined the association of mental health conditions with outcomes among patients in a multimodal treatment program. In this sample, 90 percent of the patients met criteria for one psychiatric disorder and 50 percent were diagnosed with a personality disorder. Gatchel et al. (1994) found that psychiatric diagnosis was unrelated to patients' return to work but emphasized that successful chronic pain programs should include attention to mental health issues.

Conclusion

In economic terms, chronic pain is a major factor influencing productivity and is a major contributor to health care costs. Politically, chronic pain has been plagued by controversy about whether the condition is "genuine." This suspicion by some legislators and policy makers is influenced by the finding that most chronic pain conditions do not have a clearly verifiable cause. Additionally, the high comorbidity with psychiatric conditions raises questions about whether chronic pain is a syndrome in its own right versus an expression of depression and/or anxiety. It is important to recognize that even in the absence of tissue pathology, patients genuinely do experience pain. The effectiveness of biomedical interventions such as surgery and medications are limited for chronic pain. Their limited efficacy is likely to be in part because chronic pain syndromes have a significant psychosocial component. Effective treatment of chronic pain involves a multidisciplinary approach and a matching of specific interventions to the patient's pain experience in terms of culture, immediate social context, and personality style. One of the key mechanisms that appears to underlay relaxation, self-hypnosis, biofeedback, and cognitive therapy is self-efficacy. Interventions that enhance patients' sense of control over their pain experience are most likely to be successful.

CHAPTER 9

Smoking and Smoking Cessation

You may wonder why a whole chapter is being devoted to smoking and smoking cessation. Cigarette smoking continues to be one of the major causes of premature death. Approximately 20 percent of Americans are regular smokers. In addition, in contrast to alcohol use, there are few "social smokers." Typically, addiction to nicotine occurs very quickly. Readers who are currently smokers likely began the habit in high school. It is also very likely that when you began smoking you had no intention of continuing it for multiple years. This description fits the experience of most long-term adult smokers in the United States. Smoking also raises a series of complex macrosystems issues, particularly those involving legislation to restrict tobacco and the economic interests of the tobacco industry. Smoking is a difficult habit to stop. The majority of those who quit return to smoking within weeks or months. There are, however, combinations of medications and behavioral strategies that increase the likelihood of successful smoking cessation. Finally, while smoking is dropping in most Western countries, developing economies such as China are experiencing a major surge in the number of adult smokers. There is also concern that in these countries, these new smokers do not have basic information about the impact of long-term tobacco use.

Health Risks of Smoking and Tobacco Use

Cigarette smoking and tobacco use remain major health problems in the United States and are the single most preventable cause of terminal illness. Smoking accounts for 480,000 US deaths each year (Centers for Disease Control [CDC], 2018a). Cigarette smoking accounts for approximately one out of every five deaths. Deaths from smoking associated lung cancer outweigh annual deaths from HIV, illegal drug use, alcohol use, motor vehicle injuries, suicides, and murders combined. Cigarette smoking increases the risk of multiple cancers with the most common being cancers of the lung, larynx, oral cavity, esophagus, and cervix. For male smokers, lung cancer is 22 times more likely and cancer of the oral cavity 30 times more common than for nonsmokers. Among women, more die of smoking-related lung cancer than breast cancer (CDC, 2017; 2018d). Compared with nonsmokers, the average life span of regular smokers is 14 years less (Frieden & Blakeman, 2005). For every smoking-related death, there are 30 people with a smoking-related illness (CDC, 2018b). More than 70 percent of head and neck cancers are associated with smoking, alcohol use, and their combination. Regular use of alcohol adds to smoking's cancer risk (Blot et al., 1988).

Women are not always aware of the gender-specific risks of smoking, including cervical cancer, osteoporosis, early menopause, miscarriage, and infertility.

Approximately 8 percent of women smoked at some point during pregnancy, with 21 percent who smoked during the first two trimesters quitting by the third trimester (Curtin & Matthews, 2016). Cigarette use during pregnancy is associated with greater infant mortality, low-birth-weight infants, and preterm delivery. Even pregnant women smoking five cigarettes per day had greater risk of giving birth to a low-birth-weight infant compared with nonsmoking women (Frieden & Blakeman, 2005). Smoking during pregnancy is also associated with the later development of childhood conduct disorder (Wakschlag et al., 1997) and attention deficit hyperactivity disorder (Langley, Rice, & Thapar, 2005)—preterm birth and/or low birth weight likely mediate this relationship.

While cancer is the best-known outcome of tobacco use, smokers also have elevated rates of cardiovascular disease (CDC, 2018b). Among middle-aged and older Canadians, fewer than half identified smoking as associated with increased risk of heart disease (Frieden & Blakeman, 2005). Of all cardiovascular-related deaths in the United States, 30 percent are attributed to smoking (CDC, 2018b). Even low levels of smoking elevate health risks. For example, smoking fewer than five cigarettes per day increases the danger of cardiovascular disease, including stroke (CDC, 2018b).

However, the negative effects do not solely impact smokers themselves. Indirect exposure to cigarette smoke also increases illness rates. Specifically, exposure to secondhand smoke is associated with greater risk of cancer, heart disease, and respiratory illness. Secondhand smoke is estimated to kill about 41,000 nonsmoking adults each year (CDC, 2017). Each year in the United States, secondhand smoke exposure accounts for approximately 34,000 adult deaths from coronary heart disease and 430 infant deaths from sudden infant death syndrome (SIDS) (CDC, 2017). After 30 minutes of exposure to secondhand smoke, the vasoconstriction effects are like that of a regular smoker. Exposure to environmental smoke also increases the risk of chronic respiratory disease by 25 percent and adult asthma by 50 percent. Pregnant women exposed to secondhand smoke exposure face double the risk of sudden infant death syndrome (CDC, 2017). Another concern is that exposure to secondhand smoke is associated with greater risk for middle-ear disease (chronic otitis media) (Håberg et al., 2010) among children, which, in turn, increases the risk of language delays and dyslexia.

A common misconception is that cigarettes advertised as "light" or "ultralight" pose less risk. However, these terms do not describe the nicotine content or presence of other chemicals in cigarettes but instead refer to the subjective flavor (Frieden & Blakeman, 2005). Survey findings suggest that only about 10 percent of smokers are aware of this caveat. Studies suggest that when smokers of light cigarettes attempt to quit, they are less likely to be successful (Frieden & Blakeman, 2005).

History of Cigarette Smoking

In 1900, cigarettes accounted for only 2 percent of tobacco use in the United States. Chewing tobacco accounted for 50 percent, and loose tobacco, typically smoked in pipes, accounted for 20 percent (Brandt, 2007). By 1950, 80 percent of tobacco use was in the form of cigarettes. The development of cigarettes led to a major increase in tobacco consumption. By the late 1940s, more than half of American men smoked and 20 percent of American women were smokers (Brandt, 2007). In Britain in the 1940s and 1950s, up to 80 percent of men smoked. For some time, smoking among women was often considered "unladylike." However, in cigarette advertising campaigns in the 1920s and 1930s, directed specifically at women, smoking was depicted as a sign of modernity and independence. In the 1940s, 40 to 50 percent of physicians were regular smokers. Smoking ads often portrayed physicians with testimonials such as "More doctors smoke Lucky Strikes than any other cigarette."

As noted in the section on epidemiology in Chapter 2, by the 1960s, Doll and Hill (1950; 1964) established the causal connection between smoking and lung cancer. In 1964, the US surgeon general announced with considerable publicity that smoking was a definitive cause of lung cancer. Fifty years later, a federal report concluded that smoking was definitively associated with cataracts, pneumonia, and leukemia, as well as cancers of the cervix and lips and increased risk of kidney failure (US Department of Health and Human Services, 2014). Despite this information, the prevalence of smoking in the United States, while declining significantly from the 1940s, has persistently remained in the 15 to 20 percent range.

Demographics of Smoking

At present, approximately 15 to 16 percent of the US population smokes, with higher rates among men (17.5 percent) than women (13.5 percent) (CDC, 2018a). By ethnicity, Native Americans have the highest smoking prevalence at 31.8 percent. Rates are essentially equal between non-Hispanic Whites (16.6 percent) and Blacks (16.5 percent). The smoking rate among Latinos is low relative to the general population (10.7 percent) and is particularly low among women. Asian Americans, as a group, have the lowest smoking rate (9 percent) but also exhibit considerable variability, with Korean Americans having a 20 percent smoking prevalence (CDC, 2018a).

Socially disadvantaged populations are more likely to smoke and less likely to successfully quit (Hiscock, Bauld, Amos, Fidler, & Munafò, 2012). In some developed countries, 60 percent of persons in lower socioeconomic groups smoke (Hiscock et al., 2012). As greater social disadvantage accrues, smoking rates increase. One investigation found the highest smoking rates among geographic regions with "single parent households living in public rented accommodation, with little community support, residents who have no access to a car with few occupational qualifications and high TV viewing behaviors" (Sharma, Lewis, & Szatkowski, 2010; cited in Hiscock et al., 2012, p. 108).

Multiple studies have shown that in developed countries, smoking is associated with lower income, lower levels of education, and unemployment. Social class differences appear to override employment status—unemployed blue-collar workers are more likely to continue smoking than unemployed white-collar workers. Among women, there is a definite association between social class and cessation. There have been multiple hypotheses about the association between social status and smoking, including lack of support for quitting, reduced access to nicotine replacement and smoking cessation pharmacotherapies, and lower levels of self-efficacy (Hiscock et al., 2012).

Smoking Initiation

Most adult smokers began in their teens. Between 40 and 60 percent of high school seniors have tried cigarettes at least once. In 2016, approximately 8 percent of high school and middle school students had used cigarettes in the past month—a 16 percent decline from 2011 (CDC, 2018a). However, when smokeless tobacco, hookahs, and electronic cigarettes are included, 20.2 percent of high school students reported use of tobacco or related products (CDC, 2018a). There are three major risk factors associated with initiating smoking: peers who smoke; parents who smoke; and the presence of depressed mood. The greater the number of smoking peers in an adolescent's social network, the greater the probability of the teenager initiating smoking. If you were to ask a group of young teenagers whether they expect to be smoking in 5 to 10 years, the majority would say no and that they believe they can stop when they desire. However, a high percentage do not stop smoking—a phenomenon termed "optimistic bias" (Arnett, 2000). Adults who are heavier smokers are far more likely to have started in their teens compared with adults smoking under a pack per day.

Other factors associated with initiating smoking include poor self-esteem, having no plans for additional education after high school, and having parents who did not attend college (CDC, 2018a).

While most models of addiction would suggest that one of its defining features is a withdrawal syndrome when cigarettes are unavailable, Peterson, Vander Weg, and Jaén (2015) suggest that with nicotine, withdrawal is not the defining feature. Instead, it is the experience of losing autonomy and the ability to refuse cigarettes. The addictive properties of smoking are illustrated by the finding that 25 to 30 percent of teenagers exhibited this difficulty with refusal after their first cigarette (Peterson et al., 2015).

The media also appears to influence smoking initiation. Feature films frequently include characters who smoke. Adolescents who watch movies depicting smoking are almost three times as likely to smoke (Dalton et al., 2003). Children ages 12 to 17 are twice as likely as adults to be exposed to tobacco advertising. Cigarette advertising may have an additive influence as part of the social context that includes having peers who smoke (Frohlich, Potvin, Chabot, & Corin, 2002; Frohlich, Potvin, Gauvin, & Chabot, 2002).

Arnett and Terhanian (1998) found that Marlboro and Camel ads were most popular among adolescents. Correspondingly, these were the cigarette brands adolescents were most likely to smoke (Arnett and Terhanian, 1998).

There is evidence of a genetic diathesis that may predispose some individuals to smoking. Research suggests that individuals with a specific genetic variant in dopamine transporter and dopamine receptor genes were more likely to smoke (Sullivan & Kendler, 1999). When the effects of major depressive disorder are added to this genetic predisposition, the likelihood of smoking further increases (Audrain-McGovern et al., 2004).

Mental Health Conditions and Smoking

Persons with mental illness account for 35 to 45 percent of all cigarettes consumed in the United States (CDC, 2018c). Indeed, when persons without a mental disorder are removed from the statistics, smoking rates fall to about 10 percent. Those with mental illness are two to four times as likely to smoke as those with no psychiatric history (CDC, 2018c; Vanable, Carey, Carey, & Maisto, 2003). In the United States it has been estimated that up to 90 percent of persons with schizophrenia are regular smokers. Approximately 60 percent of those diagnosed with bipolar disorder and 30 to 55 percent of those diagnosed with an anxiety disorder smoke. About 40 percent of persons with major depressive disorder are smokers (Hirshbein, 2015).

The disproportionate rates of smoking among those with mental illness are, in part, likely to stem from nicotine's physiochemical effects. Since nicotine stimulates dopamine, it contributes to greater alertness and increased heart rate and blood pressure, as well as muscle relaxation and release of endorphins—the natural opiates that reduce stress. Nicotine also reduces blood circulation to the extremities, such as the hands and feet, and suppresses appetite for carbohydrates.

The highest rates of smoking associated with a psychiatric condition are those with other substance-abuse problems—approximately 50 to 60 percent of persons with alcohol, marijuana, cocaine, or other substance abuse problems are smokers (Vanable et al., 2003). The co-occurrence of smoking with mental health and substance abuse has led to disagreement about the optimal treatment. While it had been previously suggested that smoking cessation not be initiated during treatment for alcohol or other drug abuse because the demands of quitting two or more substances simultaneously were likely to place undue pressure on the patient and reduce success rates, more recent research suggests that smoking cessation intervention does not seem to interfere with, and may actually enhance, treatment of other substance-abuse problems (Searight, 2018).

Smoking may also complicate the psychiatric and medical treatment of persons with mental illness. Major depressive disorder elevates mortality rates from vascular disease and cancer—likely further exacerbated by smoking. Since nicotine increases the rate of metabolism of many psychotropic medications, lower doses of antipsychotic and antidepressant medications may be necessary when patients stop smoking. Because of this change in drug metabolism associated with cessation, drug side effects, such as atypical motor movements in patients taking antipsychotic medication (Peterson et al., 2015), may appear. The pattern of smoking initiation and onset of psychiatric symptoms is not entirely clear. It would be understandable that persons with major depressive disorder would be more inclined to smoke because of nicotine's impact on improving mood, attention, and concentration. It is also possible that persons predisposed to psychiatric illness find that smoking helps with early symptoms of major depressive disorder, anxiety disorders, and even schizophrenia.

There is some debate in the literature about whether persons with major depressive disorder are less likely to be successful when they stop or attempt to stop smoking. From a clinical perspective, it would seem logical that the negative mood states, such as irritability, that are associated with the first 7 to 14 days of cessation would be more pronounced among those with untreated major depressive disorder. However, research has often not distinguished between persons with a single episode versus multiple episodes of chronic major depressive disorder (Hitsman, Borrelli, McChargue, Spring, & Niaura, 2003). Additionally, it has been recommended that smoking cessation be incorporated into treatment when mental health professionals are treating patients for mental health conditions. When this integrated approach is used, there are suggestions that cessation efforts may lead to better outcomes for treated mental health conditions as well as better compliance with smoking pharmacotherapy and a greater likelihood of successful smoking cessation (Hall & Prochaska, 2009; Peterson et al., 2015).

The Macrosystem: Public Health, the Cigarette Industry, and Tobacco-Control Policies

If you read newspapers and news magazines, you have an appreciation of the complexity of the economic and political issues involved with tobacco. In examining international patterns of smoking, there appear to be historical patterns reflecting shifts in demographics of smokers. Lopez, Collishaw, & Piha (1994) describe a four-stage model depicting demographic changes in smoking. In the first stage, as tobacco use is initially established in a country, men are far more likely than women to initiate smoking. In the next stage, smoking continues to increase among men, and women initiate smoking. In the third stage, smoking begins to decline, particularly among men. In the fourth stage, overall smoking continues to slowly decline. During this final phase, socioeconomic differences in smoking become visible (Lopez, Collishaw, & Piha, 1994). In many developed countries, smoking has been declining; the up-and-coming populations of new smokers are coming from developing countries such as India, China, and parts of Africa (Ng et al., 2014).

There have been three primary governmental strategies to reduce tobacco consumption. Increased taxation on tobacco products occurs primarily at the state level. Federal guidelines have restricted advertising of tobacco-related products. As you may notice, there are no tobacco ads on television. The final strategy has been to reduce the number of places that one can smoke. No-smoking ordinances in public places such as restaurants are initiated and passed at both the local municipal level as well as the state level. All of these policy interventions appear to have had some effectiveness in reducing smoking.

However, at the same time, governmental policies surrounding smoking have historically demonstrated contradictions. While federal and state governments have funded and developed many public health awareness campaigns to reduce tobacco use, there is also a legacy of federal farm subsidies that have maintained tobacco production. From 1995 to 2012, tobacco subsidies in the United States were a total of $1.5 billion. Additionally, up until about 2014, the federal government had, for the previous 10 years, required the tobacco industry to compensate farmers through a federal program for the regulation of the tobacco industry (Bomey, 2015). However, the general trend has been toward reducing production, with the acreage devoted to tobacco declining from 93,300 in 1997 to 4,268. By 2015, nearly all federal tobacco subsidies in the United States were essentially eliminated. However, as the production of tobacco in the United States has diminished, other countries are importing non-US tobacco, thus incentivizing tobacco production internationally (Bomey, 2015).

Tobacco Taxes and Related Legislation

Since Sir Walter Raleigh brought tobacco to England in the 1600s, it has been the source of considerable government revenue (Brandt, 2007). International data suggest that a 10 percent increase in cigarette price reduces smoking by about 8 percent in low- and middle-income countries and 4 percent in high-income countries (Hiscock et al., 2012). While legislation was often originally written so that the revenues generated by cigarette taxes would fund public health education smoking programs, states, often strapped financially, have used cigarette tax money for other purposes. There is evidence internationally, however, that when the revenue generated by cigarette taxes is directed toward smoking education, there are further reductions in smoking levels (Chaloupka, Yurekli, & Fong, 2012). However, while not canceling out the benefits of cigarette taxation, there is evidence that as cigarette taxes rise, black-market cigarette activity increases. In New York in 2002, the state increased the cigarette tax from $1.11 to $1.50 per pack. New York City increased its own local tax from $0.08 to $1.50. As a result, there was a $3.00 increase in the price of a pack of cigarettes in New York City. Corresponding with the tax increase, smoking rates declined by at least 2 percent. However, within a year of this tax increase, there was a reported 89 percent increase in cigarettes purchased through alternative channels. These included cigarettes purchased outside of the state, on the internet, and on the street from various sellers. It was noted that lower-income individuals who were smokers were more likely to use these alternative channels for acquiring cigarettes (Shelley, Cantrell, Moon-Howard, Ramjohn, & VanDevanter, 2007). As would be imagined, the tobacco industry has developed a wide range of strategies for countering government tobacco control efforts.

When there are state referenda and ballot initiatives directed toward increasing taxes on cigarettes, the tobacco industry responds aggressively. It is relatively rare that the industry's public messages focus on the health aspects of smoking (Laposata, Kennedy, & Glantz, 2014). Since only about one out of five Americans smoke, a significant proportion of nonsmokers would have to vote against any ballot initiative for smoking restriction or increased cigarette taxation to fail. Recognizing this, the tobacco industry's public opposition messages typically center around American values of freedom and personal independence. Rather than focusing specifically on increased taxation of cigarettes, the message conveyed is that this is another example of government intrusion and increased punitive use of taxation (Laposata, Kennedy, & Glantz, 2014). Tobacco companies also have histories of funding trade unions and may look to these organizations for support when smoking control issues are placed on the ballot (Balbach, Herzberg, & Barbeau, 2006).

Public Education

In the United States there is a text warning that is placed on all cigarette packs ("Surgeon General's Warning: Smoking causes lung cancer, heart disease, emphysema, and may complicate pregnancy"). In other countries, such as Canada, the warning is accompanied by a graphic picture depicting the consequences of smoking—for example, a photo of cancerous lungs or an individual with a stoma (hole) in their throat due to laryngeal cancer. Studies of the effects of these labels have found that among Canadians, those who had read and thought about graphic warning labels were significantly more likely to have tried to quit smoking within the previous three months (Hammond, Fong, McDonald, Cameron, & Brown, 2003).

In 2009, the federal Family Smoking Prevention and Tobacco Control Act was established in the United States. The act required pictorial warnings on cigarette packs, similar to those used in Canada. However, since that time, the implementation has been stalled by numerous court challenges. In 2012, an appeals court indicated that the Food and Drug Administration had not provided any evidence to support the principle that pictorial warnings reduce smoking (Baynes, 2012).

However, based upon similar principles, such as the role of fear in health behavior change, there has also been some evidence that smokers may defensively and unconsciously engage less with images. Harris, Mayle, Mabbott, and Napper (2007) compared smokers' and nonsmokers' reactions to graphic warning images. The participants were asked to rate how disturbing or frightening the images were and how relevant the pictures were personally. Smokers reportedly found the images no more personally relevant than nonsmokers and reported that they found them less frightening. Interestingly, up to 30 percent of smokers say they try to cover the warnings on the cigarette packages (Harris et al., 2007). However, a recent US study in which smokers were randomly assigned cigarette packs that had pictorial warnings versus text-only warnings and were followed for four weeks suggests that the pictures have impact (Brewer et al., 2016). It was found that 40 percent of those with the pictorial warnings attempted to quit during this time, compared with 34 percent of those in the text-only condition. Additionally, 5.7 percent of smokers who received the pictorial warning had quit for a week during this four-week period, compared with 3.8 percent of those receiving text-only cigarette packages (Brewer et al., 2016).

Smoking Bans

The number of settings in which smoking has been banned by legislation or institutional policy has grown dramatically in the past 25 years. Smoking bans often have begun with hospitals, later spreading to restaurants, airports, train stations, bars, stores, and educational institutions. Even some casinos, often depicted as the last bastion of public smoking, have gone to a smoke-free policy, at least in some parts of the building. While evidence is not always consistent and involves varying time frames and varying types of smoking bans, there does appear to be a modest decrease in smoking prevalence in regions with indoor smoking bans (Koh, Joossens, & Connolly, 2007). This pattern has been found both in the United States and internationally; as time since implementation of the bans increases, health benefits do appear to be associated with the smoking restrictions. Specifically, there does appear to be an association between smoking bans and smoking-related morbidity and mortality. There is also evidence suggesting that smoke-free policies have been associated with better cardiovascular and respiratory health as well as reductions in premature delivery and low-birth-weight infants (Frazer et al., 2016).

California has one of the most aggressive and broad-based tobacco control programs in the world. In addition to initiating smoking bans in most public settings in 1994, the state has a history of being very proactive with tobacco education. For some years, until a recent budgetary crisis emerged, California had one of the highest levels of state expenditures for tobacco reduction activities (Barnoya & Glantz, 2004). Recent estimates of heart disease and lung cancer suggest that smoking-related death rates in California have dropped as well (Fichtenberg & Glantz, 2000). While these efforts appear to be successful, because of state budgetary issues, revenue generated from cigarette taxes has not been consistently devoted to tobacco education. In 2012, a California referendum to increase the tax on cigarettes failed. While correlation is certainly not causation, multiple states have found significant declines in smoking associated with well-funded tobacco control programs (Farrelly, Pechacek, Thomas, & Nelson, 2008). There do appear to be consistent associations between the amount of funding states devote to tobacco education and, in conjunction with smoking bans, reductions in smoking initiation among adolescents (Lovato, Linn, Stead, & Best, 2003).

In terms of secondhand smoke, comprehensive antismoking legislation has resulted in significant reductions in childhood asthma and respiratory disorders (Faber et al., 2016). Specifically, a recent European meta-analysis found an 18.5 percent reduction in hospitalizations for lower respiratory tract infections, a 9.8 percent decline in childhood asthma hospital admissions, and a 3.7 percent reduction in preterm births (Faber et al., 2016).

In recent years, the tobacco industry's marketing expenditures have been 10 to 15 times greater than the total investment in state tobacco control efforts. The tobacco industry has often responded to referenda on smoking bans with a multi-pronged strategy. They have rallied persons working in the hospitality industry, such as restaurants, by suggesting that smoking bans will greatly cut into their business. A common opposition message is that smoking bans are another form of government regulation, which, if permitted, may seep into other areas of life and remove personal independence. For example, it has been suggested that smoking bans may increase social division and support intolerance of others. Additionally, these bans reduce freedom of choice and violate the property rights of the owners of restaurants and bars (Anderson, 2003).

The Tobacco Industry

Documents obtained through legal challenges have demonstrated that the tobacco industry has been aware of the negative effects of smoking for some time. In various industry memos, cigarettes have been referred to as a nicotine delivery system (Brandt, 2007). Terms such as "nicotine addict" appeared in industry reports as early as 1961. Additionally, internal memoranda suggest that other substances, including alkaline additives such as ammonia and increased amounts of burley, have been added to cigarettes to increase the "kick" associated with nicotine (World Health Organization, 2000). Since it is selling a product with established health risks, the cigarette industry has had to have a comprehensive, multifaceted marketing approach that responds to both scientific evidence and attempts at government regulation.

Advertising has been a staple of the tobacco industry. In the 1940s, it was common for cigarette industries to portray medical doctors in their ads. Even at that time, there was anxiety among the public about the possible effects of smoking. Advertisements announcing that a large-scale survey found that physicians "preferred Lucky Strikes" were designed to allay those concerns. Given the impact of economic factors on smoking, it is understandable that those who have a vested interest in smoking would be least in favor of large-scale smoking cessation efforts. There is evidence that cigarette companies primed young people for smoking through cartoons—between 1937 and 1997 two-thirds of children's cartoons made by five of the major production companies, including Walt Disney and Universal, included characters that smoked (Goldstein, Sobel, & Newman, 1999). Joe Camel has been recognized by more six-year-olds than Mickey Mouse (Fischer, Schwartz, Richards, Goldstein, & Rojas, 1991).

Mental Illness and Tobacco Use

The tobacco industry appears to have been aware of the association between mental illness and smoking well before mental health professionals. In the early 1980s, marketing specialists for R. J. Reynolds described tobacco users who smoke for mood enhancement and cognitive stimulation (Hirshbein, 2015). At around this same time, some tobacco companies were funding the research of well-known stress researchers such as Hans Selye, who suggested that smoking could be helpful as a diversion for reducing stress. An industry-supported marketing study concluded that it could be beneficial to market cigarettes with an emphasis on nicotine as a type of short-term therapy for depressive symptoms, as something that helped "perk you up" and facilitated problem solving. The tobacco industry was also aware of the perceived value of cigarettes for anxiety and as useful for enhancing self-control and reducing the experience of feeling overwhelmed (Hirshbein, 2015). Analysis of previously unavailable tobacco industry records indicates that tobacco companies supported, either directly with funding or indirectly, research suggesting that persons with schizophrenia were less likely to be harmed by regular tobacco use. Additionally, the industry supported the view that persons with schizophrenia benefited from tobacco. Finally, there were suggestions that the tobacco industry promoted smoking in psychiatric settings by making cigarettes available as well as by assisting with opposition to hospital smoking bans (Prochaska, Hall, & Bero, 2007).

Ethnicity, Culture, and Smoking

The review of internal tobacco industry documents also suggested that marketing strategies were being developed for specific segments of US populations. Some tobacco epidemiologists have suggested that the lower rates of smoking among African Americans—particularly African American women—as well as the lower rates of smoking among African American adolescents compared with Whites may reflect resistance to perceived tobacco company control. The attempt of R. J. Reynolds to market a cigarette specifically for the African American community, the Uptown cigarette brand, is well known. In 1990, R. J. Reynolds was planning to launch the new Uptown brand in Philadelphia. It was noted that the advertising campaign focused on placing Uptown in the context of "nightlife, entertainment and music themes" while highlighting the cigarette's premium quality—a classy product refit reflecting the "good life" (Balbach, Gassior, & Barbeau, 2003; Robinson & Sutton, 1994). Six weeks after the launch of Uptown, organized opposition within the African American community publicized R. J. Reynolds's plan. A coalition in Philadelphia forced R. J. Reynolds to withdraw Uptown before the cigarettes were on the market. Review of documents, however, indicates that R. J. Reynolds continued to market to African Americans with its emphasis on menthol. In the late 1980s, before Uptown, R. J. Reynolds had begun to focus on mentholated cigarettes. It was fairly evident that the menthol initiative program was targeting African Americans. It was noted that in one document, titled "The Black Initiative Monthly Marketing Report," "Black" was crossed out and replaced by the word "Menthol." At that time, in the general cigarette-smoking market, mentholated cigarettes constituted 29 percent of cigarette purchases. However, nearly 70 percent of African American smokers chose a menthol brand. Salem cigarettes, in particular, became the menthol brand of choice (Gardiner, 2004). Balbach and colleagues (2003) noted that the themes of nightlife, "hipness," and expensive objects continued to be used by R. J. Reynolds in service of selling mentholated cigarettes.

There do appear to be ethnic differences in cessation rates, with African Americans, Native Americans, and Hispanic Americans less likely to attempt quitting and less likely to use pharmacotherapy when they do make cessation attempts. There are suggestions that tailoring cessation programs to ethnic communities may increase success rates. For example, smoking cessation programs offered by churches may be more effective in engaging African Americans who smoke (Campbell et al., 2007; Schorling et al., 1997). However, while promising, tailored messages that are culturally based are relatively rare, and evaluation of this approach is even rarer.

As countries such as Australia and the United Kingdom have shown demonstrable declines in smoking, these gains have been offset by the rise in smoking in China. Other regions high in cigarette consumption are eastern and southern Europe (Lopez et al., 1994). Even in countries that have reduced smoking prevalence dramatically, the smokers that remain are high-volume cigarette consumers (Ng et al., 2014). It is estimated that by 2030, almost 80 percent of tobacco-related deaths will occur in low- and middle-income countries (Lopez et al., 1994). Tobacco control regulations are often absent or not enforced in many of these countries. For example, in Africa sale of single cigarettes is encouraged since it makes smoking accessible to lower-income groups. Additionally, tobacco companies have provided free cigarettes to children ages 13 to 15 and sponsored youth events (Westhead, 2000).

Smoking Cessation—Common Issues

Background for Smoking Cessation

About 70 percent of smokers report smoking 15 or more cigarettes a day. The half-life of nicotine is about 2 hours. After 6 to 8 hours of regular smoking, nicotine levels may persist 6 to 8 hours after the last cigarette. Weight gain is a concern among those who undertake smoking cessation (Pistelli, Aquilini, Carrozzi, 2016). On average, smokers weigh 7 pounds less than nonsmokers.

Smoking cessation is very difficult. The average smoker makes six to seven quit attempts before they are successful. One-year abstinence rates for smokers who quit "cold turkey" are about 12 percent (Peterson et al., 2015). Cigarettes have often become an integral part of the smoker's day-to-day life. Smoking cessation efforts are unlikely to be successful unless the context of cigarette use is fully appreciated. Smokers report that it improves their mood, attention, alertness, and concentration and often serves as a refreshing break from demanding activities. A recent qualitative study found that smoking had different meanings and functions based upon the social environment (Katainen, 2012). On the job, the "smoke break" is a way to briefly escape the work routine. Having a cigarette means having a break; not having a cigarette means not having a "true" break in the workday. Readers who have worked in the fast-food industry may have observed that smokers are more likely to take the "required" 15-minute break every four hours. During the smoke break, work is covered by nonsmokers, who often get shortchanged in terms of their own break time. Smoking is also a way of affirming social bonds—particularly in settings involving alcohol. In a study of young adults who regularly gathered for socialization, those who did not smoke were implicitly criticized by peers. Another interesting study examined how women caring for children at home used smoking. Based upon the diaries that the women kept, smoking was a way of coping—particularly in households with young children. When these women would feel overwhelmed, smoking appeared to be a way to reimpose structure or regularity upon a chaotic household (Katainen, 2012).

Assessment Prior to Undertaking Smoking Cessation

It is important to remember that most individuals who stop smoking do so on their own without any professional assistance (Peterson et al., 2014). At the same time, there is evidence that both behavioral and pharmacological therapies improve cessation rates. For clinicians who are working with smokers, it is important to understand what the client has tried in the past and the degree of success associated with these strategies.

For younger adults and adolescents, behavioral modification alone may be effective without adjunctive pharmacotherapy. With lighter smokers consuming fewer than 10 cigarettes a day, stimulus control–oriented behavioral intervention combined with relapse prevention strategies may actually be more effective than any type of pharmacotherapy. It is also important to openly discuss possible weight gain and the degree of distress that this relatively small weight gain may elicit (Pistelli et al., 2016). Rates of major depressive disorder are twice as high in females compared with males, and these rates are likely to be significantly higher among women who smoke. A particularly challenging group are those with less than a high school education. Fewer years of formal education is associated with increased prevalence of smoking and less success with smoking cessation strategies (Hymowitz, Sexton, Ockene, Grandits, & MRFIT Research Group, 1991). As noted earlier, only half of pregnant smokers quit smoking altogether, while a significant number of pregnant women reduce their number of cigarettes. Relapse rates during pregnancy range from 15 to 30 percent among those who attempt to become abstinent (McBride et al., 1999).

There are several formal questionnaires that are often used to assess levels of nicotine dependence. The Fagerstrom Scale is one of the most commonly used instruments in smoking cessation programs (Fagerstrom & Schneider, 1989). Questions include the following: "How soon after you wake up do you smoke your first cigarette?" "Which cigarette (first in the morning or any other during the day) would you most hate to give up?" "Do you smoke even if you are so ill that you are in bed most of the day?" The total Fagerstrom score has been useful in assisting clinicians' decisions about the need for pharmacotherapy for a given patient.

A less formal but very useful assessment tool is a cigarette diary. A very simple version is an index card kept with the cigarette pack, with the hours of the day listed and space to record the number of cigarettes removed from the package per hour. Often, a pattern becomes apparent—80 percent of cigarettes are smoked at home, and more than half of the day's cigarettes are smoked before 11 a.m. Additional information includes the presence of smokers in the home and in the workplace. This can provide a picture of the number of people in their social circle that are regular smokers. As will become evident below in the discussion of nicotine withdrawal, it is very helpful to know the number of prior quit attempts and length of time in days, months, or years that the individual has successfully abstained in prior efforts (Searight, 2018).

Nicotine Withdrawal

Getting through nicotine withdrawal is typically the most challenging part of smoking cessation. Nicotine withdrawal is characterized by both psychological and physical symptoms (Hughes, Higgins, & Bickel, 1994). In addition to craving, aversive mood states including irritability, anxiety, and dysphoria are common. Smokers going through withdrawal also report that their concentration and attention are poorer than when smoking. Other aspects of withdrawal include increased hunger, difficulty sleeping, and constipation. Those with ongoing GI disturbances such as ulcerative colitis may experience a brief exacerbation of their condition. It is likely that the emotional component of withdrawal is significantly more intense for persons who have ongoing mental health problems. Nicotine withdrawal in the presence of major depressive disorder could conceivably intensify the symptoms of the mood disorder. Again, this pattern lends support to the idea of incorporating cessation into the patient's mental health treatment.

The acute phase of nicotine withdrawal begins within 24 hours of the last cigarette. While subjectively, the symptoms may be experienced as interminable, the episodes of craving typically last minutes or less, and the physical, cognitive, and mood symptoms dissipate after 10 days. By three weeks after the initiation of cessation, the only symptom remaining is the craving sensation.

Similar to withdrawal from many other addictive drugs, a key to successful withdrawal and cigarette abstinence is reducing the intensity of emotional and physical discomfort. Recent research has also suggested that the craving experience, a potent factor for early relapse, can be modified through cognitive strategies. The best predictor of the degree of craving has been the number of cigarettes consumed per week. In one study, research participants who were smokers were asked to look at a picture of either a fatty food or a cigarette, and then they were told to think about the immediate as well as the long-term consequences of consuming the substance. When the "now" state was compared with the "later" state, smokers reported significantly less craving when asked to consider future consequences (Kober, Kross, Mischel, Hart, & Ochsner, 2010). In terms of application, the results suggest that it may be useful to ask individuals, as part of the cessation process, to maintain a diary where they remind themselves of the longer-term effects of smoking, such as lung cancer and the potential future impact of those conditions on family and friends.

Interventions

Pharmacotherapy

Nicotine replacement exists in the form of gum, skin patches, inhalers, nasal spray, and lozenges (Silagy, Mant, Fowler, & Lodge, 1994). Successful use of the, has the patient beginning with an optimal nicotine dose, such as 21 mg, and then gradually reducing the dose by 7 mg every 2 weeks until they are no longer using replacement. A 21 mg patch is the equivalent of one pack of cigarettes per day, with a 14 mg patch equal to half a pack. It is important to recognize that even with nicotine replacement, for multiple-pack-per-day smokers, nicotine withdrawal, while of diminished intensity, will still occur since standard nicotine replacement therapies will provide less nicotine than smoking (Fiore, Smith, Jorenby, & Baker, 1994). Research suggests that when the patch is used beyond 6 to 8 weeks, it is not useful in helping patients quit.

Another common form of nicotine replacement therapy is nicotine gum such as Nicorette (Peterson et al., 2015). One limitation of both the patch and gum is that nicotine absorbed through the skin or the GI system does not have the same level of potency as when it is obtained through smoking. It is estimated that blood levels of nicotine provided by both the patch and gum are only about 40 to 50 percent of that obtained through smoking (Peterson et al., 2015). Many patients will use both of these nicotine replacement methods over extended periods of time. While this practice was originally thought to be dangerous, it is probably not as risky as originally suggested. However, it does defeat the purpose of nicotine replacement therapy as a tool for smoking cessation.

Nicotine nasal spray is absorbed more quickly and may reduce withdrawal symptoms more rapidly than some other forms of nicotine replacement. Inhalers, similar to electronic cigarettes (discussed further below), are plastic tubes, shaped in the form of a cigarette and inhaled similarly. A nicotine cartridge is placed within the plastic inhaler (Zellweger, 2001). Proponents of nicotine inhalers have argued that hand-to-mouth motions have some reinforcement value to smokers and that the inhaler mimics this aspect of cigarette use. Research has generally found that when used alone, nicotine replacement therapy is associated with a quit rate of approximately 25 percent at 6 months, compared with quit rates of 12 to 15 percent of patients receiving placebo (Fiore et al., 1994).

While it is recommended that patients not initiate nicotine replacement therapy before their quit date, other non-nicotine replacement medications are often started in advance of quitting. The antidepressant bupropion (marketed for smoking cessation as Zyban) is initiated several weeks before the quit date so that the drug is exerting some therapeutic effect at the time of smoking cessation. Research does suggest that long-term cessation rates with bupropion alone are higher than for nicotine replacement alone (Jorenby et al., 1999). Bupropion's success rate at one year is approximately 21 percent. With both nicotine replacement and bupropion, counseling, including periodic phone support from a nurse or health care provider, increases the one-year success rate by another 5 percent.

Varenicline (Chantix) currently is the most effective pharmacotherapy for smoking cessation. However, there is one important caveat—patients must stay on the medication for this effect to occur, and Chantix has a high discontinuation rate. The effects of Chantix occur through agonist activity at the nicotine receptor sites. While dopamine release continues with Chantix, it is at a lower level than with nicotine. As a result, Chantix both reduces cigarette cravings as well as reduces the reinforcement value associated with smoking. Chantix is recommended to be used for a period of 12 weeks. One year after its initiation, Chantix has been found to have success rates of 20 to 25 percent (Jorenby et al., 2006). However, unpleasant side effects have been frequently reported for Chantix, with nausea reported in 30 to 40 percent of those taking the medication. These unpleasant gastrointestinal effects can typically be remediated if the medication is taken with food. As readers may know, the medication has been associated with nightmares, mood changes, and well-publicized instances of aggressive behavior. While cognitive and emotional reactions to Chantix do not occur in most individuals, patients with pre-existing psychiatric problems, such as major depressive disorder, may be more likely to have negative behavioral reactions to Chantix (Anthenelli et al., 2016).

When Chantix and bupropion are used together, one-year success rates have been in the 50 to 55 percent range (Issa, Abe, Moura, Santos, & Pereira, 2012). While combining with nicotine patches may seem intuitively attractive, the simultaneous use of Chantix with nicotine replacement therapy may reduce Chantix's effectiveness. Adding nicotine reduces the effectiveness of varenicline in reducing nicotine receptor activity.

Cognitive and Behavioral Strategies

Telephone counseling is occasionally provided along with pharmacotherapy. Two general strategies have been employed by these adjunctive counselors. Health professionals, such as nurses or persons trained in smoking cessation counseling, initiate contact with patients in the early phases of quitting or, alternatively, the patient initiates the phone contact themselves. Both approaches appear to have beneficial effects on top of pharmacotherapy. There are some suggestions that smoker-initiated contacts are somewhat more effective. Additionally, there appears to be a dose-response effect, with three or more calls increasing the likelihood of successful cessation (Stead, Perera, & Lancaster, 2006).

While techniques such as hypnosis often appear attractive to patients—often based upon advertisements that they have seen in popular media—when used alone, long-term effectiveness is not significantly better than quitting "cold turkey" (Law & Tang, 1995). Mindfulness meditation, in which one develops the ability to observe the symptoms of withdrawal without responding to them, was recently applied to nicotine withdrawal. This approach will be discussed further below.

The underlying assumption for most behavioral approaches to smoking cessation is that cigarette use is acquired and maintained by a combination of both classical conditioning and operant learning principles (Lazev, Herzog, & Brandon, 1999). With this as a foundation, psychologists have applied aversion principles to smoking cessation. Rapid smoking, in which one smokes cigarettes in very rapid succession—inhaling every 6 seconds until they become nauseous and feel light-headed—appears to have some success. Peterson et al. (2015) report 19 percent abstinence rates at 6 months. Another aversive procedure has been to pair vivid, unpleasant mental images with active smoking. A concrete application of aversive methods involves maintaining a jar of the contents of emptied ashtrays and added water—not only does it appear undesirable, but the smell is also extremely unpleasant. Persons are instructed to smell the contents of the jar whenever they have an urge to smoke. Aversive methods for behavior change, while possibly having some short-term effectiveness, also carry risks. Rapid smoking can provoke a heart attack in vulnerable individuals. Additionally, exclusive reliance on aversive methods does not provide the patient with the skills to address situations that might provoke relapse.

Rather than aversive or punishment-oriented applications, the most widely accepted applications of learning theory are based on removing environmental stimuli that have been paired with cigarette smoking. These cues include the smell of smoke in one's car or home, the presence of cigarettes, cigarette lighters, full ashtrays, and the presence of other smokers. Importantly, smoking seemingly may include one's spouse, close friends, and coworkers. If these members of one's social network are active smokers, it will make successful cessation more difficult to achieve.

There is research indicating that the social networks of smokers, containing persons directly known to the smoker but also those at several levels removed from the target individual, are more likely to be smokers themselves. In an early study involving social contagion theory, Christakis and Fowler (2008) found that smoking cessation appears to spread within social networks beyond the dyadic relationships between smokers. In examining smoking networks over time, it was found that there is a cascade effect in which socially connected clusters stopped smoking at about the same time. Interestingly, education appeared to be an important shared dimension among clusters that reduced smoking; the higher the level of education within a cluster, the greater the likelihood of cessation (Christakis and Fowler, 2008). The investigators also found that social clusters in which smoking persisted moved to the edges of this broader social network. Interestingly, this larger network became progressively "polarized" between 1971 and 2003 as social ties between smokers and nonsmokers diminished (Christakis & Fowler, 2008).

The stimulus control principles that maintain smoking extend to other ritualized patterns of behavior that accompany cigarette use. For example, while a growing number of bars have become smoke-free, the presence of alcohol—particularly in a familiar social context, such as weekends spent drinking beer on the patio or while watching sports with friends—is a historical context for smoking that may readily contribute to relapse.

More recently, several studies have suggested that mindfulness meditation may be a useful smoking cessation strategy by itself or in combination with pharmacotherapy. When compared with the well-regarded cognitive behavioral approach developed by the American Lung Association, participants receiving mindfulness treatment exhibited a greater reduction in cigarette use and pronounced improvement in abstinence rates at four months. At the four-month mark, abstinence rates for those receiving mindfulness treatment were 31 percent, compared with 6 percent for those receiving Freedom from Smoking cognitive behavioral treatment (Brewer et al., 2011). In applying mindfulness meditation to smoking cessation, rather than trying to suppress cravings, individuals are encouraged to accept these experiences. Formal instruction includes a body scan focusing on physical sensations in the body; loving-kindness in which positive wishes for oneself and others are practiced and often stated subvocally as a mantra; and breathing-oriented meditation with the attentional focus placed on the breath. In addition, participants are encouraged to set daily goals and perform daily activities in a mindful manner (Brewer et al., 2011).

Stages and Successful Smoking Cessation Strategies

Among patients who have decided to quit smoking, strategies specific to the preparation and action stages of the trans-theoretical model are most relevant. For those who are in the precontemplation or contemplation stages, it is often helpful to ask whether there's anything that could occur in the future that would tell them that it is time to quit (Searight, 2018). Health care providers can also address a patient's reluctance to begin cessation through motivational interviewing techniques. If the provider is skilled at expressing empathy and reflecting ambivalence, patients are likely to conclude that there is no optimal time for quitting and that the present is as good a time as any.

Preparation

In preparation, the smoker has set a definite quit date and they should inform family and friends of the date. As part of the countdown to cessation day, cigarettes should be purchased one pack at time rather than by the carton. Ashtrays and lighters should be removed from the workplace, home, and car. Their home and office should be thoroughly cleaned—often including shampooing carpets and dry-cleaning draperies. The automobile should be cleaned with particular attention to removing the smell of smoke from the interior.

A key dimension in preparing to stop smoking is anticipating situations in which there are strong temptations to smoke. Preparation also includes systematically removing or reducing stimuli associated with cigarette use; specific strategies will need to be developed to substitute new behavior for cigarette smoking. The cigarette diary, described earlier, can be very helpful to both the person trying to quit as well as any health professional working with them in identifying settings or times of the day in which cigarette consumption is greater. Armed with this information, specific strategies can be developed for these contexts.

For example, the smoke breaks that are part of the workday, the ritual of reading the morning newspaper along with a cigarette and coffee, as well as having a cigarette immediately after meals, are all contexts for which the smoker will need to develop alternative behavioral scripts (Searight, 2018). It is almost universally recommended that the individual who is trying to quit smoking encourage their significant other to quit with them. Another principle is that it is easier to discontinue a behavior if an alternative behavior is put in its place. Hard candy, gum, toothpicks, and drinking straws may all be used as substitutes for smoking, and adequate quantities should be available before the quit date.

A very simple strategy is to smoke less before the cessation date. One way this can be easily accomplished is to encourage the smoker to delay 20 to 30 minutes before smoking the first cigarette of the day. Smokers may also try smoking only two-thirds of a cigarette before putting it out. Finally, they may switch brands to one that is less desirable (Peterson et al., 2015).

Action

Pharmacotherapy combined with stimulus control and behavioral intervention should make the process less distressing, but even with a well-developed plan, unanticipated challenges are likely to arise. The most difficult period will be the first 7 to 10 days, in which nicotine withdrawal is at its peak. For those who are making their fourth or fifth attempt at cessation, the implementation of cognitive behavioral strategies is particularly important. However, if previous attempts have been successful for at least several weeks, there should be a fund of experience to predict high-risk situations for relapse. It is highly probable that certain social situations may need to be avoided for several months, such as Friday-night happy hours or joining smoking coworkers for lunch. When the social network does include smokers, it is not uncommon for them to feel guilty about their ongoing smoking habit, and they may at least indirectly attempt to sabotage their friend or coworker's quit attempt. This pressure is likely to be even more pronounced if there is a smoker in the household, such as a spouse.

For those smokers with histories of major depressive disorder, regular contact with a therapist and/or physician during the first months of cessation is likely to improve success rates. As noted earlier, it may be necessary for the dosages of antidepressant medication to be altered because of the changes in metabolism associated with smoking cessation (Hall & Prochaska, 2009).

Mindfulness practices encourage "urge surfing" when cravings arise (Bowen & Marlatt, 2009). In this approach, individuals focus on the area where they experience craving—this may be a physical feeling of fatigue or agitation or irritability. In "surfing" it is important to try to specify the bodily region in which the urges are greatest. For smokers, it is often in the mouth and nose. Second, it is important to acknowledge the cravings rather than try to suppress these physical and emotional experiences—it is often helpful to name them: "I am feeling tension in my stomach" or "I can't seem to keep my hands still." While focusing on the area of the body or the specific experience associated with craving, slow rhythmic deep breathing should be initiated. With each exhalation, notice how the urge changes. This breathing meditation should continue until the craving is reduced. Again, it is helpful for recent ex-smokers to recognize that this period is, in objective terms, usually a matter of a few minutes (Marlatt & Donovan, 2005).

As noted above, smokers who may not have social support for their efforts at cessation may benefit from contact with a smoking cessation group such as those offered through the American Cancer Society; if available, telephone-based counseling is also likely to be helpful.

Vaping and E-cigarettes

Electronic cigarettes began being sold in the United States in 2007. In 2011 the United States Food and Drug Administration indicated that e-cigarettes would be regulated as a "tobacco product" rather than a "drug delivery system." E-cigarettes are tubes with electronic devices that heat liquid to produce a vapor. A lithium battery typically powers the heating element. Usually, vaporization does not include tobacco smoke. However most e-cigarettes do include nicotine. The liquid that is vaporized has added flavoring such as cherry, chocolate, or mint.

In 2016, it was reported that 16 percent of high school students and 5.3 percent of middle school students had used e-cigarettes in the past 30 days (US Department of Health and Human Services, 2016). It is estimated that about 20 percent of cigarette smokers have tried e-cigarettes (Centers for Disease Control, 2017). There are suggestions that e-cigarettes may be a safer alternative to tobacco. While e-cigarette vapors contain some of the toxic chemicals found in cigarettes, the levels are substantially lower. However, again, e-cigarettes are not without risk (Centers for Disease Control, 2018b). Similar to tobacco, there is evidence that aerosols and nicotine are released into the environment and are inhalable by others in the vicinity. However, data suggest that this secondhand vapor is not as detrimental as being exposed to secondhand cigarette smoke.

While appearing promising as a nicotine replacement treatment for smoking cessation, e-cigarettes do not appear to be substantially more effective than other nicotine replacement therapies in eliminating cigarette smoking. When comparing nicotine patches with e-cigarettes with and without nicotine, e-cigarettes with nicotine demonstrated a slight benefit in cigarette cessation at six months (Farsalinos & Polosa, 2014).

It has been noted that those who use e-cigarettes in place of regular cigarettes inhale e-cigarettes more deeply—probably to obtain a stronger effect from nicotine. While e-cigarettes do increase the pulse and impact measures of heart function, they exert less effect than cigarettes. Finally, there do appear to be a reasonable number of smokers who use both conventional cigarettes and electronic cigarettes (Grana, Benowitz, & Glantz, 2014).

Another concern is that adolescents may initially use e-cigarettes and progress to tobacco-based cigarettes. Research suggests that those who experimented with e-cigarettes were more likely to smoke tobacco-based products and become regular users of traditional cigarettes (Dutra & Glantz, 2014). While there have been suggestions that e-cigarettes might be part of a harm reduction strategy for smoking, research to date suggests that, at present, this conclusion is unwarranted (Grana et al., 2014).

Conclusion

The effects of smoking are the most common form of preventable death in the United States. While smoking's prevalence has declined significantly and in recent years plateaued in the United States and Canada, it is becoming a major public health hazard in developing countries. As is evident, smoking is initiated and maintained by a complex biopsychosocial web of factors ranging from genetic predisposition to federal government policies and international business interests. The fact that cessation appears to be most likely when there is a combination of cognitive, behavioral, and pharmacological interventions used simultaneously supports the view that smoking is a complex biopsychosocial phenomenon. The vast majority of smokers in the United States would like to quit. Most teenagers who initiate smoking do not plan to continue the habit into adulthood. However, the low success rates of smoking cessation efforts attest to the potent addictive properties of cigarettes. While the use of e-cigarettes is being marketed as a safer replacement for cigarettes, their long-term safety remains an open question. Research to date suggests that e-cigarettes are unlikely to replace traditional cigarettes.

CHAPTER 10

Obesity, Exercise, and Eating Disorders

Eating is fraught with meaning. We are constantly in an approach-avoidance conflict regarding weight loss and food. Around the world, food is a centerpiece of daily life. Meals are when we are supposed to connect with friends and family. The sheer variety of available food continues to increase. Ben & Jerry's has had more than 1,000 flavors of ice cream. When we thought we had seen everything, something new, such as chocolate-covered bacon, comes along. I recently encountered a hamburger served between two doughnuts. However, the constant availability of enjoyable foods has been a major factor contributing to the growing problem of excess weight and obesity among Americans. Faced with these challenges, we try to "burn it off" with exercise. However, the results of exercise, even while beneficial to our overall health, do not typically yield the decline in weight that we would desire. Unfortunately, many handle the dilemmas posed by abundant food and a culture that values thinness by developing disordered eating such as in anorexia nervosa and bulimia. While the overall percentage of persons who meet a formal categorical diagnosis for an eating disorder is small, relatively speaking, "subclinical" eating disordered behavior is very common. In particular, among college-aged women, up to 1 in 4 may engage in some problematic eating and/or compensatory behavior such as self-induced vomiting.

Based on current trends, it is estimated that by 2030, 83 percent of Americans will be overweight (Hruby & Hu, 2015). Rates of obesity continue to climb in the United States, having doubled over the course of the last several decades. In 1960, only about 20 percent of US adults were considered overweight. However, by the early 1990s, at least 40 percent qualified as overweight or obese. Currently 33 percent of adults are overweight and an additional 35 percent of US adults are obese. The body mass index (BMI) is the most commonly used index of obesity. The BMI is calculated by dividing weight in kilograms by height in meters. At present, a normal BMI is in the range of 18.5 to 24.9, while overweight is reflected in a BMI between 25 and 29.9. Obesity is defined as a BMI of 30 or above. The term *overweight* is defined as weighing 10 percent or more over one's recommended weight for one's height and skeletal frame. The formal definition of obesity is weighing 20 percent or more over recommended weight. Recently, another category, extreme obesity, characterizing at least 6 percent of US adults, is present when the BMI is greater than 40.

Obesity has been a particularly intractable problem from a public health perspective. Behavioral interventions, diet, and exercise, even when combined in an intensive program, yield modest weight loss, which is often not maintained. Even surgical procedures, such as gastroplasty, are often not associated with long-term maintenance of weight loss.

Obesity's Role in Health and Illness

Obesity is an independent risk factor for a number of diseases. Obesity increases the risk of hypertension by a factor of five and is one of the six controllable factors contributing to heart disease. Other conditions linked to obesity are type 2 diabetes, kidney failure, and coronary artery disease, including elevated cholesterol and heart attack. Gallstones, asthma, and sleep apnea are also associated with being overweight (Brennan & Murphy, 2013). About 10 percent of all cancers are associated with obesity. The presence of obesity increases the cancer risk by 30 percent among those with a BMI greater than 30 and 100 percent by those with a BMI greater than 40 (Brennan & Murphy, 2013). Among those who are severely obese, life expectancy is reduced by 5 to 20 percent (Faulconbridge & Wadden, 2010). While the direction of causality is not clear, mental health conditions—specifically major depressive disorder and anxiety disorders—are also more common among those who are overweight (Martin-Rodriguez, Guillen-Grima, Martí, & Brugos-Larumbe, 2015).

Risk Factors for Being Overweight

Heritability accounts for about 35 to 55 percent of body weight. However, inheritance is complex, with an estimated 32 genetic loci for weight. Heredity also influences body shape, size, fat distribution, and metabolic rate. In twin studies, it appears that between 55 and 80 percent of BMI variance is associated with heritability. However, environmental factors do play a significant role in body weight. Eliciting this genetic predisposition depends upon a range of factors, including amount of time spent viewing television as well as level of physical activity (Hruby et al., 2016).

From an evolutionary perspective, the ability to store large amounts of body fat enhanced survival and increased the likelihood of passing genes on to the next generation. Additionally, infants with more body fat were more likely to survive during this vulnerable period. In our past history as a species, being able to store large amounts of body fat was adaptive since food was scarce and energy expenditures were high. However, in our modern era, there is easy access to an array of attractive, calorically dense foods, and the amount of physical activity required to maintain life has declined. As a result of being in what many would call an "unnatural" environment, increased body weight is understandable (Faulconbridge & Wadden, 2010). From an evolutionary perspective, there is also a genetic diathesis for maintenance of body fat and energy efficiency. This inherited predisposition is elicited in an "obesonogenic" environment featuring readily accessible and desirable food choices.

There is evidence that those who are obese are much more responsive to external food cues. While non-obese individuals will eat less after being "preloaded" with food, those who are obese, beginning in childhood, do not compensate by eating less after eating immediately before. Consider the last time you went to a buffet or smorgasbord; it is likely that you ate more than usual. We tend to eat more food when offered a larger variety of desirable foods. But there does appear to be a satiation point for even highly desirable foods. However, if a different desirable food is presented, even after previously consuming a large quantity of desirable food, we will continue to eat; this process can repeat itself multiple times.

Sensory processes also appear to be involved in eating. Brain imaging studies have found that obese individuals demonstrate greater "reward-related activation" when presented with food cues. When the sense of smell is eliminated—often due to central nervous system abnormality, a condition called anosmia—individuals tend to lose weight (Aschenbrenner et al., 2008). Additionally, persons born without the sense of smell are less likely as adults to have an elevated BMI. Neuroimaging studies indicate that the taste and smell of food activate the brain's reward systems. The brain's cortical-limbic-striatal circuit shows hyper activation in the presence of food among persons who are obese (Geliebter et al., 2006). In addition, persons who are obese do not demonstrate delay discounting. When given the choice of a specific amount of food now or an opportunity of a larger amount of food later, persons who are overweight do not wait—there is a consistent preference for immediate food reward (Weller, Cook, Avsar, & Cox, 2008). Interestingly, the hyperactivity shown in the brain circuitry remains even after an individual has lost significant weight. Two hormones, leptin and ghrelin, also play a role in food consumption and weight (Faulconbridge & Wadden, 2010). Leptin exerts its effect on the thalamus by increasing the experience of "fullness" and decreasing the desire to eat. Ghrelin is released into the gastrointestinal system (Faulconbridge & Wadden, 2010). When ghrelin levels drop, our experience of hunger increases. Metabolic rate, the process by which nutrients are incorporated and used, also plays a role in weight gain. Overall, the largest component of metabolism is resting metabolic state—the energy required to maintain basic bodily functions. Metabolism, over time, becomes more efficient. This is one of the reasons why recurrent episodes of dieting make it more difficult to lose weight.

As mentioned in Chapter 11 on sleep disorders, too little sleep appears to be associated with increased obesity risk. Women sleeping 5 hours per night or less were more likely to gain weight than those sleeping 7 or 8 hours (Patel, Mahlotra, White, Gottlieb, & Hu, 2006). As the number of shift-work jobs has increased, there has also been concern about this pattern adversely impacting sleep and, in turn, contributing to obesity. There is a positive association between shift work and weight gain (Antunes, Levandovski, Dantas, Caumo, & Hidalgo, 2010).

Compared with the 1960s, Americans today consume more dietary fat and carbohydrates as well as more total daily calories. From 1970 to 2003, the average American increased their calorie consumption by an average of 523 daily calories. Additionally, Americans eat out more often, with more than 40 percent of the family's total food budget spent on food eaten away from home (Faulconbridge & Wadden, 2010). As calorie consumption has increased, physical activity has declined. The average American now spends 15 minutes per day exercising and 170 minutes per day watching television or related media (Hruby et al., 2016).

Body Weight, Stereotypes, and Discrimination

There is considerable evidence that persons who are overweight are viewed negatively by potential employers, dating partners, and health care professionals. Research indicates links between "weight-based victimization" and depression as well as suicidal ideation among adolescents and adults. Among teenagers, weight stigma has been associated with depression and increased calorie consumption (Schvey, Puhl, & Brownell, 2011). Among adults, quality of life has been inversely associated with body mass index (Jia & Lubetkin, 2005). Weight bias is in part founded upon a view that weight is controllable and that those who are unable to maintain this control are irresponsible and lazy. As a way of countering this stigma, it has been suggested that media, such as television shows, increase positive portrayals of overweight individuals.

Health care professionals are often caught in a bind—given the growing rates of obesity and its correlates, it is important the issue be addressed with patients. Health care professionals, despite knowledge of genetic factors, have been found to openly criticize obese patients and spend less time with them, as well as provide less preventive care. Patients, even when criticism is not overt, are aware of this stigma (Wadden et al., 2000). There is also evidence that obese patients, possibly because of their concern about being stigmatized, are less likely to use the health care system (Puhl & Heuer, 2009). There is some evidence that patients who were told to lose weight actually were more likely to gain weight over time. This is congruent with research that has been done with children, in which parents who focus on weight are more likely to have children who have attitudes associated with eating disorders (Smolak, Levine, & Schermer, 1999).

Weight bias refers to social judgments associated with weight. There are a number of implicit characteristics that have come to be associated with being overweight, including laziness, dependence, and irresponsibility. Unfortunately, when they encounter someone with weight bias—for example, a health care professional—overweight individuals may experience stigma and shame. There is a misconception that this stigma and shame will motivate patients to lose weight (Clifford & Curtis, 2016). However, as suggested above, this view is misguided, and any remotely critical comments are likely to lead to reduced contact with medical professionals.

Weight-Loss Interventions

As suggested by Chapter 5 on health communication, weight-loss goals are often extremely unrealistic. The inability to achieve these goals leads to diminished self-efficacy and makes it unlikely that dietary changes will be maintained. Many people make New Year's resolutions—fewer than half of them keep those resolutions for 6 months (Norcross, Mrykalo, & Blagys, 2002). While many people enter weight-loss programs with goals of losing up to 25 to 30 percent of body weight, a 5 to 10 percent weight loss is associated with significant health benefits, including reduced risk for diabetes, hypertension, and high cholesterol (Wing et al., 2011). In one study involving a nearly 3-year follow-up, participants who underwent a "lifestyle intervention," involving an increase in physical activity to 150 minutes or more per week, exhibited a 58 percent reduced risk for developing type 2 diabetes compared with a control group. Even with additional weight gain during the follow-up, those who lost relatively small amounts had reduced risk of type 2 diabetes and cardiovascular disease at follow-up (Faulconbridge & Wadden, 2010; Wadden & Frey, 1997).

Low-Calorie Diets

One of the strategies to increase the experience of "success" with weight loss has been the very low calorie diet (VLCD). Very low calorie diets typically involve food intake of no more than 800 calories per day. However, they have been extended downward to 500 calories per day and are medically monitored. The VLCD contains all of the necessary vitamins and minerals as well as protein. However, carbohydrate may be absent or very minimal. The food typically takes the form of a powder that is mixed with water. It is usually considered appropriate only for persons with a BMI above 30. The average weight loss associated with a 10-week VLCD program was 10 pounds more than behavioral intervention alone. At 3 to 5 years after the intervention, the degree of benefit was approximately 2 pounds compared with behavioral intervention (Parretti et al., 2016).

Behavioral and Cognitive Behavioral Approaches

Comprehensive behaviorally oriented weight-loss programs include self-monitoring of caloric intake and often the type and duration of physical activity (Brennan & Murphy, 2013). Additionally, more complex self-report systems may include indicating emotional states associated with eating. Goal setting is an important element (Brennan & Murphy, 2013). However, these objectives focus primarily or solely on the number of pounds lost. Because of individual variability as well as the benefits of relatively small amounts of weight reduction, it is often more helpful for the goals to be focused on staying within specific calorie parameters for the day or week and completing specific amounts of exercise. Since eating is likely to follow principles of classical and/or operant conditioning (Brennan & Murphy, 2013), it is important to regulate eating cues. At a basic level, this means having a preset plan of food consumption for each day and also eliminating high-fat high-caloric foods from the home.

It is also helpful to have a plan for situations in which there may be a tendency to overeat or skip exercise. Cognitive patterns such as those discussed earlier with the trans-theoretical model are also important to address. Dieting is often associated with all-or-nothing thinking. Patients may begin each day with the gym and a controlled calorie diet. However, by evening, there is a sense of deprivation and hunger, which leads to overeating or eating high-calorie foods. The guilt associated with breaking the diet leads people to feel guilty, but they may try again the next day. However, these episodes erode self-confidence about one's ability to maintain a healthy eating pattern. Lapses are often associated with the attribution that weight loss is simply impossible or the changes in diet are not worth the relatively small weight reduction achieved. Again, it is more helpful for persons undertaking weight-loss programs to set realistic goals and remember that limited weight reduction is associated with significant health benefits.

Third-wave behavioral inventions such as acceptance and commitment therapy (ACT) have also been applied to weight loss. As discussed earlier, acceptance and commitment therapy has added some useful techniques to addressing healthy eating. Emotional eating appears to be particularly refractory to change. ACT suggests that emotional eating may be a form of experiential avoidance—a way to avoid feeling overwhelmed by the demands of school, work, or distress about a relationship. ACT argues that distress arises not from the aversive emotions but, instead, can be traced to our strategies of trying to deny and avoid unpleasant feelings. Eating has become a practiced way of tuning out or distracting ourselves from these feelings and thoughts while also being intrinsically rewarding. In an interesting study examining this issue, Forman et al. (2007) gave transparent boxes of Hershey's kisses to undergraduate students. They were told that they could not eat the kisses for the next two days. The investigators assigned participants to several different strategies for resisting the desire to eat the candy. One group of students was taught how to use distraction. Cognitive reappraisal was another condition (Forman et al., 2007), and a third group used ACT strategies that encouraged the students to accept their cravings. Interestingly, follow-up research suggested that the effects of acceptance were particularly pronounced among those who were more sensitive to the external food environment and persons who were more likely to engage in emotional eating (Forman, Hoffman, Juarascio, Butryn, & Herbert, 2013).

Many weight-loss programs, including self-help interventions, such as TOPS (Take Off Pounds Sensibly), have a strong interpersonal component. Meeting with a group of individuals who are also addressing weight loss and sharing struggles and success on a weekly basis can often be beneficial. There is some evidence that continued contact with group members after a formal intervention has ended is associated with maintenance of weight loss (Brennan & Murphy, 2013).

Weight-Loss Medication

There is a long history of prescription and non-prescription medications used for weight loss. The Federal Trade Commission has noted that half of the advertisements for over-the-counter weight-loss products make representations that are likely to be false. Importantly, these products are not often subject to the degree of regulation that governs prescription medication.

Prescription medications include phentermine and sibutramine. These medications, while influencing metabolism, also may reduce the experience of hunger (Brennan & Murphy, 2013). Sibutramine has been found to be effective with weight reduction; the effects are even more pronounced with the addition of behavior therapy (Wadden et al., 2005). Orlistat is a medication that inhibits absorption of dietary fat. It has been found to be effective in a dose-response pattern. When added to a diet and exercise regimen, patients taking orlistat were more likely to lose 5 percent of body weight compared with a comparison placebo group (Hauptman, Lucas, Boldrin, Collins, & Segal, 2000). Generally speaking, prescription drugs are associated with moderate weight loss. However, since these drugs are not intended for long-term use, the weight loss obtained is often not maintained. Typically, prescription weight-loss drugs such as orlistat are recommended for people with a BMI greater than 30 who have attempted other approaches to weight reduction without success.

Bariatric Surgery

Surgery has been recommended for those with a BMI of 40 or higher or a BMI of 35 or above accompanied by significant medical morbidities, such as type 2 diabetes or hypercholesterolemia. Historically, the original form of gastric bypass surgery was the Roux-Y procedure in which a small pouch is created at the base of the esophagus. The limited size of the pouch reduces food consumption markedly. The procedure also bypasses the stomach. Laparoscopic gastric banding is a related procedure that involves creating the pouch but without the bypassing of the stomach and intestine (Faulconbridge & Wadden, 2010). In addition to reducing food absorption by the gastrointestinal tract, postsurgical patients will often experience nausea if they consume foods high in fat. Early research on the procedure indicated that the majority of patients receiving these surgical procedures no longer met criteria for type 2 diabetes and/or elevated cholesterol. With the Roux-Y procedure, an average weight loss at one year of about 33 percent was reported, with maintenance weight loss of approximately 25 percent (Faulconbridge & Wadden, 2010). Death rates associated with the procedure are well below 1 percent. However, complication rates may range from 10 to 17 percent, with about 7 to 8 percent of patients requiring reoperation (Chang et al., 2014; Gloy et al., 2013).

The Macrosystem
Cultural Factors in Food Consumption: The French Paradox

There are significant international differences in rates of obesity between countries. In 2000, approximately one-third of Americans were considered obese compared with about 22 percent of citizens of the United Kingdom and only about 3 percent of Japanese. While there have been some efforts made to explain these cross-national differences on a genetic basis, it is unlikely that heredity accounts for these differences.

One of the cross-national discrepancies that has been difficult to explain is a difference between Americans and the French in terms of obesity. In the United States, rates of obesity are about five times that of France. However, French cooking, for anyone who has enjoyed it, tends to be high in fat and sugar as well as butter and cream. While the French do seem to have higher cholesterol levels than Americans, they also have a longer life span and lower rates of heart disease. Some observers have pointed to the high consumption of wine among the French. There is some evidence that wine, in moderation, may reduce the risk of coronary heart disease. Rozin, Kabnick, Pete, Fischler, & Shields (2003) and Heine (2015) suggest that there are fundamentally different attitudes toward food between France and the United States. Among the French, eating is seen as more of an aesthetic sensory experience that is intended to be enjoyable and social. When dining at McDonald's, the French spend 50 percent more time eating than Americans. They spend this extended time eating despite the fact that in France, McDonald's portion sizes are smaller.

American young women are also more preoccupied with foods that have allegedly been altered to make them healthier, such as low-fat yogurt or low-fat cream cheese. Rosencrantz and Cohen (cited in Heine, 2015) conducted a study in which subjects were asked to say whatever words came to mind in response to the word *food*. Among American women, a frequent response was "fattening," which did not appear among the French.

As noted above, a major difference between French and US diets appears to be portion size. In the United States, supersized meals and soft drinks are actually a fairly recent phenomenon historically that began in the 1970s and continues to this day. However, even the concept of a "medium-sized" order of French fries is objectively different in France versus the United States. At a McDonald's in the United States, a medium-sized order contains about 70 percent more French fries. Rozin and colleagues (2003) also found that in reviewing cookbooks, the amount of ingredients was significantly larger in American guides than it was in French ones. At most fast food chains in the United States, portion sizes for French fries, chicken nuggets, sodas, and milkshakes are now 2 to 5 times larger than when these products were initially introduced (Heine, 2015; Young & Nestle, 2002).

The Food Industry

Exposés of the food industry suggest that manufacturers may deliberately modify food content to increase consumption. A common strategy is to deliberately enhance taste through specific combinations of fat, sugar, salt, and various food additives including artificial flavor enhancers. Additionally, by removing protein and fiber, sugar can be absorbed more quickly into the bloodstream.

Some critics have argued that ultra-processed foods meet the definition of an addictive substance similar to alcohol or cigarettes. When rats are given a diet of ultra-processed foods such as cookies, cheesecake, and bacon versus standard food for these laboratory animals, the animals exposed to ultra-processed foods are much more likely to seek out food high in fat and sugar even when these foods are paired with electric shocks (Johnson & Kenny, 2010; Gearhardt et al., 2012). It has been suggested that for many people, consumption of ultra-processed foods is consistent with the definition of substance abuse/dependence: continued use of a substance despite the psychological and physical problems and the experience of having little self-control in the presence of these foods. When someone has been successful in reducing processed food intake, the risk of lapse and relapse persist. Similar to patterns found among problem gamblers, studies of brain activity among individuals with obesity indicate that in the presence of food-related cues, there is pronounced activity in neural circuits associated with reward.

Policies for Increasing Nutritional Awareness

In May 2010, the White House convened a childhood obesity task force. One of the recommendations was that foods have a front-of-package (FOP) label with nutritional information. In part because of this recommendation, the industry developed and encouraged the "Smart Choices" FOP system while the government was still studying the issue. This basic FOP information includes: calories, saturated fat, sodium, and sugar per serving. In addition, specific nutrients such as vitamin C and potassium, if present, were highlighted (Hawley et al., 2013). A symbol indicated that these foods were considered to be "better for you." While the determination of food quality was reportedly the work of a team that included industry nutritionists, scientists, academics, government regulators, and public health professionals, the program rapidly became the subject of criticism when sweetened cereals such as Coco Crispies and Fruit Loops were designated as "Smart Choices" (Brownell & Koplan, 2011). The program subsequently folded.

Surveys indicated that about two-thirds of US shoppers will use FOP labels "often" or "sometimes" in making purchase decisions. However, straightforward information such as number of calories was often misinterpreted; many shoppers erroneously assumed that the labeled calorie count was for the entire package rather than for an individual serving. Some countries use a simplified "traffic light" approach to FOP labeling—a "red light" indicates that the packaged food is unhealthy, marginal (yellow light), or healthy (green light). These labels have been found to be particularly useful for consumers with weaker arithmetic skills. In addition, if accurate, the traffic lights permit rapid decision-making about food purchases. Research suggests that the traffic light system is associated with reduced purchasing of high-calorie foods. One study found that traffic lights were more effective in reducing purchases of unhealthy foods than a 10 to 15 percent tax on unhealthy foods or financial subsidies for healthier foods (Ellison, Lusk, & Davis, 2014).

Providing consumers with this information is also useful in choosing premade foods lower in calories. When ordering lunch from a website, traffic light labels and caloric listings were found to be associated with a 10 percent reduction in calories. Adding detailed caloric information to the "traffic light" had no further impact in reducing the calories purchased (VanEpps, Downs, & Loewenstein, 2016). From the perspective of reducing obesity, it was hoped that by publicly labeling nutritional value, there would be significant impact on food selection. This impact has not been seen on a large scale, although there is some evidence of modest change in the Netherlands and New Zealand. Today, the multiple traffic light model with limited additional information about calories and nutrition appears to be preferred by consumers (Hawley et al., 2013).

As an increasing number of meals are consumed outside of the home, nutritional information is being made available in restaurants. While not as widely studied as FOP labels, restaurants with caloric information on their menus such as "the recommended daily caloric intake for men is ___ and for women is ___" did have an impact on the number of calories ordered. In a randomized study, when ordering from a restaurant menu that included calorie labels, adults consumed fewer calories than those ordering from a menu without this information (Gearhardt et al., 2012; Roberto, Larsen, Agnew, Baik, & Brownell, 2010). Additionally, there are suggestions that when this type of information is available on restaurant menus, parents' food choices for children include more reduced-calorie options.

Sugar Taxes

During his tenure as mayor of New York City, Michael Bloomberg was ridiculed for attempting to institute a "nanny state" when he proposed a ban on sales of extra-large sugary soft drinks as an approach to reducing obesity. While not successful in New York, Bloomberg has provided support to other communities, such as Philadelphia, which passed a 3 percent tax on soft drinks. Other cities that had a similar tax include Boulder, Colorado; San Francisco, California; and Cook County in Illinois. A study examining the impact of the tax in Berkeley, California, found that it was associated with a 21 percent reduction in sweetened soft drink consumption, while consumption increased by 4 percent in comparison cities. Additionally, water intake increased by 63 percent in Berkeley compared with 19 percent during the same time period in the control cities (Falbe et al., 2016).

While relative prices on fruits and vegetables significantly increased between 1979 and 2009, the price of carbonated drinks was actually below the average rise in the consumer price index (Brownell & Frieden, 2009). As suggested by the findings in Berkeley, increasing the overall price of high-sugar beverages reduces consumption. It is estimated that a penny-per-ounce tax on sugared beverages would decrease consumption by 13 percent and lead to an average weight reduction of two pounds per person per year (Brownell & Frieden, 2009). Since the habit of consuming sweetened soft drinks typically begins early in childhood, it is believed that over time, these taxes, which indirectly promote alternatives to sugared drinks, should be associated with reduced population-level obesity.

Marketing and Economic Factors

The food industry spends billions of dollars every year on various types of marketing. Newer types of marketing include advertising through cell phones and the internet as well as social media outlets such as Facebook and Twitter, which allow food companies to market their products to specific demographic groups. Studies of food ads indicate that the vast majority of ads are for high-caloric food with minimal nutrients (Gearhardt et al., 2012). Branded food products appear in 70 percent of the top box-office-earning films.

Much of food advertising is directed at children. It is estimated that children view approximately 15 food commercials for food products each day. Children are disproportionately represented in marketing efforts. Of food and beverage ads as well as websites studied, 85 percent appeared to be targeting children (Gearhardt et al., 2012; Lingas, Dorfman, & Bukofzer, 2009). The impact of "licensed characters" on the perceived value of the food is significant. Children will describe the food as tasting better if a licensed character is on the package compared with the same food in a different package. SpongeBob alone has 700 licensing partners worldwide (Gearhardt et al., 2012). At the municipal level, several California cities such as San Francisco and Santa Clara have passed ordinances requiring that children's meals including a toy meet certain nutritional standards (Gearhardt et al., 2012; Otten et al., 2014). Some countries actually have regulations limiting the types of food ads and accompanying items, such as toys, directed at children. In the United States, recommendations have been made about modifying food and beverage ads directed to children. Adoption of these standards is voluntary.

Exercise

A Brief Historical Perspective

While Hippocrates viewed moderate exercise as beneficial to health, this observation was not shared by most physicians until the mid- to late 1900s. Physicians such as Paracelsus and Galen emphasized that overexertion was likely harmful to health. In the 1700s, the Italian physician Bernardini Ramazzini, in studying the health of men employed in various occupations, noted that messengers exhibited better health status than sedentary workers such as cobblers (Paffenbarger, Blair, & Lee, 2001). Studies in the 1800s suggested that physically vigorous occupations as well as avocational interests such as hiking and swimming were associated with longer life. By the early 1900s, the US surgeon general's office reported that cardiovascular and kidney disease appeared to be less common among those engaged in physical labor. Several studies also suggested that there was a dose-response gradient such that greater physical activity was associated with longer life (Paffenbarger et al., 2001).

A classic study of the modern era is that of Morris and colleagues (Morris, Heady, Raffle, Roberts, & Parks, 1953), who examined heart attack rates among two types of transportation workers on double-decker buses: bus drivers and conductors. The conductor's role involved going back and forth and up and down stairs to collect tickets, while the driver remained sedentary. They found that rates of heart attacks were 2 to 3 times greater among bus drivers compared with conductors. When compared with drivers, conductors exhibited lower blood pressure, smaller waist sizes, and reduced rates of obesity (Paffenbarger et al., 2001). Even among drivers and conductors who smoked cigarettes—a very common habit in the 1950s and 1960s—exercise still exhibited a protective effect on mortality as well as reduced risk of cancer (Paffenbarger et al., 2001).

Nationally, only 25 percent of youth ages 12 to 15 meet the CDC criteria for moderate to vigorous physical activity for 60 minutes per day. As physical activity among children and youth has declined, sedentary activities have become more common—approximately 70 percent of 12- to 16-year-olds reported two or more hours per day watching television, playing video games, or using a computer for activities unrelated to school (Centers for Disease Control, 2016b). Television and computer use among young adolescents has been associated with overweight status, elevated blood pressure, and elevated cholesterol levels.

Adults with type 2 diabetes exhibit lower levels of physical activity than the general population. Additionally, they exhibit lower levels of self-efficacy surrounding exercise. In developing a physical activity program for persons with this condition, targeting self-efficacy for physical activity appears to be particularly important in increasing regular active exercise among this group (Dutton et al., 2009).

Exercise and Mental Health

As you may have experienced in your own life, an hour or so of vigorous exercise does improve mood—we generally feel more upbeat, less overwhelmed, and calmer after aerobic activity. Research has consistently found that exercise does improve symptoms of major depressive disorder as well as subclinical depressive symptoms (Cooney et al., 2014). While the effects of exercise are modest, and probably not strong enough to be used as a stand-alone treatment for serious major depressive disorder, there do appear to be some additive effects of exercise when combined with medication. While the benefits of exercise for treating symptoms of depression are fairly well established, the mechanism involved is less clear. There is some evidence, primarily from animal studies, that physiological mechanisms may be responsible. However, support is more consistent for psychosocial factors, including enhanced self-esteem and self-efficacy associated with exercise (Marcus, Selby, Niaura, & Rossi, 1992; Salmon, 2001). Additionally, after an episode of major depressive disorder, higher rates of physical activity are associated with reductions in relapse (Goodrich & Kilbourne, 2010). It also appears that those with the lowest pre-exercise mood achieve the greatest benefits from exercise (Goodrich & Kilbourne, 2010).

The effects for exercise on anxiety are mixed. There is evidence that for those who are lower in trait anxiety (stable anxiety that is often considered part of a person's personality), levels of regular exercise are greater (De Moor, Beem, Stubbe, Boomsma, & De Geus, 2006). However, for some conditions such as panic disorder, increased exercise and, in particular, increased heart rate may provoke panic attacks.

For many of us, experiential avoidance is a major part of our struggle regarding exercise. If our original plan was to work out first thing in the morning and we awaken feeling tired, we may let ourselves get another hour of sleep and plan to work out later in the day. Throughout the day, however, challenges emerge and we begin to tell ourselves, "I'm not sure if I'll have time to work out today; I don't think I'm going to be able to make it." And by the end of the day, "I'm just way too tired to go to the gym; I'll double up on my workout tomorrow." As discussed earlier in this book, Acceptance and Commitment Therapy (ACT) highlights core values. As such, the importance of physical activity should take precedence over current emotional and motivational states, including the gradual diminishing commitment to exercise that occurs during the day. By teaching individuals to be observers of their experience, the thoughts, feelings, and sensations that work against initiating physical activity can be viewed as transient phenomena rather than reality (Butryn, Forman, Hoffman, Shaw, & Juarascio, 2011). By recognizing and accepting states such as fatigue and hunger that might reduce commitment to exercise and defusing these experiences while remembering the value of exercise, we can effectively reduce the influence of these internal obstacles. Researchers found that adding ACT to a regular exercise program increased levels of physical activity compared with a control educational condition (Butryn et al., 2011).

Exercise and Cognitive Functioning

Attention, concentration, and short-term recall improve immediately after aerobic exercise (Perkins, Searight, & Ratwik, 2011). Lees and Hopkins (2013) found that these immediate effects on short-term memory were greater for those who had an ongoing history of regular exercise. Most of the research relating exercise to cognition has been conducted with older adults. A recent study found that regular exercise reduced the likelihood of developing symptoms of Alzheimer's disease such as decline in short-term memory (Ngandu et al., 2015). On imaging tests, there is evidence that among older adults there are increases in brain volume in neural regions associated with age-related cognitive decline. These areas of the brain actually increased in volume among older adults who exercised regularly (Colcombe et al., 2006). In addition to improved attention and concentration, more complex skills such as executive functioning (self-monitoring) and processing speed demonstrate positive associations with exercise (Smith et al., 2010). Task switching, in which there are demands to shift from one task to another then back to the original activity, is a common challenge in daily life. Young adults who engaged in regular physical activity demonstrated better performance in the face of task switching compared with those who were sedentary (Kamijo & Takeda, 2010). Similar exercise benefits on tasks requiring shifts in cognitive set have been shown for older adults (Guiney & Machado, 2013).

Developmental Benefits of Exercise for Prevention of Mental Health Conditions

Fewer than 10 percent of US high schools and elementary schools require daily physical education (Story, Nanney, & Schwartz, 2009). This pattern is unfortunate since there is growing evidence that early introduction to regular exercise may reduce development of mood disorders as well as body image distress. Both of these conditions are more common among young women. Organized exercise programs appear to have greater efficacy with pre- and early adolescent females—compared with older adolescent females—particularly in terms of increasing physical activity and improved psychological functioning (Biddle, Braithwaite, & Pearson, 2014). Programs addressing exercise as well as lifestyle issues and self-esteem appeared to be associated with enduring decreases in body mass index (Wright, Giger, Norris, & Suro, 2013), depressive symptoms (Stanton, Highland, & Tercyak, 2016), and reduced body image distress, as well as increased physical activity maintained after program completion (Biddle et al., 2014; Dobbins, Husson, DeCorby, & LaRocca, 2013). While these outcomes may appear disparate, research indicates that childhood and early adolescent risk factors for later obesity include the absence of physical activity, low self-esteem, depression, and body image discomfort. For example, without intervention, there is evidence that depressive symptoms among preadolescent girls are predictive of full-blown major depressive disorder in later adolescence (Feng et al., 2009). This pathway continues with major depressive disorder in adolescence as an independent risk factor for adult obesity for females but not for males (Richardson et al., 2003). However, there is evidence that the physical activity intervention improves self-esteem in preadolescent girls (Stanton et al., 2016) and could be a valuable form of primary prevention.

Macrosystems and Physical Activity

There is a clear association between population density, physical activity levels, and BMI. As population density increases, exercise levels increase and BMI decreases (Hruby et al., 2016). Density refers to the existence of nearby shops, restaurants, and so on. Effects of population density on BMI are also influenced by easily accessible recreation facilities. When the number of recreation and exercise facilities increases in a highly populated region, the odds of being overweight decline by more than 30 percent (Hruby et al., 2016). Those living in less populated areas are more likely to be engaged in activities such as bicycling or jogging and spend more time per week involved in these activities (Hruby et al., 2016).

Eating Disorders

Preoccupation with diet and body image in children and young adolescents is a risk factor for several eating disorders. All three of the most prevalent eating disorders—anorexia nervosa, bulimia nervosa, and binge eating disorder—have some commonalities in terms of symptoms and causal dynamics. In addition, individuals who have one of these conditions are at greater risk for developing the other two disorders. Developmentally, investigators have described how a preoccupation with body image in preadolescent girls may develop into anorexia nervosa in young adolescent females, followed by bulimia nervosa in later adolescence and early adulthood.

Anorexia Nervosa

According to the American Psychiatric Association's (2013) definition, there are three key features of anorexia nervosa: refusal to attain or maintain body weight that it is 85 percent of one's normal body weight based on age and height, distorted body image, and inadequate calorie intake. Typically resulting from inadequate calorie intake, women with anorexia will meet another one of the criteria—absence of at least three consecutive menstrual periods. Studies of body image among females with anorexia suggest that they maintain a distorted view of healthy and physically attractive body size. Persons with this condition also are very frightened of gaining weight ("fat phobic"). DSM-5 describes two types of anorexia nervosa—the restricting type, in which abnormally low weight is maintained through calorie restriction, and the binge/purge subtype, in which abnormally low body weight is maintained through compensatory behavior such as use of laxatives or vomiting or excessive exercise.

Prevalence figures for anorexia nervosa vary somewhat, from a total population prevalence of 0.5 percent to a prevalence of 1 percent of women and 0.3 percent of men (Hoek, 2006; Hoek & van Hoeken, 2003). Most researchers believe that these epidemiological figures are probably artificially low. There is also evidence that while 75 to 90 percent of cases of anorexia nervosa are female, the rates among males are growing. The typical age of onset is 14 to 18 years old. In terms of ethnicity, anorexia nervosa is found predominantly among White European females and is not nearly as common among people of African American or Asian background. However, there are reports that in countries such as China, rates of anorexia are on the rise—particularly as more countries are exposed to Western media.

Physical and Medical Effects of Anorexia Nervosa

Anorexia has pronounced physiological effects and may become a life-threatening condition. Persons with the condition develop low blood pressure and abnormally low body temperature. As the illness continues, there is often a loss of bone density. Additionally, as body temperature continues to drop, the body develops hair called lanugo—similar to the hair that newborn babies acquire to keep them warm. The skin becomes dry and develops a yellow/orange hue. Long-term mortality rates for anorexia have been cited in the 10 to 15 percent range (Birmingham, Su, Hlynsky, Goldner, & Gao, 2005); the most common proximate cause of death is heart failure as the body begins using the heart muscle for nutrition.

Comorbid Conditions

As a psychiatric condition, anorexia nervosa is typically associated with other mental health diagnoses; 50 to 60 percent of persons with anorexia nervosa have another mental health condition (Herpertz-Dahlmann et al., 2001). The most common are major depressive disorder, anxiety disorders (particularly generalized anxiety and social anxiety disorder), and personality disorders—in particular, borderline personality disorder characterized by social and emotional instability as well as avoidant personality disorder with features of rejection sensitivity and extreme discomfort in social situations, or comorbid conditions. Because of the difficulties with emotional regulation and social interaction, these conditions raise particular challenges in treating eating disorders (Martinussen et al., 2017).

Course Over Time
While anorexia is typically thought of as a disorder of teenagers, it is also a chronic condition. Fewer than half of young women who develop anorexia nervosa recover entirely. For about 30 percent of those affected, the condition is chronic over multiple years (Uher et al., 2003). Uher and colleagues found that about a third of those with anorexia nervosa improved but did not go into complete remission. Among those with chronic symptoms, approximately 15 percent died prematurely; of these deaths, half were associated with medical complications of anorexia and the other half committed suicide.

Causes
There is evidence of a genetic predisposition for anorexia nervosa; if a primary family member has the condition, there is significantly greater risk of developing any eating disorder (Fuller-Tyszkiewicz, Krawczyk, Ricciardelli, & Thompson, 2013). Research has examined the possible heritability of specific dimensions of eating disorders and found estimated heritabilities of 30 to 70 percent for body dissatisfaction and weight preoccupation (Wade, Bulik, Heath, Martin, & Eaves, 2001). In terms of brain structure, there is evidence of gray matter reductions in the temporal and occipital regions of the brain among those with anorexia nervosa. There are also reductions in the size of the hypothalamus, which is involved with appetite (Meher & Brown, 2015; Touyz, Polivy, & Hay, 2008).

Psychological explanations of anorexia suggest that the syndrome is often initiated with dieting and restriction of certain foods. Initially, high-fat foods are restricted, and over time food intake overall becomes significantly limited. Persons with anorexia have been found to be high in perfectionism (Touyz, Polivy, & Hay, 2008), which, in turn, leads them to be particularly prone to the abstinence violation effect described in Chapter 5. Additionally, those with eating disorders tend to have higher levels of anxiety and are much more self-critical. Persons with anorexia have been found to have heightened awareness of personal flaws—often these are distorted self-perceptions.

While psychodynamic theory has often been effectively refuted as an explanation for many health-related conditions, there are some elements of the theory that appear to be useful in understanding eating disorders. In anorexia nervosa, one of the key symptoms is absence of a menstrual period for three consecutive cycles. Developmental psychodynamic theorists have argued that the onset of menses means that the young woman is now an adult. However, girls prone to developing anorexia are frightened of becoming adults. By suppressing menstruation, anorectic behavior effectively maintains childhood status. It's also been argued that adolescent girls with anorexia oftentimes experience minimal independence within their families; the only domain in which they can have some control is around their body (Bruch, 1974).

Treatment

A key factor in treating anorexia is that people with the condition do not view their bodies accurately, so a young woman who is 5 feet 6 inches tall and weighs 90 pounds may still see herself as fat—a hindrance to treatment. Additionally, weight gain, while obviously important for improved health among women with anorexia, is associated with acute anxiety and unrealistic fears of becoming significantly overweight. Treatment of severe anorexia often initially takes place in the hospital. Some patients need to be medically stabilized before psychiatric treatment can be initiated. With the use of behavioral methods, particularly in a controlled setting such as an eating disorder residential program—short-term increases in weight resulting from operant principles do occur. Long-term maintenance after discharge from the program is more problematic. Family therapy appears to be an evidence-based treatment of choice for anorexia nervosa—particularly structural therapy, which addresses the overly close family dynamic characterized by minimization of any differences or conflict (Minuchin, Roseman, & Baker, 2009). In general, as the condition becomes progressively more chronic, treatment becomes less likely to be successful.

Bulimia Nervosa

While descriptions of anorexia nervosa can be found at least as far back as the 1600s, bulimia appears to have arisen in the mid-20th century. Bulimia is characterized by eating within a discrete period of time (e.g., 2 hours) an amount of food that is significantly larger than most people would eat during that same time period and in the same circumstances. Additionally, there is compensatory behavior such as self-induced vomiting, use of laxatives and/or diuretics, or excessive exercise at least once a week for three consecutive months. A key element defining bulimia nervosa is a sense of having lost control over eating during the binge episodes. Similar to persons with anorexia nervosa, self-evaluation is unduly influenced by body weight (American Psychiatric Association, 2013).

The majority of those with bulimia are female. The condition is estimated to affect 1 to 2 percent of women and 0.5 percent of men in the general population. Bulimia typically begins somewhat later than anorexia nervosa—in later adolescence or early adulthood. In the United States, bulimia is more common among White European and Asian American women.

Psychological and Physical Effects of Bulimia Nervosa

Because of the alternate episodes of binging and purging and other methods used to control weight such as laxative use, a state of physiological instability is established. Electrolyte imbalances are very common. These physiochemical abnormalities may, in turn, lead to unstable heart rhythms. The regurgitation of gastric contents through vomiting may damage the intestinal tract. Frequent vomiting also erodes teeth, and there are cosmetic dentists who directly market repair services to persons with bulimia. Also, because of the vomiting, the parotid glands, the largest of the salivary glands, become swollen. The enlarged, swollen cheeks may produce a "chipmunk-like" facial appearance. Calloused or scarred knuckles and fingers are also associated with using fingers to initiate vomiting.

Psychologically, episodes of loss of control and overeating are typically followed by intense experiences of shame and self-loathing. Since the binging and purging typically take place in secret, persons with the condition may avoid close social relationships.

Comorbid Conditions
Similar to anorexia nervosa, bulimia does not typically exist alone. About three-quarters of those with bulimia have another mental health condition. The most common comorbid condition is major depressive disorder, with anxiety disorders being second (Touyz et al., 2008). Approximately one-third of women with bulimia have a substance abuse problem, which is associated with poorer treatment outcome. As with anorexia, the presence of personality disorders is also common and complicates treatment.

Course Over Time
While it was originally believed that bulimia had a better prognosis over time than anorexia nervosa, this optimism has recently become more guarded. Recent studies have found that about a third of those with the condition will still be symptomatic a year later. Five years after original diagnosis, 15 percent met criteria for the condition. Additionally, many persons originally diagnosed with bulimia will continue to have symptoms, but not of the frequency or severity required for a formal DSM-5 diagnosis (Touyz et al., 2008).

Causes
Biological factors have been implicated in bulimia. With the finding that the likelihood of developing bulimia is 4 to 9 times greater if one has a relative with the condition, a genetic predisposition is suggested. Additionally, it has been suggested that there is a genetic basis for specific dimensions of bulimia such as dietary restraint and binge eating, with heritabilities between 45 and 70 percent (Fuller-Tyszkiewicz et al., 2013; Rozenblat et al., 2017).

In terms of the central nervous system, the inferior frontal region of the brain may be smaller in persons with the condition (Marsh et al., 2015). This neurological pattern corresponds to the experience of loss of control during binge episodes. As is the case with anorexia, most central nervous system studies of eating disorders are conducted with persons who already have the condition. Given the significant physiological disruption associated with the disorders, it is certainly conceivable that small differences in brain anatomy between those with these conditions could be the result of his behavior. There is also some evidence of serotonin dysregulation in bulimia. Support for this perspective comes from the finding that selective serotonin reuptake inhibitors do seem to reduce bulimic behavior.

Psychological explanations of bulimia suggest that those affected experience significant fears of intimacy and distrust of others. This view that others cannot be depended upon is particularly pronounced for close romantic relationships. The binging behavior represents a self-controlled way of nurturing oneself. There is anecdotal support for this perspective from family research. The families of persons who develop bulimia are often described as cold, competitive, and rejecting. There is also some evidence of a higher incidence of sexual abuse among young women who develop bulimia—again providing indirect support for the view that persons with the condition may be prone to be particularly distrustful of others (Miller et al. 1993).

Treatment

Individually oriented cognitive therapy does appear to be helpful for women with bulimia. Initial treatment efforts center around patient education, which may be directed to increasing motivation for change (Dean, Touyz, Rieger, & Thornton, 2008). The cycle of anxiety, binge eating, and purging is discussed. Individual factors such as history of child abuse, growing up in a family where weight criticism was frequent, or having been in a field such as dance or gymnastics where weight was closely monitored are incorporated into this process. Involvement of a nutritionist is also helpful. Patients should be encouraged to eat regular meals and to keep diaries including both their food intake and any compensatory behavior, as well as situational factors and feelings associated with binging and purging. Patients typically have a group of "feared" foods. These tend to be high-caloric foods that are eaten during binges. The therapist, in conjunction with a nutritionist, gradually urges the patient to introduce these foods into the diet, beginning with least and gradually progressing to most feared. Problem-solving strategies for high-risk situations are developed. Finally, in keeping with the transtheoretical model, discussions of lapse and relapse are included. Patients are encouraged to consider situations that might trigger relapse and develop strategies in advance for dealing with them. As noted earlier, serotonergic dysregulation appears to be a factor in bulimia (Mayer & Walsh, 1998). SSRI medications are associated with some degree of improvement in both bulimia and binge eating disorder. It is likely that these medications may improve mood somewhat so that the aversive mood states that trigger binging and subsequent purging are diminished.

Binge Eating Disorder

Binge eating disorder was not recognized as an official psychiatric diagnosis until the publication of the DSM-5 in 2013. As a result, less is known about the condition compared with anorexia and bulimia. The principal symptom is rapid, uncontrolled eating of large amounts of food accompanied by subsequent distress about the behavior. In terms of frequency these episodes occur twice per week for six continuous months. In contrast to bulimia, there is no compensatory behavior such as purging. Similar to bulimia, a key element is the experience of loss of control. Additionally, while overall food consumption is higher among those with binge eating disorder than bulimia, actual caloric intake during binges is lower in binge eating disorder than bulimia (Fuller-Tyszkiewicz et al., 2013).

The estimated lifetime prevalence of the condition is 2 to 3 percent. In contrast to bulimia and anorexia, binge eating disorder appears to be more equally distributed by gender, race, and ethnicity. The estimated duration of binge eating disorder is eight years (Hudson, Hiripi, Pope, & Kessler, 2007). The direct health risks associated with the condition are significantly lower than for anorexia or bulimia. The chief medical risk associated with binge eating disorder is developing the metabolic syndrome and elevated cholesterol that, in turn, increase the risk of type 2 diabetes (McElroy et al., 2016).

Since it is a relatively new diagnosis, less is known about the factors associated with binge eating disorder. The moderate effectiveness of selective serotonin reuptake inhibitors in reducing frequency of binges suggests that at the neurotransmitter level, serotonin is involved. Research suggests that emotional inhibition is a key element in binge eating. It is also associated with past history of sexual abuse.

Medication treatments demonstrating some effectiveness include selective serotonin reuptake inhibitors, lisdexamfetamine (a stimulant), and topiramate (a mood stabilizer). Cognitive behavioral therapy has shown some benefits for the condition (Berkman et al., 2015).

Eating Disorders: Immediate Social and Macrosystem Influences

Family and Social Factors

There is some evidence that families with young people who develop eating disorders are characterized by parental transmission of concern with appearance (Gardner, Stark, Friedman, & Jackson, 2000). Additionally, parental communication often centers around the child's weight, the amount of food that the child consumes, and overall diet. Parents who engage in eating for emotional regulation appear to have children who have elevated risk of the same behavior (Tan & Holub, 2015). There is also evidence that the peer group of young adults who become bulimic in early adolescence is a social network that tends to focus on diet, weight, and appearance.

Mass Media

David Epston's approach to treatment of young women with eating disorders includes attention to broader social influences. In his approach, young women are encouraged to examine the media and the ways in which television and popular magazines "recruit" women and girls into eating disorders (Lock, Epston, Maisel, & de Faria, 2005; Epston, Morris, & Maisel, 1995). Longitudinal studies from 1979 to 1988 found that 60 percent of Miss America contestants met criteria for anorexia nervosa. Currently, the average Miss America contestant is 30 pounds underweight (Bernacchi, 2017). Analyses of media have found that women in magazines and television shows popular among teenagers and young women often portray an ideal body image that is unrealistic. However, these media images become internalized, beginning as young as age five (Damiano, Paxton, Wertheim, McLean, & Gregg, 2015). The average model portrayed in the media weighs 23 percent less than the average American woman.

These media representations are also believed to contribute to objectification in which young women view themselves from the perspective of an external observer who sees them as an object evaluated on the basis of physical appearance (Dakanalis et al., 2015). Media portrayals of women's appearance encourage objectification and a distorted physical self-image. Among a sample of college women, 55 percent viewed themselves as overweight, although in reality only 6 percent were (Striegel-Moore, Silberstein, & Rodin, 1986; Touyz et al. 2008). In another survey, 94 percent of one sample of women indicated that they wanted to be smaller, and 96 percent viewed themselves as larger than the current social ideal. Particularly disturbing is that half the women in one study reported that they would rather be hit by a truck than "be fat" (Smith, 2010).

Cross-Cultural Studies of Eating Disorders

A current cross-cultural debate centers around the extent to which eating disorders are becoming more common internationally in regions such as Asia and whether increases in eating disorders in these countries reflect a Westernization effect. This Westernization effect refers to the impact of increased cultural contact with Western ideas and how they are incorporated into non-Western cultures (Pike & Dunne, 2015). The Western model of mental health, including the American Psychiatric Association's Diagnostic and Statistical Manual, is becoming the standard for mental health diagnoses around the world. However, there are concerns that this American system may not be culturally congruent with how distress is expressed in other cultures. Additionally, with more than 400 diagnoses, a large percentage of the US population could be considered mentally ill. This tendency to convert social and psychological distress into diagnosis has historically not been widely accepted outside of Western countries. For example, in Japan, severe depression, melancholia, has been seen as a type of stoic character—not necessarily undesirable. The melancholic individual was described as hard-working, exhibiting a strong loyalty to society and community and having a preference for definite rules and clear organization. This melancholic type of depression was not consistently seen as a condition needing psychiatric intervention (Kato et al., 2011). It was only relatively recently that the "modern" concept of depression treated with medication was recognized in Japan (Kato et al., 2011).

Similarly, cases of eating disorders in China and Taiwan reported in the early to mid-1990s were different from those described by the DSM. The symptoms of distorted body image and fear of becoming "fat" were not reported in these Asian countries. While food intake was restricted, patients indicated that reduced food intake was due to abdominal pain, bloating, or simply the absence of hunger. Over the past 20 years, however, cases of anorexia nervosa have increased, and the condition has become one that is consistent with Western conceptualizations of eating disorders (Pike & Dunne, 2015).

A dramatic example of the effect of Westernization on body image occurred in Fiji. Western media, including television, were not available in Fiji until the late 1990s. Studies examined young Fijian women's perception of ideal body image and eating disorder symptoms before and after the introduction of Western media. Prior to the arrival of television in the region, Fijian views of female attractiveness emphasized a heavier and more robust body type. However, within a decade of being exposed to Western television, young women expressed more body dissatisfaction and desire to lose weight. In addition, purging behavior became more common among young women (Becker, 2004; Pike & Dunne, 2015).

Eating Disordered Culture

While we typically discuss how a particular condition interacts with culture, in the case of eating disorders, there are subgroups of people with the condition who advocate for a culture devoted to promoting eating disorders. This culture can readily be encountered through "pro-ana" websites and internet message boards. Within this culture, the perfectionism that drives the disorder motivates young women as they strive to be "the best anorectic" (Warin, 2016). Those who want to be cured of their disorder may be referred to as "outside anorexics" by groups of persons with the condition. Among this group, the term "outside anorectic" has shaming connotations. Getting better and reducing eating-disorder behavior leads to losing support as an "in-crowd" anorexic, and there may also be a simultaneous loss of identity. Warin (2016) describes how anorexia has become a "religion," a "competitive sporting team," and a "fascinating game" (p. 126).

Those with anorexia become sensitive to the cues of fellow adherents of the culture—they know the difference between skinny and being a member of the anorectic "club." "'The dead look' in their eyes, the sallowness of their upper arms, and the heaviness of their gait" (Warin, 2016, p. 127) are all signs that one is part of the subculture. To be part of the club, one must be sick.

While some internet providers have blocked pro-ana websites, they are difficult to regulate. In response to these attempts, it appears that the sites have become more insular, such that members can share messages with one another while outsiders are blocked. While this may at some level seem desirable, the reduced availability of the sites to "outsiders" makes it difficult for public health educators to convey information about where to seek help to the pro-ana online community (Cassilli, Pailler, & Tubaro, 2013).

Conclusion

From a historical perspective, access to desirable food in large quantities, as is the case in Western, industrialized countries, is a fairly recent phenomenon. Evolutionary theory would suggest that histories of food shortages would predispose people to consume large quantities of available food in preparation for periods of relative scarcity. In Western countries, this pattern occurs in the context of societies that value thin bodies. The relatively recent appearance of bulimia nervosa is one in which purging to prevent weight gain captures these contradictory social and historical trends. Furthermore, the restricting type of anorexia nervosa has a history of at least 400 years, while the binging-purging variation is a relatively new phenomenon—likely prompted by the availability of large quantities of food (Keel & Klump, 2003). Bulimia became increasingly common between 1970 and 1990.

Formal diagnoses of eating disorders characterize under 15 percent of the population. Subthreshold patterns of disordered eating are much more common. For example, 20 to 25 percent of college women have some characteristics of eating disorders. This category of high-frequency behavior includes purging and binging as well as preoccupation with weight. However, these symptoms do not occur with adequate frequency or intensity to warrant a formal DSM-5 diagnosis. Treatments for obesity and clinical eating disorders often have modest and short-term effectiveness. Preventing these conditions before they arise is likely to be a better use of health care resources. However, to do so will require sustained multimodal efforts. Internationally, the early data from government programs (including legislation) that include education about food and nutrition, as well as deterrents to reduce consumption of high-calorie, low-nutrient products such as sweetened sodas, show some promise for changing habits.

CHAPTER 11

Sleep and Sleep Disorders

If you are under the age of 25 and have 8 a.m. classes, I feel for you. High school and college students often stay up late—until after midnight—but then have to get up early. As you will see later in this chapter, there is a reason why you feel like falling asleep in that 8:00 a.m. calculus class, and it is not the subject matter. With the addition of 24-hour media and cellular devices that permit both voice and text communication, it has become a challenge to turn off the external stimulation that keeps us awake. Among college students, use of cell phones late at night has been one reason why some studies suggest that up to 80 percent of college students are sleep deprived and erroneously believe that they can make up for lost sleep by sleeping in on the weekends. However, this issue is not unique to college students. Sleep disorders are increasingly common in the industrialized world. The amount of sleep Americans receive has declined by about an hour during the past 30 years.

Why Do We Sleep?

Sleep, for many, is a necessary nuisance. If we did not have to sleep, we might not feel so rushed trying to cram school, job, social life, eating, and exercising into the 16 to 18 hours we are awake. Scientists, beginning with the ancient Greeks, have debated sleep's function. Sleep has been explained in terms of evolutionary theory. Large animals require little sleep, but because of their body mass, they need the extra time for foraging for food. There may also be some adaptive value in having periods of time in which activity is limited. For some species, such as humans with their poor night vision, foraging and hunting during periods of darkness could be dangerous. Additionally, valuable energy is conserved during periods of rest. Many species, including humans to some extent, maintain some degree of awareness of external events while resting but don't initiate activity (Meddis, 1975). However, evolutionary theory is difficult to test, and it is possible to generate many plausible explanations for sleep that cannot be proved or disproved.

More recent neuroscience research suggests that sleep is a time for removing our neurophysiological "trash." Our morning feeling of being rested after a good night's sleep may be associated with the removal of neurotoxic waste from our central nervous system that builds up during the day. During sleep, the glial cells shrink so that the glymphatic system, which involves fluid moving through the spaces between the cells, is more active; research has found that this space may increase by up to 60 percent during sleep (Xie et al., 2013). If the neurotoxin theory is correct, fatigue may arise from decreased processing efficiency because of the buildup of these substances, and, as a result, additional cortical regions may become active to maintain performance (Slater et al., 2017).

The Stages of Sleep

The basis for describing sleep stages is the pattern of electrical activity on the electroencephalogram (EEG). Assessing electrical patterns of brain activity, the EEG transmits electrical activity that is converted into visual patterns of waves. In the waking stage, the EEG shows frequent low-amplitude, high-frequency waves (Carlson, 2013). However, the EEG patterns during sleep take different forms during the course of the night. EEGs are often used in sleep laboratories to monitor brain wave activity since persons with sleep disorders often show distinct patterns of brain activity that differ from the normal sleep cycle.

Sleep laboratories, originally developed to conduct research, are now very common. Patients spend the night in the sleep laboratory while they are monitored with an EEG. Electrodes may be placed on the chin to assess muscle activity (electromyogram) as well as around the eyes to assess eye movements (electrooculagram). Additionally, the laboratory has video cameras or one-way mirrors so that the patient's behavior can be directly observed. Sleep technicians take note of the amount of physical activity during sleep as well as how much time is spent asleep in each night, together with overall time in bed. Breathing and heart rate are also monitored.

Based on the EEG, when we are awake, there are two general types of wave patterns. Alpha waves are generally regular, medium-frequency waves occurring when we are awake but resting. An irregular low-amplitude pattern of waves characterizes beta activity. Beta waves dominate when we are alert and attentive or actively thinking (Carlson, 2013). REM stands for rapid eye movement. In non-REM sleep, breathing is regular, and muscle tone declines. The EEG itself shows a decrease in frequency and increase in amplitude (Peigneux, Urbain, & Schmitz, 2012). While passing through all stages of sleep requires an average of 110 minutes, the amount of time spent in the REM phase increases as we continue to sleep.

Non-REM Stages

Stage 1

This is a period of drowsiness in the transition between wakefulness and sleep. Behaviorally, individuals will not respond to some external sounds—however, reawakening is very common, and if awakened from this stage, people will often report that they were not sleeping. As the EEG pattern shows, stage 1 is characterized by a slight reduction in frequency and an increase in wave amplitude. During this time, people open and close their eyes, and their eyes may also roll upward or downward (Carlson, 2013).

This is also the period in which hypnagogic experiences are most likely to occur. These are very vivid perceptual experiences like hallucinations. While they are a characteristic of the sleep disorder narcolepsy, discussed below, they also seem to occur in about 35 percent of the general population (Ohayon, Priest, Caulet, & Guilleminault, 1996). Hypnopompic hallucinations are those that occur upon awakening and are reported by 12 percent of the general population (Ohayon et al., 1996).

Stage 2

After 10 minutes in stage one, the next stage is entered. The EEG pattern waveforms become more irregular but contain periods of theta waves of two types. Sleep spindles are low-amplitude bursts that occur two to five times a minute during stages

1 to 4. There is evidence that the activity associated with sleep spindles is important for memory consolidation (Clemens, Fabo, & Halasz, 2005). K-complexes are short bursts of high-amplitude waves occurring on the average of about one per minute. K-complexes appear to be inhibitory, and similar wave formations become progressively more common during stages 3 and 4 and are associated with deeper sleep (Tank et al., 2003). Similar to stage 1 sleep, people awakened during this phase may state that they were not asleep even though they were sleeping soundly.

Stage 3
After about 15 minutes of being in stage 2 sleep, high-amplitude irregular waves become more common. These high-amplitude waves are slower in frequency and of higher amplitude (Carlson, 2013). During this period, growth hormones are released. People are much more difficult to awaken. If suddenly woken up, they often appear confused.

Stage 4
The demarcation between stage 3 and stage 4 sleep is not clear cut. The delta waves characteristic of stage 3 become the predominant wave type in stage 4 sleep. One distinction that is made is that stage 3 contains 20 percent to 50 percent delta activity and stage 4 contains more than 50 percent delta waves. Stage 4 sleep is the deepest stage. Only loud noises will cause someone to wake up. Stage 4 sleep appears to be involved in memory consolidation. In studies in which subjects learn a set of paired words and then are allowed to take a nap or are kept awake, those who took the nap performed somewhat better on the task of remembering the pairs (Carlson, 2013). However, this was not true for visual motor memory. During stage 4 sleep, among children, bedwetting and sleepwalking occur. The slow, higher-frequency wave pattern indicates a state in which it is very difficult to awaken someone, and if awakened directly from stage 3 or 4 sleep, the person may seem confused. Stages 3 and 4 are often referred to together as "Slow Wave Sleep."

REM Sleep
After being asleep for about 90 minutes, including 45 minutes in stage 4, there is an abrupt shift in the EEG pattern (Carlson, 2013). The heart rate and respiration rate increase. There is increased flow of blood to the brain as well as increased oxygen uptake in parts of the brain that are activated. Additionally, the male penis and female clitoris become at least partially erect. The overall pattern resembles stage 2, with a relatively high number of low-amplitude, high-frequency waves. Even though the person's eyes are closed, the eyes themselves are darting back and forth beneath the eyelids. There is also a loss of nearly all muscle tone; in actuality, the muscles are paralyzed. People awakened during REM sleep almost always report that they had been dreaming. Researchers have found that when examining eye movements during REM sleep, the pattern is very similar to that which would be expected of a person who was awake and visually tracking some event (Schenck & Mahowald, 2002). The brain activity that seems to be activated during dreams is consistent with the dream content. For example, if the dream is of running away, the pattern of brain activity is similar to that when one is actually running. REM sleep appears

to be particularly important. If people are selectively deprived of REM sleep for several nights, they will show a rebound effect whereby on subsequent nights they spend more time in the REM sleep stage (Carlson, 2013). As noted earlier, while awake and alert, the EEG shows rapid, low-amplitude waves—called beta waves. This EEG pattern is similar to that seen in the REM stage; however, many of the features, such as paralysis, are not present during wakefulness.

Circadian Rhythm

Another factor contributing to sleep is our circadian rhythm, which is based upon the cycle of light and dark that we experience every day in most parts of the world. This is a daily pattern that involves both an internal clock and physiological responses to changes in external levels of light. Our circadian rhythm has a natural cycle of 25 hours. In a classic sleep study, Kleitman and a younger colleague spent 32 days in Mammoth Cave to study the effects of total darkness on the natural sleep-wake clock. The two sleep scientists attempted to regulate themselves according to a 28-hour clock. The younger scientist was able to reset his biological clock; however, Kleitman was not consistently successful (Kroker, 2007). A region of the brain, the suprachiasmatic nucleus, is sensitive to these normal light-dark changes. If this area is damaged, physiological rhythms of the body become disrupted. However, in healthy individuals, research has shown that even if kept in darkness for sustained periods of time, exposure to light seems to automatically reset the circadian clock (Carlson, 2013).

Sleep Through the Life Span

Infants sleep approximately 18 to 19 hours. There is evidence that, for infants, sleep is a period in which neural connections are established (Arnett, 2016). If not interrupted, infants will normally sleep for 4 to 6 hours and then return to sleep for another block of similar length. New parents in the United States unfortunately do not have the benefit of the 6- to 12-month maternity/paternity leave found in Western Europe and Canada. Because of the demands of employment, parents are often focused on the goal of having their infants sleep through the night. Often parents set up the infant's environment in the hope of producing longer periods of sleep. By putting them in a dark, noiseless environment and having them consume milk or formula immediately before putting them down to sleep, it is hoped that they will sleep longer. However, some researchers have suggested that the combination of being in a dark, noiseless environment together with the metabolic demands of digestion may play a role in sudden infant death syndrome. Some infants have not yet developed the reflex to turn their head when CO_2 levels increase. Sudden infant death syndrome (SIDS) is defined as the unexplained, sudden death of an infant under 12 months of age. It has been suggested that when babies are sleeping facedown and they breathe in carbon dioxide, they either wake up or reflexively turn their head. Infants succumb to sudden infant death syndrome if they are deficient in this reflex (Kinney & Thach, 2009). While central nervous system abnormalities have been suggested, an additional factor may be that the combination of feeding and stimulus-free environment leads the child to sleep more deeply, thus not waking when carbon dioxide builds up.

Between the ages of one and three, children typically have two sleep periods during the day as well as nighttime sleep. During the daytime, these episodes typically occur around 10 to 11 a.m. and 2 to 3 p.m. As children mature, these two naps become one. By the age of three, one nap is sufficient. Elementary school children typically require about 10 hours of sleep. A growing issue in the United States is increased obesity rates among children (Cappucio et al., 2008). A longitudinal study found that being a short sleeper in the third grade predicted being overweight in the sixth grade. This sleep-weight association among children has been found in multiple countries (Cappucio et al., 2008).

Our circadian rhythm is regulated by environmental cues from sunlight as well as hormones such as cortisol melatonin. Many teenagers experience a delay in the release of both cortisol and melatonin and have difficulty falling asleep before midnight (Crowley, Acebo, & Carskadon, 2007). The natural waking time is also later. This is a physiological phenomenon called the adolescent sleep phase delay. In addition, adolescents as a group do not get adequate sleep. Up to 70 percent of adolescents report seven or fewer hours sleep on an average school night (National Adolescent and Young Adult Health Information Center, 2014). Additionally, sleep patterns are irregular among adolescents and young adults, with large samples showing a two-hour discrepancy in the amount of sleep obtained on weekends versus weekdays. The time of optimal alertness is typically around 2 to 3 p.m. for teenagers. However, the start times of most high schools are not consistent with the adolescent sleep-phase delay. It is very common for high school to begin at 8 a.m. or earlier. Research on adolescent sleep problems has shown that when schools begin after about 8:30 a.m., teenagers will still go to bed at about the same time, regardless of the time at which they are supposed to get up. Attendance was better in schools with later start times (National Adolescent and Young Adult Health Information Center, 2014). Teenagers attending schools with early start times are more likely to be sleepy during the day and exhibit cognitive difficulties, including poorer attention and concentration, compared with students in later-start-time high schools (Weis 2014). In addition, when schools have delayed start times by 90 minutes, auto accidents by 16- to 18-year-olds declined by 70 percent (National Adolescent and Young Adult Health Information Center, 2014).

Additionally, there is an inverse relationship between hours of sleep and academic performance among both high school and middle school students (Shochat, Cohen-Zion, & Tzichinsky, 2014). On average, 25 percent of high school students regularly fall sleep in class (Chen, Wang, & Jeng, 2006), with an additional 22 percent routinely falling asleep during homework. Other factors that have increased daytime sleepiness among adolescents are academic workloads (which appear to increase during the course of high school) and increased screen time—particularly internet and cellular communication devices (Shochat et al., 2014)—which is also associated with a reduced likelihood of being physically active. Among adolescents, each 1-hour decrease in sleep time increased the likelihood of being overweight or obese by nearly 7 percent (Shochat et al., 2014). Among teenage females, insufficient sleep is associated with physical problems, including lower back pain, neck pain, headache, and abdominal pain.

While the adolescent phase shift is common, 7 to 10 percent of adolescents are believed to have a more significant circadian rhythm disorder. There are several strategies to address this problem. First is to gradually move bedtime to an earlier point. So if the adolescent has been going to bed at 1:30 a.m., bedtime might initially be moved to 1:15 a.m. The addition of supplemental melatonin and light stimulation may also be useful. The melatonin should be taken shortly before bedtime. Early in the morning, upon awakening, adolescents expose themselves to a high-intensity artificial light—these are actually available with programmable alarms that become progressively brighter during a span of 15 to 30 minutes.

If allowed to sleep without interruption, young adults would sleep an average of 9.2 hours. However, the median sleep time for emerging adult college students is 6 hours and 39 minutes. While it is estimated that young adults require 7.5 to 8 hours, fewer than 20 percent of this age group meet this criterion. The phase delay found among adolescents is also found among those who are 18 to 25 years old (Radek & Karpelian, 2013). Similar to adolescents, there is evidence that poor sleep is associated with greater emotional distress as well as poor academic performance (Shochat et al., 2014). However, oversleeping among first-year college students is also associated with reduced grade point average (Radek & Kaprelian, 2013). In a study of college students, it was estimated that about 45 minutes of sleep was lost per week because of waking up and checking a cell phone. In addition to the social stimulation of these devices, cellular phones expose users to direct light, which may delay sleep onset.

In later adulthood, sleep needs decline to about 7.5 hours. Among women, reproductive cycles influence sleep. During pregnancy, women are particularly sleepy during the first trimester. However, physical discomfort may impair sleep during the third trimester (Sahota, Jain, & Dhand, 2003). Sleep is also influenced by the menstrual cycle, with women being sleepier in the second half of the cycle. Menopause may be associated with hot flashes, which can interrupt sleep as well.

In middle age, sleep becomes lighter and nighttime awakenings are more frequent. It is not unusual for middle-age adults to wake up after three hours of sleep (Singer & Applebee, 2008). Because middle-aged adults have often gained weight, they may experience breathing problems during the course of sleep, which, in turn, may lead to a condition called sleep apnea, discussed in more detail below. Particularly among men, awakening may be due to a condition such as benign prostatic hypertrophy (enlarged prostate, which creates pressure to urinate more frequently).

Among older adults, deep sleep declines further and there are multiple awakenings during the night. Falling asleep typically takes somewhat longer. In Alzheimer's disease, the sleep patterns seen in normal aging are present but are more pronounced, with greater amounts of daytime and less nighttime sleep (Bliwise, 2004). Despite these sleep disruptions, during a 24-hour period, older adults usually accumulate the same amount of total sleep as younger people.

Reasons for Disrupted Sleep

During the last 50 years, the duration of sleep for Americans has declined. Some reports put the current nightly average for adults at six hours (Adenekan et al., 2013).

Sleep deprivation is associated with increased errors at work as well as traffic accidents and impaired judgment and performance. Several major industrial accidents appear to have been associated with sleep deprivation. Another sleep-related issue is working at night. About 15 million Americans work the night shift or rotate back and forth between night and day shifts. Working at night runs against our body's natural circadian rhythm (Harrington, 1994). From an evolutionary perspective, nighttime was a source of danger since humans have poor night vision. As a result, those who work night shifts are essentially walking uphill against both evolution and our circadian rhythms. Even if one is able to get adequate sleep during the day, some researchers believe that this will not make up for the effects of the circadian disruption associated with night work. Jobs such as emergency room physician or nurse, police officer, and some retail workers, as well as those involved in international business, lead to daytime fatigue, depressed mood, and slower reaction time (Harrington, 1994).

Research has suggested that nighttime work is associated with a more vulnerable immune system (Haus & Smolensky, 2006). There is growing evidence that adults who work at night and likely receive less sleep are more likely to gain weight and develop metabolic syndrome, which often leads to type 2 diabetes. Violanti et al. (2009) found that a sample of adults who worked the 8 p.m. to 4 a.m. shift had the highest prevalence of metabolic syndrome symptoms including larger waist circumference, elevated triglyceride levels, higher total cholesterol, high blood pressure, and elevated blood glucose. The subgroup who worked the 8 p.m. to 4 a.m. shift and averaged fewer than six hours sleep during a 24-hour period, four times per week, were at the highest risk of developing metabolic syndrome (Violanti et al., 2009).

Having to change one's sleep schedule can also have pronounced effects. Workers on swing shifts for extended periods reported more fatigue, poor concentration, and more depression. Even shifting one's sleep 2 to 4 hours forward or backward from the regular schedule increases fatigue, diminishes mood, and is associated with poorer performance on attention and concentration tasks (Taub & Berger, 1972; Wright, Bogan, & Wyatt, 2013).

Many students will come back from classes and decide they are too tired to study and decide it's a perfect time for a nap. Their argument is that after being renewed by sleep, studying will be much more productive. Several studies have examined the effects of short naps of 10, 20, and 30 minutes; these all indicated greater alertness and better performance. However, those who had 20- to 30-minute naps experienced a common phenomenon—sleep inertia—the desire to sleep continuously. Research suggests that 10 minutes is probably the optimal duration for a nap. Naps less than 20 minutes do not appear to have significant negative effects on nighttime sleep (Milner & Cote, 2009).

As noted above, there can be serious consequences associated with sleep deprivation. It is estimated that 200,000 traffic accidents per year are associated with sleep deprivation, and, of these, 5,000 are fatal accidents. Approximately 1 in 5 drivers reports having fallen asleep at the wheel at least once. A microsleep is a brief episode lasting seconds. If you are listening to a boring lecture, have to do a repetitive task, or have been driving for hours without stopping, it is likely you may experience these episodes lasting between 1 and 6 seconds (Koch, 2016). In a study of microsleep, participants were asked to track a target with the joystick on a computer monitor—however, it was required that they do this for a full 15 minutes. On average, there were approximately 70 microsleep episodes during the time they were playing the game. Microsleep also shows a distinct EEG pattern. During these episodes, the brain is essentially asleep for several seconds. These episodes appear to be more common among persons who are not getting adequate sleep at night. For example, in the trucking industry, single-vehicle truck accidents are much more likely at night, and it is estimated that up to 50 percent of all US trucking accidents are fatigue related (Mitler, Miller, Lipsitz, Walsh, & Wylie, 1997).

The impact of even mild disruptions in sleep schedule is dramatically illustrated when auto accidents associated with the change to daylight savings time are examined (Lambe & Cummings, 2000). During the fall, we gain an hour and "fall back," but during the spring we lose an hour as we "spring forward." The number of Monday accidents following the change to daylight savings time in the spring is significantly higher by at least 8 to 10 percent (Coren, 1996). However, during the fall there appear to be approximately 8 to 10 percent fewer accidents on the Monday following daylight savings time (Coren, 1996).

The Macrosystem: Diversity and Sleep
Culture

While sleep may be considered a shared human activity with a universal pattern, there are actually cultural and historical differences in sleep patterns (Arber, Meadows, & Venn, 2012). One classification has been the number of sleep episodes within a 24-hour period. In most Western countries, sleep is monophasic—a single block that typically occurs at night. Other places such as Spain and countries that have Spanish influence, such as Mexico, have often exhibited biphasic sleep. These are countries in which a siesta, an afternoon nap, has been common. Finally, polyphasic societies include regular napping (Arber, Meadows, & Venn, 2012). In many of these polyphasic societies, sleep often occurs in public areas. For example, in China it is not unusual to walk through a market in the afternoon and find many of the vendors asleep in their stalls. Polyphasic sleep has been common in India and other developing countries (Arber, Meadows & Venn, 2012).

The biphasic pattern was common in 19th-century Western Europe. At that time, Western Europeans often experienced two intervals of sleep with an hour of wakefulness in between. These episodes would be considered the first and second sleep, and there was a period of about an hour in between (Ekirch, 2006). After three or four hours, one would wake up, eat, be sexually active, read, or meditate quietly for about an hour and then return to sleep. This was certainly easier in times in which most productive activity stopped when the sun went down.

However, in our flat world with 24-hour technology, sleep is seen as unsalvageable time and often as time wasted. Industrialized society brought about a culture in which someone who was "tough" could function on very little sleep. Sleep was seen as an intrusion into productive work. Insomnia, in and of itself, is only considered problematic because its effects make one less productive the next day. Even though insomnia may stem from emotional reactions to work, it still is seen as a problem requiring medical attention since it interferes with one's ability to work (Henry, McClellen, Rosenthal, Dedrick, & Gosdin, 2008). Indirect support for this view is that poor sleep quality is associated with lower socioeconomic status and higher levels of unemployment (Patel, Grandner, Xie, Branas, & Gooneratne, 2010). It is not known whether the relationship between socioeconomic status and sleep is confounded by poor health among those in lower socioeconomic strata. Poor sleep quality also appears to be associated with less education as well (Patel et al., 2010).

Gender

As will be evident in the discussion of sleep disorders, women appear to have more problems with sleep than men. Some reasons hypothesized have included hormonal changes associated with menopause or pregnancy; however, rates of major depressive disorder, of which sleep disturbances are a common symptom, is also twice as common among women as men (Tamanna & Geraci, 2013). Some of the sleep disparity may be based on allocation of responsibility. Among couples with children where both partners are employed outside the home, women still take responsibility for a disproportionate share of household and childcare activities. In addition, an issue that has become increasingly common with the "sandwich generation" is that women are more likely to be caregivers of family members with degenerative illnesses such as Alzheimer's disease and Parkinson's disease (McCurry, Logsdon, Teri, & Vitiello, 2007). This includes daughters-in-law as well as daughters. There is evidence that, when compared with men in the caretaking role of an elderly parent, women still report greater distress than male spouse caregivers (Fitting, Rabins, Lucas, & Eastham, 1986). This distress may emerge as insomnia, which is more common among women.

Rumination, more common among women, is also associated with insomnia—specifically sleep onset. Rumination involves continuous processing of depressed mood coupled with self-evaluation and self-criticism (Nolen-Hoeksema & Jackson, 2001). There is evidence that delayed sleep onset is associated with rumination even when its association with depression is controlled (Pillai, Steenberg, Ciesla, Roth, & Drake, 2014). Rumination may also include anticipation of external threats such as work demands. The presence of less slow-wave sleep on EEG patterns suggests that it is the anticipation of difficulties that physiologically links rumination to impaired sleep.

Ethnicity

Within the United States, there are differences in sleep patterns by ethnicity. African Americans sleep, on average, more than a half-hour less than Whites. One study found that White European Americans slept for an average of 6.32 hours, while African Americans averaged 5.9 hours per night (Adenekan et al., 2013). African Americans also have a greater prevalence of long (9 hours or more) and short (5 hours or less) sleepers. Compared with Asian, White European, and Hispanic Americans, African Americans were least likely to report that they had a good night's sleep at least a few nights per week (Adenekan et al., 2013). Poor sleep has been raised as a factor mediating the increased risk of type 2 diabetes and cardiovascular disease among African Americans (Adenekan et al., 2013). Obesity, a factor in obstructive sleep apnea, is also more common among African Americans.

The Cross-Cultural Significance of Sleep Paralysis

Sleep paralysis occurring during the REM phase, while not troubling to most people of White European background, has significance in other cultures. Kryger (2015) describes a case of isolated sleep paralysis: A 19-year-old woman reported frightening episodes that had been occurring over the past year. During each episode, she awoke but could not move or speak for several minutes. She reported the experience of a "gnome-like" creature hovering over her bed. The young woman sensed that this gnome-like being was going to attack her. These episodes tended to have their onset about 90 minutes after the young woman fell asleep (Kryger, 2015, pp. 96–97).

While sleep paralysis is commonly reported among persons with narcolepsy (discussed below), there do appear to be forms of the condition that occur in the absence of narcolepsy. Among some individuals of Chinese background, sleep paralysis is associated with being possessed by a ghost (Wing, Lee, & Chen, 1994). Among a group of Cambodian refugees, 42 percent reported an episode of sleep paralysis in the past year. The episodes almost always included visual hallucinations and panic symptoms. Informants described some type of supernatural being that would put a hand on their chest or neck and push down on them, creating tightness in the chest and making it difficult to breathe (Hinton, Pich, Chhean, & Pollack, 2005).

In a sample of African Americans, it was found that those with histories of post-traumatic stress disorder (PTSD) were about four times as likely to report isolated sleep paralysis. In some African American communities in the Southern United States, the experience is described as a witch or devil riding on the sleeper's back (Paradis & Friedman, 2005). Finally, in Newfoundland—which, because of its status as an island some distance from the mainland, had been isolated for many years—sleep paralysis has been described as a particularly frightening experience. A phenomenon called "the old hag" seems to be associated with sleep paralysis. The experience is that one is awakened from sleep and cannot move. The body is paralyzed and people report that it feels like an old woman is sitting on their chest (Ness, 1978).

Sleep Disorders

While polysomnographic studies in a sleep laboratory are one of the most direct ways to evaluate sleep disturbance, there are a number of self-report questionnaires that are administered as well. One of the most common is the Pittsburgh Sleep Quality Index (Buysse, Reynolds, Monk, Berman, & Kupfer, 1989). In addition to asking about number of hours of sleep per night, the scale asks about difficulty sleeping because of feeling too hot or too cold or because of pain. The questionnaire also asks the respondent about their level of "enthusiasm" for completing daily tasks within the past month.

Insomnia

Definition and Prevalence

Insomnia is a persistent pattern of initiating or maintaining sleep. Insomnia can be of three types: initial—difficulty falling asleep (typically one half hour); intermittent—waking up and not being able to go back to sleep within 30 minutes; and terminal—waking up earlier than one needs to and not being able to return to sleep. Up to half of US adults reported insomnia at least a few nights a week during the past year, with 30 percent reporting some clinically significant insomnia symptoms during the past year (Ong, 2017). For most people, insomnia is considered transient and occurs for less than two weeks. However, when insomnia is more specifically defined to include impairment in daily functioning and a lack of satisfaction with the amount or quality of sleep, with medical factors that can cause insomnia ruled out, prevalence drops to approximately 6 to 10 percent of those who have clinically significant insomnia (Ong, 2017). Chronic insomnia, in which lack of sleep is associated with distress and impairment for six months or longer, does appear to be persistent—over half continue to report symptoms three years later (Ong, 2017; Ohayon, 2002). Insomnia appears to be twice as common in women as men and also increases with age. Insomnia is the second most common health complaint in outpatient settings—second only to pain. There are international differences in insomnia as well. For example, in the United States approximately 20 percent of persons ages 40 to 64 report difficulties initiating sleep. The comparable prevalence in China is approximately 9 percent, with Korean adults exhibiting similar rates (Heine, 2015).

Health Conditions Associated with Insomnia
Research has shown that 30 to 60 percent of insomnia complaints are associated with a clear medical condition (Ong, 2017; Ohayon, 2002). Insomnia as a specific condition is typically not diagnosed if it is better accounted for by a medical or psychiatric condition. There are a number of physical health conditions that can cause insomnia, such as hyperthyroidism, arthritis, or any type of chronic pain. Other conditions in which insomnia may occur include chronic lung and kidney disease, cerebrovascular disease, gastroesophageal reflux disorder, and type 2 diabetes, as well as neurological conditions such as epilepsy, Parkinson's disease, stroke, brain tumor, and Alzheimer's disease. People with major depressive disorder (MDD) often exhibit insomnia, and it is one of the nine criteria for diagnosis. While all three types of insomnia can occur with MDD, the most common type is early morning awakening. Interestingly, while it often takes weeks or several months for patients to fully benefit from antidepressant medication, sleep manipulation has provided some short-term relief for patients with depressive symptoms. In this manipulation, patients actually are deprived of sleep for a limited period of time—they are told to stay up all night—which appears to have benefits for symptoms. If these episodes of sleep deprivation are paired with exposure to sunlight or artificial light, the effect may last up to a week (Dallaspezia & Benedetti, 2014).

Medications Causing Insomnia
Some common substances that can cause insomnia include alcohol, caffeine, and chocolate. Medications that impair sleep include bronchodilators that are used for asthma, decongestants, thyroid replacement hormone for hypothyroidism, and treatments for high blood pressure. Alcohol is associated with lighter sleep and also a rebound in which awakening occurs during the latter part of the night. Caffeine is generally associated with greater time needed to fall asleep (sleep latency) and more awakenings during the night. In cases in which insomnia is believed to be associated

with a medication or medical condition, if sleep difficulties persist after effective treatment of the medical condition or removal of the offending medication, then it would be considered to be a "stand-alone" diagnosis to be treated.

Psychological Causes of Insomnia

Insomnia has been explained according to a diathesis stress model (Ong, 2017). Diatheses, or predisposing characteristics, include an overly responsive sympathetic nervous system leading to states of long-term arousal and circadian rhythm preferences (oriented toward morning or evening), as well as anxiety and tendency toward rumination. An external event will trigger acute insomnia through its interaction with these predisposing factors.

Once episodes of insomnia begin, the individual often engages in compensatory behavior such as going to bed earlier, taking naps, and using stimulants such as coffee or energy drinks during the day (Ong, 2017). The use of naps and patterns of sleeping later in the morning to make up for sleep loss are likely to disrupt normal circadian rhythms. Additionally, after several difficult nights, persons with these predisposing factors become anxious about their inability to fall asleep, which, in turn, makes it difficult to fall asleep. As a result, as it nears bedtime, the bed and associated rituals become associated with arousal (Wyatt, Cvengros, & Ong, 2011).

Other investigators have pointed to differences in perceptions of sleep among those with insomnia; insomniacs tend to overestimate the time they are awake and underestimate their sleep time (Ong, 2017; Perlis, Giles, Mendelson, Bootzin, & Wyatt, 1997). However, there is some evidence that among those with insomnia, there is more beta wave activity shown on EEGs during non-REM sleep. Beta activity, associated with wakefulness, may in part explain why these individuals underreport the amount of time they sleep or describe themselves as a "light sleeper" (Ong, 2017).

Cognitive theorists emphasize how distorted thinking about sleep interacts with the already high level of sympathetic nervous system activity and compensatory behavior (Morin, 1993). Additionally, rumination centering around the consequences of sleep loss, such as impaired work performance, becomes a factor. Harvey et al. (2014) suggest that the transition from acute to chronic insomnia involves distorted perceptions of daytime functioning and "counterproductive safety" behavior such as naps, sleeping pills, or use of stimulants during the day. In more extreme situations, the individual begins avoiding work and social functions because of perceptions of insufficient energy. As one withdraws socially, rumination tends to become more prominent, as does accompanying arousal (Hairston, Talbot, Eidelman, Gruber, & Harvey, 2010). While most of us experience insomnia occasionally, those who develop clinically significant insomnia become hyper-focused on physical experiences, their surroundings, and performance. They may become preoccupied with aspects of the environment such as noise or excess light. Additionally, persons with chronic insomnia become preoccupied with experiences of fatigue, sleepiness, feeling "foggy," and not performing as well at work or school—all of which are attributed to insufficient sleep. Common cognitive distortions associated with insomnia are "I must have at least 8 hours of sleep each night or I will not be able to function the next day" and "Insomnia can make me sick and cause a mental breakdown." These faulty beliefs about the consequences of insomnia may become extreme (Edinger, Wohlgemuth, Radtke,

TABLE 11.1. Factors Associated with Insomnia

Predispositions
Family history
"Short sleeper" trait
Sympathetic hyperarousal

Precipitants
Job stress
Marital conflict
Issues with children/extended family
Death of close family member
Change in sleep pattern due to external factors such as change in work hours, newborn baby, etc.

Psychosocial Factors
Worry about sleep
Rumination about work performance associated with sleep
Worry about falling asleep associated with bedtime
Medical conditions (e.g., pain)
Mental health conditions (depression, anxiety)
Stimulant use (caffeine, cold medication with pseudoephedrine
Depressant use (alcohol)
Pre-sleep routine
Changes in sleep-wake schedule

Marsh, & Quillian, 2001; Harvey, 2002). Reduced activity and reports of fatigue may also be inadvertently reinforced by friends, family members, and coworkers. If someone has become preoccupied with insomnia and feels tired throughout the day, this situation will likely lead to others putting reduced demands on the patient (Morgan, Gregory, Tomeny, David, & Gascoigne, 2012). In addition, persons with insomnia often will report being too tired to engage in any type of physical activity, while exercise earlier in the day may actually help the individual fall asleep. As the individual becomes deconditioned as a result of reduced physical activity, their fatigue is also likely to increase.

Insomnia Treatment

As part of treating insomnia, it is helpful to have an assessment of the individual's sleep patterns as well as changes that occur as a result of treatment. The sleep diary is probably the most common method used. The patient answers a series of questions each day about the previous night's sleep, such as "What time did you get to bed?" "How long does it take to fall asleep?" "What time did you get out of bed for the day?" and "How would you rate the quality of your sleep?" (Carney et al., 2012).

Insomnia treatment includes medical and psychological/behavioral interventions. Sleeping pills are probably the most common treatment. Approximately 10 to 20 percent of Americans over age 65 have used a sleeping pill at some point in their lives. While these medications do have some effectiveness in cases of acute insomnia, they are usually ineffective with chronic insomnia. There is a preference for short-acting medication to reduce the "morning hangover" experience. These negative effects in the morning are common with medications such as diazepam (Valium). Shorter-acting medications such is triazolam (Halcion) or temazepam (Restoril) often are helpful in getting off to sleep, but because of the drug's short half-life, many people will have insomnia later in the night. These drugs typically act on the GABA (inhibitory neurotransmitter) system. More recently developed sleep medications such as zolpidem (Ambien) and zaleplon (Sonata) are somewhat less likely to be associated with drowsiness in the morning and appear to be less disruptive to the natural phases of sleep. Because tolerance and withdrawal develop relatively quickly, these medications are not intended for long-term treatment of sleep problems. In addition, if they are stopped abruptly, rebound insomnia is likely. Many over-the-counter sleep medications include diphenhydramine (Benadryl), an antihistamine, which can cause mild cognitive impairment in older adults (Agostini, Leo-Summers, & Inouye, 2001).

For those whose circadian rhythms have been disrupted, use of light therapy—specifically 30 minutes of bright light upon awakening—may be helpful. These specialized lights, used for seasonal affective disorder, have become more readily available and less expensive in recent years.

A procedure called stimulus control is based upon the idea that insomnia is classically conditioned (Morin et al., 2006). Typically, someone will have several nights in which they have difficulty remaining asleep and then become anxious about and ruminative about sleep—which in turn maintains insomnia. The bedroom becomes a conditioned stimulus that maintains arousal. Factors that establish and maintain this connection include the practice of lying down while awake and the practice of extending sleep activity through naps or going to bed earlier and getting out of bed later to alleviate perceived sleep deficits. For stimulus control, the person should only go to bed when sleepy and use the bed only for sleeping (and romantic encounters) but not for watching television, using the computer, or talking on the phone. If unable to sleep after 30 minutes, the person should get up and move to another room. Again, while waiting to become sleepy, the individual should not use any electronic technology. Quiet reading is the most helpful. Upon beginning to feel sleepy again, the person should return to bed. If not asleep within 30 minutes, the person should repeat the procedure. Importantly, persons using sleep restriction should also try to get up at the same time every morning and not nap during the day. However, while stimulus control therapies are effective, using them as the only technique yields only about a 50 percent reduction in insomnia symptoms (Murtaugh & Greenwood, 1995).

Stimulus control is often combined with cognitive therapy. The Dysfunctional Beliefs and Attitudes About Sleep Scale (Shahid, Wilkinson, Marcu, & Shapiro, 2012) is a 28-item questionnaire. Sample items include the following: "Without an adequate night's sleep, I can hardly function the next day." "It usually shows in my physical appearance when I haven't slept well." "I am worried that I may lose control over my ability to sleep." Cognitive therapy focuses on helping the patient to logically evaluate their mistaken assumptions about sleep. Additional techniques include covering the face of the alarm clock or turning it so it is not visible and eliminating all media at least 60 minutes before bedtime. The patient is also invited to consider in more realistic terms whether and how much their functioning is impaired on a night in which they did not receive what they consider an optimal number of hours of sleep. In absolute terms, the client's impairment in functioning is actually likely to be small (if there is any at all). However, the patient is likely to exaggerate the extent of their impairment. Those treated with cognitive behavioral therapy also continue to improve in the months after formal treatment is completed.

Sleep restriction is an intervention that is best done with a professional (Spielman, Yang, & Glovinsky, 2011). Before making any changes, patients need to pay attention to the number of hours they are actually sleeping. Once that is determined—say, 4 to 5 hours per night—they should be in bed only for that time, but no less than 4 hours. No additional sleep is permitted outside these hours, and patients record their sleep regularly with a sleep log. Progressively more time is spent in bed—typically in 15-minute intervals. The procedure focuses on limiting the time in bed to time actually slept. Often, persons reporting insomnia are actually entering stage 1 sleep but misinterpret this light sleep experience as being awake. The goal is to improve sleep efficiency—meaning the percentage of time in bed spent actually sleeping. However, for persons who have excessive sleepiness during the day, other treatment should be considered since sleep restriction is likely to further impair functioning.

An intervention that has been suggested for teenagers who are having difficulty falling asleep because of rumination is to have them write their concerns on a daily basis in a "worry diary" (Dahl & Harvey, 2007; Weis, 2014). Teenagers are instructed to set aside a particular time each day during which they write in their diary about their worries. When rumination occurs while trying to fall asleep, teenagers are instructed to tell themselves that they have another place and a time to deal with their worries. The "worry diary" is often used along with guided imagery in which the teenager is encouraged to think of being by themselves and doing something relaxing (Dahl & Harvey, 2007).

Obstructive Sleep Apnea

In obstructive sleep apnea (OSA), breathing is interrupted during sleep and each episode of not breathing may last 10 to 60 seconds. There are hundreds of these episodes throughout the night. While asleep, the person often appears to be gasping for air, and during the brief awakenings, they may snort and inhale strongly. Often, this is accompanied by substantial loud snoring, night sweats, awakening with the sensation of choking, and disrupted sleep. In addition to sleepiness during the day, there is evidence of cognitive problems, particularly with attention and higher-level reasoning. In the absence of significant stimulation, such as when reading or being a passenger in a car, patients are likely to feel sleepy and often doze (Singer & Applebee, 2008). Typically, this is condition noted by a bed partner who may be somewhat frightened about these episodes of not breathing and annoyed by the snoring. The daily impact of frequent sleep apnea is excessive sleepiness and headaches in the morning, as well as impaired attention, concentration, and short-term memory. "Nodding off" during the day is very common—particularly when there is minimal external stimulation, such being a passenger in a car.

This is a relatively common condition, with an estimated 24 percent of men and 9 percent of women having obstructive sleep apnea; at least 2 percent of women and 4 percent of men with the condition report significant daytime sleepiness (Weaver & Ye, 2011). Central sleep apnea occurs when airflow is disrupted for at least 10 seconds. Among adults with this condition, there is a greater likelihood of complaining of insomnia than of being tired during the day. There is likely to be some central nervous system component to central apnea. As noted earlier, sudden infant death syndrome (SIDS) is associated with breathing disruptions and a buildup of carbon dioxide. Some cases of SIDS also appear to be associated with apnea.

Sleep apnea is typically caused by obstruction of the airway, which can occur for multiple reasons (Mannarino, Di Filippo, & Pirro, 2012). The most common reason for sleep apnea is obesity; weight loss often results in improvement. Additional causes include a particularly thick or "bull" neck, enlarged tonsils, and loss of muscle tone associated with aging. Persons with sleep apnea are at elevated risk for hypertension, stroke, and major depressive disorder. It has been estimated that up to 800,000 drivers per year are involved in obstructive sleep apnea–related accidents. About 25 percent of those with obstructive sleep apnea report falling asleep while driving (Pagel, 2009).

Treatment consists of using a machine called a constant positive airway pressure device (CPAP). CPAPs have a mask and a tube attached to the mask in the machine. The device keeps the upper airway open (Weaver & Ye, 2011). For patients who can tolerate the mask and device, regular CPAP use appears to be very effective and has been associated with decreased daytime sleepiness and improved cognitive functioning and alertness. Two other interventions that have been conducted are surgery to alter the airway and weight loss. Surgery may involve removal of tonsils and adenoids or "remodeling" throat tissue.

Narcolepsy

Although it has received a good deal of attention, narcolepsy is a relatively rare condition affecting 0.5 to 1 percent of the general population (Ohayon, Priest, Zulley, Smirne, & Paiva, 2002). Narcolepsy's major feature is sudden onset of sleep—often described as an "irresistible" desire to sleep (Dauvilliers, Arnulf, & Mignot, 2007) during waking hours (Dauvilliers & Bayard, 2011). Formal diagnosis of narcolepsy includes a 3-month period of daily episodes of the urge to sleep. The average duration of episodes of daytime sleep is approximately 10 to 20 minutes, but it can last up to several hours. From a sleep physiology perspective, narcolepsy appears to represent a sudden intrusion of REM as well as non-REM sleep during these periods. The intrusion of REM sleep is associated with an experience of paralysis and vivid dreams. While these episodes can occur in multiple situations, there is a tendency for these "sleep attacks" to occur when there is little external environmental stimulation, such as when sitting quietly or being a passenger in a car (Dauvilliers & Bayard, 2011). Unless narcolepsy is treated, persons with the condition may have up to two to six episodes per day. Narcolepsy tends to have its onset between the ages of 15 and 25. The condition is often associated with poor concentration, impaired memory, and an experience of low energy. Additionally, periods of isolated sleep paralysis, as described above, are fairly common among those with narcolepsy (Dauvilliers & Bayard, 2011).

A less common subtype of narcolepsy includes cataplexy, in which there is a sudden loss of muscle tone. A trigger for cataplexy is being exposed to an emotional situation such as suddenly being surprised or fearful. Narcolepsy appears to have a strong hereditary component, with increased episodes during pregnancy, fever, or times of emotional distress. At the level of the central nervous system, there appears to be a defect in the hypothalamus such that the amount of hypocretin regulating sleep, wakefulness, and arousal is reduced (Straub, 2016). Narcolepsy is a chronic condition in which symptoms can be controlled somewhat but not cured. As a result, most adults with narcolepsy continue to have some daily difficulty in social and occupational functioning.

Medication used for narcolepsy includes stimulant medications such as methylphenidate (Ritalin) and amphetamine-like stimulants such as modafinil. These may be used for excessive daytime sleepiness as well. Cataplexy appears to respond to antidepressant medication.

Restless Legs Syndrome

Restless legs syndrome (RLS) is the experience of needing to move one's legs and having uncomfortable, "prickly" sensations in the legs when lying down or sitting for prolonged periods. Moving the legs briefly reduces the sensations. RLS often occurs when trying to fall asleep, and it may also occur when one has to sit for prolonged periods, such as in an airplane or sitting at a desk for several hours. The estimated prevalence in the general population is about 5 percent. Research to date suggests that the condition is about 35 percent more common among women and occurs more commonly in people of White European background (Innes, Selfe, & Agarwal, 2012). The condition seems to increase in prevalence with age, with the peak age for RLS being in the 60s and 70s. One report found a 3 percent prevalence between ages 18 and 29, 10 percent prevalence among those 30 to 79, and a 19 percent prevalence among those 80 to 93 years of age (Innes et al., 2012). RLS is also more common among those with chronic medical conditions, including type 2 diabetes, hypertension, and major depressive disorders. There are indications that there is a genetic predisposition to RLS; however, there does not seem to be a single genotype associated with the condition (Winkelmann et al., 2007). There are several medications used to treat the condition. Dopamine replacement, while effective, has been found to be associated with rebound restless legs episodes later in the day. Long-acting benzodiazepines, while not relieving RLS, do help people sleep through these episodes. Additionally, persons with RLS may be advised to reduce caffeine intake and eliminate alcohol.

Periodic limb movement (PLM) is a disorder distinct from RLS but often occurs along with it. They are both forms of nocturnal myoclonus—involuntary muscle spasms. PLM occurs during sleep, with bursts of leg movement of seconds to minutes occuring multiple times throughout the night. PLM's prevalence is 5 percent of persons 30 to 50 years of age but more than 40 percent of those over age 65 (Wilt et al., 2013). These bursts of leg movements, typically occurring during the first half of the night, occur primarily during stage 2 sleep. However, they often may awaken the patient. Dopamine agonists such as levodopa have been successful in reducing these episodes (Wilt et al., 2013) but may lead to rebound episodes in the second half of the night.

Excessive Daytime Sleepiness

Excessive daytime somnolence is described as a level of sleepiness that interferes with daily activities. Up to 20 percent of the US population reports episodes of daytime sleepiness that interfere with daily functioning (Pagel, 2009). It is commonly secondary to another condition such as obstructive sleep apnea. It is presumed that the patient is obtaining an adequate number of hours of sleep. Many individuals, however, may have insufficient sleep, leading to episodes of excessive daytime somnolence, particularly in the afternoon, evening, or after meals. In addition, medical conditions as well as medications that could contribute to the condition are evaluated. Excessive daytime somnolence is not diagnosed unless the person is obtaining what is considered an adequate number of hours of sleep within a 24-hour period. A common approach to assessing this is the Epworth Sleepiness Scale (Johns, 1991). The scale asks patients to rate themselves on a scale from 0 (no chance of dozing off) to 3 (high chance of dozing off) in a series of activities, including watching television and sitting quietly after lunch without alcohol. The treatment for the condition is modafinil—a medication that is also used with narcolepsy. While modafinil is a stimulant, it has less potential for abuse than prescription amphetamines such as methylphenidate (Ritalin).

Hypersomnia

It is uncommon to find hypersomnia by itself and not a symptom of another condition such as major depressive disorder or seasonal affective disorder. Persons with hypersomnia sleep for 12 hours per day and oftentimes will also take naps. The prevalence appears to be 5 to 15 percent of the general population reporting a duration of one month (Dauvilliers & Bayard, 2011). The chief complaint of people with hypersomnia is that they do not feel refreshed when they wake up and are fatigued during the day.

Childhood Sleep Disorders

Because of continued maturation of the central nervous system, the sleep-waking cycle of children is different than for adults. There are also sleep disorders that, while known in adults, are much more common among children. Many of these are developmental in nature and remit with age. Sleep problems among children are relatively common, with up to a third of children exhibiting difficulty at some point prior to adolescence (Stores, 1996; Weis, 2014).

Bedtime Refusal

While probably not rooted in central nervous system development, children's bedtime refusals can be very disruptive to families. By the age of 6 to 7 months, infants can typically soothe themselves and upon awakening will, in a relatively short period of time, fall back to sleep. However, if the onset of sleeping becomes associated with being held by parents or being in the parents' bed, these stimuli will be classically conditioned to sleep onset and children will not be able to fall asleep without these conditions present (Weis, 2014). Infants and toddlers typically awaken for brief periods of time throughout the night as part of the normal sleep cycle. Most children engage in some type of self-soothing behavior such as hugging a stuffed animal. However, if returning to sleep from these awakenings has been conditioned to other stimuli, such as being held by parents, the 4 to 6 awakenings that young children normally experience will require parental presence to fall asleep again.

Among older children, a common pattern is to delay falling asleep—requesting another drink of water, another story read to them, or (if they are slightly older) being allowed to stay up and watch television. If parents periodically permit these exceptions, they have successfully placed the child on an intermittent reinforcement schedule that is particularly resistant to extinction. In a study in which parents were instructed to keep their child up an hour later than usual, there was evidence of poor sleep quality and poor cognitive functioning the following day (Sadeh, Gruber, & Raviv, 2003; Weis, 2014).

To prevent this pattern from worsening, it is best to address bedtime problems as early as possible. With infants, "planned ignoring" is generally effective. Parents using the strategy respond to the crying baby by deliberately "ignoring" the crying until the baby falls asleep independently. This technique is often easier said than done—particularly for new parents. Because of this challenge, a modified version has been recommended in which parents check on the crying baby every five minutes and may briefly pat them or hug them and then leave the room. If the crying continues for another five minutes, parents again check on the baby and leave, continuing this pattern until the child falls asleep. In reality, the latter strategy is perhaps more therapeutic for the parents than for the infant (Weis 2014).

Sleep (Night) Terrors

Sleep or night terrors are characterized by very abrupt awakenings in which the child appears to be extremely frightened. Children often scream, appear terrified, and may show symptoms similar to a panic attack with increased autonomic activity such as being flushed, having a rapid heart rate, and gasping for air. The prevalence of sleep terrors in children is 1.5 to 3 percent (Weis, 2014). Sleep terrors generally occur after several hours of sleeping and do not occur during the REM stage. These events commonly occur during stages 3 and 4 of the sleep cycle. The child appears very frightened but does not report dreams or any other internal experience associated with the awakening. Sleep terror episodes will typically have a duration of 10 to 30 minutes, after which the child readily returns to sleep. The child typically has no recollection of the event the next day. Sleep terrors are a syndrome in and of themselves and are not symptomatic of any other psychological condition (Weis, 2014). These episodes peak in frequency at ages three and four, usually remit over the course of development, and typically disappear in later childhood, certainly by adolescence. Sleep terrors appear to be more common among children who exhibit sleepwalking as well as enuresis (bedwetting).

Nightmare Disorder

Nightmares are not uncommon among children. Between 2 and 11 percent of children indicate they have frequent nightmares, and up to an additional 30 percent report that they have occasional nightmares (Weis, 2014). Up to 50 percent of preschool children have nightmares; however, the prevalence drops to about 10 percent by adolescence. Nightmares usually occur during REM sleep; children who are experiencing nightmares can be readily awakened. Typically, if asked immediately upon awakening, children having nightmares can describe the content of the dream, in contrast to children having night terrors. Younger children tend to dream about monsters, while slightly older children often report dreams of wild animals or storms. Among children who have repeated nightmares characterized by themes of threats to their own survival or security, other emotional issues such as an anxiety disorder may be present. For example, nightmares are fairly common in posttraumatic stress disorder. Typically, children can provide a very detailed account of the dream and are quite alert and oriented upon awakening, unlike when they have sleep terrors. As noted above, another factor distinguishing nightmares from night terrors is that in contrast to night terrors, frequent nightmares among older children and adolescents often are associated with psychosocial stressors.

Somnambulism (Sleepwalking)

Sleepwalking, like night terrors, is an arousal disorder. Sleepwalking is most common between ages 4 and 8 years. About a third of children will occasionally sleepwalk. These events typically occur early in the evening during non-REM, slow-wave sleep (Weis, 2014). It is believed that somnambulism commonly occurs when a child is transitioning from slow-wave sleep to the beginning of the first REM phase of the night. Somnambulism also is of brief duration. During sleepwalking episodes, children are not responsive to parental questions or directions and experience amnesia for the event the next day (Weis, 2014). During the episode, they often have a blank stare, are very difficult to awaken, and are unresponsive to others. If awoken, they are confused. On occasion, sleepwalking children may engage in dangerous behavior such as turning on the stove or leaving the house. There does appear to be a hereditary predisposition for night terrors as well as somnambulism. If both parents have one of these conditions, it is twice as likely that one of their children will develop either somnambulism or sleep terrors (Kales et al., 1980). It has been suggested that children with these conditions have less mature central nervous system development and over time develop the ability to inhibit both arousal and movement.

While somnambulism is almost exclusively a childhood condition, several medications, such as those used for seizures, have been implicated in somnambulism episodes in young adults (Varkey & Varkey, 2003). There have also been reports of violence and self-injury by adults during sleepwalking episodes (Kavey, Whyte, Resor, & Gidro-Frank, 1990).

Conclusion

Our knowledge of sleep has expanded greatly in the past 50 years. Additionally, the field of sleep disorders continues to develop, with sleep laboratories for assessment purposes being established at a growing number of health care sites. As is evident from this chapter, problems with sleeping are very common in the general population as well as across the life span. With the development of the internet, 24-hour businesses, and media outlets with round-the-clock news, there has been an encroachment upon the number of hours that we sleep. As our world has become flatter, time spent sleeping may seem wasted. It is safe to say that the average US adult does not obtain enough sleep and is likely offsetting their fatigue and associated attention and concentration difficulties with coffee and various caffeinated beverages and energy drinks. As noted, the average number of hours of sleep during the week appears to be about six in the United States—about two hours fewer than is recommended for most adults. It will be interesting to see whether sleep, time continues to drop and whether conditions related to impaired sleep, such as cardiovascular disease and auto/industrial accidents, rise in frequency. For students who find this chapter interesting, the sleep disorders field is expanding—psychologists, physicians, and technicians will be needed to staff the growing number of sleep disorder centers.

CHAPTER 12

Psychosexual Disorders

Sexuality is a sensitive area, and one in which there is still a good deal of misinformation. In the United States, education around sexuality often depends upon parents' attitudes toward the subject as well as how specific school systems address or do not address the topic. While there is often an unspoken question—"Am I normal?"—when it comes to sexuality, a specific criterion for normality is hard to come by. There is also a reluctance to ask parents or professionals about sexuality since the topic may be embarrassing and many young adults want to portray an image of being knowledgeable in this area. Unfortunately, inadequate or erroneous information about sexuality often leads to anxiety and self-doubt when sexual situations arise. While this chapter contains information about conditions labeled as "sexual dysfunctions," it is to be remembered that there is wide variation in sexual behavior and desire. In many respects, the important criterion in determining whether a sexual performance issue is a problem is the degree of distress that it creates for the individual or the relationship.

The discussion of sexuality and the psychosexual disorders in this chapter may seem mechanical. One of the criticisms of sex therapy is that it often seems to remove sexuality from emotional intimacy between partners. To paraphrase the family therapist Carl Whitaker, sexual organs are present, but the people have not caught up to them yet (Whitaker & Bumberry, 1988). This is an important dimension, and as a clinical psychologist who has used some of the techniques discussed in this chapter with couples, in reality it is not possible to separate sexuality from the overall climate of a relationship. High levels of conflict, poor communication skills, and an absence of respect and genuine friendship for one's partner readily override physiological responses.

The Sexual Response Cycle

Most contemporary sex researchers and therapists still rely on the work of William Masters and Virginia Johnson, who pioneered the field. Masters, an obstetrician, became interested in sexuality through working with women having difficulty conceiving. While Masters and Johnson's research methods are considered somewhat controversial (anonymous women and men wearing masks and having sex in a laboratory while being observed and physiologically monitored), their work in describing the normal sexual response cycle, categorizing and describing specific psychosexual disorders, and developing treatments is still considered groundbreaking, foundational work (Maier, 2009).

Masters and Johnson (1966) described a sexual response pattern with somewhat similar stages for men and women, although there was greater variability in the stages for women. The original four stages of the sexual response cycle and their key physical dimensions are:

1. *Excitement*—increased muscle tension, increased heart rate, possible flushing of the skin; for women, there is swelling of the clitoris, initial lubrication, and swelling of the inner labia. For men, penile erection occurs.
2. *Plateau*—intensification of the sensations and physiological reactions (e.g., breathing, heart rate, blood pressure); for women, vagina continues to swell and vaginal walls become dark purple.
3. *Orgasm*—lasting just a few seconds; characterized by involuntary muscle contractions and possible muscle spasms. For men, muscle contractions of the penis lead to ejaculation; for women, the muscles of the vagina contract.
4. *Resolution*—physiological functions regularly return to normal.

Some women are capable of additional orgasms. However, men have a refractory period—essentially a recovery time after orgasm during which they cannot have another orgasm. While men have a single orgasm, women may have one of three patterns during the orgasm phase: arousal without orgasm, a single orgasm, or in some instances multiple orgasms.

Some sex therapists view Masters and Johnson's four-stage model as incomplete or limiting. The critics suggest that prior to sexual excitement is a state of desire, characterized by motivation to seek out sexually related stimuli, including one's partner. Kaplan (1995) describes three basic stages: *desire*, *excitement* (which includes Masters and Johnson's first and second stages), and *orgasm*. It has also been noted that a significant number of women may not necessarily experience a spontaneous desire for sex but do respond positively to initiation of sexual activity (Meana, 2012). Research has found that, among women, sexual desire and arousal are not necessarily distinct experiences (Basson, 2006). Additionally, more commonly among women than men, motivation for sex may not necessarily be centered on sexual arousal but instead may be guided by a desire for emotional closeness (Meana, 2012). However, despite these very reasonable criticisms, the diagnosis of psychosexual problems in the DSM system still reflects the Masters and Johnson model of sexuality.

Sensate Focus

In terms of treatment, several of the categories of both male and female sexual dysfunction benefit from a technique developed by Masters and Johnson called sensate focus. Originally, sensate focus was based upon counter-conditioning principles (Weiner & Avery-Clark, 2014). Masters and Johnson emphasized the role that anxiety plays in diminishing or inhibiting normal sexual responsiveness. The anxiety may stem from several factors. Many adults have conflicting feelings regarding sexual expression—often associated with negative messages about sexuality received as a child and adolescent. In some instances, particularly in cases of adults with histories of childhood sexual abuse or adult sexual assault, sexual activity may be experienced as traumatic. For males, performance-related anxiety may be powerful enough to override normal sexual excitement with resulting erectile dysfunction.

The overall goals of sensate focus are to reduce the performance demands of sex, improve communication around sexuality, and reduce anxiety. There are multiple variations on this technique. It essentially involves "non-demand pleasuring." Both partners undress and caress each other, typically beginning with touching non-genital areas. In the classic Masters and Johnson approach, couples were instructed not to have sex for the first several weeks even if they became aroused. They were also instructed to give their partner feedback about types of touch that felt good to them. Sensate focus shares mindfulness's emphasis of being in the present and attending to immediate sensory experience.

Wincze and Weisberg (2015) describe a four-stage process with some variations on the classical Masters and Johnson approach. First, non-genital pleasuring—the couple are dressed in comfortable clothing and engage in non-sexual physical contact such as massaging or holding hands. Removing the performance element from sexuality helps couples appreciate that they can enjoy physical contact with one another that is not necessarily sexual. In the second stage, partners are encouraged to touch genitals and breasts and give feedback about touching—noting the types of touch that are enjoyable and those that are not. If stages 1 and 2 are successfully completed, the couple moves toward intercourse. One technique that is often used in the transition to intercourse is that the receptive partner—typically the female—is on top of her partner so she can better control the depth of penetration and the amount of time spent in penetration (Wincze & Weisberg, 2015).

Again, the tendency for psychosexual disorders to be compartmentalized from other relationship dimensions often leads to a narrow focus on sexual response without adequate attention to other aspects of the relationship. In a relatively early study of sensate focus for sexual dysfunction, outcome was highly predicted by the couple's quality of marital communication at the outset of treatment. Those couples with better communication skills responded better to sensate focus (Hawton, Catalan, & Fagg, 1992).

Erectile Dysfunction

Erectile dysfunction (ED) was recognized as a common problem early in the development of sex therapy. The DSM-5 defines ED as featuring at least one of these key symptoms: (1) difficulty obtaining erections; (2) difficulty maintaining an erection; and (3) decrease in erectile rigidity. To meet criteria for diagnosis, this problem must be present for six months and characterize approximately 75 to 100 percent of episodes of sexual activity (American Psychiatric Association, 2013).

While it is estimated that maybe half of all men experience erectile difficulty at some point in their lives, this appears to be a function of age. Approximately 10 percent of men under 35 will have periodic episodes of ED, while up to 50 percent—65 percent of men over 50—report difficulties initiating or maintaining an erection (Benet & Melman, 1995; Carbone & Seftel, 2002; Rowland, 2012).

Erectile dysfunction is a condition in which a thorough medical history is essential before initiating sex therapy. Difficulties with erections are particularly common in men with type 2 diabetes and cardiovascular disease. There has been controversy regarding the impact of normal age-related declines in testosterone. While testosterone may well decline, much of the research and clinical practice of having men take synthetic testosterone is based upon investigations suggesting that certain medications that reduce testosterone are associated with reduced sexual interest and functioning. Alcohol as well as several kinds of medication—some antihypertensive medicines and the current, second-generation antidepressant medications (SSRIs)—are associated with sexual difficulties. In addition to type 2 diabetes, metabolic syndrome (defined by abdominal obesity, dyslipidemia, hypertension, and hyperglycemia) may contribute to the problem. There is evidence that metabolic syndrome is associated with decreased blood flow to the penis (Traish, Guay, Feeley, & Saad, 2009). This condition can be treated through lifestyle changes including regular exercise and changes in diet.

Psychologically oriented sex therapists emphasize the role of performance anxiety. Sexual functioning is readily affected by patterns of classical conditioning. Anxiety about performing sexually paradoxically suppresses sexual function. Cognitive theorists point out that men with recent experiences of erectile dysfunction will become anxious when sexual intercourse is anticipated. The spectator phenomenon appears to be an important factor contributing to sexual performance anxiety among many men. This phenomenon occurs when men, while in sexual situations with a partner, are evaluating their performance from the perspective of an external observer. Needless to say, this pattern increases performance anxiety. There is an expectation of failure followed by sadness and a sense of helplessness. This anxiety and accompanying cognitions soon become associated with having sex (Wiederman, 2001).

With the availability of medications such as Viagra and Cialis, the emphasis on psychological intervention has declined. Even with pharmacotherapy, it is useful to conduct a psychosocial assessment, including developing an understanding of the patient's view of the problem as well as their knowledge about typical sexual functioning. The best-known pharmacological interventions today include sildenafil (Viagra), tadalafil (Cialis), and vardenafil (Levitra). These drugs, known as PDE-5 inhibitors, act primarily by increasing blood flow to the penis (Gresser & Gleiter, 2002). However, psychosocial factors also interact with PDE-5 inhibitors; these medications are less effective when there is an ongoing history of sexual or marital conflict or lack of desire (Rosen, Miner, & Wincze, 2014).

Female Sexual Interest/Arousal Disorder

From the perspective of Masters and Johnson's mapping of the sexual response cycle, interest and arousal are distinct. With women, arousal historically has been physiologically defined as consisting of vaginal vasocongestion and lubrication. However, as noted above, for women, arousal and interest are often merged. As such, it is difficult for researchers and clinicians to distinguish between desire and arousal. Women themselves often do not distinguish between the two states (Kaplan, 1995). The DSM-5 definition of female sexual interest/arousal disorder requires that women have three of six symptoms: (1) minimal interest in sex; (2) few erotic thoughts; (3) lack of initiation of sexual activity; (4) minimal to no pleasure during sex; (5) lack of emergence of sexual desire or interest during sex; (6) reduced physical sexual sensations. The pattern should be persistently present for six months, with some of the symptoms present in at least 75 percent of sexual encounters.

While this is a relatively new diagnosis and epidemiological data are minimal, the prevalence of some of the symptoms has been studied. Given the heterogeneity of criteria in the definition, it should not be a surprise that prevalence rates also vary widely, from 22 percent indicating episodes of little sexual interest—with more than 10 percent reporting low sexual desire for six months or longer—and 40 percent reporting lack of interest for at least a month (Brotto & Luria, 2015). As with other DSM-5 diagnoses, symptoms must be associated with psychological distress. However, it is noted that many women are not particularly distressed by this condition, and when distress is factored in as an additional criterion, rates fall to 8 percent or below (Brotto & Luria, 2015). There is evidence that the distress associated with reduced desire is much greater among younger than older females.

Composite measures of genital sensation suggest that the absence of physiologically related sexual response occurs in about 12 percent of women, ages 16 to 44. However, it is important to keep in mind that age plays a significant role in physiological responsiveness. For example, vaginal dryness becomes increasingly common after menopause.

The specific etiology for this condition has been elusive. However, it is likely that reduced sexual desire stems from a constellation of factors, with some of them playing a larger role depending upon the woman's age and psychosocial history.

Hormonal factors have been implicated with related declines in estrogen as well as androgens. In women, levels of androgens peak in the 20s and drop significantly by age 40. Estrogen markedly declines after menopause. Physiologically, it is noted that lubrication problems increase with age and become more pronounced after menopause (Graziottin & Leiblum, 2005). Among premenopausal women, sexual interest increases near the time of ovulation.

Major depressive disorder, which is twice as common among women as men, is also a significant contributor to low sexual desire, with approximately one-third of premenopausal women reporting major depressive disorder (Clayton, DeRogatis, Rosen, & Pyke, 2012). Additionally, reductions in sexual responsiveness are common side effects of SSRI antidepressants.

In terms of psychosocial precipitants, current life stressors, negative views toward sex from upbringing, and a history of sexual trauma increase the likelihood of reduced sexual desire and interest. Research does suggest that for women, sexual responsiveness is influenced by a much greater range of factors than is the case for men. For example, Meana (2012) found that among women with hypoactive sexual desire, a substantial number, upon becoming mothers, stopped viewing themselves as "sexual beings." Cross-cultural studies suggest that there are significant variations in female sexual desire depending upon how sexuality is viewed culturally. Guilt around sexuality and religiosity also appear to play a role in sexual desire.

Medical treatments have included artificial testosterone. Psychosocial interventions have been employed, including sensate focus and masturbation (Meana, 2012). Recently, mindfulness meditation has been applied (Silverstein, Brown, Roth, & Britton, 2011). Given the heterogeneity of symptoms, women with very different physical and psychological processes would be given the same diagnosis. This might include an absence of sexual fantasies or thoughts about sex with normal physical responses. However, women may have an interest in sex and experience sexual fantasies but have little in the way of physiological response or pleasurable physical sensations.

Hypoactive Sexual Desire in Men

For men, in the DSM-5, the criteria for hypoactive sexual desire were carried forward from the previous DSMIV-TR. As noted above, for women, the diagnosis has been revised with the addition of reduced sexual interest (Meana & Steiner, 2014). This distinction is likely to reflect clinical reality in that hypoactive sexual desire is an infrequent presenting problem for men. Additionally, hypoactive sexual desire among women, versus men, has been the subject of more research and development of treatments. In keeping with this lack of information, prevalence rates for this condition among men are not well established and have ranged from 0 to 40 percent. Approximately 15 percent of men report a lack of sexual interest lasting for at least two months. There is some evidence that this figure increases to 25 to 40 percent with age (Krakowsy & Grober, 2016; Rowland, 2012; Wincze & Weisberg, 2015). The extent to which this issue creates subjective distress for men is not known. Anecdotally, it is often a partner who initiates treatment for the condition.

Suspected causes have included biological factors such as low testosterone, which, however, has not been found to consistently correlate with sexual interest. While results are variable, testosterone replacement may increase sexual desire (Schiavi, White, Mandeli, & Levine, 1997). Again, antidepressant medications such as selective serotonin reuptake inhibitors reduce sexual interest and (in some men) precipitate erectile dysfunction, which in turn may contribute to reduced interest in being sexually active. Finally, medical conditions such as ulcerative colitis and inflammatory bowel disease are associated with marked reductions in sexual desire. Moreover, some of the medications used to treat inflammatory bowel disease may reduce testosterone levels (Rowland, 2012).

Again, while research is limited, there are suggestions that psychosocial factors outweigh the significance of biological factors in terms of low desire among men. Up to half of men with low sexual desire reported depressive symptoms, with a similar percentage reporting anxiety (Meana & Steiner, 2015; Rowland, 2012). Similar to women, exposure to negative attitudes toward sexuality, either culturally or familially, may increase performance anxiety, which, in turn, decreases interest. Finally, having a partner who has diminished interest in sex may contribute to the condition.

PDE-5 inhibitors such as Viagra counter the effects of the enzyme cGMP, which relaxes smooth muscle and allows an inflow of blood to the penis. Indirectly, these medications may increase the sex drive. PDE-5 inhibitors are not indicated for men with cardiac problems and may be associated with nasal congestion, headaches, and muscle aches (Gresser & Gleiter, 2002; Rowland, 2012).

Meana and Steiner (2014) note that low sexual desire might actually reflect hidden sexual desire. In some instances, sexual desires are maintained, but not for a current long-term partner. Additionally, sexual interest may be directed to masturbation, pornography, or an extramarital partner. With pornography's ready availability through the internet, patterns of pornography use should be examined. Often, the retreat into pornography may be because of performance anxiety or general fears of intimacy. However, pornography often portrays unrealistic patterns of sexual activity, which may dampen interest in activity with one's partner (Manning, 2006). When these issues are present, a therapist should address them directly with the couple together.

Problems with Ejaculation

There are two types of problems with ejaculation reported by men—premature and delayed. Premature ejaculation may occur together with erectile dysfunction. Premature ejaculation may be secondary to psychogenic ED (ejaculating rapidly for fear of losing one's erection) (Rosen, Miner, & Wincze, 2014).

Premature (Early) Ejaculation

In considering the diagnosis of premature ejaculation, the question arises: Who defines what is premature? Masters and Johnson diagnosed the condition relative to the female partner: "When a man cannot control his ejaculatory process . . . to satisfy his partner in at least 50 percent of coital encounters." Since many women do not have an orgasm with intra-penile penetration, this is not a terribly satisfactory definition. In Kinsey's early studies, 75 percent of the men surveyed indicated that they ejaculated within two minutes of intravaginal stimulation. DSM-5 defines "Premature (Early) Ejaculation" as the inability to control orgasm and ejaculation in less than a minute after vaginal penetration. This pattern should exist for six months and be present in 75 to 100 percent of coital encounters. Again, the problem should result in significant distress or dissatisfaction/tension between partners (American Psychiatric Association, 2013).

The DSM-5 definition only applies to vaginal sex; there is no time frame on other types of sexual activity that results in a male orgasm. According to the DSM definition, one minute is not sufficient time for a woman to reach orgasm.

Population prevalence rates reflect varying definitions of "premature," with up to 30 percent of males reporting it based on self-report (Montorsi, 2005). However, when more rigorous quantitative measures are used, rates decline to between 1 percent and 3 percent (Rowland, 2012). The unfortunate use of the term "premature" was recognized in the DSM-5 revision, with the term "early" being added in parentheses. The average time of ejaculation upon penetration is between 1 and 10 minutes. Unfortunately, particularly for men who compare themselves with actors in pornographic films, there is often a belief that anything short of 15 to 30 minutes is premature.

Biological explanations for the condition have included a genetic predisposition. Research suggests that genetics may be a predisposing factor for premature ejaculation (Santtila et al., 2010). The mechanism by which genes lead to this condition is likely to involve the serotonin system. Activation of the serotonin 5-HT2C receptor delays ejaculation, and activation of the 5-HT1A receptor makes ejaculation occur sooner. This pattern in laboratory animals is consistent with the experience of delayed ejaculation or the inability to ejaculate as a common side effect of SSRIs when used to treat depression. Other causes are likely to include relative sexual (in)experience as well as hypersensitivity of the penis to stimulation (Rowland, 2012). Additionally, ejaculation can be considered a conditioned response—frequent masturbation under time constraints may be a factor in this regard.

Dapoxetine, while not approved for use in the United States, is a short-acting SSRI that has been used to treat premature ejaculation in Europe (de Carufel, 2016; Waldinger, 2015). Additionally, some physicians have capitalized on the side effects of selective serotonin reuptake inhibitors, one of which is delayed ejaculation.

Topical anesthetics such as lidocaine, which reduce penile sensitivity, have demonstrated some effectiveness (Waldinger, 2015).

Psychosocial treatments include sensate focus, which is often coupled with the "squeeze technique" popularized by Masters and Johnson. In implementing this technique with a couple, the woman may manually masturbate the male partner until he is close to orgasm but not at the point of ejaculatory inevitability (the moment right before ejaculation when the man has no voluntary control over ejaculation) (Masters & Johnson, 1970). At that point, she gently squeezes the base of the penis. This technique is repeated and may also be built into intercourse. Wincze and Weisberg (2015) also encourage the couple to continue to have sex after ejaculation. Also, men who do ejaculate rapidly often are able to obtain a second erection within a reasonable period of time and then may have intercourse again for a more sustained period.

Delayed Ejaculation

Physiologically, while men tend to experience ejaculation and orgasm as unified, in reality these are distinct processes. Ejaculation is the expulsion of semen, while orgasm refers to the genital sensations and subjective sense of pleasure associated with rhythmic muscle contractions. Delayed ejaculation, again, is the difficulty or inability to achieve orgasm despite adequate desire and stimulation. In the previous DSM-IV-TR, the label "male orgasmic disorder" was applied to this condition. DSM-5 indicates that the following must occur in about 75 to 100 percent of episodes of partnered sexual activity: (1) delayed ejaculation; (2) infrequent ejaculation or its absence; (3) symptoms must be at least six months' duration; (4) the individual does not desire the delay; (5) ejaculatory delay is not explained by a mental disorder, relationship distress, or a physiological reason. Delayed ejaculation is further subdivided into lifelong versus acquired, in which "acquired" refers to delayed ejaculation in the context of an extended period of normal sexual functioning. Additionally, the delay may be generalized or situational. Generalized ejaculatory delay includes all sexual partners as well as activity such as masturbation. Situational delay is specific to a partner or context. As was the case with premature ejaculation, the issue of what constitutes a delay is unsettled. A large international study found that the time to ejaculation with intravaginal sex averaged 8 minutes, a median of 5.4 minutes and a large standard deviation of 7.1 minutes (Althof et al., 2010). The formal diagnosis of the condition, however, is more subjective, and, as with most natural phenomena, ejaculatory delay exists on a continuum, with some men ejaculating very quickly and others being delayed. A similar set of explanations has been invoked for delayed ejaculation as for premature ejaculation. Wincze and Weisberg (2015) suggest that there is a genetic component with serotonin involved. Aging may also be a factor, which in turn reflects a decline in testosterone levels and possible reductions in sensory nerve conduction.

As noted earlier, spectating can impair sexual functioning. There are also suggestions that men who have specific masturbatory styles to which they have been conditioned and which are not approximated by the partner may develop this condition. Recently it was suggested that the availability of internet pornography permits men to have a very wide array of specialized stimuli for masturbation—experiences that partnered sex cannot replicate. Finally, hostility toward one's partner as well as ambivalence about being in the relationship may also be contributory.

Female Orgasmic Disorder

As noted earlier, there is some variation in the normal female response cycle. It is also important to recognize that some women may not achieve orgasm but do experience desire, pleasure, arousal, and sexual satisfaction. While Freud famously wrote about the superiority of the vaginal orgasm, occurring during intra-penile penetration, and viewed it as superior to clitoral orgasm, most researchers disagree; clitoral stimulation is typically required for orgasm (Meana, 2012).

According to the DSM-5, female orgasmic disorder is characterized by a persistent pattern of delay or absence of orgasm in the context of a normal excitement phase. To give the diagnosis, the clinician must make a judgment that the woman's orgasmic response is less than would be expected for the woman's age, level of sexual experience, and adequacy of sexual stimulation received. The orgasmic problems must cause significant individual or interpersonal distress (American Psychiatric Association, 2013). The condition has been further subdivided into subtypes based on whether it is lifelong or acquired. In the latter case, difficulties with orgasm occur after a period of normal sexual functioning. Additionally, anorgasmia may be generalized—occurring across situations—or situational, in which anorgasmia is limited to specific types of stimulation or specific partners. For example, women who do not experience orgasm with a partner but who do so with self-stimulation would not meet criteria for the condition.

Prevalence rates for the condition vary widely—ranging from 3 percent to 34 percent (Graham, 2010). When anorgasmia is defined by a persistent inability to achieve orgasm, the prevalence is more than 20 percent; however, when subjective distress is added to the criteria, prevalence rates fall to 3.4 percent. Other surveys suggest that for many women, the emotional closeness associated with sex may be of greater importance than experiencing orgasm (Graham, 2010). It has been estimated that 9 percent of women do not ever experience orgasm (Graham, 2010).

Evidence of a possible genetic disposition as well as personality traits such as introversion and reduced openness to new experiences have been suggested as possible causal factors. Relationship issues may also be prominent (Donahey, 2010). In particular, for women who have a history of being orgasmic in the context of a long-term relationship and abruptly develop anorgasmia, interpersonal factors should be examined in detail. Resentment toward one's partner, extramarital affairs, and other issues may certainly play a role in orgasmic responsiveness (Donahey, 2010). Other relationship factors may include a partner lacking sensitivity to female sexuality or having problems with ejaculatory control.

In terms of treatment, sensate focus has been recommended. Additionally, among women who find it acceptable, directed masturbation does appear to have reasonable support for its effectiveness. There is evidence that self-directed masturbation increases the likelihood that women will be orgasmic—both alone and with a partner (Graham, 2010; Meana, 2012). In a large sample of American women ages 18 to 60, 53 percent reported using vibrators on at least one occasion (Herbenick et al., 2009). Vibrator use has been associated with improved female sexual functioning (Meana, 2012). While medications such as sildenafil (Viagra), estrogen, and testosterone have been employed as treatments, the effect sizes and quality of available studies are too limited to draw broad conclusions. Sildenafil may offset sexual side effects of antidepressant medication (Nurnberg et al., 2008). Flibanserin, which increases dopamine levels, was touted as the female Viagra. However, its effectiveness appears modest (Thorp et al., 2012). It may also be necessary for a therapist to dispel misinformation about sexual response (Meana, 2012). Clitoral stimulation is typically required, and it may not be provided through coitus. Again, use of SSRI medication for major depressive disorder has been established as a frequent cause of anorgasmia in women who have previously been orgasmic. In order to satisfactorily address the patient's depressive symptoms, it may be helpful to change to a less serotonergic agent such as bupropion (Meana, 2012).

Genito-Pelvic Pain/Penetration Disorder

While some reports of genital pain among men exist, nearly all of the research and clinical descriptions of this condition focus on women. The DSM-5 merged two previously distinct conditions—dyspareunia and vaginismus—into a single diagnostic category. Vaginismus is an involuntary muscle spasm on the outer part of the labia that makes it difficult for the penis to penetrate. The DSM-5 definition of genito-pelvic pain/penetration disorder requires that one of the following problems be persistently present for six months: (1) difficulty with vaginal penetration during intercourse; (2) pain during intercourse or attempted intercourse; (3) anticipatory anxiety about experiencing pain during intercourse. Vulvovaginal or pelvic pain prior to intercourse may lead to involuntary tightening of the muscles of the pelvic floor during attempted penetration. As a result, sexual intercourse is either infrequent or absent. The patient must also experience distress about the symptoms. Compared with the other female sexual dysfunctions, the painful symptoms are more likely to cause distress. In addition, the difficulties with sexual intercourse may contribute to significant relationship conflicts.

Prevalence rates vary widely, from 7 percent to 45 percent among older women and 14 percent to 34 percent of younger women (van Lankveld et al., 2010). When the six-month time frame and associated distress are present along with one of the DSM-5 symptoms, prevalence is estimated to be 1 to 3 percent (Bergeron, Rosen, & Pukall, 2014; Meana, 2012). There are suggestions that this condition may follow a bimodal distribution, with higher prevalence in late adolescence and early adulthood and a second increase in the postmenopausal period. Additionally, the postpartum year appears to be associated with an increase in painful intercourse. Genital pain also occurs outside sexual contact, with 25 percent or more of adolescent girls indicating that tampon insertion was painful (Landry & Bergeron, 2009).

Among possible causes, medical conditions including fibroids, cystitis, pelvic inflammatory disease, and endometriosis should be considered when painful intercourse is reported (Bergeron, Rosen, & Pukall, 2014). Reduced estrogen is also a commonly cited biological cause. Again, as was the case with anorgasmia, there does appear to be the possibility of a genetic predisposition, with dopamine receptor genes suspected of having significance (Meana, 2012). Histories of significant psychosocial trauma are more common among women with penetration disorder and pelvic pain than in the general population (Meana, 2009). One investigation found that rates of sexual abuse were six times greater and physical abuse four times greater among women with genito-pelvic pain/penetration disorder (Bergeron, Rosen, & Pukall, 2015; Meana, 2012).

Consistent with the dopamine hypothesis, flibanserin (aka female Viagra) increases levels of dopamine and has been used to treat this condition—however, without consistent results. Vaginal dilation, in which the woman inserts a progressively larger set of dilators over time, has been found useful to women who are accepting of this approach. The dilators are used in a graduated approach such that the woman should feel comfortable and relaxed with a particular size before moving to a larger one (Meana, 2012). Optimally, this approach should be supervised by a psychologist or sex therapist. Cognitive behavioral therapies to address distorted beliefs about sexuality and to manage pain have been found helpful. Borg, de Jong, and Schultz (2010) found that women with both vaginismus and dyspareunia had higher levels of "disgust associations" with sex. However, these cognitive associations are experienced as automatic, and once elicited by sexual stimuli, are likely to interfere with normal physiological arousal processes (Borg, de Jong, & Schultz, 2010). This is essentially a conditioned response that is not easily overridden and explains why this condition is so challenging to treat. Anticipatory anxiety about pain further increases vaginal tension prior to attempting intercourse. Mindfulness-based treatment with focus on the present moment rather than rehearsing thoughts may also disrupt some of the distracting cognitions that increase pain during attempted intercourse (Rosenbaum, 2013).

Cross-Cultural Issues in Sexuality

Sexual practices as well as attitudes toward sexuality vary widely across cultures. The labeling and definition of sexual dysfunction as well as methods for treatment were primarily developed in the United States. The extent to which the United States is a permissive society when it comes to sexuality is complex. When rates of premarital sex and numbers of sexual partners in the United States are compared with countries in Asia and the Middle East, the US population appears to be particularly sexually active. However, when compared with other Western countries such as Canada and much of Northern Europe, the United States appears to be more conflicted around matters of sexuality. For example, many regions of the United States have publicly funded sex education programs that focus on abstinence and do not describe various methods of contraception. This pattern may well be a factor in the higher teen pregnancy rate in the United States compared with other countries (Arnett, 2016). Research does suggest that contraception use during one's most recent episode of sexual activity is higher among European than US adolescents (Darroch, Singh, & Frost, 2001).

There are also differences in attitudes toward premarital sexual activity. Within many Islamic communities, loss of virginity outside of marriage is seen as a serious infraction that reflects negatively on one's family of origin and may precipitate a young woman becoming a victim of suicide or homicide (Yaşan, Essizoglu, & Yildirim, 2009). In a group of Turkish university students, approximately 40 percent of men and 6 percent of women reported having premarital sexual experiences. The majority of the males who had premarital sex had done so in an interaction with a sex worker. Rates of self-reported masturbation were similarly skewed by sex, with 11 percent of females and 88 percent of men reporting engaging in the practice (Yaşan, Essizoglu, & Yildirim, 2009). In Malaysia, premarital sex rates have been reported to be about 3 percent for women and 8 percent for men (Lee, Chen,

Lee, and Kaur, 2006). In Iran, 0.6 percent of women and 16 percent of men, and 98.2 percent of women in Morocco have had no sexual intercourse before marriage (Douki, Zineb, Nacef, & Halbreich, 2007).

Not a great deal is known about sexual dysfunction in non-Western cultures. In a sample of Ghanaian women, Amidu and colleagues (Amidu et al., 2010b) reported a lifetime sexual dysfunction rate of 73 percent. The most common conditions were sexual dissatisfaction (77.7 percent), anorgasmia (72.4 percent), and sexual infrequency (71.4 percent). The women reported a desire that intercourse last 8 to 19 minutes, which is twice as long as that considered appropriate by many sex therapists (Amidu et al., 2010b). The prevalence of vaginismus in the study was 68 percent—comparable to rates found in a sample of 200 "infertile" women in Iran (Tayebi & Ardakani, 2009). Among a Turkish sample attending a psychiatric clinic specializing in sexual issues, nearly 60 percent of the women reported vaginismus and nearly 40 percent of the men reported premature ejaculation (Yaşan & Gürgen, 2008).

Among men in Ghana, the overall rate of self-rated sexual dysfunction was 66 percent (Amidu et al., 2010a). The most commonly reported area of "sexual dysfunction" was infrequency (70 percent), followed by premature ejaculation (65 percent), and "impotence" (60 percent). In this large male sample, respondents perceived an intravaginal ejaculatory time of 7 to 25 minutes as being normal—above what is generally seen as common in Western countries.

In examining cultural influences on sexual behavior, it is often difficult, and probably would be artificial, to separate sexuality from religious and cultural belief systems. Most major world religions include guidelines for sexual behavior. In their original research, Masters and Johnson (1970) found an association between strong religious upbringing in Judaism, Catholicism, or Protestantism and sexual practices. Those without a formal religious affiliation reported more frequent sexual experiences, a greater number of partners, and more frequent masturbation. Additionally, more frequent attendance at religious services was found to be associated with fewer partners and a later age for initial sexual intercourse. In the Turkish sample noted above, a higher degree of commitment to one's religious faith was associated with lower rates of masturbation and sexual activity (Yaşan & Gürgen, 2008).

Wincze and Weisberg (2015) also suggest that rates of sexual dysfunction may reflect the status of women in non-Western countries. Rates of female sexual dysfunction appear to be significantly higher in countries with greater restrictions placed on women, such as arranged marriages and the inability to own property and drive (Wincze & Weisberg, 2015). In the Turkish sample of clinic attendees, more than 25 percent of the women, but only about 2 percent of the men, had been married without their consent (Yaşan & Gürgen, 2008). It is likely that this cultural practice around marriage plays a role in sexual functioning.

Conclusion

To reiterate a comment from the introduction to this chapter, sexual relationships are often a sensitive barometer of levels of trust and emotional closeness between partners. While there is some recognition that communication skills should be a component of effective sex therapy, treatment approaches for sexual dysfunction continue to be dominated by a "mechanical" perspective on sexuality. For persons without a history of adequate education regarding sexuality, learning about these basic physiological mechanics may be very helpful. Treatments appear to be particularly effective for premature ejaculation and erectile dysfunction. For women, particularly when the standard is experiencing orgasm, treatments may be less consistently effective. However, as noted, there is quite a disparity between self-reports of orgasmic frequency or its absence and levels of associated distress. While these patterns suggest that an emotionally close, healthy relationship is an important element of sexual satisfaction, the increased biological focus in treating sexual dysfunction suggests that sexuality will continue to be viewed as a mechanistic experience, with less attention paid to developing emotional intimacy.

CHAPTER 13

The Future Direction of Health and Health Care

If you follow the news, you are aware that the future of health care in the United States and many countries around the world is changing dramatically—a process that is likely to accelerate. There are several factors currently operating that are changing health care delivery and will continue to do so for the next several decades. Rates of mental illness in Western countries continue to rise. It is now estimated that more than 50 percent of the US population will meet criteria for a mental health condition at some point in their lives. Among college students, the likelihood of having a formally diagnosable psychiatric condition during a university career is about 45 percent. There is growing evidence that mental health conditions and medical conditions are not isolated and split off into separate domains, as Descartes argued, but rather influence one another.

With the shift from infectious disease to chronic illnesses, medical care will increasingly be targeting lifestyle factors as the most effective targets for intervention. Despite the statistics indicating that the average body weight is increasing along with associated conditions such as type 2 diabetes and that obesity is on the rise in nearly all segments of the population, including preschoolers, average weight in the US population has yet to plateau. As the life span increases in industrialized countries, we will live longer—however, it is certainly not a foregone conclusion that we will live better. The longer we live, the greater the likelihood of multiple forms of physical deterioration and illnesses such as cancer, which increase in probability with age. While we have discussed the impact of our increasingly "flat world" on our health and medical care, the implications of increased internationalization are not entirely clear. However, one change that is evident is that infectious diseases, rather than requiring multiple months or years to be transmitted from one continent to another, as was the case in the days of Christopher Columbus, can now be transmitted in a matter of days or even hours.

The Interface of Physical and Mental Health

As the rates of psychiatric illness continue to rise precipitously in Western countries and are increasingly recognized in developing nations (Watters, 2010), there is also greater appreciation of the role that psychiatric illness plays in physical conditions and, in particular, chronic health conditions. As was evident in the chapters on chronic pain and physician-patient communication, major depressive disorder is a particularly salient predictor of the course of many medical conditions, including cardiovascular disease, chronic obstructive pulmonary disease, and type 2 diabetes, among others, as well as of adherence with medical treatment.

Medical patients with concomitant mental illness absorb 20 to 40 percent of the total US health care budget (Kroenke & Unützer, 2017). It has been estimated that about 90 percent of patients with mental health conditions are seen in the medical sector alone and that at least 60 percent of these patients receive no treatment for their mental health condition (Kroenke & Unützer, 2017).

Among persons with serious mental illness, physical health is significantly worse than for the general population. Persons with schizophrenia have more medical hospitalizations and a reduced life span of about 15 to 20 years (Corrigan et al., 2017; Hausswolff-Juhlin, Bjartveit, Lindström, & Jones, 2009). The issues associated with significant mental illness are likely to interact with psychosocial factors associated with health, including housing and access to care. As the severity of mental health symptoms increases, there is a corresponding increase in the likelihood of having a non-psychiatric medical condition (Niles et al., 2015). While it is well known that there is an association between BMI (body mass index) and medical illness, the association between symptoms of depression and anxiety and physical health is even greater (Niles et al., 2015).

Both major depressive and bipolar illness are increasingly recognized as major contributors to poorer physical health. For example, persons with bipolar disorder have the highest health costs of any mental health diagnosis. Much of this financial burden stems from medical rather than psychiatric conditions. Even when direct effects of psychiatric illness such as suicide are controlled, the mortality rate of those with mental illness is twice as high as those without a mental health condition. Psychiatric illness is associated with a loss of approximately 10 years of life. About two-thirds of these deaths are due to "natural causes" (Walker, McGee, & Druss, 2015).

Unipolar depression (major depressive disorder) appears to be an independent risk factor for the development of type 2 diabetes. While body mass index and family history are associated with new onset diabetes, the predictive effects of depression remain even after these established factors are controlled. Additionally, while some antidepressants are associated with weight gain, the predictive effect of major depressive disorder still remains after pharmacotherapy is taken into account (Campayo et al., 2010). By implication, aggressive treatment of depression in persons at risk for type 2 diabetes may be able to prevent the development of this metabolic condition (Campayo et al., 2010).

Among persons with bipolar disorder, cardiovascular disease is the leading cause of premature death (Goldstein et al., 2015). Bipolar disorder has an independent effect on the development of the condition, over and above factors such as physical activity. Among adults, rates of cardiovascular disease are three times higher among those with major depressive disorder compared with persons without a psychiatric diagnosis. In addition, the presence of depression was associated with earlier onset of cardiovascular disease by about 5 to 7 years (Goldstein et al., 2015). Recent research has found that unipolar and bipolar mood disorders have been found to be predictive of cardiovascular disease and atherosclerosis in adolescents (Goldstein et al., 2015).

There is also increased awareness by health care professionals of the direct interaction between the mental health and medical domains. Patients with bipolar disorder who also have thyroid dysfunction are more likely to develop the difficult-to-treat rapid-cycling form of the disorder in which depression and mania alternate in brief periods of time (Comer, 2015).

The symptoms of anxiety disorders often mimic medical conditions. For example, panic attacks often feature many of the same symptoms as a heart attack. In both conditions, patients experience chest pain, shortness of breath, and dizziness—symptoms are of such a severity that patients seek emergency treatment (Searight, 1999). Generalized anxiety disorder is characterized by muscle tension and soreness as well as problems with attention and concentration. However, the picture is further complicated by the fact that among persons with cardiovascular disease and some respiratory diseases such as asthma, rates of anxiety disorders are higher than in the general population. For example, panic disorder was 4.5 times more common among adults with asthma compared to those without the condition (Feldman et al., 2016). Additionally, the presence of panic disorder has been found to be associated with poorer patient control over asthma symptoms. Patients with asthma who had higher levels of anxiety sensitivity also had more emergency department visits (Favreau, Bacon, Labrecque, & Lavoie, 2014).

Since the mid-1980s, most health insurance companies have segregated—"carved out"—mental health coverage from that of medical conditions. Mental health insurance coverage is typically managed by a separate company with its own regulations and patient reimbursement limits distinct from that for other medical conditions. While legislation toward parity in covering both medical and psychiatric conditions has been implemented as law, these two areas remain segregated. As is evident from the above, optimal care would involve integration of medical and mental health treatment. In the past decade, there have been some health centers that have been successful in providing integrated care.

Collaborative and Integrated Health Care

One of the reasons for the relatively high cost of care in the United States compared with other countries is that our use of health services is very fragmented. There is often an overlap in the care provided by various health professionals working with a patient as well as redundant medical testing. Beginning with changes in funding health care in the 1980s, a growing emphasis was placed on the role of the patient's primary care physician as a care coordinator.

The Affordable Care Act (ACA) established as policy a concept that had been encouraged by primary care physician organizations for the previous 15 to 20 years—the medical home. The ACA's version of the medical home includes: (1) a consistent personal physician for each patient; (2) a "whole person" orientation (emphasizing attention to psychosocial aspects of patient care); (3) integration and coordination of care; (4) evidence-based treatments and use of health information technology such as electronic medical records to assist with continuous improvement; (5) improved access to care; and (6) revising reimbursement systems to recognize the value of patient-centered care (Lyon, Markus, & Rosenbaum, 2010).

The ACA has brought renewed attention to integrated mental health–medical care models. These approaches have varying structures but emphasize centralization of care—typically with a primary care provider at the hub who coordinates or directly provides both mental health and medical care. When referring to mental health and primary medical care, the terms "integrated care" and "collaborative care" are often used interchangeably (Dobmeyer, 2017).

Behavioral health's affiliation with primary care medicine is the most common form of "whole person" care. As well as addressing lifestyle modifications such as smoking cessation or reducing alcohol use, collaborative care models, in which mental health professionals function as consultants to physicians and other allied health professionals such as nurse practitioners and/or directly treat patients, have been clearly demonstrated to be more effective in improving mental health conditions than traditional primary care (Dobmeyer, 2017). Collaborative approaches have also been used with specific patient groups, including older adults, pregnant women, and neurology and oncology patients, as well as those with chronic pain and type 2 diabetes (Kroenke & Unützer, 2017). However, at present, most collaborative care occurs between office settings rather than within a single practice. Unfortunately, when patients have to see a behavioral specialist in a separate geographic setting—even if it is across the hall—they are less likely to follow up (Searight, 2010).

The colocated model, with physicians and behavioral health specialists practicing in the same office setting, addresses this problem. This approach was initiated by the Veterans Administration Health System approximately 10 years ago. Involving a team of nurses, primary care physicians, and clinical psychologists, all care takes place on-site and psychologists typically consult with physicians and nursing staff but also provide direct patient care. For more complicated psychiatric conditions, patients are referred to the VA mental health clinics (Kroenke & Unützer, 2017).

This approach to patient care has been present, to some extent, in the United Kingdom for some time. Recently, there has been a major push to improve integrated care in general practice in Great Britain. There is currently a plan to place 3,000 more mental health therapists in general practitioners' (primary care physicians') office settings along with 1,500 more clinical pharmacists. To support this initiative, the National Health Service (NHS) has collected data on the high levels of comorbidity between psychiatric and physical illness as well as the heavy health care utilization by patients with medically unexplained syndromes (Russell, 2018).

Research on collaborative care has yielded positive results. Collaborative care has been found to be associated with better diabetic control as well as improvements in depression (Chwastiak et al., 2017). Patients with coronary heart disease and major depressive disorder managed in a collaborative care setting demonstrated greater reduction in systolic blood pressure, had their hypertensive medications adjusted more frequently for optimal benefit, and reported better quality of life as well as greater satisfaction with care. Counseling, directed toward lifestyle modification and depression, was provided by nurses with supervision by medical specialists, including a psychiatrist as well as a psychologist (Katon et al., 2010). Among patients with type 2 diabetes, integrated care was associated with better medication adherence as well as more favorable laboratory test results (Dobmeyer, 2017).

Rather than a traditional 50-minute psychotherapy hour, mental health professionals in primary care settings often see patients in 15- to 20-minute segments (Dobmeyer, 2017). These brief mental health contacts within a primary care practice have been found to be associated with reduced patient alcohol use as well as improved sleep. Additionally, by being colocated, the behavioral health specialist may consult with primary care physicians about cases. This consultation, occurring without directly seeing the patient, may be adequate for addressing some mental health concerns.

Cost effectiveness has been an issue with integrated care. Since the insurance provider for the patient's medical care is separate from that for mental health care, there are financial disincentives for collaboration. Historically, insurance for mental health care has typically denied payment to both primary care physicians and mental health professionals for addressing problems such as smoking, diet, and exercise from a behavioral health perspective. Even though the addition of behavioral health services leads to reductions in inappropriate health service utilization as well as increased adherence—and, as a result, reduced health care costs—insurance companies have traditionally not been fiscally supportive of this model. There is a time lag for the economic benefits to occur; it has been suggested that the cost savings may lag about 3 to 4 years behind collaborative care initiation (Kroenke & Unützer, 2017). In one large care study, for every dollar spent on evaluation and treatment of depression, six dollars were saved (Unützer et al., 2008).

For collaborative care involving mental health professionals and primary care providers to become common in the United States, reimbursement structures would have to be significantly revised. Mental health care was "carved out" of medical care beginning at least 30 years ago. Carved-out mental health care means that mental health services are billed, monitored, and reimbursed separately from medical services. One possible approach has been bundled payments (Miller et al., 2017). This reimbursement system has been used with surgical procedures and delivering babies. In the bundled model, the charge is for the treatment package, including hospitalization, medication, and any medical tests or X-rays. The bundled approach discourages physicians from ordering unnecessary tests and does encourage cost-effective care. Additionally, the charge for a bundled package of services can readily include behavioral health care. For example, there may be a flat bundled charge for a year of managing a type 2 diabetic patient that would include nutritional counseling, primary care visits, medication, and mental health care.

Recently, Medicare began to permit payments for behavioral services by health care providers (Press et al., 2017). This new set of reimbursement categories includes having a behavioral health care manager meet with the patient directly. This "manager" could be a psychologist but could also be a family physician. This change in reimbursement would permit primary care physicians to bill for their counseling time, which historically has not been covered.

Increased Attention to the Psychosocial in Medical Care

Psychosocial "Vital Signs"

The biopsychosocial model, while having its share of critics, has infiltrated much of medical education (Searight, 2016). The Institute of Medicine (IOM) has recommended that three types of information—sociological, psychosocial, and health behavior—be routinely included in patients' medical records. For example, the IOM suggests the following information for the sociological dimension: (1) residential address, (2) race/ethnicity, (3) education, and (4) overall financial status. At the psychosocial level, three areas should be assessed: (1) depression, (2) social integration, and (3) domestic violence. The third dimension, health behaviors, reflects topics that this book has addressed in detail: physical activity, tobacco use, alcohol use, and so on (Matthews, Adler, Forrest, & Stead, 2016).

Influenced by the IOM, psychologists in health care settings recently tried to systematize the biopsychosocial model by encouraging inclusion of psychosocial "vital signs" (Matthews et al., 2016) and expanding upon the IOM recommendations for patients. In reality, these three dimensions interact and it is difficult to firmly demarcate boundaries between sociological, psychological, and health behaviors.

Drawing upon social epidemiology, Marcus and colleagues (Marcus, Echeverria, Holland, Abraido-Lanza, & Passannante, 2016) point out that social integration and neighborhood economic status are health "risk factors" in a similar vein as cigarette smoking. There is a growing body of research finding associations between the specific location of one's residence and health status. The recent use of geographic coding with geospatial maps illustrates these associations (Matthews et al., 2016). Other dimensions that have been suggested for a fuller sociological picture of the patient include country of origin, having adequate food, having safe housing, and military deployment.

Marcus et al. (2016) describe how the levels of social integration and financial status of a neighborhood interact. The authors found that while low social integration was associated with elevated mortality, neighborhood alone did not predict death rates. However, the combination of low social integration and living in an economically deprived area was associated with further increases in mortality rates. Survival rates are 50 percent higher among persons with good versus poor or nonexistent social relationships (Holt-Lunstad, Smith, & Layton, 2010; Matthews et al., 2016). These factors also interact and are likely additive. In examining patients who had a heart attack, the psychosocial factors, taken together with sociological indicators, were more predictive of the acute event than hypertension and diabetes (Matthews et al., 2016; Yusuf et al., 2004). Domestic violence is frequent enough that patients should be routinely asked whether they feel safe at home. Pregnancy is a risk factor for domestic assault on women.

There has been interest in including some form of brief personality assessment—conscientiousness and optimism are traits that appear to influence health status. Self-efficacy, or the belief in one's ability to achieve specific outcomes, was also of interest to the IOM but at present does not have adequate support for the medical record. Finally, in terms of health behaviors, dietary patterns, health literacy, and sexual behavior were areas of interest that warranted further study (Matthews et al., 2016).

Brief Models of Counseling for Busy Physicians

At least 50 percent of all mental health care in the United States is provided by primary care physicians (Searight, 2018). There are multiple reasons for this pattern, including patient comfort with their physician, difficulties accessing specialty mental health care, and perceived stigma associated with seeking care in the mental health sector. Patients also report greater satisfaction with their health care when physicians include attention to psychosocial issues. However, primary care physicians' patient encounters average between 13 and 20 minutes (Searight, 2019). As well as addressing mental health and counseling patients about smoking, alcohol use, and diet, physicians must also address acute or chronic physical problems within this time frame.

Recognizing these constraints, while also appreciating that if a patient's primary care physician does not provide basic mental health care and health risk counseling, no one else will, brief counseling strategies have been developed specifically for the primary care setting (Searight, 2007; 2018). The BATHE technique was introduced more than 25 years ago to primary care physicians in a book titled *The Fifteen Minute Hour* (Stuart & Lieberman, 2015). BATHE is an acronym for a series of questions and statements that the physician asks in a specific order. The BATHE questions in order are as follows: *Background*: "What is going on in your life?" *Affect*: "How do you feel about the situation?" *Troubles*: "What troubles you the most about the situation?" *Handling*: "How are you handling (coping with) the situation?" *Empathy*: a simple empathic statement such as "That sounds like a very difficult situation."

There are several brief, yet effective, strategies for counseling about health risk behavior. FRAMES is an acronym for a brief protocol to counsel patients about alcohol and drug use (Searight, 2007; 2018). *Feedback*: effective feedback is concrete—blood pressure, laboratory tests such as those assessing liver function. *Responsibility*: "Is this something that you want to a change? It's up to you." *Advice*: "The best way to get your liver back to normal is to stop or at least cut down on your drinking." *Menu of options*: "There are several strategies that have worked well for patients who want to stop drinking. . . ." *Empathy*: "I am sure that at first this will be difficult and fighting the craving to drink will be a challenge, but you will get better at it over time." *Self-efficacy*: "You really do want to feel better and know that cutting down on alcohol will be necessary for that to happen. You are determined to be successful and know what you have to do to stop drinking" (Fleming, Barry, Manwell, Johnson, & London, 1997).

As noted earlier, motivational interviewing (MI) was originally developed for substance-abuse treatment. However, physicians and nurses in primary care and even in specialty areas have found the social psychological principles effective for patient behavior change. As a result, MI has been adapted to nutritional counseling as well as to working with patients with diabetes, chronic pain, and patient management of heart failure. It has even been adapted to more acute problems such as leg ulcerations (Anstiss, 2009).

As noted above, the importance of physician-patient communication and rapport is increasingly recognized outside of primary care, and brief counseling strategies are now used by some medical specialists. For example, the BATHE protocol (Stuart & Lieberman, 2015) was recently adapted to the presurgical anesthesiology interview: *Background*: "What brings you in today?" *Affect*: "How are you feeling about the upcoming surgery?" *Troubles*: "What about the surgery worries you the most?" *Handling*: "How are you coping with (or managing) your feelings about the surgery?" *Empathy*: "It's perfectly normal to be nervous about surgery. Let me explain what will happen on the day of your surgery" (DeMaria, DeMaria, Silvay, & Flynn, 2011).

Health care professionals in multiple specialties are also paying more attention to the "teachable moment"—time-limited situations in which the patient's motivation for change may temporarily be higher. One example of this is the application of motivational interviewing in the emergency department setting. It is estimated that about 7 to 8 percent of emergency department visits are alcohol related (McDonald, Wang, & Camargo, 2004). Traffic accidents, falls, and physical fights are all more likely under the influence of alcohol. Given that these emergency department patients are likely to be in some distress because of an incident related to excessive alcohol use, they may be particularly amenable to cutting down on alcohol use. There have been several studies demonstrating that brief applications of motivational interviewing in the emergency department have been associated with reduced drinking at follow-up periods of multiple months to a year (Bernstein et al., 2007; Monti et al., 2007). Even 5-minute versions of MI provided by regency department physicians have demonstrated some benefit.

Professionalism and Patient-Centered Care

The Accreditation Council for Graduate Medical Education (2018) established a set of core competencies for residency education in all medical specialties. One of these core competencies is "Professionalism" (Huffmyer & Kirk, 2017). Standards for professionalism are now part of graduate medical education in specialties as diverse as pediatrics, anesthesiology, surgery, and pathology. One of the objectives with professionalism is effective communication. This dimension includes physician-patient communication and sensitivity to the psychosocial context in which illness and medical treatment occur, as well as cultural literacy. In addition, medical educators are recognizing that physicians need to be able to communicate effectively with their peers as well as other members of their "team." The team may be composed of nurses, physical therapists, occupational therapists, speech therapists, technicians, and so on. As noted earlier in this book, ineffective communication appears to be a key dimension associated with medical errors. The development of medical ethics as a viable discipline also highlights the importance of dimensions of health care that extend well beyond pathophysiology (Searight & Barbarash, 1994).

Health Care Navigators

Coordinating care between primary care providers, specialty physicians, mental health professionals, physical therapists, and other health care providers is a challenge for many patients. In addition, many quite intelligent patients do not have up-to-date knowledge about available health insurance plans, coverage for specific types of care, and medication. In order to assist patients with health care decision-making about insurance plans, coverage for various procedures and medical tests, and negotiating the network of specialists to which patients are referred, a new profession has arisen—the health care navigator. While navigators were specifically included in the Affordable Care Act, they have been in place for some time in oncology practices, where they helped patients navigate cancer treatments such as radiation, chemotherapy, or surgery. With respect to cancer care, early navigators addressed prevention and treatment as well as survival. In addition, they helped clarify doctors' orders and medications. Patients also experienced navigators as a source of social support—particularly when they were of the same cultural background or if they had had similar health conditions such as breast cancer.

Navigator programs have been seen as potentially useful in reducing health care disparities. For example, among a sample of Native American patients, adherence with a recommended mammogram was more common among those with peer navigator assistance (Buhransstipanov et al., 2010). In some instances, bilingual navigators serve as language interpreters in medical encounters for patients with limited English proficiency.

More recently, health care navigators have assisted those who were obtaining insurance through newly established "Obamacare" exchanges. Even when health care insurance is made available without significant expense, going through the process of establishing coverage is daunting for many who need coverage. Navigators are knowledgeable about various health insurance policies, as well as the types of coverage that patients of different ages and with different conditions typically need. However, since they typically are not employees of insurance companies, navigators do not have conflicts of interest and can assist patients without a sales agenda.

Navigators may also be assigned to patient panels within a particular health care system and serve as a conduit for primary care physicians, mental health professionals, pharmacists, social workers, medical assistants, and other staff working with the patient. Complicated patients, such as those with concurrent psychiatric illness and medical conditions, are likely to have an array of unmet physical health, mental health, and basic psychosocial needs such as food and housing. Navigators have been able to help patients with psychiatric conditions obtain these basic services.

A recent study involving navigators assisting persons with significant mental illnesses such as schizophrenia and bipolar disorder found that navigators, in addition to improving the housing and insurance coverage status of persons with severe mental illness, were associated with improvement in physical and mental health symptoms (Corrigan et al., 2017). Among another group of patients who frequently appeared in the hospital emergency department for acute psychiatric problems, those working with a navigator were much more likely to maintain follow-up appointments and establish themselves with both mental health and primary care providers. Patients who did not benefit from navigators' assistance tended to be those with dual diagnoses—a psychiatric condition and a concomitant substance abuse diagnosis (Griswold, Homish, Pastore, & Leonard, 2010).

Internationalization: The Flat World Continues to Flatten

In a thought-provoking book, Watters (2010) describes how America's psychiatric conditions are being exported around the world. He describes the case of a young girl in Hong Kong who had intentionally lost a good deal of weight due to not eating and passed out on the street. The case received a good amount of popular attention. This attention then led to the view that there was an undiagnosed near epidemic of eating disorders among young girls in countries where they had not been previously diagnosed. As mentioned in the section in Chapter 10 on eating disorders, anorexia nervosa was not the same condition in these early cases in Asia as in the United States—the issues with body image distortion were absent. Once the label "anorexia nervosa" appeared and the DSM criteria for the condition became better known, the symptoms of young Asian women began to resemble those in the United States. Watters (2010) argues that through the widespread adoption of the American Psychiatric Association's definitions of mental disorder, the United States has exported a form of hyperindividualism centered on excessive introspection. Once the DSM announces its list of symptoms for a diagnosis, these conditions arise in countries where they did not previously exist (Watters, 2010). The United States models the "correct way" to have a psychiatric condition.

The availability of direct international flights to and from a growing number of cities throughout the United States provides more avenues for new biologically infectious agents to enter the country and spread rapidly. It has been suggested that someone with an infection can carry disease to any other part of the world within 36 hours. In many instances, the travel time is less than the incubation period of the illness. Therefore, one can leave home newly infected and arrive at a foreign destination still not experiencing any symptoms but able to infect others. While we make distinctions between local and global disease, this distinction is becoming less meaningful.

The spring 2018 cholera outbreak in Yemen, with an estimate of more than 800,000 cases, was a warning of the domino effect of political collapse and social breakdown. The main cause of cholera, as was the case in John Snow's London, is poor sanitation. In Yemen, this situation was in part attributable to sanitation workers not being paid and garbage piling up on the streets. The government stopped funding the public health department a year earlier in the midst of an ongoing civil war. Because of the flow of refugees and air travel, these politically based health crises can directly or indirectly impact developed countries very quickly.

Increased migration from less developed to developed countries exposes residents of developed countries to conditions that had previously been eradicated. In Germany this year, health officials reported increased rates of chickenpox, cholera, hantavirus, leprosy, measles, rubella, whooping cough, and tuberculosis—all diseases that were close to nonexistent in the country. In one situation, an asylum seeker from Yemen potentially infected more than 50 German children with a highly contagious and treatment-resistant form of tuberculosis. In developing countries, up to 40 percent of tuberculosis cases are multidrug resistant (Kern, 2018).

The Aging of the Population and the Maximization of Life

As discussed throughout this book, a high percentage of current US deaths are associated with "lifestyle" factors. While some of these have diminished, such as smoking cigarettes, other factors, such as obesity and inadequate physical activity, continue to increase. However, the chronic illnesses associated with these risk factors do not result in acute death. Obesity, for example, may contribute to type 2 diabetes, while smoking contributes to chronic obstructive pulmonary disease.

There are symptomatic treatments for these conditions, and patients can live for many years with them.

Research has suggested that the upper end of the human life span is around 120 years. A limiting factor is biological; the Hayflick limit is the maximum number of times that cells can divide—a figure believed to be around 50 and placing the absolute maximum human life span at around 120 years.

The life span in developed countries has continued to rise. With this increase, a number of social and economic questions associated with health care have become increasingly pressing. Research indicates that for an average individual in the United States, 75 to 90 percent of their total health expenditures will occur in the last 6 months of their life.

Kaufman (2015), an anthropologist, observed a number of encounters between older patients with cancer and their physicians. Kaufman noted that once a surgical procedure or other treatment such as radiation therapy had been established as the evidence-based treatment of choice for a particular condition and was authorized by Medicare, it was typically recommended without attention to the patient's advanced age or life circumstances.

What follows is an exchange between an 80-year-old man recently diagnosed with bladder cancer and a physician encouraging the patient to pursue aggressive treatment.

> Physician: "You don't have that many other medical conditions. There is nothing I can see to keep you from living until 90 or even 100. . . . We need to decide between surgery and radiation. . . . So your options are surgery, then radiation. . . . I wouldn't recommend external beam radiation only but external beam and brachytherapy. You have external beam radiation for five weeks, then the seeds. You'd be on the hormones two years. . . . On the hormone therapy, you have to be careful to do cardio exercises and weightlifting because the hormones affect the bones. Another problem with radiation is that it causes scar tissue in the bladder which heightens the risk of bladder cancer ten years out." (Kaufman, 2015, p. 75)

The patient responded, "But I'm eighty! 10 years out!" The patient asked what would happen if he did nothing and was told, "You wouldn't know for some time, maybe 5 to 10 years before it's a clinical problem" (Kaufman, 2015, p. 75).

Based on mortality statistics, the oncologist is correct—while White males have an average life expectancy in the upper 70s to 80 years range, statistically speaking, if one reaches the age of 80, the life expectancy is nearly 90 (Kaufman, 2015). Once a procedure becomes more common, such as putting in a stent for a 90-year-old, it eventually will not seem unusual. Certainly if one is willing to undergo an increasing number of medical procedures such as surgery in later years and, if unable to eat and drink, consents to artificial hydration and nutrition, the life span can be extended. The question then becomes "What sort of life is it?"

Conclusion

While the future is hard to predict, there are reasons to be hopeful but also worried about health and medical care in the years ahead. The biopsychosocial approach to health, while not embraced in its entirety, has exerted an influence on medical education as well as the clinical and economic aspects of patient care. Young adults reading this book are likely to see an expansion of patient navigators as well as other professional roles to assist with reducing disparities and providing more efficient and less costly medical care. However, medical technology and the pharmaceutical industry will continue to provide us with seemingly better, yet more expensive, innovations to improve the quality and length of our lives. The question remains, however: Will living longer add satisfaction and meaning to our existence?

References

Abadie, R. (2010). *The professional guinea pig: Big pharma and the risky world of human subjects.* Durham, NC: Duke University Press.

Abraham, C., Conner, M., Jones, F., & O'Connor, D. (2016). *Health psychology.* London, UK: Routledge.

Abraham, T. M., Pencina, K. M., Pencina, M. J., & Fox, C. S. (2015). Trends in diabetes incidence: The Framingham Heart Study. *Diabetes Care, 38*(3), 482–487.

Abrams, B. M. (2013). Medication overuse headaches. *Medical Clinics, 97*(2), 337–352.

Accreditation Council for Graduate Medical Education (ACGME). (2018). Common program requirements. https://www.acgme.org/What-We-Do/Accreditation/Common-Program-Requirements.

Adenekan, B., Pandey, A., McKenzie, S., Zizi, F., Casimir, G. J., & Jean-Louis, G. (2013). Sleep in America: Role of racial/ethnic differences. *Sleep Medicine Reviews, 17*(4), 255–262.

Adler, R., & Cohen, N. (1993). Psychoneuroimmunology: Conditioning and stress. *Annual Review of Psychology, 44*(1), 53–85.

Agency for Healthcare Research and Quality. (2011). *National health care quality and disparities report.* Washington, DC: US Dept. of Health and Human Services.

Agency for Healthcare Research and Quality. (2015). *Health care innovations for Hispanic population.* Washington, DC: US Dept. of Health and Human Services. https://innovations.ahrq.gov/issues/2015/10/21/health-care-innovations-hispanic-populations.

Agostini, J. V., Leo-Summers, L. S., & Inouye, S. K. (2001). Cognitive and other adverse effects of diphenhydramine use in hospitalized older patients. *Archives of Internal Medicine, 161*(17), 2091–2097.

Aiello, J. R., Baum, A., & Gormley, F. P. (1981). Social determinants of residential crowding stress. *Personality and Social Psychology Bulletin, 7*(4), 643–649.

Aiken, L. S., West, S. G., Woodward, C. K., & Reno, R. R. (1994). Health beliefs and compliance with mammography-screening: Recommendations in asymptomatic women. *Health Psychology, 13*(2), 122–129.

Ainsworth, M. D. S., Blehar, M., Waters, E., & Wall, S. (1978). *Patterns of attachment: A psychological study of the strange situation.* Hillsdale, NJ: Lawrence Erlbaum.

Ajzen, I. (1991). The theory of planned behavior. *Organizational Behavior and Human Decision Processes, 50*(2), 179–211.

Ajzen, I., & Fishbein, M. (1977). Attitude-behavior relations: A theoretical analysis and review of empirical research. *Psychological Bulletin, 84*(5), 888–918.

Åkerblom, S., Perrin, S., Fischer, M. R., & McCracken, L. M. (2015). The mediating role of acceptance in multidisciplinary cognitive-behavioral therapy for chronic pain. *Journal of Pain, 16*(7), 606–615.

Albarracin, D., Johnson, B. T., Fishbein, M., & Muellerleile, P. A. (2001). Theories of reasoned action and planned behavior as models of condom use: A meta-analysis. *Psychological Bulletin, 127*(1), 142–161.

Albers, A. B., Siegel, M., Chen, D. M., Biener, L., & Rigotti, N. A. (2007). Effect of smoking regulations in local restaurants on smokers' anti-smoking attitudes and quitting behaviours. *Tobacco Control, 16*(2), 101–106.

Alexander, F. (1950). *Psychosomatic medicine.* New York, NY: W. W. Norton.

Alp, M. H., Court, J. H., & Grant, A. K. (1970). Personality pattern and emotional stress in the genesis of gastric ulcer. *Gut, 11*(9), 773–777.

Althof, S. E., Abdo, C. H., Dean, J., Hackett, G., McCabe, M., McMahon, C. G., . . . & Broderick, G. A. (2010). International Society for Sexual Medicine's guidelines for the diagnosis and treatment of premature ejaculation. *Journal of Sexual Medicine, 7*(9), 2947–2969.

Amante, D. J., Hogan, T. P., Pagoto, S. L., English, T. M., & Lapane, K. L. (2015). Access to care and use of the internet to search for health information: Results from the US National Health Interview Survey. *Journal of Medical Internet Research, 17*(4).

Amato, P. R. (2000). The consequences of divorce for adults and children. *Journal of Marriage and Family, 62*(4), 1269–1287.

American Psychiatric Association (1994). *The diagnostic and statistical manual of mental disorders* (4th Ed.) (DSM-IV). Washington, DC: American Psychiatric Association.

American Psychiatric Association. (2013). *Diagnostic and statistical manual of mental disorders* (DSM-5). Washington, DC: American Psychiatric Publications.

American Psychological Association. (2015). *Stress in America: Paying with our health.* Washington, DC: American Psychological Association.

Amidu, N., Owiredu, W. K., Woode, E., Addai-Mensah, O., Gyasi-Sarpong, K. C., & Alhassan, A. (2010a). Prevalence of male sexual dysfunction among Ghanaian populace: Myth or reality? *International Journal of Impotence Research, 22*(6), 337–342.

Amidu, N., Owiredu, W. K., Woode, E., Addai-Mensah, O., Quaye, L., Alhassan, A., & Tagoe, E. A. (2010b). Incidence of sexual dysfunction: A prospective survey in Ghanaian females. *Reproductive Biology and Endocrinology, 8*(1), 106.

Anderson, J. W., Liu, C., & Kryscio, R. J. (2008). Blood pressure response to transcendental meditation: A meta-analysis. *American Journal of Hypertension, 21*(3), 310–316.

Anderson, K., Jue, S., & Madaras-Kelly, K. (2008). Identifying patients at risk for medication mismanagement: Using cognitive screens to predict a patient's accuracy in filling a pillbox. *The Consultant Pharmacist*, 23(6), 459–472.

Anderson, M. (2015). Technology device ownership: 2015. Pew Research Center. http://www.pewinternet.org/2015/10/29/technology-device-ownership-2015/.

Anderson, W. (2003). Smoking and property rights. *MISES Daily*, June 3. https://mises.org/library/smoking-and-property-rights.

Andersson, G. B. (1999). Epidemiological features of chronic low-back pain. *The Lancet*, 354(9178), 581–585.

Andreasen, A. R. (1995). *Marketing social change: Changing behavior to promote health, social development, and the environment.* San Francisco, CA: Jossey-Bass.

Angel, I., Carey, M., & Gould, H. (1996). Intrathecal morphine pump as a treatment option in chronic pain of nonmalignant origin. Paper# 755. *Neurosurgery*, 39(3), 651.

Angulo, F. J., & Jones, T. F. (2006). Eating in restaurants: A risk factor for foodborne disease? *Clinical Infectious Diseases*, 43(10), 1324–1328.

Anstiss, T. (2009). Motivational interviewing in primary care. *Journal of Clinical Psychology in Medical Settings*, 16(1), 87–93.

Anthenelli, R. M., Benowitz, N. L., West, R., St. Aubin, L., McRae, T., Lawrence, D., . . . & Evins, A. E. (2016). Neuropsychiatric safety and efficacy of varenicline, bupropion, and nicotine patch in smokers with and without psychiatric disorders (EAGLES): A double-blind, randomised, placebo-controlled clinical trial. *Lancet*, 387(10037), 2507–2520.

Anthony, J. C., LeResche, L., Niaz, U., von Korff, M. R., & Folstein, M. F. (1982). Limits of the "Mini-Mental State" as a screening test for dementia and delirium among hospital patients. *Psychological Medicine*, 12(2), 397–408.

Antoni, M. H., Lutgendorf, S. K., Cole, S. W., Dhabhar, F. S., Sephton, S. E., McDonald, P. G., . . . & Sood, A. K. (2006). The influence of bio-behavioural factors on tumour biology: Pathways and mechanisms. *Nature Reviews Cancer*, 6(3), 240–248.

Antunes, L. C., Levandovski, R., Dantas, G., Caumo, W., & Hidalgo, M. P. (2010). Obesity and shift work: Chronobiological aspects. *Nutrition Research Reviews*, 23(1), 155–168.

Apaydin, E. A., Chen, P. G., & Friedberg, M. W. (2018). Differences in physician income by gender in a multiregion survey. *Journal of General Internal Medicine*, 1–8.

Arber, S., Meadows, R., & Venn, S. (2012). Sleep and society. In C Morin and C. Espie (Eds.), *The Oxford handbook of sleep and sleep disorders* (pp. 223–247). Oxford, UK: Oxford University Press.

Armitage, C. J. (2009). Is there utility in the transtheoretical model? *British Journal of Health Psychology*, 14(2), 195–210.

Arnett, J. J. (2000). Optimistic bias in adolescent and adult smokers and nonsmokers. *Addictive Behaviors*, 25(4), 625–632.

Arnett, J. J. (2016). *Human development: A cultural approach.* (2nd edition). New York, NY: Pearson.

Arnett, J. J., & Terhanian, G. (1998). Adolescents' responses to cigarette advertisements: Links between exposure, liking, and the appeal of smoking. *Tobacco Control*, 7(2), 129–133.

Aschenbrenner, K., Hummel, C., Teszmer, K., Krone, F., Ishimaru, T., Seo, H. S., & Hummel, T. (2008). The influence of olfactory loss on dietary behaviors. *The Laryngoscope*, 118(1), 135–144.

Ashforth, B. E. (1989). The experience of powerlessness in organizations. *Organizational Behavior and Human Decision Processes*, 43(2), 207–242.

Atkinson, J. H., Slater, M. A., Patterson, T. L., Grant, I., & Garfin, S. R. (1991). Prevalence, onset, and risk of psychiatric disorders in men with chronic low back pain: A controlled study. *Pain*, 45(2), 111–121.

Atlas, S. J., Keller, R. B., Robson, D., Deyo, R. A., & Singer, D. E. (2000). Surgical and nonsurgical management of lumbar spinal stenosis: Four-year outcomes from the Maine lumbar spine study. *Spine*, 25(5), 556–562.

Atlas, S. J., Keller, R. B., Wu, Y. A., Deyo, R. A., & Singer, D. E. (2005). Long-term outcomes of surgical and nonsurgical management of lumbar spinal stenosis: 8 to 10 year results from the Maine lumbar spine study. *Spine*, 30(8), 936–943.

Atli, A., Theodore, B. R., Turk, D. C., & Loeser, J. D. (2010). Intrathecal opioid therapy for chronic nonmalignant pain: A retrospective cohort study with 3-year follow-up. *Pain Medicine*, 11(7), 1010–1016.

Audrain-McGovern, J., Rodriguez, D., Tercyak, K. P., Cuevas, J., Rodgers, K., & Patterson, F. (2004). Identifying and characterizing adolescent smoking trajectories. *Cancer Epidemiology and Prevention Biomarkers*, 13(12), 2023–2034.

Aveyard, P., Lawrence, T., Cheng, K. K., Griffin, C., Croghan, E., & Johnson, C. (2006). A randomized controlled trial of smoking cessation for pregnant women to test the effect of a transtheoretical model-based intervention on movement in stage and interaction with baseline stage. *British Journal of Health Psychology*, 11(2), 263–278.

Aviv, R. (2017, April 3). The trauma of facing deportation. *New Yorker*.

Axelsson, M., Brink, E., Lundgren, J., & Lötvall, J. (2011). The influence of personality traits on reported adherence to medication in individuals with chronic disease: An epidemiological study in West Sweden. *PloS One*, 6(3), e18241.

Baird, G., Charman, T., Baron-Cohen, S., Cox, A., Swettenham, J., Wheelwright, S., & Drew, A. (2000). A screening instrument for autism at 18 months of age: A 6-year follow-up study. *Journal of the American Academy of Child & Adolescent Psychiatry*, 39(6), 694–702.

Baker, R. B. (2009). The travails and triumphs of publishing the first global history of medical ethics. *Health Progress*, 65–70.

Balbach, E. D., Gasior, R. J., & Barbeau, E. M. (2003). RJ Reynolds' targeting of African Americans: 1988–2000. *American Journal of Public Health*, 93(5), 822–827.

Balbach, E. D., Herzberg, A., & Barbeau, E. M. (2006). Political coalitions and working women: How the tobacco industry built a relationship with the Coalition of Labor Union Women. *Journal of Epidemiology & Community Health*, 60(suppl 2), ii27–ii32.

Balint, M. (1957). Psychotherapy and the general practitioner—I. *British Medical Journal*, 1(5011), 15.

Ballantyne, J. C., & Sullivan, M. D. (2015). Intensity of chronic pain—the wrong metric? *New England Journal of Medicine*, 373(22), 2098–2099.

Bandura, A. (1978). The self system in reciprocal determinism. *American Psychologist*, 33(4), 343–358.

Bandura, A. (2004). Health promotion by social cognitive means. *Health Education & Behavior*, 31(2), 143–164.

Bandura, A. (2009). Social cognitive theory of mass communication. In J. Bryant & D. Zillman (Eds.). *Media effects: Advances in theory and research* (2nd ed., pp. 121–153). Hillsdale, NJ: Lawrence Erlbaum.

Bandura, A. (2010). Modeling. In *The Corsini Encyclopedia of Psychology* (Vol. 4, pp. 1–3). New York, NY: John Wiley & Sons.

Bandura, A., Ross, D., & Ross, S. A. (1961). Transmission of aggression through imitation of aggressive models. In B. Marlowe & A. S. Canestari (Eds.), *Educational psychology in context: Readings for future teachers*. Thousand Oaks, CA: Sage.

Barker, K. K. (2008). Electronic support groups, patient-consumers, and medicalization: The case of contested illness. *Journal of Health and Social Behavior*, 49(1), 20–36.

Barnoya, J., & Glantz, S. (2004). Association of the California tobacco control program with declines in lung cancer incidence. *Cancer Causes & Control*, 15(7), 689–695.

Baron-Cohen, S., Allen, J., & Gillberg, C. (1992). Can autism be detected at 18 months? The needle, the haystack, and the CHAT. *British Journal of Psychiatry*, 161, 839–843.

Barro, R. J. (2000). Inequality and growth in a panel of countries. *Journal of Economic Growth*, 5(1), 5–32.

Barsky, A. J. (2001). The patient with hypochondriasis. *New England Journal of Medicine*, 345(19), 1395–1399.

Barsky, A. J., & Ahern, D. K. (2004). Cognitive behavior therapy for hypochondriasis: A randomized controlled trial. *Journal of the American Medical Association*, 291(12), 1464–1470.

Barsky, A. J., & Borus, J. F. (1995). Somatization and medicalization in the era of managed care. *Journal of the American Medical Association*, 274(24), 1931–1934.

Barsky, A. J., Wyshak, G., & Klerman, G. L (1990). The somatosensory amplification scale and its relationship to hypochondriasis. *Journal of Psychiatric Research*, 24, 323–334.

Basson, R. (2006). Sexual desire and arousal disorders in women. *New England Journal of Medicine*, 354(14), 1497–1506.

Batty, G. D., Russ, T. C., Stamatakis, E., & Kivimäki, M. (2017). Psychological distress in relation to site specific cancer mortality: Pooling of unpublished data from 16 prospective cohort studies. *British Medical Journal*, 356, j108.

Baum, A., & Davis, G. E. (1980). Reducing the stress of high-density living: An architectural intervention. *Journal of Personality and Social Psychology*, 38(3), 471–481.

Baum, A., Mapp, K., & Davis, G. E. (1978). Determinants of residential group development and social control. *Environmental Psychology and Nonverbal Behavior*, 2(3), 145–160.

Baumeister, R. F., & Tierney, J. (2012). *Willpower: Rediscovering the greatest human strength*. New York, NY: Penguin.

Baumeister, R. F., & Vonasch, A. J. (2015). Uses of self-regulation to facilitate and restrain addictive behavior. *Addictive Behaviors*, 44, 3–8.

Baynes, T. (2012, May 19). Graphic cigarette label constitutional, court rules. *Huffington Post*. https://www.huffingtonpost.com/2012/03/19/graphic-cigarette-warning-labels_n_1364429.html.

Beach, M. C., Saha, S., Korthuis, P. T., Sharp, V., Cohn, J., Wilson, I., . . . & Moore, R. (2010). Differences in patient–provider communication for Hispanic compared to non-Hispanic white patients in HIV care. *Journal of General Internal Medicine*, 25(7), 682–687.

Beck, A. H. (2004). The Flexner report and the standardization of American medical education. *Journal of the American Medical Association*, 291(17), 2139–2140.

Beck, A. T. (1979). *Cognitive therapy of depression*. New York, NY: Guilford Press.

Becker, A. E. (2004). Television, disordered eating, and young women in Fiji: Negotiating body image and identity during rapid social change. *Culture, Medicine and Psychiatry*, 28(4), 533–559.

Becker, U., Deis, A., Sorensen, T. I., Gronbaek, M., Borch-Johnsen, K., Muller, C. F., . . . & Jensen, G. (1996). Prediction of risk of liver disease by alcohol intake, sex, and age: A prospective population study. *Hepatology*, 23(5), 1025–1029.

Beckman, H. B., & Frankel, R. M. (1984). The effect of physician behavior on the collection of data. *Annals of Internal Medicine*, 101(5), 692–696.

Beecher, H. K. (1956). Relationship of significance of wound to pain experienced. *Journal of the American Medical Association*, 161(17), 1609–1613.

Beecher, H. K. (1966). Ethics and clinical research. *New England Journal of Medicine*, 274, 1354–1360.

Bellah, R. N., Madsen, R., Sullivan, W. M., Swidler, A., & Tipton, S. M. (2007). *Habits of the heart: Individualism and commitment in American life*. Berkeley, CA: University of California Press.

Bendick, J. (2002). *Galen and the gateway to medicine*. Bathgate, ND: Bethlehem Books.

Benet, A. E., & Melman, A. (1995). The epidemiology of erectile dysfunction. *The Urologic Clinics of North America*, 22(4), 699–709.

Benson, H., & Klipper, M. Z. (1992). *The relaxation response*. New York, NY: HarperCollins.

Benson, H., Marzetta, B., Rosner, B., & Klemchuk, H. (1974). Decreased blood-pressure in pharmacologically treated hypertensive patients who regularly elicited the relaxation response. *The Lancet*, 303(7852), 289–291.

Ben-Zeev, D., Brenner, C. J., Begale, M., Duffecy, J., Mohr, D. C., & Mueser, K. T. (2014). Feasibility, acceptability, and preliminary efficacy of a smartphone intervention for schizophrenia. *Schizophrenia Bulletin*, 40(6), 1244–1253.

Bergeron, S., Rosen, N. O., & Pukall, C. R. (2014). Genital pain in women and men: It can hurt more than your sex life. In Y. M. Binik & S. K. Hall (Eds.), *Principles and practice of sex therapy* (pp. 159–176). New York, NY: Guilford Press.

Berkman, N. D., Brownley, K. A., Peat, C. M., Lohr, K. N., Cullen, K. E., Morgan, L. C., . . . & Bulik, C. M. (2015). *Management and outcomes of binge-eating disorder*. Rockville, MD: Agency for Healthcare Research and Quality.

Bernacchi, D. L. (2017). Bulimia nervosa: A comprehensive analysis of treatment, policy, and social work ethics. *Social Work*, 62(2), 174–180.

Bernstein, E., Bernstein, J., Feldman, J., Fernandez, W., Hagan, M., Mitchell, P., . . . & Lee, C. (2007). An evidence-based alcohol screening, brief intervention and referral to treatment (SBIRT) curriculum for emergency department (ED) providers improves skills and utilization. *Substance Abuse: Official Publication of the Association for Medical Education and Research in Substance Abuse*, 28(4), 79–92.

Bertakis, K. D., Azari, R., Helms, L. J., Callahan, E. J., & Robbins, J. A. (2000). Gender differences in the utilization of health care services. *Journal of Family Practice*, 49(2), 147–152.

Bertalanffy, L. v. (1968). *General systems theory*. New York, NY: George Braziller.

Bertalanffy, L. v. (1969). General systems theory and psychiatry—an overview. *General Systems Theory and Psychiatry*, 32(4), 33–46.

Bhutta, Z. A. (2013). Conflict and polio: Winning the polio wars. *Journal of the American Medical Association*, 310(9), 905–906.

Biddle, S. J., Braithwaite, R., & Pearson, N. (2014). The effectiveness of interventions to increase physical activity among young girls: A meta-analysis. *Preventive Medicine*, 62, 119–131.

Binkiewicz-Glińska, A., Bakuła, S., Tomczak, H., Landowski, J., Ruckemann-Dziurdzińska, K., Zaborowska-Sapeta, K., & Kiebzak, W. (2015). Fibromyalgia syndrome: A multidisciplinary approach. *Psychiatr Pol*, 49(4), 801–810.

Birmingham, C. L., Su, J., Hlynsky, J. A., Goldner, E. M., & Gao, M. (2005). The mortality rate from anorexia nervosa. *International Journal of Eating Disorders*, 38(2), 143–146.

Blackhall, L. J., Murphy, S. T., Frank, G., Michel, V., & Azen, S. (1995). Ethnicity and attitudes toward patient autonomy. *Journal of the American Medical Association*, 274(10), 820–825.

Blagg, C. R. (1998). Development of ethical concepts in dialysis: Seattle in the 1960s. *Nephrology*, 4(4), 235–238.

Bliwise, D. L. (2004). Sleep disorders in Alzheimer's disease and other dementias. *Clinical Cornerstone*, 6(1), S16–S28.

Blot, W. J., McLaughlin, J. K., Winn, D. M., Austin, D. F., Greenberg, R. S., Preston-Martin, S., . . . & Fraumeni, J. F. (1988). Smoking and drinking in relation to oral and pharyngeal cancer. *Cancer Research*, 48(11), 3282–3287.

Blum, D. (2011, March 24). The radium girls. *Wired*. https://www.wired.com/2011/03/the-radium-girls/.

Blumenthal, D. (2006). Employer-sponsored health insurance in the United States—origins and implications. *New England Journal of Medicine*, 355(1), 82–88.

Blumenthal, D., & Collins, S. R. (2014). Health care coverage under the Affordable Care Act—a progress report. *New England Journal of Medicine*, 371, 275–281.

Blyth, F. M., March, L. M., & Cousins, M. J. (2003). Chronic pain-related disability and use of analgesia and health services in a Sydney community. *Medical Journal of Australia*, 179(2), 84–87.

Boardman, T., Catley, D., Grobe, J. E., Little, T. D., & Ahluwalia, J. S. (2006). Using motivational interviewing with smokers: Do therapist behaviors relate to engagement and therapeutic alliance? *Journal of Substance Abuse Treatment*, 31(4), 329–339.

Bolier, L., Haverman, M., Westerhof, G. J., Riper, H., Smit, F., & Bohlmeijer, E. (2013). Positive psychology interventions: A meta-analysis of randomized controlled studies. *BMC Public Health*, 13(1), 119.

Bomey, N. (2015, September 2). Thousands of farmers stopped growing tobacco after deregulation payouts. *USA Today*.

Bonham, V. L., Sellers, S. L., & Neighbors, H. W. (2004). John Henryism and self-reported physical health among high-socioeconomic status African American men. *American Journal of Public Health*, 94(5), 737–738.

Bonica, J. J. (1974). Acupuncture anesthesia in the People's Republic of China: Implications for American medicine. *Journal of the American Medical Association*, 229(10), 1317–1325.

Borg, C., de Jong, P. J., & Schultz, W. W. (2010). Vaginismus and dyspareunia: Automatic vs. deliberate disgust responsivity. *Journal of Sexual Medicine*, 7(6), 2149–2157.

Borland, R., Partos, T. R., Yong, H. H., Cummings, K. M., & Hyland, A. (2012). How much unsuccessful quitting activity is going on among adult smokers? Data from the International Tobacco Control Four Country cohort survey. *Addiction*, 107(3), 673–682.

Boulware, L. E., Cooper, L. A., Ratner, L. E., LaVeist, T. A., & Powe, N. R. (2016). Race and trust in the health care system. *Public Health Reports*, 118(4), 358–365.

Bowen, S., & Marlatt, A. (2009). Surfing the urge: Brief mindfulness-based intervention for college student smokers. *Psychology of Addictive Behaviors*, 23(4), 666–671.

Boyce, W. T., Chesney, M., Alkon-Leonard, A., Tschann, J., Adams, S., Chesterman, B., Cohen, F., Kaiser, P., Folkman, S., & Wara, D. (1995). Psychobiologic reactivity to stress and childhood respiratory illnesses: Results of two prospective studies. *Psychosomatic Medicine*, 57, 411–422.

Boyle, P. J., Feng, Z., & Raab, G. M. (2011). Does widowhood increase mortality risk? Testing for selection effects by comparing causes of spousal death. *Epidemiology*, 22(1), 1–5.

Bramadat, P. (2017). Introduction: Seeking a better conversation. In P. Bramadat, M. Guay, J. A. Bettinger, & R. Roy (Eds.), *Public health in the age of anxiety: Religious and cultural roots of vaccine hesitancy in Canada* (pp. 5–15). Toronto, ON: University of Toronto Press.

Brandt, A. M. (2007). *The cigarette century: The rise, fall, and deadly persistence of the product that defined America*. Cambridge, MA: Basic Books.

Brennan, L., & Murphy, K. (2013). The role of psychology in overweight and obesity management. In M. Caltabiano & L. A. Ricciardelli (Eds.), *Applied topics in health psychology* (pp. 303–316). West Sussex, UK: John Wiley & Sons.

Breslau, N., Lipton, R. B., Stewart, W. F., Schultz, L. R., & Welch, K. M. A. (2003). Comorbidity of migraine and depression investigating potential etiology and prognosis. *Neurology*, 60(8), 1308–1312.

Breslau, N., Schultz, L. R., Stewart, W. F., Lipton, R. B., Lucia, V. C., & Welch, K. M. A. (2000). Headache and major depression: Is the association specific to migraine? *Neurology*, 54(2), 308–308.

Brewer, J. A., Mallik, S., Babuscio, T. A., Nich, C., Johnson, H. E., Deleone, C. M., . . . & Carroll, K. M. (2011). Mindfulness training for smoking cessation: Results from a randomized controlled trial. *Drug and Alcohol Dependence*, 119(1–2), 72–80.

Brewer, N. T., Chapman, G. B., Gibbons, F. X., Gerrard, M., McCaul, K. D., & Weinstein, N. D. (2007). Meta-analysis of the relationship between risk perception and health behavior: The example of vaccination. *Health Psychology*, 26(2), 136–145.

Brewer, N. T., Hall, M. G., Noar, S. M., Parada, H., Stein-Seroussi, A., Bach, L. E., . . . & Ribisl, K. M. (2016). Effect of pictorial cigarette pack warnings on changes in smoking behavior: A randomized clinical trial. *JAMA Internal Medicine*, 176(7), 905–912.

Brody, G. H., Yu, T., Chen, E., Miller, G. E., Kogan, S. M., & Beach, S. R. (2013). Is resilience only skin deep? Rural African Americans' socioeconomic status–related risk and competence in preadolescence and psychological adjustment and allostatic load at age 19. *Psychological Science*, 24(7), 1285–1293.

Bronfenbrenner, U. (2005). Ecological systems theory (1992). In U. Bronfenbrenner (Ed.), *Making human beings human: Bioecological perspectives on human development* (pp. 106–173). Thousand Oaks, CA: Sage.

Brotto, L., & Luria, M. (2015). Sexual arousal/interest disorder in women. In Y. M. Binik & K. S. Hall (Eds.), *Principles and practice of sex therapy* (5th ed., pp. 17–41). New York, NY: Guilford Press.

Brown, B. B. (1977). *Stress and the art of biofeedback*. New York, NY: Harper & Row.

Brown, R. P., & Gerbarg, P. L. (2009). Yoga breathing, meditation, and longevity. *Annals of the New York Academy of Sciences*, 1172(1), 54–62.

Brown, T. N., Williams, D. R., Jackson, J. S., Neighbors, H. W., Torres, M., Sellers, S. L., & Brown, K. T. (2000). "Being black and feeling blue": The mental health consequences of racial discrimination. *Race and Society*, 2(2), 117–131.

Brownell, K. D., & Frieden, T. R. (2009). Ounces of prevention—the public policy case for taxes on sugared beverages. *New England Journal of Medicine*, 360(18), 1805–1808.

Brownell, K. D., & Koplan, J. P. (2011). Front-of-package nutrition labeling—an abuse of trust by the food industry? *New England Journal of Medicine*, 364(25), 2373–2375.

Brownson, R. C., Baker, E. A., Housemann, R. A., Brennan, L. K., & Bacak, S. J. (2001). Environmental and policy determinants of physical activity in the United States. *American Journal of Public Health*, 91(12), 1995–2003.

Brownson, R. C., Housemann, R. A., Brown, D. R., Jackson-Thompson, J., King, A. C., Malone, B. R., & Sallis, J. F. (2000). Promoting physical activity in rural communities: Walking trail access, use, and effects. *American Journal of Preventive Medicine*, 18(3), 235–241.

Brownson, R. C., Tabak, R. G., Stamatakis, K. A., & Glanz, K. (2015). Implementation, dissemination and diffusion of public health interventions. In

K. Glanz, B. Rimer, & K. Viswanath (Eds.), *Health behavior: Theory, research, and practice* (5th ed., pp. 301–326). San Francisco, CA: Jossey-Bass.

Bruch, H. (1974). *Eating disorders: Obesity, anorexia nervosa, and the person within*. New York, NY: Routledge & Kegan Paul.

Bruckner, T. A., Saxton, K. B., Anderson, E., Goldman, S., Brudney, K., & Dobkin, J. (1991). Resurgent tuberculosis in New York City. *American Review of Respiratory Disease*, 144, 745–749.

Bruckner, T. A., Saxton, K., Anderson, E., Goldman, S., & Gould, J. B. (2009). From paradox to disparity: Trends in neonatal death among very low weight black and white infants, 1989–2004. *Journal of Pediatrics*, 155, 482–487.

Bruhn, J. G., & Wolf, S. (2013). *The Roseto story: An anatomy of health*. Norman, OK: University of Oklahoma Press.

Bryant, A. S., Nakagawa, S., Gregorich, S. E., & Kuppermann, M. (2010). Race/ethnicity and pregnancy decision making: The role of fatalism and subjective social standing. *Journal of Women's Health*, 19(6), 1195–1200.

Bulloch, A., Williams, J., Lavorato, D., & Patten, S. (2014). Recurrence of major depressive episodes is strongly dependent on the number of previous episodes. *Depression and Anxiety*, 31(1), 72–76.

Burbaum C., Stresing, A.-M., Fritzsche K., Auer, P., Wirsching, M., Lucius-Hoene, G. (2010). Medically unexplained symptoms as a threat to patients' identity? A conversation analysis of patients' reactions to psychosomatic attributions. *Patient Education and Counseling*, 79(2), 207–217.

Burhansstipanov, L., Dignan, M. B., Schumacher, A., Krebs, L. U., Alfonsi, G., & Apodaca, C. C. (2010). Breast screening navigator programs within three settings that assist underserved women. *Journal of Cancer Education*, 25, 247–252.

Burns, J. W., Kubilus, A., Bruehl, S., Harden, R. N., & Lofland, K. (2003). Do changes in cognitive factors influence outcome following multidisciplinary treatment for chronic pain? A cross-lagged panel analysis. *Journal of Consulting and Clinical Psychology*, 71(1), 81–91.

Burns, L. C., Ritvo, S. E., Ferguson, M. K., Clarke, H., Seltzer, Z. E., & Katz, J. (2015). Pain catastrophizing as a risk factor for chronic pain after total knee arthroplasty: A systematic review. *Journal of Pain Research*, 8, 21–32.

Burton, M. J., Glasziou, P. P., Chong, L. Y., & Venekamp, R. P. (2014). Tonsillectomy or adenotonsillectomy versus non-surgical treatment for chronic/recurrent acute tonsillitis. *Cochrane Database of Systematic Reviews*, 2014(11).

Burton, M. J., Pollard, A. J., Ramsden, J. D., Chong, L. Y., & Venekamp, R. P. (2014). Tonsillectomy for periodic fever, aphthous stomatitis, pharyngitis and cervical adenitis syndrome (PFAPA). *Cochrane Database of Systematic Reviews*, 2014(9).

Butryn, M. L., Forman, E., Hoffman, K., Shaw, J., & Juarascio, A. (2011). A pilot study of acceptance and commitment therapy for promotion of physical activity. *Journal of Physical Activity and Health*, 8(4), 516–522.

Buysse, D. J., Reynolds, C. F., III, Monk, T. H., Berman, S. R., & Kupfer, D. J. (1989). The Pittsburgh Sleep Quality Index: A new instrument for psychiatric practice and research. *Psychiatry Research*, 28(2), 193–213.

Bynum, W. (2008). *The history of medicine: A very short introduction*. Oxford, UK: Oxford University Press.

Calhoun, J. B. (1962). Population density and social pathology. *Scientific American*, 206(2), 139–149.

Calzada, E. J., Fernandez, Y., & Cortes, D. E. (2010). Incorporating the cultural value of respeto into a framework of Latino parenting. *Cultural Diversity and Ethnic Minority Psychology*, 16(1), 77–86.

Campayo, A., De Jonge, P., Roy, J. F., Saz, P., De la Cámara, C., Quintanilla, M. A., . . . & Lobo, A. (2010). Depressive disorder and incident diabetes mellitus: The effect of characteristics of depression. *American Journal of Psychiatry*, 167(5), 580–588.

Campbell, D. (2015, January 24). Overcrowded hospitals kill 500. *The Guardian*. https://www.theguardian.com/uk-news/2015/jan/24/overcrowded-hospitals-deaths.

Campbell, D. (2017, January 13). 193,000 NHS patients a month waiting beyond target time for surgery. *The Guardian*. https://www.theguardian.com/society/2017/jan/13/193000-nhs-patients-a-month-waiting-beyond-target-for-surgery.

Campbell, D. T. (1979). Assessing the impact of planned social change. *Evaluation and Program Planning*, 2(1), 67–90.

Campbell, D. T. (1991). Methods for the experimenting society. *Evaluation Practice*, 12(3), 223–260.

Campbell, M. K., Hudson, M. A., Resnicow, K., Blakeney, N., Paxton, A., & Baskin, M. (2007). Church-based health promotion interventions: Evidence and lessons learned. *Annual Review of Public Health*, 28, 213–234.

Cannon, W. B. (2002). "Voodoo" death. *American Journal of Public Health*, 92(10), 1593–1596.

Cantwell, M. F., McKenna, M. T., McCray, E., & Onorato, I. M. (1998). Tuberculosis and race/ethnicity in the United States: Impact of socioeconomic status. *American Journal of Respiratory and Critical Care Medicine*, 157(4), 1016–1020.

Capanoglu, M., Dibek Misirlioglu, E., Toyran, M., Civelek, E., & Kocabas, C. N. (2015). Evaluation of inhaler technique, adherence to therapy and their effect on disease control among children with asthma using metered dose or dry powder inhalers. *Journal of Asthma*, 52(8), 838–845.

Cappuccio, F. P., Taggart, F. M., Kandala, N. B., Currie, A., Peile, E., Stranges, S., & Miller, M. A. (2008). Meta-analysis of short sleep duration and obesity in children and adults. *Sleep*, *31*(5), 619–626.

Carbone, J. D., & Seftel, A. D. (2002). Erectile dysfunction. Diagnosis and treatment in older men. *Geriatrics*, *57*(9), 18–24.

Carley, J. A., Karp, J. F., Gentili, A., Marcum, Z. A., Reid, M. C., Rodriguez, E., . . . & Weiner, D. K. (2015). Deconstructing chronic low back pain in the older adult: Step by step evidence and expert-based recommendations for evaluation and treatment: Part IV, depression. *Pain Medicine*, *16*(11), 2098–2108.

Carlson, N. R. (2013). *Physiology of behavior*. Harlow, UK: Pearson Publishers.

Carney, C. E., Buysse, D. J., Ancoli-Israel, S., Edinger, J. D., Krystal, A. D., Lichstein, K. L., & Morin, C. M. (2012). The consensus sleep diary: Standardizing prospective sleep self-monitoring. *Sleep*, *35*(2), 287–302.

Carpenter, C. J. (2010). A meta-analysis of the effectiveness of health belief model variables in predicting behavior. *Health Communication*, *25*(8), 661–669.

Carter, N. L., & Beh, H. C. (1989). The effect of intermittent noise on cardiovascular functioning during vigilance task performance. *Psychophysiology*, *26*(5), 548–559.

Carter, R. E. (1984). Family reactions and reorganization patterns in myocardial infarction. *Family Systems Medicine*, *2*(1), 55.

Carver, C. S., & Connor-Smith, J. (2010). Personality and coping. *Annual Review of Psychology*, *61*, 679–704.

Carver, C. S., & Scheier, M. F. (2014). Dispositional optimism. *Trends in Cognitive Sciences*, *18*(6), 293–299.

Carver, C. S., Scheier, M. F., & Weintraub, J. K. (1989). Assessing coping strategies: A theoretically based approach. *Journal of Personality and Social Psychology*, *56*(2), 267–283.

Casilli, A. A., Pailler, F., & Tubaro, P. (2013). Online networks of eating-disorder websites: Why censoring pro-ana might be a bad idea. *Perspectives in Public Health*, *133*(2), 94–95.

Cassell, J. (2005). *Life and death in intensive care*. Philadelphia, PA: Temple University Press.

Catley, M. J., Gibson, W., Wand, B. M., Meads, C., & O'Connell, N. E. (2015). Transcutaneous electrical nerve stimulation (TENS) for chronic pain—an overview of Cochrane reviews (Protocol). *Cochrane Database of Systematic Reviews*, *2015*(9).

Catz, S. L., Kelly, J. A., Bogart, L. M., Benotsch, E. G., & McAuliffe, T. L. (2000). Patterns, correlates, and barriers to medication adherence among persons prescribed new treatments for HIV disease. *Health Psychology*, *19*(2), 124–133.

Caughey, A. B., Cheng, Y. W., Stotland, N. E., Washington, A. E., & Escobar, G. J. (2010). Maternal and paternal race/ethnicity are both associated with gestational diabetes. *American Journal of Obstetrics and Gynecology*, *202*(6), 616-e1.

Centers for Disease Control and Prevention. (2013). NCHS: Death rates and life expectancy. https://data.cdc.gov/browse?q=life%20expectancy%20by%20race&sortBy=reelvance.

Centers for Disease Control and Prevention. (2016a). CDC estimates 1 in 68 school-aged children have autism; no change from previous estimate. https://www.cdc.gov/media/releases/2016/p0331-children-autism.html.

Centers for Disease Control and Prevention. (2016b). Adverse childhood experiences (ACEs). https://www.cdc.gov/violenceprevention/acestudy/index.html.

Centers for Disease Control and Prevention. (2016c). HIV and transgender communities. https://www.cdc.gov/hiv/pdf/policies/cdc-hiv-transgender-brief.pdf.

Centers for Disease Control and Prevention. (2017). Second hand smoke facts. https://www.cdc.gov/tobacco/data_statistics/fact_sheets/secondhand_smoke/general_facts/index.htm.

Centers for Disease Control and Prevention. (2018a). Burden of tobacco use in the U.S. https://www.cdc.gov/tobacco/campaign/tips/resources/data/cigarette-smoking-in-united-states.html.

Centers for Disease Control and Prevention. (2018b). Health effects of smoking. https://www.cdc.gov/tobacco/data_statistics/fact_sheets/health_effects/effects_cig_smoking/index.htm.

Centers for Disease Control and Prevention. (2018c). Tobacco use among adults with mental illness and substance use disorder. https://www.cdc.gov/tobacco/disparities/mental-illness-substance-use/index.htm.

Centers for Disease Control and Prevention. (2018d). Tobacco use and pregnancy. https://www.cdc.gov/reproductivehealth/MaternalInfantHealth/TobaccoUsePregnancy/index.htm.

Centers for Disease Control and Prevention. (2018e). HPV vaccination coverage data. https://www.cdc.gov/hpv/hcp/vacc-coverage/index.html.

Chaloupka, F. J., Yurekli, A., & Fong, G. T. (2012). Tobacco taxes as a tobacco control strategy. *Tobacco Control*, *21*(2), 172–180.

Chan, C. W., & Peng, P. (2011). Failed back surgery syndrome. *Pain Medicine*, *12*(4), 577–606.

Chang, S. H., Stoll, C. R., Song, J., Varela, J. E., Eagon, C. J., & Colditz, G. A. (2014). The effectiveness and risks of bariatric surgery: An updated systematic review and meta-analysis, 2003–2012. *JAMA Surgery*, *149*(3), 275–287.

Charles, C., Whelan, T., & Gafni, A. (1999). What do we mean by partnership in making decisions about treatment? *British Medical Journal*, *319*, 780–782.

Chen, M. Y., Wang, E. K., & Jeng, Y. J. (2006). Adequate sleep among adolescents is positively associated with health status and health-related behaviors. *BMC Public Health*, *6*(1), 59.

Cherkin, D. C., Deyo, R. A., Battié, M., Street, J., & Barlow, W. (1998). A comparison of physical therapy, chiropractic manipulation, and provision of an educational booklet for the treatment of patients with low back pain. *New England Journal of Medicine, 339*(15), 1021–1029.

Christakis, N. A., & Fowler, J. H. (2008). The collective dynamics of smoking in a large social network. *New England Journal of Medicine, 358*(21), 2249–2258.

Chwastiak, L. A., Jackson, S. L., Russo, J., DeKeyser, P., Kiefer, M., Belyeu, B., . . . & Lin, E. (2017). A collaborative care team to integrate behavioral health care and treatment of poorly-controlled type 2 diabetes in an urban safety net primary care clinic. *General Hospital Psychiatry, 44*, 10–15.

Clark, D. A., & Beck, A. T. (2011). *Cognitive therapy of anxiety disorders: Science and practice.* New York, NY: Guilford Press.

Clark, M. A., Rakowski, W., Ehrich, B., Rimer, B. K., Velicer, W. F., Dube, C. E., . . . & Goldstein, M. (2002). The effect of a stage-matched and tailored intervention on repeat mammography. *American Journal of Preventive Medicine, 22*(1), 1–7.

Clarke, J. (1996). *Health, illness, and medicine in Canada.* Toronto, ON: Oxford University Press.

Claxton, G., Rae, M., Panchal, N., Damico, A., Whitmore, H., Kenward, K., & Osei-Anto, A. (2012). Health benefits in 2012: Moderate premium increases for employer-sponsored plans; young adults gained coverage under ACA. *Health Affairs, 31*(10), 2324–2333.

Clayton, A. H., DeRogatis, L. R., Rosen, R. C., & Pyke, R. (2012). Intended or unintended consequences? The likely implications of raising the bar for sexual dysfunction diagnosis in the proposed DSM-V revisions: 1. For women with incomplete loss of desire or sexual receptivity. *Journal of Sexual Medicine, 9*(8), 2027–2039.

Clemens, Z., Fabo, D., & Halasz, P. (2005). Overnight verbal memory retention correlates with the number of sleep spindles. *Neuroscience, 132*(2), 529–535.

Clements, K., & Turpin, G. (1996). The life events scale for students: Validation for use with British samples. *Personality and Individual Differences, 20*(6), 747–751.

Clifford, D., & Curtis, L. (2016). *Motivational interviewing in nutrition and fitness.* New York. NY: Guilford Press.

Cockerham, W. C. (1997). The social determinants of the decline of life expectancy in Russia and Eastern Europe: A lifestyle explanation. *Journal of Health and Social Behavior, 38*(2), 117–130.

Cockerham, W. C. (2015). *Medical sociology.* New York, NY: Routledge.

Codori, A. M., & Brandt, J. (1994). Psychological costs and benefits of predictive testing for Huntington's disease. *American Journal of Medical Genetics Part A, 54*(3), 174–184.

Cohen, R. (1992, February 10). Among growing crime, Zurich closes a park it reserved for drug addicts. *New York Times.*

Cohen, S., Hamrick, N., Rodriguez, M. S., Feldman, P. J., Rabin, B. S., & Manuck, S. B. (2002). Reactivity and vulnerability to stress-associated risk for upper respiratory illness. *Psychosomatic Medicine, 64*(2), 302–310.

Cohen, S., Kamarck, T., & Mermelstein, R. (1983). A global measure of perceived stress. *Journal of Health and Social Behavior, 24*(4), 385–396.

Cohen, S., & Lichtenstein, E. (1990). Partner behaviors that support quitting smoking. *Journal of Consulting and Clinical Psychology, 58*(3), 304–309.

Cohen, W. J. (1985). Reflections on the enactment of Medicare and Medicaid. *Health Care Financing Review, 1985*(Suppl), 3.

Colcombe, S. J., Erickson, K. I., Scalf, P. E., Kim, J. S., Prakash, R., McAuley, E., . . . & Kramer, A. F. (2006). Aerobic exercise training increases brain volume in aging humans. *Journals of Gerontology Series A: Biological Sciences and Medical Sciences, 61*(11), 1166–1170.

Comer, R. (2015). *Abnormal psychology.* New York, NY: Worth.

Conrad, P. (2008). *The medicalization of society: On the transformation of human conditions into treatable disorders.* Baltimore, MD: Johns Hopkins University Press.

Cook, L. (2015, January 28). U.S. education: Still separate and unequal. *U.S. News and World Report online.* https://www.usnews.com/news/blogs/data-mine/2015/01/28/us-education-still-separate-and-unequal.

Cooney, G. M., Dwan, K., Grieg, C. A., Lawler, D. A., Rimer, J. A., Waugh, F. R., McMurdo, M., & Mead, G. E. (2014). Exercise for depression. *Journal of the American Medical Association, 311*(23), 2432–2433.

Coontz, S. (1992). *The way we never were.* New York, NY: Basic Books.

Cooper, L. A., Roter, D. L., Carson, K. A., Beach, M. C., Sabin, J. A., Greenwald, A. G., & Inui, T. S. (2012). The associations of clinicians' implicit attitudes about race with medical visit communication and patient ratings of interpersonal care. *American Journal of Public Health, 102*(5), 979–987.

Cooper, L. A., Roter, D. L., Johnson, R. L., Ford, D. E., Steinwachs, D. M., & Powe, N. R. (2003). Patient-centered communication, ratings of care, and concordance of patient and physician race. *Annals of Internal Medicine, 139*(11), 907–915.

Cooper, R. S., Rotimi, C. N., & Ward, R. (1999). The puzzle of hypertension in African-Americans. *Scientific American, 280*(2), 56–63.

Coren, S. (1996). Daylight savings time and traffic accidents. *New England Journal of Medicine, 334,* 924–925.

Corrigan, P. W., Kraus, D. J., Pickett, S. A., Schmidt, A., Stellon, E., Hantke, E., & Lara, J. L. (2017). Using peer navigators to address the integrated health care needs of homeless African Americans with serious mental illness. *Psychiatric Services, 68*(3), 264–270.

Costa P. T., Jr., & McCrae, R. R. (1992). Four ways five factors are basic. *Personality and Individual Differences, 13*(6), 653–665.

Coston, B. M. (2014). Women's health, health care utilization, and experience of intimate partner violence.

In V. Harvey & T. Housel (Eds.), *Health care disparities and the LGBT population* (pp. 167–188). Lanham, MD: Lexington.

Creed, F., & Barsky, A. (2004). A systematic review of the epidemiology of somatisation disorder and hypochondriasis. *Journal of Psychosomatic Research*, 56(4), 391–408.

Crowley, S. J., Acebo, C., & Carskadon, M. A. (2007). Sleep, circadian rhythms, and delayed phase in adolescence. *Sleep Medicine*, 8(6), 602–612.

Curtin, S., & Matthews, T. (2016). Smoking prevalence and cessation before and during pregnancy: Data from the birth certificate, 2014. *National Vital Statistics Report*, 65, 1–13.

Curtin, S. C., & Hoyert, D. L. (2017). Maternal morbidity and mortality: Exploring racial/ethnic differences using new data from birth and death certificates. In M. Hoque, B. Pecotte, & M. McGehee (Eds.), *Applied demography and public health in the 21st century* (pp. 95–113). New York, NY: Springer.

Dahl, J., Luciano, C., & Wilson, K. (2005). *Acceptance and commitment therapy for chronic pain*. Oakland, CA: New Harbinger Publications.

Dahl, J., & Lundgren, T. (2006). Acceptance and commitment therapy (ACT) in the treatment of chronic pain. In R. A. Baer (Ed.), *Mindfulness-based treatment approaches: Clinician's guide to evidence base and applications* (pp. 285–306). Burlington, MA: Academic Press.

Dahl, J., Wilson, K. G., & Nilsson, A. (2004). Acceptance and commitment therapy and the treatment of persons at risk for long-term disability resulting from stress and pain symptoms: A preliminary randomized trial. *Behavior Therapy*, 35(4), 785–801.

Dahl, R. E., & Harvey, A. G. (2007). Sleep in children and adolescents with behavioral and emotional disorders. *Sleep Medicine Clinics*, 2(3), 501–511.

Dakanalis, A., Carrà, G., Calogero, R., Fida, R., Clerici, M., Zanetti, M. A., & Riva, G. (2015). The developmental effects of media-ideal internalization and self-objectification processes on adolescents' negative body-feelings, dietary restraint, and binge eating. *European Child & Adolescent Psychiatry*, 24(8), 997–1010.

Dallaspezia, S., & Benedetti, F. (2014). Sleep deprivation therapy for depression. In P. Meerlo, R. M. Benca, & T. Abel (Eds.), *Sleep, neuronal plasticity and brain function* (pp. 483–502). Berlin, Germany: Springer.

Dalton, M. A., Sargent, J. D., Beach, M. L., Titus-Ernstoff, L., Gibson, J. J., Ahrens, M. B., . . . & Heatherton, T. F. (2003). Effect of viewing smoking in movies on adolescent smoking initiation: A cohort study. *The Lancet*, 362(9380), 281–285.

Damiano, S. R., Paxton, S. J., Wertheim, E. H., McLean, S. A., & Gregg, K. J. (2015). Dietary restraint of 5-year-old girls: Associations with internalization of the thin ideal and maternal, media, and peer influences. *International Journal of Eating Disorders*, 48(8), 1166–1169.

D'Amico, E. J., & Fromme, K. (1997). Health risk behaviors of adolescent and young adult siblings. *Health Psychology*, 16(5), 426–432.

Daniels, K., Daugherty, J. D., & Jones, J. (2014, December). Current contraceptive status among women aged 15–44: United States, 2011–2013. *NCHS Data Brief*. http://i2.cdn.turner.com/cnn/2016/images/10/04/contraceptive.use.stats.pdf.

Darroch, J. E., Singh, S., & Frost, J. J. (2001). Differences in teenage pregnancy rates among five developed countries: The roles of sexual activity and contraceptive use. *Family Planning Perspectives*, 33(6), 244–281.

Dauvilliers, Y., Arnulf, I., & Mignot, E. (2007). Narcolepsy with cataplexy. *The Lancet*, 369(9560), 499–511.

Dauvilliers, Y., & Bayard, S. (2011). Narcolepsy and hypersomnia. In C. M. Morin & C. A. Espie (Eds.), *The Oxford handbook of sleep and sleep disorders* (pp. 690–706). Oxford, UK: Oxford University Press.

Davidoff, F., Haynes, B., Sackett, D., & Smith, R. (1995). Evidence based medicine. *British Medical Journal*, 310(6987), 1085.

Davidson, J. A., Rosales, A., Shillington, A. C., Bailey, R. A., Kabir, C., & Umpierrez, G. E. (2015). Improving access to shared decision-making for Hispanics/Latinos with inadequately controlled type 2 diabetes mellitus. *Patient Preference and Adherence*, 9, 619–625.

Davison, K. A., Negrato, C. A., Cobas, R., Matheus, A., Tannus, L., Palma, C. S., . . . & Araújo, N. B. (2014). Relationship between adherence to diet, glycemic control and cardiovascular risk factors in patients with type 1 diabetes: A nationwide survey in Brazil. *Nutrition Journal*, 13(1), 19.

Dawber, T. R., Kannel, W. B., Revotskie, N., Stokes III, J., Kagan, A., & Gordon, T. (1959). Some factors associated with the development of coronary heart disease—six years' follow-up experience in the Framingham Study. *American Journal of Public Health and the Nation's Health*, 49(10), 1349–1356.

de Bustinza, V. (2016, November–December). How early Islamic science advanced medicine. *National Geographic History*. https://www.nationalgeographic.com/archaeology-and-history/magazine/2016/11-12/muslim-medicine-scientific-discovery-islam/.

de Carufel, F. (2016). *Premature ejaculation: Theory, evaluation and therapeutic treatment*. London, UK: Routledge.

De Kruif, P. (1996). *Microbe hunters*. New York, NY: Houghton Mifflin Harcourt.

de Lissovoy, G., Rice, T., Ermann, D., & Gabel, J. (1986). Preferred provider organizations: Today's models and tomorrow's prospects. *Inquiry*, 23(1), 7–15.

De Moor, M. H. M., Beem, A. L., Stubbe, J. H., Boomsma, D. I., & De Geus, E. J. C. (2006). Regular exercise, anxiety, depression and personality: A population-based study. *Preventive Medicine*, 42(4), 273–279.

de Vries, S. T., Keers, J. C., Visser, R., de Zeeuw, D., Haaijer-Ruskamp, F. M., Voorham, J., & Denig, P. (2014). Medication beliefs, treatment

complexity, and non-adherence to different drug classes in patients with type 2 diabetes. *Journal of Psychosomatic Research*, 76(2), 134–138.
Dean, H. Y., Touyz, S. W., Rieger, E., & Thornton, C. E. (2008). Group motivational enhancement therapy as an adjunct to inpatient treatment for eating disorders: A preliminary study. *European Eating Disorders Review*, 16(4), 256–267.
Dedeli, O., & Kaptan, G. (2013). Spirituality and religion in pain and pain management. *Health Psychology Research*, 1(3), e29.
DeLongis, A., Coyne, J. C., Dakof, G., Folkman, S., & Lazarus, R. S. (1982). Relationship of daily hassles, uplifts, and major life events to health status. *Health Psychology*, 1(2), 119–136.
DeLongis, A., Folkman, S., & Lazarus, R. S. (1988). The impact of daily stress on health and mood: Psychological and social resources as mediators. *Journal of Personality and Social Psychology*, 54(3), 486–495.
DeMaria, S., Jr., DeMaria, A. P., Silvay, G., & Flynn, B. C. (2011). Use of the BATHE method in the preanesthetic clinic visit. *Anesthesia & Analgesia*, 113(5), 1020–1026.
Dennison, C. R., McEntee, M. L., Samuel, L., Johnson, B. J., Rotman, S., Kielty, A., & Russell, S. D. (2011). Adequate health literacy is associated with higher heart failure knowledge and self care confidence in hospitalized patients. *Journal of Cardiovascular Nursing*, 26(5), 359–367.
DeSilver, D. (2018). Global inequality: How the U.S. compares. The Pew Research Center. http://www.pewresearch.org/fact-tank/2013/12/19/global-inequality-how-the-u-s-compares/.
DeWall, C. N., MacDonald, G., Webster, G. D., Masten, C. L., Baumeister, R. F., Powell, C., . . . & Eisenberger, N. I. (2010). Acetaminophen reduces social pain: Behavioral and neural evidence. *Psychological Science*, 21(7), 931–937.
Dewe, P. (1991). Primary appraisal, secondary appraisal and coping: Their role in stressful work encounters. *Journal of Occupational and Organizational Psychology*, 64(4), 331–351.
Dewhurst, K. (1966). *Dr. Thomas Sydenham (1624–1689): His life and original writings*. Berkeley, CA: University of California Press
Deyo, R. A. (1994). Magnetic resonance imaging of the lumbar spine—terrific test or tar baby? *New England Journal of Medicine*, 331(2), 115–116.
Deyo, R. A. (2002a). Diagnostic evaluation of LBP: Reaching a specific diagnosis is often impossible. *Archives of Internal Medicine*, 162(13), 1444–1447.
Deyo, R. A. (2002b). Cascade effects of medical technology. *Annual Review of Public Health*, 23(1), 23–44.
Deyo, R. A., Loeser, J. D., & Bigos, S. J. (1990). Herniated lumbar intervertebral disk. *Annals of Internal Medicine*, 112(8), 598–603.
Deyo, R. A., Nachemson, A., & Mirza, S. K. (2004). Spinal-fusion surgery—the case for restraint. *The Spine Journal*, 4(5), S138–S142.
Dijkstra, A., Conijn, B., & De Vries, H. (2006). A match–mismatch test of a stage model of behaviour change in tobacco smoking. *Addiction*, 101(7), 1035–1043.
DiMatteo, M. R. (2004). Variations in patients' adherence to medical recommendations: A quantitative review of 50 years of research. *Medical Care*, 42(3), 200–209.
DiMatteo, M. R., Haskard-Zolnierek, K. B., & Martin, L. R. (2012). Improving patient adherence: A three-factor model to guide practice. *Health Psychology Review*, 6(1), 74–91.
DiMatteo, M. R., Lepper, H. S., & Croghan, T. W. (2000). Depression is a risk factor for noncompliance with medical treatment: Meta-analysis of the effects of anxiety and depression on patient adherence. *Archives of Internal Medicine*, 160(14), 2101–2107.
Direito, A., Dale, L. P., Shields, E., Dobson, R., Whittaker, R., & Maddison, R. (2014). Do physical activity and dietary smartphone applications incorporate evidence-based behaviour change techniques? *BMC Public Health*, 14(1), 646.
Dobbins, M., Husson, H., DeCorby, K., & LaRocca, R. L. (2013, February). School-based physical activity programs for promoting physical activity and fitness in children and adolescents aged 6 to 18. *The Cochrane Database of Systematic Reviews*, 2013(2).
Dobmeyer, A. (2017). *Psychological treatment of medical patients in integrated primary care*. Washington, DC: American Psychological Association.
Doerflinger, R., & Gomez, C. (2017). Kill the pain not the patient: Palliative care versus assisted suicide. United States Conference of Catholic Bishops. http://www.usccb.org/about/pro-life-activities/respect-life-program/killing-the-pain.cfm.
Dolezsar, C. M., McGrath, J. J., Herzig, A. J., & Miller, S. B. (2014). Perceived racial discrimination and hypertension: A comprehensive systematic review. *Health Psychology*, 33(1), 20–34.
Doll, R. (1998). Epidemiological evidence of the effects of behaviour and the environment on the risk of human cancer. In M. Schwab, H. Rabe, K. Munk, & P. H. Hofschneider (Eds.), *Genes and environment in cancer* (pp. 3–21). Berlin, Germany: Springer.
Doll, R., & Hill, A. B. (1950). Smoking and carcinoma of the lung. *British Medical Journal*, 2(4682), 738–748.
Doll, R., & Hill, A. B. (1964). Mortality in relation to smoking: Ten years' observations of British doctors. *British Medical Journal*, 1(5395), 1399–1410.
Donahey, K. M. (2010). Female orgasmic disorder. In S. B. Levine & C. Risen (Eds.), *Handbook of clinical sexuality for mental health professionals* (pp. 181–192). New York, NY: Routledge.
Dornan, T. (2005). Osler, Flexner, apprenticeship and "the new medical education." *Journal of the Royal Society of Medicine*, 98(3), 91–95.
Dorsher, P. T. (2011). Acupuncture for chronic pain. *Techniques in Regional Anesthesia & Pain Management*, 15(2), 55–63.

Douki, S., Zineb, S. B., Nacef, F., & Halbreich, U. (2007). Women's mental health in the Muslim world: Cultural, religious, and social issues. *Journal of Affective Disorders, 102*(1), 177–189.

Doyal, L. (1997). The rationing debate: Rationing within the NHS should be explicit: The case for. *British Medical Journal, 314*(7087), 1114.

Dressler, W. W., Bindon, J. R., & Neggers, Y. H. (1998). John Henryism, gender, and arterial blood pressure in an African American community. *Psychosomatic Medicine, 60*(5), 620–624.

Drinker, P. A., & McKhann, C. F. (1986). The iron lung. *Journal of the American Medical Association, 255*(11), 1476–1480.

Drossman, D. A. (1998). Gastrointestinal illness and the biopsychosocial model. *Psychosomatic Medicine, 60*(3), 258–267.

Drossman, D A. (2013). 2012 David Sun lecture: Helping your patient by helping yourself—how to improve the patient-physician relationship by optimizing communication skills. *The American Journal of Gastroenterology, 108*(4), 521.

Duncan, D. T., & Hatzenbuehler, M. L. (2014). Lesbian, gay, bisexual, and transgender hate crimes and suicidality among a population-based sample of sexual-minority adolescents in Boston. *American Journal of Public Health, 104*(2), 272–278.

Dunn, J. E. (1975). Cancer epidemiology in populations of the United States—with emphasis on Hawaii and California—and Japan. *Cancer Research, 35*(11 Part 2), 3240–3245.

Durkin, S. J., Biener, L., & Wakefield, M. A. (2009). Effects of different types of antismoking ads on reducing disparities in smoking cessation among socioeconomic subgroups. *American Journal of Public Health, 99*(12), 2217–2223.

Duse, G., Davià, G., & White, P. F. (2009). Improvement in psychosocial outcomes in chronic pain patients receiving intrathecal morphine infusions. *Anesthesia & Analgesia, 109*(6), 1981–1986.

Duster, T. (2004). *Backdoor to eugenics*. New York, NY: Routledge.

Dutra, L. M., & Glantz, S. A. (2014). Electronic cigarettes and conventional cigarette use among US adolescents: A cross-sectional study. *JAMA Pediatrics, 168*(7), 610–617.

Dutton, G. R., Tan, F., Provost, B. C., Sorenson, J. L., Allen, B., & Smith, D. (2009). Relationship between self-efficacy and physical activity among patients with type 2 diabetes. *Journal of Behavioral Medicine, 32*(3), 270–277.

Eastwood, M. A. (2017). Heisenberg's uncertainty principle. *QJM: An International Journal of Medicine, 110*(5), 335–336.

Eccleston, C., & Crombez, G. (2007). Worry and chronic pain: A misdirected problem solving model. *Pain, 132*(3), 233–236.

Eccleston, C., Morley, S. J., & Williams, A. D. C. (2013). Psychological approaches to chronic pain management: Evidence and challenges. *British Journal of Anaesthesia, 111*(1), 59–63.

Eddy, D. M. (1983). Finding cancer in asymptomatic people. Estimating the benefits, costs and risks. *Cancer, 51*(S12), 2440–2445.

Edinger, J. D., Wohlgemuth, W. K., Radtke, R. A., Marsh, G. R., & Quillian, R. E. (2001). Does cognitive-behavioral insomnia therapy alter dysfunctional beliefs about sleep? *Sleep, 24*(5), 591–599.

Edwards, L. (2014). *In the kingdom of the sick: A social history of chronic illness in America*. New York, NY: Bloomsbury.

Edwards, R. R., Dworkin, R. H., Sullivan, M. D., Turk, D. C., & Wasan, A. D. (2016). The role of psychosocial processes in the development and maintenance of chronic pain. *Journal of Pain, 17*(9), T70–T92.

Ekirch, A. R. (2006). *At day's close: Night in times past*. New York, NY: W. W. Norton.

Elderkin-Thompson, V., & Waitzkin, H. (1999). Differences in clinical communication by gender. *Journal of General Internal Medicine, 14*(2), 112–121.

Elias, M. F., Elias, P. K., Sullivan, L. M., Wolf, P. A., & D'Agostino, R. B. (2003). Lower cognitive function in the presence of obesity and hypertension: The Framingham heart study. *International Journal of Obesity, 27*(2), 260–268.

Ellis, H. (2002). *A history of surgery*. Cambridge, UK: Cambridge University Press.

Ellison, B., Lusk, J. L., & Davis, D. (2014). The impact of restaurant calorie labels on food choice: Results from a field experiment. *Economic Inquiry, 52*(2), 666–681.

Elmore, J. G., Barton, M. B., Moceri, V. M., Polk, S., Arena, P. J., & Fletcher, S. W. (1998). Ten-year risk of false positive screening mammograms and clinical breast examinations. *New England Journal of Medicine, 338*(16), 1089–1096.

Ely, J. W., Osheroff, J. A., Ebell, M. H., Bergus, G. R., Levy, B. T., Chambliss, M. L., & Evans, E. R. (1999). Analysis of questions asked by family doctors regarding patient care. *British Medical Journal, 319*(7206), 358–361.

Emanuel, E. (2014). *Reinventing American health care: How the Affordable Care Act will improve our terribly complex, blatantly unjust, outrageously expensive, grossly inefficient, error prone system*. New York, NY: Public Affairs.

Emanuel, E. J., & Gudbranson, E. (2018). Does medicine overemphasize IQ? *Journal of the American Medical Association, 319*(7), 651–652.

Emons, W. H., Meijer, R. R., & Denollet, J. (2007). Negative affectivity and social inhibition in cardiovascular disease: Evaluating type-D personality and its assessment using item response theory. *Journal of Psychosomatic Research, 63*(1), 27–39.

Engel, G. L. (1959). "Psychogenic" pain and the pain-prone patient. *American Journal of Medicine, 26*(6), 899–918.

Engel, G. L. (1977). The need for a new medical model: A challenge for biomedicine. *Science, 196*(4286), 129–136.

Engler, B. (2013). *Personality theories*. Belmont, CA: Wadsworth.

Epston, D., Morris, F., & Maisel, R. (1995). A narrative approach to so-called anorexia/bulimia. *Journal of Feminist Family Therapy, 7*(1–2), 69–96.

Esparza-Romero, J., Valencia, M. E., Urquidez-Romero, R., Chaudhari, L. S., Hanson, R. L., Knowler, W. C., . . . & Schulz, L. O. (2015). Environmentally driven increases in type 2 diabetes and obesity in Pima Indians and non-Pimas in Mexico over a 15-year period: The Maycoba Project. *Diabetes Care, 38*, 2075–2082.

Eysenck, H. J. (1994). Cancer, personality and stress: Prediction and prevention. *Advances in Behaviour Research and Therapy, 16*(3), 167–215.

Eysenck, H. J. (2017). *The biological basis of personality*. London, UK: Routledge.

Faber, T., Been, J. V., Reiss, I. K., Mackenbach, J. P., & Sheikh, A. (2016). Smoke-free legislation and child health. *NPJ Primary Care Respiratory Medicine, 26*, 16067.

Fagerstrom, K. O., & Schneider, N. G. (1989). Measuring nicotine dependence: A review of the Fagerstrom Tolerance Questionnaire. *Journal of Behavioral Medicine, 12*(2), 159–182.

Falbe, J., Thompson, H. R., Becker, C. M., Rojas, N., McCulloch, C. E., & Madsen, K. A. (2016). Impact of the Berkeley excise tax on sugar-sweetened beverage consumption. *American Journal of Public Health, 106*(10), 1865–1871.

Farrelly, M. C., Pechacek, T. F., Thomas, K. Y., & Nelson, D. (2008). The impact of tobacco control programs on adult smoking. *American Journal of Public Health, 98*(2), 304–309.

Farsalinos, K., & Polosa, R. (2014). Safety evaluation and risk assessment of electronic cigarettes as tobacco cigarette substitutes: A systematic review. *Therapeutic Advances in Drug Safety, 5*(2), 67–86.

Faulconbridge, L. F., Wadden, T. A. (2010). Managing the obesity epidemic. In J. Suls, K. W. Davidson, & R. K. Kaplan (Eds.), *Handbook of health psychology and behavioral medicine* (pp. 508–526). New York, NY: Guilford Press.

Favreau, H., Bacon, S. L., Labrecque, M., & Lavoie, K. L. (2014). Prospective impact of panic disorder and panic-anxiety on asthma control, health service use, and quality of life in adult patients with asthma over a 4-year follow-up. *Psychosomatic Medicine, 76*(2), 147–155.

Feldman, J. M., Matte, L., Interian, A., Lehrer, P. M., Lu, S. E., Scheckner, B., . . . & Shim, C. (2016). Psychological treatment of comorbid asthma and panic disorder in Latino adults: Results from a randomized controlled trial. *Behaviour Research and Therapy, 87*, 142–154.

Felitti, V. J., Anda, R. F., Nordenberg, D., Williamson, D. F., Spitz, A. M., Edwards, V., . . . & Marks, J. S. (1998). Relationship of childhood abuse and household dysfunction to many of the leading causes of death in adults: The adverse childhood experiences (ACE) study. *American Journal of Preventive Medicine, 14*(4), 245–258.

Feng, X., Keenan, K., Hipwell, A. E., Henneberger, A. K., Rischall, M. S., Butch, J., . . . & Babinski, D. E. (2009). Longitudinal associations between emotion regulation and depression in preadolescent girls: Moderation by the caregiving environment. *Developmental Psychology, 45*(3), 79–808.

Fenster, J. M., & Fenster, J. M. (2001). *Ether day: The strange tale of America's greatest medical discovery and the haunted men who made it*. New York, NY: HarperCollins Publishers.

Fernando, R. L., Nettleton, D., Southey, B. R., Dekkers, J. C. M., Rothschild, M. F., & Soller, M. (2004). Controlling the proportion of false positives in multiple dependent tests. *Genetics, 166*(1), 611–619.

Fichtenberg, C. M., & Glantz, S. A. (2000). Association of the California Tobacco Control Program with declines in cigarette consumption and mortality from heart disease. *New England Journal of Medicine, 343*(24), 1772–1777.

Fichtenberg, C. M., & Glantz, S. A. (2002). Effect of smoke-free workplaces on smoking behaviour: Systematic review. *British Medical Journal, 325*(7357), 188–195.

Finer, L. B., & Zolna, M. R. (2011). Unintended pregnancy in the United States: Incidence and disparities, 2006. *Contraception, 84*(5), 478–485.

Finneran, C., & Stephenson, R., (2013). Intimate partner violence among men who have sex with men: A systematic review. *Trauma, Violence, & Abuse, 14*(2), 168–185.

Fiore, M. C., Smith, S. S., Jorenby, D. E., & Baker, T. B. (1994). The effectiveness of the nicotine patch for smoking cessation: A meta-analysis. *Journal of the American Medical Association, 271*(24), 1940–1947.

Fischer, M. A., Stedman, M. R., Lii, J., Vogeli, C., Shrank, W. H., Brookhart, M. A., & Weissman, J. S. (2010). Primary medication non-adherence: Analysis of 195,930 electronic prescriptions. *Journal of General Internal Medicine, 25*(4), 284–290.

Fischer, P. M., Schwartz, M. P., Richards, J. W., Goldstein, A. O., & Rojas, T. H. (1991). Brand logo recognition by children aged 3 to 6 years: Mickey Mouse and Old Joe the Camel. *JAMA, 266*(22), 3145–3148.

Fishbein, M. (Ed.). (1967). *Readings in attitude theory and measurement*. New York, NY: John Wiley & Sons.

Fitting, M., Rabins, P., Lucas, M. J., & Eastham, J. (1986). Caregivers for dementia patients: A comparison of husbands and wives. *The Gerontologist, 26*(3), 248–252.

Flack, J. M., Ference, B. A., & Levy, P. (2015). Hypertension in African Americans. In K. C. Ferdinand (Ed.), *Hypertension in high risk African Americans* (pp. 233–249). New York, NY: Humana Press.

Flegal, K. M., Kruszon-Moran, D., Carroll, M. D., Fryar, C. D., & Ogden, C. L. (2016). Trends in obesity among adults in the United States, 2005 to 2014. *Journal of the American Medical Association, 315*(21), 2284–2291.

Flegal, K. M., & Troiano, R. P. (2000). Changes in the distribution of body mass index of adults and children in the US population. *International Journal of Obesity, 24*(7), 807–818.

Fleming, M. F., Barry, K. L., Manwell, L. B., Johnson, K., & London, R. (1997). Brief physician advice for problem alcohol drinkers: A randomized controlled trial in community-based primary care practices. *Journal of the American Medical Association, 277*(13), 1039–1045.

Fletcher-Lartey, S., Yee, M., Gaarslev, C., & Khan, R. (2016). Why do general practitioners prescribe antibiotics for upper respiratory tract infections to meet patient expectations: A mixed methods study. *BMJ Open, 6*(10), e012244.

Flor, H., Turk, D. C., & Scholz, O. B. (1987). Impact of chronic pain on the spouse: Marital, emotional and physical consequences. *Journal of Psychosomatic Research, 31*(1), 63–71.

Flores, G. (2006). Language barriers to health care in the United States. *New England Journal of Medicine, 355*(3), 229–231.

Flores, G., Laws, M. B., Mayo, S. J., Zuckerman, B., Abreu, M., Medina, L., & Hardt, E. J. (2003). Errors in medical interpretation and their potential clinical consequences in pediatric encounters. *Pediatrics, 111*(1), 6–14.

Fongwa, M. N., Cunningham, W., Weech-Maldonado, R., Gutierrez, P. R., & Hays, R. D. (2008). Reports and ratings of care: Black and white Medicare enrollees. *Journal of Health Care for the Poor and Underserved, 19*(4), 1136–1147.

Fordyce, W. E., Fowler, R. S., Lehmann, J. F., & Delateur, B. J. (1968). Some implications of learning in problems of chronic pain. *Journal of Chronic Diseases, 21*(3), 179–190.

Fordyce, W. E., Fowler, R., Lehmann, J. F., Delateur, B. J., Sand, P. L., & Trieschmann, R. B. (1973). Operant conditioning in the treatment of chronic pain. *Archives of Physical Medicine and Rehabilitation, 54*(9), 399–408.

Fordyce, W. E., Lansky, D., Calsyn, D. A., Shelton, J. L., Stolov, W. C., & Rock, D. L. (1984). Pain measurement and pain behavior. *Pain, 18*(1), 53–69.

Fordyce, W. E., Shelton, J. L., & Dundore, D. E. (1982). The modification of avoidance learning pain behaviors. *Journal of Behavioral Medicine, 5*(4), 405–414.

Fordyce, W. E., & Steger, J. C. (1979). Chronic pain. In O. Pomerleau & J. P. Brady (Eds.), *Behavioral medicine: Theory and practice* (pp. 125–153). Baltimore, MD: Williams & Wilkins.

Forhan, S. E., Gottlieb, S. L., Sternberg, M. R., Xu, F., Datta, S. D., McQuillan, G. M., . . . & Markowitz, L. E. (2009). Prevalence of sexually transmitted infections among female adolescents aged 14 to 19 in the United States. *Pediatrics, 124*(6), 1505–1512.

Forman, E. M., Hoffman, K. L., Juarascio, A. S., Butryn, M. L., & Herbert, J. D. (2013). Comparison of acceptance-based and standard cognitive-based coping strategies for craving sweets in overweight and obese women. *Eating Behaviors, 14*(1), 64–68.

Forman, E. M., Hoffman, K. L., McGrath, K. B., Herbert, J. D., Brandsma, L. L., & Lowe, M. R. (2007). A comparison of acceptance- and control-based strategies for coping with food cravings: An analog study. *Behaviour Research and Therapy, 45*(10), 2372–2386.

Foster, G. D., Wadden, T. A., Vogt, R. A., & Brewer, G. (1997). What is a reasonable weight loss? Patients' expectations and evaluations of obesity treatment outcomes. *Journal of Consulting and Clinical Psychology, 65*(1), 79–85.

Fox, R. C. (2017). *Spare parts: Organ replacement in American society*. New York, NY: Routledge.

Frank, G., Blackhall, L. J., Michel, V., Murphy, S. T., Azen, S. P., & Park, K. (1998). A discourse of relationships in bioethics: Patient autonomy and end-of-life decision making among elderly Korean Americans. *Medical Anthropology Quarterly, 12*(4), 403–423.

Fraser Institute (2017). Waiting Your Turn: Wait Times for Health Care in Canada, 2017 Report. https://www.fraserinstitute.org/studies/waiting-your-turn-wait-times-for-health-care-in-canada-2017.

Frazer, K., Callinan, J. E., McHugh, J., van Baarsel, S., Clarke, A., Doherty, K., & Kelleher, C. (2016, February). Legislative smoking bans for reducing harms from secondhand smoke exposure, smoking prevalence and tobacco consumption. *The Cochrane Database System Review*.

Fredrickson, B. L. (2001). The role of positive emotions in positive psychology: The broaden-and-build theory of positive emotions. *American Psychologist, 56*(3), 218–226.

Fredrickson, B. L. (2005). The broaden-and-build theory of positive emotions. *Philosophical Transactions of the Royal Society B: Biological Sciences, 359*(1449), 1367.

Fredrickson, B. L., & Branigan, C. (2005). Positive emotions broaden the scope of attention and thought-action repertoires. *Cognition & Emotion, 19*(3), 313–332.

Frieden, T. R., & Blakeman, D. E. (2005). The dirty dozen: 12 myths that undermine tobacco control. *American Journal of Public Health, 95*(9), 1500–1505.

Friedman, E. (2011). The law that changed everything—and it isn't the one you think. *Hospitals and Health Networks Online.* http://emilyfriedman.com/columns/2011-04-05-emtala.html.

Friedman, L. S., Hedeker, D., & Richter, E. D. (2009). Long-term effects of repealing the national maximum speed limit in the United States. *American Journal of Public Health, 99*(9), 1626–1631.

Friedman, M., & Rosenman, R. H. (1959). Association of specific overt behavior pattern with blood and cardiovascular findings: Blood cholesterol level, blood clotting time, incidence of arcus senilis, and clinical coronary artery disease. *Journal of the American Medical Association, 169*(12), 1286–1296.

Friedman, T. (2007). *The world is flat 3.0.* New York, NY: Picador.

Frohlich, K. L., Potvin, L., Chabot, P., & Corin, E. (2002). A theoretical and empirical analysis of context: Neighbourhoods, smoking and youth. *Social Science & Medicine, 54*(9), 1401–1417.

Frohlich, K. L., Potvin, L., Gauvin, L., & Chabot, P. (2002). Youth smoking initiation: Disentangling context from composition. *Health & Place, 8*(3), 155–166.

Fukuda, H., & Mizobe, M. (2017). Impact of nonadherence on complication risks and healthcare costs in patients newly-diagnosed with diabetes. *Diabetes Research and Clinical Practice, 123*, 55–62.

Fuller-Tyszkiewicz, M., Krawczyk, R., Ricciardelli, L., & Thompson, J. K. (2013). Eating and weight-related disorders. In M. V. Spiers, P. A. Geller, & J. D. Kloss (Eds.), *Women's Health Psychology* (pp. 173–198). Hoboken, NJ: John Wiley & Sons.

Funk, S. C. (1992). Hardiness: A review of theory and research. *Health psychology, 11*(5), 335–345.

Gaertner, J., Elsner, F., Pollmann-Dahmen, K., Radbruch, L., & Sabatowski, R. (2004). Electronic pain diary: A randomized crossover study. *Journal of Pain Symptom Management, 28*(3), 259–267.

Galanti, G. A. (2002). *Caring for patients from different cultures.* Philadelphia, PA: University of Pennsylvania Press.

Galea, S., Tracy, M., Hoggatt, K. J., DiMaggio, C., & Karpati, A. (2011). Estimated deaths attributable to social factors in the United States. *American Journal of Public Health, 101*(8), 1456–1465.

Galvez, M. P., Morland, K., Raines, C., Kobil, J., Siskind, J., Godbold, J., & Brenner, B. (2008). Race and food store availability in an inner-city neighbourhood. *Public Health Nutrition, 11*(6), 624–631.

Gardiner, P. S. (2004). The African Americanization of menthol cigarette use in the United States. *Nicotine & Tobacco Research, 6*(Suppl_1), S55–S65.

Gardner, R. M., Stark, K., Friedman, B. N., & Jackson, N. A. (2000). Predictors of eating disorder scores in children ages 6 through 14: A longitudinal study. *Journal of Psychosomatic Research, 49*(3), 199–205.

Gaskin, D. J., & Richard, P. (2012). The economic costs of pain in the United States. *Journal of Pain, 13*(8), 715–724.

Gatchel, R. J. (2005). *Clinical essentials of pain management.* Washington, DC: American Psychological Association.

Gatchel, R. J., McGeary, D. D., McGeary, C. A., & Lippe, B. (2014). Interdisciplinary chronic pain management: Past, present, and future. *American Psychologist, 69*(2), 119–130.

Gatchel, R. J., Polatin, P. B., Mayer, T. G., & Garcy, P. D. (1994). Psychopathology and the rehabilitation of patients with chronic low back pain disability. *Archives of Physical Medicine and Rehabilitation, 75*(6), 666–670.

Gates, G. J. (2011). *How many people are lesbian, gay, bisexual and transgender?* Los Angeles, CA: The Williams Institute of the University of California, Los Angeles School of Law.

Gearhardt, A. N., Bragg, M. A., Pearl, R. L., Schvey, N. A., Roberto, C. A., & Brownell, K. D. (2012). Obesity and public policy. *Annual Review of Clinical Psychology, 8*, 405–430.

Geliebter, A., Ladell, T., Logan, M., Schweider, T., Sharafi, M., & Hirsch, J. (2006). Responsivity to food stimuli in obese and lean binge eaters using functional MRI. *Appetite, 46*(1), 31–35.

Geyman, J. P. (2015). *How Obamacare is unsustainable: Why we need a single-payer solution for all Americans.* Copernicus Healthcare. http://copernicus-healthcare.org/.

Gilfillan, R. J., Tomcavage, J., Rosenthal, M. B., Davis, D. E., Graham, J., Roy, J. A., . . . & Weikel, K. M. (2010). Value and the medical home: Effects of transformed primary care. *The American Journal of Managed Care, 16*(8), 607–661.

Gillespie, C. (2013). Guinea pig meat salmonella outbreak sickens 81 in Minneapolis. *Food Poisoning Bulletin.* https://foodpoisoningbulletin.com/2013/guinea-pig-meat-salmonella-outbreak-sickens-81-in-minneapolis.

Gilson, L. (2003). Trust and the development of health care as a social institution. *Social Science & Medicine, 56*(7), 1453–1468.

Gladwell, M. (2006). *The tipping point: How little things can make a big difference.* New York, NY: Little, Brown.

Glover, N. G., Sylvers, P. D., Shearer, E. M., Kane, M. C., Clasen, P. C., Epler, A. J., . . . & Jakupcak, M. (2016). The efficacy of focused Acceptance and Commitment Therapy in VA primary care. *Psychological Services, 13*(2), 156.1541–1559.

Gloy, V. L., Briel, M., Bhatt, D. L., Kashyap, S. R., Schauer, P. R., Mingrone, G., . . . & Nordmann, A. J. (2013). Bariatric surgery versus non-surgical treatment for obesity: A systematic review and meta-analysis of randomised controlled trials. *British Medical Journal, 347*, f5934.

Goetz, S. (2013). Salmonella outbreak linked to N.C. Holiday Inn sickened 100, final report says. *Food Safety News.* https://www.foodsafetynews.com/2013/07/salmonella-outbreak-linked-to-north-carolina-holiday-sickened-100-final-report-says/.

Goldstein, A. O., Sobel, R. A., & Newman, G. R. (1999). Tobacco and alcohol use in G-rated children's animated films. *Journal of the American Medical Association, 281*(12), 1131–1136.

Goldstein, B. I., Carnethon, M. R., Matthews, K. A., McIntyre, R. S., Miller, G. E., Raghuveer, G., . . . & McCrindle, B. W. (2015). Major depressive disorder and bipolar disorder predispose youth to accelerated atherosclerosis and early cardiovascular disease: A scientific statement from the American Heart Association. *Circulation, 132*(10), 965–986.

Goodale, I. L., Domar, A. D., & Benson, H. (1990). Alleviation of premenstrual syndrome symptoms with the relaxation response. *Obstetrics and Gynecology 75*(4), 649–655.

Goodman, R. D., & Goodman, B. (1999). The lost children of Rockdale County. *Frontline.* https://www.pbs.org/wgbh/pages/frontline/shows/georgia/.

Goodrich, D. E., & Kilbourne, A. M. (2010). A long time coming: The creation of an evidence base for physical activity prescription to improve health outcomes in bipolar disorder. *Mental Health and Physical Activity, 3*(1), 1.

Gottman, J. M. (2013). *Marital interaction: Experimental investigations.* New York, NY: Elsevier.

Gottman, J. M., & Notarius, C. I. (2002). Marital research in the 20th century and a research agenda for the 21st century. *Family Process, 41*(2), 159–197.

Gould, J. B. (2009). From paradox to disparity: Trends in neonatal death in very low birth weight non-Hispanic black and white infants, 1989–2004. *Journal of Pediatrics, 155*(4), 482–487.

Goyal, M., Haythornthwaite, J., Levine, D., Becker, D., Vaidya, D., Hill-Briggs, F., & Ford, D. (2010). Intensive meditation for refractory pain and symptoms. *Journal of Alternative and Complementary Medicine, 16*(6), 627–631.

Goyal, M., Singh, S., Sibinga, E. M., Gould, N. F., Rowland-Seymour, A., Sharma, R., . . . & Ranasinghe, P. D. (2014). Meditation programs for psychological stress and well-being: A systematic review and meta-analysis. *JAMA Internal Medicine, 174*(3), 357–368.

Graham, C. A. (2010). The DSM diagnostic criteria for female orgasmic disorder. *Archives of Sexual Behavior, 39*(2), 256–270.

Grana, R., Benowitz, N., & Glantz, S. A. (2014). E-cigarettes: A scientific review. *Circulation, 129*(19), 1972–1986.

Granath, J., Ingvarsson, S., von Thiele, U., & Lundberg, U. (2006). Stress management: A randomized study of cognitive behavioural therapy and yoga. *Cognitive Behaviour Therapy, 35*(1), 3–10.

Grant, J. M., Mottet, L. A., Tanis, J., Herman, J. L., Harrison, J., & Keisling, M. (2010). *National transgender discrimination survey report on health and health care.* Washington, DC: National Center for Transgender Equality and the National Gay and Lesbian Task Force.

Graziottin, A., & Leiblum, S. R. (2005). Biological and psychosocial pathophysiology of female sexual dysfunction during the menopausal transition. *Journal of Sexual Medicine, 2*(s3), 133–145.

Greeff, A. P., & Conradie, W. S. (1998). Use of progressive relaxation training for chronic alcoholics with insomnia. *Psychological Reports, 82*(2), 407–412.

Green, A. R., Carney, D. R., Pallin, D. J., Ngo, L. H., Raymond, K. L., Iezzoni, L. I., & Banaji, M. R. (2007). Implicit bias among physicians and its prediction of thrombolysis decisions for black and white patients. *Journal of General Internal Medicine, 22*(9), 1231–1238.

Greenwald, A. G., McGhee, D. E., & Schwartz, J. L. (1998). Measuring individual differences in implicit cognition: The implicit association test. *Journal of Personality and Social Psychology, 74*(6), 1464.

Gresser, U., & Gleiter, C. H. (2002). Erectile dysfunction: Comparison of efficacy and side effects of the PDE-5 inhibitors sildenafil, vardenafil and tadalafil-review of the literature. *European Journal of Medical Research, 7*(10), 435–446.

Griffith, M. A., Dubow, E. F., & Ippolito, M. F. (2000). Developmental and cross-situational differences in adolescents' coping strategies. *Journal of Youth and Adolescence, 29*(2), 183–204.

Griggs, J. J., Sorbero, M. E., Stark, A. T., Heininger, S. E., & Dick, A. W. (2003). Racial disparity in the dose and dose intensity of breast cancer adjuvant chemotherapy. *Breast Cancer Research and Treatment, 81*(1), 21–31.

Griswold, K. S., Homish, G. G., Pastore, P. A., & Leonard, K. E. (2010). A randomized trial: Are care navigators effective in connecting patients to primary care after psychiatric crisis? *Community Mental Health Journal, 46*(4), 398–402.

Groopman J. (2010, February 11). Health care: Who knows best? *New York Review of Books, 57*(2).

Groopman, J., & Hartzband, P. (2017, July 13). Putting patients ahead of profits. *New York Review of Books, 64*(12).

Gu, J., Strauss, C., Bond, R., & Cavanagh, K. (2015). How do mindfulness-based cognitive therapy and mindfulness-based stress reduction improve mental health and wellbeing? A systematic review and meta-analysis of mediation studies. *Clinical Psychology Review, 37,* 1–12.

Guiney, H., & Machado, L. (2013). Benefits of regular aerobic exercise for executive functioning in healthy populations. *Psychonomic Bulletin & Review, 20*(1), 73–86.

Guo, G., Jia, K. R., Shi, Y., Liu, X. F., Liu, K. Y., Qi, W., . . . & Zou, Q. M. (2009). Psychological stress enhances the colonization of the stomach by Helicobacter pylori in the BALB/c mouse. *Stress, 12*(6), 478–485.

Gutgsell, T., Walsh, D., Zhukovsky, D. S., Gonzales, F., & Lagman, R. (2003). A prospective study of the pathophysiology and clinical characteristics of pain in a palliative medicine population. *American Journal of Hospice and Palliative Medicine, 20*(2), 140–148.

Haza, C., & Shaver, P. (1987). Romantic love conceptualized as an attachment process. *Journal of Personality and Social Psychology, 52*(3), 511–524.

Haas, J. S., Earle, C. C., Orav, J. E., Brawarsky, P., Keohane, M., Neville, B. A., & Williams, D. R. (2008). Racial segregation and disparities in breast cancer care and mortality. *Cancer, 113*(8), 2166–2172.

Håberg, S. E., Bentdal, Y. E., London, S. J., Kvaerner, K. J., Nystad, W., & Nafstad, P. (2010). Prenatal and postnatal parental smoking and acute otitis media in early childhood. *Acta Paediatrica, 99*(1), 99–105.

Hagger, M. S., Chatzisarantis, N. L., & Biddle, S. J. (2002). A meta-analytic review of the theories of reasoned action and planned behavior in physical activity: Predictive validity and the contribution of additional variables. *Journal of Sport and Exercise Psychology, 24*(1), 3–32.

Hairston, I. S., Talbot, L. S., Eidelman, P., Gruber, J., & Harvey, A. G. (2010). Sensory gating in primary insomnia. *European Journal of Neuroscience, 31*(11), 2112–2121.

Haley, J. (1987). *Problem-Solving Therapy*. San Francisco: Jossey-Bass.

Hall, J. A., & Roter, D. L. (2002). Do patients talk differently to male and female physicians? A meta-analytic review. *Patient Education and Counseling, 48*(3), 217–224.

Hall, P. A., & Fong, G. T. (2015). Temporal self-regulation theory: A neurobiologically informed model for physical activity behavior. *Frontiers in Human Neuroscience, 9*, 117.

Hall, S. M., & Prochaska, J. J. (2009). Treatment of smokers with co-occurring disorders: Emphasis on integration in mental health and addiction treatment settings. *Annual Review of Clinical Psychology, 5*, 409–431.

Hallett, C. (2005). The attempt to understand puerperal fever in the eighteenth and early nineteenth centuries: The influence of inflammation theory. *Medical History, 49*(1), 1–28.

Hamine, S., Gerth-Guyette, E., Faulx, D., Green, B. B., & Ginsburg, A. S. (2015). Impact of mHealth chronic disease management on treatment adherence and patient outcomes: A systematic review. *Journal of Medical Internet Research, 17*(2).

Hammond, D., Fong, G. T., Borland, R., Cummings, K. M., McNeill, A., & Driezen, P. (2007). Text and graphic warnings on cigarette packages: Findings from the international tobacco control four country study. *American Journal of Preventive Medicine, 32*(3), 202–209.

Hammond, D., Fong, G. T., McDonald, P. W., Cameron, R., & Brown, K. S. (2003). Impact of the graphic Canadian warning labels on adult smoking behaviour. *Tobacco Control, 12*(4), 391–395.

Hanson, J. D., Larson, M. E., & Snowdon, C. T. (1976). The effects of control over high intensity noise on plasma cortisol levels in rhesus monkeys. *Behavioral Biology, 16*(3), 333–340.

Harrington, J. M. (1994). Shift work and health: A critical review of the literature on working hours. *Annals of the Academy of Medicine, Singapore, 23*(5), 699–705.

Harris, P. R., Mayle, K., Mabbott, L., & Napper, L. (2007). Self-affirmation reduces smokers' defensiveness to graphic on-pack cigarette warning labels. *Health Psychology, 26*(4), 437–446.

Hartzband, P., & Groopman, J. (2009). Money and the changing culture of medicine. *New England Journal of Medicine, 360*(2), 101–103.

Hartzband, P., & Groopman, J. (2016). Medical Taylorism. *New England Journal of Medicine, 374*(2), 106–108.

Harrison, A. E., & Silenzio, V. M. (1996). Comprehensive care of lesbian and gay patients and families. *Primary Care: Clinics in Office Practice, 23*(1), 31–46.

Harvey, A. G. (2002). A cognitive model of insomnia. *Behaviour Research and Therapy, 40*(8), 869–893.

Harvey, A. G., Bélanger, L., Talbot, L., Eidelman, P., Beaulieu-Bonneau, S., Fortier-Brochu, É., . . . & Mérette, C. (2014). Comparative efficacy of behavior therapy, cognitive therapy, and cognitive behavior therapy for chronic insomnia: A randomized controlled trial. *Journal of Consulting and Clinical Psychology, 82*(4), 670–83.

Harvey, J. N. (2015). Psychosocial interventions for the diabetic patient. *Diabetes, Metabolic Syndrome and Obesity: Targets and Therapy, 8*, 29–43.

Harvey, J. N., & Lawson, V. L. (2009). The importance of health belief models in determining self-care behaviour in diabetes. *Diabetic Medicine, 26*(1), 5–13.

Hauptman, J., Lucas, C., Boldrin, M. N., Collins, H., & Segal, K. R. (2000). Orlistat in the long-term treatment of obesity in primary care settings. *Archives of Family Medicine, 9*(2), 160–167.

Haus, E., & Smolensky, M. (2006). Biological clocks and shift work: Circadian dysregulation and potential long-term effects. *Cancer Causes & Control, 17*(4), 489–500.

Hausswolff-Juhlin, V., Bjartveit, M., Lindström, E., & Jones, P. (2009). Schizophrenia and physical health problems. *Acta Psychiatrica Scandinavica, 119*(s438), 15–21.

Hawley, K. L., Roberto, C. A., Bragg, M. A., Liu, P. J., Schwartz, M. B., & Brownell, K. D. (2013). The science on front-of-package food labels. *Public Health Nutrition, 16*(3), 430–439.

Hawton, K., Catalan, J., & Fagg, J. (1992). Sex therapy for erectile dysfunction: Characteristics of couples, treatment outcome, and prognostic factors. *Archives of Sexual Behavior*, 21(2), 161–175.

Hay, J. (1931). A British Medical Association lecture on the significance of a raised blood pressure. *British Medical Journal*, 2(3679), 43–47.

Hayes, S. C., & Shenk, C. (2004). Operationalizing mindfulness without unnecessary attachments. *Clinical Psychology: Science and Practice*, 11(3), 249–254.

Hayes, S. C., Strosahl, K. D., & Wilson, K. G. (2012). *Acceptance and commitment therapy*. New York, NY: Guilford Press.

Haynes, R. B., Taylor, D. W., & Sackett, D. L. (Eds.). (1979). *Compliance in health care*. Baltimore, MD: Johns Hopkins University Press, 1979

Hazan, C., & Shaver, P. (1987). Romantic love conceptualized as an attachment process. *Journal of Personality and Social Psychology*, 52(3), 511–524.

Heim, C., & Binder, E. B. (2012). Current research trends in early life stress and depression: Review of human studies on sensitive periods, gene–environment interactions, and epigenetics. *Experimental Neurology*, 233(1), 102–111.

Heine, S. (2015). *Cross-Cultural Psychology* (3rd ed.). New York, NY: W. W. Norton.

Helman, C. G. (1987). Heart disease and the cultural construction of time: The type A behaviour pattern as a Western culture-bound syndrome. *Social Science & Medicine*, 25(9), 969–979.

Henry, D., McClellen, D., Rosenthal, L., Dedrick, D., & Gosdin, M. (2008). Is sleep really for sissies? Understanding the role of work in insomnia in the US. *Social Science & Medicine*, 66(3), 715–726.

Herbenick, D., Reece, M., Sanders, S., Dodge, B., Ghassemi, A., & Fortenberry, J. D. (2009). Prevalence and characteristics of vibrator use by women in the United States: Results from a nationally representative study. *Journal of Sexual Medicine*, 6(7), 1857–1866.

Herbert, J. D., & Brandsma, L. L. (2015). Understanding and enhancing psychological acceptance. In Lynn, S. J. O'Donohue, W. T., & Lilenfeld, S. O. (Eds.), *Health, happiness, and well-being: Better living through psychological science* (pp. 62–88). Los Angeles, CA: Sage.

Herbert, J. D., & Forman, E. M. (2013). Caution: The differences between CT and ACT may be larger (and smaller) than they appear. *Behavior Therapy*, 44(2), 218–223.

Herbig, P. A., & Palumbo, F. A. (1994). Karoshi: Salaryman sudden death syndrome. *Journal of Managerial Psychology*, 9(7), 11–16.

Herpertz-Dahlmann, B., Hebebrand, J., Müller, B., Herpertz, S., Heussen, N., & Remschmidt, H. (2001). Prospective 10-year follow-up in adolescent anorexia nervosa—course, outcome, psychiatric comorbidity, and psychosocial adaptation. *Journal of Child Psychology and Psychiatry and Allied Disciplines*, 42(5), 603–612.

Herzlinger, R. E., & Parsa-Parsi, R. (2004). Consumer-driven health care: Lessons from Switzerland. *Journal of the American Medical Association*, 292(10), 1213–1220.

Hill, A. B. (1965). The environment and disease: Association or causation? *Proceedings of the Royal Society of Medicine*, 58, 295–300.

Hilsman, R., & Garber, J. (1995). A test of the cognitive diathesis-stress model of depression in children: Academic stressors, attributional style, perceived competence, and control. *Journal of Personality & Social Psychology*, 69, 370–380.

Hinote, B. P., & Wasserman, J. A. (2016). *Social and behavioral science for health professionals*. Lanham, MD: Rowman & Littlefield.

Hinton, D. E., Pich, V., Chhean, D., & Pollack, M. H. (2005). "The ghost pushes you down": Sleep paralysis-type panic attacks in a Khmer refugee population. *Transcultural Psychiatry*, 42(1), 46–77.

Hirshbein, L. D. (2015). *Smoking privileges: Psychiatry, the mentally ill, and the tobacco industry in America*. New Brunswick, NJ: Rutgers University Press.

Hiscock, R., Bauld, L., Amos, A., Fidler, J. A., & Munafò, M. (2012). Socioeconomic status and smoking: A review. *Annals of the New York Academy of Sciences*, 1248(1), 107–123.

Hitsman, B., Borrelli, B., McChargue, D. E., Spring, B., & Niaura, R. (2003). History of depression and smoking cessation outcome: A meta-analysis. *Journal of Consulting and Clinical Psychology*, 71(4), 657–663.

Hoar, M. (2015). *Racial microaggressions: Relationship to cardiovascular reactivity and affect among Hispanic/Latinos and non-Hispanic whites*. Dallas, TX: University of North Texas Press.

Hoek, H. W. (2006). Incidence, prevalence and mortality of anorexia nervosa and other eating disorders. *Current Opinion in Psychiatry*, 19(4), 389–394.

Hoek, H. W., & van Hoeken, D. (2003). Review of the prevalence and incidence of eating disorders. *International Journal of Eating Disorders*, 34(4), 383–396.

Hoffman, B. (2008). Health care reform and social movements in the United States. *American Journal of Public Health*, 98(Supplement_1), S69–S79.

Hollenbach, J. P., Schifano, E. D., Hammel, C., & Cloutier, M. M. (2017). Exposure to secondhand smoke and asthma severity among children in Connecticut. *PloS One*, 12(3), e0174541.

Holmes, T. H., & Rahe, R. H. (1967). The social readjustment rating scale. *Journal of Psychosomatic Research*, 11(2), 213–218.

Holt-Lunstad, J., Smith, T. B., & Layton, J. B. (2010). Social relationships and mortality risk: A meta-analytic review. *PLoS Medicine*, 7(7), e1000316.

Honjo, K. (2004). Social epidemiology: Definition, history, and research examples. *Environmental Health and Preventive Medicine*, 9(5), 19–199.

Hooley, J. M. (2007). Expressed emotion and relapse of psychopathology. *Annual Review of Clinical Psychology*, 3, 329–352.

Howell, E. A., Hebert, P., Chatterjee, S., Kleinman, L. C., & Chassin, M. R. (2008). Black/white differences in very low birth weight: Neonatal mortality rates among New York City hospitals. *Pediatrics*, 121(3), e407-e415.

Hruby, A., & Hu, F. B. (2015). The epidemiology of obesity: A big picture. *Pharmacoeconomics*, 33(7), 673–689.

Hruby, A., Manson, J. E., Qi, L., Malik, V. S., Rimm, E. B., Sun, Q., . . . & Hu, F. B. (2016). Determinants and consequences of obesity. *American Journal of Public Health*, 106(9), 1656–1662.

Hudson, J. I., Hiripi, E., Pope, H. G., & Kessler, R. C. (2007). The prevalence and correlates of eating disorders in the National Comorbidity Survey Replication. *Biological Psychiatry*, 61(3), 348–358.

Huffmyer, J. L., & Kirk, S. E. (2017). Professionalism: The "forgotten" core competency. *Anesthesia and Analgesia*, 125(2), 378.

Hufford, M. R., Witkiewitz, K., Shields, A. L., Kodya, S., & Caruso, J. C. (2003). Relapse as a nonlinear dynamic system: Application to patients with alcohol use disorders. *Journal of Abnormal Psychology*, 112(2), 219–227.

Hughes, J. R., Higgins, S. T., & Bickel, W. K. (1994). Nicotine withdrawal versus other drug withdrawal syndromes: Similarities and dissimilarities. *Addiction*, 89(11), 1461–1470.

Hughes, L. S., Clark, J., Colclough, J. A., Dale, E., & McMillan, D. (2017). Acceptance and Commitment Therapy (ACT) for Chronic Pain. *Clinical Journal of Pain*, 33(6), 552–568.

Hunter, J., & Maunder, R. (Eds.). (2015). *Improving patient treatment with attachment theory: A guide for primary care practitioners and specialists.* New York, NY: Springer.

Hunter, M., & Philips, C. (1981). The experience of headache: An assessment of the qualities of tension headache pain. *Pain*, 10(2), 209–219.

Hustvedt, A. (2011). *Medical muses: Hysteria in nineteenth-century Paris.* New York, NY: W. W. Norton.

Huta, V., & Waterman, A. S. (2014). Eudaimonia and its distinction from hedonia: Developing a classification and terminology for understanding conceptual and operational definitions. *Journal of Happiness Studies*, 15(6), 1425–1456.

Hymowitz, N., Sexton, M., Ockene, J., Grandits, G., & MRFIT Research Group. (1991). Baseline factors associated with smoking cessation and relapse. *Preventive Medicine*, 20(5), 590–601.

Imai, M. (2012). *Gemba Kaizen: A commonsense approach to a continuous improvement strategy.* New York, NY: McGraw Hill.

Ingraham, C. (2018, May 21). Millions of U.S. citizens don't speak English to one another. That's not a problem. *Washington Post*.

Innes, K. E., Selfe, T. K., & Agarwal, P. (2012). Restless legs syndrome and conditions associated with metabolic dysregulation, sympathoadrenal dysfunction, and cardiovascular disease risk: A systematic review. *Sleep Medicine Reviews*, 16(4), 309–339.

Insel, K., Morrow, D., Brewer, B., & Figueredo, A. (2006). Executive function, working memory, and medication adherence among older adults. *Journals of Gerontology Series B: Psychological Sciences and Social Sciences*, 61(2), P102–P107.

Isaac, M. L., & Paauw, D. S. (2014). Medically unexplained symptoms. *Medical Clinics*, 98(3), 663–672.

Issa, J. S., Abe, T. O., Moura, S., Santos, P. C., & Pereira, A. C. (2012). Effectiveness of coadministration of varenicline, bupropion, and serotonin reuptake inhibitors in a smoking cessation program in the real-life setting. *Nicotine & Tobacco Research*, 15(6), 1146–1150.

Itz, C. J., Willems, P. C., Zeilstra, D. J., & Huygen, F. J. (2016). Dutch multidisciplinary guideline for invasive treatment of pain syndromes of the lumbosacral spine. *Pain Practice*, 16(1), 90–110.

James, S. A. (1994). John Henryism and the health of African-Americans. *Culture, Medicine and Psychiatry*, 18(2), 163–182.

Jauhar, S. (2008, January 1). Explain a medical error? Sure. Apologize too? *New York Times*.

Jayson, S. (2014, February 11). Teens feeling stress and many not managing it well. *USA Today*.

Jegindø, E. M. E., Vase, L., Jegindø, J., & Geertz, A. W. (2013). Pain and sacrifice: Experience and modulation of pain in a religious piercing ritual. *International Journal for the Psychology of Religion*, 23(3), 171–187.

Jenkins, C. D., Rosenman, R. H., & Friedman, M. (1967). Development of an objective psychological test for the determination of the coronary-prone behavior pattern in employed men. *Journal of Chronic Diseases*, 20(6), 371–379.

Jenni, M. A., & Wollersheim, J. P. (1979). Cognitive therapy, stress management training, and the type A behavior pattern. *Cognitive Therapy and Research*, 3(1), 61–73.

Jensen, M. P. (2009). Hypnosis for chronic pain management: A new hope. *Pain*, 146(3), 235–237.

Jensen, M. P. (2010). *Hypnosis for chronic pain management.* New York, NY: Oxford University Press.

Jewkes, R. K., Dunkle, K., Nduna, M., & Shai, N. (2010). Intimate partner violence, relationship power inequity, and incidence of HIV infection in young women in South Africa: A cohort study. *The Lancet*, 376(9734), 41–48.

Jia, H., & Lubetkin, E. I. (2005). The impact of obesity on health-related quality-of-life in the general adult US population. *Journal of Public Health*, 27(2), 156–164.

Johannes, C. B., Le, T. K., Zhou, X., Johnston, J. A., & Dworkin, R. H. (2010). The prevalence of chronic pain in United States adults: Results of an Internet-based survey. *Journal of Pain, 11*(11), 1230–1239.

Johns, M. W. (1991). A new method for measuring daytime sleepiness: The Epworth sleepiness scale. *Sleep, 14*(6), 540–545.

Johnson, C. C., Kennedy, C., Fonner, V., Siegfried, N., Figueroa, C., Dalal, S., . . . & Baggaley, R. (2017). Examining the effects of HIV self-testing compared to standard HIV testing services: A systematic review and meta-analysis. *Journal of the International AIDS Society, 20*(1).

Johnson, N. (2001). Tobacco use and oral cancer: A global perspective. *Journal of Dental Education, 65*(4), 328–339.

Johnson, P. J., Ghildayal, N., Ward, A. C., Westgard, B. C., Boland, L. L., & Hokanson, J. S. (2012). Disparities in potentially avoidable emergency department (ED) care: ED visits for ambulatory care sensitive conditions. *Medical Care, 50*(12), 1020–1028.

Johnson, P. M., & Kenny, P. J. (2010). Dopamine D2 receptors in addiction-like reward dysfunction and compulsive eating in obese rats. *Nature Neuroscience, 13*(5), 635.

Johnson, S. K. (2008). *Medically unexplained illness: Gender and biopsychosocial implications.* Washington, DC: American Psychological Association.

Johnston, M., & Vögele, C. (1993). Benefits of psychological preparation for surgery: A meta-analysis. *Annals of Behavioral Medicine, 15*(4), 245–256.

Jonsen, A. R. (2007). The God squad and the origins of transplantation ethics and policy. *Journal of Law, Medicine, and Ethics, 35*, 238–240.

Jorenby, D. E., Hays, J. T., Rigotti, N. A., Azoulay, S., Watsky, E. J., Williams, K. E., . . . & Varenicline Phase 3 Study Group. (2006). Efficacy of varenicline, an α4β2 nicotinic acetylcholine receptor partial agonist, vs placebo or sustained-release bupropion for smoking cessation: A randomized controlled trial. *Journal of the American Medical Association, 296*(1), 56–63.

Jorenby, D. E., Leischow, S. J., Nides, M. A., Rennard, S. I., Johnston, J. A., Hughes, A. R., . . . & Fiore, M. C. (1999). A controlled trial of sustained-release bupropion, a nicotine patch, or both for smoking cessation. *New England Journal of Medicine, 340*(9), 685–691.

Juckett, G. (2013). Caring for Latino patients. *American Family Physician, 87*(1), 48–54.

Kabat-Zinn, J. (1994). *Wherever you go, there you are.* New York, NY: Hyperion.

Kabat-Zinn, J. (2003). Mindfulness-based interventions in context: Past, present, and future. *Clinical Psychology: Science and Practice, 10*(2), 144–156.

Kachan, D., Olano, H., Tannenbaum, S. L., Annane, D. W., Mehta, A., Arheart, K. L., . . . & Lee, D. J. (2017). Peer Reviewed: Prevalence of Mindfulness Practices in the US Workforce: National Health Interview Survey. *Preventing Chronic Disease, 14*.

Kales, A., Soldatos, C. R., Bixler, E. O., Ladda, R. L., Charney, D. S., Weber, G., & Schweitzer, P. K. (1980). Hereditary factors in sleepwalking and night terrors. *British Journal of Psychiatry, 137*(2), 111–118.

Kamijo, K., & Takeda, Y. (2010). Regular physical activity improves executive function during task switching in young adults. *International Journal of Psychophysiology, 75*(3), 304–311.

Kamper, S. J., Apeldoorn, A. T., Chiarotto, A., Smeets, R. J. E. M., Ostelo, R. W. J. G., Guzman, J., & van Tulder, M. W. (2015). Multidisciplinary biopsychosocial rehabilitation for chronic low back pain: Cochrane systematic review and meta-analysis. *BMJ, 350*, h444.

Kandasamy, R., & Price, T. J. (2015). The pharmacology of nociceptor priming. In H.-G. Schaible (Ed.), *Pain Control* (pp. 15–37). Berlin, Germany: Springer.

Kannel, W. B., Gordon, T., & Schwartz, M. J. (1971). Systolic versus diastolic blood pressure and the risk of coronary heart disease: The Framingham Study. *American Journal of Cardiology, 27*, 335–342.

Kanner, A. D., Coyne, J. C., Schaefer, C., & Lazarus, R. S. (1981). Comparison of two modes of stress measurement: Daily hassles and uplifts versus major life events. *Journal of Behavioral Medicine, 4*(1), 1–39.

Kaplan, H. S. (1995). *The sexual desire disorders: Dysfunctional regulation of sexual motivation.* New York, NY: Routledge.

Kaplan-Myrth, N. (2007). Interpreting people as they interpret themselves: Narrative in medical anthropology and family medicine. *Canadian Family Physician, 53*(8), 1268–1269.

Katainen, A. (2012). Smoking and workers' autonomy: A qualitative study on smoking practices in manual work. *Health, 16*(2), 134–150.

Kato, P. M. (2010). Video games in health care: Closing the gap. *Review of General Psychology, 14*(2), 113–121.

Kato, T. A., Shinfuku, N., Fujisawa, D., Tateno, M., Ishida, T., Akiyama, T., . . . & Balhara, Y. P. S. (2011). Introducing the concept of modern depression in Japan: An international case vignette survey. *Journal of Affective Disorders, 135*(1), 66–76.

Katon, W., Egan, K., & Miller, D. (1985). Chronic pain: Lifetime psychiatric diagnoses. *American Journal of Psychiatry, 142*(10), 1156–1160.

Katon, W. J., Lin, E. H., Von Korff, M., Ciechanowski, P., Ludman, E. J., Young, B., . . . & McCulloch, D. (2010). Collaborative care for patients with depression and chronic illnesses. *New England Journal of Medicine, 363*(27), 2611–2620.

Katon, W. J., & Walker, E. A. (1998). Medically unexplained symptoms in primary care. *Journal of Clinical Psychiatry, 59*(Suppl 20), 15–21.

Kaufman, S. (2015). *Ordinary medicine: Extraordinary treatments, longer lives, and where to draw the line.* Chapel Hill, NC: Duke University Press.

Kavey, N. B., Whyte, J., Resor, S. R., & Gidro-Frank, S. (1990). Somnambulism in adults. *Neurology, 40*(5), 749–749.

Kawachi, I., & Kennedy, B. P. (1997). Socioeconomic determinants of health: Health and social cohesion: Why care about income inequality? *British Medical Journal, 314*(7086), 1037.

Kawachi, I., & Subramanian, S. V. (2014). Income inequality. In L. Berkman, I. Kawachi, & M. M. Glymour (Eds.), *Social epidemiology* (126–152). New York, NY: Oxford University Press.

Keel, P. K., & Klump, K. L. (2003). Are eating disorders culture-bound syndromes? Implications for conceptualizing their etiology. *Psychological Bulletin, 129*(5), 747–769.

Kelder, S. H., Hoelscher, D., & Perry, C. L. (2015). How individuals, environments, and health behaviors interact. In K. Glanz, B. K. Rimer, K. Viswanath (Eds.), *Health behavior: Theory, research, and practice* (pp. 159–182). San Francisco, CA: Jossey-Bass.

Keller, A., Hayden, J., Bombardier, C., & van Tulder, M. (2007). Effect sizes of non-surgical treatments of non-specific low-back pain. *European Spine Journal, 16*(11), 1776–1788.

Keller, R. B., Atlas, S. J., Singer, D. E., Chapin, A., Mooney, N., Patrick, D., & Deyo, R. A. (1996). The Maine lumbar spine study: I. Background and concepts. *Spine 21*, 1769–1776.

Kelly, A. B., Halford, W. K., & Young, R. M. (2002). Couple communication and female problem drinking: A behavioral observation study. *Psychology of Addictive Behaviors, 16*(3), 269–271.

Kern, S. (2018). Migrant crisis reaches Spain. Gatestone Institute. https://www.gatestoneinstitute.org/10840/spain-migrant-crisis.

Kerns, R. D., Rosenberg, R., & Jacob, M. C. (1994). Anger expression and chronic pain. *Journal of Behavioral Medicine, 17*, 57–67.

Kessels, L. T., Ruiter, R. A., & Jansma, B. M. (2010). Increased attention but more efficient disengagement: Neuroscientific evidence for defensive processing of threatening health information. *Health Psychology, 29*(4), 346–354.

Kessler, D., Heath, I., Lloyd, K., Lewis, G., & Gray, D. P. (1999). General practice cross sectional study of symptom attribution and recognition of depression and anxiety in primary care. Commentary: There must be limits to the medicalisation of human distress. *British Medical Journal, 318*(7181), 436–440.

Kevles, B. (1997). *Naked to the bone: Medical imaging in the twentieth century.* New Brunswick, NJ: Rutgers University Press.

Khaw, K. T., Wareham, N., Bingham, S., Welch, A., Luben, R., & Day, N. (2008). Combined impact of health behaviours and mortality in men and women: The EPIC-Norfolk prospective population study. *PLoS Medicine, 5*(1), e12.

Khaw, K. T., Wareham, N., Luben, R., Bingham, S., Oakes, S., Welch, A., & Day, N. (2001). Glycated haemoglobin, diabetes, and mortality in men in Norfolk cohort of European Prospective Investigation of Cancer and Nutrition (EPIC-Norfolk). *BMJ, 322*(7277), 15.

Kiecolt-Glaser, J. K., Fisher, L. D., Ogrocki, P., Stout, J. C., Speicher, C. E., & Glaser, R. (1987). Marital quality, marital disruption, and immune function. *Psychosomatic Medicine, 49*(1), 13–34.

Kiecolt-Glaser, J. K., & Glaser, R. (1995). Psychoneuroimmunology and health consequences: Data and shared mechanisms. *Psychosomatic Medicine, 57*(3), 269–274.

Kiecolt-Glaser, J. K., Glaser, R., Strain, E. C., Stout, J. C., Tarr, K. L., Holliday, J. E., & Speicher, C. E. (1986). Modulation of cellular immunity in medical students. *Journal of Behavioral Medicine, 9*(1), 5–21.

Kiecolt-Glaser, J. K., McGuire, L., Robles, T. F., & Glaser, R. (2002). Emotions, morbidity, and mortality: New perspectives from psychoneuroimmunology. *Annual Review of Psychology, 53*(1), 83–107.

Kiecolt-Glaser, J. K., & Newton, T. L. (2001). Marriage and health: His and hers. *Psychological Bulletin, 127*(4), 472–503.

Kiecolt-Glaser, J. K., & Wilson, S. J. (2017). Lovesick: How couples' relationships influence health. *Annual Review of Clinical Psychology, 13*, 421–443.

Kim, P., Evans, G. W., Chen, E., Miller, G., & Seeman, T. (2018). How socioeconomic disadvantages get under the skin and into the brain to influence health development across the lifespan. In N. Halfon, C. B. Forrest, R. M. Lerner, & E. M. Faustman (Eds.), *Handbook of life course health development* (pp. 463–497). New York, NY: Springer.

Kimmel, P. L., Fwu, C. W., Abbott, K. C., Ratner, J., & Eggers, P. W. (2016). Racial disparities in poverty account for mortality differences in US Medicare beneficiaries. *SSM-Population Health, 2*, 123–129.

Kimmel, P. L., Fwu, C. W., & Eggers, P. W. (2013). Segregation, income disparities, and survival in hemodialysis patients. *Journal of the American Society of Nephrology, 24*(2), 293–301.

Kinetz, E. (2001, June 24). Gershwin diagnosis: It ain't necessarily so. *New York Times.*

King, D. K., Glasgow, R. E., Toobert, D. J., Strycker, L. A., Estabrooks, P. A., Osuna, D., & Faber, A. J. (2010). Self-efficacy, problem solving, and social-environmental support are associated with diabetes self-management behaviors. *Diabetes Care, 33*(4), 751–753.

Kinney, H. C., & Thach, B. T. (2009). The sudden infant death syndrome. *New England Journal of Medicine, 361*(8), 795–805.

Kinnunen, J. (1996). Gabriel Tarde as a founding father of innovation diffusion research. *Acta Sociologica, 39*(4), 431–442.

Kirchner, T. R., Shiffman, S., & Wileyto, E. P. (2012). Relapse dynamics during smoking cessation: Recurrent abstinence violation effects and lapse-relapse progression. *Journal of Abnormal Psychology, 121*(1), 187–197.

Klein, R. (2006). The troubled transformation of Britain's National Health Service. *New England Journal of Medicine, 355*, 409–415.

Kleinman, A. (1988). *The illness narratives: Suffering, healing, and the human condition.* New York, NY: Basic Books.

Ko, K. M., Mak, D. H., Chiu, P. Y., & Poon, M. K. (2004). Pharmacological basis of "Yang-invigoration" in Chinese medicine. *Trends in Pharmacological Sciences, 25*(1), 3–6.

Kobasa, S. C. (1979). Stressful life events, personality, and health: An inquiry into hardiness. *Journal of Personality and Social Psychology, 37*(1), 1–11.

Kobasa, S. C., Maddi, S. R., & Kahn, S. (1982). Hardiness and health: A prospective study. *Journal of Personality and Social Psychology, 42*(1), 168–177.

Kober, H., Kross, E. F., Mischel, W., Hart, C. L., & Ochsner, K. N. (2010). Regulation of craving by cognitive strategies in cigarette smokers. *Drug and Alcohol Dependence, 106*(1), 52–55.

Koch, C. (2016, November 1). Sleeping while awake. *Scientific American Mind.* https://www.scientificamerican.com/article/sleeping-while-awake/.

Koh, H. K., Joossens, L. X., & Connolly, G. N. (2007). Making smoking history worldwide. *New England Journal of Medicine, 356*(15), 1496–1498.

Kohler-Hausmann, J. (2007). "The crime of survival": Fraud prosecutions, community surveillance and the original "welfare queen." *Journal of Social History, 41*(2), 329–354.

Kolb, B. (2018). Overview of factors influencing brain development. In R. Gibb & B. Kolb (Eds.), *The neurobiology of brain and behavioral development* (pp. 51–79). London, UK: Academic Press.

Kominski, G. (2013). The Patient Protection and Affordable Care Act of 2010. In G. Kominski (Ed.). *Changing the U.S. health care system.* San Francisco, CA: Jossey-Bass.

Kondo, N., Sembajwe, G., Kawachi, I., van Dam, R. M., Subramanian, S. V., & Yamagata, Z. (2009). Income inequality, mortality, and self rated health: Meta-analysis of multilevel studies. *British Medical Journal, 339*, b4471.

Koyama, A., Miyake, Y., Kawakami, N., Tsuchiya, M., Tachimori, H., & Takeshima, T. (2010). Lifetime prevalence, psychiatric comorbidity and demographic correlates of "hikikomori" in a community population in Japan. *Psychiatry Research, 176*(1), 69–74.

Krakowsky, Y., & Grober, E. D. (2016). Hypoactive sexual desire in men. In L. I. Lipshultz, A. W. Pastuszak, A. T. Goldstein, A. Giraldi, & M. A. Perelman (Eds.), *Management of sexual dysfunction in men and women* (pp. 171–187). New York, NY: Springer.

Kramer, P. D., & Brody, E. B. (1994). Listening to Prozac: A psychiatrist explores antidepressant drugs and the remaking of the self. *Journal of Nervous and Mental Disease, 182*(6), 362.

Kravitz, R. L., Helms, L. J., Azari, R., Antonius, D., & Melnikow, J. (2000). Comparing the use of physician time and health care resources among patients speaking English, Spanish, and Russian. *Medical Care, 38*(7), 728–738.

Kremer, E., Atkinson, J. H., & Ignelzi, R. J. (1981). Measurement of pain: Patient preference does not confound pain measurement. *Pain, 10*(2), 241–248.

Kressin, N. R., & Petersen, L. A. (2001). Racial differences in the use of invasive cardiovascular procedures: Review of the literature and prescription for future research. *Annals of Internal Medicine, 135*(5), 352–366.

Krieger, T., Altenstein, D., Baettig, I., Doerig, N., & Holtforth, M. G. (2013). Self-compassion in depression: Associations with depressive symptoms, rumination, and avoidance in depressed outpatients. *Behavior Therapy, 44*(3), 501–513.

Kripalani, S., Yao, X., & Haynes, R. B. (2007). Interventions to enhance medication adherence in chronic medical conditions: A systematic review. *Archives of Internal Medicine, 167*(6), 540–549.

Krishnan, K. R. R., France, R. D., Pelton, S., McCann, U. D., Davidson, J., & Urban, B. J. (1985). Chronic pain and depression. I. Classification of depression in chronic low back pain patients. *Pain, 22*(3), 279–287.

Kroenke, K., & Mangelsdorff, D. (1989). Common symptoms in ambulatory care: Incidence, evaluation, therapy and outcome. *American Journal of Medicine, 86*, 262–286.

Kroenke, K., & Unützer, J. (2017). Closing the false divide: Sustainable approaches to integrating mental health services into primary care. *Journal of General Internal Medicine, 32*(4), 404–410.

Kroker, K. (2007). *The sleep of others and the transformations of sleep research.* Toronto, ON: University of Toronto Press.

Kross, E., Berman, M. G., Mischel, W., Smith, E. E., & Wager, T. D. (2011). Social rejection shares somatosensory representations with physical pain. *Proceedings of the National Academy of Sciences, 108*(15), 6270–6275.

Kryger, M. (2015). *Kryger's sleep medicine review* (2nd ed.). Philadelphia, PA: Elsevier.

Ku, L., & Flores, G. (2005). Pay now or pay later: Providing interpreter services in health care. *Health Affairs, 24*(2), 435–444.

Kuhn, E., Greene, C., Hoffman, J., Nguyen, T., Wald, L., Schmidt, J., . . . & Ruzek, J. (2014). Preliminary evaluation of PTSD Coach, a smartphone app for post-traumatic stress symptoms. *Military Medicine, 179*(1), 12–18.

Kumar, K., Taylor, R. S., Jacques, L., Eldabe, S., Meglio, M., Molet, J., . . . & Buchser, E. (2008). The effects of spinal cord stimulation in neuropathic pain are sustained: A 24-month follow-up of the prospective randomized controlled multicenter trial of the effectiveness of spinal cord stimulation. *Neurosurgery, 63*(4), 762–770.

Kumar, K., Toth, C., Nath, R., & Laing, P. (1998). Epidural spinal cord stimulation for treatment of chronic pain—some predictors of success: A 15-year experience. *Surgical Neurology, 50*(2), 110–121.

Kushel, M. B., Perry, S., Bangsberg, D., Clark, R., & Moss, A. R. (2002). Emergency department use among the homeless and marginally housed: Results from a community-based study. *American Journal of Public Health, 92*(5), 778–784.

La Ferrara, E., Chong, A., & Duryea, S. (2012). Soap operas and fertility: Evidence from Brazil. *American Economic Journal: Applied Economics, 4*(4), 1–31.

Lambe, M., & Cummings, P. (2000). The shift to and from daylight savings time and motor vehicle crashes. *Accident Analysis & Prevention, 32*(4), 609–611.

Landry, T., & Bergeron, S. (2009). How young does vulvo-vaginal pain begin? Prevalence and characteristics of dyspareunia in adolescents. *Journal of Sexual Medicine, 6*(4), 927–935.

Langley, K., Rice, F., & Thapar, A. (2005). Maternal smoking during pregnancy as an environmental risk factor for attention deficit hyperactivity disorder behaviour: A review. *Minerva Pediatrica, 57*(6), 359–371.

Laposata, E., Kennedy, A. P., & Glantz, S. A. (2014). When tobacco targets direct democracy. *Journal of Health Politics, Policy and Law, 39*(3), 537–564.

Larkin, C., & Searight, H. R. (2014). A systematic review of cultural preferences for receiving medical "bad news" in the United States. *Health, 6*(16), 2162.

Larson, J. S., & Muller, A. (2002). Managing the quality of health care. *Journal of Health and Human Services Administration*, 261–280.

Lasser, K. E., Himmelstein, D. U., & Woolhandler, S. (2006). Access to care, health status, and health disparities in the United States and Canada: Results of a cross-national population-based survey. *American Journal of Public Health, 96*(7), 1300–1307.

Latimer, W. W., Ernst, J., Hennessey, J., Stinchfield, R. D., & Winters, K. C. (2004). Relapse among adolescent drug abusers following treatment: The role of probable ADHD status. *Journal of Child & Adolescent Substance Abuse, 13*(3), 1–1.

Lavarreda, S. A., & Brown, E. R. (2013). Public Health Insurance. In G. F. Kominski (Ed.), *Changing the US health care system: Key issues in health services policy and management* (pp. 157–190). San Francisco, CA: Jossey-Bass.

Lavery, L. A., Ashry, H. R., van Houtum, W., Pugh, J. A., Harkless, L. B., & Basu, S. (1996). Variation in the incidence and proportion of diabetes related amputations in minorities. *Diabetes Care, 19*(1), 48–52.

Law, M., & Tang, J. L. (1995). An analysis of the effectiveness of interventions intended to help people stop smoking. *Archives of Internal Medicine, 155*(18), 1933–1941.

Lawler, K. A., & Schmied., L. A. (1992). A prospective study of women's health: The effects of stress, hardiness, locus of control, type A behavior, and physiological reactivity. *Women and Health, 19*(1), 27–41.

Lay, C., & Silverman, S. (1996). Trait procrastination, anxiety, and dilatory behavior. *Personality and Individual Differences, 21*(1), 61–67.

Lay, C. H., & Schouwenburg, H. C. (1993). Trait procrastination, time management, and academic behavior. *Journal of Social Behavior and Personality, 8*(4), 647–662.

Lazare, A., Putnam, S. M., & Lipkin, M. (1995). Three functions of the medical interview. In S. A. Cole & J. Bird (Eds.), *The medical interview* (pp. 3–19). New York, NY: Springer.

Lazarus, R. S., & Folkman, S. (1984). Coping and adaptation. In W. D. Gentry (Ed.), *The handbook of behavioral medicine* (pp. 282–325). New York, NY: Guilford Press.

Lazev, A. B., Herzog, T. A., & Brandon, T. H. (1999). Classical conditioning of environmental cues to cigarette smoking. *Experimental and Clinical Psychopharmacology, 7*(1), 56–63.

Lee, D. C., Long, J. A., Sevick, M. A., Stella, S. Y., Athens, J. K., Elbel, B., & Wall, S. P. (2016). The local geographic distribution of diabetic complications in New York City: Associated population characteristics and differences by type of complication. *Diabetes Research and Clinical Practice, 119*, 88–96.

Lee, L. K., Chen, P. C. Y., Lee, K. K., & Kaur, J. (2006). Premarital sexual intercourse among adolescents in Malaysia: A cross-sectional Malaysian school survey. *Singapore Medical Journal, 47*(6), 476.

Lee, R. U., & Radin, J. M. (2016). A population-based epidemiologic study of adult-onset narcolepsy incidence and associated risk factors, 2004–2013. *Journal of the Neurological Sciences, 370*, 29–34.

Lee, V. J., Tan, S. C., Earnest, A., Seong, P. S., Tan, H. H., & Leo, Y. S. (2007). User acceptability and feasibility of self-testing with HIV rapid tests. *Journal of Acquired Immune Deficiency Syndromes, 45*(4), 449–453.

Lees, C., & Hopkins, J. (2013). Peer reviewed: Effect of aerobic exercise on cognition, academic achievement, and psychosocial function in children: A systematic review of randomized control trials. *Preventing Chronic Disease, 10*. doi:10.5888/pcd10.130010.

Leger, K. A., Charles, S. T., Ayanian, J. Z., & Almeida, D. M. (2015). The association of daily physical symptoms with future health. *Social Science & Medicine, 143*, 241–248.

Leon, D. A., Chenet, L., Shkolnikov, V. M., Zakharov, S., Shapiro, J., Rakhmanova, G., . . . & McKee, M. (1997). Huge variation in Russian mortality rates 1984–94: Artefact, alcohol, or what? *The Lancet, 350*(9075), 383–388.

Lepani, K. (2012). *Islands of love, islands of risk: Culture and HIV in the Trobriands*. Nashville, TN: Vanderbilt University Press.

Lerman, C., Trock, B., Rimer, B. K., Jepson, C., Brody, D., & Boyce, A. (1991). Psychological side effects of breast cancer screening. *Health Psychology, 10*(4), 259–267.

Leserman, J., Li, Z., Drossman, D. A., & Hu, Y. J. (1998). Selected symptoms associated with sexual and physical abuse history among female patients with gastrointestinal disorders: The impact on subsequent health care visits. *Psychological Medicine, 28*(2), 417–425.

Lespérance, F., Frasure-Smith, N., Juneau, M., & Théroux, P. (2000). Depression and 1-year prognosis in unstable angina. *Archives of Internal Medicine, 160*(9), 1354–1360.

Lespérance, F., Frasure-Smith, N., Talajic, M., & Bourassa, M. G. (2002). Five-year risk of cardiac mortality in relation to initial severity and one-year changes in depression symptoms after myocardial infarction. *Circulation, 105*(9), 1049–1053.

Levenstein, S., Rosenstock, S., Jacobsen, R. K., & Jorgensen, T. (2015). Psychological stress increases risk for peptic ulcer, regardless of *Helicobacter pylori* infection or use of nonsteroidal anti-inflammatory drugs. *Clinical Gastroenterology and Hepatology, 13*(3), 498–506.

Levinson, W., Roter, D. L., Mullooly, J. P., Dull, V. T., & Frankel, R. M. (1997). Physician-patient communication: The relationship with malpractice claims among primary care physicians and surgeons. *Journal of the American Medical Association, 277*(7), 553–559.

Lewallen, S., & Courtright, P. (1998). Epidemiology in practice: Case-control studies. *Community Eye Journal, 11*(28), 57–58.

Lewis, M. A., DeVellis, B., & Sleath, B. (2002). Interpersonal communication and social influence. In K. Glanz, B. K. Rimes, & F. M. Lewis (Eds.), *Health behavior and health education: Theory, research, and practice* (pp. 363–402). San Francisco, CA: Jossey-Bass.

Lichtenstein, P., Holm, N. V., Verkasalo, P. K., Iliadou, A., Kaprio, J., Koskenvuo, M., . . . & Hemminki, K. (2000). Environmental and heritable factors in the causation of cancer—analyses of cohorts of twins from Sweden, Denmark, and Finland. *New England Journal of Medicine, 343*(2), 78–85.

Liddle, H. A., & Dakof, G. A. (1995). Efficacy of family therapy for drug abuse: Promising but not definitive. *Journal of Marital and Family Therapy, 21*(4), 511–543.

Lin, K. M. (1983). Hwa-Byung: A Korean culture-bound syndrome? *American Journal of Psychiatry, 140*(1), 105–107.

Linder-Pelz S. (1982). Social psychological determinants of patient satisfaction: A test of five hypotheses. *Social Science and Medicine, 16*, 583–589.

Lingas, E. O., Dorfman, L., & Bukofzer, E. (2009). Nutrition content of food and beverage products on Web sites popular with children. *American Journal of Public Health, 99*(S3), S587–S592.

Liss, D. T., & Baker, D. W. (2014). Understanding current racial/ethnic disparities in colorectal cancer screening in the United States: The contribution of socioeconomic status and access to care. *American Journal of Preventive Medicine, 46*(3), 228–236.

Liu, Y., Croft, J. B., Chapman, D. P., Perry, G. S., Greenlund, K. J., Zhao, G., & Edwards, V. J. (2013). Relationship between adverse childhood experiences and unemployment among adults from five US states. *Social Psychiatry and Psychiatric Epidemiology, 48*(3), 357–369.

Lock, A., Epston, D., Maisel, R., & de Faria, N. (2005). Resisting anorexia/bulimia: Foucauldian perspectives in narrative therapy. *British Journal of Guidance & Counselling, 33*(3), 315–332.

López, A., Sanderman, R., & Schroevers, M. J. (2016). Mindfulness and self-compassion as unique and common predictors of affect in the general population. *Mindfulness, 7*(6), 1289–1296.

Lopez, A. D., Collishaw, N. E., & Piha, T. (1994). A descriptive model of the cigarette epidemic in developed countries. *Tobacco Control, 3*(3), 242–247.

Lovato, C., Linn, G., Stead, L. F., & Best, A. (2003). Impact of tobacco advertising and promotion on increasing adolescent smoking behaviours. *Cochrane Database Systems Review, 2003*(4).

Lowe, C. F., Horne, P. J., Tapper, K., Bowdery, M., & Egerton, C. (2004). Effects of a peer modelling and rewards-based intervention to increase fruit and vegetable consumption in children. *European Journal of Clinical Nutrition, 58*(3), 510–522.

Luthra, S. (2018, February). States are advancing bills designed to lower drug costs with importation plans. *Scientific American*. https://www.scientificamerican.com/article/states-are-advancing-bills-designed-to-lower-drug-costs-with-importation-plans/.

Lynch, J. W., Smith, G. D., Kaplan, G. A., & House, J. S. (2000). Income inequality and mortality: Importance to health of individual income, psychosocial environment, or material conditions. *British Medical Journal, 320*(7243), 1200–1204.

Lyon, M., Markus, A. R., & Rosenbaum, S. J. (2010). Affordable Care Act, medical homes, and childhood asthma: A key opportunity for progress. Geiger Gibson/RCHN Community Health Foundation Research Collaborative. Paper 53. https://hsrc.himmelfarb.gwu.edu/sphhs_policy_ggrchn/53.

MacCoun, R. J. (1998). Toward a psychology of harm reduction. *American Psychologist, 53*(11), 1199–1208.

Mackenzie, C. S., Gekoski, W. L., & Knox, V. J. (2006). Age, gender, and the underutilization of mental health services: The influence of help-seeking attitudes. *Aging and Mental Health, 10*(6), 574–582.

Mackenzie, E. R., Taylor, L., Bloom, B. S., Hufford, D. J., & Johnson, J. C. (2003). Ethnic minority use of complementary and alternative medicine (CAM): A national probability survey of CAM utilizers. *Alternative Therapies in Health and Medicine, 9*(4), 50.

MacKinnon, J. C. (2004). The arithmetic of health care. *Canadian Medical Association Journal, 171*(6), 603–604.

MacPherson, H., Sinclair-Lian, N., & Thomas, K. (2006). Patients seeking care from acupuncture practitioners in the UK: A national survey. *Complementary Therapies in Medicine, 14*(1), 20–30.

Madsen, M. V., Gøtzsche, P. C., & Hróbjartsson, A. (2009). Acupuncture treatment for pain: Systematic review of randomised clinical trials with acupuncture, placebo acupuncture, and no acupuncture groups. *British Medical Journal, 338*, a3115.

Maier, T. (2009). *Masters of sex: The life and times of William Masters and Virginia Johnson, the couple who taught America how to love*. New York, NY: Basic Books.

Malloy, K. M., & Milling, L. S. (2010). The effectiveness of virtual reality distraction for pain reduction: A systematic review. *Clinical Psychology Review, 30*(8), 1011–1018.

Malone, R. E., & Dohan, D. (2000). Emergency department closures: Policy issues. *Journal of Emergency Nursing, 26*(4), 380–383.

Mannarino, M. R., Di Filippo, F., & Pirro, M. (2012). Obstructive sleep apnea syndrome. *European Journal of Internal Medicine, 23*(7), 586–593.

Manning, J. (2014). Coming out conversations and gay/bisexual men's sexual health: A constitutive model study. In V. L. Harvey & T. H. Housel (Eds.), *Health care disparities and the LGBT population* (pp. 27–54). Lanham, MD: Lexington Books.

Manning, J. C. (2006). The impact of internet pornography on marriage and the family: A review of the research. *Sexual Addiction & Compulsivity, 13*(2–3), 131–165.

Manteuffel, M., Williams, S., Chen, W., Verbrugge, R. R., Pittman, D. G., & Steinkellner, A. (2014). Influence of patient sex and gender on medication use, adherence, and prescribing alignment with guidelines. *Journal of Women's Health, 23*(2), 112–119.

Marcum, Z. A., Sevick, M. A., & Handler, S. M. (2013). Medication nonadherence: A diagnosable and treatable medical condition. *Journal of the American Medical Association, 309*(20), 2105–2106.

Marcus, A. F., Echeverria, S. E., Holland, B. K., Abraido-Lanza, A. F., & Passannante, M. R. (2016). The joint contribution of neighborhood poverty and social integration to mortality risk in the United States. *Annals of Epidemiology, 26*(4), 261–266.

Marcus, B. H., Selby, V. C., Niaura, R. S., & Rossi, J. S. (1992). Self-efficacy and the stages of exercise behavior change. *Research Quarterly for Exercise and Sport, 63*(1), 60–66.

Margalit, R. S., Roter, D., Dunevant, M. A., Larson, S., & Reis, S. (2006). Electronic medical record use and physician-patient communication: An observational study of Israeli primary care encounters. *Patient Education and Counseling, 61*(1), 134–141.

Marks, E. M., & Hunter, M. S. (2015). Medically unexplained symptoms: An acceptable term? *British Journal of Pain, 9*(2), 109–114.

Marlatt, G. A. (1985). Relapse prevention: Theoretical rationale and overview of the model. In G. Marlatt & J. R. Gordon (Eds.), *Relapse prevention: A self-control strategy for the maintenance of behavior change* (pp. 3–70). New York, NY: Guilford Press.

Marlatt, G. A. (1996). Taxonomy of high-risk situations for alcohol relapse: Evolution and development of a cognitive-behavior model. *Addiction, 91*(Suppl 12), S37–49.

Marlatt, G. A., & Donovan, D. M. (2005). *Relapse prevention: Maintenance strategies in the treatment of addictive behaviors*. New York, NY: Guilford Press.

Marlatt, G. A., & Witkiewitz, K. (2002). Harm reduction approaches to alcohol use: Health promotion, prevention, and treatment. *Addictive Behaviors, 27*(6), 867–886.

Marmot, M. (2005). Social determinants of health inequalities. *The Lancet, 365*(9464), 1099–1104.

Marmot, M. G., Stansfeld, S., Patel, C., North, F., Head, J., White, I., . . . & Smith, G. D. (1991). Health inequalities among British civil servants: The Whitehall II study. *The Lancet, 337*(8754), 1387–1393.

Marsh, R., Stefan, M., Bansal, R., Hao, X., Walsh, B. T., & Peterson, B. S. (2015). Anatomical characteristics of the cerebral surface in bulimia nervosa. *Biological Psychiatry, 77*(7), 616–623.

Martin-Rodriguez, E., Guillen-Grima, F., Martí, A., & Brugos-Larumbe, A. (2015). Comorbidity associated with obesity in a large population: The APNA study. *Obesity Research & Clinical Practice, 9*(5), 435–447.

Martinussen, M., Friborg, O., Schmierer, P., Kaiser, S., Øvergård, K. T., Neunhoeffer, A. L., . . . & Rosenvinge, J. H. (2017). The comorbidity of personality disorders in eating disorders: A meta-analysis. *Eating and Weight Disorders-Studies on Anorexia, Bulimia and Obesity, 22*(2), 201–209.

Martland, H. S. (1931). The occurrence of malignancy in radioactive persons: A general review of data gathered in the study of the radium dial painters, with special reference to the occurrence of osteogenic sarcoma and the inter-relationship of certain blood diseases. *American Journal of Cancer, 15*(4), 2435–2516.

Mason, A. E., & Sbarra, D. A. (2012). Romantic separation, loss, and health: A review of moderators. In M. Newman & N. A. Roberts (Eds.), *Handbook of health and social relationships* (pp. 95–120). Washington, DC: American Psychological Association.

Masters, W. H., & Johnson, V. E. (1966). *Human sexual response*. New York, NY: Ishi Press Intl.

Masters, W., & Johnson, V. (1970). *Human sexual inadequacy*. Boston, MA: Little Brown & Co.

Matthews, K. A., Adler, N. E., Forrest, C. B., & Stead, W. W. (2016). Collecting psychosocial "vital signs" in electronic health records: Why now? What are they? What's new for psychology? *American Psychologist, 71*(6), 497–504.

Mauksch, L. B. (2017). Questioning a taboo: Physicians' interruptions during interactions with patients. *Journal of the American Medical Association, 317*(10), 1021–1022.

May, A. L., Freedman, D., Sherry, B., Blanck, H. M., & Centers for Disease Control and Prevention (CDC). (2013). Obesity—United States, 1999–2010. *MMWR Surveillance Summary, 62*(Suppl 3), 120–128.

Mayer, L. E., & Walsh, B. T. (1998). The use of selective serotonin reuptake inhibitors in eating disorders. *Journal of Clinical Psychiatry, 59*, 28–34.

Mazumder, B., & Miller, S. (2016). The effects of the Massachusetts health reform on household financial distress. *American Economic Journal: Economic Policy, 8*(3), 284–313.

McBride, C. M., Curry, S. J., Lando, H. A., Pirie, P. L., Grothaus, L. C., & Nelson, J. C. (1999). Prevention of relapse in women who quit smoking during pregnancy. *American Journal of Public Health, 89*(5), 706–711.

McCabe, M. S., Varricchio, C. G., Padberg, R., & Simpson, N. (1995, May). Women's health advocacy: Its growth and development in oncology. *Seminars in Oncology Nursing, 11*(2), 137–142.

McConnaughy, E. A., Prochaska, J. O., & Velicer, W. F. (1983). Stages of change in psychotherapy: Measurement and sample profiles. *Psychotherapy: Theory, Research & Practice, 20*(3), 368–375.

McCormick, R. A., & Taber, J. I. (1988). Attributional style in pathological gamblers in treatment. *Journal of Abnormal Psychology, 97*(3), 368–370.

McCracken, L. M., & Vowles, K. E. (2014). Acceptance and commitment therapy and mindfulness for chronic pain: Model, process, and progress. *American Psychologist, 69*(2), 178–187.

McCracken, M., Olsen, M., Chen, M. S., Jemal, A., Thun, M., Cokkinides, V., . . . & Ward, E. (2007). Cancer incidence, mortality, and associated risk factors among Asian Americans of Chinese, Filipino, Vietnamese, Korean, and Japanese ethnicities. *CA: A Cancer Journal for Clinicians, 57*(4), 190–205.

McCurry, S. M., Logsdon, R. G., Teri, L., & Vitiello, M. V. (2007). Sleep disturbances in caregivers of persons with dementia: Contributing factors and treatment implications. *Sleep Medicine Reviews, 11*(2), 143–153.

McDaniel, M. A., Einstein, G. O., Stout, A. C., & Morgan, Z. (2003). Aging and maintaining intentions over delays: Do it or lose it. *Psychology and Aging, 18*(4), 823–835.

McDonald, A. J., Wang, N., & Camargo, C. A. (2004). US emergency department visits for alcohol-related diseases and injuries between 1992 and 2000. *Archives of Internal Medicine, 164*(5), 531–537.

McDougall, J. A., Madeleine, M. M., Daling, J. R., & Li, C. I. (2007). Racial and ethnic disparities in cervical cancer incidence rates in the United States, 1992–2003. *Cancer Causes & Control, 18*(10), 1175–1186.

McElroy, S. L., Hudson, J., Ferreira-Cornwell, M. C., Radewonuk, J., Whitaker, T., & Gasior, M. (2016). Lisdexamfetamine dimesylate for adults with moderate to severe binge eating disorder: Results of two pivotal phase 3 randomized controlled trials. *Neuropsychopharmacology, 41*(5), 1251.

McEwen, B. S., & Stellar, E. (1993). Stress and the individual: Mechanisms leading to disease. *Archives of Internal Medicine, 153*(18), 2093–2101.

McGill, D., & Pearce, J. K. (2005). British families. In M. McGoldrick, K. Pearce, & J. Giordano (Eds.), *Ethnicity and family therapy* (pp. 457–479). New York, NY: Guilford Press.

McGinnis, J. M., & Foege, W. H. (1993). Actual causes of death in the United States. *Journal of the American Medical Association, 270*(18), 2207–2212.

McTavish, S., Moore, S., Harper, S., & Lynch, J. (2010). National female literacy, individual socio-economic status, and maternal health care use in sub-Saharan Africa. *Social Science & Medicine, 71*(11), 1958–1963.

McWilliams, L. A., & Bailey, S. J. (2010). Associations between adult attachment ratings and health conditions: Evidence from the National Comorbidity Survey Replication. *Health Psychology, 29*(4), 446–453.

McWilliams, L. A., Cox, B. J., & Ennis, M. W. (2003). Mood and anxiety disorders associated with chronic pain: An examination in a nationally representative sample. *Pain, 106*(1–2), 127–133.

Meana, M. (2009). Painful intercourse: Dyspareunia and vaginismus. *Journal of Family Psychotherapy, 20*(2–3), 198–220.

Meana, M. (2012). *Sexual dysfunction in women*. Boston, MA: Hogrefe Publishing.

Meana, M., & Steiner, E. T. (2014). Hidden disorder/hidden desire: Presentations of low sexual desire in men. In Y. M. Binik & K. S. K. Hall (Eds.), *Principles and practice of sex therapy* (pp. 42–60). New York, NY: Guilford Press.

Mechanic, D. (2004). The rise and fall of managed care. *Journal of Health and Social Behavior, 45*(Suppl), 76–86.

Meddis, R. (1975). On the function of sleep. *Animal Behaviour, 23*, 676–691.

MediConnect (2018). Medical tourism facilitator. https://medicaltourismfacilitator.com/facilitator/mediconnect/400.

Mehler, P. S., & Brown, C. (2015). Anorexia nervosa—medical complications. *Journal of Eating Disorders, 3*(1), 11.

Melzack, R. (1975). The McGill Pain Questionnaire: Major properties and scoring methods. *Pain, 1*(3), 277–299.

Melzack, R. (2001). Pain and the neuromatrix in the brain. *Journal of Dental Education, 65*(12), 1378–1382.

Melzack, R., & Wall, P. D. (1965). Pain mechanisms: A new theory. *Science, 150*(3699), 971–979.

Merrill, R. M. (2016). *Introduction to epidemiology*. Burlington, MA: Jones & Bartlett.

Merskey, H. (1994). PART III pain terms: A current list with definitions and notes on usage. In *Classification of chronic pain: Descriptions of chronic pain syndromes and definitions of pain terms* (pp. 207–214). Washington, DC: IASP Press.

Metersky, M. L., Hunt, D. R., Kliman, R., Wang, Y., Curry, M., Verzier, N., . . . & Moy, E. (2011). Racial disparities in the frequency of patient safety events: Results from the National Medicare Patient Safety Monitoring System. *Medical Care, 49*(5), 504–510.

Meyerowitz, B. E., & Chaiken, S. (1987). The effect of message framing on breast self-examination attitudes, intentions, and behavior. *Journal of Personality and Social Psychology, 52*(3), 500–510.

Mikail, S. F., Henderson, P. R., & Tasca, G. A. (1994). An interpersonally based model of chronic pain: An application of attachment theory. *Clinical Psychology Review, 14*(1), 1–16.

Mikhail, B. I. (1994). Hispanic mothers' beliefs and practices regarding selected children's health problems. *Western Journal of Nursing Research, 16*(6), 623–638.

Miller, B. F., Ross, K. M., Davis, M. M., Melek, S. P., Kathol, R., & Gordon, P. (2017). Payment reform in the patient-centered medical home: Enabling and sustaining integrated behavioral health care. *American Psychologist, 72*(1), 55–68.

Miller, D. A., McCluskey-Fawcett, K., & Irving, L. M. (1993). The relationship between childhood sexual abuse and subsequent onset of bulimia nervosa. *Child Abuse & Neglect, 17*(2), 305–314.

Miller, W., & Munoz, R. (1982). *How to control your drinking: A practical guide to responsible drinking* (Revised ed.). Albuquerque, NM: University of New Mexico Press.

Miller, W. R. (1983). Motivational interviewing with problem drinkers. *Behavioral Psychotherapy, 11*, 147–172.

Miller, W. R., & Rollnick, S. (2002). *Motivational interviewing: Preparing people for change* (2nd ed.). New York, NY: Guilford Press.

Miller, W. R., & Rose, G. S. (2009). Toward a theory of motivational interviewing. *American Psychologist, 64*(6), 527–537.

Milner, C. E., & Cote, K. A. (2009). Benefits of napping in healthy adults: Impact of nap length, time of day, age, and experience with napping. *Journal of Sleep Research, 18*(2), 272–281.

Mintz, S., & Kellogg, S. (1989). *Domestic revolutions: A social history of American family life*. New York, NY: Simon and Schuster.

Minuchin, S., Rosman, B. L., & Baker, L. (2009). *Psychosomatic families: Anorexia nervosa in context*. Cambridge, MA: Harvard University Press.

Mischel, W. (1999). Personality coherence and dispositions in a cognitive-affective personality system (CAPS) approach. In D. Cervone & Y. Shoda (Eds.), *The coherence of personality: Social-cognitive bases of consistency, variability, and organization* (pp. 37–60). New York, NY: Guilford Press.

Mischel, W., & Ayduk, O. (2004). Willpower in a cognitive-affective processing system: The dynamics of delay of gratification. In R. F. Baumeister & K. D. Vohs (Eds.), *Handbook of self-regulation: Research, theory, and applications* (pp. 99–129). New York, NY: Guilford Press.

Mistler, B. J., Reetz, D., Krylowicz, B., & Barr, V. (2013). *Association for University and College Counseling Center Directors Annual Survey: Reporting period September 1, 2011 through August 31, 2012*. https://www.aucccd.org/support/Monograph_2012_AUCCCD%20Public.pdf.

Mitler, M. M., Miller, J. C., Lipsitz, J. J., Walsh, J. K., & Wylie, C. D. (1997). The sleep of long-haul truck drivers. *New England Journal of Medicine, 337*(11), 755–762.

Moher, M., Hey, K., & Lancaster, T. (2005). Workplace interventions for smoking cessation. *Cochrane Database of Systematic Reviews, 2005*(2), CD003440.

Mold, J. W., & Stein, H. F. (1986). The cascade effect in the clinical care of patients. *New England Journal of Medicine, 314*, 512–514.

Montano, D. E., & Kasprzyk, D. (2015). Theory of reasoned action, theory of planned behavior, and the integrated behavioral model. In K. Glanz, B. K. Rimer, & K. Viswanath (Eds.), *Health behavior: Theory, research and practice* (pp. 95–124). San Francisco, CA: Jossey-Bass.

Montgomery, M., & McCrone, S. H. (2010). Psychological distress associated with the diagnostic phase for suspected breast cancer: Systematic review. *Journal of Advanced Nursing, 66*(11), 2372–2390.

Monti, P. M., Barnett, N. P., Colby, S. M., Gwaltney, C. J., Spirito, A., Rohsenow, D. J., & Woolard, R. (2007). Motivational interviewing versus feedback only in emergency care for young adult problem drinking. *Addiction, 102*(8), 1234–1243.

Montorsi, F. (2005). Prevalence of premature ejaculation: A global and regional perspective. *Journal of Sexual Medicine, 2*, 96–102.

Montoya, M. (2011). *Making the Mexican diabetic: Race, science, and the genetics of inequality*. Berkeley, CA: University of California Press.

Moody, H., Darden, J. T., & Pigozzi, B. W. (2016). The racial gap in childhood blood lead levels related to socioeconomic position of residence in metropolitan Detroit. *Sociology of Race and Ethnicity, 2*(2), 200–218.

Moon, R. Y., Oden, R. P., Joyner, B. L., & Ajao, T. I. (2010). Qualitative analysis of beliefs and perceptions about sudden infant death syndrome in

African-American mothers: Implications for safe sleep recommendations. *Journal of Pediatrics*, *157*(1), 92–97.

Moon, R. Y., & Task Force on Sudden Infant Death Syndrome. (2016). SIDS and other sleep-related infant deaths: Evidence base for 2016 updated recommendations for a safe infant sleeping environment. *Pediatrics*, *138*(5), e20162940.

Moore, L., & Thompson, F. (2015). Adults meeting fruit and vegetable intake recommendations—United States, 2013. *Morbidity & Mortality Weekly Report*, *64*(26), 709–713.

Moosavi, A., & Ardekani, A. M. (2016). Role of epigenetics in biology and human diseases. *Iranian Biomedical Journal*, *20*(5), 246.

Morgan, K., Gregory, P., Tomeny, M., David, B. M., & Gascoigne, C. (2012). Self-help treatment for insomnia symptoms associated with chronic conditions in older adults: A randomized controlled trial. *Journal of the American Geriatrics Society*, *60*(10), 1803–1810.

Morin, C. M. (1993). *Insomnia: Psychological assessment and management*. New York, NY: Guilford Press.

Morin, C. M., Bootzin, R. R., Buysse, D. J., Edinger, J. D., Espie, C. A., & Lichstein, K. L. (2006). Psychological and behavioral treatment of insomnia: Update of the recent evidence (1998–2004). *Sleep*, *29*(11), 1398–1414.

Morley, S., Eccleston, C., & Williams, A. (1999). Systematic review and meta-analysis of randomized controlled trials of cognitive behaviour therapy and behaviour therapy for chronic pain in adults, excluding headache. *Pain*, *80*(1–2), 1–13.

Morra, L. F., & Strauss, G. P. (2016). Severity of hypertension predicts the generalized neurocognitive deficit in schizophrenia. *Schizophrenia Research*, *176*(2), 527–528.

Morris, J. N., Heady, J. A., Raffle, P. A. B., Roberts, C. G., & Parks, J. W. (1953). Coronary heart-disease and physical activity of work. *The Lancet*, *262*(6796), 1111–1120.

Morrison, R. S., Wallenstein, S., Natale, D. K., Senzel, R. S., & Huang, L. L. (2000). "We don't carry that"—failure of pharmacies in predominantly nonwhite neighborhoods to stock opioid analgesics. *New England Journal of Medicine*, *342*(14), 1023–1026.

Morrissey, E. C., Durand, H., Nieuwlaat, R., Navarro, T., Haynes, R. B., Walsh, J. C., & Molloy, G. J. (2017). Effectiveness and content analysis of interventions to enhance medication adherence and blood pressure control in hypertension: A systematic review and meta-analysis. *Psychology & Health*, *32*(10), 1195–1232.

Moser, D. K., & Dracup, K. (1996). Is anxiety early after myocardial infarction associated with subsequent ischemic and arrhythmic events? *Psychosomatic Medicine*, *58*(5), 395–401.

Moser, M. (2006). Historical perspectives on the management of hypertension. *Journal of Clinical Hypertension*, *8*(8 Suppl 2), 15–20.

Mossialos, E., Wenzl, M., Osborn, R., & Anderson, C. (2017). *International profiles of health care systems*. New York, NY: The Commonwealth Fund.

Mucci, L. A., Hjelmborg, J. B., Harris, J. R., Czene, K., Havelick, D. J., Scheike, T., . . . & McIntosh, C. (2016). Familial risk and heritability of cancer among twins in Nordic countries. *Journal of the American Medical Association*, *315*(1), 68–76.

Murdock, B. B., Jr. (1962). The serial position effect of free recall. *Journal of Experimental Psychology*, *64*(5), 482–488.

Murray, C. D., Pettifer, S., Howard, T., Patchick, E. L., Caillette, F., Kulkarni, J., & Bamford, C. (2007). The treatment of phantom limb pain using immersive virtual reality: Three case studies. *Disability and Rehabilitation*, *29*(18), 1465–1469.

Murtagh, D. R., & Greenwood, K. M. (1995). Identifying effective psychological treatments for insomnia: A meta-analysis. *Journal of Consulting and Clinical Psychology*, *63*(1), 79–89.

Myers, L. B., & Midence, K. (1998). *Adherence to treatment in medical conditions*. Reading, UK: Harwood Academic.

Myers, L. L. (2010). Health risk behaviors among adolescents in the rural South: A comparison of race, gender, and age. *Journal of Human Behavior in the Social Environment*, *20*(8), 1024–1037.

Myint, P. K., Luben, R. N., Wareham, N. J., Bingham, S. A., & Khaw, K. T. (2009). Combined effect of health behaviours and risk of first ever stroke in 20,040 men and women over 11 years' follow-up in Norfolk cohort of European Prospective Investigation of Cancer (EPIC Norfolk): Prospective population study. *British Medical Journal*, *19*(338), b349.

Nader, R. (1965). *Unsafe at any speed: The designed-in dangers of the American automobile*. New York, NY: Grossman.

Nair, K. V., Miller, K., Park, J., Allen, R. R., Saseen, J. J., & Biddle, V. (2010). Prescription co-pay reduction program for diabetic employees. *Population Health Management*, *13*(5), 235–245.

National Adolescent and Young Adult Health Information Center. (2014). *A guide to evidence-based programs for adolescent health*. San Francisco, CA: University of California–San Francisco.

National Institute of Mental Health (2018). Major depression. https://www.nimh.nih.gov/health/statistics/major-depression.shtml.

Nelson, H. D., Tyne, K., Naik, A., Bougatsos, C., Chan, B. K., & Humphrey, L. (2009). Screening for breast cancer: An update for the US Preventive Services Task Force. *Annals of Internal Medicine*, *151*(10), 727–737.

Ness, R. C. (1978). The old hag phenomenon as sleep paralysis: A biocultural interpretation. *Culture, Medicine and Psychiatry*, *2*(1), 15–39.

Nestoriuc, Y., Martin, A., Rief, W., & Andrasik, F. (2008). Biofeedback treatment for headache disorders: A comprehensive efficacy review. *Applied Psychophysiology and Biofeedback*, *33*(3), 125–140.

Neuman, W. (2018, April 16). City orders Sims statue removed from Central Park. *New York Times*.

Newsham, D. (2000). Parental non-concordance with occlusion therapy. *British Journal of Ophthalmology, 84*, 957–962.

Ng, M., Freeman, M. K., Fleming, T. D., Robinson, M., Dwyer-Lindgren, L., Thomson, B., . . . & Murray, C. J. (2014). Smoking prevalence and cigarette consumption in 187 countries, 1980–2012. *Journal of the American Medical Association, 311*(2), 183–192.

Ng, W. S., Agarwal, P. K., Sidiki, S., MacKay, L., Townend, J., & Blanco, A. A. (2010). The effect of socioeconomic deprivation on severity of glaucoma at presentation. *British Journal of Ophthalmology, 94*(1), 85–87.

Ngandu, T., Lehtisalo, J., Solomon, A., Levälahti, E., Ahtiluoto, S., Antikainen, R., . . . & Lindström, J. (2015). A 2 year multidomain intervention of diet, exercise, cognitive training, and vascular risk monitoring versus control to prevent cognitive decline in at-risk elderly people (FINGER): A randomised controlled trial. *The Lancet, 385*(9984), 2255–2263.

Nguyen, S. N., Von Kohorn, I., Schulman-Green, D., & Colson, E. R. (2012). The importance of social networks on smoking: Perspectives of women who quit smoking during pregnancy. *Maternal and Child Health Journal, 16*(6), 1312–1318.

Nichols, K. H., Rice, M., & Howell, C. (2011). Anger, stress and blood pressure in overweight children. *Journal of Pediatric Nursing, 26*(5), 446–455.

Nieuwlaat, R., Wilczynski, N., Navarro, T., Hobson, N., Jeffery, R., Keepanasseril, A., . . . & Sivaramalingam, B. (2014). Interventions for enhancing medication adherence. *Cochrane Database of Systematic Reviews, 20*(11).

Nikolajsen, L., & Christensen, K. F. (2015). Phantom limb pain. In R. Tubbs, E. Rizk, M. Shoja, et al. (Eds.). *Nerves and Nerve Injuries* (pp. 23–34). Waltham, MA: Academic Press.

Nikolajsen, L., & Jensen, T. (2015). Phantom limb pain. *British Journal of Anaesthesia, 87*, 107–116.

Niles, A. N., Dour, H. J., Stanton, A. L., Roy-Byrne, P. P., Stein, M. B., Sullivan, G., . . . & Craske, M. G. (2015). Anxiety and depressive symptoms and medical illness among adults with anxiety disorders. *Journal of Psychosomatic Research, 78*(2), 109–115.

Nimmon, L., & Stenfors-Hayes, T. (2016). The "handling" of power in the physician-patient encounter: Perceptions from experienced physicians. *BMC Medical Education, 16*(1), 114.

Nimnuan, C., Hotopf, M., & Wessely, S. (2001). Medically unexplained symptoms: An epidemiological study in seven specialities. *Journal of Psychosomatic Research, 51*(1), 361–367.

Nimnuan, C., Rabe-Hesketh, S., Wessely, S., & Hotopf, M. (2001). How many functional somatic syndromes? *Journal of Psychosomatic Research, 51*(4), 549–557.

Noble, L. M. (1998). Doctor-patient communication and adherence to treatment. In L. B. Myers & K. Midence (Eds.), *Adherence to treatment in medical conditions* (pp. 51–82). Amsterdam, Netherlands: Harwood Academic Publishers.

Nolen-Hoeksema, S., & Jackson, B. (2001). Mediators of the gender difference in rumination. *Psychology of Women Quarterly, 25*(1), 37–47.

Norcross, J. C., Mrykalo, M. S., & Blagys, M. D. (2002). Auld lang syne: Success predictors, change processes, and self-reported outcomes of New Year's resolvers and nonresolvers. *Journal of Clinical Psychology, 58*(4), 397–405.

Notzon, F. C., Komarov, Y. M., Ermakov, S. P., Sempos, C. T., Marks, J. S., & Sempos, E. V. (1998). Causes of declining life expectancy in Russia. *Journal of the American Medical Association, 279*(10), 793–800.

Nour, N. M. (2009). Child marriage: A silent health and human rights issue. *Reviews in Obstetrics and Gynecology, 2*(1), 51.

Novotney, A. (2014, September). Students under pressure. *Monitor on Psychology*, 37–41.

Nurnberg, H. G., Hensley, P. L., Heiman, J. R., Croft, H. A., Debattista, C., & Paine, S. (2008). Sildenafil treatment of women with antidepressant-associated sexual dysfunction: A randomized controlled trial. *Journal of the American Medical Association, 300*(4), 395–404.

Obama, B. (2016). United States health care reform: Progress to date and next steps. *Journal of the American Medical Association, 316*(5), 525–532.

Obenchain, T. G. (2016). *Genius belabored: Childbed fever and the tragic life of Ignaz Semmelweis*. Tuscaloosa, AL: University of Alabama Press.

Obradović, J., Bush, N. R., Stamperdahl, J., Adler, N. E., & Boyce, W. T. (2010). Biological sensitivity to context: The interactive effects of stress reactivity and family adversity on socioemotional behavior and school readiness. *Child Development, 81*(1), 270–289.

O'Connor, D. B., & Shimizu, M. (2002). Sense of personal control, stress and coping style: A cross-cultural study. *Stress and Health: Journal of the International Society for the Investigation of Stress, 18*(4), 173–183.

OECD Health Statistics (2017). http://www.oecd.org/els/health-systems/health-data.htm.

O'Farrell, T. J., & Fals-Stewart, W. (2003). Alcohol abuse. *Journal of Marital and Family Therapy, 29*(1), 121–146.

Offenbaecher, M., Bondy, B., Jonge, S. D., Glatzeder, K., Krüger, M., Schoeps, P., & Ackenheil, M. (1999). Possible association of fibromyalgia with a polymorphism in the serotonin transporter gene regulatory region. *Arthritis & Rheumatism: Official Journal of the American College of Rheumatology, 42*(11), 2482–2488.

Ogilvie, G., Anderson, M., Marra, F., McNeil, S., Pielak, K., Dawar, M., . . . & Patrick, D. M. (2010). A population-based evaluation of a publicly funded, school-based HPV vaccine program in British Columbia, Canada: Parental factors associated with HPV vaccine receipt. *Plos Medicine, 7*(5), e1000270.

Ohayon, M. M. (2002). Epidemiology of insomnia: What we know and what we still need to learn. *Sleep Medicine Reviews, 6*(2), 97–111.

Ohayon, M. M., Priest, R. G., Caulet, M., & Guilleminault, C. (1996). Hypnagogic and hypnopompic hallucinations: Pathological phenomena? *British Journal of Psychiatry, 169*(4), 459–467.

Ohayon, M. M., Priest, R. G., Zulley, J., Smirne, S., & Paiva, T. (2002). Prevalence of narcolepsy symptomatology and diagnosis in the European general population. *Neurology, 58*(12), 1826–1833.

Olsen, O., & Gøtzsche, P. C. (2001). Cochrane review on screening for breast cancer with mammography. *The Lancet, 358*(9290), 1340–1342.

Ong, J. C. (2017). *Mindfulness-based therapy for insomnia*. Washington, DC: American Psychological Association.

Orchard, A. (2013, August 12). The Lordstown strike. Walter Reuther Library, Wayne State University. http://reuther.wayne.edu/node/10756.

Orel, N. A. (2014). Investigating the needs and concerns of lesbian, gay, bisexual, and transgender older adults: The use of qualitative and quantitative methodology. *Journal of Homosexuality, 61*(1), 53–78.

OrganDonor.gov. (2018). Organ donation statistics. https://www.organdonor.gov/.

Oshinsky, D. M. (2005). *Polio: An American story*. New York, NY: Oxford University Press.

Otten, J. J., Saelens, B. E., Kapphahn, K. I., Hekler, E. B., Buman, M. P., Goldstein, B. A., . . . & King, A. C. (2014). Peer reviewed: Impact of San Francisco's toy ordinance on restaurants and children's food purchases, 2011–2012. *Preventing Chronic Disease, 11*, (E122).

Paffenbarger, R. S., Jr., Blair, S. N., & Lee, I. M. (2001). A history of physical activity, cardiovascular health and longevity: The scientific contributions of Jeremy N. Morris, DSc, DPH, FRCP. *International Journal of Epidemiology, 30*(5), 1184–1192.

Pagel, J. F. (2009). Excessive daytime sleepiness. *American Family Physician, 79*(5), 391–396.

Pantalone, D., Haldeman, D., & Martell, C. (2018). Health care issues facing lesbian, gay, bisexual, and transgender individuals. In O. J. Sahler, J. E. Carr, J. B. Frank, & J. Nunes (Eds.), *The behavioral sciences and health care* (4th ed., pp. 163–174). Boston MA: Hogrefe.

Paradis, C. M., & Friedman, S. (2005). Sleep paralysis in African Americans with panic disorder. *Transcultural Psychiatry, 42*(1), 123–134.

Parretti, H. M., Jebb, S. A., Johns, D. J., Lewis, A. L., Christian-Brown, A. M., & Aveyard, P. (2016). Clinical effectiveness of very-low-energy diets in the management of weight loss: A systematic review and meta-analysis of randomized controlled trials. *Obesity Reviews, 17*(3), 225–234.

Parsons, T. (1951). Illness and the role of the physician: A sociological perspective. *American Journal of Orthopsychiatry, 21*(3), 452–460.

Patel, N. P., Grandner, M. A., Xie, D., Branas, C. C., & Gooneratne, N. (2010). "Sleep disparity" in the population: Poor sleep quality is strongly associated with poverty and ethnicity. *BMC Public Health, 10*(1), 475.

Patel, S. R., Malhotra, A., White, D. P., Gottlieb, D. J., & Hu, F. B. (2006). Association between reduced sleep and weight gain in women. *American Journal of Epidemiology, 164*(10), 947–954.

Payer L. (1988). *Medicine and culture: Varieties of treatment in the United States, Germany, and France*. New York, NY: Henry Holt.

Pedersen, C. A., Ascher, J. A., Monroe, Y. L., & Prange, A. J. (1982). Oxytocin induces maternal behavior in virgin female rats. *Science, 216*(4546), 648–650.

Peel Ontario Department of Public Health. (2018). Host responsibilities. http://www.peelregion.ca/health/responsible/alcohol/mocktails.htm.

Peeno, L. (1996, May 30). Congressional testimony. http://www.hospicepatients.org/drpeenotestimony.html.

Peigneux, P., Urbain, C., & Schmitz, R. (2012). *Sleep and the brain*. Oxford: Oxford University Press.

Pence, G. (2017). *Medical ethics: Accounts of groundbreaking cases* (8th ed.). New York, NY: McGraw Hill.

Pennebaker, J. W., Kiecolt-Glaser, J. K., & Glaser, R. (1988). Disclosure of traumas and immune function: Health implications for psychotherapy. *Journal of Consulting and Clinical Psychology, 56*(2), 239–245.

Pennebaker, J. W., & Smyth, J. M. (2016). *Opening up by writing it down: How expressive writing improves health and eases emotional pain*. New York, NY: Guilford Press.

Penzien, D. B., Rains, J. C., Lipchik, G. L., & Creer, T. L. (2004). Behavioral interventions for tension-type headache: Overview of current therapies and recommendation for a self-management model for chronic headache. *Current Pain and Headache Reports, 8*(6), 489–499.

Pergolizzi, J. V., Jr., Mercadante, S., Echaburu, A. V., Eynden, B. V. D., Fragoso, R. M. D. F., Mordarski, S., . . . & Slama, O. (2009). The role of transdermal buprenorphine in the treatment of cancer pain: An expert panel consensus. *Current Medical Research and Opinion, 25*(6), 1517–1528.

Perkins, S., Searight, H. R., & Ratwik, S. (2011). Walking in a natural winter setting to relieve attention fatigue: A pilot study. *Psychology, 2*(8), 777.

Perlis, M. L., Giles, D. E., Mendelson, W. B., Bootzin, R. R., & Wyatt, J. K. (1997). Psychophysiological insomnia: The behavioural model and a neurocognitive perspective. *Journal of Sleep Research, 6*(3), 179–188.

Peters, S., Goldthorpe, J., McElroy, C., King, E., Javidi, H., Tickle, M., & Aggarwal, V. R. (2015). Managing chronic orofacial pain: A qualitative study of patients', doctors', and dentists' experiences. *British Journal of Health Psychology, 20*(4), 777–791.

Peterson, A., Takiya, L., & Finley, R. (2003). Meta-analysis of trials of interventions to improve medication adherence. *American Journal of Health Systems Pharmacy, 60*, 657–665.

Peterson, A., Vander Weg, W., & Jaén, C. (2015). *Nicotine and tobacco dependence.* Boston, MA: Hogrefe and Huber.

Pezalla, E. J., Rosen, D., Erensen, J. G., Haddox, J. D., & Mayne, T. J. (2017). Secular trends in opioid prescribing in the USA. *Journal of Pain Research, 10,* 383–387.

Phillips, C. V., & Goodman, K. J. (2004). The missed lessons of Sir Bradford Hill. *Epidemiologic Perspectives & Innovations, 1*(1), 3.

Picariello, F., Ali, S., Moss-Morris, R., & Chalder, T. (2015). The most popular terms for medically unexplained symptoms: The views of CFS patients. *Journal of Psychosomatic Research, 78*(5), 420–426.

Pike, K. M., & Dunne, P. E. (2015). The rise of eating disorders in Asia: A review. *Journal of Eating Disorders, 3*(1), 33.

Pillai, V., Steenburg, L. A., Ciesla, J. A., Roth, T., & Drake, C. L. (2014). A seven day actigraphy-based study of rumination and sleep disturbance among young adults with depressive symptoms. *Journal of Psychosomatic Research, 77*(1), 70–75.

Pillsbury, B. L. (1978). "Doing the month": Confinement and convalescence of Chinese women after childbirth. *Social Science & Medicine. Part B: Medical Anthropology, 12,* 11–22.

Pincus, T., Burton, A. K., Vogel, S., & Field, A. P. (2002). A systematic review of psychological factors as predictors of chronicity/disability in prospective cohorts of low back pain. *Spine, 27*(5), E109–E120.

Pistelli, F., Aquilini, F., & Carrozzi, L. (2016). Weight gain after smoking cessation. *Monaldi Archives for Chest Disease, 71*(2).

Polatin, P. B., Kinney, R., Gatchel, R. J., Lillo, E., & Mayer, T. G. (1993). Psychiatric illness and chronic low-back pain. The mind and the spine—which goes first? *Spine, 18*(1), 66–71.

Pollock, G. H. (1961). Mourning and adaptation. *International Journal of Psycho-Analysis, 42,* 341–361.

Porter, J., & Jick, H. (1980). Addiction rare in patients treated with narcotics. *New England Journal of Medicine, 302*(2), 123.

Poss, J., & Jezewski, M. A. (2002). The role and meaning of susto in Mexican Americans' explanatory model of type 2 diabetes. *Medical Anthropology Quarterly, 16*(3), 360–377.

Poulsen, P., Kyvik, K. O., Vaag, A., & Beck-Nielsen, H. (1999). Heritability of type II (non-insulin-dependent) diabetes mellitus and abnormal glucose tolerance: A population-based twin study. *Diabetologia, 42*(2), 139–145.

Powe, B. D. (1995). Fatalism among elderly African Americans. Effects on colorectal cancer screening. *Cancer Nursing, 18*(5), 385–392.

Powell, L. H., Shahabi, L., & Thoresen, C. E. (2003). Religion and spirituality: Linkages to physical health. *American Psychologist, 58*(1), 36–52.

Press, M. J., Howe, R., Schoenbaum, M., Cavanaugh, S., Marshall, A., Baldwin, L., & Conway, P. H. (2017). Medicare payment for behavioral health integration. *New England Journal of Medicine, 376*(5), 405–407.

Price, J. H. (2014). Adherence barriers to andtidepressants among the urban female Latino population. *Ethnomed.* http://ethnomed.org/clinical/mental-health/adherence-barriers-to-antidepressants-among-an-urban-female-latino-population.

Price-Wise, G. (2008). Language, culture, and medical tragedy: The case of Willie Ramirez. *Health Affairs Blog.* https://www.healthaffairs.org/do/10.1377/hblog20081119.000463/full/.

Prochaska, J. J., Hall, S. E., Delucchi, K., & Hall, S. M. (2014). Efficacy of initiating tobacco dependence treatment in inpatient psychiatry: A randomized controlled trial. *American Journal of Public Health, 104*(8), 1557–1565.

Prochaska, J. J., Hall, S. M., & Bero, L. A. (2007). Tobacco use among individuals with schizophrenia: What role has the tobacco industry played? *Schizophrenia Bulletin, 34*(3), 555–567.

Prochaska, J. O. (1994). Strong and weak principles for progressing from precontemplation to action on the basis of twelve problem behaviors. *Health Psychology, 13*(1), 47–51.

Prochaska, J. O., & DiClemente, C. C. (1982). Transtheoretical therapy: Toward a more integrative model of change. *Psychotherapy: Theory, Research & Practice, 19*(3), 276–288.

Prochaska, J. O., DiClemente, C. C., & Norcross, J. C. (1992). In search of how people change: Applications to addictive behaviors. *American Psychologist, 47*(9), 1102–1114.

Prochaska, J. O., Velicer, W. F., Rossi, J. S., Goldstein, M. G., Marcus, B. H., Rakowski, W., . . . & Rossi, S. R. (1994). Stages of change and decisional balance for 12 problem behaviors. *Health Psychology, 13*(1), 39–46.

Puhl, R. M., & Heuer, C. A. (2009). The stigma of obesity: A review and update. *Obesity, 17*(5), 941–964.

Pun, S. P., Coates, V., & Benzie, I. F. (2009). Barriers to the self-care of type 2 diabetes from both patients' and providers' perspectives: Literature review. *Journal of Nursing and Healthcare of Chronic Illness, 1*(1), 4–19.

Puskarich, C. A., Whitman, S., Dell, J., Hughes, J. R., Rosen, A. J., & Hermann, B. P. (1992). Controlled examination of effects of progressive relaxation training on seizure reduction. *Epilepsia, 33*(4), 675–680.

Puskas, C. M., Kaida, A., Miller, C. L., Zhang, W., Yip, B., Pick, N., . . . & Hogg, R. S. (2017). The adherence gap: A longitudinal examination of men's and women's antiretroviral therapy adherence in British Columbia, 2000–2014. *AIDS, 31*(6), 827–833.

Quinn, C. C., Clough, S. S., Minor, J. M., Lender, D., Okafor, M. C., & Gruber-Baldini, A. (2008). WellDoc mobile diabetes management randomized controlled trial: Change in clinical and behavioral outcomes and patient and physician satisfaction. *Diabetes Technology & Therapeutics, 10*(3), 160–168.

Quinn, G. P., Sanchez, J. A., Sutton, S. K., Vadaparampil, S. T., Nguyen, G. T., Green, B. L., . . . & Schabath, M. B. (2015). Cancer and lesbian, gay, bisexual, transgender/transsexual, and queer/questioning (LGBTQ) populations. *CA: A Cancer Journal for Clinicians, 65*(5), 384–400.

Raco, M. (2017). This is what we know about HPV, the vaccine and its backlash. *Global News* (October 18). https://globalnews.ca/news/3805478/this-is-what-we-know-about-hpv-the-vaccine-and-its-backlash/.

Radek, K. S., & Kaprelian, J. (2013). Emerging adult sleep quality: Health and academic performance factors of assessment. *Journal of Sleep Disorders and Therapy* 2(112).

Randall, V. R. (1995). Slavery, segregation and racism: Trusting the health care system ain't always easy—an African American perspective on bioethics. *Saint Louis University Public Law Review, 15*, 191.

Ravussin, E., Valencia, M. E., Esparza, J., Bennett, P. H., & Schulz, L. O. (1994). Effects of a traditional lifestyle on obesity in Pima Indians. *Diabetes Care, 17*(9), 1067–1074.

Raynor, D. K. (1998). The influence of written information on patient knowledge and adherence to treatment. In L. Myers & K. Midence (Eds.), *Adherence to treatment in medical conditions* (pp. 83–111). Amsterdam, Netherlands: Harwood Academic Publishers.

Redelmeier, D. A., & Singh, S. M. (2001). Survival in Academy Award–winning actors and actresses. *Annals of Internal Medicine, 134*(10), 955–962.

Reding, N. (2010). *Methland: The death and life of an American small town*. New York, NY: Bloomsbury Publishing USA.

Rendall, M. S., Weden, M. M., Favreault, M. M., & Waldron, H. (2011). The protective effect of marriage for survival: A review and update. *Demography, 48*(2), 481–506.

Resnicow, K., & Blackburn, D. (2005). Motivational interviewing in medical settings. *Obesity Management, 1*(4), 155–159.

Reverby, S. M. (2011). "Normal exposure" and inoculation syphilis: A PHS "Tuskegee" doctor in Guatemala, 1946-1948. *Journal of Policy History, 23*(1), 6–28.

Reynolds, S., Searight, H. R., & Ratwik, S. (2014). Adult attachment styles and rumination in the context of intimate relationships. *North American Journal of Psychology, 16*(3), 495–506.

Rich, E. C., Crowson, T. W., & Harris, I. B. (1987). The diagnostic value of the medical history: Perceptions of internal medicine physicians. *Archives of Internal Medicine, 147*(11), 1957–1960.

Richards, W. (1971). The fortification illusions of migraines. *Scientific American, 224*(5), 88–97.

Richardson, L. P., Davis, R., Poulton, R., McCauley, E., Moffitt, T. E., Caspi, A., & Connell, F. (2003). A longitudinal evaluation of adolescent depression and adult obesity. *Archives of Pediatrics & Adolescent Medicine, 157*(8), 739–745.

Richter, R. (2015). Among teens, sleep deprivation an epidemic. Stanford Medicine News Center. https://med.stanford.edu/news/all-news/2015/10/among-teens-sleep-deprivation-an-epidemic.html.

Rider, G. N., McMorris, B. J., Gower, A. L., Coleman, E., & Eisenberg, M. E. (2018, February). Health and care utilization of transgender and gender nonconforming youth: A population-based study. *Pediatrics*, e20171683.

Riedel, S. (2005). Edward Jenner and the history of smallpox and vaccination. *Baylor University Medical Center Proceedings, 18*(1), 21–25.

Rimer, B. K., & Brewer, N. T. (2015). Introduction to health behavior theories that focus on individuals. In K. Glanz, B. K. Rimer, & K. Viswanath (Eds.), *Health behavior: Theory, research and practice* (5th ed., pp. 67–74). San Francisco, CA: Jossey-Bass.

Roberto, C. A., Larsen, P. D., Agnew, H., Baik, J., & Brownell, K. D. (2010). Evaluating the impact of menu labeling on food choices and intake. *American Journal of Public Health, 100*(2), 312–318.

Roberts, J., & Mitchell, L. (2017). "It's your body, your decision": An anthropological investigation of HPV vaccine hesitancy. In P. Bramadat, M. Guay, J. A. Bettinger, & R. Roy (Eds.), *Public health in the age of anxiety: Religious and cultural roots of vaccine hesitancy in Canada* (pp. 293–320). Toronto, ON: University of Toronto Press.

Robinson, J. K., Altman, J. S., & Rademaker, A. W. (1995). Socioeconomic status and attitudes of 51 patients with giant basal and squamous cell carcinoma and paired controls. *Archives of Dermatology, 131*(4), 428–431.

Robinson, R. G., & Sutton, C. D. (1994). The coalition against Uptown cigarettes. *Making news, changing policy: Case studies of media advocacy on alcohol and tobacco issues*. Rockville, MD: University Research Corporation and the Marin Institute for the Prevention of Alcohol and Other Drug Problems, Center for Substance Abuse Prevention.

Rodin, J., & Baum, A. (1978). Crowding and helplessness: Potential consequences of density and loss of control. In J. Rodin & A. Baum (Eds). *Human*

response to crowding (pp. 389–401). Hillsdale, NJ: Lawrence Erlbaum.
Rogers, E. M. (2004). A prospective and retrospective look at the diffusion model. *Journal of Health Communication, 9*(Suppl 1), 13–19.
Rollnick, S., & Miller, W. R. (1995). What is motivational interviewing? *Behavioural and Cognitive Psychotherapy, 23*(4), 325–334.
Rollnick, S., Miller, W. R., & Butler, C. C. (2008). *Motivational interviewing in health care: Helping patients change behavior.* New York, NY: Guilford Press.
Roseboom, T., de Rooij, S., & Painter, R. (2006). The Dutch famine and its long-term consequences for adult health. *Early Human Development, 82*(8), 485–491.
Rosen, R. C., Miner, M. M., & Wincze, J. P. (2014). Erectile dysfunction: Integration of psychological and medical approaches. In Y. M. Binik & K. S. Hall (Eds.), *Principles and practice of sex therapy* (5th ed., pp. 61–86). New York, NY: Guilford Press.
Rosenbaum, D. (1984, March 5). Chrysler, hit hard by costs, studies health care system. *New York Times*.
Rosenbaum, T. Y. (2013). An integrated mindfulness-based approach to the treatment of women with sexual pain and anxiety: Promoting autonomy and mind/body connection. *Sexual and Relationship Therapy, 28*(1–2), 20–28.
Rosenblum, A., Marsch, L. A., Joseph, H., & Portenoy, R. K. (2008). Opioids and the treatment of chronic pain: Controversies, current status, and future directions. *Experimental and Clinical Psychopharmacology, 16*(5), 405–416.
Rosengren, D. B. (2017). *Building motivational interviewing skills: A practitioner workbook.* New York, NY: Guilford Press.
Rosenstock, I. M. (1974). The health belief model and preventive health behavior. *Health Education Monographs, 2*(4), 354–386.
Rosenthal, E. (2013, August 3). In need of a new hip, but priced out of the U.S. *New York Times*.
Ross, N. A., Wolfson, M. C., Dunn, J. R., Berthelot, J. M., Kaplan, G. A., & Lynch, J. W. (2000). Relation between income inequality and mortality in Canada and in the United States: Cross sectional assessment using census data and vital statistics. *British Medical Journal, 320*(7239), 898–902.
Roter, D. L., Hall, J. A., & Aoki, Y. (2002). Physician gender effects in medical communication: A meta-analytic review. *Journal of the American Medical Association, 288*(6), 756–764.
Roter, D. L., Hall, J. A., Kern, D. E., Barker, L. R., Cole, K. A., & Roca, R. P. (1995). Improving physicians' interviewing skills and reducing patients' emotional distress: A randomized clinical trial. *Archives of Internal Medicine, 155*(17), 1877–1884.
Roter, D. L., Stewart, M., Putnam, S. M., Lipkin, M., Stiles, W., & Inui, T. S. (1997). Communication patterns of primary care physicians. *Journal of the American Medical Association, 277*(4), 350–356.
Rothenberg, R. B., Sterk, C., Toomey, K. E., Potterat, J. J., Johnson, D., Schrader, M., & Hatch, S. (1998). Using social network and ethnographic tools to evaluate syphilis transmission. *Sexually Transmitted Diseases, 25*(3), 154–160.
Rowland, D. L. (2012). *Sexual dysfunction in men.* Cambridge, MA: Hogrefe.
Rozenblat, V., Ong, D., Fuller-Tyszkiewicz, M., Akkermann, K., Collier, D., Engels, R. C., . . . & Kiive, E. (2017). A systematic review and secondary data analysis of the interactions between the serotonin transporter 5-HTTLPR polymorphism and environmental and psychological factors in eating disorders. *Journal of Psychiatric Research, 84*, 62–72.
Rozin, P., Kabnick, K., Pete, E., Fischler, C., & Shields, C. (2003). The ecology of eating: Smaller portion sizes in France than in the United States help explain the French paradox. *Psychological Science, 14*(5), 450–454.
Ruesch, J., & Bateson, G. (1949). Structure and process in social relations. *Psychiatry, 12*(2), 105–124.
Ruiter, R. A., Kessels, L. T., Peters, G. J. Y., & Kok, G. (2014). Sixty years of fear appeal research: Current state of the evidence. *International Journal of Psychology, 49*(2), 63–70.
Russell, P. (2018, August 28). GPs should house mental health services within practices. MedScape. https://www.medscape.com/viewarticle/901257.
Rustøen, T., Wahl, A. K., Hanestad, B. R., Lerdal, A., Paul, S., & Miaskowski, C. (2004). Prevalence and characteristics of chronic pain in the general Norwegian population. *European Journal of Pain, 8*(6), 555–565.
Rutledge, T., & Hogan, B. E. (2002). A quantitative review of prospective evidence linking psychological factors with hypertension development. *Psychosomatic Medicine, 64*(5), 758–766.
Ryan, B., & Gross, N. C. (1943). The diffusion of hybrid seed corn in two Iowa communities. *Rural Sociology, 8*(1), 15.
Ryff, C. D., Singer, B. H., & Love, G. D. (2004). Positive health: Connecting well-being with biology. *Philosophical Transactions of the Royal Society B: Biological Sciences, 359*(1449), 1383–1394.
Sabido, M. (2003). The origins of entertainment-education. In A. Singhal, M. J. Cody, E. M. Rogers, & M. Sabido (Eds.), *Entertainment-education and social change* (pp. 83–96). New York, NY: Routledge.
Sabin, J. A., Rivara, F. P., & Greenwald, A. G. (2008). Physician implicit attitudes and stereotypes about race and quality of medical care. *Medical Care, 46*(7), 678–685.
Sackett, D. L. (1997). *Evidence-based medicine: How to practice and teach EBM.* Philadelphia, PA: WB Saunders Company.

Sadeh, A., Gruber, R., & Raviv, A. (2003). The effects of sleep restriction and extension on school-age children: What a difference an hour makes. *Child Development, 74*(2), 444–455.

Saha, S., Komaromy, M., Koepsell, T. D., & Bindman, A. B. (1999). Patient-physician racial concordance and the perceived quality and use of health care. *Archives of Internal Medicine, 159*(9), 997–1004.

Sahota, P. K., Jain, S. S., & Dhand, R. (2003). Sleep disorders in pregnancy. *Current Opinion in Pulmonary Medicine, 9*(6), 477–483.

Saito, T., & Angles, J. (2013). *Hikikomori: Adolescence without end*. Minneapolis, MN: University of Minnesota Press.

Sallin, K., Lagercrantz, H., Evers, K., Engström, I., Hjern, A., & Petrovic, P. (2016). Resignation Syndrome: Catatonia? Culture-Bound? *Frontiers in Behavioral Neuroscience, 10*(7). doi: 10.3389/fnbeh.2016.00007.

Salmon, P. (2001). Effects of physical exercise on anxiety, depression, and sensitivity to stress: A unifying theory. *Clinical Psychology Review, 21*(1), 33–61.

Salmon, P., & Calderbank, S. (1996). The relationship of childhood physical and sexual abuse to adult illness behavior. *Journal of Psychosomatic Research, 40*(3), 329–336.

Sampson, R. J., & Winter, A. S. (2016). The racial ecology of lead poisoning: Toxic inequality in Chicago neighborhoods, 1995–2013. *Du Bois Review: Social Science Research on Race, 13*(2), 261–283.

Sanger-Katz, M. (2014, July 23). Two Americas on health care, and danger of further division. *New York Times*.

Sansone, R. A., & Sansone, L. A. (2012). Antidepressant adherence: Are patients taking their medications? *Innovations in Clinical Neuroscience, 9*(5–6), 41.

Santo, K., Richtering, S. S., Chalmers, J., Thiagalingam, A., Chow, C. K., & Redfern, J. (2016). Mobile phone apps to improve medication adherence: A systematic stepwise process to identify high-quality apps. *Journal of Medical Internet Research, 4*(4), e132.

Santtila, P., Jern, P., Westberg, L., Walum, H., Pedersen, C. T., Eriksson, E., & Kenneth Sandnabba, N. (2010). The dopamine transporter gene (DAT1) polymorphism is associated with premature ejaculation. *Journal of Sexual Medicine, 7*(4, pt. 1), 1538–1546.

Sapolsky, R. (2004). *Why don't zebras get ulcers?* New York, NY: Henry Holt and Company.

Sarafino, E. P., & Smith, T. W. (2011). *Health psychology: Biopsychosocial interactions* (7th ed.). New York, NY: John Wiley & Sons.

Schanzer, B., Dominguez, B., Shrout, P. E., & Caton, C. L. (2007). Homelessness, health status, and health care use. *American Journal of Public Health, 97*(3), 464–469.

Scheier, M. F., & Carver, C. S. (2003). Self-regulatory processes and responses to health threats: Effects of optimism on well-being. In J. Suls & K. A. Wallston (Eds.), *Social psychological foundations of health and illness* (pp. 395–428). Malden, MA: Blackwell.

Schenck, C. H., & Mahowald, M. W. (2002). REM sleep behavior disorder: Clinical, developmental, and neuroscience perspectives 16 years after its formal identification in SLEEP. *Sleep: Journal of Sleep and Sleep Disorders Research, 25*(2), 120–138.

Scher, L. S., Maynard, R. A., & Stagner, M. (2006, December 19). Interventions intended to reduce pregnancy-related outcomes among adolescents. *Campbell Systematic Reviews*.

Schiavi, R. C., White, D., Mandeli, J., & Levine, A. C. (1997). Effect of testosterone administration on sexual behavior and mood in men with erectile dysfunction. *Archives of Sexual Behavior, 26*(3), 231–241.

Schlesinger, M. (2002). A loss of faith: The sources of reduced political legitimacy for the American medical profession. *The Milbank Quarterly, 80*(2), 185–235.

Schmidt, H., Voigt, K., & Emanuel, E. J. (2013). The ethics of not hiring smokers. *New England Journal of Medicine, 368*(15), 1369–1371.

Schneider, E. C., Zaslavsky, A. M., & Epstein, A. M. (2002). Racial disparities in the quality of care for enrollees in Medicare managed care. *Journal of the American Medical Association, 287*(10), 1288–1294.

Schorling, J. B., Roach, J., Siegel, M., Baturka, N., Hunt, D. E., Guterbock, T. M., & Stewart, H. L. (1997). A trial of church-based smoking cessation interventions for rural African Americans. *Preventive Medicine, 26*(1), 92–101.

Schouwenburg, H. C., & Lay, C. H. (1995). Trait procrastination and the big-five factors of personality. *Personality and Individual Differences, 18*(4), 481–490.

Schulman, K. A., Berlin, J. A., Harless, W., Kerner, J. F., Sistrunk, S., Gersh, B. J., . . . & Eisenberg, J. M. (1999). The effect of race and sex on physicians' recommendations for cardiac catheterization. *New England Journal of Medicine, 340*(8), 618–626.

Schultz, J. H., & Luthe, W. (1969). *Autogenic training* (Vol. 1). New York, NY: Grune & Stratton.

Schvey, N. A., Puhl, R. M., & Brownell, K. D. (2011). The impact of weight stigma on caloric consumption. *Obesity, 19*(10), 1957–1962.

Schwartz, B. (2015). The paradox of choice. In S. Joseph (Ed.), *Positive psychology in practice: Promoting human flourishing in work, health, education, and everyday life* (2nd ed., pp. 121–138). Hoboken, NJ: John Wiley & Sons.

Scofea, L. A. (1994). The development and growth of employer-provided health insurance. *Monthly Labor Review, 117*(3), 3–10.

Scull, A. (2009). *Hysteria: The biography*. Oxford, UK: Oxford University Press.

Searfoss, A. R. (2013). Review of William Lauinger's *Well-Being and Theism: Linking Ethics to God*. *International Journal of Wellbeing, 3*(2).

Searight, H. R. (1994). Psychosocial knowledge and allopathic medicine: Points of convergence and departure. *Journal of Medical Humanities*, 15(4), 221–232.

Searight, H. R. (1999). *Behavioral medicine: A primary care approach*. Philadelphia, PA: Taylor & Francis.

Searight, H. R. (2007). Efficient counseling techniques for the primary care physician. *Primary Care: Clinics in Office Practice*, 34(3), 551–570.

Searight, H. R. (2010). *Practicing psychology in primary care*. Boston, MA: Hogrefe.

Searight, H. R. (2014). *Family of origin therapy and cultural diversity*. New York, NY: Taylor & Francis.

Searight, H. R. (2016). The biopsychosocial model: "Reports of my death have been greatly exaggerated." *Culture, Medicine, and Psychiatry*, 40(2), 289–298.

Searight, H. R. (2017). Clinical and ethical issues in working with a foreign language interpreter. *Journal of Health Services Psychology*, 43, 79–82.

Searight, H. R. (2018). Behavior change. In M. Smith, S. Schraeger, & V. WinklerPrins (Eds.), *Essentials of family medicine* (7th ed.). Baltimore, MD: Lippincott, Williams, and Wilkins.

Searight, H. R. (2019, in press). Evidence based approaches for efficient counseling in primary care. *American Family Physician*.

Searight, H. R., & Armock, J. A. (2013). Foreign language interpreters in mental health: A literature review and research agenda. *North American Journal of Psychology*, 15(1), 17–38.

Searight, H. R., & Barbarash, R. A. (1994). Informed consent: Clinical and legal issues in family practice. *Family Medicine*, 26(4), 244–249.

Searight, H. R., & Gafford, J. (2005). Cultural diversity at the end of life: Issues and guidelines for family physicians. *American Family Physician*, 71(3), 515–522.

Searight, H. R., & Meredith, T. (2019, in press). Physician deception and telling the truth about medical "bad news": History, ethical perspectives, and cultural issues. In T. Docan-Morgan (Ed.), *Palgrave Handbook of Deceptive Communication*. New York, NY: Palgrave Macmillan.

Searight, H. R., & Noce, J. J. (1988). Towards a systemic model of health care compliance: Rationale and interview protocol. *Journal of Strategic and Systemic Therapies*, 7(1), 42–53.

Seeman, T. E., Singer, B. H., Rowe, J. W., Horwitz, R. I., & McEwen, B. S. (1997). Price of adaptation—allostatic load and its health consequences: MacArthur studies of successful aging. *Archives of Internal Medicine*, 157(19), 2259–2268.

Seligman, M. E. P., Ernst, R. M., Gillham, J., Reivich, K., & Linkins, M. (2009). Positive education: Positive psychology and classroom interventions. *Oxford Review of Education*, 35(3), 293–311.

Seligman, M. E. P., Steen, T. A., Park, N., & Peterson, C. (2005). Positive psychology progress: Empirical validation of interventions. *American Psychologist*, 60, 410–421.

Selye, H. (1973). The evolution of the stress concept: The originator of the concept traces its development from the discovery in 1936 of the alarm reaction to modern therapeutic applications of syntoxic and catatoxic hormones. *American Scientist*, 61(6), 692–699.

Shahar, E., Whitney, C. W., Redline, S., Lee, E. T., Newman, A. B., Javier Nieto, F., . . . & Samet, J. M. (2001). Sleep-disordered breathing and cardiovascular disease: Cross-sectional results of the Sleep Heart Health Study. *American Journal of Respiratory and Critical Care Medicine*, 163(1), 19–25.

Shahid, A., Wilkinson, K., Marcu, S., & Shapiro, C. M. (Eds.). (2012). Dysfunctional Beliefs and Attitudes About Sleep Scale (DBAS). In *STOP, THAT and one hundred other sleep scales* (pp. 145–147). New York, NY: Springer.

Shanafelt, T. D., Dyrbye, L. N., Sinsky, C., Hasan, O., Satele, D., Sloan, J., & West, C. P. (2016). Relationship between clerical burden and characteristics of the electronic environment with physician burnout and professional satisfaction. In *Mayo Clinic Proceedings*, 91(7), 836–848.

Shankland, S. (2016, October 24). Refugees cling to Wi-Fi in the jungle of Calais. https://www.cnet.com/news/refugees-cling-to-wi-fi-calais-jungle-france-refugee-crisis/.

Sharma, A., Lewis, S., & Szatkowski, L. (2010). Insights into social disparities in smoking prevalence using Mosaic, a novel measure of socioeconomic status: An analysis using a large primary care dataset. *BMC Public Health*, 10(1), 755.

Shelley, D., Cantrell, M. J., Moon-Howard, J., Ramjohn, D. Q., & VanDevanter, N. (2007). The $5 man: The underground economic response to a large cigarette tax increase in New York City. *American Journal of Public Health*, 97(8), 1483–1488.

Shkolnikov, V., McKee, M., & Leon, D. A. (2001). Changes in life expectancy in Russia in the mid-1990s. *The Lancet*, 357(9260), 917–921.

Shkolnikov, V. M., & Nemtsov, A. (1997). The anti-alcohol campaign and variations in Russian mortality. In J. L. Bobadilla, C. A. Costello, & F. Mitchell (Eds.), *Premature death in the new independent states* (pp. 239–248). Washington, DC: National Academies Press.

Shochat, T., Cohen-Zion, M., & Tzischinsky, O. (2014). Functional consequences of inadequate sleep in adolescents: A systematic review. *Sleep Medicine Reviews*, 18(1), 75–87.

Siegel, M., & Donner, T. H. (1998). Pretesting messages and materials. In E. A. Resnick & M. Siegel (Eds.), *Marketing public health: Strategies to promote social change* (pp. 415–446). Frederick, MD: Aspen Publishers.

Silagy, C., Mant, D., Fowler, G., & Lodge, M. (1994). The effectiveness of nicotine replacement therapies in smoking cessation. *Online Journal of Current Clinical Trials*, 113(7,906).

Silvers, A., Rhodes, R., & Battin, M. P. (2015). Introduction. In *Physician assisted suicide* (pp. 1–8). New York, NY: Routledge.

Silverstein, R. G., Brown, A. C. H., Roth, H. D., & Britton, W. B. (2011). Effects of mindfulness training on body awareness to sexual stimuli: Implications for female sexual dysfunction. *Psychosomatic Medicine*, 73(9), 817–825.

Simmons, J. P., Nelson, L. D., & Simonsohn, U. (2011). False-positive psychology: Undisclosed flexibility in data collection and analysis allows presenting anything as significant. *Psychological Science*, 22(11), 1359–1366.

Sims, M., Diez-Roux, A. V., Gebreab, S. Y., Brenner, A., Dubbert, P., Wyatt, S., . . . & Taylor, H. (2016). Perceived discrimination is associated with health behaviours among African-Americans in the Jackson Heart Study. *Journal of Epidemiology and Community Health*, 70(2), 187–194.

Singer, C. M., & Applebee, G. A. (2008). Sleep disorders. In M. Feldman & J. Chistensen (Eds.), *Behavioral medicine: A guide for clinical practice* (3rd ed.). New York, NY: McGraw-Hill.

Singer, M. (2015). *Anthropology of infectious disease*. Walnut Creek, CA: Left Coast Press.

Singhal, A., & Rogers, E. (2012). *Entertainment-education: A communication strategy for social change*. New York, NY: Routledge.

Sirois, B. C., & Burg, M. M. (2003). Negative emotion and coronary heart disease: A review. *Behavior Modification*, 27(1), 83–102.

Sirois, F. M., Melia-Gordon, M. L., & Pychyl, T. A. (2003). "I'll look after my health, later": An investigation of procrastination and health. *Personality and Individual Differences*, 35(5), 1167–1184.

Skinner, C. S., Tiro, J., & Champion, V. L. (2015). The health belief model. In K. Glanz, B. K. Rimer, & K. Viswanath (Eds.), *Health behavior: Theory, research and practice* (pp. 75–94). San Francisco, CA: Jossey-Bass.

Skloot, R. 2010. *The immortal life of Henrietta Lacks*. New York, NY: Crown Publishers.

Skoyen, J. A., Kogan, A. V., Novak, S. A., & Butler, E. A. (2013). Health behavior and emotion regulation in couples. In M. Newman and M. Newman (Eds.), *Health and social relationships: The good, the bad, and the complicated*. Washington, DC: American Psychological Association.

Slater, J. D., Chelaru, M. I., Hansen, B. J., Beaman, C., Kalamangalam, G., Tandon, N., & Dragoi, V. (2017). Focal changes to human electrocorticography with drowsiness: A novel measure of local sleep. *Journal of Neuropsychiatry and Clinical Neurosciences*, 29(3), 236–247.

Smith, D. D. (2005). The history of mesothelioma. In H. Pass, N. Vogelzang, & M. Carbone (Eds.), *Malignant mesothelioma: Advances in pathogenesis, diagnosis, and translational therapies* (pp. 3–20). New York, NY: Springer.

Smith, E. M., Johnson, S. R., & Guenther, S. M. (1985). Health care attitudes and experiences during gynecologic care among lesbians and bisexuals. *American Journal of Public Health*, 75(9), 1085–1087.

Smith, G. D., Hart, C., Hole, D., MacKinnon, P., Gillis, C., Watt, G., Blane, D., & Hawthorne, V. (1998). Education and occupational social class: Which is the more important indicator of mortality risk? *Journal of Epidemiology & Community Health*, 52(3), 153–160.

Smith, G. D., Hart, C., Upton, M., Hole, D., Gillis, C., Watt, G., & Hawthorne, V. (2000). Height and risk of death among men and women: Aetiological implications of associations with cardiorespiratory disease and cancer mortality. *Journal of Epidemiology & Community Health*, 54(2), 97–103.

Smith, G. D., Hart, C., Watt, G., Hole, D., & Hawthorne, V. (1998). Individual social class, area-based deprivation, cardiovascular disease risk factors, and mortality: The Renfrew and Paisley Study. *Journal of Epidemiology & Community Health*, 52(6), 399–405.

Smith, M. C. (1991). *A social history of the minor tranquilizers: The quest for small comfort in the age of anxiety*. Philadelphia, PA: Haworth Press.

Smith, O. (2010, October 21). Campaign targets "fat talk," negative body images. CNN. http://www.cnn.com/2010/LIVING/10/21/no.fat.talk.week/index.html.

Smith, P. J., Blumenthal, J. A., Hoffman, B. M., Cooper, H., Strauman, T. A., Welsh-Bohmer, K., . . . & Sherwood, A. (2010). Aerobic exercise and neurocognitive performance: A meta-analytic review of randomized controlled trials. *Psychosomatic Medicine*, 72(3), 239.

Smith, T. W. (1992). Hostility and health: Current status of a psychosomatic hypothesis. *Health Psychology*, 11(3), 139–150.

Smith, W. A. (2000). Social marketing: An evolving definition. *American Journal of Health Behavior*, 24(1), 11–17.

Smitherman, T. A., Penzien, D. B., Rains, J. C., Nicholson, R. A., & Houle, T. T. (2015). *Headache* (Advances in Psychotherapy: Evidence-Based Practice). Cambridge, MA: Hogrefe.

Smolak, L., Levine, M. P., & Schermer, F. (1999). Parental input and weight concerns among elementary school children. *International Journal of Eating Disorders*, 25(3), 263–271.

Snow, M. G., Prochaska, J. O., & Rossi, J. S. (1992). Stages of change for smoking cessation among former problem drinkers: A cross-sectional analysis. *Journal of Substance Abuse*, 4(2), 107–116.

So, H. W., & Cheung, F. M. (2005). Review of Chinese sex attitudes and applicability of sex therapy for Chinese couples with sexual dysfunction. *Journal of Sex Research*, 42(2), 93–101.

Sommers, B. D., Long, S. K., & Baichker, K. (2014). Changes in mortality after Massachusetts health

care reform: A quasi-experimental study. *Annals of Internal Medicine*, 160(9), 585–593.
Spiegel, D., Kraemer, H., Bloom, J., & Gottheil, E. (1989). Effect of psychosocial treatment on survival of patients with metastatic breast cancer. *The Lancet*, 334(8668), 888–891.
Spielman, A. J., Yang, C. M., & Glovinsky, P. B. (2011). Sleep restriction therapy. In M. Perlis., M. Aloia, & B. Kuhm (Eds.), *Behavioral treatments for sleep disorders* (pp. 9–19). London, UK: Elsevier.
Springer, D. (2016, September 28). "Death spiral"? ObamaCare problems making coverage harder to afford, find. Fox News. http://www.foxnews.com/politics/2016/09/28/death-spiral-obamacare-problems-making-coverage-harder-to-afford-find.html.
Stanton, C. A., Highland, K. B., & Tercyak, K. P. (2016). Tobacco use experimentation, physical activity, and risk of depression among multiethnic urban preadolescents. *Journal of Early Adolescence*, 36(3), 372–387.
Starr, P. (2008). *The social transformation of American medicine: The rise of a sovereign profession and the making of a vast industry*. New York, NY: Basic Books.
Starr, P. (2013). *Remedy and reaction: The peculiar American struggle over health care reform*. New Haven, CT: Yale University Press.
Stead, L. F., Perera, R., & Lancaster, T. (2006). Telephone counselling for smoking cessation. *Cochrane Database of Systematic Reviews*, 3(3).
Stein, H. F. (1982). The annual cycle and the cultural nexus of health care behavior among Oklahoma wheat farming families. *Culture, Medicine and Psychiatry*, 6(1), 81–99.
Stein, H. F. (1990). *American medicine as culture*. Boulder, CO: Westview Press.
Stein, H. F., & Mold, J. W. (1988). Stress, anxiety, and cascades in clinical decision-making. *Stress and Health*, 4(1), 41–48.
Steinberg, K. K., Thacker, S. B., Smith, S. J., Stroup, D. F., Zack, M. M., Flanders, W. D., & Berkelman, R. L. (1991). A meta-analysis of the effect of estrogen replacement therapy on the risk of breast cancer. *Journal of the American Medical Association*, 265(15), 1985–1990.
Stern, A. M., & Markel, H. (2005). The history of vaccines and immunization: Familiar patterns, new challenges. *Health Affairs*, 24(3), 611–621.
Stetter, F., & Kupper, S. (2002). Autogenic training: A meta-analysis of clinical outcome studies. *Applied Psychophysiology and Biofeedback*, 27(1), 45–98.
Stores, G. (1996). Practitioner review: Assessment and treatment of sleep disorders in children and adolescents. *Journal of Child Psychology and Psychiatry*, 37(8), 907–925.
Story, M., Nanney, M. S., & Schwartz, M. B. (2009). Schools and obesity prevention: Creating school environments and policies to promote healthy eating and physical activity. *The Milbank Quarterly*, 87(1), 71–100.
Straub, R. O. (2016). *Health psychology: A biopsychosocial approach*. New York, NY: Macmillan.
Strawbridge, W. J., Cohen, R. D., Shema, S. J., & Kaplan, G. A. (1997). Frequent attendance at religious services and mortality over 28 years. *American Journal of Public Health*, 87, 957–961.
Striegel-Moore, R. H., Silberstein, L. R., & Rodin, J. (1986). Toward an understanding of risk factors for bulimia. *American Psychologist*, 41, 246–263.
Strik, J. J., Denollet, J., Lousberg, R., & Honig, A. (2003). Comparing symptoms of depression and anxiety as predictors of cardiac events and increased health care consumption after myocardial infarction. *Journal of the American College of Cardiology*, 42(10), 1801–1807.
Strosahl, K. (1998). Integrating behavioral health and primary care services: The primary mental health care model. In A. Blount (Ed.), *Integrated primary care: The future of medical and mental health collaboration* (pp. 139–166). New York, NY: W. W. Norton.
Stuart, M. R., & Lieberman, J. A. (2015). *The fifteen minute hour: Therapeutic talk in primary care*. Boca Raton, FL: CRC Press.
Suarez, E. C., & Williams, R. B. (1989). Situational determinants of cardiovascular and emotional reactivity in high and low hostile men. *Psychosomatic Medicine*, 51, 414–418.
Subramanyam, M. A., James, S. A., Diez-Roux, A. V., Hickson, D. A., Sarpong, D., Sims, M., . . . & Wyatt, S. B. (2013). Socioeconomic status, John Henryism and blood pressure among African-Americans in the Jackson heart study. *Social Science & Medicine*, 93, 139–146.
Substance Abuse and Mental Health Services Administration. (2018). Adverse childhood experiences. https://www.samhsa.gov/capt/practicing-effective-prevention/prevention-behavioral-health/adverse-childhood-experiences.
Sullivan, G. M., & Feinn, R. (2012). Using effect size—or why the p value is not enough. *Journal of Graduate Medical Education*, 4(3), 279–282.
Sullivan, M. J., Thorn, B., Haythornthwaite, J. A., Keefe, F., Martin, M., Bradley, L. A., & Lefebvre, J. C. (2001). Theoretical perspectives on the relation between catastrophizing and pain. *Clinical Journal of Pain*, 17, 52–64.
Sullivan, P. F., & Kendler, K. S. (1999). The genetic epidemiology of smoking. *Nicotine & Tobacco Research*, 1(Suppl 2), S51–S57.
Suwa, M., & Suzuki, K. (2013). The phenomenon of "hikikomori" (social withdrawal) and the sociocultural situation in Japan today. *Journal of Psychopathology*, 19, 191–198.
Svensdottir, V., Eriksen, H. R., & Reme, S. E. (2012). Assessing the role of cognitive behavioral therapy in the management of chronic nonspecific back pain. *Journal of Pain Research*, 5, 371–380.

Swan, W. (Ed.). (2016). *Handbook of gay, lesbian, bisexual, and transgender administration and policy.* Boca Raton, FL: CRC Press.

Szumilas, M. (2010). Explaining odds ratios. *Journal of the Canadian Academy of Child and Adolescent Psychiatry, 19*(3), 227.

Tamanna, S., & Geraci, S. A. (2013). Major sleep disorders among women. *Southern Medical Journal, 106*(8), 470–478.

Tan, C. C., & Holub, S. C. (2015). Emotion regulation feeding practices link parents' emotional eating to children's emotional eating: A moderated mediation study. *Journal of Pediatric Psychology, 40*(7), 657–663.

Tank, J., Diedrich, A., Hale, N., Niaz, F. E., Furlan, R., Robertson, R. M., & Mosqueda-Garcia, R. (2003). Relationship between blood pressure, sleep K-complexes, and muscle sympathetic nerve activity in humans. *American Journal of Physiology-Regulatory, Integrative and Comparative Physiology, 285*(1), R208–R214.

Tannenbaum, M. B., Hepler, J., Zimmerman, R. S., Saul, L., Jacobs, S., Wilson, K., & Albarracín, D. (2015). Appealing to fear: A meta-analysis of fear appeal effectiveness and theories. *Psychological Bulletin, 141*(6), 1178–1204.

Taub, J. M., & Berger, R. J. (1973). Performance and mood following variations in the length and timing of sleep. *Psychophysiology, 10*(6), 559–570.

Tayebi, N., & Ardakani, S. M. Y. (2009). Incidence and prevalence of the sexual dysfunctions in infertile women. *European Journal of General Medicine, 6*(2), 74–77.

Taylor, S. E. (1983). Adjustment to threatening events: A theory of cognitive adaptation. *American Psychologist, 38*(11), 1161–1173.

Taylor, S. E. (2006). Tend and befriend: Biobehavioral bases of affiliation under stress. *Current Directions in Psychological Science, 15*(6), 273–277.

Taylor, S. E. (2009). *Health psychology* (6th Edition). New York, NY: McGraw-Hill.

Taylor, S. E. (2014). *Health psychology* (9th Edition). New York, NY: McGraw-Hill.

Taylor, S. E., Lichtman, R. R., & Wood, J. V. (1984). Attributions, beliefs about control, and adjustment to breast cancer. *Journal of Personality and Social Psychology, 46*(3), 489–502.

Teasdale, J. D. (1988). Cognitive vulnerability to persistent depression. *Cognition & Emotion, 2*(3), 247–274.

Teo, A. R. (2010). A new form of social withdrawal in Japan: A review of hikikomori. *International Journal of Social Psychiatry, 56*(2), 178–185.

Thomas, S. B., & Quinn, S. C. (1991). The Tuskegee Syphilis Study, 1932 to 1972: Implications for HIV education and AIDS risk education programs in the black community. *American Journal of Public Health, 81*(11), 1498–1505.

Thorp, J., Simon, J., Dattani, D., Taylor, L., Kimura, T., Garcia, M., Jr., . . . & DAISY Trial Investigators. (2012). Treatment of hypoactive sexual desire disorder in premenopausal women: Efficacy of flibanserin in the DAISY study. *Journal of Sexual Medicine, 9*(3), 793–804.

Todd, K. H., Samaroo, N., & Hoffman, J. R. (1993). Ethnicity as a risk factor for inadequate emergency department analgesia. *Journal of the American Medical Association, 269*(12), 1537–1539.

Tomes, N. (2016). *Remaking the American patient: How Madison Avenue turned patients into consumers.* Chapel Hill, NC: University of North Carolina Press.

Toussaint, L., Worthington, E., & Williams, D. R. (Eds.). (2015). *Forgiveness and health: Scientific evidence and theories relating forgiveness to better health.* New York, NY: Springer.

Touyz, S., Polivy, J., & Hay, P. (2008). *Eating disorders.* Boston, MA: Hogrefe and Huber.

Traish, A. M., Guay, A., Feeley, R., & Saad, F. (2009). The dark side of testosterone deficiency: I. Metabolic syndrome and erectile dysfunction. *Journal of Andrology, 30*(1), 10–22.

Tran, J., Tran, R., & White, J. R. (2012). Smartphone-based glucose monitors and applications in the management of diabetes: An overview of 10 salient "apps" and a novel smartphone-connected blood glucose monitor. *Clinical Diabetes, 30*(4), 173–178.

Travis, F., Haaga, D. A., Hagelin, J., Tanner, M., Nidich, S., Gaylord-King, C., . . . & Schneider, R. H. (2009). Effects of transcendental meditation practice on brain functioning and stress reactivity in college students. *International Journal of Psychophysiology, 71*(2), 170–176.

Traylor, A. H., Schmittdiel, J. A., Uratsu, C. S., Mangione, C. M., & Subramanian, U. (2010). Adherence to cardiovascular disease medications: Does patient-provider race/ethnicity and language concordance matter? *Journal of General Internal Medicine, 25*(11), 1172–1177.

Troxel, W. M., Matthews, K. A., Gallo, L. C., & Kuller, L. H. (2005). Marital quality and occurrence of the metabolic syndrome in women. *Archives of Internal Medicine, 165*(9), 1022–1027.

Truog, R. D., Kesselheim, A. S., & Joffe, S. (2012). Paying patients for their tissue: The legacy of Henrietta Lacks. *Science, 337*(6090), 37–38.

Tsugawa, Y., Jena, A. B., Figueroa, J. F., Orav, E. J., Blumenthal, D. M., & Jha, A. K. (2017). Comparison of hospital mortality and readmission rates for Medicare patients treated by male vs. female physicians. *JAMA Internal Medicine, 177*(2), 206–213.

Tumolo, M. (2014). Political action as a health-giving activity: Transforming silence into language and activism. In V. Harvey & T. Housel (Eds.), *Health care disparities and the LGBT population* (pp. 189–201). Lanham, MD: Lexington.

Turk, D. C., & Burwinkle, T. M. (2005). Clinical outcomes, cost-effectiveness, and the role of psychology in treatments for chronic pain sufferers. *Professional Psychology: Research and Practice*, 36(6), 602–610.

Turner, J. A. (1982). Comparison of group progressive-relaxation training and cognitive-behavioral group therapy for chronic low back pain. *Journal of Consulting and Clinical Psychology*, 50(5), 757–765.

Turner, J. A., Holtzman, S., & Mancl, L. (2007). Mediators, moderators, and predictors of therapeutic change in cognitive-behavioral therapy for chronic pain. *Pain*, 127(3), 276–286.

Twal, W. O., Wahlquist, A. E., & Balasubramanian, S. (2016). Yogic breathing when compared to attention control reduces the levels of pro-inflammatory biomarkers in saliva: A pilot randomized controlled trial. *BMC Complementary and Alternative Medicine*, 16(1), 294.

Uher, R., Brammer, M. J., Murphy, T., Campbell, I. C., Ng, V. W., Williams, S. C., & Treasure, J. (2003). Recovery and chronicity in anorexia nervosa: Brain activity associated with differential outcomes. *Biological Psychiatry*, 54(9), 934–942.

Unützer, J., Katon, W. J., Fan, M. Y., Schoenbaum, M. C., Lin, E. H., Della Penna, R. D., & Powers, D. (2008). Long-term cost effects of collaborative care for late-life depression. *The American Journal of Managed Care*, 14(2), 95–100.

Urquidez-Romero, R., Esparza-Romero, J., Chaudhari, L. S., Begay, R. C., Giraldo, M., Ravussin, E., . . . & Valencia, M. E. (2014). Study design of the Maycoba Project: Obesity and diabetes in Mexican Pimas. *American Journal of Health Behavior*, 38(3), 370–378.

US Department of Health and Human Services. (2014). *The health consequences of smoking—50 years of progress: A report of the surgeon general*. Atlanta, GA: US Department of Health and Human Services, Centers for Disease Control and Prevention, National Center for Chronic Disease Prevention and Health Promotion, Office on Smoking and Health.

US Department of Health and Human Services. (2016). *E-cigarette use by youth and young adults: A report from the Surgeon General*. Atlanta, GA: US Department of Health and Human Services, Centers for Disease Control and Prevention, National Center for Chronic Disease Prevention and Health Promotion, Office on Smoking and Health.

US Department of State. (2018). International Women of Courage Awards. https://www.state.gov/s/gwi/index.htm.

Vable, A. M., Subramanian, S. V., Rist, P. M., & Glymour, M. M. (2015). Does the "widowhood effect" precede spousal bereavement? Results from a nationally representative sample of older adults. *American Journal of Geriatric Psychiatry*, 23(3), 283–292.

van Lankveld, J. J., Granot, M., Schultz, W. C. W., Binik, Y. M., Wesselmann, U., Pukall, C. F., . . . & Achtrari, C. (2010). Women's sexual pain disorders. *Journal of Sexual Medicine*, 7(1), 615–631.

Van Tilburg, M. A., Levy, R. L., Walker, L. S., Von Korff, M., Feld, L. D., Garner, M., . . . & Whitehead, W. E. (2015). Psychosocial mechanisms for the transmission of somatic symptoms from parents to children. *World Journal of Gastroenterology*, 21(18), 5532.

van Tulder, M. W., Ostelo, R., Vlaeyen, J. W., Linton, S. J., Morley, S. J., & Assendelft, W. J. (2000). Behavioral treatment for chronic low back pain: A systematic review within the framework of the Cochrane Back Review Group. *Spine*, 25(20), 2688–2699.

Vanable, P. A., Carey, M. P., Carey, K. B., & Maisto, S. A. (2003). Smoking among psychiatric outpatients: Relationship to substance use, diagnosis, and illness severity. *Psychology of Addictive Behaviors*, 17(4), 259–265.

Vance, C. G., Dailey, D. L., Rakel, B. A., & Sluka, K. A. (2014). Using TENS for pain control: The state of the evidence. *Pain Management*, 4(3), 197–209.

Vance, S. R., Ehrensaft, D., & Rosenthal, S. M. (2014). Psychological and medical care of gender nonconforming youth. *Pediatrics*, 134(6), 1184–1192.

Vandenbroucke, J. P. (2001). In defense of case reports and case series. *Annals of Internal Medicine*, 134(4), 330–334.

VanEpps, E. M., Downs, J. S., & Loewenstein, G. (2016). Calorie label formats: Using numeric and traffic light calorie labels to reduce lunch calories. *Journal of Public Policy & Marketing*, 35(1), 26–36.

Varkey, B. M., & Varkey, L. M. (2003). Topiramate induced somnabulism and automatic behaviour. *Indian Journal of Medical Sciences*, 57(11), 508–510.

Velicer, W. F., Fava, J. L., Prochaska, J. O., Abrams, D. B., Emmons, K. M., & Pierce, J. P. (1995). Distribution of smokers by stage in three representative samples. *Preventive Medicine*, 24(4), 401–411.

Ventola, C. L. (2011). Direct-to-consumer pharmaceutical advertising: Therapeutic or toxic? *Pharmacy and Therapeutics*, 36(10), 661–684.

Vickers, A. J., & Linde, K. (2014). Acupuncture for chronic pain. *Journal of the American Medical Association*, 311(9), 955–956.

Violanti, J. M., Burchfiel, C. M., Hartley, T. A., Mnatsakanova, A., Fekedulegn, D., Andrew, M. E., . . . & Vila, B. J. (2009). Atypical work hours and metabolic syndrome among police officers. *Archives of Environmental & Occupational Health*, 64(3), 194–201.

Virani, S. S., Woodard, L. D., Ramsey, D. J., Urech, T. H., Akeroyd, J. M., Shah, T., . . . & Petersen, L. A. (2015). Gender disparities in evidence-based statin therapy in patients with cardiovascular disease. *The American Journal of Cardiology*, 115(1), 21–26.

Virginia Commonwealth University. (2016, September 26). Mapping life expectancy. https://societyhealth.vcu.edu/work/the-projects/mapping-life-expectancy.html.

Viswanathan, M., Golin, C. E., Jones, C. D., Ashok, M., Blalock, S. J., Wines, R. C., Coker-Schwimmer, E. J., Rosen, D. L., Sista, P., & Lohr, K. N. (2012). Interventions to improve adherence to self-administered medications for chronic diseases in the United States: A systematic review. *Annals of Internal Medicine*, 157, 785–795.

Vize, R. (2015, April 24). Rationing care is a fact of life for the NHS. *The Guardian*. https://www.theguardian.com/healthcare-network/2015/apr/24/rationing-care-fact-of-life-nhs.

Volpp, K. G., & Bundorf, M. K. (1999). Consumer protection and the HMO backlash: Are HMOs to blame for drive-through deliveries? *Inquiry*, 36(1), 101–109.

Vowles, K. E., & McCracken, L. M. (2008). Acceptance and values-based action in chronic pain: A study of treatment effectiveness and process. *Journal of Consulting and Clinical Psychology*, 76(3), 397–407.

Wadden, T. A., Anderson, D. A., Foster, G. D., Bennett, A., Steinberg, C., & Sarwer, D. B. (2000). Obese women's perceptions of their physicians' weight management attitudes and practices. *Archives of Family Medicine*, 9(9), 854–860.

Wadden, T. A., Berkowitz, R. I., Womble, L. G., Sarwer, D. B., Phelan, S., Cato, R. K., . . . & Stunkard, A. J. (2005). Randomized trial of lifestyle modification and pharmacotherapy for obesity. *New England Journal of Medicine*, 353(20), 2111–2120.

Wadden, T. A., & Frey, D. L. (1997). A multicenter evaluation of a proprietary weight loss program for the treatment of marked obesity: A five-year follow-up. *International Journal of Eating Disorders*, 22(2), 203–221.

Wade, T. D., Bulik, C. M., Heath, A. C., Martin, N. G., & Eaves, L. J. (2001). The influence of genetic and environmental factors in estimations of current body size, desired body size, and body dissatisfaction. *Twin Research and Human Genetics*, 4(4), 260–265.

Wailoo, K. (2014). *Pain: A political history*. Baltimore, MD: Johns Hopkins University Press.

Wakschlag, L. S., Lahey, B. B., Loeber, R., Green, S. M., Gordon, R. A., & Leventhal, B. L. (1997). Maternal smoking during pregnancy and the risk of conduct disorder in boys. *Archives of General Psychiatry*, 54(7), 670–676.

Walberg, P., McKee, M., Shkolnikov, V., Chenet, L., & Leon, D. A. (1998). Economic change, crime, and mortality crisis in Russia: Regional analysis. *BMJ*, 317(7154), 312–318.

Waldinger, M. D. (2015). Pharmacotherapy for premature ejaculation. *Expert Opinion on Pharmacotherapy*, 16(17), 2615–2624.

Walker, E. R., McGee, R. E., & Druss, B. G. (2015). Mortality in mental disorders and global disease burden implications: A systematic review and meta-analysis. *JAMA Psychiatry*, 72(4), 334–341.

Walker, L. S., Garber, J., & Greene, J. W. (1991). Somatization symptoms in pediatric abdominal pain patients: Relation to chronicity of abdominal pain and parent somatization. *Journal of Abnormal Child Psychology*, 19(4), 379–394.

Walker, L. S., Garber, J., Smith, C. A., Van Slyke, D. A., & Claar, R. L. (2001). The relation of daily stressors to somatic and emotional symptoms in children with and without recurrent abdominal pain. *Journal of Consulting and Clinical Psychology*, 69(1), 85–91.

Wanic, R., & Kulik, J. (2011). Toward an understanding of gender differences in the impact of marital conflict on health. *Sex Roles*, 65(5–6), 297–312.

Ward, B. W., Dahlhamer, J. M., Galinsky, A. M., & Joestl, S. S. (2014). Sexual orientation and health among US adults: National Health Interview Survey, 2013. *National Health Statistics Report*, 77, 1–10.

Ward, J. L., & Viner, R. M. (2017). The impact of income inequality and national wealth on child and adolescent mortality in low and middle-income countries. *BMC Public Health*, 17, 429.

Ware, N. C., & Kleinman, A. (1992). Culture and somatic experience: The social course of illness in neurasthenia and chronic fatigue syndrome. *Psychosomatic Medicine*, 54(5), 546–560.

Warin, M. (2016). Relatedness in anorexia. In Manderson, L., Cartwright, E., & Hardon, A. (Eds.), *The Routledge Handbook of Medical Anthropology* (pp. 125–128). New York, NY: Routledge.

Warshaw, P. R., & Davis, F. D. (1985). Disentangling behavioral intention and behavioral expectation. *Journal of Experimental Social Psychology*, 21(3), 213–228.

Washington, D. M., Curtis, L. M., Waite, K., Wolf, M. S., & Paasche-Orlow, M. K. (2018). Sociodemographic factors mediate race and ethnicity-associated childhood asthma health disparities: A longitudinal analysis. *Journal of Racial and Ethnic Health Disparities*, 5(5), 928–938.

Washington, H. A. (2006). *Medical apartheid: The dark history of medical experimentation on Black Americans from colonial times to the present*. New York, NY: Doubleday Books.

Watters, E. (2010). *Crazy like us: The globalization of the American psyche*. New York, NY: Free Press.

Weaver, T., & Ye, L. (2011). Sleep related breathing disorders. In C. M. Morin & C. A. Espie (Eds.), *The Oxford handbook of sleep and sleep disorders* (pp. 666–689). New York, NY: Oxford University Press.

Webster, C. (2002). *The National Health Service: A political history*. New York, NY: Oxford University Press.

Weiner, L., & Avery-Clark, C. (2014). Sensate focus: Clarifying the Masters and Johnson's model. *Sexual and Relationship Therapy*, 29(3), 307–319.

Weingarten, S. (2000). Translating practice guidelines into patient care: Guidelines at the bedside. *Chest*, 118(2), 4S–7S.

Weinstein, J. N., Lurie, J. D., Olson, P., Bronner, K. K., Fisher, E. S., & Morgan, M. T. S. (2006). United

States trends and regional variations in lumbar spine surgery: 1992–2003. *Spine*, *31*(23), 2707–2714.

Weis, R. (2014). *Abnormal child psychology*. Thousand Oaks, CA: Sage.

Weiss, S. C., Emanuel, L. L., Fairclough, D. L., & Emanuel, E. J. (2001). Understanding the experience of pain in terminally ill patients. *The Lancet*, *357*(9265), 1311–1315.

Weller, R. E., Cook, E. W., III, Avsar, K. B., & Cox, J. E. (2008). Obese women show greater delay discounting than healthy-weight women. *Appetite*, *51*(3), 563–569.

Wellisch, D. K., & Yager, J. (1983). Opinion: Is there a cancer-prone personality? *CA: A Cancer Journal for Clinicians*, *33*(3), 145–153.

Wells, B. L., & Horm, J. W. (1992). Stage at diagnosis in breast cancer: Race and socioeconomic factors. *American Journal of Public Health*, *82*(10), 1383–1385.

Westhead, J. (2000, September 20). UK tobacco firm targets African youth. BBC. http://news.bbc.co.uk/2/hi/uk_news/933430.stm.

Whitacre, C. C. (2001). Sex differences in autoimmune disease. *Nature Immunology*, *2*(9), 777.

Whitaker, C., & Bumberry, W. (1988). *Dancing with the family*. New York, NY: Routledge.

Whitman, S. M. (2007). Pain and suffering as viewed by the Hindu religion. *Journal of Pain*, *8*(8), 607–613.

Wiech, K., & Tracey, I. (2009). The influence of negative emotions on pain: Behavioral effects and neural mechanisms. *Neuroimage*, *47*(3), 987–994.

Wiederhold, M., & Wiederhold, B. (2007). Virtual reality and interactive simulation for pain distraction. *Pain Medicine*, *8*(Suppl 3), S182–S188.

Wiederman, M. W. (2001). "Don't look now": The role of self-focus in sexual dysfunction. *The Family Journal*, *9*(2), 210–214.

Willes, K., & Allen, M. (2014). The importance of sexual orientation disclosure to physicians for women who have sex with women. In V. Harvey & T. Housel (Eds.), *Health care disparities and the LGBT population* (pp. 9–26). Lanham, MD: Lexington.

Wilt, T. J., MacDonald, R., Ouellette, J., Khawaja, I. S., Rutks, I., Butler, M., & Fink, H. A. (2013). Pharmacologic therapy for primary restless legs syndrome: A systematic review and meta-analysis. *JAMA Internal Medicine*, *173*(7), 496–505.

Wincze, J. P., & Weisberg, R. B. (2015). *Sexual dysfunction: A guide for assessment and treatment*. New York, NY: Guilford Press.

Wing, R. R., Lang, W., Wadden, T. A., Safford, M., Knowler, W. C., Bertoni, A. G., . . . & Look AHEAD Research Group. (2011). Benefits of modest weight loss in improving cardiovascular risk factors in overweight and obese individuals with type 2 diabetes. *Diabetes Care*, *34*(7), 1481–1486.

Wing, Y. K., Lee, S. T., & Chen, C. N. (1994). Sleep paralysis in Chinese: Ghost oppression phenomenon in Hong Kong. *Sleep*, *17*(7), 609–613.

Wingood, G. M., & DiClemente, R. J. (1997). The effects of an abusive primary partner on the condom use and sexual negotiation practices of African-American women. *American Journal of Public Health*, *87*(6), 1016–1018.

Winkelmann, J., Schormair, B., Lichtner, P., Ripke, S., Xiong, L., Jalilzadeh, S., . . . & Trenkwalder, C. (2007). Genome-wide association study of restless legs syndrome identifies common variants in three genomic regions. *Nature Genetics*, *39*(8), 1000.

Winkleby, M. A., Jatulis, D. E., Frank, E., & Fortmann, S. P. (1992). Socioeconomic status and health: How education, income, and occupation contribute to risk factors for cardiovascular disease. *American Journal of Public Health*, *82*(6), 816–820.

Witt, C. M., Jena, S., Selim, D., Brinkhaus, B., Reinhold, T., Wruck, K., . . . & Willich, S. N. (2006). Pragmatic randomized trial evaluating the clinical and economic effectiveness of acupuncture for chronic low back pain. *American Journal of Epidemiology*, *164*(5), 487–496.

Witte, K., & Allen, M. (2000). A meta-analysis of fear appeals: Implications for effective public health campaigns. *Health Education & Behavior*, *27*(5), 591–615.

Wolfe, F. (1989). Fibromyalgia: The clinical syndrome. *Rheumatic Diseases Clinics of North America*, *15*(1), 1–18.

Wong, C., Harrison, C., Britt, H., & Henderson, J. (2014). Patient use of the internet for health information. *Australian Family Physician*, *43*(12), 875–877.

World Health Organization. (2000). *Tobacco company strategies to undermine tobacco control activities at the World Health Organization*. Geneva, Switzerland: World Health Organization. http://www.who.int/tobacco/publications/industry/who_inquiry/en/.

World Health Organization. (2008). What is the WHO definition of health? http://www.who.int/suggestions/faq/en/.

World Health Organization. (2010). WHO vaccine-preventable diseases: Monitoring system, 2010 global summary. http://apps.who.int/immunization_monitoring/globalsummary.

Wright, K., Giger, J. N., Norris, K., & Suro, Z. (2013). Impact of a nurse-directed, coordinated school health program to enhance physical activity behaviors and reduce body mass index among minority children: A parallel-group, randomized control trial. *International Journal of Nursing Studies*, *50*(6), 727–737.

Wright, K. P., Bogan, R. K., & Wyatt, J. K. (2013). Shift work and the assessment and management of shift work disorder (SWD). *Sleep Medicine Reviews*, *17*(1), 41–54.

Wyatt, J., Cvengros, J., & Ong, J. (2011). Clinical assessment of sleep-wake complaints. In C. M. Morin & C. A. Espie (Eds.), *The Oxford handbook of sleep and sleep disorders* (pp. 383–404). Oxford, UK: Oxford University Press.

Xie, L., Kang, H., Xu, Q., Chen, M. J., Liao, Y., Thiyagarajan, M., . . . & Takano, T. (2013). Sleep drives metabolite clearance from the adult brain. *Science, 342*(6156), 373–377.

Yang, B. H., Bray, F. I., Parkin, D. M., Sellors, J. W., & Zhang, Z. F. (2004). Cervical cancer as a priority for prevention in different world regions: An evaluation using years of life lost. *International Journal of Cancer, 109*(3), 418–424.

Yaşan, A., Essizoglu, A., & Yildirim, E. A. (2009). Predictor factors associated with premarital sexual behaviors among university students in an Islamic culture. *International Journal of Sexual Health, 21*(3), 145–152.

Yaşan, A., & Gürgen, F. (2008). Marital satisfaction, sexual problems, and the possible difficulties on sex therapy in traditional Islamic culture. *Journal of Sex & Marital Therapy, 35*(1), 68–75.

Ye, S., Krupka, D. J., & Davidson, K. W. (2012). Diagnosing medication non-adherence in a patient with myocardial infarction. *Frontiers in Psychology, 3*, 267, 1–6.

Yitzhaki, S. (1979). Relative deprivation and the Gini coefficient. *The Quarterly Journal of Economics, 93*(2), 321–324.

Young, L. R., & Nestle, M. (2002). The contribution of expanding portion sizes to the US obesity epidemic. *American Journal of Public Health, 92*(2), 246–249.

Yusuf, S., Hawken, S., Ôunpuu, S., Dans, T., Avezum, A., Lanas, F., . . . & Lisheng, L. (2004). Effect of potentially modifiable risk factors associated with myocardial infarction in 52 countries (the INTERHEART study): Case-control study. *The Lancet, 364*(9438), 937–952.

Zang, E. A., & Wynder, E. L. (1996). Differences in lung cancer risk between men and women: Examination of the evidence. *Journal of the National Cancer Institute, 88*(3–4), 183–192.

Zborowski, M. (1952). Cultural components in responses to pain. *Journal of Social Issues, 8*(4), 16–30.

Zellweger, J. P. (2001). Anti-smoking therapies. *Drugs, 61*(8), 1041–1044.

Ziegler, R. G., Hoover, R. N., Pike, M. C., Hildesheim, A., Nomura, A. M., West, D. W., . . . & Hyer, M. B. (1993). Migration patterns and breast cancer risk in Asian-American women. *JNCI: Journal of the National Cancer Institute, 85*(22), 1819–1827.

Zijdenbos, I. L., de Wit, N. J., van der Heijden, G. J., Rubin, G., & Quartero, A. O. (2009, January 21). Psychological treatments for the management of irritable bowel syndrome. *Cochrane Database of Systematic Reviews, 2009*(1).

Zola, I. K. (1966). Culture and symptoms—an analysis of patient's presenting complaints. *American Sociological Review, 31*(5), 615–630.

Zuvekas, A. (1990). Community and migrant health centers: An overview. *Journal of Ambulatory Care Management, 13*(4), 1–12.

Zwart, J. A., Dyb, G., Hagen, K., Ødegård, K. J., Dahl, A. A., Bovim, G., & Stovner, L. J. (2003). Depression and anxiety disorders associated with headache frequency. The Nord-Trøndelag Health Study. *European Journal of Neurology, 10*(2), 147–152.

Index

A

abstinence: as standard, issues with, 122; violation effect, 122
acceptance and commitment therapy (ACT), 178–79; and exercise, 246; for pain, 211–12; for weight loss, 239–40
access to health care: disparities in, 75; sexual orientation and, 83
acculturation, 74; and health status, 87
ACES. *See* Adverse Childhood Experiences Survey
ACT. *See* acceptance and commitment therapy
action: in smoking cessation, 232; transtheoretical model on, 118–19
acupuncture, 197, 206
adaptation, diffusion of innovation theory on, 115
addiction, nicotine and, 223
adherence, 142–51; ethnicity and, 97–98; interventions for, 149; term, 142–43
adolescents: and contraception, 289; and eating disorders, 248, 249; and e-cigarettes, 232–33; and exercise, 245, 247; overweight, 237–38; and sleep, 261–62; and smoking, 218; and smoking cessation, 226; worry diary for, 271
adrenaline, 155
adverse childhood experiences, 163; costs of, 172
Adverse Childhood Experiences Survey (ACES), 163
Affordable Care Act (Obamacare), 8–9, 42, 63–65, 129, 295, 300; and electronic medical records, 134; issues with, 64–65; principles of, 63
African Americans: causes of death among, 86; discrimination and health status, 87; disparities in health care, 84–85; history of health care, 93–96; quality of health care, 88–89; and sleep, 265, 266; and smoking, 217, 224–25
age: and adherence, 144; and restless legs syndrome, 273; and sleep, 260–62, 267
aging population, 302–3
agreeableness, 145
alarm, stress model and, 156
alcohol use: and erectile dysfunction, 282; sexual orientation and, 81; and sleep, 267
Alexander, F., 12
allostatic load, 156–57
Alzheimer's disease screening, 28
Ambien. *See* zolpidem
amblyopia, 143
American Medical Association, 48–49
American Psychiatric Association, 248
amitriptyline, 204
analysis of variance (ANOVA), 27
anamnesis, 2
anesthesia, 48
anger, and pain, 190
anorexia nervosa, 248–50; causes of, 249; definition of, 248; treatment of, 250
anosmia, 237
antidepressant medications: adherence among Latinas, 97–98; and erectile dysfunction, 282; for fibromyalgia, 204; for smoking cessation, 228–29
anxiety: and anorexia nervosa, 249; and cardiovascular disease, 166; and erectile dysfunction, 280, 282; exercise and, 246; and fibromyalgia, 185; and migraine, 187; and physical health, 295; and sexual response, 280–81; and smoking, 219
apps: for adherence, 149; for behavior change, 126–27
arousal, 280, 282–83
asbestos, 33–34
Asian-Pacific Islanders: causes of death among, 86; and disparities in health care, 84–85; and health care system, 98; and smoking, 217
aspirin, 204
asthma, racial disparities in, 85
attachment patterns, 6–7
attitudes, TRA/TPB on, 107–8
aura, 187
auscultation, and physical diagnosis, 45–46
autism spectrum disorder screening, 30
autogenic training, 175
autonomic nervous system, 155
aversion, and smoking cessation, 229–30
Avicenna, 44
avoidant coping, 162

B

balance billing, 60
Balint, Michael, 67
Bandura, Albert, 110–11
bariatric surgery, 240–41
barriers, health belief model on, 103–4
base rate, and statistical significance, 27–30
Bateson, G., 7
BATHE technique, 299
bedtime refusal, 274–25
Beecher, Henry, 54, 189, 196
behavior change: cyber media and, 126–27; health communication and, 101–27; individually focused models of, 116–27; telenovelas and, 111–12
behavior intention, TRA/TPB on, 107
behavior therapy. *See* cognitive (behavioral) therapy
Benadril. *See* diphenhydramine
benefits, health belief model on, 103
Benson, Herbert, 177
Bertalanffy, Ludwig von, 8
bias: participant, 32; in physicians, 89–90
binge eating disorder, 252–53
biofeedback, 175–76; for pain, 209
biopsychosocial model, 9–10, 297–98
biphasic sleep, 264
bipolar disorder: and physical health, 294; and smoking, 219

347

Blacks. *See* African Americans
Bloomberg, Michael, 243
Blue Cross Blue Shield, 56
body mass index (BMI), 5, 235; heritability of, 27, 236; population density and, 247
Bonica, J. J., 197
borderline personality disorder, 249
Bradford Hill criteria, 37–38
brain-gut connection, 11–12
breast cancer screening, 28–29
Brenna, Brenda, 198
Bronfenbrenner, Urie, 8
bulimia nervosa, 250–52; causes of, 251; treatment of, 252
bupropion (Zyban), 228, 229
Buxton, Peter, 94–95

C

Campbell Collaboration, 42
Canada, health care in, 68–70
cancer: heritability of, 27; and nutrition, 35; pain in, 188; psychosomatic medicine and, 13; stress and, 167–68
Cannon, Walter, 155–56
CAPS model, 144–45
cardiovascular disease: smoking and, 216; stress and, 165–67
cascade effect, 10
case-control studies, 32–34
case reports, 31
cataplexy, 273
catastrophization, 189–90
causality: epidemiology and, 24–25, 37–38; reciprocal, 10–11
cell theory, 46
challenge, and stress, 164
Chantix. *See* varenicline
Charcot, J.-M., 45
Checklist for Autism in Toddlers (CHAT), 30
childbirth, traditional beliefs on, 98
childhood health conditions, racial disparities in, 85
children: and exercise, 245; and sleep, 261; sleep disorders in, 274–76; and weight issues, 244
chlorpromazine, 53
cholera, 47, 302
chronic disease: disparities in, 74–75; gender and, 78
chronic pain, 183–213; definition of, 184; disorders related to, 185–88; explanations of, 188–94; history of, 184–85; multimodal/multidisciplinary program for, 212–13; prevalence of, 183; treatment approaches, 202–13
Cialis. *See* tadalafil
cigarette diary, 227
cigarette smoking. *See* smoking
circadian rhythm, 260
clinical interview, 132; importance of, 131; for pain, 201–2

clinical medicine, 129–52
Clinton, Bill, 63, 95
Clinton, Hillary, 63
cocaine, 52
Cochrane Reviews, 39, 40–41
coercive power, 146
cognitive (behavioral) therapy, 177–78; for bulimia nervosa, 252; for chronic pain, 207–12; for genito-pelvic pain/penetration disorder, 289; for illness anxiety disorder, 138; for insomnia, 270–71; for smoking cessation, 229–31; third-wave, 211–12; for weight loss, 239–40
cognitive functioning: and adherence, 144; exercise and, 246–47
cognitive perspectives, on pain, 189–90
cohort studies, 34–35
coining, 98
collaborative health care, 295–97
colocated model, 296
commitment, and stress, 164
communication: and adherence, 145–48; brief counseling models for, 298–300; in clinical interview, 131; effective, 101–27; of medical mistakes, 134–35. *See also* clinical interview; public service announcements
communities, 15; and coping, 171
community health centers, 54
compliance: definition of, 142. *See also* adherence
complications, ethnicity and, 87–88
concordance, 4
connectors, diffusion of innovation theory on, 115
conscientiousness, 145
constant positive airway pressure (CPAP) device, 272
consumer movement, 53–55
contact tracing, 23–24
contraception, race and, 95
control, and stress, 161, 164
conversion disorder, 137
coping, 153–82; active versus passive, 211; smoking and, 226; styles of, 162–63
corporate policies, and health behavior, 151
cost, in diffusion of innovation theory, 115
counseling: brief models of, 298–300; for smoking cessation, 229
couples, 13–14; and pain, 193; and stress, 169–70
CPAP device. *See* constant positive airway pressure device
cross-sectional studies, 31–32
CT scans, 51
cues to action, health belief model on, 104
cultural issues/values, 14–15; American medicine and, 92–93; Asian, 98; and eating disorders, 253–54; and end-of-life decision making, 35; Hispanic, 96–98; and illness and treatment, 92–98; and pain, 194–95; and physical symptoms, 141; and physiological reactivity, 155–56; and sexuality, 289–90; and sleep, 264–65; and smoking, 224–25; and stress, 173–74; and weight issues, 241–42

cupping, 98
cyber media, and health behavior change, 126–27
Cymbalta. *See* duloxetine

D

Dapoxetine, 285
death: causes of, race and, 86; and stress, 169
defusion, 178–79
delayed ejaculation, 286
depression: and cardiovascular disease, 166; exercise and, 245–46; incidence of, 180; and migraine, 187. *See also* major depressive disorder
Descartes, René, 184
desire, 280; in men, 284
Deyo, R. A., 10, 28
diabetes, 4, 5–6; gestational, ethnicity and, 88. *See also* type 2 diabetes
dialysis, 51, 53–54
diathesis, 4–7
diathesis-stress model, 5–7, 25–27, 154; and insomnia, 268
diazepam (Valium), 53, 270
DiClemente, C. C., 117
diets, 239; and eating disorders, 249
diffusion of innovation theory, 114–16
diphenhydramine (Benadril), 270
disability, politics of, 195–96
discrepancy, motivational interviewing and, 124
discrimination, and health status, 87
disease, versus illness, 2–4
diseases of affluence, 49
disparities in health care, 73–99; economic, 75–77; educational, 77–78; evidence for, 84–85; specific conditions, 86–90
diversity: and disparities in health care, 73–99; and medical conditions, 86–90; and sleep, 264–66; and stress, 172–74. *See also* cultural issues/values; ethnicity; gender
divorce, and stress, 169–70
DNA, 11
Doll, Richard, 37
dopamine, 4, 218, 219, 229, 273, 288–89
dose-response relationship, 36, 37
Douglas, Tommy, 68
duloxetine (Cymbalta), 204
Duster, T., 73
Dysfunctional Beliefs and Attitudes About Sleep Scale, 270–71
dyspareunia, 288, 289

E

E. coli. See Escherichia coli
ear infections, smoking and, 216
eating disorders, 247–55; culture of, 254–55
eating issues, 235–55
EBM. *See* evidence-based medicine
e-cigarettes, 232–33

economic issues, 15–16; disparities in, 75–77; and non-adherence, 151; and weight issues, 244
ecosystems, 8–9
Edmonton-Zagreb vaccine, 95
educational disparities, 77–78
ejaculation: delayed, 286; premature, 285–86
elder care, 265
electronic medical records, 115–16, 134
emergency departments, 62
Emergency Medical Treatment and Active Labor Act (EMTALA), xiv, 62
emotional eating, 239–40
emotional state, and stress, 161–62
emotion-focused coping, 162
empathy, motivational interviewing and, 123, 124
employer-based health insurance, 56–57; mandate for, 71
employment policies, and health behavior, 151
EMTALA. *See* Emergency Medical Treatment and Active Labor Act
end-of-life decision making, 35
endorphins, 205, 206
Engel, George, 9, 11, 130
environmental cues, and smoking cessation, 230
environmental stressors, 27, 168
EPIC cohort, 35
epidemiology, 21–42; investigatory designs in, types of, 30–35; overview of, 21–22; social, 15, 36–37; terminology in, 24–25
epigenetics, 11
Epston, David, 253
Epworth Sleepiness Scale, 274
erectile dysfunction, 281–82
Escherichia coli, 21
estrogen, 158
ethnicity: and disparities in health care, 84–85; and medical conditions, 86–90; and pain, 194; and sleep, 265–66; and smoking, 217, 224–25
eudaimonia, 180–81
evidence-based medicine (EBM), 38–42; health interventions in larger systems, 41–42; issues in, 41; principles of, 39
evil eye, 97
excessive daytime sleepiness, 274
excitement, and sexual response cycle, 280
exercise, 244–47; history of, 244–45
exhaustion, stress model and, 156
exposure, definition of, 24
extraversion, 145
Eysenck, H. J., 167

F

factitious disorder, 137
Fagerstrom Scale, 226
failed back surgery syndrome, 203, 204
false positives, 28–29
families, 13–14; and eating disorders, 253
familismo, 96

family medicine, 130
Family Smoking Prevention and Tobacco Control Act, 221–22
fear: and adherence, 147–48; and health behavior, 106–7; and smoking, 222
fibromyalgia, 136, 185; medications for, 204
fight-or-flight response, 155–56; and pain, 192
Fishbein, M., 107, 108
Fleming, Alexander, 52
Flexner, Abraham, 49
flibanserin, 288, 289
fluoxetine (Prozac), 204
FOCUS (app), 127
food-borne illness, 22
food industry, 242, 244
FOP labels. *See* front-of-package labeling
Fordyce, Wilbert, 185, 188, 207
forgiveness, 182
FRAMES strategy, 299
Framingham Heart Study, 34–35
Fredrickson, B. L., 161–62
French paradox, 241–42
Freud, Sigmund, 137, 287
Friedman, M., 165
Friedman, Thomas, 17
front-of-package (FOP) labeling, 242–43

G

Galen, 44, 244
gastric banding, 241
Gatchel, R. J., 190, 207, 213
gate control model, 185, 190–92; politics of, 197–98
gender: and health care disparities, 78–80; of physician, and outcomes, 79, 133; and restless legs syndrome, 273; and sleep, 265, 267; and smoking, 215–17, 220; and stress, 169, 172; term, 74, 78
gender-nonconforming individuals, 83–84
general adaptation syndrome, 156
generalized anxiety disorder, 295
general practitioners (GPs), 130
genetic factors, and smoking, 218
genito-pelvic pain/penetration disorder, 288–89
germ theory, 46
Gershwin, George, 12
gestational diabetes, ethnicity and, 88
ghrelin, 237
Giardia lamblia, 22
Gini coefficient, 75–76
global system, 8, 17–18
Gottman, John, 14
Gottman, Julie, 14
government policies, and smoking, 220–23
GPs. *See* general practitioners
gratitude, 182
Great Britain, health care in, 67–68, 296
Guatemala syphilis study, 95

H

Halcion. *See* triazolam
Haley, Jay, 193
happiness, 180–81
hardiness, 164
hardy type A personality, 26
harm reduction, 125–26
Hassles Scale, 160
Hay, John, 52
Hayflick limit, 303
headache, 186–87; treatment of, 211
health behavior information, 297–98
health belief model (HBM), 102–7; analysis of, 104–6
health care, 43–71; collaborative and integrated, 295–97; costs of, 57–59; future direction of, 293–304; history of, 43–53; international comparisons, 65–71; quality of, disparities in, 88–89; recommendations for, 71; sexual orientation and, 83
health care navigators, 300–301
health insurance, 56–65; costs of, 57–59
health maintenance organizations (HMOs), 58–59
Heisenberg, Werner, 10
Hela cells, 95
hemophilia, 26
heritability, 4, 27
heroin, 52, 200
Hikikomori, 16
Hill, Bradford, 37–38
Hippocrates, 43–44, 184, 244
Hispanics: causes of death among, 86; and health care system, 96–98; quality of health care, 88, 89. *See also* Latinos
HIV: health communication on, 103, 105; self-testing for, 29–30
HMOs. *See* health maintenance organizations
Holmes, T. H., 159
homeostasis, 155
hospitals, history of, 45–46
HPV vaccine, 150
hwa byung, 98
hypersomnia, 274
hypertension: discrimination and, 87; stress and, 166–67
hypnagogic experiences, 258
hypnosis, 209–10, 229
hypochondriasis. *See* illness anxiety disorder

I

Iacocca, Lee, 57
IBS. *See* irritable bowel syndrome
illness, 2–4; characteristics of, and adherence, 148; diathesis-stress models and, 5–7; stress and, 165–68
illness anxiety disorder (hypochondriasis), 137–38
imaging techniques, 50–51
immune system: night work and, 263; stress and, 157
incidence, definition of, 24

income inequality, 75–76
individualism, 92–93
individual mandate, 71
infancy: race and disparities in health care, 85; sleep in, 260, 275
infant mortality, racial disparities in, 85, 88
informational power, 146
informed consent, 54
innovation, diffusion of, 114–16
insomnia, 264, 266–67; definition of, 266–67; factors associated with, 269t; prevalence of, 267; treatment of, 269–71; among women, 265, 267
inspection, and physical diagnosis, 45
Institute of Medicine (IOM), 297–98
insulin resistance, 4
integrated health care, 295–97
internationalization, 301–2
internet: and eating disorders, 254, 255; and medicalization, 141–42; and pain medication, 199
interpersonal skills, 133
interpersonal systems, 13–14
interpretation: accuracy, 91–92; definition of, 90
interviewing skills, 133
intimate partner violence, sexual orientation and, 82
IOM. *See* Institute of Medicine
iron lung, 51
irritable bowel syndrome (IBS), 11–12, 136

J

Japan, 16; melancholia in, 254; stress in, 173
Jauhar, S., 135
Jenkins Activity Schedule, 165
Jenner, Edward, 46
Jensen, M. P., 210
John Henryism, 77
Johnson, Lyndon B., 59
Johnson, Virginia, 279–80, 285, 290
journaling, 180

K

Kabat-Zinn, Jon, 178
Kaizen, transtheoretical model on, 118
karoshi (Salary Man Sudden Death Syndrome), 173
Kaufman, S., 303
Kevorkian, Jack, 198
Kleinman, Arthur, 141
Koch, Robert, 47
Kolff, Wilhelm, 51
Komen Foundation, 114

L

Lacks, Henrietta, 95
Laennec, René, 46
lanugo, 248
Latinos: and disparities in health care, 84–85; and smoking, 217; term, 74. *See also* Hispanics
lead exposure, racial disparities in, 85

Leeuwenhoek, Antony van, 46
legal issues, 54
legitimate power, 146
leptin, 237
lesbian, gay, bisexual, and transgender (LGBT) individuals: and health care disparities, 80–84; population, 81
Levitra. *See* vardenafil
lidocaine, 205, 286
life expectancies, 49, 66; ethnicity and, 90; future of, 293; gender and, 78; geographic region and, 75; maximization of, 302–3; in Russia, 15–16
light therapy, 270
Limbaugh, Rush, 199
linguistic diversity, 90–92
lisdexamfetamine, 253
Lister, Joseph, 48
low-calorie diets, 239
lower back pain, 186
lung cancer, 215

M

macrosystems: and adherence, 150–51; definition of, 8; and eating disorders, 253–55; EBM health interventions in, 41–42; examples of, 15–16; and pain, 195–200; and physical activity, 247; and sleep, 264–66; and smoking, 220–24; and stress, 168–72; and weight issues, 241–44
magnetic resonance imaging (MRI), 51
Maharishi Yogi, 176
maintenance, transtheoretical model on, 119
major depressive disorder, 26; cardiovascular disease and, 166; exercise and, 245–46; and fibromyalgia, 185; incidence of, 180; and insomnia, 267; and physical health, 294; and sexual issues, 283; and smoking, 219
malingering, 136–37
mammograms, 29
marketing principles, and health communication, 112–14
Masters, William, 279–80, 285, 290
masturbation, 283, 285, 286, 287
mavens, diffusion of innovation theory on, 115
maximizers, 181
McEwen, B. S., 157
McGill Pain Questionnaire, 200–201
media: and eating disorders, 253; and health behavior change, 126–27
mediators, of stress, 160–65
Medicaid, 59, 60–61
medical education, 48–49
medical home, 134, 295
medicalization, 3, 141–42
medically unexplained symptoms (MUS), 135–41; diagnostic criteria, 140; gender and, 79; most common complaints, 140f; primary care physician and, 139–41; psychiatric approach to, 136–39

medical mistakes, communicating, 134–35
medical profession, 49–50; challenges to, 53–55
medical travel, 18
Medicare, 59–60, 297
medications, 52–53; and insomnia, 267–68; for pain, 204–5; for smoking cessation, 228–29; for weight loss, 240
meditation, 176–77
men: causes of death among, 86; and erectile dysfunction, 281–82; and hypoactive desire, 284; and sexual response cycle, 279–80; and stress, 172. See also gender
mental health: and anorexia nervosa, 248–49; exercise and, 245–46; gender-nonconforming individuals and, 84; integrated care and, 295–97; and non-adherence, 145; and pain, 202; and physical, future of, 293–95; sexual orientation and, 82; and smoking, 218–20, 224
meridian theory, 206
mesosystem: definition of, 8; examples of, 14–15
mesothelioma, 33–34
meta-analysis, 40
metabolic syndrome, and erectile dysfunction, 282
methamphetamine use, 9–10
methylphenidate, 273, 274
MI. See motivational interviewing
microsleeps, 263–64
microsystems: definition of, 8; examples of, 11–13
migraine headaches, 186–87; treatment of, 211
Miller, William, 123
mindfulness, 177; and cognitive intervention, 178; for genito-pelvic pain/penetration disorder, 289; for smoking cessation, 229–32
Mini Mental Status Examination, 28
mistakes, medical, communicating, 134–35
modafinil, 273, 274
moderators, of stress, 160–65
Montoya, M., 73
morphine, 52; pumps, 204–5
motivational interviewing (MI), 123–25, 299; philosophy of, 123–24; skills in, 124–25
MRI. See magnetic resonance imaging
multidisciplinary approach, for pain, 212–13
Munchausen syndrome, 137
MUS. See medically unexplained symptoms

N

Nader, Ralph, 53
naps, 263, 268
narcolepsy, 272–73
narrative, 2–3, 6
National Health Service (NHS), 67–68, 296
national political issues, 15–16
Native Americans: causes of death among, 86; and disparities in health care, 84–85; navigator programs and, 301; and smoking, 217
navigator programs, 300–301

neurasthenia, 141
neuromatrix model, 192
neuroticism, 145
NHS. See National Health Service
nicotine: addiction to, 223; replacements, 228, 233; withdrawal from, 227
nightmare disorder, 276
night terrors, 275
Nixon, Richard, 41, 58
nociceptors, 191
non-adherence, 143–45; economic causes of, 151; patient factors in, 144–45. See also adherence
nonbinary individuals, 84
noncardiac chest pain, 136
norepinephrine, 158
nutrition: and cancer, 35; labeling, 242–43

O

Obama, Barack, 64
Obamacare. See Affordable Care Act
obesity: cultural beliefs and, 93; ethnicity and, 87, 96; future of, 293; and health, 236; prevalence of, 235; sleep and, 261; stereotypes and discrimination, 237–38
obstructive sleep apnea, 271–72
odds ratio, 25
older adults, and sleep, 262
openness, 145
operant model, 117, 178; and pain, 185, 188–89
opiates, 204
opioids, history of, 198–200
opposition, diffusion of innovation theory on, 115
optimism, 163–64
organ transplantation, 51–52
orgasm, 280; female orgasmic disorder, 2587–288
orlistat, 240
Osler, William, 49
overweight: prevalence of, 235; risk factors for, 236–37; stereotypes and discrimination, 237–38
oxycodone (Percocet), 52, 196
oxytocin, 158

P

Pacific Islanders. See Asian-Pacific Islanders
pain: definition of, 183–84; intractable, 198; mechanism of, 191; prevalence of, 183; as social metaphor, 193; as vital sign, 198–200. See also chronic pain
pain diary, 201
palliative care, 199
palpation, and physical diagnosis, 45
Pancini, Filippo, 47
panic disorder, 185, 246, 295
Paracelsus, 44–45, 244
parasympathetic nervous system, 155
Parsons, Talcott, 2
participant bias, 32
Pasteur, Louis, 46–47

paternalistic medicine, 54
patient-centered care, 300
Patient's Bill of Rights, 54–55
Pearson, Lester, 69
Peeno, Linda, 58–59
penicillin, 52
perceived control, TRA/TPB on, 108–9
Perceived Stress Scale, 159
Percocet. *See* oxycodone
percussion, and physical diagnosis, 45
performance anxiety, 165, 280, 282
periodic limb movement, 273–74
peripheral nervous system, 155
personalismo, 96–97
personality assessment, 298
personality disorders, and anorexia nervosa, 249
personality factors, 26, 265–68; and adherence, 144–45; and coping, 163–65
pessimism, 163–64
PET. *See* positron emission tomography
pharmaceutical industry, 52–53; and medicalization, 142
phentermine, 240
physical diagnosis, 45–46
physical therapy (PT), 206
physician(s): education of, 48–49; gender of, and outcomes, 79; interpersonal skills of, 133; and non-adherence, 145–48; professionalization of, 49–50; rating sites, 134; social power of, 145–46
physician-assisted suicide, 198
physician-patient interaction: brief counseling models for, 298–300; ethnic disparities in, 89–90; good versus poor, 132–33; linguistic diversity and, 91–92; and non-adherence, 145–48
Pima Indians, 5–6
Pittsburgh Sleep Quality Index, 266
place, social marketing on, 113–14
plateau, and sexual response cycle, 280
polio, 47
politics: and gate control theory, 197–98; and pain, 195–200
polyphasic sleep, 264
population density, and BMI, 247
pornography, 284, 286
positive psychology, 180–82
positron emission tomography (PET), 51
posttraumatic stress disorder, and sleep paralysis, 266
poverty, 36, 61
power, types of, 146
PPOs. *See* professional provider organizations
pranayama, 176
prayer, 14
precontemplation, transtheoretical model on, 117–18
pregnancy: race and disparities in health care, 85; unintended, 143
premature ejaculation, 285–86
preparation: in smoking cessation, 231; in transtheoretical model, 118

prevalence: definition of, 24; and statistical significance, 27–30
price, social marketing on, 113–14
primary care, definition of, 130–31
primary care physician, 58, 129–30; and medically unexplained syndromes, 139–41
problem-focused coping, 162
Prochaska, J. O., 117
procrastination, 164–65
product, social marketing on, 113
professionalism, 300
professional provider organizations (PPOs), 59
progressive relaxation, 174–75; for pain, 209
promotion, social marketing on, 113–14
Prozac. *See* fluoxetine
pseudo seizures, 137
psychiatric approach, to medically unexplained symptoms, 136–39
psychodynamic theory, on anorexia nervosa, 249
psychological treatment, for chronic pain, 207–12
psychoneuroimmunology, 157
psychosexual disorders, 279–91
psychosocial factors: medical care and, 297–300; and pain, 193
psychosomatic medicine, 12–13
PT. *See* physical therapy
PTSD Coach (app), 127
public education: on nutrition, 242–43; on smoking, 221–22
public health, and smoking, 220–24
public service announcements: fear as motivator in, 106–7; on race and disease, effects, 73; on SIDS, 85
Pure Food and Drug Act, 52

Q

qualitative research, 35

R

race: and disparities in health care, 84–85; term, 73. *See also specific race*
radium, 33
Rahe, R. H., 159
Raleigh, Walter, 220
Ramazzini, Bernardini, 244
Reagan, Ronald, 197
reasonable medical practitioner standard, 54
reciprocal causality, 10–11
reciprocal determinism, 110
referent power, 146
refractory period, 280
relapse: prevention of, 120–23; risk factors for, 121
relationships, 13–14; conflict in, 169–70; and pain, 193; workplace, 171
relative risk, 25
relaxation response, 177
religion, 14–15; and pain, 195, 199; and sexuality, 290
REM sleep, 258–60

repetition, diffusion of innovation theory on, 115
residential segregation, 75
resignation syndrome, 173–74
resilience, 181
resistance: motivational interviewing and, 124; and stress, 156
resolution, and sexual response cycle, 280
respeto, 97
restless legs syndrome, 273
Restoril. *See* temazepam
risk factors, 24–27; ethnicity and, 87–88
Ritalin, 273, 274
Robin Hood index, 36–37
role ambiguity, 170–71
Röntgen, Wilhelm, 50
Roosevelt, Franklin, 47, 56
Rosenman, R. H., 165
Roux-Y procedure, 241
Ruesch, J., 7
rumination, 190, 265, 268
Russia, 15–16

S

Sabin, Albert, 47
Sackett, D. L., 38
Salary Man Sudden Death Syndrome. *See* karoshi
salesmen, diffusion of innovation theory on, 115
Salk, Jonas, 47
sandwich generation, 265
satisfiers, 181
schema, 6
S-CHIP. *See* State Children's Health Insurance Program
schizophrenia, 4–5, 26; and physical health, 294; and smoking, 219
Schleiden, Theodor, 46
Schultz, Johan, 175
Schwann, Matthias, 46
Schweiker, Richard, 197
scientific medicine, 50–53
screening tests, 28–30; ethnicity and, 88
secondary gain, 188–89
secondhand smoke, 216
selective serotonin reuptake inhibitors (SSRIs): for eating disorders, 252; and sexual disorders, 282, 285, 288
self-compassion, 179
self-efficacy, 298; health belief model on, 104; motivational interviewing and, 124; social cognitive model on, 111; transtheoretical model on, 119
Selye, Hans, 156, 224
Semmelweis, Ignaz, 47–48, 114–15
sensate focus, 280–81, 286–87
sertraline (Zoloft), 204
severity, health belief model on, 103
sex, term, 74, 78
sexuality, 279–91

sexually transmitted diseases, 23–24; in developing countries, gender and, 80; sexual orientation and, 81
sexual orientation, and health care disparities, 80–84
sexual response cycle, 279–80
shen kui, 98
shiftwork, 170; and sleep, 263; and weight gain, 237
shock, stress model and, 156
Shopen, Michael, 18
sibutramine, 240
sick role, 2
SIDS. *See* sudden infant death syndrome
sildenafil (Viagra), 282, 284, 287–88
Sims, J. Marion, 94
Skinner, B. F., 117, 185, 188
sleep, 257–77; and obesity, 237; reasons for, 257; stages of, 258–60
sleep deprivation, reasons for, 262–64
sleep disorders, 266–74
sleep paralysis, 266
sleep restriction, 271
sleep terrors, 275
sleep walking, 276
smoking, 215–33; bans on, 222–23; corporate policies and, 151; demographics of, 217; gender and, 79; health communication on, 106, 108–9; health risks of, 215–16; history of, 216–17; initiation of, 218; sexual orientation and, 81; transtheoretical model on, 117–20
smoking cessation, 225–33; assessment before, 226–27; relapse prevention, 120–23; social cognitive model on, 111; stages in, 231–32
Snow, John, 46
social cognitive model, 110–12
social contagion theory, 230
social epidemiology, 15, 36–37
social factors: and eating disorders, 253–55; and smoking, 226, 230
social influence theory, and adherence, 145–46
social marketing, 112–14; definition of, 113
Social Readjustment Rating Scale, 159–60
social support: and adherence, 148–49; and smoking cessation, 232; and weight loss, 240
socioeconomic status: and disease, 36; and health care disparities, 75–77; and smoking, 217
sociological information, 297–98
somatic nervous system, 155
somatic symptom disorder, 138–39
somatosensory amplification, 139
somnambulism, 276
Sonata. *See* zaleplon
specialist physicians, 131
spinal stimulators, implantable, 203–4
squeezing technique, 286
SSI. *See* Supplemental Security Income
SSRIs. *See* selective serotonin reuptake inhibitors
stages of change model, 117–20

State Children's Health Insurance Program (S-CHIP), 61
statistical significance, 27–30
sterilization, race and, 95–96
stimulus control, 270
stress, 153–82; assessment of, 159–60; definition of, 154–58; gender and, 78–79; and illness, 165–68; mediators/moderators of, 160–65; smoking and, 224, 226
stressors: characteristics of, 161; history of exposure to, 163; and insomnia, 269*t*
stress reduction, 174–82
striving for upward mobility, and health outcomes, 77
Student Stress Scale, 160
subjective norms, TRA/TPB on, 108
substance abuse, and smoking, 219
sudden infant death syndrome (SIDS), 216, 260, 272; racial disparities in, 85
sugar taxes, 243–44
suicide, physician-assisted, 198
Supplemental Security Income (SSI), 60, 194, 195, 197, 207
surgery: bariatric, 240–41; history of, 47–48; for pain, 203
susceptibility, health belief model on, 102–3
susto, 97
Sweden, 173–74
swing shifts, 263
Switzerland, health care in, 66–67
Sydenham, Thomas, 45
sympathetic nervous system, 155
symptoms, 2–4
syphilis, 23–24, 45, 54
systematic reviews, 40
systems perspective, 1–19; Bertalanffy on, 8; biopsychosocial model, 9–10; Bronfenbrenner on, 8; complexity and, 7–11; example of, 18–19, 19*t*

T

tadalafil (Cialis), 282
Tarde, Gabriel, 115
task switching, exercise and, 246–47
taxes, on tobacco, 220–21
team approach, for pain, 212–13
teens. *See* adolescents
telenovelas, and behavior change, 111–12
temazepam (Restoril), 270
temperomandibular joint dysfunction, 136
tend and befriend response, 158
TENS. *See* trans-electrical nerve stimulation
tension headaches, 186–87; treatment of, 211
termination, transtheoretical model on, 119
testosterone, 281–83, 287
thalidomide, 33
theory of reasoned action/theory of planned behavior (TRA/TPB), 107–10; analysis and research on, 109–10
TM. *See* transcendental meditation

tobacco industry, 223–25
tobacco use: health risks of, 215–16. *See also* smoking; smoking cessation
Tomes, N., 50
topiramate, 253
traditional medicine, 97–98
trait reactivity, 164
transactional model, 158
transactional theory, on coping skills, 162
transcendental meditation (TM), 176
trans-electrical nerve stimulation (TENS), 205–6
transgender individuals, 83–84
translation, definition of, 90
transtheoretical model, 117–20
TRA/TPB. *See* theory of reasoned action/theory of planned behavior
triazolam (Halcion), 270
t-tests, 27
tuberculosis, 86
Tuskegee syphilis study, 54, 94–95
Twain, Mark, 154
type 2 diabetes, 4, 5–6; and erectile dysfunction, 281; and exercise, 245; major depressive disorder and, 294
type A personality, 26; and cardiovascular disease, 165–66
type C personality, 167
type D personality, 26

U

ulcers, 12–13
undertreatment, 75
uninsured, 61–62
Uplifts Scale, 160

V

vaccines, 46–47; Canada and, 69–70; decision making on, 150–51; ethnicity and, 88, 95
vaginismus, 288, 289, 290
Valium. *See* diazepam
values: and health care systems, 70–71; of patient versus provider, 134. *See also* cultural issues/values
vaping, 232–33
vardenafil (Levitra), 282
varenicline (Chantix), 228–29
ventilators, 51
very low calorie diet (VLCD), 239
Vesalius, 44
veterans, and pain, 196
Viagra. *See* sildenafil
vital signs, psychosocial, 297–99
von Frey, M., 185

W

Wailoo, K., 196
wait times: Canadian system and, 69; NHS and, 68
weight bias, 238

weight gain, smoking cessation and, 226
weight loss: interventions for, 238–41; social cognitive model on, 111
Westernization, and eating disorders, 253–54
Whitaker, Carl, 279
Whites: causes of death among, 86; quality of health care, 88–89; and sleep, 265; and smoking, 217
withdrawal, from nicotine, 227
women: causes of death among, 86; and genito-pelvic pain/penetration disorder, 288–89; and orgasmic disorder, 287–288; and sexual interest/arousal disorder, 282–83; and sexual response cycle, 279–80; and smoking, 215–17, 220; and stress, 172. *See also* gender
women's movement, 54
work ethic, 195–96
workmen's compensation, 136, 141, 186, 188, 194
workplace stress, 170–71; and pain, 193–94
World Health Organization, 2, 66, 127; on costs of non-adherence, 143
worry diary, 271
wounded soldiers, and pain, 196
writing: for insomnia, 271; and pain assessment, 201; and stress, 180, 182

X

X-rays, 50–51

Y

yoga breathing, 176
youth. *See* adolescents

Z

zaleplon (Sonata), 270
Zborowski, M., 194
Zoloft. *See* sertraline
zolpidem (Ambien), 270
Zyban. *See* bupropion